ISBN 978-0-260-04831-8
PIBN 10924393

THE

# NEW MONTHLY

# MAGAZINE

AND

# *LITERARY JOURNAL.*

---

## VOL. VIII.

## ORIGINAL PAPERS.

---

## LONDON:

PRINTED FOR HENRY COLBURN AND CO.

---

## 1823.

LONDON:

PRINTED BY S. AND R. BENTLEY, DORSET-STREET.

# CONTENTS

### OF

## THE EIGHTH VOLUME.

# CONTENTS.

# CONTENTS.

THE

# NEW MONTHLY MAGAZINE.

## ORIGINAL PAPERS.

### SKETCHES OF THE IRISH BAR.—NO. VI.

#### *Mr. O'Connell.*

IF any one of you, my English readers, being a stranger in Dublin, should chance, as you return upon a winter's morning from one of the " small and early" parties of that raking metropolis, that is to say, between the hours of five and six o'clock, to pass along the south side of Merrion Square, you will not fail to observe that among those splendid mansions, there is one evidently tenanted by a person whose habits differ materially from those of his fashionable neighbours. The half-opened parlour-shutter, and the light within, announces that some one dwells there whose time is too precious to permit him to regulate his rising with the sun's. Should your curiosity tempt you to ascend the steps, and, under cover of the dark, to reconnoitre the interior, you will see a tall able-bodied man standing at a desk, and immersed in solitary occupation. Upon the wall in front of him there hangs a crucifix. From this, and from the calm attitude of the person within, and from a certain monastic rotundity about his neck and shoulders, your first impression will be, that he must be some pious dignitary of the Church of Rome absorbed in his matin devotions. But this conjecture will be rejected almost as soon as formed. No sooner can the eye take in the other furniture of the apartment, the book-cases clogged with tomes in plain calf-skin binding, the blue-covered octavos that lie about on the tables and the floor, the reams of manuscript in oblong folds and begirt with crimson tape, than it becomes evident that the party meditating amidst such objects must be thinking far more of the law than the prophets. He is, unequivocally, a barrister, but apparently of that homely, chamber-keeping, plodding cast, who labour hard to make up by assiduity what they want in wit—who are up and stirring before the bird of the morning has sounded the retreat to the wandering spectre—and are already brain-deep in the dizzying vortex of mortgages and cross-remainders, and mergers and remitters ; while his clients, still lapped in sweet oblivion of the law's delay, are fondly dreaming that their cause is peremptorily set down for a final hearing. Having come to this conclusion, you push on for home, blessing your stars on the way that you are not a lawyer, and sincerely compassionating the sedentary drudge whom you have just detected in the performance of his cheerless toil. But should you happen in the course of the same day to stroll down to the Four Courts, you will be not a little surprised to find the object of your pity miraculously transferred from the severe recluse of the morning into one of the most bustling, important, and joyous personages in that busy scene. There you will be sure to

see him, his countenance braced up and glistening with health and
spirits—with a huge, plethoric bag, which his robust arms can scarcely
sustain, clasped with paternal fondness to his breast—and environed
by a living palisade of clients and attorneys, with outstretched necks,
and mouths and ears agape, to catch up any chance-opinion that
may be coaxed out of him in a colloquial way, or listening to what the
client relishes still better, for in no event can they be slided into a bill
of costs, the counsellor's bursts of jovial and familiar humour, or, when
he touches on a sadder strain, his prophetic assurances that the hour of
Ireland's redemption is at hand.   You perceive at once that you have
lighted upon a great popular advocate, and if you take the trouble to
follow his movements for a couple of hours through the several Courts,
you will not fail to discover the qualities that have made him so—his
legal competency—his business-like habits—his sanguine temperament,
which renders him not merely the advocate but the partisan of his
client—his acuteness—his fluency of thought and language—his unconquerable good humour—and, above all, his versatility.   By the
hour of three, when the judges usually rise, you will have seen him go
through a quantity of business, the preparation for, and performance of
which, would be sufficient to wear down an ordinary constitution, and
you naturally suppose that the remaining portion of the day must of
necessity be devoted to recreation or repose : but here again you will
be mistaken ; for should you feel disposed, as you return from the
Courts, to drop in to any of the public meetings that are almost daily
held for some purpose, or to no purpose, in Dublin, to a certainty
you will find the counsellor there before you, the presiding spirit of
the scene, riding in the whirlwind, and directing the storm of popular
debate, with a strength of lungs, and redundancy of animation, as if he
had that moment started fresh for the labours of the day.   There he
remains, until, by dint of strength or dexterity, he has carried every
point ; and from thence, if you would see him to the close of the day's
" eventful history," you will, in all likelihood, have to follow him to a
public dinner, from which, after having acted a conspicuous part in
the turbulent festivity of the evening, and thrown off half a dozen
speeches in praise of Ireland, he retires at a late hour to repair the
wear and tear of the day by a short interval of repose, and is sure to
be found before dawn-break next morning at his solitary post, recommencing the routine of his restless existence.   Now, any one who has once
seen, in the preceding situations, the able-bodied, able-minded, acting,
talking, multifarious person I have been just describing, has no occasion to enquire his name—he may be assured that he is, and can be no
other than " Kerry's pride and Munster's glory," the far-famed and
indefatigable Daniel O'Connell.

Mr. O'Connell was born about eight and forty years ago, in that
part of the united kingdoms of Ireland and Kerry, called Kerry.  He
is said to be descended in a mathematically and morally straight line
from the ancient kings of Ivera.*   The discrowned family, however,
have something better than the saddening boast of regal descent to
prop their pride.   His present ex-majesty of Ivera, Mr. Daniel
O'Connell's uncle, has a territorial revenue of four or five thousand a

---

* One of the kingdoms of the county of Kerry.

year to support the dignity of his traditional throne; while the numerous princes of the blood, dispersed through the dominions of their fathers, in the characters of tenants in fee-simple, opulent lease-holders, or sturdy mortgagees in possession, form a compact and powerful squirearchy, before whose influence the proud "descendants of the stranger" are often made to bow their necks, in the angry collisions of county politics. The subject of the present notice is understood to be the heir-apparent to his uncle's possessions. These he must soon enjoy, for his royal kinsman has passed his 90th year. In the mean time he rules in his own person an extensive tract among the Kerry hills; of little value, it is said, in point of revenue, but dear to the possessor, as the residence of the idol of his heart, and in truth almost the only tenant on three-fourths of the estate—

"The mountain-nymph, sweet Liberty."

Mr. O'Connell was originally intended for the Church, or more strictly speaking, for the Chapel. He was sent, according to the necessities of the time, to be educated at St. Omer—for in those days the wise government of Ireland would not allow the land of Protestant ascendancy to be contaminated by a public school of Catholic theology. Dr. Duigenan was compelled to permit the detested doctrines to be freely preached; but to make the professors of them good subjects, he shrewdly insisted that they should still, as of old, be forced to cross the seas, and lay in a preliminary stock of Irish loyalty at a foreign university. But the dread of indigenous theology was not peculiar to that great man. I observe that some of our statesmen of the present year have discovered that *all* the disasters of Ireland have been caused by an invisible establishment of Jesuits, and must continue until the omnipotence of Parliament shall expel the intruders—a felicitous insight into cause and effect, resembling that of the orthodox crew of a British packet, who having discovered, during a gale of wind, that a Methodist preacher was among the passengers, at once made up their minds that the fury of the tempest would never abate until the vessel should be exorcised by heaving the non-conformist overboard. I have not heard what occasioned Mr. O'Connell to change his destination. He probably had the good sense to feel that he had too much flesh and blood for a cloister; and the novelty of a legal career to a Catholic (for the Bar had just been opened to his persuasion) must have had its attractions. He accordingly left St. Omer with its casuistry and fasting and vesper hymns, to less earthly temperaments; and having swallowed the regular number of legs of mutton at the Middle Temple, was duly admitted to the Irish Bar in Easter Term 1798. The event has justified his choice. With all the impediments of his religion and his politics, his progress was rapid. He is now, and has been for many years, as high in his profession as it is possible for a Catholic to ascend.

Mr. O'Connell, if not the ablest, is certainly the most singular man at the Irish Bar. He is singular, not merely in the vigour of his faculties, but in their extreme variety and apparent inconsistency; and the same may be said of his character. The elements of both are so many and diverse, that it would seem as if half a dozen varieties of the human species, and these not always on the best terms with each other, had been capriciously huddled together into a single frame to make up his strange and complex identity; and hence it is, that, though I spoke of him heretofore as a favourable subject for a sketch, I find the task of accurate delineation to be far less easy than I anticipated. I have the man before me, and willing enough, it would appear, that his features should be commemorated; but, like the poor artist that had to deal with the frisky philosopher of Ferney, with all my efforts I cannot keep him steady to any single posture or expression. I see him distinctly at one moment a hard-headed working lawyer, the next a glowing politician, the next an awful theologian; his features now sunk into the deepest shade of patriotic anguish, now illuminated, no one can tell why, as for the celebration of a national triumph. A little while back I caught him in his character of a sturdy reformer, proclaiming the constitution, and denouncing the vices of courts and kings, and he promised me that he would keep to *that*; but before I had time to look about me, there he was, off to the levee! be-bagged and be-sworded like any oppressor of them all, playing off his loyal looks and anti-radical bows, as if he was to be one of Mr. Blake's next Baronets, or as if he had not sufficiently proved his attachment to the throne by presenting his majesty with a crown of Irish laurel on the beach of Dunleary. Such a compound can be described only by enumerating its several ingredients; and even here I am not sure that my performance, if rigidly criticized, may not turn out, like my subject, to be occasionally at variance with itself. I shall begin with (what in other eminent lawyers is subordinate) his individual and extra-professional peculiarities; for in O'Connell these are paramount, and act a leading part in every scene, whether legal or otherwise, of his complicated avocations.

His frame is tall, expanded, and muscular; precisely such as befits a man of the people—for the physical classes ever look with double confidence and affection upon a leader who represents in his own person the qualities upon which they rely. In his face he has been equally fortunate; it is extremely comely. The features are at once soft and manly; the florid glow of health and a sanguine temperament is diffused over the whole countenance, which is national in the outline, and beaming with national emotion. The expression is open and confiding, and inviting confidence; there is not a trace of malignity or wile—if there were, the bright and sweet blue eyes, the most kindly and honest-looking that can be conceived, would repel the imputation. These popular gifts of nature O'Connell has not neglected to set off by his external carriage and deportment—or, perhaps, I should rather say, that the same hand which has moulded the exterior has supersaturated the inner man with a fund of restless propensity, which it is quite beyond his power, as it is certainly beside his inclination, to controul. A large portion of this is necessarily expended upon his legal avocations; but the labours of the most laborious of professions cannot tame him into repose: after deducting the daily drains of the study and the Courts, there remains an ample residuum of animal spirits and ardour for occupation, which go to form a distinct, and I might say, a predominant character—the political chieftain. The existence of this overweening vivacity is conspicuous in O'Connell's manners and movements, and being a popular, and more particularly a national quality, greatly recommends him to the Irish people—" Mobilitate viget" —

Body and soul are in a state of permanent insurrection. See him in the streets, and you perceive at once that he is a man who has sworn that his country's wrongs shall be avenged. A Dublin jury (if judiciously selected) would find his very gait and gestures to be high treason by construction, so explicitly do they enforce the national sentiment, of "Ireland her own, or the world in a blaze." As he marches to Court, he shoulders his umbrella as if it were a pike. He flings out one factious foot before the other, as if he had already burst his bonds, and was kicking the Protestant ascendancy before him; while ever and anon a democratic, broad-shouldered roll of the upper man is manifestly an indignant effort to shuffle off "the oppression of seven hundred years." This intensely national sensibility is the prevailing peculiarity in O'Connell's character; for it is not only when abroad and in the popular gaze that Irish affairs seem to press upon his heart: the same Erin-go-bragh feeling follows him into the most technical details of his forensic occupations. Give him the most dry and abstract position of law to support—the most remote that imagination can conceive from the violation of the Articles of Limerick, or the Rape of the Irish Parliament, and ten to one but he will contrive to interweave a patriotic episode upon those examples of British domination. The people are never absent from his thoughts. He tosses up a bill of exceptions to a judge's charge in the name of Ireland, and pockets a special retainer with the air of a man that dotes upon his country. There is, perhaps, some share of exaggeration in all this; but much less, I do believe, than is generally suspected, and I apprehend that he would scarcely pass for a patriot without it; for, in fact, he has been so successful, and looks so contented, and his elastic, unbroken spirits are so disposed to bound and frisk for very joy—in a word, he has naturally so bad a face for a grievance, that his political sincerity might appear equivocal, were there not some clouds of patriotic grief or indignation to temper the sunshine that is for ever bursting through them.

As a professional man, O'Connell is, perhaps, for general business, the most competent advocate at the Irish Bar. Every requisite for a barrister of all-work is combined in him; some in perfection—all in sufficiency. He is not understood to be a deep scientific lawyer. He is, what is far better for himself and his clients, an admirably practical one. He is a thorough adept in all the complicated and fantastic forms with which Justice, like a Chinese monarch, insists that her votaries shall approach her. A suitor advancing towards her throne, cannot go through the evolutions of the indispensable *Ko-tou* under a more skilful master of the ceremonies. In this department of his profession, the knowledge of the practice of the Courts, and in a perfect familiarity with the general principles of law that are applicable to questions discussed in open Court, O'Connell is on a level with the most experienced of his competitors; and with few exceptions, perhaps with the single one of Mr. Plunkett, he surpasses them all in the vehement and pertinacious talent with which he contends to the last for victory, or, where victory is impossible, for an honourable retreat. If his mind had been duly disciplined, he would have been a first-rate reasoner and a most formidable sophist. He has all the requisites from nature—singular clearness, promptitude, and acuteness. When occasion requires, he evinces a metaphysical subtlety of perception

which nothing can elude. The most slippery distinction that glides
across him, he can grasp and hold " pressis manibus," until he pleases
to set it free.   But his argumentative powers lose much of their effect
from want of arrangement.   His thoughts have too much of the impatience of conscious strength to submit to an orderly disposition.   Instead of moving to the conflict in compact array, they rush forward
like a tumultuary Insurgent mass, jostling and overturning one another
in the confusion of the charge; and though finally beating down all
opposition by sheer strength and numbers, still reminding us of the far
greater things they might have achieved had they been better drilled.
But O'Connell has by temperament a disdain of every thing that is
methodical and sedate.   You can see this running through his whole
deportment in Court.   I never knew a learned personage who resorted
so little to the ordinary tricks of his vocation.   As he sits waiting till
his turn comes to "blaze away," he appears totally exempt from the
usual throes and heavings of animo-gestation.   There is no hermeti-
cally-sealing of the lips, as if nothing less could restrain the fermentation within ; there are no trances of abstraction, as if the thoughts had
left their home on a distant voyage of discovery ; no haughty swellings
of the mind  into alto-relievos on the  learned brow ;—there is nothing
of this about O'Connell.   On the contrary, his countenance and manners impress you with the notion, that he looks forward to the coming
effort as to a pastime in which he takes delight.  'Instead of assuming
the "Sir Oracle," he is all gaiety and good-humour, and seldom fails
to  disturb  the  gravity of the  proceedings  by a series  of disorderly
jokes, for which he is duly rebuked by his antagonists with a solemnity
of indignation that provokes a repetition of the offence; but his insub-
ordinate levity is, for the most part, so redeemed  by his *imperturbable*
good-temper, that even the judges, when compelled to interfere and
pronounce him out of order, are generally shaking their sides as heartily
as the most enraptured of his admirers in the galleries.   In the midst,
however, of this seeming carelessness, his mind is in reality attending
with the keenest vigilance to the subject-matter of discussion ; and the
contrast is often quite amusing.   While his eyes are wantoning round
the Court in search of an object to be knocked down by a blow of his
boisterous playfulness, or, in a more serious mood, while he is sketch-
ing on the margin of his brief the outline of an impossible republic, or
running through a rough calculation of the number of Irishmen capable
of bearing pikes according to the latest returns of the population, if
the minutest irregularity or misstatement is attempted on the other side,
up he is sure to start with all imaginable alertness, and, reassuming the
advocate, puts forward his objection with a degree of vigour and per-
spicuity which manifests that his attention had not wandered for an instant from the business before him.
     Mr. O'Connell is in particular request in jury-cases.   There he is in
his element.  Next to the " harp of his country," an Irish jury is the
instrument on which he delights to play; and no one better understands
its qualities and compass.   I have already glanced at his versatility.
It is here that it is displayed.   His  powers  as  a Nisi-prius  advocate
consist not so much in the perfection of any of the qualities necessary
to the art of persuasion, as in the number of them that he has at command, and the skill with which he selects and adapts them to the exi-

gency of each particular case. He has a thorough knowledge of human nature, as it prevails in the class of men whom he has to mould to his purposes. I know of no one that exhibits a more quick and accurate perception of the essential peculiarities of the Irish character. It is not merely with reference to their passions that he understands them, though here he is pre-eminently adroit. He can cajole a dozen of miserable corporation-hacks into the persuasion that the honour of their country is concentred in their persons. His mere acting on such occasions is admirable : no matter how base and stupid, and how poisoned by political antipathy to himself he may believe them to be, he affects the most complimentary ignorance of their real characters. He hides his scorn and contempt under a look of unbounded reliance. He addresses them with all the deference due to upright and high-minded jurors. He talks to them of "the eyes of all Europe," and the present gratitude of Ireland, and the residuary blessings of posterity, with the most perfidious command of countenance. In short, by dint of unmerited commendations, he belabours them into the belief that, after all, they have some reputation to sustain, and sets them chuckling with anticipated exultation at the honours with which a verdict according to the evidence is to consecrate their names. But, in addition to the art of heating the passions of his hearers to the malleable point, O'Connell manifests powers of observation of another, and, for general purposes, a more valuable kind. He knows that strange modification of humanity, the Irish mind, not only in its moral but in its metaphysical peculiarities. Throw him upon any particular class of men, and you would imagine that he must have lived among them all his life, so intuitively does he accommodate his style of argument to their particular modes of thinking and reasoning. He knows the exact quantity of strict logic which they will bear or can comprehend. Hence, (where it serves his purpose) instead of attempting to drag them along with him, whether they will or no, by a chain of unbroken demonstration, he has the address to make them imagine that their movements are directed solely by themselves. He pays their capacities the compliment of not making things too clear. Familiar with the habitual tendencies of their minds, he contents himself with throwing off rather materials for reasoning than elaborate reasonings—mere fragments, or seeds of thought, which, from his knowledge of the soil in which they drop, he confidently predicts will shoot up and expand into precisely the conclusions that he wants. This method has the disadvantage, as far as personally regards the speaker, of giving the character of more than his usual looseness and irregularity to O'Connell's jury-speeches ; but his client, for whom alone he labours, is a gainer by it—directly in the way I have been stating, and indirectly for this reason, that it keeps the jury in the dark as to the points of the case in which he feels he is weak. By abstaining from a show of rigorous demonstration, where all the argument is evidently upon his side, he excites no suspicion by keeping at an equal distance from topics which he could not venture to approach. This, of course, is not to be taken as O'Connell's invariable manner, for he has no invariable manner, but as a specimen of that dexterous accommodation of particular means to a particular end, from which his general powers as a Nisi-prius advocate may be inferred. And so too of the tone in which he labours to extort a verdict ;

for though when compelled by circumstances, he can be soft and soothing, as I have above described him, yet on other occasions, where it
can be done with safety, he does not hesitate to apprise a jury, whose
purity he suspects, of his real opinion of their merits, and indeed, not
unfrequently, in the roundest terms defies them to balance for an instant between their malignant prejudices and the clear and resistless
justice of the case.

There is one, the most difficult, it is said; and certainly the most
anxious and responsible part of an advocate's duties, in which O'Connell is without a rival at the Irish Bar—I allude to his skill in conducting defences in the Crown Court.  His ability in this branch of his
profession illustrates one of those inconsistencies in his character to
which I have already adverted.  Though habitually so bold and sanguine, he is here a model of forethought and undeviating caution.  In
his most rapid cross-examinations, he never puts a dangerous question.
He presses a witness upon collateral facts, and beats him down by
argument and jokes and vociferation; but wisely presuming his client
to be guilty until he has the good luck to escape conviction, he never
affords the witness an opportunity of repeating his original narrative,
and perhaps, by supplying an omitted item, of sealing the doom of the
accused.

O'Connell's ordinary style is vigorous and copious, but incorrect.
The want of compactness in his periods, however, I attribute chiefly
to inattention.  He has phrase in abundance at command, and his ear
is sensible of melody.  Every now and then he throws off sentences
not only free from all defect, but extremely felicitous specimens of
diction.  As to his general powers of eloquence, he rarely fails, in a
case admitting of emotion, to make a deep impression upon a jury; and
in a popular assembly he is supreme.  Still there is much more of eloquence in his manner and topics than in his conceptions.  He unquestionably proves, by occasional bursts, that the elements of oratory, and
perhaps of the highest order, are about him; but he has had too many
pressing demands of another kind to distract him from the cultivation
of this the rarest of all attainments, and accordingly I am not aware
that any of his efforts, however able and successful, have deserved, as
examples of public speaking, to survive the occasion.  His manner,
though far from graceful, is earnest and impressive.  It has a steady
and natural warmth, without any of that snappish animation in which
gentlemen of the long robe are prone to indulge.  His voice is powerful, and the intonations full and graduated.  I understand that when
first he appeared at the Bar, his accent at once betrayed his foreign
education.  To this day there is a remaining dash of Foigardism in his
pronunciation of particular words; but, on the whole, he has brought
himself, as far as delivery is concerned, to talk pretty much like a
British subject.

It was my original intention to have dwelt in some detail upon
O'Connell, as a popular leader, but I have no longer space, and I
could scarcely effect my purpose without plunging into that " sea of
troubles," the present politics of Ireland : yet a word or two upon the
subject before I have done.  Indeed, in common fairness, I feel bound
to correct any depreciating inferences that may be drawn from the
tone of levity in which I may have glanced at some traits of his public

deportment, and which I should have hesitated to indulge in, if I had not given him credit for the full measure of good-humour and good sense, that can discriminate at once (should these pages meet his eye) between an inoffensive sally and a hostile sneer.

O'Connell has been now for three and twenty years a busy actor upon an agitated scene. During that period no public character has been more zealously extolled, or more cordially reviled. Has the praise or blame been excessive, or has either been undeserved? Has he been a patriot, or an incendiary? for, such are the extreme points of view in which the question of his merits has been discussed by persons, too impassioned and too interested in the result to pronounce a sound opinion upon it. To one, however, who has never been provoked to admire or hate him to excess, the solution may not be difficult. After reviewing the whole of O'Connell's career as a politician, an impartial observer will be disposed to say of him, that he was a man of a strong understanding and of stronger feelings, occupied incessantly, and almost always without due preparation, upon questions where it would have perplexed the wisest to discern the exact medium between disgraceful submission and factious importunity—that by necessity a partisan, he has been steady to his cause, and consistent in his ultimate object, though many times inconsistent in the adoption of the means to obtain it; and that now in the long run, after all the charges of violence and indiscretion that have been heaped upon him, it is questioned by some of the clearest understandings in England, whether, in the present state of political morals, a more courtly policy than O'Connell's either is, or was ever, calculated to advance the interests of his body. But leaving his political incentives aside, and referring solely to the personal provocations to which he is daily exposed, I should say, that it would be utterly unnatural in such a man to be other than violent. To O'Connell, as a barrister, his disqualification is a grievous injustice. It is not in theory alone that it operates. It visits him in the practical details of his professional life, and in forms the most likely to gall a man of conscious powers and an ambitious temperament. He has the mortification of being incessantly reminded, that for years past his fortunes have been absolutely at a dead stop, while he was constantly condemned to see men who started with him and after him, none of them his superiors, many of them far beneath him, partially thrust before him, and lifted into stations of honour and emolument to which he is forbidden to aspire. The stoutest adversary of Papal encroachments must admit, that there is something irritating in this; for my part, instead of judging harshly of the spirit in which he retaliates, I rather honour the man for the energy with which he wrestles to the last with the system that would keep him down; and if now and then his resistance assumes such a form as to be in itself an evil, I am not sorry, for the sake of freedom and humanity, to see it proved that intolerant laws cannot be enforced without inconvenience. But in general (to speak the truth) O'Connell's vengeance is not of a very deadly description. He is, after all, a man of a kindly and forgiving nature; and where the general interests of his country are not concerned, is disposed to resent his personal wrongs with great command of temper. His forbearance in this respect is really creditable to him, and the more so as it meets with no return.

The admirers of King William have no mercy for a man, who, in his seditious moods, is so provoking as to tell the world that their idol was " a Dutch adventurer." Then his intolerable success in a profession where many a stanch Protestant is condemned to starve, and his fashionable house in Merrion-square, and a greater eye-sore still, his dashing revolutionary equipage, green carriage, green liveries, and turbulent Popish steeds, prancing over a Protestant pavement to the terror of Protestant passengers—a nuisance that in the good old times would have been put down by Act of Parliament—these and other provocations of equal publicity, have exposed this learned culprit to the deep and irrevocable detestation of a numerous class of his Majesty's hating subjects in Ireland. And the feeling is duly communicated to the public. The loyal press of Dublin teems with the most astounding imputations upon his character and motives. As a dish for the periodical libellers of the day, O'Connell is quite a cut-and-come-again, from the crazy Churchman, foaming over the apprehended fall of tithes, down to the political striplings of the College, who, instead of trying their youthful genius upon the cardinal virtues, or " the lawfulness of killing Cæsar," devote their hours of classic leisure to the more laudable task of demonstrating, for the comfort of the Orange lodges, that " Counsellor O'Connell carries on a treasonable correspondence with Captain Rock." But the Counsellor, who happens to know a little more of the law of high treason than his accusers, has the good sense to laugh at them and their threats of the hangman. Now that all practical attempts upon life have been abandoned*, he bears the rest with true Christian patience and contempt ; and whenever any of his defamers recant " *in extremis*" and die good Catholics, as the most bigoted among them are said to do, if the fact be duly certified by his friend Mr. Denis Scully†, who has quite an instinct for collecting materials touching this portion of secret history, O'Connell, I am assured, not only forgives them all their libels, but contributes liberally towards setting on foot a few expiatory masses for their souls.

---

* I allude to what was really a shocking occurrence.—A Corporation has been defined to be " a thing having neither a body to be kicked nor a soul to be damned." With this definition before him, Mr. O'Connell did not imagine that he exceeded the limits of public debate in calling the Dublin Corporation a " beggarly Corporation." One of its most needy members, however, either volunteered or was incited to think otherwise, and called upon the speaker to apologize or fight. To Mr. O'Connell, a life of vital importance to a numerous family, and of great importance to the best part of the Irish public, the alternative was dreadful. He saw the ferocity of the transaction in its full light, but he committed his conduct to the decision of his friends, and a duel ensued. The aggressor was killed. Had the result been different, his claims would probably not have been overlooked by the patrons of the time (1815) ; at least such is understood to have been the expectation under which he provoked his fate.

† The Catholic barrister, a gentleman quite clever and important enough to be treated of apart. For the present, I shall merely record of him that one of his favourite theories is, that no rank Orangeman ever " dies game." He can tell you the exact moment when Doctor Duigenan began to roar out for a priest. He has a large stock of mortuary anecdotes illustrating his general doctrine, and he relates them with true Sardonic vivacity.

## THE DESTROYING ANGEL.

THE sun had set on a fearful day,
When the banner'd hosts of Assyria lay
On the battle-field stretch'd in the soldier's sleep,
In number the sands on the shore of the deep,
   And fierce in security.

They had vaunted their strength in their chariots' might,
They had boasted to level on Lebanon's height
The tall cedar-trees—at their conquests wide
Over nations laid waste in the march of their pride,
   Israel had blench'd with affright.

From her city towers she had look'd o'er the plain,
Where the swarm of her foes heaved like waves on the main;
She had seen in the sunbeams an harvest of spears,
And the tramp of the horsemen had burst on her ears—
   To combat or fly was vain.

" My arm," said the Lord, " shall the foemen engage,
I will bridle his mouth and his ire assuage—
I will send him a remnant in number away,
And the king of Assyria shall fly from his prey,
   And the spoiler forget his rage."

'Twas night, and no moon had lit up the sky,
The hosts, wrapp'd in dreams, thought no danger nigh,
The sentinel only his bright arms wore,
While the darkness wax'd greater more and more
   As the noon of night pass'd by.

The silence is fear-struck as night's noon comes by !
And a sound like the wing of an eagle on high,
That shook 'mid the stillness his pennons strong,
With a rush like an autumn-blast sweeping along,
   Smote the hearers fearfully.

The Angel of Death o'er the arm'd hosts is flying,
The Simoom from his wing their hearts-blood is drying,
From the slumber of life into death they have past,
And his is the march like a rustling blast,
   Their prowess and strength defying.

Swifter far than the flash 'mid the tempest's roar,
He deliver'd the terrible message he bore;
And myriads lay breathless and rotting ere day
Lit the stranger to mark the Assyrian array
   Like grass upon Galilee's shore.

There is silence of horror all over the plain—
There are few that arise from that couch of the slain ;—
And they wander in fear 'mid the festering dead,
And they shout, but no comrade lifts his head—
   They shout, and they shout in vain.

There the steed and his rider, the chief of the sword,
Are melted away by the breath of the Lord ;
And the purple Sennacherib is wailing his power,
For whose bosom of pride in prosperity's hour
   The wine-cup of wrath is pour'd.

There are none that the burial-rites prepare
For the thousands that cover the green earth there ;
The living have fled to their far country,
The unsepulchred dead are the vultures' prey,
   And wolves the carnival share.

## PROSPECTUS OF A NEW WORK.

*" Ætherias, lascive, cupis volitare per auras,*
*I, fuga; sed poteras tutior esse domi."*　　　MARTIAL.

### *To the Editor of the New Monthly Magazine.*

SIR,—I have always been of opinion that a large part of the labours of man are lost, both to the individual and to society, from their not having been directed to some certain and well-defined scope. For this reason, from the moment I first entered College (now, alas! five-and-thirty years ago), I determined to look about me, and fix upon some useful object, suited to my feelings and capacities, upon which I might concentrate all my powers, and produce something that might at once prove serviceable to my species, and procure me a name that may shine conspicuous when the art of the brass-founder shall be forgotten, and a medal or a bronze no longer remain in existence.

I am a man, Sir, of much patient industry, of some shrewdness of remark, of profoundly retentive memory, and of extensive reading,—qualities of which I the less hesitate to boast, because they are pledges of my fitness for the task I have undertaken, and because it is in strict compliance with the received custom among the learned of the last age—the "mighty dead"—to announce themselves with a becoming confidence. If Horace and Ovid, indeed, were justified in singing of themselves, " *Exegi monumentum*" and " *Jamque opus*," &c. on account of their poetry, how much more may a Gesner, a Baxter, or a Heinsius boast, whose labours have prevented these (so called) immortal works from perishing; who have restored these dilapidated " monuments," have explained their inscriptions, and rendered them intelligible to schoolboys and undergraduates : and here I may be permitted to remark, that this present age, which has added to the stores of English literature three first-rate poets, (Southey, Wordsworth, and the anonymous author of a MS. volume of Latin poetry *penès me*), to say nothing of the *minora sidera*, Byron, Campbell, Moore, &c. &c. it has, in its immense fertility, brought to light not one Commentator.

Influenced by this reflection, and by the natural bent of my own genius, I no sooner knew myself, (*e cœlo descendit*, &c. &c.), than I determined to embark my hopes and my fortunes in the composition of a great literary work suited to my peculiar talents. My parents, indeed, were anxious that I should have entered upon some of the active professions, and figured in the busy haunts of men, a lawyer, a divine, or a physician. But what, Sir, are theologians or physicians? Men who confine themselves to one limited study, who survey nature in one only of its numerous aspects, and who, binding themselves to a single end, scarcely ever are found even to accomplish that. The lawyers are still worse : their reading lies wholly in a circle which nobody thinks of entering but themselves ; and " *scire tuum nihil est ;*" the knowledge which you cannot display to others is only so much ignorance. A lawyer, Sir, ranks with a conjuror ; more feared than estimated ; worshipped only by the ignorant and the credulous, and carefully avoided by all who have the slightest regard for their quiet or their purse. My multifarious reading, which has extended over the whole range of literature, qualified me for nobler pursuits, and my ambition, or rather my instinct, led me to emulate the Bentleys, the Stevenses, and the Burmans, those universal geniuses, who threw the light of their erudition into the most tenebrous holes and corners of their author's obscurity.

No sooner, then, had I attained the qualification of *Dominus* on the College boards, than I plunged deep into criticism, and determined to give my days and nights to the illustration of some learned author. The classic "world was all before me where to choose;" but the choice was not easy. An esteemed author was not upon any terms to be had, who was not already so towsled and mumbled by the critics, as not to leave a "*sed*" or a "*que*" to the ingenuity of the present day; while an obscure and valueless writer would plunge his commentator into his own obscurity, and effectually impede him in his flight to immortality. For, though a commentator is intrinsically more worthy than his original, as the precious gums and essences are more valuable than the lifeless mass they embalm, still it is vain to comment, when men will not read. The old stock of authors was exhausted; the new discoveries of unrolled Pompeian MSS. and of Palimpsestic parchments had not yet furnished fresh matter of research: and I was upon the point of abandoning my schemes, and of embarking in some of the less useful walks of life—wasting my hours in chemistry or natural philosophy—when chance put into my hands, from among the MSS. of Trinity College, Cambridge, an invaluable and inedited fragment of Greek poetry, of which I shall only say, that it is the original of the celebrated English poem, which begins

"Three children sliding on the ice,"

and which has been translated by some vile plagiary, and passed, unacknowledged in the literary world, as his own.

As your lady readers do not understand Greek, I shall quote in what follows the English version alone. But, for the benefit of the learned, I shall throw the Greek text into a note.[*]

No sooner was I in possession of this treasure, than I set about illustrating it; and having arranged the text to my own satisfaction, I enriched it, during the course of thirty years exclusive application, with a series of illustrations which leave little or nothing to desire.

---

[*] Κρυσταλλοπηκτους τρεπτυχοι κοροι βοας
Ωρα, θερους, ψαιροντες ενταρσοις ποσι,
Διναις επιπτον, δια δη πιπτειν φιλει,
Απαντες· επ᾽ εφευγον οἱ λελαμμενοι.
Αλλ᾽ ειπερ ησαν εγκεκλεισμενοι μοχλοις,
Η ποσιν ολισθαινοντες εν ξιφφ ποδῳ
Χρυσιν αν εθελησ᾽ περιδοσθαι οταθμων
Ει μη μερος τι των νεων εσωζεται.
Αλλ᾽ ω τοκεις, ὁσοις μεν οντα τυγχανει,
'Οσοις δε μη, βλαστημματ᾽ ευτεχνου σπορας,
Ην εντυχεις ευχησθε τας θυραξ ὁδους,
Τοις πασιν, ευσφας εν δομοις φυλασσετε.

This beautiful *morceau* has been attributed to Professor Porson; but if the internal evidence of style did not prove its antiquity, the parchment and character of the MS. at least assign it six centuries of existence.

The precise number of volumes the work will occupy I am not prepared exactly to state; but the extent may be guessed with some approximation towards accuracy by any one acquainted with the manner in which such subjects are usually handled, when he shall have perused the sketch which I propose now to lay before your readers of that portion of my labours which is as yet ready for the press.

PROGRAM.

The first line of this wonderfully philosophic and profound specimen of Pythagorean lore (for such it is) embraces a great variety of subjects for elucidation, of which I propose to treat in the order of their occurrence.

" Three (1) children (2) sliding (3) on the ice (4)."

(1) THREE.—Beginning at the beginning, I propose to enter at large upon the consideration of the number three, which, from the remotest antiquity, has obtained a mysterious and recondite signification; as is abundantly proved (omitting other instances) by the three heads of Cerberus; the triple goddess Diana; Isis, Osiris, and Horus; the three wise men of the East; the three dynasties, and three consuls of France; the rule of three; the three dimensions of matter; the three angles of a triangle; the three Fates; the three witches in Macbeth; the three estates of the realm; the " three jolly pidgeons ;" Shadrach, Meshech, and Abednego; and the Three Gentlemen of Verona. I have diligently collated the poets for their use of this number ; such as the " *Ter conatu loqui,*" " *Trois fois heureux,*" and " Thrice to thine, thrice to mine, and thrice again to make up nine ;" which last quotation introduces a few parenthetic observations on the multiples of three, and of that odd fraction the circulating decimal ·9—which at the same time is, and is not, one. In reference also to the " triple tree," I have read through a most voluminous collection of the last speeches of the most celebrated " *patibulaires,*" from which the reader will find copious extracts. I have also a word or two, *en passant*, on Mr. Canning's " Loves of the Triangles," a new translation of the Welsh Triads, and a critical history of the Three per cents. distinguishing the Consols from the Reduced, with a table of interest, a memoir of the house of Rothschild, notices of inscriptions in the *grand livre* of France, an engraving of Cobbett's gridiron, and a " Catalogue Raisonnée" of the authors on the great question of currency.

(2) CHILDREN.—On this word will be noted, *inter alia*, the Abbé Quillet's Callipædia; the Pædotrophia of St. Marthe, physician to Henry III. of France; the Cyropædia of Xenophon; Fenelon's Telemachus; and the Chevalier Ramsay's Travels of Cyrus. Notices will be given, likewise, of Peter the Wild Boy, and other wild children; of *Les enfans trouvés*, and foundling hospitals of most European nations; the Garry Owen boys; the Bluecoat boys; the children in the wood; the young Roscius and Miss Clara Fisher; the Lancastrian system; Pestalozzi and Fellenburg; the " *Così al egro*" of Tasso, which he stole from Lucretius—a theft the less excusable as Lucretius has twice repeated the simile, *totidem verbis*, to mark it the more certainly as his own. In order more completely to illustrate this portion of the text,

I shall give remarks on second childhood, or old age; remarks on Shakspeare's and Churchill's ages of man, the golden age, the Augustan age, the middle ages; Lord Byron's "Age of Bronze," with an original treatise on the use and abuse of that happy exordium, "In this (as the case may be) learned, pious, sceptical, revolutionary, or degenerate age."

(3) SLIDING.—Upon sliding I shall introduce a dissertation on the antiquity of the practice, and an inquiry into the invention of scates; a secret history of sliding panels and doors covered with tapestry, taken from the most approved and authorized novels; observations on sliding rules, sliding boys, *atalanches*, and "*versi sdruccioli!*" notes on eels, sophists, political rats, and other slippery animals; including memoirs of Ch—t—br—nd, the B——m family, and Mother L——; some account of the slips at the theatres, and in the dock-yards, *lapsus linguæ*, the slips of my aunt Dinah not original (Sterne's plagiarism), on backslidings and "*faux pas*" in general, with an account of the newest method of soaping a pig's tail.

(4) ICE.—This is a word of much obscurity, and requires ample illustration. I shall notice only a few of the points which will be touched upon in this part of my work. The chemical history of ice, with the most approved theory of heat; on icebergs, glaciers, and voyages to the North Pole; memoirs of the Humane Society, and lives of persons drowned in the Serpentine; on ice-creams, Roman punch (*glacé*), French dramatic poetry, iced champaigne, artificial frigorific mixtures, the late Lord Londonderry's speeches in Parliament, &c. &c. with a new receipt for making cool-cup; account of a burning-glass of ice; the ice palace on the Neva, and Moore's Holy Alliance; the burning of Moscow, the retreat through Russia, and the surgical treatment of frost-bitten limbs; on the *Iceni*, or men of Kent, an *excursus*.

The second line of this extraordinary poem furnishes no less occasion for research than the first.

"All on (5) a summer's (6) day (7)."

(5) ALL ON.—Rise, progress, and fall of this phrase in English poetry, with philological researches, and etymologies; the "*tractatus de omnibus rebus et quibusdam aliis;*" the inscriptions "put on" and "put off," on our way-sides, mistaken by foreigners for a remnant of Catholic superstition, and supposed to refer to the hat; spirituous compound called "All sorts" not to be confounded with omnium or scrip; "All the talents;" "All Lombard-street to an egg-shell;" treatise on the use of "On," in epitaphs and epigram writing; outline of modern ON-tology; memoirs of Tommy ON-slow; "On, Stanley, on!" stolen from the "*en avant*" of the French, &c. &c.

(6) SUMMER.—I shall here touch on Thomson's and Delille's Seasons, with citations from all known poets, descriptive of the four quarters of the year; on seasoning, with anecdotes of the cook's oracles, *Le Cuisinier François*, *L'Almanach des Gourmands*, and a life of Hannah Glasse; notes on Bologna sausages, "*jambon de Westphalie*," partridge pye, &c. &c. That highly seasoned dish, a mock pig, will introduce an inquiry into the antiquity of sucking-pigs, with the whole

law of tithes : Esau's sale of his estate for a mess of pottage typical of modern Amphitryonism ; Lucullus's hall of Apollo ; Apicius, Sir W. C—t—s, &c. &c. ; of speaking in season and out of season ; of seizin and livery, with notices of the lives of John Doe and Richard Roe.

(7) DAY.—Distinction between an astronomical and natural day ; rent-day, pay-day, and "*le quart d'heur de Rabelais ;*" the day of judgment ; on wedding and birth-days, and the different modes of keeping them, and on Burns' "Allhallow Eve ;" on daybooks and ledgers ; on lack-a-day, well-a-day, and on "Daylight," a term in symposiacs. Michael Angelo's "Day" and "Night" in the *Chiesa di San Lorenzo* in Florence ; on Day and Martin's blacking, and the Dey of Algiers ; Beaumarchais' Follies of a Day, or "La Folle journée ;" Mr. Day and "Sandford and Merton ;" a fair day and a "day after the fair ;" meteorological remarks on the weather ; on daily journals with distinctive characters, and *(obiter)* of the weekly press ; Examiner and John Bull ; Saxons did not reckon by days, and why ? Daisy, or day's eye, (the *Bellis perennis* of Linnæus,) not to be confounded with dandelion ; Burns' beautiful ode on it ; on turning night into day, and on settling-days at the Stock Exchange ; on lame ducks ; on saints' days, days of yore, and the "golden days of good Queen Bess." On night ; poetical descriptions ; *Gherardo da Notte ;* of midnight, and (incidentally) of ghosts and witches, with true histories ; Hogarth's "Night ;" Mr. Knight's peas ; his improver engravings ; of the Knights Templars, of Knight the actor, and of Peg Nicholson's Knights ; of Moore's Almanack, Poor Robin, the Zodiac of Tentyra, and of Bullock's Museum.

Such, Mr. Editor, is a brief outline of my first three volumes, embracing, as you will perceive, the first two lines of the fragment. These I propose to publish, *statim*, as a sample of the whole, with title-pages, indexes, dedication, laudatory verses, and testimonies of authors ; a treatise on the art of criticism, engraved portraits of the three children, ichnography of the icepool, and a facsimile of each of the young gentlemen's hand-writing, taken from an old slate found in a neglected corner of the Rev. Timothy Twig-their-bottom's far-famed "seminary :" likewise the original music of the song, supposed to be either by Birde, or by Locke, the composer of the music of Macbeth ; engraved specimens of the title-pages of various editions, and conjectural emendations of doubtful passages.

If this first specimen meet with the desired success, the rest will be immediately forthcoming, as I have only to search the Vatican and Bodleian libraries, and the Bibliothèque du Roi at Paris, to complete the work.

Your making this prospectus known through the medium of your invaluable Miscellany will much oblige

Your obedient and very humble Servant,

JULIUS CÆSAR SCALIGER GRUB, M.A. & F.R.S.

## ON MUSIC.

**No. 4.**—*With reference to the principles of the Beautiful in that Art.*

THESE guides* we intend to follow faithfully and strictly in our remarks on the fourth and last point to be considered in vocal composition, viz. *verbal expression.* Under character we understood the general nature and feeling which pervades a poem *in toto.* Verbal expression regards the appropriate musical utterance of every successive sentence in a poetical text. It might aptly be termed musical diction ; its functions are quite similar to those of declamation in oratory.

Correctness of verbal expression is a most important requisite in vocal composition ; and yet, strange to tell, it is more or less neglected by the greater part of composers, nay it is scarcely dreamed of by many. Hundreds are quite satisfied if they have devised an air of agreeable melody and harmony, tolerably corresponding with the *metre* of the text. The words are held so cheap that some vocal composers, rather than lose the momentary inspiration of a *motivo,* are in the habit of storing them up ready made against any poetry that subsequent chance may throw into their way. No wonder, then, that the fit often should resemble that of a Monmouth-street suit. In this manner the musical annals of England point out a whole, and indeed a favourite opera, composed about twenty years ago, the greater part of the music of which was ready made before the words were thought of.

Some of these latitudinarian vocalists may ask, perchance,—What does it matter whether

"Darest thou thus upbraid a lover ?"

be set one way or another, so that the musical phrase run smooth and tasteful ? and we may be called upon to prove altogether that there exist any laws for verbal expression, and that those laws rest upon solid and not imaginary grounds.

We accept the challenge ! There does exist a law, *one* law only ; it is in few words :

"Sing as thou speakest !"

All the varied and manifold inflexions of the voice employed by a good speaker, its alternate ascent and descent, its emphases, its louder intonations, and softer under-tones, not only lie within the reach of Music, but derive additional and higher charms from that art.

A text, which is to be set to music, ought, therefore, first of all to be rehearsed with appropriate and correct enunciation and declamation ; the composer ought to watch scrupulously the alternate rising and falling of the voice, and especially to mark those words which require peculiar stress of elocution. All these peculiarities his melody ought to imitate as much as possible. But in what manner is this imitation to be effected ?

Upon ascent and descent we need not waste words. They are produced in Music precisely as in common parlance, subject, however, to the general laws of melody and musical metre. The near affinity between declamation and Music is illustrated by the well-known story of the Roman orator, who placed a slave with a flute behind the rostrum, in order to be guided by musical aid in the modulation of his voice. But

---

* Nature and an attentive observation of mankind.

how are we to impart, musically, peculiar stress and emphasis to a word? This may be effected in three different ways. 1st. By assigning to the emphatic words comparatively higher notes. 2dly. By throwing the emphatic syllable into the accented part of the bar (although this expedient applies as much and more to the metre of the text). And 3dly. By increased loudness *(forte)*.

All these expedients are, as they should be, merely direct imitations of nature. By way of illustrating the first, and most essential and legitimate of these three resources, let us recur to the above line, "Darest thou thus upbraid a lover?" It is susceptible of various modes of declamation, all equally proper, according to the sense which the speaker may intend to convey. Of this more presently. But suppose, for example, we wished to read it

Darest thou thus upbraid a lover?

Here we readily perceive, that "thus" is intonated comparatively high. The line, in this sense, might therefore appropriately be melodized as follows—

Darest thou thus upbraid a    lover?

But if it were wished to throw the emphasis upon the first word, viz.

Darest thou thus, &c.?

the following musical phrase would suggest itself—

Darest thou thus up - braid a    lover?

Were the declamation this—

Darest thou thus upbraid a lover?

Darest thou thus upbraid a    lover?

Without multiplying examples, it is obvious that this single line is susceptible of as many distinct shades of signification as it has words. Upon each of the five words stress may be laid in the declamation, according to the implied meaning; and just so may each of the five words receive a high and emphatic note in five different melodies.

A similar train of reflection will suggest the propriety of setting the Music to sentences of interrogation in *ascent;* because in asking questions we generally modulate the voice from grave to acute. The Italian, indeed, has no other mode of rendering a phrase interrogatory.

" He has finished the work," and " Has he finished the work ?" is expressed by the same words, " *Ha finito l'opera*," with this difference, that in the question the voice ascends strongly.

Will you come to the bower ?

T. Moore.

Know'st thou the land ?

Beethoven.

Since in a question the phrase terminates, as it were, in an unfinished, suspensive manner, it is, moreover, desirable, generally speaking, that the melody, independently of its ascending, should not conclude the question with a tonic cadence, which breathes too much repose.

The great use of *piano* and *forte, crescendo, diminuendo, &c.* in assisting verbal expression must be self-evident ; the employment of these resources being, like those above-mentioned, absolutely borrowed from the ordinary rules of declamation, although, without any reference to those rules, certain alternations of loud and subdued sounds tend of themselves to produce variety, and, like the due dispensation of light and shade in a painting, to throw, as it were, a chiaroscuro over the harmonic picture, so pleasing at all times, that in instrumental pieces, the composer not unfrequently puts down his *f*'s and *p*'s quite arbitrarily, merely to effect variety. You might often exchange the *p*'s for the *f*'s, and *vice versa*, without much detriment. Not so in vocal compositions. Here the *forte* is appropriately employed for spirited determined sentences and words of vigour ; the *piano* or the *sottovoce* for soft and mild expressions, the *crescendo* for cases of rhetorical climax, the *calando, diminuendo, morendo, &c.* for decreasing strength, expiring accents of love, grief, &c. All this is so natural, that we deem it quite unnecessary to add quotations from classic works to illustrate what must be obvious to every one. If the reader will open, at random, any opera of Mozart, he is sure to meet with ample instances of the judicious use of the *piano* and *forte*. In Cimarosa and Rossini, he will likewise find abundant elucidation.

Even of subdued murmurs and mutterings, numerous examples may be found. An apt instance occurs in Cimarosa's duet (Matrimonio Segreto) between the old man and the lover, when the latter offers a great sum to be permitted to marry the younger instead of the elder sister. The father pauses, reflects, and then mutters to himself, " Qui risparmio del bell' oro, e si salva anche il decoro*."—All *piano* upon one single note. A similar instance presents itself in the beautiful

---

* Here I save my gold and credit.

terzett, "Ah soccorso, son' ferito" (Don Giovanni) where Leporello in an under-tone, mutters out his comment and horror at the murder of the old Commendatore, just perpetrated by the nefarious libertine, his master.

Some of our readers will be surprised, when we state that the employment of the *piano* and *forte,* and of the different gradations of loudness within or beyond these, is, comparatively speaking, of modern invention. In the compositions of about a hundred years ago, we seek in vain for the marks *p* or *f* or for any other directions regarding the strength of the sounds. In fact, at that time every thing was played with equal force, or, at most, the little musical colouring, which then appeared desirable or practicable, was entirely left to the discretion of the performer. It would be difficult to conceive how such a simple and yet powerful means of producing effect, and aiding expression, should not have suggested itself at an earlier period, if the performance of *mediocre* players, or of amateurs of fifty years practice, did not occasionally afford practical proof of the possibility of such neglect. The celebrated Jomelli was the first who began to imagine and prescribe various tints of musical colouring, and to bring them into some sort of method. Since his time, however, this branch of executive Music has been so much enlarged and improved, that it is at this time scarcely possible to conceive any shade of expression, which does not form part of our musical terminology. There is still a certain vagueness in the usual directions as to the positive degree of force intended, many of the terms being absolutely relative ; but we should not be surprised to see this uncertainty brought, in time, under mathematical controul, by the invention of a musical Phonometer, to indicate the precise strength of sound, in the same manner as the Metronome fixes the precise duration of musical time.

Upon the foregoing subject of musical emphasis we might fill many pages with a variety of curious and interesting remarks, were it not that our limits and immediate object compel us to content ourselves with touching slightly and briefly upon matters, which a professional treatise alone could be expected to expand and develope.

But before we conclude our remarks upon verbal expression, we would wish to add a few words concerning its abuse in Music. This abuse is often encountered in compositions adapted to " depictive" poetry, describing physical phenomena, peculiar sounds, motions, &c. such as thunder, lightning, the rolling of waves, the howlings of the wind, the babbling of brooks, rustling of leaves, the roaring of wild beasts, warbling of birds, the crawling of serpents, the galloping of steeds, &c. Of all these, and innumerable other natural appearances, composers have attempted direct imitations, the vouchers for which we could quote without difficulty.

The question, whether such imitations are the legitimate province of the composer, whether they are accordant with the principles of the beautiful, is a delicate and difficult one. If we consult our own feelings, we should candidly say, that some of these attempts at the musical picturesque have afforded us considerable pleasure, while others, and by far the greater part, appeared to us trifling conceits full of quaintness and littleness.

Among the favourable specimens we would place foremost, the

accompaniments expressive of the placid undulation of the sea, in the beautiful terzett, "Soave sia il vento" (Così fan' tutte)—the beating of the oars preceding the first appearance of Selim, in Il Turco in Italia—a similar approach of the skiff, in La Donna del Lago—the approach of the Jew pedlar, in La Gazza Ladra—and some few other cases of the like description.

On the other hand, we derived no gratification from several imitations of the chirping of birds in some English songs, from the numerous and varied attempts at the picturesque of all sorts in Haydn's Creation, in which all manner of sounds and things are musically pencilled out, not excepting chaos and primitive darkness itself.

We are far from the presumption of forming from our individual likings and dislikes a standard of the Beautiful in this matter : our opinion, however, must necessarily be founded on these. This opinion we give candidly and unpretendingly, leaving it to others to judge whether it coincides with their own observations and feelings.

It seems to us, in the first place, that imitations of this kind ought to be used with a very sparing hand. If they present themselves once or twice in a whole opera, or in any evening's performance, it is quite enough. We consider them altogether as mechanical expedients, forming licences in the art. Hence, if they are imitations ever so apt, and in themselves unobjectionable, their frequent recurrence is likely to have a detrimental effect. They are, after all, but fanciful attempts at approximation, of doubtful comprehension, and calculated to divert the mind from the more direct and legitimate aims of the art. We conceive, in the next place, that the more insignificant the object of the imitation is, the more trifling the result will be, and the less ought it to be attempted. Little minds will generally be found to resort to the picturesque in Music more freely, and it is little minds that more particularly find entertainment in listening to it, because it is more tangible to a narrow intellect, than the nobler sublimities of the art. They are the same people that will value a picture, not for its composition, grouping, or the expression in the countenance, but on account of the charming fidelity in the imitation of the Brussels lace, the truth in the representation of a china basin, or a copper fish-kettle. A purely imitative piece of Music, therefore, would seem to stand in the same relation to a noble and classic composition, as a Dutch painting of grapes, carrots, and onions, to a Madonna and Child of Raphael.

It is on these grounds, probably, that musical imitations are less objectionable in humorous compositions. When we have a mind to be ludicrous, we do not stick at trifles. In this manner we have seen the musical picturesque successfully applied to imitate sneezing and other strange sounds; and the genius of the sublime Beethoven (*quandoque dormitans*) has with consummate art typified, not only the parabolic 'leaps of a frisky flea, but even the ultimate doom usually inflicted on that offending race.

LONDON LYRICS.

*Time and Love.*

An artist painted Time and Love :
Time with two pinions spread above,
   And Love without a feather :
Sir Harry patronized the plan,
And soon Sir Hal and Lady Anne
   In wedlock came together.

Copies of each the dame bespoke :
The artist, ere he drew a stroke,
   Reversed his old opinions,
And straightway to the fair one brings
Time in his turn devoid of wings,
   And Cupid with two pinions.

" What blunder 's this ?" the lady cries.
" No blunder, Madam," he replies,
   " I hope I'm not so stupid.
Each has his pinions, in his day,
Time, before marriage, flies away,
   And, after marriage, Cupid."

---

*Surnames.*

Men once were surnamed from their shape or estate,
   (You all may from History worm it)
There was Lewis the Bulky, and Henry the Great,
   John Lackland, and Peter the Hermit.
But now, when the door-plates of Misters and Dames
   Are read, each so constantly varies
From the owner's trade, figure, and calling, Surnames
   Seem given by the rule of contraries.

Mr. Box, though provoked, never doubles his fist,
   Mr. Burns in his grate has no fuel,
Mr. Playfair won't catch me at hazard or whist,
   Mr. Coward was wing'd in a duel.
Mr. Wise is a dunce, Mr. King is a Whig,
   Mr. Coffin's uncommonly sprightly,
And huge Mr. Little broke down in a gig
   While driving fat Mrs. Golightly.

Mrs Drinkwater 's apt to indulge in a dram,
   Mrs. Angel 's an absolute fury,
And meek Mr. Lyon let fierce Mr. Lamb
   Tweak his nose in the lobby of Drury.
At Bath, where the feeble go more than the stout,
   (A conduct well worthy of Nero)
Over poor Mr. Lightfoot, confined with the gout,
   Mr. Heaviside danced a Bolero.

Miss Joy, wretched maid, when she chose Mr. Love,
   Found nothing but sorrow await her :
She now holds in wedlock, as true as a dove,
   That fondest of mates, Mr. Hayter.
Mr. Oldcastle dwells in a modern-built hut,
   Miss Sage is of madcaps the archest ;
Of all the queer bachelors Cupid e'er cut
   Old Mr. Younghusband 's the starchest.

Mr. Child, in a passion, knock'd down Mr. Rock,
    Mr. Stone like an aspen-leaf shivers,
Miss Poole used to dance, but she stands like a stock,
    Ever since she became Mrs. Rivers.
Mr. Swift hobbles onward, no mortal knows how,
    He moves as though cords had entwined him,
Mr. Metcalfe ran off, upon meeting a cow,
    With pale Mr. Turnbull behind him.

Mr. Barker's as mute as a fish in the sea,
    Mr. Miles never moves on a journey,
Mr. Gotobed sits up till half-after-three,
    Mr. Makepiece was bred an attorney.
Mr. Gardener can't tell a flower from a root,
    Mr. Wilde with timidity draws back.
Mr. Ryder performs all his journeys on foot,
    Mr. Foote all his journeys on horseback.

Mr. Penny, whose father was rolling in wealth,
    Kick'd down all the fortune his dad won,
Large Mr. Le Fever's the picture of health,
    Mr. Goodenough is but a bad one.
Mr. Cruickshank stept into three thousand a year,
    By shewing his leg to an heiress :—
Now I hope you'll acknowledge I've made it quite clear
    Surnames ever go by Contraries.

---

### ROUGE ET NOIR.

——— "Could I forget
What I have been, I might the better bear
What I am destined to. I'm not the first
That have been wretched—but to think how much
I have been happier !"———     SOUTHERN.

NEVER shall I forget that accursed 27th of September : it is burnt in upon the tablet of my memory ; graven in letters of blood upon my heart. I look back to it with a strangely compounded feeling of horror and delight ; of horror at the black series of wretched days and sleepless nights of which it was the fatal precursor ; of delight at that previous career of tranquillity and self-respect which it was destined to terminate—alas, for ever !

On that day I had been about a fortnight in Paris, and in passing through the garden of the Palais Royal had stopped to admire the beautiful *jet-d'eau* in its centre, on which the sun-beams were falling so as to produce a small rainbow, when I was accosted by my old friend Major E——, of the Fusileers. After the first surprises and salutations, as he found that the business of procuring apartments and settling my family had prevented my seeing many of the Parisian *lions*, he offered himself as my Cicerone, proposing that we should begin by making the circuit of the building that surrounded us. With its history and the remarkable events of which it had been the scene I was already conversant ; but of its detail and appropriation which, as he assured me, constituted its sole interest in the eyes of the Parisians, I was completely ignorant.

After taking a cursory view of most of the sights above ground in this multifarious pile, I was conducted to some of its subterraneous wonders,—to the Café du Sauvage, where a man is hired for six francs a night to personate that character, by beating a great drum with all the grinning, ranting, and raving of a madman;—to the Café des Aveugles, whose numerous orchestra is entirely composed of blind men and women;—and to the Café des Variétés, whose small theatre, as well as its saloons and labyrinths, are haunted by a set of Sirens not less dangerous than the nymphs who assailed Ulysses. Emerging from these haunts, we found that a heavy shower was falling; and while we paraded once more the stone gallery, my friend suddenly exclaimed, as his eye fell upon the numbers of the houses—" one hundred and fifty-four!—positively we were going away without visiting one of the ——" gaming-houses was the meaning of the term he employed, though he expressed it by a word that the fashionable preacher never mentioned to " ears polite."—" I have never yet entered," said I, " a Pandæmonium of this sort, and I never will:—I refrain from it upon principle;—' Principiis obsta;' I am of Dr. Johnson's temperament, I can practise abstinence, but not temperance; and every body knows that prevention is better than cure."—" Do you remember," replied E——, " what the same Dr. Johnson said to Boswell—' My dear Sir, clear your mind of cant;' I do not ask you to play; but you must have often read, when you were a good little boy, that ' Vice to be hated needs but to be seen,' and cannot have forgotten that the Spartans sometimes made their slaves drunk, and shewed them to their children to inculcate sobriety. Love of virtue is best secured by a hatred of its opposite: to hate it you must see it; besides, a man of the world should see every thing."—" But it is so disreputable," I rejoined.—" How completely John-Bullish!" exclaimed E——. " Disreputable! why I am going to take you to an establishment recognised, regulated, and taxed by the Government, the upholders of religion and social order, who annually derive six millions of francs from this source of revenue; and as to the company, I promise you that you shall encounter men of the first respectability, of all sects and parties, for in France every one gambles at these salons,—except the devotees, and they play at home."—He took my arm, and I walked upstairs with him, merely ejaculating as we reached the door—"Mind, I don't play."

Entering an ante-room, we were received by two or three servants, who took our sticks and hats, for which we received tickets, and by the number suspended around I perceived that there was a tolerably numerous attendance within. *Roulette* was the game to which the first chamber was dedicated. In the middle of a long green table was a circular excavation, resembling a large gilt basin, in whose centre was a rotatory apparatus turning an ivory ball in a groove, which, after sundry gyrations, descended to the bottom of the basin where there was a round of little numbered compartments or pigeon-holes, into one of which it finally settled, when the number was proclaimed aloud. Beside this apparatus there was painted on the green baize a table of various successive numbers, with divisions for odd and even, &c. on which the players deposited their various stakes. He who was in the compartment of the proclaimed number was a winner, and if he had singled out that individual one, which of course was of very rare occurrence, his deposit was doubled I know not how many times. The odd or even declared their own fate: they were lost or doubled. This altar of chance had but few votaries, and merely stopping a moment to admire the handsome decorations of the room we passed on into the next.

This, whispered my companion, for there was a dead silence in the apartment, although the long table was entirely surrounded by people playing,—this is only the silver room; you may deposit here as low as a five franc piece: let us pass on to the next, where none play but those who will risk bank-notes or gold. Casting a passing glance at these comparatively humble gamesters, who were, however, all too deeply absorbed to move their eyes from the cards, I followed my conductor into the sanctuary of the gilded Mammon.

Here was a Rouge et Noir table, exactly like the one I had just quitted. In its centre was a profuse display of gold in bowls and rouleaus, with thick piles of bank notes, on either side of which sat a partner of the bank and an assistant, the dragon guards of this Hesperian fruit. An oblong square, painted on each end of the green table, exhibited three divisions, one for Rouge, another for Noir, and the centre was for the stakes of those who speculated upon the colour of the first and last card, with other ramifications of the art which it would be tedious to describe. Not one of the chairs around the table was unoccupied, and I observed that each banker and assistant was provided with a *rateau*, or rake, somewhat resembling a garden hoe, several of which were also dispersed about, that the respective winners might withdraw the gold without the objectionable intervention of fingers. When the stakes are all deposited, the dealer, one of the bankers in the centre, cries out—" Le jeu est fait," after which nothing can be added or withdrawn; and then taking a packet of cards from a basket full before him, he proceeds to deal. Thirty-one is the number of the game: the colour of the first card determines whether the first row be black or red : the dealer turns up till the numbers on the cards exceed thirty-one, when he lays down a second row in the same manner, and whichever is nearest to that amount is the winning row. If both come to the same, he cries " Après," and recommences with fresh cards, but if each division should turn up *thirty-one*, the bank takes half of the whole money deposited, as a forfeit from the players. In this consists their certain profit, which has been estimated at ten per cent. upon the total stakes. If the red loses, the banker on that side rakes all the deposits into his treasury; if it wins, he throws down the number of Napoleons or notes necessary to cover the lodgments made by the players, each one of whom rakes off his prize, or leaves it for a fresh venture. E—— explained to me the functions of the different members of the establishment—the Inspector, the Croupier, the Tailleur, the Messieurs de la chambre, &c. and also the meaning of the ruled card and pins which every one held before him, consulting it with the greatest intenseness, and occasionally calling to the people in attendance for a fresh supply. This horoscope was divided by perpendicular lines into columns, headed with an alternate R. and N. for Rouge and Noir, and the pin is employed to perforate the card as each colour wins, as a groundwork for establishing some calculation in that elaborate delusion termed the doctrine of Chances. Some, having several of these records before them, closely pierced all over, were summing up the results upon paper, as if determined to play a game of chance without leaving any thing to hazard; and none seemed willing to adventure without having some species of sanction from these Sibylline leaves.

An involuntary sickness and loathing of heart came over me as I contemplated this scene, and observed the sofas in an adjoining room, which the Parisians, who turn every thing into a joke, have christened " the hospital for the wounded." There, thought I to myself, many a wretch has thrown himself down in anguish and despair of soul, cursing himself and the world with fearful imprecations, or blaspheming in that silent bitterness of spirit which is more terrific than words. I contrasted the gaudy decorations and panelled mirrors that surrounded me with the smoky and blackened ceiling, sad evidence of the nocturnal lamps lighted up at the shrine of this Baal, and of the unhallowed worship prosecuted through the livelong night. Turning to the window, I beheld the sun shining from the bright blue sky, the rain was over, the birds were singing in the trees, and the leaves fluttering in the wind; the external gaiety giving the character of an appalling antithesis to the painful silence, immovable attitudes, and spell-bound looks of the care-worn figures within. One man, a German, was contending against a run of ill-luck with a dogged obstinacy that was obviously making deep inroads upon his purse and his peace; for though his face was invisible from being bent over his perforated card, the drops of perspiration standing upon his forehead betrayed the inward agitation. All the losers were struggling to suppress emotions which still revealed themselves by the working of some disobedient muscle, the compression of the lips, the sardonic grin, or the glaring wrath of the eye; while the winners belied their assumed indifference by flushed cheeks and an expression of anxious triumph. Two or three forlorn operators, who had been *cleaned out*, as the phrase is, and condemned to idleness, were eyeing their more fortunate neighbours with a leer of malignant envy; while the bankers and their assistants, in the certainty of their profitable trade, exhibited a calm and watchful cunning, though their features, pale and sodden, betrayed the effect of confinement, heated rooms, and midnight vigils. E—— informed me that the frequenters of these houses were authorized to call for refreshments of any description, but no one availed himself of the privilege; the " auri sacra fames," the pervading appetite of the place, had swallowed up every other. The very thought revolted me. What! eat and drink in this arena of the hateful passions; in this fatal room, from which many a suicide has rushed out to grasp the self-destroying pistol, or plunge into the darkness of the wave! in this room, which is denounced to heaven by the widow's tears and the orphan's maledictions! Revolving these thoughts in my mind, I surveyed once more the faces before me, and could not help exclaiming— What a hideous study of human nature!

"As we have employed so much time," said E——, "in taking the latitude, or rather the longitude of these various phizzes, we shall be expected to venture something: I will throw down a Napoleon, as a sop to Cerberus, and will then convoy you home."—" Nay," replied I, " it was for my instruction we came hither; the lesson I have received is well worth the money, so put down this piece of gold, and let us begone." —" Let us at least wait till we have lost it," he resumed; " and in the mean time we will take our places at the table." I felt that I blushed as I sat down, and was about to deposit my offering hap hazard, when my companion stopped my hand, and, borrowing a perforated card, bade me remark, that the red and black had zig-zagged, or won alternately for fourteen times; and that there had subsequently been a long run upon the black, which would now probably cross over to the other colour; from all which premises he deduced that I should venture upon the red: which I accordingly did. Sir Balaam's devil who " now tempts by making rich, not making poor," was, I verily believe, hovering over my devoted head at that instant; my deposit was doubled, and I was preparing to decamp with my two Naps, when my adviser insisted upon my not balking my luck, as there would probably be a run upon the red, and I suffered my stake to remain, and go on doubling until I had won ten or twelve times in succession. "Now," cried E——, "I should advise you to pocket the affront, and be satisfied." Adopting his counsel, I could hardly believe his assertion, or my own eyes, when he handed me over bank-notes to the amount of twenty thousand francs, observing that I had made a tolerably successful *debût* for a beginner.

Returning home in some perturbation and astonishment of mind, I resolved to prepare a little surprise for my wife; and spreading the bank notes upon the table with as much display as possible, I told her, upon her entering the room, how I had won them; and enquiring whether Aladdin with his wonderful lamp could have spent two or three hours more profitably, I stated my intention of appropriating a portion of it to her use in the purchase of a handsome birthday present. In a moment the blood rushed to her face, and as quickly receded, leaving it of an ashy paleness, when she spurned the notes from her, exclaiming with a solemn terror—"I would as soon touch the forty pieces of silver for which Judas betrayed his master." Her penetrating head instantly saw the danger to which I had exposed myself, and her fond heart as quickly gave the alarm to her feelings; but in a few seconds she threw her arms around me, and ejaculated as the tears ran down her cheek—"Forgive me, my dear Charles, pardon my vehemence, my ingratitude; I *have* a present to ask, a boon to implore—promise that you will grant it me."—"Most willingly," I rejoined, "if it be in my power."—"Give me then your pledge, never to play again." —"Cheerfully," continued I, for I had already formed that resolution. She kissed me with many affectionate thanks, adding that I had made her completely happy. I believe it, for at that moment I felt so myself.

Many men who are candid and upright in arguing with others, are the most faithless and jesuitical of casuists in chopping logic with themselves. Let no one trust his head in a contest with the heart; the former, suppressing or perverting whatever is disagreeable to the latter, will assume a demure and sincere conviction, while it has all along been playing booty, and furnishing weapons to its adversary. The will must be honest if we wish the judgment to be so. A tormenting itch for following up my good luck, as I termed it, set me upon devising excuses for violating my pledge to my wife, and no shuffling or quibbling was too contemptible for my purpose. I had promised never to play again—" *at that house*," or if I had not actually said so, I meant to say so: there could be no forfeiture of my word, therefore, if I went to another. Miserable sophistry! yet, wretched as it was, it satisfied my conscience for the moment,—so easily is a weak man deluded into criminal indulgence. Fortified with such valid arguments, I made my *debût* at the Salon des Etrangers, and after a two hours sitting, had the singular good luck to return home a winner of nearly as much as I had gained on the first day. Success for once made me moderate; in the humility of my prosperous play, I resolved only to continue till I had won ten thousand pounds, when I would communicate my adventures to my wife with a solemn abjuration of the pursuit in future; and as I considered myself in possession of the certain secret of winning whatever I pleased, I took credit to myself for my extreme moderation. From Frascati, the scene of my third attempt, by a lucky, or rather unlucky fatality, which my subsequent experience only renders the more wonderful, I retired with a sum exceeding the whole of my previous profits, when, like the tiger who is rendered insatiate by the taste of blood, I instantly became ravenous for larger riches; and already repenting the paltry limitation of the day before, determined on proceeding until I had doubled its amount. Another day's luck, and even this would have been spurned, for neither Johnson's Sir Epicure Mammon, nor Massinger's Luke, nor Pope's Sir Balaam, underwent a more rapid developement of the latent devils of ambition. Indistinct visions of grandeur floated before my eyes; my senses already seemed to be steeped in a vague magnificence; and after hesitating, in a sort of waking dream, between Wanstead House and Fonthill, one of which I held to be too near, and the other too distant from London, I dwelt complacently on the idea of building a mansion at some intermediate station, which should surpass the splendour of both. Sleep presenting to me the same images through a magnifying glass, I went forth next morning to the accomplishment of my destiny with an exaltation of mind little short of delirium.

Weak and wicked reveries!—a single turn of Fortune's wheel reduced me, not to reason, but to an opposite extreme of mortification and despondence. A run of ill-luck swept away in one hour more than half my gains, and unfortunately losing my temper still faster than my money, I kept doubling my stakes in the blindness of my rage, and quitted the table at night, not only lightened of all my suddenly acquired wealth, but loser of a considerable sum besides. I could now judge by experience of the bitterness of soul that I had lately inflicted upon those who had lost what I had won, and inwardly cursed the pursuit whose gratifications could only spring from the miseries of others; but so far from abandoning this inevitable see-saw of wretchedness, I felt as if I had been defrauded of my just property, and burnt with the desire of taking my revenge. The heart-sickening detail of my infirmity, my reverses, and my misery, need not be followed up. Suffice it to say, that a passion, a fury, an actual phrenzy of play absorbed every faculty of my soul; mine was worse than a Promethean fate; I was gnawed and devoured by an inward fire which nothing could allay. Alas! not even poverty and the want of materials could quench it. In my career of prosperity, I felt not the fraud I was practising upon my wife, for I meant to make my peace with ten or twenty thousand pounds in my hand, and a sincere renunciation of gaming in my heart; but now that I was bringing ruin upon and my children, the sense of my falsehood and treachery embittering the anguish of my losses, plunged me into an unutterable re. morse and agony of soul. Still I wanted courage to make the fatal revelation, and at last only imparted it to her in the cowardice of impending disgrace.

Madame Deshoulières says very truly, that gamesters begin by being dupes and end by being knaves; and I am about to confirm it by an avowal to which nothing should have impelled me but the hope of deterring others by an exposure of my own delinquency. A female relation had remitted me seven hundred pounds to purchase into the French funds, with which sum in my pocket I unfortunately called at the Salon des Etrangers in my way to the stock-broker's, and my evil genius suggesting to me that there was a glorious opportunity of recovering my heavy losses, I snatched the notes from my pocket, threw them on the table just before the dealer began——and lost! Stunned by the blow, I went home in a state of calm despair, communicated the whole to my wife in as few words as possible, and ended by declaring that she was a beggar, and her husband disgraced for ever. " Not yet, my dear Charles," replied the generous woman, her eyes beaming with an affectionate forgiveness,—" not yet; we may still exclaim with the French King after the battle of Pavia, we have lost every thing but our honour ;—and, while we retain *that*, our losses are but as a grain of sand. We may be depressed by fortune, but we can only be disgraced by ourselves. As to this seven hundred pounds —take my jewels—they will sell for more than is required ; and if our present misfortunes induce you to fly from Paris, and abandon this fatal pursuit, they will assuredly become the greatest blessings of our life."

No reproach ever passed her lips, or lingered in her eye; nor did I fail to observe the delicacy which, mingling up her own fate with mine, strove to soothe my feelings, by disguising my individual guilt under the cloak of a joint misfortune. Noble-minded woman! Mezentius himself could not have devised a more cruel fate than to tie thee to a soul so dead to shame, and so defunct in gratitude as mine !

Will not the reader lothe and detest me, even worse than I do myself, when I inform him, that in return for all this magnanimity I had the detestable baseness to linger in Paris, to haunt the gaming-table, to venture the wretched drainings of my purse in the *silver* room, to become an habitual borrower of paltry sums under pledges of repayment which I knew I had not the means of redeeming, and to submit tamely to the indignity of palpable cuts from my acquaintance in the public streets? From frequently encountering at the salons, I had formed a slight friendship with Lord T——, Lord F——, Sir G—— W——, Colonel T——, and particularly with poor S——t, before he had consummated the ruin of his fine fortune, and debilitated his frame by paralysis brought on by anxiety; and I was upon terms of intimacy with others of my countrymen, who with various success, but much more ample means than myself, were making offerings to the dæmon of *Rouge et Noir.* Should this brief memoir fall beneath the eye of any of my quondam friends, they may not impossibly derive benefit from its perusal : at all events they may be pleased to know that I have not forgotten their kindnesses. I am aware that I abused their assistance, and wore out their patience; but I never anticipated the horror to which the exhaustion of my own means, and the inability to extort more from others, would reduce me. The anguish of my losses, the misery of my degradation, the agony of mind with which I reflected upon my impoverished wife and family, were nothing, absolutely nothing, compared to the racking torment of being compelled to refrain from gambling. It sounds incredible, but it is strictly true. To sit at the table with empty pockets and see others playing, was absolutely insupportable. I envied even the heaviest losers—could I have found an antagonist, I would have gambled for an eye, an arm, a leg, for life itself. A thousand devils seemed to be gnawing at my heart—I believe I was mad—I even hope I was.

Yes; I have tasked myself to detail my moral degradation and utter prostration of character; with a fidelity worthy of Rousseau himself, and I feel it a duty not to shrink from my complete exposure. After a night passed in the state of mind I have been describing, in one of those haunts which I was justly entitled to denominate a Hell, I wandered out at daybreak towards the Pont de Jena, as if I could cool my parched lips and burning brain by the heavy shower that was then falling. As the dripping rustics passed me on their market-horses, singing and whistling, their happiness, seeming to be a mockery of my wretchedness, filled me with a malignant rage. By the time I had reached the bridge, the rain had ceased, the rising sun, glancing upon the river threw a bloom over the woods in the direction of Sèvres and St. Cloud, and the birds were piping in the air. Ever a passionate admirer of Nature, her charms stole me for a moment from myself, but presently my thoughts reverting from the heaven without to the hell within, I gnashed my teeth, and fell back into a double bitterness and despair of soul.

I have always been a believer in sudden and irresistible impulses; an idea which will not appear ridiculous to those who are conversant with the records of crime. A portrait of Sarah Malcolm the murderess, which I had seen many years ago in the possession of Lord Mulgrave, leading me to the perusal of her trial and execution in the Newgate Calendar, induced me to give perfect credit to the averment, that the idea of the crime came suddenly into her head without the least solicitation, and that she felt driven forward to its accomplishment by some invisible power. Similar declarations from many other offenders offer abundant confirmation of the same fact; and it will be in the recollection of many, that the murderer of Mr. and Mrs. Bonar at Chiselhurst repeatedly declared that he had never dreamt of the enormity ten minutes before its commission, but that the thought suddenly rushed into his mind, and pushed him forward to the bloody deed. Many people cannot look over a precipice without feeling tempted to throw themselves down; I know a most affectionate father who never approaches a window with his infant child without being haunted by solicitations to cast it into the street; and a gentleman of unimpeachable honour, who if he happens, in walking the highway, to see a note-case or handkerchief emerging from a passenger's pocket, is obliged to stop short or cross over the way, so vehemently does he feel impelled to withdraw them. These "toys of desperation," generated in the giddiness of the mind at the bare imagination of any horror, drive it to commit the reality as a relief from the fearful vision, upon the same principle that delinquents voluntarily deliver themselves up to justice, because death itself is less intolerable than the fear of it. Let it not be imagined that I am seeking to screen any of these unhappy men from the consequences of their hallucination; I am merely asserting a singular property of the mind, of which I myself am about to record a frightful confirmation.

Standing on the bridge, and turning away my looks from the landscape in that despair of heart which I have described, my downcast eyes fell upon the waters gliding placidly beneath me. They seemed to invite me to quench the burning fire with which I was consumed; the river whispered to me with a distinct utterance that peace and oblivion were to be found in its Lethean bed:—every muscle of my body was animated by an instant and insuperable impulse; and within half a minute from its first maddening sensation, I had climbed over the parapet, and plunged headlong into the water!—The gushing of waves in my ears, and the rapid flashing of innumerable lights before my eyes, are the last impressions I recollect. Into the circumstances of my preservation I never had the heart to enquire: when consciousness revisited me, I found myself lying upon my own bed with my wife weeping beside me, though she instantly assumed a cheerful look, and told me that I had met with a dreadful accident, having fallen into the river when leaning over to examine some object beneath. That she knows the whole truth I am perfectly convinced, but we scrupulously avoid the subject, by an understood, though unexpressed compact.' It is added in her mind to the long catalogue of my offences, never to be alluded to, and, alas! never to be forgotten. She left my bedside for a moment to return with my children, who rushed up to me with a cry of joy; and as they contended for the first kiss, and enquired my health with glistening eyes, the cruelty, the atrocity of my cowardly attempt struck with a withering remorse upon my heart.—O villain! villain!                                        C—— L——.

---

## SONNET FROM PETRARCH.

*" Nè per sereno cielo, ir vaghe stelle."*

NOT the bright firmament of stars above,
  Nor goodly vessels gliding o'er the main,
  Nor warlike prowess of the knightly train,
Nor wild beasts gaily sporting through the grove,
Nor news of long'd-for joy, nor song of love
  In sweetest numbers, or in loftiest strain,
  Nor by the sparkling fountain and green plain
Singing of gentle ladies praise to move:
Nor these, nor all the joys that earth contains
  Again can reach this heart of mine, that lies
  Buried with her, who to my longing eyes
Was life and light; now wearied with life's chains,
  I call on death again with her to be,
  Whom, better had I never lived to see.

---

## ACTORS AND THEATRICALS.

In England alone actors have occupied somewhat of that consideration in society to which they are entitled. Not that we are by any means a theatrical people, but the dictates of good sober sense have shewn us that there is no reason why the professor of a liberal and ingenious art should be undervalued upon the stale plea of custom. It is here a received rule, to a given extent, that "worth makes the man," or, to be more explicit, that the honourable character and conduct of an individual is more looked to than his profession, provided, indeed, he be not poor, for that is an "unconquerable bar" to social notice. There is feeling and good sense in this discrimination, as far as it goes; it is worthy the better portion of the better class of English society. I say "better portion," because Lord Chesterfield observes that "people of the first quality can be as silly, ill-bred, and worthless, as people of meaner degree;" and there are some of the higher orders of English society, high only in pride and fortune, that have about as correct a notion of the claims of intellect upon them, as an Esquimaux would have of the nature of Newton's Fluxions, were he questioned respecting them. But though actors are held in far more estimation here than in foreign countries, still many have a ridiculous prejudice against the profession, which they should overcome.

This sort of prejudice, though very unreasonable, is of old standing. The ancients, it is well known, held the profession of an actor in disesteem; but there are certain contradictions respecting them which it would be difficult to clear up. Lucian says that a great knowledge of music, poetry, rhetoric, and philosophy, were necessary, to succeed on the stage in his time. Now, this being the case, it is singular that the respect universally paid to persons versed in these arts should not have operated in favour of those so accomplished in them. We know very little of the ancient stage, but what we do know leads us to believe that tragedy was exhibited on it more in the way of declamation than as an imitation of nature. A large portion of the ancient stage entertainments consisted of mimicry and antics, the professors of which had, perhaps, no great claim to respect, and the comedy of the ancients was of a low kind. They used masques in their stage performances, which must have effectually concealed the different changes of countenance produced by every attempt at expression; and this gives us additional reason to believe that certain regulated gestures and a well-toned voice, with a recitation, rather than acting as we now understand it, were all the ancients valued in a performer. The accounts which have come down to us, however, tend to shew that some actors of good morals and attainments were held in esteem by the highest ranks in Rome, as in the example of Roscius, of whom Cicero speaks so highly. It is therefore probable, that the majority of performers were low, dissolute mimics, and that the censure cast upon the whole corps had its exceptions among the higher classes of tragedians. Modern acting differs from the ancient, in its requiring greater originality, and a certain natural genius, to succeed. The power of representation of the different emotions of the mind, for which we value an actor, was no part of the qualification they deemed necessary for the stage. Their tragedy, with the chorus, could we hear it performed now, would not, it is likely, though we were perfect masters of the language, arouse our feelings more than the simple reading. It was strictly national, and the taste for it must have been acquired by education. It appears to me, that our stage performances are of a much higher order, and the performers also, because they are more universally interesting, and the scene is kept nearer to nature. Poetry should speak a universal language, and the stage should speak it too. Let us suppose the insanity of Orestes exhibited by a performer in a mask, who recites the character with a well-regulated tone and emphasis: it is obvious that he would add but little comparative effect to the poetry of the author. Suppose the same piece performed by Garrick or Kean, their acting would be felt and understood, wherever the language was comprehended, because nature shews the same emotions every where under similar causes of excitement. There is a poetical feeling necessary for a modern actor. He must be imaginative, and have an acquaintance with the deep secrets of the mind, which cannot be taught him by art. The actor of the ancients was, perhaps, more the being of study and artifice. Such we may conjecture, for we can conjecture only, is the difference between the two; and if so, the advantage is certainly on the side of the moderns.

In Catholic countries, actors have always been treated with great contumely. The priests and monks formerly promoted the performance of mysteries and other superstitious representations, because it supported the influence of their doctrines, and tended to rivet more firmly the bonds of mental slavery; but they refused acts of common charity, and even burial rites, to the unhappy performers in return. Such is priestcraft: they who reprobated stage-players on the score of a vicious profession, preached the holiness and infallibility of Popes who committed incest and sealed their crimes with blasphemy,* The latest instance of bigot zeal exerted against the inanimate body of a performer in France, was after the return of the Bourbons in Jan. 1815, when the funeral of Madame Raucourt, on arriving at the burying-ground of Père La Chaise, at Paris, was refused the rite of burial by the minister, who wished to restore, with the temporal, the spiritual customs of old times. The indignant populace, highly to its honour, compelled the priest to do his duty by force; and such was the popular effervescence, that the experiment of a second refusal will hardly be ventured on again in that city.

We may congratulate ourselves on the increase of our stock of "harmless amusement," and the superior excellence of our actors, from the liberal view we now take of the profession. Since Garrick appeared, a theatrical race, fostered by the public, of honourable lives and highly talented, have unfolded to us, better than a thousand commentators could do it, the noble conceptions of our dramatic writers. Theatrical talent has increased with the consideration it has received in society. We are now in a third era of histrionic excellence within fourscore years: the first beginning with Garrick, the second with Kemble, Cooke, and Mrs. Siddons, and the third with Kean, Young, and others. In no era of our stage history has the aggregate of

* For example, Pope Alexander VI. who lived in a state of incest with his sister, and had her painted as a Madonna!

talent on the boards surpassed the present. Of this, Drury-lane is a sufficient proof. An actress like Mrs. Siddons is, perhaps, wanting, and may never be supplied; but from Kean and Young to the most inferior characters, there is, at Drury-lane, power and *matériel* such as none of our theatres have before exhibited at the same moment. The tragedies of Shakspeare, that we have been told would not half fill a house during the rage for the " gorgons, hydras, and chimeras dire," of melodrama, have been played to overflowing benches. Othello and Iago have not cloyed the public taste, which, it now clearly appears, is not so vicious as some blundering managers have been interested in representing it, to cover their own deficiencies.

I confess I love the theatre, for I have received impressions there which no words from human lips have ever produced any where else. I have leaned on the benches, in forgetfulness of all around me but the scene, and, wrapped in a world of ideality, stored up sensations that will, by and by, feed the thoughts of declining years. The tones of the actor's voice blended themselves with the words of the poet so forcibly, that his name has become associated with them, and I can scarcely remember the one without recalling the other. Kemble's unequalled delivery of certain passages when playing Penruddock, his pathos and heart-thrilling tones, softened into mellowness by intervening time, still come over my mind like a romantic music. It may be, therefore, that I am somewhat prejudiced in favour of the profession, but it is clear to me that I have no attachment for it which is not grounded in reason and reflection; and it demands very much more than what is understood in the term " worldly custom," to convince me I am erroneous in my view of the subject. In all professions there are worthy and unworthy members; but the tragedian, who ranks high in public favour, must be a gifted man, and is therefore entitled to respect. If of unimpeachable character, hard indeed is his lot if be be not equal to a shopkeeper or an attorney in estimation—he who must unite judgment with personal and intellectual qualifications—he who must be a student of the works of genius and the expounder of them to the world, whose pursuit calls into exercise the most vigorous faculties of the mind, and is neither mean and pettifogging on the one hand, nor a tame retailing of ledger-accounts and sordid bargaining on the other. The preference bestowed on riches, the meanest but most influential of possessions, must not be suffered to contravene the truth. The actor who instructs and amuses the public, and who stands well in public opinion, is a being far higher in the intellectual scale than the stockjobber with his plum, or the city gripeall who has amassed his million for the future dissipation of his heirs. There is, too, a reason why actors should be duly estimated in society, arising from a claim on our sympathies. They who delight us through life, leave no marks behind of all their toils to please, of their peculiar excellences and the attractions that commanded the applauses of thousands. The poet, the author, the sculptor, dies and leaves unperishable records of his labours; the soldier's achievement is preserved in history;— but the actor consigns no legacy to posterity. His glory is as evanescent as the clap of the multitude, and perishes with himself; he is, therefore, on the score of generosity, entitled to the more consideration when living, in proportion as his lot in this respect is unfelicitous.

In regard to moral worth, I believe we have seen as much of it among the professors of the stage as among an equal number in other walks of life; and there has been this advantage on the side of the most peccable, that their vices have seldom been varnished by hypocrisy. They were for ever in the public gaze, and the smallest speck was magnified in proportion; but it was never their custom to disguise, under the specious veil of canting, any errors into which they had unhappily fallen; and this is of itself almost a redeeming virtue. On the other side, let the conduct of many actors of both sexes that have been public favourites, be scrutinised even by malevolence, and what will be found registered against them? They have in moral worth been equal to other individuals in society that are respected, and their claims on this score have been tacitly allowed, particularly among actresses. Away, then, with what remains of this unworthy prejudice!

Perhaps some grounds for dislike to the profession may have appeared in the tendency of certain pieces brought on the boards, and the passages offensive to good morals which they contain. This is not the fault of the actor, but of the author, censor, and manager. As a whole, the character of our actors is infinitely beyond the morality of our theatre. We owe much to the stage, but it must be allowed that its secondary class of writers have not made it so instructive or moral as they might have done. Some of the lighter pieces which live but for a moment, are the production of authors who write for the galleries, and have nothing in point of reputation to lose. It is not the piece which holds up to admiration certain points of character in a thief or a murderer that will produce an evil effect on society. Public opinion has stamped both the one and the other of these characters with infamy. In spite of what has been said respecting Macheath, for example, it is highly improbable that any one ever became a robber from seeing the character performed. It is holding up to the admiration of the vulgar, unmingled with reprobation, lesser scoundrels whose vices are not held in equal detestation, being offences against good manners rather than breaches of laws universally recognized, that is to be condemned. "Tom and Jerry" is a piece of this class. Had its coarse exhibition of low-lived vices been kept to a picture of vice duly satirized and turned into ridicule, it might have done good. But it is easy to see that where blackguardism and folly are exhibited without due reprobation, the ignorant and vulgar of every rank in life will admire the hero of the tale, when his habits and opinions are in unison with their own, and he is made an object of admiration rather than contempt. Our guardians of the night and police magistrates can bear testimony to this truth. Next to the author, the censor intervenes, who ought, if such an interference should be tolerated at all, to have an eye on the indecencies and immoral tendencies of the works of obscure stage-writers. His notions of morality, however, are generally merged in his politics. He is, in fact, only a political automaton, and it is difficult to say whether he could be any thing else without much increasing the mischief of his office; for who could set bounds to puritanical curtailments and alterations which would be as likely to exceed reasonable limits as to keep within them? Yet while such an office exists, a little more attention to this subject might not be misplaced. Still he is so much the creature of accident, as to office, that he may or may not have grasp of mind enough, little as it requires, to comprehend the true drift of a dramatic piece: he may see it free from sentences of constructive sedition, and think his duty executed. I am astonished how such a play as "The Hypocrite" is tolerated in the present day. In a dramatic view it is unnatural and absurd ; morality it has none. It is forced in every way, and it would be worthy the good sense of the managers of the great theatres to consign it to well-merited oblivion, instead of suffering its disgusting indecencies to flush the cheeks of the better part of their audiences. Its late reappearance was in very bad taste on Mr. Elliston's part. This play was written to satirize Whitfield, who, with his contemporary and friend Wesley, were virtuous, well-meaning, but enthusiastic men, of blameless conduct and irreproachable lives. However erroneous they might be deemed, on points where all can be but matter of opinion, they did infinite good in reforming the morals and softening the brutality of the lower classes, from the colliers of Walsall to the miners of the West. Their labours were, as Lord Chatham would say, more those of a college of fisher-men than of a conclave of bishops or cardinals. Notwithstanding their aberration from the statute faith, they were just and conscientious men. Are such men fit objects of disgusting satire in the present enlightened times ? Ought not the good sound sense of an English audience (the best censor in a free country) to put down that which no excellence of acting can sanction ?

We should wish to see all theatrical reform effected by public taste, rather than by any other mode. How often, after being delighted with the exhibition of a noble tragedy, that has elevated the mind to lofty feeling, and roused to mental activity every latent virtue—how often are we disgusted by an afterpiece calculated to eradicate the good impression the tragedy has produced, indebted to *double entendre* for wit, and to the slang of St. Giles's for phraseology. Now that Drury-lane Theatre is all that can be wished as to elegance of building, accommodation of the audience, and excellence of its company—now that it stands once more the first of our histrionic exhibitions—now that the public fill the house to suffocation on the acting of legitimate tragedy by Kean and Young—it becomes the manager to fix on a firm basis a national standard of taste in his department for our other theatres to imitate. We could wish to see there the selection of tragedy and comedy made from among the best-written and most pure in the language, and a stern rejection of all mawkish trash, under whatever name introduced. The afterpieces should include none but such as have sterling merit in writing, real wit, and a perfect freedom from those indelicacies and jurations resorted to by sterile writers to fill an hiatus or wind up the climax of a stupid sentence. We could wish to see some of our sound old tragedies, and our old genteel comedy, preserved from desuetude. A singleness of object, on the part of a manager possessing freedom of thought, and a bold reliance on common sense rather than on recorded opinion, might effect much good, and complete a theatre that we might justly be proud to array in *all things* against any in a foreign country—a *Théâtre Anglais*, where a pure national literature, excellence of acting, and a due regard to decorum, may save us the trouble of apologizing to strangers for faults which *they* do not tolerate, and give them a clear idea of a drama adhering to the verity of existing things, and carrying to the summit of perfection the effect of the romantic or Shakspearian school, which must finally, in every country, take the uppermost place as the mirror of nature. Let Mr. Elliston think originally in this respect, and complete the good work he has entered upon ; for he has given us a novel and high treat by uniting the excellences of our two most distinguished actors in one piece—let him purify the stage of every thing objectionable on the score of taste, and leave behind him a name as the perfecter of our theatrical exhibitions, in propriety*, costume, style, judgment, and morals. There is one difficulty, however, for him to overcome, which, it must be confessed, is embarrassing, namely, the subjugation of the gallery audience to a well-regulated conduct. The pit was formerly the place of the critic, affording, from its situation, the greatest facility of hearing and judging. The applause or censure of the pit decided every thing; it was the mean between the aristocracy of the boxes, and the radicalism of the galleries. At present the pit is generally filled with a respectable but uncritical audience. The amateurs of the performance are scattered through the boxes, in solitary observation. The tempered and judicious censure or applause once displayed by the pit is exchanged for the ignorant howlings and noisy interruptions of the galleries. Inferior actors, particularly in the more vulgar parts, play to the galleries, that now possess such a petty sovereignty over the whole house as it would be a slur on the audience to tolerate, were they not without a remedy to help themselves. Many reasonable alterations, for which a manager would be greeted with applause, would be overruled by the rabble. Farcewriters and melodram-compounders interlard their abortive productions with the vilest diction, to catch the never-failing applause of the " gods," as they are styled. Thus the gallery is, at present, nearly the dictator of the house,—a state of affairs which it is difficult for a manager to alter. The gallery is vast in size, and its receipts are a great object in an expensive establishment ; but its clamours operate against the interest of the other parts of the house, and its subjugation to the rules of good order seems a work indispensable to complete success. To hope better things from an amelioration of manners in the class that frequents the galleries is an idle expectation; to submit to it for ever will be a stigma both on the manager and the other parts of the house. Some have proposed to divide the gallery longitudinally, and thus prevent a concerted system of action. In what mode that good can be effected, which, unless effected, gives no hope of perfecting our theatrical exhibitions, is matter worthy the serious consideration of all who feel the charm of rational entertainment, and hold in estimation the pleasures of imagination and poesy. Thousands now do not visit the theatre at all, who, if these objections were removed, would be frequent visitants. The theatre, they justly observe, should be a school of the purest language, and a scene of decorum and refinement; it should be visited as an intellectual feast, in which " no crude surfeit reigned." This subject, which involves the real interest of the drama, has not often enough been brought before the

---

* Why will Mr. Kean persist in playing Othello as a sooty woolly-headed negro? —it is no reason for one of his genius that tragedians have erred before him.

public, nor efforts commensurate to its importance been attempted to change it.

I write this with no knowledge of any manager personally, and with no wish to exalt the manager of Drury-lane above his merits. He has effected much for the public gratification, but much yet remains to be done. It is still farther in his favour, that he has shewn his willingness to give a fair trial to the production of every author that has apparently any chance of success. This is praiseworthy, and adds another laurel to his theatrical crown; but he must leave the author to his own judgment, and not shackle him by restraints. A practice has lately arisen of writing for an actor, and getting a play up with a character purposely drawn for him to sustain. Such a production never can be a happy one either for author or manager, and can only be of temporary interest. It is the actor's place to study the poet, not the poet the actor. In late times, among other strange things, we have seen most extraordinary acknowledgments put forth by authors to performers, indicating that the latter have, occasionally at least, pretensions humiliating to the pride of authorship, which the world would never have guessed, but for the confession—a confession no less novel and astounding to contemporaries than to ourselves. We are gravely told of an actor (Mr. Macready), in the dedication of "Julian," lately performed at Covent-garden, that his powers have inspired, and his taste "has fostered the tragic dramatists of the age !!" A piece of information, then first communicated to them, of which they had lived in unfelicitous ignorance, and would have so continued to live but for this important disclosure. "Elegance and luxuriance of praise" are revived from old Dryden's days,—this is to the full as bad as "your Lordship in satire and Shakspeare in tragedy!"

I fear I have occupied more space than I ought in thus noticing, in a desultory way, subjects which would seem to demand more methodic details. Those, however, who love the theatre, will agree in thinking that what remains to be done is so obvious, that the task of execution is alone wanting, and that this rests with the manager who possesses sufficient originality of mind to act by the rules of good taste alone in the improvement of our dramatic entertainments.*                    Y.

---

## INVOCATION TO THE CUCKOO.

O PURSUIVANT and Herald of the Spring !
   Whether thou still dost dwell
   In some rose-laurell'd dell
Of that charm'd Island whose magician king
   Bade all its rocks and caves,
   Woods, winds, and waves,
Thrill to the dulcet chant of Ariel,
   Until he broke the spell
And cast his wand into the shuddering sea,—
   O hither, hither fleet,
   Upon the south wind sweet,
And soothe us with thy vernal melody !

---

* As one step, let the text of Shakspeare be forthwith restored in his plays, and the interpolated trash rejected which has so long disgraced the representation of some of his best works.

Or whether to the redolent Azores,
  Amid whose tufted sheaves
  The floral Goddess weaves
Her garland, breathing on the glades and shores
  Intoxicating air,
  Truant! thou dost repair:—
Or lingerest still in that meridian nest,
  Where myriad piping throats
  Rival the warbler's notes,
The saffron namesake of those Islands blest,—
  O hither, hither wing
Thy flight, and to our longing woodlands sing!

Or in those sea-girt gardens dost thou dwell,
  Of plantain, cocoa, palm,
  And that red tree whose balm
Fumed in the holocausts of Israel;
  Beneath Banana shades,
  Guava, and fig-tree glades,
Painting thy plumage in the sapphirine hue
  Thrown from the heron blue,
Or rays of the prismatic parroquet,—
  O let the perfumed breeze
  From those Hesperides
Waft thee once more our eager ears to greet!

For lo! the young leaves flutter in the South,
  As if they tried their wings,
  While the bee's trumpet brings
News of each bud that pouts its honied mouth;
  Blue-bells, yellow-cups, jonquils,
  Lilies wild and daffodils,
Gladden our meads in intertangled wreath:
  The sun enamour'd lies,
  Watching the violet's eyes
On every bank, and drinks their luscious breath:
  With open lips the thorn
  Proclaims that May is born,
And darest thou, bird of Spring, that summons scorn?

Cuckoo! Cuckoo! O welcome, welcome notes!
  Fields, woods, and waves rejoice
  In that recover'd voice,
As on the wind its fluty music floats.
  At that elixir strain,
  My youth resumes its reign,
And life's first Spring comes blossoming again:
  O wondrous bird! if thus
  Thy voice miraculous
Can renovate my spirit's vernal prime,
  Nor thou, my Muse, forbear
  That ecstasy to share,
I laugh at Fortune, and defy old Time.

## THE VILLAGE BELLS.

Funera plango; fulgura frango, Sabbata pango,
Excito lentos, dissipo ventos, paco cruentos.

Laudo Deum verum, plebem voco, conjugo clerum,
Defunctos ploro, pestem fugo, festa decoro.

*Monkish Inscriptions on Bells.*

I HAD wandered for a long time, one summer's morning, through the successive copses and thinly-wooded glades that constitute the remains of Sherwood Forest, pondering upon the days of old, when their deeper and more extensive shades echoed to the horn of Robin Hood, and that romantic outlaw might have started from the thickets through which I was strolling, clad in Lincoln green and accoutred with bow and arrow, to challenge me for intruding upon his leafy haunts, when I observed that the trees growing gradually thinner opened at length upon a small lawn, in the centre of which was a piece of water, dotted along its banks with a few straggling oaks. Throwing myself down upon its margin, I was struck with the marvellous transparency of the limpid element, which resembled a mirror spread out upon the grass, reflecting every object of this sequestered nook with a precision that actually confused apprehension by its very clearness. Never was so perfect a piece of mimicry. The blue depths of heaven, with the rich colours and majestic motion of the slowly-sailing clouds, were not only copied in the hemisphere beneath me, but a goat, that had climbed an overhanging crag by my side, saw himself so perfectly represented below that he made every demonstration of attack with his butting head, as if preparing to leap down upon his shadowy opponent. A squirrel seemed to be running up to me out of the water upon the trunk of a reflected tree, upon whose extreme branches a thrush sat piping, as if singing to me from the bottom of the little lake. Other tenants of the air, as they fluttered above, were seen reflected in the wave beneath, while fishes now and then darted like meteors athwart these commingled birds and boughs and skies, as if the elements and their respective inhabitants were all confused together. As I perused this cross-reading of Nature with a complacent admiration, the rising breeze wafted towards me from a neighbouring village the melodious chime of its bells, with the echoes of which I had not only been familiar in my boyish days, but had often stolen into the belfry to awaken them myself, though I never merited the appellation of a scientific ringer. I turned my listless steps towards the church, as the sound died away upon the wind, and again at intervals threw its music upon the air, musing upon the almost-forgotten feelings with which I had listened to the same mellow tones in my childhood,—anticipating the period, now rapidly approaching, when I should lie in the earth beneath them, deaf to their loudest peals—and whispering to myself in the beautiful words of Moore

" That other bards would walk these dells,
   And listen to the evening bells ;"—

when I fell into a train of thought upon the great sympathy and connexion that exists between these sonorous chroniclers and the public

history of the country, as well as the successive stages and leading incidents of every man's private life.

In the absence of any other national music, let us not disdain to appropriate to ourselves that which is undoubtedly our exclusive property—the art of ringing changes upon church bells, whence England
has been sometimes termed "the ringing island." Although it be
simply a melody, the construction of regular peals is susceptible of
considerable science in the variety of interchange, and the diversified
succession of consonances in the sounds produced. Many of them
bear the names of their composers, who thus bid fair to be rung down
to the latest posterity; and that the exercise of taking part in a peal
has never been deemed an ignoble amusement, is attested by the fact,
that we have several respectable associations for practising and perpetuating the art, particularly one known by the name of the College
Youths, of which Sir Matthew Hale, Lord Chief Justice of the King's
Bench, was, in his youthful days, a member. Exclusively of the delight arising from the melody itself as it floats along, gladdening hill
and dale, tower and hamlet, what can be sweeter or more soothing
than all the associations of thought connected with a merry peal of
village bells? Announcing the Sabbath-morning—the common day of
rest, when we all cease from our toils, they remind us that the humblest of those whose lot is labour, will now betake themselves in decent garb and with cheerful looks to the Temple, where all the children
of the Great Parent, without distinction of rank, assemble together to
offer up their general thanksgivings. Nothing can be more natural
than the words which Cowper has put into the mouth of Alexander
Selkirk, to express the desolation and solitude of the uninhabited island
on which he had been cast.

> " The sound of the church-going bell,
>     These valleys and rocks never heard;
>  Never sigh'd at the sound of a knell,
>     Or smiled when a Sabbath appear'd."

Of all the public duties which bells are called upon to perform, the
most puzzling and embarrassing must be the due apportionment of
their fealty to the old and new monarch, when the former—dies, we
were going to say, but kings never die;—when he ceases to reign, and
is under the necessity of laying in the dust the head which has worn a
crown. Death is a sad radical: Horace assures us, that even in his
days it was a matter of perfect indifference to the ghastly destroyer
whether he aimed his dart at the towers of kings, or the hovels of the
peasantry; and in these revolutionary times we may be sure that he
has lost nothing of his Carbonari spirit. Bells, however, acknowledge
the authority of the powers that be; their suffrages obey the influence
of the clergy, tolerably shrewd calculators of the most beneficial chances
of loyalty, and yet the brazen mourners must sometimes be in a sad
dilemma between their sorrow for the loss of the old, and their joy at
the accession of the new king. Like Garrick between Tragedy and
Comedy, we may imagine them quite at a loss which expression to assume, whether to toll a knell or ring a peal, or strike a serio-comic
chord between the two. Affection for the dead might be construed

into disaffection for the living, but a reigning sovereign has so much more power of patronage than a defunct one, that they generally obey the injunction of the royal Henry to his impatient heir,

> " Go, bid the merry bells ring to thine ear
> That thou art crowned, not that I am dead."

Could the bells of even this sequestered village church, said I to myself, recall to us with their iron tongues the various and often contradictory occasions, when the passions of man have called forth their echoes, what a humiliating record of human nature would they present! Accession of king after king, public tumult and struggle, curfew and tocsin, civil and foreign war, victories and peace, generation upon generation knelled into the church-yard, and again a new king or a new war, and fresh victories and another peace, forming but a recommencement of the old circle of events, ever new and yet the same, ever passing away and recurring, in which Nature perpetually moves! Like all other public history, they would announce to us little but suffering and crime; for tranquillity, happiness, and virtue seek not to be trumpeted forth by their brazen clarion: and even if they unfolded to us the annals of private life, how often would they have to tell us of fleeting joys and enduring sorrow, of sanguine hopes and bitter disappointment!

Reaching the gate of the church-yard, as this reflection passed through my mind, the first monument I encountered was that of my relative Sir Ralph Wyvill. How well do I remember the morning of his marriage! The ringers loved him, for he would sometimes mingle in their sport. They pulled the ropes with the lusty and willing arms of men who had quaffed his ale and pocketed his money; the bells threw their wide mouths up into the air, and as they roared the glad tidings to the earth, till every hill-top echoed back the sound, they seemed to cry out to the Heavens—

> " Ring out ye, crystal spheres,
> And let your silver chime
> Move in melodious time,
> And let the base of Heaven's deep organ blow."

From every octagon brick chimney of the ancient hall, wreaths of smoke streaked the clear sunshine,—cheerful evidence of the old English hospitality and the extensive preparations for the marriage-feast that were operating within:—friends and relatives were seen interchanging shakes of the hand and cordial congratulations; servants were bustling about in new liveries and huge nosegays;—the smart postilions, with white favours in their caps, were cracking their whips and their jokes at the gate;—the train of carriages with be-ribboned and be-flowered coachmen, made a goodly and glittering show;—gossips and rustics, in their holiday-clothes, clustered about the church-doors and windows;—

> " Quips and cranks and wanton wiles,
> Nods and becks and wreathed smiles,"

flickered upon every countenance; and every tongue prophesied that the happy couple would be permanently blessed, for the bridegroom was young and rich, the maiden fond and fair. Such, however, are

predictions with which every wedding is solemnised; and if the
visions of the future prove too often illusory, it is to be at-
l to the general lot of humanity, rather than to any inherent
in the marriage system.

ough he seemed to possess all the constituents of conjugal hap-
the sanguine auguries of Sir Ralph's friends were speedily fal-
; he parted from his wife, and returned with new ardour to his
loves—the bottle and the chase. On his wedding-day I had seen
. in this very church-yard, step from his carriage flushed with
h and vigour, an elastic specimen of manly beauty. Living to
him crippled, gouty, and infirm, I at last beheld him borne once
to this same spot, and methinks I now hear the deepest-mouthed
one very bells that had rung out such a merry peal on his mar-
, "swinging slow with solemn roar" its sad and solitary toll for
burial—Dong! dong! dong! dong!—What a contrast did the
scene present! Every shutter was closed in the windows of the old
hall—its chimneys were cold and smokeless—the whole house looked
forlorn and desolate, as if there were no living thing within it. The
once jovial master of that ancient mansion was borne slowly from its
gate beneath the sable plumes of a hearse; the gay carriage and the
four noble horses, of which he was so proud, followed, as if in mockery
of his present state, the servants attesting, by better evidence than their
mourning liveries, the sincerity of their grief; a sad procession of
coaches with the customary trappings of woe brought up the rear;
sorrow was upon every face; the villagers spoke to one another in
whispers; a hushing silence reigned among the assemblage, only
broken by the deep toll of the passing bell; and thus did I follow the
body to the family sepulchre, and heard the hollow rattling of the sand
and gravel as they were cast down upon the coffin-lid of the corpse that
was once Sir Ralph Wyvill.

There is not a dell or cover, a woodland or plain for many miles
around, that has not echoed to his Stentorian view hallo! nay even the
church itself and the hollow mansions of the dead, for he was no re-
specter of localities, have rung with the same cry. Where is that
tongue now? The huntsman might wind his horn, the whole pack
give cry, and the whole field unite their shouts at the very mouth of
his vault, without awakening the keen sportsman who sleeps in its deep
darkness. That tongue, whose loud smack pronounced a fiat upon
claret, from which there was no appeal—what is it now?—a banquet
for the worm until both shall be reconverted into dust. And perhaps,
ere those bells shall have rung in another new year, and awakened a
new race of candidates for the grave, the hand that traces these thoughts,
and the eye that reads them, may be laid also in the earth, withered—
decompounded—dust!

## A DAY IN LONDON.

A COUNTRY gentleman, whose habits are retired, uniform, quiet, a withal somewhat studious, on being occasionally hurried up to Lond is always much more vividly impressed with the various objects of singular scene presented by the metropolis, than those can be w reside almost all the year round in town, and whose senses are con quently accustomed and blunted to the stimulus of its imposing mo ments and its noises. This is precisely my own case. Although stranger to the multitudinous capital, my latter years have been p in a tranquil and distant part of England, whilst occasional calls duty summon me, for a few days, to endure the sounds and sights, a to respire the thick and tepid atmosphere of town. The first idea one of these journeys is always highly disagreeable to me; and, fo few days before I leave home, I feel a more than usually tender tachment to those objects which endear it to me, and lament, to a d gree that I fear would be considered absurd, the interruption of ch rished habits of regularity, and the necessity of a temporary absence from scenes and persons familiar to me, and even not always without the power of annoying me. As I generally travel by coach, I look forward with pain to the weary hours I am to pass on my journey,

    " Remote, unfriended, melancholy, *slow ;*"

and see in their termination in London nothing that has power to charm. I know not how to account for it, but the approach to, and entrance into London, invariably depresses me. This strange feeling is independent of external circumstances; for I have entered London in youth and health, and not without the power to command its pleasures; but ever as I have approached its barriers, I have seemed to enter the fatal city which was to afford me a gloomy grave. Yet, of all horrors, God preserve me from that of being hurled into the earth by a London sexton, or buried by a London clergyman!—I speak *this*, as Brutus speaks of the Tarquins, "*from the bottom of my soul.*"

With the exception of one or two entrances, an arrival in London is preceded by an hour's journey through scenes in which wretchedness and vanity are displayed in colours the most painful to the eye of reflection that can be imagined: the whole picture floats before me at this moment:—The scanty gentility of the better sort of houses; the lugubrious blackness of the few unhappy trees, placed, as in derision, among masses of hasty brick-work; the porter-houses; the coach-stands with their complement of watermen, half-pay coachmen, and regular pickpockets; the coffee-shops; the rows of brokers' stalls, each with a seductive pile of squalid finery, and withal the gaudy starvation of exotic women; and the dingy multitudes of men in worn-out black coats, all full of a London look of important wretchedness; and, mingled with these, pompous equipages; pale proud faces, physiognomies fresh from the very heart of the city, marking the wealthy who seem to be driving away into semi-rural life, as if to save their lives:— these, with the noise, the crowd, the dull, dispiriting, and carbonaceous atmosphere; glimpses of long streets of busy interested life; thousands of people, not one among whom would care if one died of apoplexy on the spot, and most of whom would rather like the excitement of

ch a spectacle:—all this is oppressive to a degree that cannot be
scribed, and causes an absolute gasping of the inward soul for the
ness of rural life and human innocence. These are things which,
withstanding the hurry with which he is driven to some pestiferous
ch-hotel, with its dungeon-offices below and prison-galleries above,
which the sun never yet shone for one bright hour, make his first
ments in London hateful to the country gentleman. The character
man is, indeed, altogether worked out unfavourably in London, and
e vast city seems to receive you as if only to devour you. Talent,
is true, is highly cultivated and richly rewarded; the intellectual
ulties are fully developed and splendidly exercised; whatever is
nd in conception, or extensive in operation, is boldly undertaken
d skilfully performed; but the good feelings of our nature, the
rm, social, uncalculating, and friendly propensities, find no favour-
le soil. Even in the higher classes there is not, from want of time,
perhaps from the eternal occupation of a town-life, that warmth of
ling which prevails in the peaceful and elegant mansions of the
untry; whilst, in the middle classes, all that is interested and vain,
nd in the lower, all that is wicked, foolish and vulgar, is brought
rth more prominently and disgustingly: ignorance is more presuming, profligacy more gloried in, villainy more open and avowed;
and in all, from the very highest to the lowest, forgetfulness of friends
ranks among the dignified virtues which adorn prosperity. Some are
absorbed in dissipation, others in the pursuit of gain, others in the promotion of profligacy, and many in the refinement and perfection of
every kind of fraud, artifice, and crime; whilst feeling and reflection
are lost in *whirl*, and noise, and hurry, and never-ending toil. Thus,
at least, it painfully appears to the visitant from the country, on his
arrival; and it is not until he is extricated, or drawn a little out of the
nucleus of the town, just far enough to feel the fanning benefit of a
west wind, and to know that he yet continues to live in a world where
sometimes the sky and sometimes the sun is seen, that he begins to
breathe, the asthma under which his heart and lungs have laboured so
painfully is relieved, and he lives to comfort or to happiness once more.
The disagreeable impressions fade rapidly away, and so far from London
then appearing a place without pleasures, and those of the highest and
most ennobling description, he finds himself perplexed with their variety, and perhaps somewhat at a loss to determine how many may be
comprehended in the brief space of two or three long and busy days.
Who is there, indeed, with *any* taste for *any* thing, with any knowledge
or admiration of any art, or any science, or any occupation, or any
amusement, that does not admire London? It is in London that the
perfection and utmost refinement of human industry and human talent
may be contemplated in works, various, endless, and irresistibly-at-
tractive. If there be any music in the soul, London is the temple of
divinest harmony; there, and there only, the finest singers, and those
who touch instruments of music with inspired fingers, may be nightly
heard. If there is any fondness for the arts, nowhere in England
can that fondness be so fully gratified: the finest works of sculpture
and painting, the most ingenious contrivances, and the most beautiful
works of genius, are all to be found in London, produced or collected
by an industry which seems almost supernatural. If eloquence moves

us, in London we may listen to that which is " almost divine :" the p
lic meeting, the lecture, the courts of law, the churches, and, above
the Senate, exhibit it in forms more perfect and animating than
aided imagination can have prepared us for, or at least realize
dreams which our acquaintance with the orators of ancient days
given birth to, and display to us, with every overpowering accom
niment, the riches and splendours of human intellect.   The very
like that of Rome, is classical, in spite of the *mal'aria* from the east
marshes :  for it was breathed by those whose eloquence, whose w
dom, whose wit, whose patriotism, have adorned and dignified
annals in the successive ages of British history : and as regards i
teresting relics of antiquity, they lie on every side, disregarded on *j*
count of their very multiplicity.   Nor is it a small matter  to fi
oneself actually in the same town with ———, and ———, and ———
men whose names and deeds furnish the remotest provinces with co
versation but seem yet obscurely viewed so long as we remain in tl
country.   I walk out, I meet a gentleman in a blue coat and black cr
vat, with an umbrella under his arm—it is the great Duke of ———
I see another on horseback, it is the Marquis of ——— :   here
Mr. ———, who shakes the senate with his brilliant and powerf
oratory ; here a poet, actually alive and walking about among commo
men : that gentleman in the chariot is a Judge, the next a Bishop, tl
third a celebrated physician, and the tall gentleman who walks so fa
is no less a person than Sir ——— ———.   All this is very astonishing t
a country gentleman.

If I am alone in London, I consider myself emancipated from th
mechanical regularities of a country life, without thinking it at all ne
cessary to conform to the habits of town ; I therefore get up and go t
bed when I choose, and in short, for a day or two, do exactly as I please.
Being .obliged to hurry to distant points in that contiguous world of
houses, my way is to *walk* in all the gentlemanly parts of the town, for
in those I always feel a peculiar amplification of my own respectability ; whereas, if I walk into the city and come at all near the Exchange, I seem to become a sort of person whom every banker's clerk
heartily despises ; and when I have occasionally walked in that inconceivable part of London near Bagnigge Wells, or in the middle of the
parish of St. Giles, I have not felt any positive or comfortable conviction of being the same gentleman that I was : in those vicinities, therefore, I shelter myself in a coach, happy, like other men, when I *meet*
with one which does not set me reflecting on cutaneous disorders, or
the driver of which puts me in no fear of assassination.   As I fly
through the streets to accomplish the long journeys which the remote
residences of friends always renders necessary, and pay my visits in
succession to men whom I remember living out of London, once amia-
bly imprudent and full of human feelings, but who are now all so
much alike that it is difficult to distinguish one from another, all asking
the same questions, all too much hurried to sit down and be idle and
agreeable, all inviting one to dinner, and all, on the refusal, (for I
always refuse,) shaking hands, apologizing, and straightway forgetting
all that concerns us ;—as I hurry through these visits of duty and
ceremony, I every now and then dive into exhibitions and museums,
and plunge into bazaars and shops of all descriptions, on all sorts of

trifling and luckily-remembered commissions; but, of all things, the collections of sculpture and painting, and natural history, detain me most and delight me longest in London. The other day, for instance, I saw the Wapeti, and lingered long near those singularly beautiful, elegant, and engaging animals. A turn to the right brought me before Mr. Haydon's picture of Lazarus: the cant of criticism, if I wished to employ it, is not in my power, and to say the truth, I have a sort of horripilation all over me when a writer or a *talker* mentions a picture, assuring myself of so much light and shade, tint and colour, expression and effect, grouping and drapery, that I shall be well nigh dead before he has murdered his subject:—but not the most casual lounger in the room where this picture is exhibited can fail to be struck with that wonderful conception, *the face of Lazarus.* It is unearthly, but not unnatural; it is appalling, and yet the eye turns to it again and again; it is death *yet*, indeed, but death as no man ever saw it—not death *approaching*, but death *departing:* the dark and terrible insensibility of the grave is yielding to the life and light of the upper world; the awful preparation for the perfect dissolution of the corporeal frame is visibly suspended; and the spectator sees at once that the features have been impressed by the hand of death, and that life is restored.

It happened that on the same day I looked in upon the *Chapeau de Paille*, and the scene presented by the exhibition-room was very amusingly different from that in which Lazarus was shown. I had visited Lazarus in the morning, some half-dozen gentlemen were there, but no man spoke a syllable; the tomb of Lazarus himself was scarcely more silent. I visited Rubens's fair dream at four o'clock, the room was crowded with ladies and gentlemen, and every body was talking; the lips of the lovely picture alone were not in motion, although the eyes were eloquent, as if animated by a living soul. I had heard of the faults of this *chef-d'œuvre*, and recognized them, but for my more intimate acquaintance with the picture I am indebted to a council of fair and loquacious ladies who stood near me; through whose observations I became fully convinced of all the meaning of the *chapeau* itself, and became more awake to the defects of the ear and the fingers, and to the indescribably sweet expression of the countenance; above all, I became aware of a fact, not I think before noticed, but yet indisputably true, that the pictured fair is represented with a *goître*. In future I shall always attend exhibitions in company with ladies; their perceptions are delicate and acute, and their organs of speech easily acted upon through the agency of the mind: but, on the whole, of this picture of Rubens—this his *chef-d'œuvre*, if so it be—I scarcely know what to say: I dare neither confess how much I was pleased with it, nor say all I thought about it: in truth, I am free to confess I know not what to make of it, and shall therefore leave it to the regular critics.

It is a reproach not uncommon in the mouths of foreigners, that an Englishman regulates all the amusements, and even all the employments of the day, by a constant and accurate reference to the hour of dinner. In this respect I confess myself *un véritable Anglais*, one with whom dinner is a habit, and who in default thereof could never, in any climate, or season, or company, deceive himself by grapes, or chesnuts, into a belief that he had actually and *bona fide* got any dinner unless the due ceremonials had been observed. Never, or very seldom, as I said before, accepting London invitations to dinner, I generally dine in the neighbourhood of the theatres, and most frequently at the Piazza, though somewhat more, I think, on account of the sound and honour of the thing than from any particular predilection for the place, for the large room invariably reminds me of some dark, cheerless, and *restored* cathedral, of which the head waiter and his pursuivants, in full canonicals, are strikingly like the Dean and Chapter. There is a certain coffee-house in that neighbourhood, the name of which is not so well calculated to adorn a narrative, but into which I often look for the face of some friend or other, who, like myself, knows its advantages, and like myself may be at a loss now and then when in London to know what to do with some hour, or half-hour, which intervenes between two engagements, an undefined blank in the plan of the day or night. It is one of the very few coffee-houses now remaining in which I find any thing which I can compare with the glorious coffee-house hours of the days of the Spectator; being resorted to by men of a certain station, and of considerable acquirements; who yet, for the most part, hang loosely upon society, and are not chained to localities by wives, children, or any set occupation or regular and daily routine of duties; whose exertions are occasional, and whose hours of relaxation often recur:—they live, for the most part, among the brilliant, the noble, and the gay; partake of the varied information of professional men, but without professional prejudices, because they are of no profession; and are men of discursive habits, tastes, and fancies; of easy manners, good spirits, well-informed minds, and lively conversation. The last time I was there, about half-a-dozen of this description were collected together, and the subjects of their discourse were various, but all treated with infinite ability, and occasionally with infinite humour. An author ventured to state his projects concerning a new publication, and was liberally and cheeringly encouraged. One of the party was going to Circassia, another to Ireland, another to the House of Commons, and remarks wandered, and witticisms scintillated, between the two poles of the world. My attention was chiefly directed to a tall thinnish gentleman, just past the middle point of life; his hair, eyes, and eyebrows were dark; his countenance singularly expressive, not altogether without a slight tragic cast, or perhaps more properly indicative, whether truly or not I know not, of high-wrought and romantic feeling; and his voice was peculiarly agreeable and gentlemanly. I judge much of men, and of women too, by their voices; the muscles of the face may, by long practice, be subdued to any habitual expression; physiognomy is fallacious; the organs of the head are easily concealed; but I am assured by all my experience, that the tone of the voice has a constant affinity with the tone of the mind. The gentleman I describe had, moreover, a brown coat on; and, although it was evening, his independence of what is called fashion was demonstrated by his being dressed in top-boots. He alternately contributed to the conversation, and leaned back in his arm chair as if to sleep; and all this with so easy and indolent an air that I was quite convinced he could be no other than an author; indeed, I half suspected him of being a poet. On enquiring his name I learnt he was Sir L—— S——, so long and so curiously distinguished in the circles of fashion. I am always deeply affected by contemplations of the silent lapse of time, and the changes effected by it: the "Eheu fugaces" of Horace is the title to a volume of recollections, each with its moral attached to it. This, then, was he who had tried every changeful variety of fashion, until invention was exhausted and vanity satiated, and who had proved, more than any man now living, the fatigue of fashionable folly, and the emptiness of the most elaborate and ingenious affectation; but who, outliving his "young days of folly," had shewn, by subsiding into the agreeable and well-informed gentleman, that beneath this frothy exterior there had always been a purer stream of sense which his shallower imitators dreamt not of, and without which it is impossible to believe that life would have been supportable to him when youth was no more! Having stept into the coffee-house on this occasion for half an hour before the play began, I left my company somewhat unwillingly, and proceeded to Drury-lane.

I could say nothing of the theatres that would not be uninteresting to those who live in London: theatrical criticism is their province, and I have no wish to invade it. If I were to say that the performances were tediously protracted, the fault might be ascribed to my rustic hours; if I thought the ladies who sung at the oratorio reminded people more of the joys of this unhappy world than of the joys of a better, it might be ascribed to my being a country gentleman. Yet the voice of Braham was as the voice of a friend, and did "good like a medicine;" I laughed at Liston as I had often laughed before; and I will not be deterred from expressing my admiration of Miss Clara Fisher; her pretty figure, her sweet and plaintive voice, and her subdued drollery and archness, reminded me of the days in which Mrs. Jordan used alternately to make me weep and laugh:—the remembrance of that delightful woman is now altogether sad, and the circumstances of her latter days are among the few subjects on which I can never speak or think without departing from the natural and customary moderation of my character.

By one of those chances which never fall out but in London, two of my most particular friends came into the very box in which I had taken my seat. When I say they were my friends, I mean as far as the most opposite habits of life can allow; *they* living almost all the year round in London, and having little relish and less taste for any thing out of it. Country gentlemen are always led into the *lobby*: perhaps it is the effect of the transition from youth to middle age, but I could not help fancying its attractions were diminished and its grosser features increased since I saw it before. After the performances I was persuaded to accompany my two friends to O——'s, which, it seems, is a famous supper-house, and which was filled, soon after we reached it, by men of fashion and of name. The arrangements, however, were by no means calculated to fortify the stomach. Nothing appeared genteel but the company; the tables were slopped, the lights were dim, the waiters were slow, the knives were wiped, the glasses were dull, and the chops, after much clamorous request on the part of the claimants, were not half-cooked. Yet to this splendidly wretched apartment numbers of young men, whose genteel appearance is unquestionable, are in the habit of resorting nightly, in hopes of destroying some part of that time which for ever weighs upon and threatens to overwhelm them; eternally pursuing a phantom of pleasure, with weariness for their associate. A young gentleman from Nottinghamshire (who had been convincing his faculties with Scotch whiskey for some time very assiduously, and imagined he was well qualified in oratory,) having made a tolerably argumentative speech on a question that was mooted by another, those present availed themselves very readily of so good a pretext for ringing with their glasses, thumping the table, and using all the polite methods of signifying approbation; and, kindling into enthusiasm with their own noise, at last voted him president for the night, conducted him with all solemnity to a leathern chair, and called for a toast and a song. A stout, good-looking gentleman, with brown and copious whiskers, wearing his hat on one side, and generally keeping a pipe in his mouth, gave us some songs in a style superior to any thing I had ever heard in private company. He was a Captain F——: he seemed popular in the assembly; had frequently, I was told, filled the president's chair, and was indeed, with many, the principal attraction to the house. Yet I could not help feeling surprise that a man accustomed during any part of the four and twenty hours to the life of a gentleman, should like to descend at night into such an equivocal company—a foolish reflection, which could only have been made by a country gentleman. Towards morning it became difficult to sing a *solo*, from the propensity of the hearers to take part in whatever they heard. My two friends could not sing, but they had become by this time so loquacious that I pleaded even more fatigue than I felt, and retired to my hotel, comparing as I went the turbulent scene I had just quitted, with the peaceful state of my distant home at the same hour, inwardly complaining of the weariness, staleness, flatness, and unprofitableness of the hours I had spent at O——'s, and determining to spend the next day at least entirely in my own way.

A sleepy, dropsical-looking waiter received me, and led me along a labyrinth of passages to my bed-room, from which I had the satisfaction of feeling assured that, in case of fire, I could not make my escape. However, I had not long amused myself with "thick-coming fancies" of being burnt to death, before I fell into a delightful sleep, to dream of the busy and infatuated multitudes that had bewildered my senses during the day.

———

### THE GODS OF GREECE. FROM SCHILLER.

FAIR beings of the fable-land!
How bless'd the race of mortal birth,
When ye resign'd to Joy's light hand
The leading-strings of earth!
When your delightful worship reign'd,
How different all!—below—above—
While yet the world with flowers enchain'd
Thy temple—God of Love!

When Fiction wove th' enchanting robe,
Whose lovely colours Truth conceal,
A livelier spirit fill'd the globe;
All felt, what none again shall feel.
To clasp her charms on Love's warm breast
Man gave to Nature added grace:
On the tranced eye, all, all impress'd
A Godhead's sacred trace.

Where now—as sages teach their lore—
A senseless fire-ball wheels its way,
Then, the gold-chariot onward bore
The God whose splendour gives the day.
On every height an Oread sprung,
Each tree a Dryad's native home,
And from their urns fair Naiads flung
The streamlet's silvery foam.

This guardian Laurel screen'd the maid,
That silent stone was Niobe,
Here Philomel attuned the glade,
There Syrinx' reed breathed melody.
Here Venus, vainly, on this mount
Bewail'd her beauteous paramour,
There Ceres wept in yonder fount
Her child in Pluto's power.

For earthly race the gods above
Heaven and their nectar-feasts forsook,
Nor Phœbus self, to win his love,
Disdain'd the shepherd's crook.
Men—heroes—gods—alike all felt
How sweet Love's equalizing power;
And mortals with immortals dwelt
In Amathusia's bower.

Stern gravity and harsh control
From your kind rites were cast aside;
Joy swell'd each pulse, bliss thrill'd each soul,
For bliss was with your power allied.
A holy light round Beauty play'd,
Nor gods 'mid joys imagined shame,
When the coy Muse a blush betray'd,
And Graces fann'd the flame.

Like palaces your temples shone,
Heroic games your glory raised,
Where wav'd o'er Isthmian feasts the crown,
And nigh the goal the chariot blazed.
The dance, that lured the soul, enwreathed
Its maze your radiant altars round,
And coronals that victory breathed
Your fragrant tresses crown'd.

Evoe's Thyrsus waved in air,
And the yoked panthers proudly drew
The God of Joy, the young, the fair,
Where Fauns and Satyrs forward flew.
Around him leap the Mænades,
Their gambols of the gay grape told,
While down the host's brown cheek, the lees
Of the drain'd goblet roll'd.

Then the dim eye that swam in death
No ghastly skeleton discern'd,
But when a kiss caught life's last breath,
His torch a genius downward turn'd.
E'en the stern Judge who ruled in hell
Was kin to earthly parentage,
And on the Thracian's plaintive shell
Reposed the Furies' rage.

Then in Elysium's blissful grove
Gay shades the joys of life renew'd :
There Love relink'd the chain of Love,
The charioteer his course pursued.
There Linus sung his wonted strain,
Admetus press'd Alcestes' heart ;
Orestes found his friend again,
The Lemnian chief his dart.

Then nobler gifts the hero braced
Who toil'd on Virtue's rugged road :
And some, by deeds sublimer graced,
Climb'd highest Heav'n—the guests of God.
To the Deliverer of the dead
The gods their brows in silence bent :
And o'er the pilot's stormy bed
The Twins their radiance sent.

Fair World ! where art thou ? bloom again,
Bloom thou again young Nature's prime !
Ah ! lives alone in fairy strain
A trace of thy fictitious Time.
How desolate earth's drear domains !
Beams on my sight no god portray'd,
Ah ! of each living form remains
The disenchanted shade.

The beauteous blossoms fade and fall,
Cut by the North wind's shivering blast,
One to enrich, one, Lord of all,
That world, and its immortals past.
Sorrowing I seek thee, star by star,
Thou, Cynthia ! there no more art found ;
Through woods, o'er waves, I call afar,
My words alone resound.

Reckless of gifts, herself provides,
Nor glorying in her power to bless,
Blind to the god her course that guides,
Nor happier for my happiness ;
Regardless of her Maker's praise,
Like the dead stroke that beats the hour,
Ungoded Nature but obeys
Dull gravitation's power.

Again her fetters to unbind,
Nature each day but delves her tomb,
And moons that round one axle wind,
Ceaseless their self-wheel'd toils resume.
Back to their home of fable-birth
The idle Deities repair,
While grown beyond their guidance, earth
Self-balanced, hangs in air,

They won 't—'twas Nature's mortal day :
Of grandeur and of grace bereft,
All hues, all harmonies decay,
A word, devoid of soul, is left.
They hover, Pindus' heights among,
From Time's o'erwhelming deluge free :
What must immortal live in song,
In life must mortal be.

### THE PHYSICIAN.—NO. VIII.

*Of the Influence of the Imagination on Bodily Health.*

NONE of the faculties of the mind present phenomena so singular and so contradictory as the imagination. This faculty, given to us as our kindest friend in this mortal life, often so poor in reality—to which we owe a relish for existence, comfort in the hours of affliction, and the enhancement of our happiness—through which we acquire a lively sense for the good and the fair, for truth and virtue, so long as we can keep it within due bounds—is liable, when it exceeds them, to become the most cruel of tyrants, robbing us of peace, happiness, nay even of life itself. It is, therefore, one of the most important maxims of our morals, to be continually upon our guard against its vagaries, and to order matters so as always to maintain a certain ascendancy over it. But this rule is not less important for our physical nature, as I shall demonstrate in this paper by some remarks on its powerful influence, and particularly by a circumstance which occurred in my own experience.

Numberless are the gradations through which that extraordinary disease which affects the imagination proceeds, as well as the masks which it assumes. From the first momentary conception that we feel something as real which does not exist, to absolute insanity, or the total derangement of the mind, there are innumerable stages, founded on the degree of the disease, on its causes and on the peculiar constitution of the patient. A great portion of what are commonly called hypochondriac or hysteric attacks, and nervous complaints, originate solely in a diseased imagination. People are accustomed to laugh at such sufferings when they are known to proceed from this cause; but their mirth is exceedingly ill-timed. I know not, in truth, a more dreadful and more real disease, than that in which the essence of our being itself suffers; for it is ten times as easy to bear a *real* evil as an *imaginary* one. In the former case I have always resources left within myself;—and with some effort of the powers of my soul, it is always possible for me to consider the evil as something distinct from and foreign to myself;—in the latter, the only thing that can afford me consolation and encouragement, my soul, is itself diseased, and my sufferings are actually a part of my being. In real evils, if the fundamental cause be removed, we may look forward with confidence to relief; but in the other case, the complaint of the soul must be combated and cured, and here the most efficacious remedies are of no avail, unless they operate upon the imagination.

In such unfortunate persons the real feelings are every moment confounded with their reveries; they see nothing aright, because they are accustomed to look at every thing in the mirror of their imagination alone. They come at length to such a pass, as either no longer to trust their senses, and thus live in continual contradiction with themselves, or become a ball, with which the imagination plays the most extravagant games; and present phenomena, that, to the sober rational mind, appear wholly incomprehensible. In this way, then, it is possible for one to fancy himself a barley-corn and in constant danger of being swallowed by the fowls; for a second to consider himself as one of the persons of the Godhead; for a third to be firmly convinced that he is made of glass and cannot be touched without breaking; and for a fourth to imagine himself the knave of spades, and that he ought to take special care to keep out of the way of the king.

Hence arises the extraordinary disease, which causes people to see themselves double, and of which I witnessed a remarkable instance, where the second self was inexpressibly troublesome, appearing every where and at very unseasonable times to the wretched original, and reducing him by its incessant annoyance almost to despair: and yet, be it observed, this was a man who possessed his perfect understanding, and was extremely regular and clever in business. It is not, however, to be denied, that the cause of this phenomenon is sometimes independent of ourselves, and may originate in a particular refraction of the rays of light, as is proved by the example of a celebrated anatomist. He was engaged one evening in his laboratory, where the atmosphere was filled with effluvia from a great quantity of anatomical preparations and subjects. Happening to raise his eyes, he perceived his own figure sitting at the opposite extremity of the room. He rose to examine the phenomenon more minutely, and went towards it, but it disappeared: on returning to his former place, he again saw it. He went to another corner, from which it was again invisible. In short, he ascertained that it depended entirely on the angle of incidence of the rays of light, and that, consequently, the apparition owed its existence to the vapours in the room, which, with the aid of the evening sun, acted like a mirror.

Through the influence of the imagination, dreams and presentiments may prove fatal: and I have always considered it as one of the most dangerous symptoms, when a patient or his friends have informed me that he has shortly before had a dream or a token of his death, or that he has seen an apparition, which has announced that he had not long to live. This was, on the one hand, a positive proof that the disease is deeply, very deeply seated in such a person, and that before it actually broke out, his nervous system and the source of his conceptions must have been greatly deranged, in order to admit of such vivid fancies: and on the other hand, I could reckon upon it with the greater confidence, that the firm conviction of death would render the disease more formidable and the remedies less efficient, and that in particular it would paralyse the curative energies of nature, without which all the skill of the physician is totally useless.

Hence, also, actual diseases may, through the influence of the imagination, be aggravated by the most unusual and dangerous symptoms, nay be produced solely by it. In such cases the physician is not likely to find much assistance in books; nor must he expect much success from any attempt to prove to the patient that his disorder is wholly imaginary. The only thing that can extricate him from the dilemma is a lucky thought, some method of diverting the imagination to a different object, or which at least is capable of rendering its consequences innoxious, or of neutralizing its convictions by means of themselves.

It is well known how a man was cured who fancied that he was dead, and refused all sustenance. His friends deposited him with all due formalities in a dark cellar. One of them caused himself soon afterwards to be carried into the same place in a coffin, containing a plentiful supply of provisions, and assured him that it was customary to eat and drink in that world, as well as in the one which they had just left. He suffered himself to be persuaded, and recovered.—Another, who imagined that he had no head, (a notion that is not so common as the reverse) was speedily convinced of the real existence of his head, by a heavy hat of lead which was set upon it, and which by its pressure, made him feel for the first time, during a long period, that he actually possessed this necessary appendage.—But the most dangerous state of all is, when the imagination fixes upon things, the lively representation of which may finally induce their realization. Of this sort was a case which fell under my own professional experience, and which affords one of the most striking proofs of the power of an overstrained imagination.

A youth of sixteen, of a weakly constitution and delicate nerves, but in other respects quite healthy, quitted his room in the dusk of the evening, but suddenly returned, with a face pale as death and looks betraying the greatest terror, and in a tremulous voice told a fellow-student who lived in the same room with him, that he should die at nine o'clock in the morning of the day after the next. His companion naturally considered this sudden transformation of a cheerful youth into a candidate for the grave as very extraordinary : he enquired the cause of this notion, and, as the other declined to satisfy his curiosity, he strove at least to laugh him out of it. His efforts, however, were unavailing. All the answer he could obtain from his comrade was, that his death was certain and inevitable. A number of well-meaning friends assembled about him, and endeavoured to wean him from his idea by lively conversation, jokes, and even satirical remarks. He sat among them with a gloomy, thoughtful look, took no share in their discourse, sighed, and at length grew angry when they began to rally him. It was hoped that sleep would dispel this melancholy mood ; but he never closed his eyes, and his thoughts were engaged all night with his approaching decease. Early next morning I was sent for. I found, in fact, the most singular sight in the world—a person in good health making all the arrangements for his funeral, taking an affecting leave of his friends, and writing a letter to his father, to acquaint him with his approaching dissolution, and to bid him farewell. I examined the state of his body, and found nothing unusual but the paleness of his face, eyes dull and rather inflamed with weeping, coldness of the extremities, and a low contracted pulse—indications of a general cramp of the nerves, which was sufficiently manifested in the state of his mind. I endeavoured, therefore, to convince him, by the most powerful arguments, of the futility of his notion, and to prove that a person whose bodily health was so good, had no reason whatever to apprehend speedy death : in short, I exerted all my eloquence and my professional knowledge, but without making the slightest impression. He willingly admitted that I, as a physician, could not discover any cause of death in him ; but this, he contended, was the peculiar circumstance of his case, that without any natural cause, merely from an unalterable decree of fate, his death must ensue ; and though he could not expect us to share this conviction, still it was equally certain that it would be verified by the event of the following day. All that I could do, therefore, was to tell him, that under these circumstances I must treat him as a person labouring under a disease, and prescribe medicines accordingly. "Very well," replied he, "but you will see not only that your medicines will not do me any good, but that they will not operate at all."

There was no time to be lost, for I had only twenty-four hours left to effect a cure. I therefore judged it best to employ powerful remedies in order to release him from this bondage of his imagination. With this view a very strong emetic and cathartic were administered, and blisters applied to both thighs. He submitted to every thing, but with the assurance that his body was already half dead, and the remedies would be of no use. Accordingly, to my utter astonishment, I learned when I called in the evening, that the emetic had taken but little or no effect, and that the blisters had not even turned the skin red. He now triumphed over our incredulity, and deduced from this inefficacy of the remedies the strongest conviction that he was already little better than a corpse. To me the case began to assume a very serious aspect. I saw how powerfully the state of the mind had affected the body, and what a degree of insensibility it had produced; and I had just reason to apprehend that an imagination, which had reduced the body to such extremity, was capable of carrying matters to still greater lengths.

All our inquiries, as to the cause of his belief, had hitherto proved abortive. He now disclosed to one of his friends, but in the strictest confidence, that the preceding evening, on quitting his room, he had seen a figure in white, which beckoned to him, and at the same moment a voice pronounced the words:—"The day after to-morrow, at nine in the morning, thou shalt die!" and the fate thus predicted nothing could enable him to escape. He now proceeded to set his house in order, made his will, and gave particular directions for his funeral, specifying who were to carry and who to follow him to the grave. He even insisted on receiving the sacrament—a wish, however, which those about him evaded complying with. Night came on, and he began to count the hours he had yet to live, till the fatal nine the next morning, and every time the clock struck, his anxiety evidently increased. I began to be apprehensive for the result; for I recollected instances in which the mere imagination of death had really produced a fatal result. I recollected also the feigned execution, when the criminal, after a solemn trial, was sentenced to be beheaded, and when, in expectation of the fatal blow, his neck was struck with a switch, on which he fell lifeless to the ground, as though his head had been really cut off: and this circumstance gave me reason to fear that a similar result might attend this case, and that the striking of the hour of nine might prove as fatal to my patient as the blow of the switch on the above-mentioned occasion. At any rate the shock communicated by the striking of the clock, accompanied by the extraordinary excitement of the imagination and the general cramp, which had determined all the blood to the head and the internal parts, might produce a most dangerous revolution, spasms, fainting-fits, or hæmorrhages; or even totally overthrow reason, which had already sustained so severe an attack.

What was then to be done? In my judgment every thing depended on carrying him, without his being aware of it, beyond the fatal moment ; and it was to be hoped that as his whole delusion hinged upon this point, he would then feel ashamed of himself and be cured of it. I therefore placed my reliance on opium, which, moreover, was quite appropriate to the state of his nerves, and prescribed twenty drops of landanum with two grains of hen-bane to be taken about midnight. I directed, that if, as I hoped, he overslept the fatal hour, his friends should assemble round his bed, and on his awaking, laugh heartily at his silly notion, that, instead of being allowed to dwell upon the gloomy idea, he might be rendered thoroughly sensible of its absurdity. My instructions were punctually obeyed: soon after he had taken the opiate, he fell into a profound sleep, from which he did not awake till about eleven o'clock the next day. " What hour is it ?" was his first question on opening his eyes; and when he heard how long he had overslept his death, and was at the same time greeted with loud laughter for his folly, he crept ashamed under the bedclothes, and at length joined in the laugh, declaring that the whole affair appeared to him like a dream, and that he could not conceive how he could be such a simpleton. Since that time he has enjoyed the best health, and has never had any similar attack.

Many instances are known of persons who, though not ill, have predicted their death in one or in a few days, and have died exactly at the time which they foretold. In former ages, when it was the fashion with the great to keep an astrologer and to consult the stars respecting the time of their death, many illustrious personages expired in the year and month predicted by their soothsayers, and the belief in their prophetic faculty was thereby not a little strengthened. In this, however, I find nothing extraordinary, and, indeed, contemporary writers explain the matter in a perfectly natural way. The good folks actually died of the prophecy; and this is one of the cases in which the prediction of a thing is the only cause why it really happens. It requires more than ordinary levity or strength of mind, to be told by a person whom we regard as possessing superior intelligence, that it is a mathematical certainty that we shall die at a stated time, without being shocked and filled with anxiety for the result. Every day that brings us nearer to the dreaded moment must augment our uneasiness, and the derangement of health inseparably connected with it. Fear is the most subtle, the most fatal of poisons : it paralyses all the faculties ; it destroys the noblest energies of our nature, and keeps the nervous system in a state of such constant tension, that it cannot but be considered, if not as itself a disease, at least as the most dangerous foundation for diseases. Should we be attacked in this mood with any slight indisposition, it may be exceedingly aggravated by the depression of the spirits and the prostration of the animal powers; and in this manner a cold may degenerate into a most malignant, nay fatal, nervous fever. Thus it is, that in times of general calamity, in epidemic diseases, and in long sieges, fear so dreadfully augments the mortality, because each is apprehensive of experiencing the same fate which he sees diffused far and wide around him.

I knew an instance of a man, who was by no means superstitious, and for whom some person had, in his youth, done the disservice to cast his nativity and to predict the year of his death. He laughed at the prophecy till the specified year arrived; he then began to be manifestly more pensive, and the idea which had formerly been a subject of mirth became an incessant torment to him. Without betraying his real cause of alarm, he went from one physician to another to consult them on the state of his health, and to stifle the voice of imagination by the opinions of the faculty. He resorted to all sorts of preservatives; every conceivable cause of disease was obviated; and the ominous year only wanted a month of its completion, when he was seized with an ordinary fever, and at the same time with the horrors of death. The whole virulence of the disease was thereby determined to the head and nerves, and on the fifth day he was carried off by apoplexy.

I mean not to assert that there may not be cases in which the soul has a real presentiment, nay a decided certainty, of approaching dissolution. These occur chiefly in lingering disorders, when the vital powers decline by slow degrees, and the inward feeling of our physical existence may in a manner calculate daily the sum of the loss. Here a presentiment of the period when the little remaining store must be completely exhausted, when the oil in the lamp shall be quite burned out, seems to be possible enough. I shall never forget a friend, who was so reduced by pulmonary consumption that a breath seemed capable of extinguishing the feeble flame, and whose dissolution was every moment expected. He was himself a physician; and in this agonising state he fixed the duration of his life at twenty-four hours, desired his watch to be hung up to his bed, counted every hour, and with steadfast look accompanied the hand to the completion of the twenty-fourth, when he closed his eyes for ever.

From the influence of the imagination, it is easy to conceive how diseases, especially those of the mind and the nerves, may have their periods, and be, in the strictest sense of the term, the fashion. Every age has, it is well known, its peculiar form and mode of thinking, and its own prevailing ideas, which at length become identified with ourselves. Nothing is more natural than that this form should communicate itself to our feelings, and particularly express itself in diseases of the nerves and of the representative faculty. To this is added a secret sympathy of the imagination, by means of which even defects and diseases of the mind easily excite imitation, and become really catching. By way of illustration, I need instance only the contagious influence of yawning. In this manner we may account for it why certain diseases of this class should be generally prevalent for a time, and then disappear; and why others, though the physical causes are the same, yet never appear again in the same form.

There are many remarkable instances of this kind. How long did the disease which manifested itself in the notions of witchcraft, and persons being possessed by the devil, prevail universally!—and yet, merely through a change in our way of thinking, and the different direction given to the imagination, it has gone quite out of fashion. People were so accustomed to regard every wicked thought as the suggestion of the devil, and every unusual sound at night as his voice, and to believe him to be continually behind the scenes, that at length this idea became the predominant one; the imagination was incessantly occupied with it; and hence unusual inward feelings of illness might easily be taken, by those to whom they occurred, for Satanic impulses and agency, and they seriously believed themselves to be bewitched and possessed. It is astonishing what firm hold this conviction had taken of some, and how they retained it even on the scaffold and at the stake. We find incontestable evidence that many were as certain of their guilt as their judges; and that the judges, as well as the unfortunate wretches condemned by them, were seized, in fact, with one and the same disease. The only difference was, that those were active, and these passive. It is, indeed, a pleasing occupation to compare the symptoms of those diseases attributed to infernal agency with the nervous complaints of our days, and the then way of thinking with the present; for it teaches us to admire the progress of natural philosophy and of the cultivation of the human mind, and gives us some idea of the blessed influence of genuine illumination.

One of the most singular fashionable diseases was that which caused people to believe themselves to be transformed into beasts. We find traces of it in the remotest antiquity. It is not improbable that many of the mythological fables may have originated in this source. The celebrated instance of King Nebuchadnezzar might have had a similar origin, and his extraordinary history may be reduced to this, that, deranged with inordinate pride, he fancied himself a brute, ran away, and with this notion actually lived several years among the beasts of the field, till at length, cured perhaps by the air and herbage, he recovered his reason and returned to his residence. But this disease was not properly in fashion till the 12th, 13th, and 14th century, when it received the distinctive appellation of *Lycanthropy*. In those times there were numbers of people who were sometimes seized with the extraordinary paroxysm of fancying themselves to be wolves. It was in fact a state of ecstasy or trance, in which the more delicate nervous system of the nineteenth century would perhaps have heard the voices of angels. Living at that time among wolves, people heard those animals howling, assumed in imagination the nature of wolves, and in idea acted accordingly. When they came to themselves, they related all that they had been doing in their dreams, just as if it had really happened. Many were even affected to such a degree, that they not only had visions, but actually ran away, wandered about for several days together in the forests, stealing lambs, devouring them raw, and conducting themselves exactly like wolves. At length this infatuation increased to such a pitch, that people firmly believed not merely that a man could fancy himself a wolf, but that he could actually transform himself into one. Hence the writers of those times gravely relate, that whole flocks of such *wolf-men* prowled about the country, that whole villages were seized with this mania, and that when a person killed a wolf, he could never be sure whether it was a real wolf or a man in the shape of a wolf; nay, it was even observed that the wounds inflicted on a supposed wolf very often appeared afterwards on the person of a man. At length it was deemed advisable to attribute this species of insanity also to the agency of the Devil, to anathematize the poor wolf-men, and to burn all that could be caught; and as the wolves themselves meanwhile gradually became more rare, and the imagination ceased to be so much engaged with them, this singular infatuation at length subsided entirely.

## THE WILD HUNTSMAN.

THY rest was deep at the slumberer's hour,
  If thou didst not hear the blast
Of the savage horn, from the Mountain-tower,*
  When the Wild Night-Huntsman past,
And the roar of the stormy chase went by,
Through the dark unquiet sky!

The deer sprang up from their mossy beds,
  When they caught the piercing sounds,
And the oak-boughs crash'd to their antler'd heads,
  As they flew from the viewless hounds;
And the falcon soar'd from her craggy height,
Away through the rushing night!

From the chieftain's hand the wine-cup fell,
  At the castle's festive board,
And a sudden pause came o'er the swell
  Of the harp's triumphal chord.
And the Minnesinger's † joyous lay
In the hall died fast away.

The convent's chaunted rite was stay'd,
  And the hermit dropp'd his beads,
And the forest rang through its deepest shade,
  With the neigh of the phantom steeds;
And the church-bells peal'd to the rocking blast,
As the Wild Night-Huntsman past!

The storm hath swept with the chase away,
  There is stillness in the sky;
But the mother looks on her son to-day,
  With a troubled heart and eye,
And the maiden's brow hath a shade of care,
'Midst the gleam of her golden hair!

The Rhine flows bright, but its waves ere long
  Must hear a voice of war,
And a clash of spears our hills among,
  And a trumpet from afar;
And the brave on a bloody turf must lie,
For the Huntsman hath gone by!‡

F. H.

---

  * The ruined Castle of Rodenstein, whence the Wild Huntsman is supposed to issue with his train, and traverse the air to the opposite Castle of Schnellerts.
  † Minnesinger, love-singers; the wandering minstrels of Germany were so called.
  ‡ It is a popular belief in the Odenwald, that the passing of the Wild Huntsman announces the approach of war.

## BEGGARS EXTRAORDINARY.—PROPOSALS FOR THEIR SUPPRESSION.

> I'm bubbled, I'm bubbled.
> Oh, how I am troubled.
> Bamboozled and bit!
> *Beggar's Opera.*

*Salve magna parens!* All hail to the parent Society for the Suppression of Mendicity!—so far from impugning its merits, I would applaud them to the very echo that should applaud again, always thanking Heaven that it was not established before the days of Homer, Belisarius, and Bampfylde Moore Carew, in which case we should have had three useful fictions the less, and lost three illustrations that have done yeoman's service in pointing many a moral, and tagging as. many tales. That I reverence the existing Association, and duly appreciate its benevolent exertions, is best evidenced by my proposal for a Branch or Subsidiary Company, not to interfere with duties already so fully and zealously discharged, but to take cognizance of various classes of sturdy beggars who do not come within the professed range of the original Institution. Mendicity is not confined to the asking of alms in the public streets; it is not the exclusive profession of rags and wretchedness, of the cripple and the crone, but is openly practised by able-bodied and well-dressed vagrants of both sexes, who, eluding the letter of the law while they violate its spirit, call loudly for the interference of some such repressive establishment as that which I am now advocating. When I inform you, Mr. Editor, that I live by my wits, you will at once comprehend the tenuity of my circumstances; and when I hint that I enact the good Samaritan to the best of my slender ability in all such cases as fall within my own observation, you will not wonder that I should wish to provide some sort of amateur Bridewell for such personages as my neighbour Miss Spriggins.

This lady is universally acknowledged to be one of the very best creatures in the world, which is the reason, I suppose, why she never married, there being no instance, out of the records of Dunmow, of any wife of that description. Her unoccupied time and affections followed the usual routine in such cases made and provided, that is to say, she became successively a bird-breeder, a dog-fancier, a blue-stocking, and lastly, the Lady Bountiful, not of our village only, (that I could tolerate,) but of the whole district, in which capacity she constitutes a central depôt for all the misfortunes that really happen, and a great many of those that do not. Scarcely a week elapses that she does not call upon me with a heart-rending account of a poor old woman who has lost her cow, a small farmer whose haystack has been burnt down, a shopkeeper whose premises have been robbed of his whole stock, or a widow who has been left with seven small children, the eldest only six years old, and that one a cripple; and the poor mother likely to add to the number in a few weeks; upon which occasions the subscription list is produced, beginning with the name of Sir David Dewlap, the great army contractor, and followed by those of nabobs, bankers, merchants, and brokers, (for I live but a few miles westward of London,) by whom a few pounds of money can no more be missed from their pockets than the same quantity of fat from their sides. My visitant, knowing the state of my purse, is kind

enough to point out to my observation that some have given so low as
a half-sovereign; but then she provokingly adds that even Mr. Tag,
a brother scribbler in the village, has put his name down for ten shillings, and surely a person of my superior talents———. Here she
smirks, and bows, and leaves off; and, partly in payment for her compliment, partly to prove that I can write twice as well as Mr. Tag, I
find it impossible to effect my ransom for less than a sovereign. Thus
does this good creature torment me in every possible way; first, by
bringing my feelings in contact with all the miseries that have occurred
or been trumped up in the whole county; and, secondly, by compelling
me to disbursements which I am conscious I cannot afford. Nor have
I even the common consolations of charity, for, feeling that I bestow
my money with an ill-will, from false pride or pique, I accuse myself
at once of vanity and meanness, of penury and extravagance. This
most worthy nuisance and insatiable beggar is the very first person I
should recommend to the notice of the proposed Society; and I hope
they will be quick, or I shall myself be upon her list. *I* shall be soon
suppressed if she is not.

That the clergyman of the parish should put me in spiritual jeopardy whenever he preaches a charity sermon, threatening me with all
sorts of cremation if I do not properly contribute to the collection, is
a process to which I can submit patiently:—for though his fulminations may be alarming, his is not the power that can enforce them.
But I do hold it to be a downright breach of the peace that Sir David
Dewlap aforesaid, and Doctor Allbury, should take their station on
each side of the church-door, thrusting in one's face a silver plate, in
such cases quite as intimidating as a pistol, and exclaiming in looks
and actions, if not in words—"Stand and deliver!" The former is
the bashaw of the village, whose fiat can influence the reception or
exclusion of all those who mix in the better sort of society, while his
custom can mar or make half the shopkeepers of the place. The
latter is our principal house-proprietor, and really, Mr. Editor, quarter-
day comes round so excessively quick, that it is never quite convenient
to be out of the good graces of one's landlord. It is precisely on
account of the undue influence they can thus exercise, that they undertake this species of legal extortion and robbery, for it deserves no
better name. Is it not as bad to put us in mental or financial, as in
bodily fear? and is it not a greater offence when practised on the
Lord's highway—(the churchyard), than even on the King's? Every
farthing thus given, beyond what would otherwise have been bestowed,
is so much swindled out of our pockets, or torn from us by intimidation,
unless we admit the possibility of compulsory free-will offerings. I
am a Falstaff, and hate to give money, any more than reasons, upon
compulsion: I submit, indeed, but it is an involuntary acquiescence.
The end, I may be told, sanctifies the means: charity covereth 'a multitude of sins;—true: but undue influence and extortion on the one
side, hypocrisy and heart-burning on the other—these are not charity,
nor do they hold any affinity with that virtue whose quality is not
strained, "but droppeth as the gentle dew from heaven." Does the
reader recollect a fine old grizzle-headed Silenus-faced demi-Hercules
of a cripple, who, with short crutches, and his limbless trunk on a kind
of sledge, used to shovel briskly along the streets of London? Dis-

daining to ask an alms, this counterpart of the Elgin Theseus would glance downwards at his own mutilated form, and upwards at the perfect one of the passengers, to whom he left it to draw the inference; and if this silent appeal failed to extract even a sympathising look, he would sometimes, in the waywardness of his mighty heart, wish " that the Devil might have them," (as who shall say he will not?)· In his paternal pride ·he had sworn to give a certain sum as a marriage-portion to his daughter; it was nearly accomplished, and he was stumping his painful rounds for its completion, when he was assailed by certain myrmidons as a vagabond, and, after a Nemæan resistance, was laid in durance vile. Was not *his* an end that might indeed sanctify the means? And shall a man like this be held a beggar by construction, when such symbolic mendicants and typical pickpockets as Sir David Dewlap and Doctor Allbury may hold their plates at our throats, and rob us with impunity? No—if I have any influence with the new Society, one of its earliest acts shall be the commitment of these Corinthian caterers to Bridewell, that they may dance a week's saraband together to the dainty measure of the Tread-Mill.

There is another class of eleemosynaries, who would be indignant at the appellation of Almsmen, since they make an attack upon your purse under the independent profession of *Borrowers*, while they are most valorous professors also (but most pusillanimous performers) of repayment. If they be gentry of whom one would fairly be quit for ever, I usually follow the Vicar of Wakefield's prescription, who was accustomed to lend a great coat to one, an old horse to a second, a few pounds to a third, and seldom was troubled by their reappearance. If they be indifferent parties, whom one may reasonably hope to fob off with banter and evasion, I quote to them from Shakspeare—

" Neither a borrower nor a lender be,
   For loan oft loses both itself and friend,
   And borrowing dulls the edge of husbandry."

Be they matter-of-fact fellows who apprehend not a joke, I shew them my empty purse, which, Heaven knows, is no joke to me, while it is the best of all arguments to them. But be they men of pith and promise, friends whom I well esteem and would long preserve, I refuse them at once, for these are companions whom I cannot afford to lose, and whom a loan would not long allow me to keep. Those who may be cooled by a refusal would have been alienated by an acquiescence. Friendship, to be permanent, must be perfectly independent; for such is the pride of the human heart, that it cannot receive a favour without a feeling of humiliation, and it will almost unconsciously harbour a constant wish to lower the value of the gift by diminishing that of the donor. Ingratitude is an effort to recover our own esteem by getting rid of our esteem for a benefactor; and when once self-love opposes our love of another, it soon vanquishes its adversary. We esteem benefactors as we do tooth-drawers, who have cured us of one pain by inflicting another. For the rich I am laying down no rules; they may afford to lose their friends as well as money, for they can command more of each; we who stand under the frown of Plutus must be economists of both, and it is for the benefit of such classes that I would have the whole brotherhood of mendicants, calling themselves borrowers, sentenced to the House of Correction—not till they had

paid their debts, for that would be equivalent to perpetual imprisonment, but until they had sincerely forgiven their old friends for lending them money, and placed themselves in a situation to acquire new
ones by a promise never to borrow any more.

A fourth description of beggars, not less pestilent in their visita-
tions, are the fellows who are constantly coming to beg that you will
lend them a book, which they will faithfully return in eight or ten
days, for which you may substitute *years*, and be no nearer to the recovery of your property. It is above that period since some of my
friends have *begged* the second volume of Tom Brown's Works, the
first of Bayle's Dictionary, Phineas Fletcher's Purple Island, and
various others whose absence creates many a " hiatus valde deflendus"
in my bookshelves, which, like so many open mouths, cry aloud to
heaven against the purloiners of odd volumes and the decimators of
sets. Books are a sort of feræ naturæ to these poachers that have
" nulla vestigia retrorsum ;" they pretend to have forgotten where they
borrowed them, and then claim them as strays and waifs. You may
know the number of a man's friends by the vacancies in his library,
and if he be one of the best fellows in the world, his shelves will assuredly be empty. Possession is held to be nine points in law, but
with friends of this class unlawful possession is the best of all titles,
for print obliterates property, *meum* and *tuum* cannot be bound up in
calf or morocco, and honour and honesty cease to be obligatory in all
matters of odd volumes. Beggars of this quality might with great
propriety be sent to the counting-houses of the different prisons and
penitentiaries, where their literary abilities might be rendered available by employing them as *book-keepers*, a business in which they
have already exhibited so much proficiency. One day for every oc-
tavo, two for a quarto, and three for every folio of which they could
not give a satisfactory account, would probably be deemed an adequate punishment.

The last species of mendicants whom I should recommend to the
new Suppression Society, and whom, judging by my own experience, I
should pronounce the most unfortunate and unreasonable of any, are
the young and old ladies, from the boarding-school Miss to the Dowager Blue Stocking, who, in the present rage for albums and autographs,
ferret out all unfortunate writers, from the Great Unknown, whom
every body knows, down to the illustrious obscure whom nobody
knows, and beg them—just to write a few lines for insertion in their
repository. If they will even throw out baits to induce so mere a min-
now as myself to nibble at a line, what must they do for the Tritons
and Leviathans of literature! Friends, aunts, cousins, neighbours,
all are put in requisition, and made successively bearers of the neat
morocco-bound begging-book. Surely, Mr. Higginbotham, you will
not refuse *me* when I know you granted the same favour to Miss Bar-
nacles, Miss Scroggs, Mrs. Scribbleton, and many others. Besides it
is so easy for *you* to compose a few stanzas.—Gadzooks ! these folks
seem to think one can write sense as fast as they talk nonsense—that
poetry comes spontaneously to the mouth, as if we were born impro-
visatori, and could not help ourselves. I believe, however, that few
will take the trouble to read that which has not occasioned some trouble to write ; and even if their supposition were true, we have the

authority of Dr. Johnson for declaring that no one likes to give away that by which he lives :—" You, Sir," said he, turning to Thrale, " would rather give away money than beer." And to come a begging of such impoverished wits as mine—*Corpo di Bacco!* it is robbing the Spittal—putting their hands in the poor-box—taking that " which nought enriches them, and makes me poor indeed"—doing their best to create a vacuum, which Nature abhors : and as to assuming that compliance costs nothing, this is the worst mendicity of all, for it is even begging the question. No, Mr. Editor, I cannot recommend to the new Society any extension of indulgence towards offenders of this class. The ladies, old and young, should be condemned to Bridewell, (not that I mean any play upon the word,) there to be dieted upon bread and water until they had completely filled one another's albums with poetry of their own composing ; after which process I believe they might be turned loose upon society without danger of their resuming the trade of begging. Other mendicant nuisances occur to me, for whose suppression the proposed Institution would be held responsible ; but I have filled my limits for the present, and shall therefore leave them to form the subject of a future communication.

---

### VALKYRIUR SONG.*

The Sea-King woke from the troubled sleep
 Of a vision-haunted night,
And he look'd from his bark o'er the gloomy deep,
 And counted the streaks of light ;
  For the red sun's earliest ray
  Was to rouse his bands that day,
 To the stormy joy of fight !

But the dreams of rest were still on earth,
 And the silent stars on high,
And there waved not the smoke of one cabin-hearth
 'Midst the quiet of the sky ;
  And along the twilight-bay
  In their sleep the hamlets lay,
 —For they knew not the Norse were nigh !

The Sea-King look'd o'er the tossing wave,
 He turn'd to the dusky shore,
And there seem'd, through the arch of a tide-worn cave,
 A gleam, as of snow, to pour.
  And forth, in watery light,
  Moved phantoms, dimly white,
 Which the garb of woman wore.

Slowly they moved to the billow-side,
 And the forms, as they grew more clear,
Seem'd each on a tall pale steed to ride,
 And a cloudy crest to rear,
  And to beckon with faint hand
  From the dark and rocky strand,
 And to point a gleaming spear !

---

* The Valkyriur, the Fatal Sisters, or Choosers of the Slain, in Northern Mythology.

Then a stillness on his spirit fell,
  Before th' unearthly train,
For he knew Valhalla's daughters well,
  The Choosers of the Slain !
    And a sudden-rising breeze
    Bore across the moaning seas
  To his ear, their lofty strain.

" 'There are songs in Odin's Hall,
For the brave, ere night to fall !
Doth the great sun hide his ray ?
—He must bring a wrathful day !
Sleeps the falchion in its sheath ?
—Swords must do the work of death !
Regner ! Sea-King ! *thee* we call !
—There is joy in Odin's Hall.

" At the feast and in the song
Thou shalt be remember'd long !
By the green Isles of the flood
Thou hast left thy track in blood !
On the earth and 'midst the sea,
There are those will speak of thee !
'Tis enough—the war-gods call !
—There is mead in Odin's Hall !

" Regner ! tell thy fair-hair'd bride
She must slumber at thy side !
Tell the brother of thy breast *
Ev'n for him thy grave hath rest !
Tell the raven-steed which bore thee,
When the wild-wolf fled before thee,
He, too, with his lord must fall !
—There is room in Odin's Hall !

" Lo ! the mighty sun looks forth !
Arm ! thou leader of the north !
Lo ! the mists of twilight fly !
We must vanish, thou must die !
By the sword, and by the spear,
By the hand that knows not fear,
Sea-King ! nobly shalt thou fall !
—There is joy in Odin's Hall !"

There was arming heard on land and wave,
  When afar the sunlight spread,
And the phantom-forms of the tide-worn cave
  With the twilight mists were fled.—
    But at eve, the kingly hand
    Of the battle-axe and brand
  Lay cold, on a pile of dead !                    F. H.

---

* When a northern chief fell gloriously in battle, his obsequies were honoured
with all possible magnificence.  His arms, gold and silver, war-horse, domestic
attendants, and whatever else he held most dear, were placed with him on the
pile.  His dependents and friends frequently made it a point of honour to die with
their leader, in order to attend on his shade in the palace of Odin.  And lastly, his
wife was generally consumed with him on the same pile.—*Mallet's Northern Anti-
quities.*

## *Dulwich College.* *

THERE are several Teniers' here, and two or three that require particular mention. First, however, as a better opportunity may perhaps not occur, I will state what strikes' me as being the distinguishing differences between this extraordinary artist, and his no less extraordinary living rival—Wilkie; for this is not one of those comparisons that are entitled to be ranked as " odious ;"—on the contrary, it can hardly fail to heighten our conception of the merits of both the subjects of it, if (as I think) it is calculated to illustrate those merits, and render them more obvious.—It is a mistake to consider either of these artists as comic painters. They are nothing less. I do not recollect a joke in any picture by either of them. They are painters of human life—at least of a certain class of it; and if the scenes that occur in and distinguish that class are of a smiling character—good : but the artists choose them, not because they bear that character generally—but *because they are there.* They are painters of truth ;—and because such is the truth, they paint it—not because the truth is such. If the truth had been different, their pictures would have been different. Without knowing any thing of the personal character of either, I should judge them both, the one to have been, and the other to be, steady, serious, severe, pains-taking men—almost incapable of enjoying a joke, much less of inventing one. They are painters of facts and of things, not of sentiments, and ideas, and opinions; and as Nature is no joker, so they are none. Not that, if society or circumstances throw a joke in their way, they have any objection to pick it up; but they never think of going out of their way to find one. In fact they are conscientious to a fault; like Mr. Crabbe, the poet. They think that whatever is fit to be done, is fit to be painted; and their *choice* of subject is confined to a class, and to nothing else.

There is, however, this grand difference between Teniers and Wilkie;—that the one is a painter of the *real* truth, and the other of the *ideal:* for Wilkie's pictures are as ideal, in the true sense of that term, as the finest of the antiques are ;—that is to say, they are as much founded in the absolute truth of Nature, yet as little to be seen there in point of fact. Every one of Teniers' scenes *has* happened; but not one of Wilkie's ever did or could happen; though there is no reason to be given why they should not. In short, the scenes of the one are absolutely *true to nature*, and consistent with it in all their parts; but the other's are *nature itself.*

Perhaps it may still farther illustrate the relative merits of these two extraordinary artists, if I say that, if Wilkie has more individual *expression* than Teniers, the latter has much more *character ;*—that if the scenes of the former are more entertaining and exciting, those of the latter are more satisfying ;—that if Wilkie's affect us more like a capital performance on the stage, Teniers' are felt and remembered more as actual scenes that have passed before us in real life ;—that, in fact, Wilkie's are admirable as *pictures*, but that Teniers' are the things

---

* Continued from page 557.

F 2

themselves. A foreigner who was acquainted with the works of Teniers at the time the Dutch boors were such as he represents them, and who went to visit the country with the remembrance of these works in his mind, must have felt at first as if he had got among a world created by Teniers' pencil, and animated by some strange magic. But this could never happen with respect to Wilkie's pictures. We might chance to fall in with one of Wilkie's *figures,*—for they must all either be or have been in existence; but we may look in vain for one of his *pictures,* any where but on his canvass;—whereas Teniers' pictures might be seen every hour in the day, in every town and village in Holland. And the reason of this difference is, simply, that the one is laborious and scrupulous to a degree in selecting, and consorting, and combining; while the other did not select at all. This, too, may in some measure account for the extraordinary facility of hand of the one, as compared with that of the other, and also the extraordinary number of his pictures that we meet with; for it might almost be said that, as Wilkie has painted nothing but what he has seen, so Teniers saw nothing but what he painted.

As I have no scruple in placing these two extraordinary artists on a general level in point of acquired skill as well as of natural power, I will add, that what Wilkie wants of the freedom and facility of touch of his dead rival, and the exquisite truth, purity, and transparency of colouring, he at least compensates for in his conception and execution of individual expression. The *quantity* of expression that he is capable of throwing into a face, without in the slightest degree overstepping the " modesty of nature," has never yet been equalled by any artist, living or dead, whose works are at present extant.

Apologizing, to those who think it necessary, for this short digression from our immediate subject, I now return to the second room of the Dulwich Gallery, and proceed to notice the remarkable pictures, nearly in the order in which they occur;—first pointing out the *Chaff-cutter* (156) as perhaps the finest (though not the most striking or ambitious) picture of Teniers in this collection. But all the others may be regarded as excellent examples, in their different ways, of his characteristic qualities, both of handling and of expression.—Nos. 106 and 118 strike me as being two of the very best pictures of Vandyke that I have ever seen, in the ideal style. The delineation of Nature—refined, but yet real nature—was his forte; but still he has painted a few ideal works that are exceedingly fine—and these must be ranked among the number. 118—a *Madonna and Child,* is the best. It has all the glow of Rubens without his coarseness; or rather all the refinement of Guido without his coldness. The upturned gaze of the mother is intense. She is feeding her mind from above with high and holy thoughts. And the attitude and character of the child express the very nobility of Nature. It seems to have fed from the same fount with its divine mother, but through *her* medium—to have sucked in its mental as well as bodily life from her breast. There is a repetition of this picture at the Cleveland Gallery; but I think the one before us is the finer of the two. Here are also two other admirable works by the same master;—portraits of the Earl of Pembroke (163), and the Archduke Albert (196); both displaying that look of conventional nobility that no one could give like Vandyke. Immediately over the latter of these hangs a capital picture by Velasquez; full of truth and spirit (195).

It represents the little Prince of Asturias, when a child of six or seven years of age, on a great trampling war-horse—sitting as upright as a dart, and as bold as if he felt the future general within him. His little legs scarcely reach half way down the horse's side, and his hands can hardly grasp the reins; and yet you feel that he has a perfect command over the animal he is riding. This is a very singular picture, and is well worth particular attention.—Returning for a moment to the second room, I would point out two pictures that are among the very finest in this collection. One of them (149) is by Rubens, and is (strangely enough) called "Saint Barbara fleeing from her Persecutors." It is very small, and a mere sketch; and it represents a female figure ascending some steps, followed by a man. But what I would particularly point out is the effect of motion which is given to the two figures—or which they are, in fact, so contrived as to give to each other. No one could manage this like Rubens, and *he* has nowhere managed it more finely than in this little sketch—struck off, no doubt, in a few happy moments, and as a mere study or amusement. You may look at this picture till you fairly see the figures move, and expect that they will presently disappear.—The other (144) is one of Rembrandt's very finest efforts, and is perhaps the most purely poetical picture he ever produced. The effect that light seemed to produce, not only on the mind but the hand of this painter, is truly astonishing. In all other things he was a common man; but when an extraordinary or even a common effect of light was his subject, he became at once a poet. The picture before us is called Jacob's Dream; and it may be safely stated that the subject, poetical and imaginative as it is, was never before so poetically or imaginatively treated. The picture is quite small, and an upright one; and nearly all over it, except the centre, is spread a thick black gloom—deep as the darkness of night, and yet so transparent that you see, or seem to see, down into it, as if you were looking into deep water. In one corner of this darkness lies Jacob, on the ground, sleeping—his arms stretched above his head, and one knee bent up, in the most inartificial attitude that can be conceived, and altogether representing a rude shepherd-boy. Round about him, and along the front of the foreground, are scratched in a few straggling shrubs, *with the wrong end of the pencil:* these are merely scratched out of the brown ground while it was wet—not painted in afterwards. In fact the picture consists but of two colours—or rather it has no colours at all, but consists merely of light and shade. All this dark part of the picture is exceedingly fine. There is an admirable keeping and consistency about it, looking at it only with a view to itself, as the immediate *scene* in which the awful dream takes place. But, as a contrast to heighten the impression we receive from the representation of the dream itself, its effect is prodigious. This representation occupies the centre part of the picture; and as a delineation of *super*-natural appearances and things, I conceive it to be finer than any thing within the same space in existence. In the upper part of the sky an intense light is bursting forth, and it descends slantwise and widening as it descends, till it reaches the sleeping youth—gradually decreasing in splendour as it recedes from its apparent source; and at different intervals of this road of light, winged figures are seen descending. In the whole circle of art there are not to be pointed out more unequivocal strokes of genius than these figures. They are as purely poetical *creations* as any thing that ever proceeded even from the pen. They are like nothing that was ever seen or described. All the angels that I have ever before seen depicted or described are but winged mortals; but these angels are no more like mortals than they are like any thing else. They are altogether of the air, airy; and if they must be likened to any thing, it is to birds; though we probably gain this association simply on account of their having *wings* like birds—for they resemble them in nothing else: they are not *flying*, but gliding down perpendicularly, as if borne up on the surface of the collected rays of light; and their outspread wings seem used only to keep them in this erect position as they descend. I conceive this picture · to be worthy the deepest study and attention, and that the more it is studied the more its extraordinary merit will be discovered and admitted.

The first picture calling for particular attention in the centre or third room is 176, A Girl at a Window, by the same artist  This is as purely natural and forcible a head as Rembrandt ever painted. It must have been a study from nature; for there is an absolute *truth* about it that no memory or invention could have given. It is taken from the lowest class of life; and there is a very particular character about it, which is sometimes observable in that class at an early age; namely, that, judging from the face merely, you can scarcely determine whether it belongs to a male or female. The character of expression depicted in the human face, is so entirely owing to the habits of thought and feeling arising from the circumstances in which we are placed, that, in the very lowest classes of life, and at an early age, before the sexual qualities become developed, you frequently see faces that exhibit no mark of sex whatever; and others (as in the instance before us) in which females, from associating indiscriminately with males, and partaking in the same sports and pursuits, acquire the same expression of countenance. The picture before us might just as well have been called "*Boy* at a Window," as Girl.

Near to the above are two very pleasing and characteristic specimens of Watteau—the gay, the graceful, the genteel, the gallánt (not the gállant) Watteau—(185 and 191), a *Bál champetre*, and a *Fête champetre*. For a natural style of depicting all that is *un*natural in manners and appearance, commend me to Watteau. He not only places us in the midst of the affected airs and courtly graces of the times of Louis XIV., but he makes us admire them. To see one of his out-of-door scenes, and not to wish ourselves in the midst of it, is impossible,— though it consist of ladies in hooped petticoats and ostrich-plumed heads, seated on the green grass, beneath green trees, talking to gentlemen with rosettes in their shoes, and flowing perriwigs on their heads —or couples of these respectively, "moving a measure" to the minuet in Ariadne, as if they had the fear of a French dancing-master before their eyes, or had read Mr. Wordsworth's poems, and were therefore cautious not to tread upon the daisies—so mincingly do they move! It is impossible to conceive of any thing less *in keeping* than the airs and graces of a court thus shewing themselves off in the very presence of that Nature which belies them all, and one breath of which, perfumed with sweet flowers, ought to be able to blow them all away in a moment,— substituting in their place that free, fresh, and unpremeditated gaiety of heart, that involuntary effusion of pure animal spirit, which vents itself in "nods, and becks, and wreathed smiles,"—in off-hand jollity, and heedless joyance—in any thing rather than courtly courtesies and cold common-places. And yet there is no denying that the art of Watteau contrives in some way or other to reconcile together Nature and its antithesis, and we seem to like each the better for its friendly union with the other. The Art, we think, cannot be wholly denaturalised that can thus willingly take Nature by the hand; and the Nature must be rich and pure indeed, that can afford to undergo this marriage with Art. No. 191 is by far the best of these two pictures, and may be regarded as a very fair example of Watteau's best style.

In Nos. 194, 195, and 196, we have three admirable portraits together; the first, Rubens's mother, by Rubens; the second, by Velasquez, of the Prince Asturias; and the third, by Vandyke, in his finest manner, the Archduke Albert. The only other picture in this room that I shall notice particularly, is one by Murillo,—though I confess that there are several others of great merit and interest. But if I were not to be *very* select in my strictures on this admirable collection, I should notice almost every picture of the three hundred and fifty that it contains, and thus write a volume instead of a short paper. And, to say the truth, I should desire nothing better in the way of authorship (as far as it respects myself, and the pleasant occupation it would afford me) than to be called upon to furnish a volume on this one Gallery alone; so rich, varied, and select are its contents.

No. 217 (Jacob and Rachel, by Murillo,) is a charming work, full of sweetness, tenderness, and grace—but the grace of nature alone, not of society—the grace that is inspired by present sentiment, not by habit or by art. "And Jacob kissed Rachel, and lifted up his voice, and wept." Both figures are in a kneeling posture,—Rachel bending forward to receive the kiss, which Jacob is proffering with uplifted lips, as if it were a vow to Heaven. It may be fancy,—but to me the face of Rachel seems intended to resemble, in lamb-like innocence and simplicity, the younglings of her father's flock. She may be supposed to have looked upon them till their beauty has passed into her face, and become a part of it. The undefined outline which Murillo gave to all his works of this class, has a very pleasing effect here,—blending all the different parts together, and suffering each to become as it were a portion of the other, and at the same time giving an airy softness to the whole.

In the fourth room, the most striking and valuable works are unquestionably the Poussins; and I know not where else to find so admirable a selection of them. Better single pictures of him may be found elsewhere; but nowhere so many fine ones collected together: for though there are a vast number of his larger gallery pictures at the Louvre, I hold this latter class of his works to be altogether inferior to the class to which the pictures here belong. Probably the best picture here by this artist is No. 287, called The Education of Jupiter. It is, in point of expression, not so fine in parts as one or two others. But, as a whole, and for colouring, composition, and expression united, it is certainly a fine work. Nothing can be more complete in itself than every separate portion of it, and at the same time each portion is finely consistent with all the others; and it is *this*, in particular, which

seems to entitle a work to the term classical. The centre group is
finely imagined, and most happily executed. The infant, in particular,
is drawn with infinite spirit, and yet with perfect nature and truth.
So, also, is the one lying down in the right-hand corner: and the colouring of this one is exquisite. The two single figures behind—the
one standing by the tree, and the other lying in a reclining attitude—
are also admirable. There is an *air* about them that no one but Poussin
ever gave. This picture is among his most highly-finished productions—much more so than any of the others in the present collection. Perhaps the one next in merit and value to the foregoing is
No. 209—a Poet drinking in inspiration from a cup presented to him
by the hand of Apollo. The youthful god is drawn in an easy, but
not very graceful attitude, holding a small shallow cup to the lips of
the poet, who is drinking the inspiring draught with all his faculties, of
mind as well as body. The expression of this figure is exceedingly
fine. There are also several little winged figures scattered about this
picture, which add to the imaginative character of it, without producing
any of that deteriorating effect which these kind of figures usually do,
when introduced injudiciously—as they almost always are. Here they
seem to typify the winged thoughts that are necessarily attendant on
the favoured of Apollo.

In the same rich and intense style in point of expression, but more
dashing and spirited in the handling, and more deep and sombre in the
colouring, is 225—The Education of Bacchus. The god is depicted
as an infant, attended by Satyrs, Nymphs, &c. who are giving him the
juice of the grape to drink, while one is filling the cup from above
as fast as he drains it. The expression of the child in this picture is
finely contrasted with, and at the same time finely resembles, that of the
poet in the other picture. The one is drinking as ardently as the
other; but the expression of the poet has much of intellect mixed
with it, while that of the child is purely animal. I do not mean to
say that this latter expression is appropriate, supposing the picture to
be what its name indicates. I conceive this name to have been given
it without any sufficient reason, and that it merely represents a Bac-
chanalian scene, in which the sport is made to consist in teaching the
children to drink, and in watching its effect upon them. The child
is drinking exactly in the manner that any other thirsty animal drinks
—*swilling*—poking its nose and lips into the cup as a horse does
into a water-trough. This is exceedingly fine as representing the
mere animal feeling of a child under such circumstances; but it is not
so, if that child is intended for the infant god. And, I repeat, though
not less ardent and intense than the expression of the poet in the
other picture, it is of a totally different character. The other expressions in this picture,—of the nymphs, satyrs, &c. who are watching
the sport,—are highly appropriate and fine.

The Jupiter and Antiope, as it is named (though again, as I think,
without adequate reason,) is a disagreeable picture, but yet, in many
respects, exceedingly fine. The sleeping nymph is indeed sleeping—
not merely in her eyes, but in all her frame. There is the protruding
lips, the total absence of consciousness, and consequently the total
freedom from the restraints of custom, and the sense of being the
subject of observation, which is always apparent, even in women, when

they sleep—but which is so seldom depicted in works of art. In most sleeping figures you have only to fancy their eyes open, and they are awake—but here all the faculties are asleep. The figure of Jupiter (so called) is drawn and coloured with great *gusto*; but it is highly disagreeable and inappropriate nevertheless.

The rest of the Poussins in this Gallery I must leave to the general admiration of the spectator. They call for particular study and attention, and pages might be written on the merits and defects of every one of them.

Here are two excellent specimens of Salvator Rosa; a small upright landscape (226), and Soldiers Gaming (236). The characteristic air of the soldier who is looking on—upright, firm, self-poised, Roman—is admirable. We have also a capital portrait by this artist, of a " Young Man drawing" (270).

In this part of the collection there are several other excellent, and indeed first-rate pictures in their respective styles, which I cannot pass over silently, and which yet I must not attempt to do more than name, and recommend to the particular attention of the spectator and student. But it is the less necessary to notice them at any length, as their merits are for the most part exactly similar to those of others by the same artists, which I have had occasion to examine in detail in my former papers, or which I shall have more eligible opportunities of attending to hereafter. Conspicuous among these are four delightful Claudes. 246, The Embarkation of St. Paul from the port of Ostia, though much smaller than the two Embarkations in Mr. Angerstein's collection, is similar in style to them, and not much inferior in merit. 248, a Landscape, divided in the centre in his favourite manner, by three trees, with a tower on the left hand, and the blue distant hills blending with the blue sky,—is exquisite. There are some figures introduced which are better than usual, and from these the picture is called Jacob and Laban. 257, is another sea-port, of the same character as 246. 252, is one of a very rare kind for this artist. It is full of figures, and represents the Campo Vacino, at Rome. The distance of this recedes finely, and the sky is all his own. There are two or three other pictures by this artist, of different degrees of merit.

251, is a Venus and Adonis, said to be by Titian; but it is not in that condition to enable one to feel any certainty as to its being really by him. It is a repetition of that by the same artist, noticed in Mr. Angerstein's collection, and it differs scarcely at all from that in point of composition, but is inferior in colouring, and in its state of preservation. 228, is an admirable portrait, by Rubens, of a Venetian lady; painted probably at the time he was in Italy, and studying the works of Titian; for it has more of that artist's intellectual style of expression, and less of his own florid colouring, than even his portraits usually had. 243, is a St. Cecilia, by Guercino; and 299 and 253 are Holy Families, by Andrea del Sarto. They are all very pleasing works, and in some degree characteristic of their authors; but neither of them are of sufficient importance to afford an eligible opportunity of enquiring into the general merits of these two excellent painters. The same may be said of 295, by Caravaggio. It is rich, racy, and full of spirit; but does not afford scope for any particular description—being nothing more than a single head. All these are in the fourth room.

We now proceed to the fifth and last, and perhaps the richest—
for it contains one picture alone that is above all price. Let us examine this at once; for we cannot properly attend to the other excellent works which this department of the Gallery contains, unless we
first in some degree dismiss this one from our thoughts for a moment
—but to dismiss or by any means get rid of it entirely, after having
once seen it, is impossible. I allude to Murillo's wonderful picture of
" Spanish Peasant Boys" (322). Murillo was a man of a very extraordinary capacity, since he could see with equal clearness, and express with equal force and facility, the two extremes of natural appearances, as far as these are connected with the human form and
character.; for it is so far alone that he appears to have studied them.
By these two extremes I mean, on the one hand, the absolute and unadorned truth, as it may be supposed to present itself to an eye purged
of all human imperfections, and divorced from all human associations
—*the truth, as it is* IN ITSELF; and, on the other hand, the'same truth,
heightened and etherealized by being looked at through a veil cast over
the senses by the heart and the affections, and at the same time coloured.
by the misty lights that fall upon it from the fancy and the imagination, through the medium of accidental or purposed associations—*the
truth, as it is* IN US. The almost miraculous picture before us, is an
example of what I mean by the first of these; and many of his scriptural pieces are examples of the second : and in each case, however
strangely they may differ from each other, I conceive that what is presented to us is *the* truth, and nothing else,—as far as regards its purposes and effects. This is undoubtedly a dangerous faculty for one
and the same person to possess ; and Murillo has occasionally proved
it to be so[*]—but perhaps less than most others would have done. It
enables him to perform either or both of the miracles ascribed to the
mortal and the immortal minstrel of old ;—it not only permits him to
" raise a mortal to the skies," but to " bring an angel down." And it
is a little singular that, in a certain class of his works, Murillo does in
some degree effect *both* of these ends at the same time. In the best of
his Assumptions of the Virgin, Holy Families, &c. the mortals are all
angelic, and the angels are all mortals. What I mean is, that, in the
mere mortal persons represented, there is, mixed up with their mortality, an air, an emanation of divinity,—as if they had gained a foretaste of their future state, and were already beatified ; and in the divine persons there is, mixed up with their divinity, a merely human—
frequently an *individual*—expression, as if they could not, or would
not, wholly assoil themselves from their connexion with the earth.
For my own part, I believe this to be the chief, if not the only charm
of Murillo's pictures of this class,—setting aside their great harmony
as well as sweetness of colouring : for they have no particular merit
of design or composition ; and the expressions of the faces include
scarcely any thing of intellectual superiority over those that we meet
in our every-day intercourse with real life ;—they have none whatever
of the divine purity and poetical elevation of Raffaelle's—none of the
intense sweetness and intellectual grace of Correggio's—none of the

---

[*]. I allude to certain pictures of his that were formerly at the Louvre, but are
now removed to the places from whence they came.

passionate softness of Guido's—none, even, of that rich vitality, that infinite life of mind, which half redeems the coarse realities of Rubens. But I am, in the present instance, to speak of perhaps the finest specimen in existence of Murillo's other class of works ; his Spanish Beggar Boys,—as it should be called—for such they are—not Peasants. The picture is upright, and not large, and it represents two boys ; one half-lying on the ground, and looking up at his companion with an intense and yet vacant expression of pleasure in his face ; while the other is standing munching a great piece of bread that he can scarcely hold in his mouth, and looking sulkily down at him on the ground, as if displeased at the cause of the other's pleasure. The merit of these two faces consists in the absolute, the undisguised, and unadorned truth of their expression, and its wonderful force and richness ; and also in the curious characteristicness of it. By the *truth* of expression, I mean the fidelity with which the painter *has* represented what he *intended* to represent ; and by its characteristicness, I mean the adaptation of that expression to the circumstances. The persons represented are in that class and condition of life in which the *human* qualities of man scarcely develope themselves at all ; in which he can scarcely be regarded in any other light than the most sagacious of the *animal* tribe of beings. Accordingly, the expressions of these boys respectively—rich, vivid, and distinct as they are—are almost entirely animal. There is nothing in the least degree *vulgar* about them ; for vulgarity is a quality dependent on society ; and these have no share in society, and consequently are without any of its results, good or bad. In fact, their wants and feelings are merely animal, and the expressions which these give rise to are correspondent. The delight of the one is that of the happy colt sporting on its native common ; and the sulkiness of the other is that of the ill-conditioned cub growling over its food. At the feet of the boy who is eating stands a dog, looking up expectantly ; and there is nearly as much expression in *his* countenance as there is in either of the others. I would not lay much stress on this ; but does it not seem to have been introduced purposely, that we might compare the expression of this *third* animal with that of the two others, and see that there is, and that there is intended to be, little difference between the different expressions, except in degree, and that they are all alike animal ? I conceive this picture to be, in its way, entirely faultless, and to have required as rare a faculty to produce it—(as *rare*, but not as valuable)—as perhaps any thing else in the art. The companion picture to it (324), on a nearly similar subject, is excellent, but not to be compared with this.—237, in the last room (which I omitted to notice there, in order that I might connect it with these) is also an admirable work in exactly the same class. It is a portrait of a Spanish Girl with Flowers ; and has the same marvellous truth and reality with the above. For a face that is not intended to include any particular kind of expression, but merely a general vivacity of eye and feature, I have never seen any thing surpassing it.—In the pictures numbered 326, the Infant Saviour with a Lamb, and 334, Assumption of the Virgin, the reader may see examples of what I have described as Murillo's other style of painting. The child, in the Assumption, is most exquisite. They are, however, not among his finest works of this class ; and indeed I know not where any are to be found in England at all equal to some that exist in different churches in Spain,—several of which were formerly at the Louvre.

"A Musical Party" (329) is a charming specimen of Giorgione's tasty and gallant manner of treating subjects of this kind. The feather in her cap is not more negligently gay and graceful in its air, than is the lady of this picture.—In the centre of this last room, at the end, and forming the most conspicuous object in this gallery, is a very fine picture by Guido,—The Martyrdom of St. Sebastian. Its merit, however, consists chiefly in the design and colouring—there being, as usual, little tragic expression in it. There is great depth and richness in the shadows; and the centre part, where the bright light falls, is very finely coloured as well as drawn—though the flesh is rather too marbly to give the effect of life.

The only other picture I can trust myself to notice (for this paper has already run to twice the length that I intended any of them to reach) is 354—"A Cardinal blessing a Priest," by Paul Veronese. This picture, though including but two figures, is a capital specimen of that sacerdotal dignity of style of which this painter was so fond, and in which he excelled all his rivals. The Catholics of his day ought to have canonized him; for he did more by his works to draw respect upon their religion than half its saints have by their miracles. Nothing can be finer than the air, attitude, and expression of the cardinal, in this picture, as he bends over the kneeling priest, blessing him. He does it with an air that bespeaks an entire confidence in the efficacy of the act, as well as a consciousness of the dignity attendant on the privilege of performing it.

---

## A FOREIGN SOLDIER'S FAREWELL TO HIS ENGLISH MISTRESS.

WHY bleeds a heart once haughty, wild,
To be from England's shores exiled?
Are home and friends the endearing band?
No, these are in a distant land.

Is 't fear that on my heart lays hold?
I am not cast in coward mould—
I've braved the battle man to man,
And borne my banner in the van.

Why do I shudder then and weep,
To mount you bark and plough the deep?
Whose stormy waves I lightly mind,
Heart-wreck'd in leaving thee behind!

Farewell! O met by fatal chance!
As eyes struck by the lightning's glance
See light no more: thus blind shall be
My soul to beauty, losing thee.

C.

## BEING IN LOVE.

I HAVE often been in love, and often been disappointed by the intervention of some untoward circumstance, which before I was too deeply linked for my heart to disenthral itself, broke the chain, and restored me to liberty. I never was a blind lover, nor could I be accused of inconstancy. I never fell in love without a wariness, the lack of which has been the ruin of far better men than myself. This arose, I hope it will pardon the avowal, from too exalted an opinion of the sex. I once thought a portion of it to be faultless, and in my foolish judgment had almost decided that the errors of mortality belonged exclusively to man. When I found some peccadillo in the fair object of my regard of very little consequence in itself, I suspected others of greater magnitude to be still concealed, and made haste to stifle my incipient passion. This I effected by the aid of a notion of perfectibility which I conscientiously believed to exist in woman, and I was determined should be found in her with whom I was to enjoy the consummation of mortal happiness. The false opinions of youth are frequently preservatives from evil, and I am indebted to my erroneous notions of female optimism for my escape from an early and too green state of matrimony. Every instance of disappointment in this way, while it acted as a fresh stimulus in my search of the perfect being that existed only in my fancy, increased my caution in my advances. I was consequently no sooner " off with the old love," as the song says, " than I was on with the new." I was in love from sixteen to twenty-six at least half a dozen times. I remember one instance when I had advanced very far in my progress, even to what M. Beyle * calls, in his fanciful way, the *seconde crystallization*, when the mind passes and repasses between the ideas of the lady's perfectibility, " her love for me, and what I must do to obtain a proof of her affection." One of the most enduring sins of woman is coquetry ; it may almost be said to commence in the cradle and linger beyond the wane of beauty. I had never dreamed of such a failing ; my own ingenuousness was so apparent that I imagined its notoriety would operate as a safeguard, and that where deceit was not even dreamt of, it would never be used in return. The first fair object of my love visited at a mansion to which I had never been invited, and in that mansion she accepted the admiration of another lover, and fed her vanity with the double incense offered from two honourable hearts at the same moment. It is but justice to declare that this failing is rarer with the male sex. Few men ever pay court with apparent sincerity to two ladies at the same time; but how many of the latter encourage a plurality of admirers without feeling a sincere attachment for any ! In my case a misdirected *billet-doux* discovered my mistress's perfidy. I enclosed it in a note to my rival, congratulating him on his sharing with me the smiles of the writer ; and though it by no means disclosed more than the advance of love on the lady's side to the *seconde crystallization* above alluded to, it exhibited a state of maturity that taught me it was of longer standing than my own. I sincerely loved, but, as I had not quite arrived at that point which hermetically seals up the eyes to all but the perfectibility

---

* See his work entitled L'Amour.

of the object beloved, *l'amour propre* dictated that I should banish the
fair hypocrite from my heart. I succeeded in doing so, but it cost me
many an hour spent like Jaques' "in a melancholy of mine own." I
was ultimately revenged on the lady, by witnessing the loss of both
her lovers. Since that time she has passed the noon of life and beauty
in the tantalizing state denominated "single blessedness." Thus the
deity of love often avenges his outraged regality.

But wherefore, I hear the reader exclaim, detail your love adventures
to me? I crave his pardon: if he be an unhappy *celibataire* who knows
nothing about being in love, let him skip my lucubration, and leave it
for the benefit of those who in time past have, or may at present be in
that enjoying state—to the young, the wise, and the susceptible. Being
in love then, to begin, by way of definition, is a state of pleasing excitement which nature and social life have created by mutual concessions
to accommodate the intercourse of the sexes to the refinements of civilization. To avoid the intensity of natural passion and the rapidity of
its approaches, slow advances, like those of an engineer towards a fortress, have been introduced. We must proceed *pas et pas.* In making
these it is that all the hazards, pleasures, and pains, in M. Beyle's
nomenclature, during the formation of *crystallizations,* happen. It was
a considerable time after my previous disappointment that I again
found myself advanced about two thirds of the way, to use simile still,
to the fortress of which I hoped to obtain possession, and every thing
seemed to indicate the fulfilment of my expectations. I had passed
safely through the palpitating feelings which are experienced at
receiving "first impressions." I had seen with triumph, that what the
ladies denominate "particular attentions," were as gratefully received
as I conjectured virgin coyness would allow them to be. My happiness seemed advancing to fruition; flowing on like an unruffled
stream, reflecting the brightness of heaven and the luxuriant scenery of
earth. I had even ventured twice to impress a kiss on the lips of the
blushing girl at those opportune moments, of which, when chance gives
them, lovers know how to take the advantage. All the visions of a para-
disiacal state danced before my sight in a long vista of years. A second
time I knew what it was to be in love. How I went down the dance!
—how my intoxicated heart poured out its gushing torrent of delight
on meeting, after a short interval of absence! Absence sharpens love's
appetite—hence the old and sound advice:

 "When you woo a maid you should seldom come in sight,"

because fancy becomes active during absence, and is so ingrossed with
the perfection of the beloved object, that it leaves no space for any other
occupation.

Being in love may produce different feelings according to the temperament of the individual; but its pleasures and anxieties are of much
the same character in all. Sometimes, as a farce-writer says, "it is the
very devil of torment;" at others, it is a state of unvarying complacency.
With the sanguine, it is, when thwarted, a whirlwind of raging
storms. With some cold constitutions, its pleasures and pains exist in a
state of negation. With myself it was a stimulant to activity. I was
never long at rest: it kept me in a kind of bodily ebriety that admitted only of marching and countermarching. It drove sleep from
my eyelids, and gave me a horror of immobility greater than I can

well express. Yet it was a state of delightful sensation when all went
on prosperously. In love there is no room for any interloping intru-
sive desire, any craving after something novel to relieve the *ennui* of
life. All is complete,—all is satisfaction,—there is ''

> No craving void left aching in the breast.

One object absorbs and fixes every thought and action; we live and
move but to think and hope and desire the idol to whose worship we
have devoted ourselves.

M——, for that was the name of my second mistress, received the
congratulations of her acquaintance on her acceptation of a lover, and
infidel indeed would he have been thought who credited that we were
not the most faithful of enamoratos. But I found too soon that M——
was devoid of sensibility—she was without passion, and while I was the
ardent lover that burned with an unquenchable flame, I found that
its light fell upon an iceberg that was incapable of receiving or reflecting the warmth that love had thrown upon it. There are many constitutions in the world physically cold that would not be conjectured
so from appearances. They marry and have families because others
marry and have families around them, and jog through life as Prior
says, " in a kind of—as it were." Now this coldness in M—— first
caused fear on my part that I was not really beloved. *Le doubt fait*
led to an endeavour to clear up all. I found my mistress's love was
strictly antarctical—it was as frigid as the ice at Melville Island, and I
became chilled by her indifference, though I am convinced she loyed
me as well as she was capable of loving at all. Love in my view consisted in " mutual and partaken bliss." I never had an idea of an
affection in which I could not confer as well as receive pleasure. Day
by day attachment diminished, but its progressive retrocession effected
no change in the conduct of M——, and this more and more lessened
my regard for her. We parted at last, on her side apparently,

> —— without the least regret
> As though that we had never met;

while I felt alternately sorrow and satisfaction at my escape. M——
was the nymph of Pygmalion—the ivory statue of beauty, that felt
nothing of the warmth it inspired. Peace to all such fair beings, who
are best fitted for lovers like themselves, to live and die in the passive-
ness of congealed feeling and of unimpassioned existence. Of all
earthly things, this neutrality between life and death, this foe to the
energy of love's divinity, this " death of each day's life," is most repel-
ling. The errors of passion admit of palliation; there is in them the
seeds of all that is great and good. When duly regulated, they are a
" rich compendium of bright essences; an extract of all that is valuable, good, and lovely in the universe." Without their incitement there
can be nothing excellent—virtue itself is but the phosphorescence of
stagnation.

One may have the misfortune of being in love by making a wrong
estimate of the disposition of the object that first impresses us. We
are exceedingly apt to interpret in our own favour every thing which
tends to confirm our wishes. A glance of pure curiosity is construed
into a token of tenderness, and a conversation that will admit of the
kind construction of one sentence in support of our hopes, is treasured

as indisputable evidence of the correctness of our views. This may be called ' being in love by presumption.' If a lady discover the mistake of any one in this regard, let him not hope she will be generous enough to undeceive him, she will infallibly run him deeper into the mire, and make his disembarrassment a matter of greater difficulty. I had the misfortune to suffer once in this way myself. The signs by which I judged, did not appear a moment doubtful, and I pushed matters pretty rapidly, till an *eclaircissement* on the lady's side was unavoidable. How was I surprised on her informing me that she had never dreamed of any thing beyond friendship, and that I was much mistaken if I thought that myself or any of my sex had made the slightest impression on her heart—a few weeks after, she clandestinely married her father's clerk.

But I will not tediously detail all my love-adventures until I was fixed for life with one who, if not perfect according to my early ideas of woman, afforded me more happiness, I am convinced, than a faultless being could have done ; and will consider a little the state of being in love in its general character. Being in love, like being in debt, is to be in a state of apprehension. From the first developement in our hearts of that sensation which informs us that an object is not indifferent to us, to the moment of certainty, there is a perpetual irritation that makes what may be styled the fever of the passion, which, as medical men would say, takes a variety of character, from the slower kind of temperate climates, to the intense paroxysms of tropical ones. The high-spirited man, warm in constitution and full of ardour, will generally find love a tropical affection ; while the lover of a thin, diluted blood will be scarcely sensible of the insidious advances of his disorder. I imagine that love among the Quakers must be of the latter kind, and that all must proceed by chronometer movements, or, at least, that the Quakers possess the art of keeping down the tokens of what they style ' carnal impressions' in a way most edifying even for divines in some other sects. A Quaker in love seems to subdue all the exacerbations of this most ungovernable passion, by moving, regardless of heel and spur, in an easy, tranquil, " cheek by jowl" pace. His eyes rarely turn upon the straight-laced object of his regard, unless under cover of the most inviolable stealth ; he groans his love upon tip-toe in the tabernacle, having first planned it with a scale and compass right mathematically, and with all the squareness of his sect. Perhaps he only feels what is called physical love, which he has an uncommon power of regulating, and is a stranger to that arising from sentiment, passion, or vanity. However he contrives it, love with him seems a very different thing from what it is with the rest of the world. A Parson in love appears only to keep the philosophy of the thing in view, as an Irishman does the proceeds of the lady's fortune rather than the fair dame herself. With some, being in love is merely a matter of calculation and contract ; with others, it is a register of sighs and melancholy, of romantic sentiments and impracticable expectations. Part of the anxieties of this important period in human existence arise out of the conventional forms of society. The state of nature knows nothing but physical love ; the other genera have sprung from refinement. Accordingly the most whimsical things have prevailed in love-affairs, invented, perhaps, to season the approaches of the lover with variety. One man advances as certain that love expires

with the first kiss; he therefore prudently avoids saluting his mistress
with his lips for a dozen years. A second confounds the means with
the end, imagines the state of being in love is the happiest, and looks
upon what the lover of passion hails as the summit of his wishes—the
possession of his mistress—as the first step of love's decline. Another
is so fastidious in his views, and possesses so much of what phrenolo-
gists would call "adorativeness" in his pericranium, that being in
love, with him, (and oftentimes bending at a shrine at which no mortal
being but himself would feel inclined to bow the knee,) is an act of
complete devotion. Thus, much of love depends upon imagination
rather than upon any thing positive; for there are instances of being in
love with an imaginary object, as in some singularly constituted dispositions with a statue, like the Parisian girl who fell in love with the
Apollo Belvidere.

The epoch of being in love, notwithstanding all, is the most agreeable in the whole course of life. The soul has then no craving to
gratify. Existence is at its highest premium, for it is then we are
farthest from indifference. He who is in love cherishes life, and but
enjoys it the better for little drawbacks in other affairs, which only
heighten love's relish when we return to it. It is a better and pleasanter thing than money-getting, or courtiership, or sullen study,
or maddening ambition, or a thousand gasping desires that engross us wholly without our feeling satisfaction in their pursuit. These
are solitary objects; being in love is participated with another, and
therefore it is a more social pleasure. The romantic tinge which often
colours our conduct, is an agreeable characteristic; it increases the attraction, and confers a hallowed charm upon the passion. Being in
love is a restraint upon evil feelings—a situation favourable to virtue.
The love of woman is a corrective of our perverse natures, and, while
its season lasts, always mends the heart. Let an unbiassed and discriminating *centenaire* answer what part of life he could look back upon
with the most kindly feelings—what portion of his departed years he
most cherished in his remembrance, and he would doubtless answer,
the time when he was in love. The memory of that delicious season,
its little adventures, its hopes, fears, and enjoyments, always come
over us with a rush of pleasing warmth, a sunbeam piercing the clouds
of departed time, and irradiating for a moment our tottering steps and
grey hairs. Being in love mingles us with the better things of life,
keeps beautiful forms perpetually before the eye, gives us pleasing
dreams, elevates the spirits, and exalts our views. It tempers our
harsher dispositions with the gentleness of beauty, and subdues our
proudest pretensions to the government of tears and caresses of mildness and persuasion. He who has never been in love is a miserable
blockhead, who is ignorant of the highest joy this distempered life
possesses for mortals. Being in love is, in fact, a sort of millenium
far above all life's other good. I would desire no better state than
that of being in love for a thousand years; and, as Quin wished he
had a mouth from England to Nova Scotia, and every inch of the way
palate, that he might fully enjoy John Dory, I would demand the temperament of youth from seventeen to twenty-five for the above space
of time, and all its ardent susceptibility to heighten my long season of
innocence and happiness.                                        Y. I.

### QUENTIN DURWARD.

*"What! will the line stretch out to the crack of doom?*
*Another yet! a seventh!"* MACBETH.

NOTWITHSTANDING the amusement which the "Novels by the author of Waverley" afford in the perusal, the astounding rapidity with which they succeed to each other gives—the *reviewer* at least, something more to do than is absolutely pleasant. The New Monthly Magazine is not more regular in its periodic appearances than these works; yet the necessity of reading whatever bears the signature, or rather the enigma, of their author, is absolute; and this necessity, we must confess, has more than once given birth within us to a movement of impatience and waspishness on the announcement of "Another Novel from the great Unknown," something analogous to that betrayed by Macbeth, in the passage which serves as our motto at the head of the page. Latterly also, to make matters worse, these announcements have so enchained themselves one within the other, that it has been impossible to engage them single-handed, or to encounter the perusal of one production without the appalling consciousness that its younger brother is "in the press," ready to pounce upon us the moment that the work in hand shall have done its business with the public. Thus the labour of the reader is brought to resemble that of the Danaides; and the "never-ending, still beginning" task occasions a flutter of the nerves, which requires all the charm of this author's dialogue and description to dissipate and appease.

Determined to "strike whilst the iron is hot,"—or, to use a proverb more congenial to July weather, "to make hay while the sun shines," and resolved, like good Queen Elizabeth, with her prayer-loving subjects, to give his readers "*enough of it*," the author of Waverley does not neglect the harvest of his popularity: and the expedition with which he conducts his movements, seems to indicate that, like some popular engravers, he must employ many assistants, to whose labours, after due touching up and polishing, he puts his own all-powerful signature—a letter of recommendation to the whole reading public of Great Britain, Germany, and France.

Every thing about these works, in truth, is singular. The dexterity, with which the friends of the "great poet of the north" contrive to keep the public unsatisfied respecting his share in their production,—the number of extrinsic causes, (dramatizing, illustrating by engravings, music, and subsidiary publications, &c. &c.) that are brought to bear in support of their popularity,—the intrinsic interest they possess,—and the nature and management of the means which are made to produce this interest, no less than the rapidity of their succession,—all combine to render their appearance one of the most striking phænomena in the literature of the present age, and a marked sign of the times in which we live.

Those who are unacquainted with *the business* of novel-writing, imagine that nothing more is necessary than to sit down before a ream of paper, and pour forth the products of a teeming brain, with about the same degree of effort that it requires to assure some "Dear Cousin" in the country that "all at home are well," and that we are, "with best love to enquiring friends," the said dear Cousin's "very affec-

tionate and obedient servant."—The reverse of all this is, however, the
case. The quantity of reading in history, geography, chronology, an-
tiquities, and even in arts and sciences, necessary to give consistency,
probability, and colouring to a work of imagination, requires, with the
most industrious, the labour of months, before a pen is put to paper for
the immediate purpose of composition.*

For the " getting up," as the stage-manager would call it, of Quentin
Durward, for instance, besides a diligent search through the historians,
through Commines, Brantome, Jean de Troyes, and the rest of the
memoir-writers, an immense quantity of Scottish lore must have been
collected in order to trick out the Scotch guard in all the verisimili-
tudes of names, families, manners, and domestic anecdote. The
trifling scene of the false herald alone, could not be detailed without a
more intimate acquaintance with the pseudo-science of blazonry than
usually falls to the lot of any man, save a German Baron, or a thorough-
paced and inveterate antiquarian.

Those who profess the faith, or the heresy, that Sir Walter Scott is
the author of these works, relate that he " writes" them during his
hours of attendance in the courts : but, besides the ingenuity he must
practise to hide his operations from the notice of the public, by which he
is at those times surrounded, he must possess the more wonderful property of knowing by intuition facts, of which others obtain the knowledge by the most intense application. Sir Walter Scott is not only
represented as a man of official occupation, as a politician actively par-
ticipating in the wrangling polemics of the Edinburgh parties, but as a
very convivial and social member of a remarkably social community,
as a bustling farmer, and a constant improver of his favourite demesne at Abbotsford. That, amidst all these associations, he should
be the sole " Author of Waverley" and of its successors, seems next to
a physical impossibility. The mere mechanical task of putting together the materials of a three-volume novel, after they have been
collected,—supposing the book to be written *currente calamo*, without
reconsideration or recopying,—would occupy months of exclusive and
laborious application; and this is a necessity which no genius can
avert, a labour no talent can abbreviate. In this respect, some little
advantage of habit apart, Sir W. Scott and the writers of the Leadenhall press are on a perfect equality. If this gentleman, therefore, is the
" Brazen mask" of the literary pantomime of hide and seek, it amounts
almost to demonstration that he is powerfully assisted by a knot of
subaltern drudges; and that he does little more than select the story,
dispose the plan, write particular scenes, and give that sort of finish to
the whole, which preserves to the book the unity of its colouring.† It
has indeed been asserted respecting the " Pirate,"—we know not with
what truth,—that it is the exclusive production of a certain member of

* It has been the custom of our popular novelist to commence by drawing up a
map of the scene of action, in the same way that a general would trace a geogra-
phical sketch of his intended campaign.
† The Editor of the New Monthly Magazine sanctions the publication of this
theory for the amusement of his readers, but begs not to be made responsible for
believing it.

Sir Walter's family; and that it received only the revision and the adoption of the " Author of Waverley."

Some probability perhaps is added to this hypothetical notion by a marked difference observable at the first glance over the different novels in the single particular of character. In the earlier, and more appropriately called " Scotch Novels," there is often displayed an intense degree of moral interest, in which the majority of the later productions are comparatively deficient. The death of the heroic Jacobites in Waverley, the strongly conceived, and finely shaded contrasts of the Serjeant and Burley, the whole description of the fanatic march, and the scene of torturing the preacher in " Old Mortality," possess an unspeakable grasp on our sympathy; for they abound with traits of humanity, in its striking and important modifications. Rob Roy is a master's sketch of a fine, bold, generous disposition, worked upon and demoralized by the force of events; and even the Baillie's eccentricities are set off with such touches of nature and feeling as often remind us—what more *can* we say?—of Shakspeare himself. Of this excellence a smaller degree exists in the more recent productions ; in which the characters differ from each other, chiefly in the shades of that weakness, or of that wickedness, which are common to them all.

In Quentin Durward, partly perhaps from the selection of the age and scene, the defect of character is singularly discoverable. Throughout all the novels, indeed, the author has shewn a stronger disposition to pourtray external nature, than to study and develope the workings of internal moral feeling and truth. Even when he enters deepest into pathos and intellectual character, his effort is always connected with a view rather to please us with the picturesque, than to sublimate our ethical principles. But in his later productions, he seems to sacrifice more than ever to picturesque effect, and he even exercises his ingenuity in giving relief to the most degraded characters which history exhibits, and in shedding the lights of an innocent and humorous peculiarity over the deepest and darkest shades of vice and crime. That the author of these novels, whoever he may be, is a devoted tory, will be no matter of new information to any of his readers; and on the ground of simple and abstracted opinion, it would be illiberal to quarrel with him. That he should even have glossed over the political offences of a Charles and a James, in order to paint those heroes of legitimacy under the traits of an amiable and gossiping privacy, may not be thought to exceed that measure of misrepresentation which the temper of our times, heated by incessant conflict and mutual injustice, appears to tolerate; but when he selects as a fit object for pencilling, and adornment the infamous Louis XI., and when he dwells with a minute and complacent satisfaction on Tristrem l' Hermite, and the two canting and jesting buffoons, his subaltern executioners, we cannot help objecting to a taste and moral tact, apparently at variance with the mind which conceived and delineated a Jenny Deans.

With all the fascination which the author's vividness of genius throws over the characters of this story, there is still something in them all that is repulsive to a mind of moral and contemplative sensibility. Quentin himself, though he has energy and decision, is an adventurer and a mercenary, who offers his courage and his sinews to the furtherance of the most atrocious and perfidious tyranny that the barbarism of modern Europe has produced, with an indifference which, however natural in the feudal aristocrat of the Scotland of those days, ought to disqualify him for the attachment of a heart of civilized times. The band of Scottish archers, which he sought to join from so vast a distance, in addition to the characteristics of cruelty and licentiousness common to all mercenaries, was marked for avoidance by its recent treachery in quitting the service of Charles VII. and joining the party of his rebellious and unnatural son, for a round sum of money. This circumstance should have made a deep impression on the mind of an ingenuous boy of gentle culture, whose love for his own parents must have been exalted by their bloody and unrevenged death; and the little coquetting squeamishness introduced to palliate the hero's conduct, serves only to place his moral obtuseness in a stronger light, Even Charles the Bold, whose chivalrous and unsuspecting frankness might have afforded some bright lights to the picture, is by a felicitous exercise of the author's colouring, shaded down below the tone of his ferocious rival, whose gloomy criminality shews like philosophy, as it is set off by the mere animal impulses which are made to actuate the conduct of the Duke of Burgundy.

Much of this moral defect, it is true, may perhaps follow unconsciously from the author's obstinate determination to defend indefensible points of history, to diminish the keen sensibility of the public to political truth, and to generate that indifference to public interests which is favourable to the propagation of the Tory creed. The romantic and picturesque points of feudality brought forward on the canvass may serve to beget a distaste for the colder and sterner aspects of a civilized and philosophical æra; and state criminals, portrayed with dramatic effect, and ornamented with the mock jewelry of candle-light virtues, may be made to engender a pernicious tolerance for political offenders; but, to produce this effect, the reader must be hurried forward, as over a quaking marsh, which affords no permanent footing for his steps; events must be presented with something of the vagueness of a dream; visions must succeed to visions, with a rapidity that leaves no pause for reflection; the imagination must alone be kept alert, and judgment be drugged into a diseased and unnatural slumber. Still, however, the later publications of the Author of Waverley are more surcharged with this defect, which we feel ourselves thus called upon to censure, than is necessary for the object that seems in a great degree to influence his writings; and a shade of probability arises, that the excess may be the work of coarser and clumsier spirits, which, in imitating their original and following the plan he has chalked out for them, have caricatured his system, and introduced faults which the master's hand has been unable to correct.

But, whatever inference may be drawn from the author's increased appetite for painting mankind under their worst aspects, it is a circumstance that becomes more striking at each succeeding publication. The system of decorating despotism is persevered in with unabated vigour, and each new novel is a special pleading in favour of passive obedience. We are not without apprehension that these observations may appear to some persons to be harsh and excessive. But let it be recollected against what evil we protest—against the misfortune of the greatest genius of the age conveying false impressions to the public of the great political concerns of man—of his blunting the sympathies of youth with the cause of human civilization, and begetting a precocious indifference to public interests. The licentiousness of the old novels was open to view; but the mischief of which we complain is more dangerous because it is more concealed. A certain public functionary is said to have written a History of England for children, in which the Revolution is purposely omitted. This act of bad faith is comparatively trifling to that of distorting facts, misrepresenting characters, and accustoming the mind to the contemplation of political vice unaccompanied by censure, or rather dressed out in the garb of amiability and goodness.

This is no imaginary offence. Its reality was well illustrated the other day in a member of our own family. A young female, of considerable liveliness, and talent beyond her years, who had just finished the perusal of Quentin Durward, being asked which of the characters she liked best, replied without hesitation, "Louis XI; he is such a pleasant gentleman." That this was a legitimate deduction in a child from the pages she had been reading, will not be disputed; and what can be more deplorable than the total confusion of right and wrong thus produced? Nor is it enough to say these works are not intended for youth; for youth will read them; and not only so, but even those of riper years will find it difficult to resist their influence, unless their moral principles are the result of a stronger character, and a deeper thought, than are often to be found among the general mass of novel-reading mankind.

We have dwelt on these generalities at some length, because we consider them important; and because the popularity of our author exempts us from the necessity of analytical criticism. Quentin Durward every body has read, or every body will read; and it is as useless to anticipate the pleasure of perusal by a bald abstract, as it is superfluous to fatigue our readers by an idle repetition. For the encouragement of those who have not yet commenced the perusal, we may say that it is altogether superior to its immediate predecessors, the scenes are more connected, the events more naturally conducted, the *denouement* better. The author has broken new ground, and seems invigorated by the freshness of his subject. For the rest, this novel possesses all the merits and defects of its brethren. It is formed on the same *cadre*, has the same tendencies, the same sort of adventure, the same vigour of picture-writing. One circumstance is peculiar;—the palpable, and perhaps careless, departure from the truth of history. The transactions which occasioned the imprisonment of Louis at Peronne * were many years antecedent to the murder of the Bishop of Liege, by William de la Mache †. In the insurrection which caused Louis's arrest, W. de la Mache's name is not mentioned; and his introduction as an agent in the story, seems only for the purpose of an additional gibe at popular revolutions. Again, when he did murder the Bishop, it was his son and not himself he named as the successor. The bearer of Charles the Bold's defiance to Louis in the castle of Plessis was the "Sire de

---

* 1468. † 1482.

Chimay, and not the Sire de Cordés, an historical personage." (See Anquetil.) Inbercourt, who is represented as first hearing of the siege of Tongres from Durward, was present at it himself, and was taken prisoner with the Bishop. Cardinal Baluc's confinement in his own iron cage, at Loches, was posterior to the King's captivity in Peronne. The false herald sent to England by Louis, and alluded to in the conference, is also an anachronism. These deviations from historic truth are material blemishes in the story. The author of an historic novel may omit facts, or add to them inventions which are in keeping with what is known. But he is not at liberty to distort the truth by a transfer of events and personages, by which, under the disguise of amusement, he gives false impressions, unsettles men's notions, and renders in a great degree nugatory, one of the most laborious and useful of human studies.

---

## THE PARISIAN CARNIVAL.

We have been told from high authority that there is a step between the sublime and the ridiculous. It is, however, a barefaced falsehood—there is no such thing. Sublime and ridiculous are one and the same—co-existent qualities, of different complexions, perhaps, as looked at in different lights, but blending and blooming together, like the green and pink shades in a shot poplin. Be it known, then, to all whom it may concern, subscribers, correspondents, and contributors, that I, Thomas Tryatall, Esquire, long time a man about town, once of a fair independence and always of fair fame, an *observateur des modes* from fancy, and a recorder of my remarks for the love of fun, an amateur of fashion and a dabbler in literature, finding from the pressure of the times that my purse was squeezed into symptoms of a delicate decline, that my estate was quite out at elbows, and my best coat shewing marks of sympathy therewith—seeing, in short, (to quit a threadbare subject) that a visit to France would be very refreshing to my constitution, and being anxious to get into good habits, accepted the very liberal offers of my friends the proprietors of this miscellany, that I should quit my lodgings in Piccadilly, take a trip to Paris for my own pleasure and our common profit, and establish myself as a kind of periodical lecturer on the fashions, follies, and fooleries—nice distinctions, mark ye—of this celebrated metropolis.

My first business, after I had shaken off the dust of the Diligence, was to look out for a tailor, knowing the importance of appearances, as well as old Quarles himself, who tells us in his "Enchiridion" that "the body is the shell of the soul; apparell is the huske of that shell; the huske often tells you what the kernel is." Now should this quotation seem to insinuate that all the secret of my character lies in a nutshell, I shall only observe, *par parenthèse*, that many people might find it deuced hard in the cracking; and to make it still more so to Parisian penetration, I was resolved to disguise myself in French costume. Decked out, then, at a day's notice in a Polish frock, black velvet vest, with a white, a pink, and a blue one, respectively of silk, inside, Hussar pantaloons, boots *à la Wellington*, and brazen spurs— French every bit of me, brass from head to foot, as a body might say— I sallied forth to present my recommendatory credentials to the friend of my friends the proprietors, M. Le Visomte de Vaurien, who had been represented to me as one of a family wonderfully well known in France, a man of fashion, literature, science, taste, talent, &c. &c. &c. a sort of second Crichton in short, who had spent many years in England during the emigration, and was attached *à la folie* to all that was British, and to the ancient *regime* at home.

" A pleasant sort of person this," thought I, as I approached his residence, " to lead a young fellow like me through the labyrinths of learning and pleasure;" for I intended to be at all in the ring, as we say familiarly at the club. Arrived at the street to which my friend the proprietor's hand-writing on the back of the letter pointed like a finger-post, I was not very favourably struck by its appearance. It was in the heart of the town, narrow, dark, and dirty ; but, knowing the ways of Paris, I did not much mind all that. " No. 18, *le voila!*" said I, entering the *porte-cochère* of a gloomy but good-looking house. Then pulling up my shirt-collar and adjusting my hair, I marched up to the landing-place of the *premier étage*, cast an inquisitive glance at the coat of arms on the pannels of a huge old family coach standing in the *remise*, and was in the act of seizing the bell-cord, when a withered old hag shot forth her visage from a dismal little den in the *entresol* below, screaming " *Diable donc ! ou allez vous ?*" " *Qui, moi?*" replied I rather indignantly, " *Je vais chez M. le Viscomte, Madame !*" " *Monsieur le Viscomte ! Qui est cela ?*" An odd question that, thought I. I cannot surely be wrong. " *Le Viscomte de Vaurien, Madame!*" " *Viscomte ! Bah ! et c'est là que vous le cherchez ! montez au sixieme.*" " *Au sixieme !*" sighed I, looking up the dismal staircase, so high that it seemed, like Jacob's ladder, to lead to a glimpse of Heaven, which twinkled through a sky-light at top. I drew a long breath of preparation for the ascent, and heard the old witch mutter below : " *Diable l'emporte ! c'est toujours comme cela vous passez partout à gauche et à droite, sans rien demander à la portière, vous autres Anglais.*" " *Vous autres Anglais !*" echoed I. " Rat it, that's too bad, though—she has found me out, in spite of my frock, waistcoats and pantaloons. But never mind, one positively can't get rid of the Bond-street lounge, that's all. *Au sixieme ! Courage !*"

Landed at length at the summit, breathless and panting, my head dizzied by a glance over the banisters into the interminable chasm below me, I leaned for a moment against the wall, and pulled a greasy bit of faded pink ribbon that hung dangling beside a filthy little door. " *Qui est là ?*" demanded a feeble voice. " *Moi,*" replied I. " Aha ! an Englishman; wait, wait one leetel bit, Saer," answered the voice, in a tone of gaiety. I waited as desired, confounded beyond measure to find that the very pronunciation of one syllable had betrayed me for the second time. While I pondered on this, the door opened, and a black silk night-cap popped itself out. A sallow wizened face was under it, and the head it covered was borne upon a narrow pair of shoulders, clothed in a short brown woollen jacket, appended to pantaloons of the same, forming stockings as well, and ending at the feet in a shabby pair of yellow morocco-leather slippers. " Walk in, Saer, walk·in, Saer," said the wearer of this strange costume and still stranger phiz. He would have measured about five feet and an inch or so, and looked a good half-century old. His upper lip was horribly embrowned with snuff, and he seemed to have but two or three straggling teeth in his head. "Is your master at home?" asked I. "My Got, Saer! vat you take me for? I am my master." "I beg your pardon, Sir," cried I, "I should wish to see the Viscomte de Vaurien." "Why dat is me, my dear Saer. Walk in, walk in, Saer." As he did not seem to wince at my mistake, my "withers were unwrung;" but you may imagine, ladies, my mortification while I contemplated the figure and the abode of my anticipated Cicerone. I shall not touch your sensibility on my account by detailing the appearance of Vaurien's garret. A truckle-bed, two tottering chairs, a broken deal-table, a tarnished mahogany basin-stand, with gilded porcelain basin and water-jug cracked and chipped, and standing for show like Goldsmith's celebrated row of broken tea-cups. These, and such like commodities, are not matters to enter into a description meant for the brightest eyes of England. I therefore draw the blanket (there being neither veil nor curtain at hand) over the mysteries of the Viscomte's abode.

A few minutes made us quite known to each other. He read my letter with attention, shook my hand with warmth, professed himself my most faithful friend and devoted servant, and finished many pleasant sayings by begging me, with an air of great *nonchalance,* to sit down while he took his breakfast. That was soon despatched, for it consisted only of a little cup of coffee without cream, which had stood simmering in a pipkin by the fire, and a small roll, of about the length and consistency of a dried herring, which lay on a shelf with the Viscount's dressing-apparatus. His repast required none of the usual appurtenances of a breakfast-table, and being quickly finished, he begged me to excuse his then making his toilette. Delighted at an opportunity of being initiated into the manœuvres of a *petit-maître de Paris,* I willingly accorded his pardon. He began by throwing off his black cap, and displaying a head completely covered with *papillotes,* which he, without shame or ceremony, pulled coolly from their respective curls, and folded up in readiness for the service of the night. At first sight of him I thought he had been bald, for not a straggling hair wandered on his temples. Now he had a profusion of dark-brown ringlets ; and had I not seen the progress of de-*cap*-itation I would have sworn he had put on a wig, so that he was just as far from natural appearance one way as the other. "Pardon, for two little moments," cried he, squeezing my hand in both of his, as he popped into a closet close by the head of his bed. In two minutes he was back, but no more like what he was before he entered, than I like Hercules. His transformation was magical—it was "Hyperion to a Satyr." A rosy flush spread over his face, and seemed faintly fading on the tips of his nose and chin, like setting sunbeams on the peaks of a mountain. A pair of false whiskers of the same pattern as his side-locks, curled upon his cheeks ; and his mouth displayed a regular row of well-set teeth ; while his head, in its whole *ensemble,* might be really supposed to have just glided gently off the shoulders of a good-looking fellow of thirty or thereabouts.

I started back. He laughed. "Ha, ha! *vous ne me connaissez pas,*"

said he, slapping me on the shoulder, " my dear saer, you must not
vonder at all dis.   Ve Frenchmen are enough philosophers to care
ver little for appearances in de house, and to know dat 'tis ever ting in
de street."   I was so amazed at the metamorphosis, and so pleased
with the aphorism, which put me so much in mind of myself and old
Quarles, that I did not closely observe the process of his dressing,
which I should otherwise have faithfully reported.   I followed him
with my eyes as he went on, but saw him indistinctly, and heard him
chatter without minding what he said.   When I recovered from my
reverie, I observed him full-dressed all but his coat, wiping the cracked
gilt basin with a towel, and placing it carefully in its proper stand.
" *Allons!*" cried he, as he finally settled his collar before the looking-
glass, and stood revealed in all the perfumed bloom of a dashing
dandy.   " Now, Saer, shall we go out see de masks on de Boulevards?"   " Masks!" exclaimed I ; " why, it isn't carnival time, is
it?"   " To be sure 'tis," replied he, " dis is *Mardi gras*, de gayest of
de gay days.   Noting but pleasure, and fun, and hosh-posh."   I may
be allowed to mention here, that the Viscomte is very proud of his
English, and loses no occasion for displaying his familiarity with the
niceties of the language, among which, " hosh-posh" is a particular
favourite.

· I·was electrified at hearing that the Carnival was really going on,
for the whole appearance of Paris was so *sombre*, so muddy, and misty,
that I could not imagine any approximation to gaiety in the place or
the people.   " *Ah, vous verrez, vous verrez bientôt,*" said the Viscomte,
as we descended the stone staircase, picking our steps in its perpetual
twilight, and directing our course by the iron banisters.   Once fairly
on the Boulevard, my friend seemed quite in his element; and though
I looked down on him from an elevation of nearly a dozen inches, and
thought myself at most times a tolerable specimen of style, I confess
there was something in his swaggering air, fine complexion, floating
curls, and the red ribbon at his button-hole, that seemed to throw me
into the shade.   He talked English loudly all the time, proud of displaying his accomplishment to the ears of his countrymen ; and his observations were amusing enough.   The day was gloomy, cold; and comfort-
less—yet the world was out.   During the hour and half which I had
spent in the Viscomte's garret, all Paris seemed to have been suddenly
infected with the wish for a walk, ride, or drive.   The pathway was
thronged with pedestrians ; many a mounted exquisite was cantering
on the centre of the pavement, between the rows of carriages going in
opposite directions, in horizontal analogy to the movements of two
buckets·in a well.   These carriages, of all sorts and descriptions, open
and close, cut a poor figure to a man accustomed to the equipages of
*the Park.*   There was scarcely one from Long Acre to be seen.   They
were almost all French, gaudy, shabby, and flimsy.   It appeared that
though all Paris was there, yet the confounded weather kept all the
decent horses at home, for such a sorry collection of jaded hacks were
never before exhibited in a Christian country.   The masks were few
and vile.   Now and then a barouche hove in sight, crammed with
clumsy harlequins, miserable mountebanks without a joke, or two or
three stupid caricatures of old women, in " feathery furs and studded
stomachers, tippets, cardinals, hoods, and ruffles."   A pretended

peasant, here and there, rode silently along; but there was nothing like frolic, or humour, or happiness. The Viscomte pointed out to me some well-known characters in the carriages which passed; among others, in his sky-blue chariot, Viscount d'A——, the romance-writer, who has described in Ipsiboé, the heroine of his last work, a better masquerade figure than the whole Carnival could produce. " Chargée de plumes, de fourrures, de fleurs, de pierreries, et de gaze, enveloppée d'un mantel à triple collet, et sa robe bordée d'images." Such was the favourite costume of " la douce fille des eaux dormantes." I, in my turn, told my companion the names of a few of my country-men; but I saw none who combined notoriety with the ludicrous, except the celebrated Squire Hold'emtight, who, mounted on the dicky of a calèche, covered with a huge box-coat, whipped along a pair of pitiful hacks, and (puffing his red and bloated cheeks against the wind) gave occasion to a group near me to holloa out " *Voilà! Voilà le bœuf gras!*"—and I certainly never saw a finer specimen of John Bullism.

While the file of carriages was thus dragging, like a wounded snake or an alexandrine, " its slow length along," and every face seemed the index of a melancholy or a dissatisfied mind, the sound of martial music struck upon my ear, and presently several regiments of infantry in full order of march, moved along the Boulevards from the direction of the Tuileries, where they had been just passed in review, prepara-tory to their departure for Spain. A train of artillery followed—the heavy rolling of the guns over the pavement mixing with the clash of the military bands, bringing to the mind a rush of awful combina-tions touching the tremendous probabilities in which these troops were going to be the actors. There they were, mingled with the fantastic fooleries of the crowd—the motley crew of masks and mockeries—heavy hearts and dreary apprehensions. I gazed at the scene with a sarcastic smile and an involuntary shudder; and exclaimed as we turned down the Rue de la Paix (Napoleon's triumphal pillar staring me in the face), " No, no, there is no step between the sublime and the ridiculous!"                                                             T. T.

---

### SELECT SOCIETY,

*With Observations on the modern Art of Match-making.*

Dulce sodalitium!

Connubio jungam stabili, propriumque dicabo.

Ir society be the end and object of civilization, it must be confessed that we English of the 19th century are in a very barbarous condition. Never was an intercourse with the world clogged with so many impe-diments as at the present moment; never did good company cost so much pains to arrive at, and never did it afford so little in return. God be with the good times, when the sole *capacity* required to figure among men was that of a two-gallon cask, and when we were sure to get on with the females at the expense of a little " evil-speaking, lying, and slandering." Then, alas! *any body* was company for *every body*; and the first lord of the land did not think shame, *faute de mieux*, to take up with the conversation of his butler, or his game-keeper, over a tankard; while the young ladies, *faute de tout*, danced "Bobbing Joan," with the rest of the domestics, in the servants' hall. But now-a-days folks are grown so confoundedly precise,—or, to use their own word, so *select*, forsooth, in their society, that a man requires fresh qualifications for every house he enters. The rigour of the Vienna aristocracy of the first class is not more unbending to the *bourgeoisie*, nor more uncompromising in a quartering, than our pretenders to *selection*, in their several degrees. A stranger might as well attempt to "work his way" into a Freemasons' lodge without the sign, as one of the profane to find favour in the eyes of a *coterie* without its specific qualification. That the supreme *bon ton* of the supreme *bon genre* should be a little particular is but right, seeing the number and pertinacity of the intruders. Almack's has nothing of the "*facilis descensus Averni*," nor should it. On the contrary, to get *out* of Newgate or the Fleet is less difficult than to get *in* to the rooms in King-street; and this I take to be a merciful dispensation of "*their Selectnesses*" the Committee; since none but those bred to the trade are capable of standing the *quietude* of *extremely* refined manners, which is just one degree less than that of the tomb. But high rank and *bon ton* do not stand alone in this pretension. We have it running through all the classes and predicaments of society, from the Four-in-hand Club to Mrs. Hourglass's "tea and tracts," the amateur concert at the Jew's Harp, near Whitechapel, and our friend's blue stocking association in Houndsditch. Even the footmen of the House of Lords, we are told, keep clear of the borough-mongers and country puts of the lower house.

This selection is *bore* enough for those who have (to use a French phrase "germain to the matter") found their *assiette* in society; but to him who is not yet placed, it is a source of bitter disappointment. Shortly after leaving the University, on my arrival in London, I was asked to dine at the house of one of our country neighbours, who, having been nominated M.P. had moved to town. This struck me as an eligible opening for making my way in good company, and I accepted the invitation with eagerness. Upon entering the drawing-room, I soon found that I was the only person not of "the house." Adam Smith, David Ricardo, and Mons. Say, would have been mere fourth-form boys to this quintessential selection of the "collective wisdom." The conversation was wholly "of the shop;" but, though I do sometimes read the papers, I was very soon completely nonplused, and at once made up my mind to bound my ambition to acquiring the reputation of a good listener.

Sauntering down the street, something out of spirits at this discomfiture, I was attracted by the lights in my aunt Lady Mary Mildew's drawing-room; and arriving at the door just as Mr. ——— the bookseller was "bundling out" a coach-load of literary lions for her ladyship's inspection, I determined to step in and see "what was going on." I had not been long in the room, when my aunt introduced me to a good-looking but rather prim young lady, as newly arrived from Cambridge. Being a tolerably good French and Italian scholar, and having a bowing acquaintance with our best English writers, I thought I should find myself pretty much *au fait* to the young lady's indigo; and I entered the list with some spirit, in the determination to make good my claim to a place among the blues, and to set myself off to advantage. But here again I was utterly thrown out: I could not tell my fair questioner whether Lady Iodina Crucible was "*intellectuel*," I had omitted to attend Mr. Sapphic's lecture at the Institution, I mistook the author of the Fall of Jerusalem for the American Addison, I was two novels behind hand with the "Great Unknown," Sydney Sm—th passed without returning my bow, and I totally failed in naming the authors of the two "crack" articles of the current Quarterly. Need I add that I was, after five minutes effort at conversation, deserted by my companion, whose contemptuous dejection of countenance, as she whispered her next neighbour, and glanced her eye hastily at my person, convinced me that I was already black-balled, at least by this member of Lady Mary's squad of Selects.

Hurrying down stairs, with the speed of a detected pickpocket, I stumbled upon Tom Headlong, of Jesus, the 'Squire's nephew of Headlong Hall; who found much favour in my sight by voting my aunt a quiz, and her party the blue devils; and on this account he had the less difficulty in carrying me to the club, of which I had just been elected a member. There, I thought, I should at least be welcome; for my credit is good, and my money as acceptable as another's. But all is vanity and vexation of spirit. Notwithstanding that Newmarket is within fourteen miles of Cambridge, my ignorance of the technicalities of a horse-race was sufficient to exclude me from the conversation of the night, which ran almost exclusively upon Epsom. My ominous silence on this interesting topic boded me no good. Then I could not name the odds at some point of the game, when asked; I mistook the round in which Gas had his "*lights doused*;" was totally out about his opponent's head being "in chancery." In short, I shewed myself up as a complete Spooney, fell out of the conversation, and was left to eat my supper in silence with what appetite I might.

The next disappointment I encountered was at the house of a maiden relation, whom I had not seen for some years. The memory of her good-natured and unpretending simplicity, of her moderate endowments, and still more moderate acquirements, assured me that I might make myself "quite at home" with her. On arriving at her house I found a formidable circle of Quaker-looking ladies, in the midst of which stood a spruce and punctiliously dressed gentleman in black, who somehow or other brought to my mind a certain necessary personage in a sabbath of witches. My entrance interrupted the reading of some book, and as my fair relation came forward to greet me, I could not but observe that though her reception was friendly, it was more measured and subdued than childish recollections induced me to expect. After the customary inquiries after absent friends, &c. the conversation seemed to lapse into a train of ideas inspired by the now suspended "readings." Its subject seemed to me religious, but it was so wrapped up in something between technical jargon and cant, as to be nearly unintelligible; and I sunk by degrees into a reverie, in which my unfitness for society, and very imperfect education, formed a prominent and a painful part.

Mortified by such repeated failures I began to lower my expectations, and to look no higher than the forming one amongst those cyphers which swell the sum total of a " squeeze," fill up door-ways and staircases, and obstruct the king's highway by their attendant carriages. But, " *non cuivis homini*," it is not every one's lot to enter at once even this numerous corps. In order to be asked every where, one must be seen every where, and known to every body ; and there are those who after spending a fortune in ices and wax-lights, are, at the end of a twenty years' struggle, only just creeping on. To be distinguished in this " *genre*," and to carry the place by a *coup de main*, is morally impossible ; because where nothing is expected, where no qualification is required, there is no advantage-ground afforded for attracting the attention of an " admiring public."

As a last resource, I determined to advance myself by the merits of my dancing-master, to ride into society on a " *demiqueue de chat*," and to wind myself round the hearts of my friends by a " *chaine Angloise.*" But this also is not to be done at will ; for it requires much patience and more intrigue to get enlisted into a set, or to be received in morning practising-parties. As, however, I am an eldest son, and the family estate is unembarrassed, my probation, in this particular, was considerably shortened. The sort of society to which I was thus introduced was not altogether " *le bon genre.*" It was made up, for the most part, of what are called " respectable families ;" i. e. families whose easy circumstances, Heaven knows how acquired, prevent their ranking absolutely as *nobody*, without very distinctly proving that they are *any body* :—East India baronets, military and civic knights, the small fry of country gentlemen, (who spend a year's revenue in a two months' visit to London or to some fashionable watering-place, living all the rest of the year in their lair at Clodpole-hall, as Cobbett would call it) together with those successful mercantile families and speculators, who, according to the same authority, are elbowing the said country gentlemen out of their estates. Though pleasure and dissipation are the objects of some of these personages in mixing with the world, and seem to be so with all, yet the *fonde* of the society consists of a class who unite business with amusement ; or rather, under the guise of pleasure, carry on an unremitting effort to strike a great stroke in life. These are the mothers who have marriageable daughters to dispose of, and whose views upon the persons of bachelors are any thing but disinterested.

Being myself, as I have already hinted, one of those enviable young men who have " every qualification for making the married state happy," I was eagerly seized on as a proper victim of this systematic conspiracy of mothers to get off their daughters ; and I soon got a pretty near insight into the whole affair. Very few houses indeed are opened to a regular ball, or even to " an early dance," in which there is not a daughter or a niece to be disposed of. The money lavished on gaudy decorations, soups, wild fowl, ices, and champaign, is therefore merely put out at usance, to be returned in a good settlement ; insomuch that, the more apparently wanton the profusion, the closer may be deemed the calculation : seeming hospitality being nothing on earth but a well-baited trap.

On these occasions every body is asked for something ; Lords. Baronets, &c. for their titles : dragoons for their regimentals : frightful old women in blue gowns and silver tissue turbans, for their sons and heirs ; handsome married women to draw the men ; ugly girls as foils ; and pretty girls because the ball cannot go on without them. Some are invited to make up a card-table for the rich dowager mother of an heir at law : some because they have an air of fashion, or write " Albany" on their card. Every thing, in short, is measured, to the minutest particular that can proceed or retard the great event, which is the mainspring of the whole.

Although it is a part of good policy in a hawking mamma, to fly her girls generally at all young fellows or old fellows of decent fortune, yet she has, for the most part, some individual in view, who is more particularly the object of pursuit : and it is truly astonishing how uniformly that favoured individual finds himself, in spite of himself, in contact with the " young lady" who has him in chase. Tall, thin, pale girls are my aversion ; yet for two months I was nightly haunted by such a spectre, who forced me to ask her to dance by " meeting my eye in an early hour of the debate," by planting herself assiduously at my side, and engaging me in a series of innocent questions at the first preparatory scrape of the violins. Somehow or other I was always obliged, too, to hand her down to supper, and consequently to sit beside her at the table. From this persecution I fortunately escaped by a lucky *équivoque*, which seemed to hint that I was engaged to a girl in the country, whose estate joins ours ; and the next evening, I had the happiness to see the stately galley bear down on another prize.

It is a curious, but a melancholy sight, to behold the long rows of overdressed girls, many of them, I hope, unconscious of the purpose for which they are thus launched on society,—with their fidgety, anxious mothers, settling from time to time their hair and dress, nodding disapprobation, or smiling encouragement (as the puppet contradicts or favours the purpose in hand by her carriage and demeanour) and having no eyes, no ears but for the one object of painful solicitude. Still more melancholy is it to witness the last struggles of an unfortunate " *abandonata*," whose tenth season is passing in vain, with " nobody coming to marry her, nobody coming to woo-oo-oo- !" (I hope the reader can whistle the tune for that last desponding monosyllable)—while each causeless giggle, intended to display a dimple, bears evidence of another accident in the " human face divine," which I forbear to name ; and a profusion of finery eclipses charms, that it is no longer prudence to expose to the broad glare of lamps and wax-lights.

When a gudgeon is observed to rise freely to the bait, he is asked to dinner, and engaged on riding-parties in the mornings. A luncheon also is regularly set out as a rallying-point for young men, whose appetites are often more *ductile* than their passions. Hearts are thus ensnared through the medium of cold tongue and bread and butter, and a sure love-potion is Madeira and soda-water. When all else fails, the good old lady herself hints very plainly her reasonable expectations, and strives hard to carry an hesitating swain by a barefaced innuendo.

As I have my own reasons for not giving into these schemes, and prefer taking a wife (when I shall take one) from purer sources, I have ever been more annoyed than flattered by such distinctions. And this probably has made me feel the more keenly the general ill-effects on society arising from these maternal intrigues, in which the married and the poor go for nothing. If one, belonging to either of these classes, engages a girl's attention and distracts her from the business of the night, you may see the mother prowling about with fretful uneasiness, like a cat whose kitten is in the paws of some unlucky urchin, and at last fairly breaking in on the conversation to hurry her daughter away from the troublesome interloper. I have felt the deepest compassion for many a worthy fellow, whose accomplishments, talents, and virtues should have made him a most desirable match, thus warned off the premises like an unqualified sportsman, and treated with contempt in the quarter in which contempt is most insufferable, merely for the want of a little dross. Where these practices are carrying on in a family, all agreeable and instructive conversation is banished the house. Even in the most intimate sociality, the necessity of knocking up a quadrille to the piano-forte, or of engaging the musical misses in the display of their acquirements, cuts short all sweet converse. All the dust of the carpet is beaten into your eyes and throat, your ears are stunned, your person pushed about the narrow room, or you are condemned to listen for the five thousandth time to " *Bid me discourse,*" and a " *Di tanti palpiti,*" sung in that time and tune which it pleaseth fortune, or the no less capricious tempers of the melodious exhibitants.

For these and a thousand other reasons, which for brevity I must now omit, it becomes a point of prudence and good policy to adopt a plan that shall consign matrimony, like all other trades, to the forenoon, and to the commercial part of the city, leaving the haunts of pleasure and the hours of recreation to their legitimate purposes. In France, marriage is transacted " by private contract." The unmarried whey faces are kept in the back-ground, and talking does not spoil conversation in the saloons. This arrangement, however, in which the young folks are not "brought out," is too foreign for our habits, and cannot be recommended. But nothing could be more convenient than the erection of an Exchange exclusively appropriated to matrimonial speculation. The neighbourhood of Mark-lane would afford a good site, as country gentlemen might then dispose of their corn and their children at the same time. Or a room might be hired in the Auction-mart, or at Tattersall's, for the purpose. The fitting up of show-rooms or Bazaars in the neighbourhood of Bond-street might have its utility, in which each girl might be ticketed, and " no second price be taken." This would answer the better, as in Bazaars "no credit can possibly be given," and " no goods are returned after they have left the shop." Subservient to this scheme, registers might be opened, by which an inspector might at a glance know how far any number in the catalogue would suit. By such arrangements we might have our evenings to ourselves ; and mammas, their daughters, and young gentlemen of good expectations, might each and all enjoy the delights of social intercourse, undisturbed by anxious speculation, and unbarassed by the dread of spring-guns and steel-traps in concerts, dances, and opera suppers. As things are now conducted, we must marry in one's own defence, and run the risk of perpetual annoyance at home in order to obtain some chance of a little tranquil enjoyment abroad. This certainly requires reform, and something might be done in the shape of a rider to some of the many marriage acts which are daily passing the two houses of Parliament. Let the members look to it, at their leisure.

C. M.

### NEW SOCIETY OF LITERATURE.

THE project of a Royal Society of Literature which so long lay mysteriously in embryo, has again presented itself to the world, or, to use parliamentary language, assumed somewhat of "a tangible shape." Never was the origin of a society, which might naturally be expected to receive its concoction among the most celebrated literati of the country, so obscure or so little known to those interested in its proceedings. Vacillation and uncertainty have marked its progress hitherto, and whether the present announcement of its constitution is to be regarded as the final result of the deliberations of its founders, or to be considered only as an initiament to be followed by another interval of silence ere its transactions be again visible to the public eye, remains for time to decide. Its commencement has been any thing but auspicious; and if the future be to be judged by the past, the hopes of its founders are likely to suffer disappointment from the very nature of the course they have been pursuing.

A recent announcement of the transactions of a meeting held on the 17th of June, has disclosed to the community the operations which have consumed two or three years in completing. A reference is easily made to these at length in some of the diurnal publications. It appears that a president (the Bishop of St. David's), eight vice-presidents, a council of sixteen fellows,* a treasurer, librarian, and secretary, have been elected. Very few of these individuals can be considered immediately connected with literature. The Society is described as being " under the patronage and endowed by the munificence of his Majesty King George the Fourth, for the advancement of literature—by the publication of inedited remains of ancient literature, and of such works, as may be of great intrinsic value, but not of that popular character which usually claims the attention of publishers—by the promotion of discoveries in literature—by endeavours to *fix the standard*, as far as is practicable, and to preserve the purity of our language, by the critical improvement of our lexicography—by the reading, at public meetings, of interesting papers on history, philosophy, poetry, philology, and the arts, and the publication of such of those papers, as shall be approved of, in the society's transactions—by the *assigning of honorary rewards* to works of *great literary merit*, and to important discoveries in literature; and by establishing a correspondence with learned men in foreign countries, for the purpose of literary inquiry and information." The two prizes, of one hundred and of fifty pounds, first proposed to be given for literary compositions, are changed into two gold medals of fifty guineas each, to be adjudged annually to persons of eminent literary merit. The society consists of fellows and associates : of the last are two classes—royal associates and associates of the society ; the former to be elected from among the latter. Ten of these associates are to receive one hundred a year each from the privy purse, and ten others a like sum from the funds of the society. There are also to be honorary associates. The persons elected as associates are to

---

* In the council of the Society, we believe, the Reverend Mr. Croly is the only one widely known as a literary character ; and to that gentleman's merits as an author we are ardently disposed to hear testimony.

give testimonials of good moral character, and to assist in the promotion of "truth, social order, and loyalty—*loyalty* in its genuine sense,
not only of personal devotion to the sovereign, but of attachment to the
*laws* and institutions of the country." Such is a brief *exposé* of the
present structure of the society.

Some of the objects before enumerated, such as the publication of
inedited works of ancient literature, the "reading interesting papers
on history, &c." and a foreign correspondence for the "purpose of
literary inquiry, &c." are unobjectionable things in themselves, and
calculated in the aggregate rather to do good than harm; but it may be
justly doubted whether individual industry has left any thing in these
respects to be performed. The other designs of the society are more
open to objection, and are not so well calculated to begin a memorable
era in British literature as its founders expect, even if its achievements
equal those which the celebrated Academy of France has accomplished
for that nation. His Majesty's munificence and good intentions no one
will feel inclined to dispute, but it may be justly a question whether
their display would not have been more advantageous to the cause of
literature, if the stipends had been conferred by royal selection, rather
than through the intervention of any society however constituted.
This mode would at least have afforded a guarantee for the impartial
fulfilment of the royal wishes, and show that the cabals of a society did
not interfere in the distribution. For notwithstanding any professions,
and sincere professions, perhaps, of the founders of this society, it will
inevitably, if it endure, become an instrument of party. All former
societies have uniformly become so; and therefore, though they might
have been advantageous in the dawn of a national literature they are
worse than useless, nay decidedly mischievous, when established during
its meridian splendour, as is the case in the present instance. The
Academy of France has uniformly been the corrupt tool of the government, and is deservedly sunk into disrepute. It injured the national
literature by attempting to "fix a standard" in each department, by
which all writers were to be circumscribed, at a time when, from the
great names connected with it, its influence was all-powerful. It chilled
the ardour of genius, cramped attempts at novelty, and endeavoured
to crush writers that had the independence to contravene any of its
arbitary or pedantic enactments. One source of its power arose from
'he comparatively unenlightened era of its establishment and the celebrated men that were successively enrolled on its list, under a government which, till a recent period, suffered no independent feeling to
exist among the people. In its best times it was a thing of feud, corruption, and abject servility; grovelling courtiers, bigoted priests,
and vain nobles, being among its members. Thus its reputation was
sustained on the shoulders of a few gifted individuals. It was the
creature of despotism, that so well understands how to turn all similar
institutions to its own aggrandisement.

But to return to the new Society, projected it may be with the most
laudable intentions—is it at all probable, that in a nation like England,
where letters have reached the proudest elevation, unsustained by
caballing academies or royal donations, that at this moment literary
men will bow the head to the *dicta* of any association whatever? Can
it be supposed that in this most enlightened age, when independence

of every sort is in the highest estimation, writers will place themselves in abeyance from a body in which scarcely a name of celebrity in the national literature has appeared, feeling and knowing that public opinion can confer on them, without shackle or compromise of any kind, lasting reputation and pecuniary advantages adequate to their toils, and far greater than any society can offer. The very soul of a high literature is freedom, a freedom owning no authority but the tribunal of the whole nation. No academy in this country will be held in sufficient respect by the public to keep the power in its hands of bestowing eminence on an author by its plaudits, or of sending him into obscurity by its censures. His glorious independence of mind and pen, his obedience to the dictates of his conscience alone, and the pride of principle, render him very justly jealous of any set of men who would seek to extend their influence over his opinions, or make him the means of propagating theirs. It may be asserted as a truth, that the society in its corporate capacity will have no weight with the better class of English writers, let the political tenets of the latter be what they may. In an early announcement of its intentions, it was observed, that without royal protection "literature would continue neutral or adverse to the service of the country." Here was a pretty plain hint to authors what its advocates thought of our present literature, and hence may be inferred one of the main objects kept in view in its formation. But the literature of this country has attained its magnificence of growth without royal protection, or any other protection than its own irresistible claims afforded. Its professors nurtured it for ages, often amid penury and distress, until it reached a flourishing maturity and spread itself abroad—the admiration of the world, too firmly rooted to require the support of thrones, and too full of vitality to be withered by the insidious care of academies or societies. Is the noblest memento of Britain's glory so vile a thing, that it may be turned or twisted to the use of any faction possessing political power, as Tory, Whig, or Radical, might deem it " adverse to the service of the country"? Does it not look, after acknowledgements so put forth, as if it had been said by the society, " when British literature was emerging from obscurity, it might well be left to force its way in neglect, but now it is become a mighty instrument in governing mankind—now its glory is gone abroad into all corners of the earth, we must offer it our patronage, enlist it on our side, and finally endeavour to control it." But it is too late; no bonds will hold its giant limbs, no art confine its proud and towering spirit. It is no longer a suppliant, gazing on· coronets and patrons for a haughty protection; but a laurelled victor, going " forth conquering and to conquer." Our literary genius, like our constitution, is essentially free, and, while it flourishes, must remain so. Our better class of writers will not enter a society, where unanimity cannot exist, and the future fate of which may be easily foreseen. Let us suppose Mr. —— feeling inclined to present an hexameter ode to the society, and to take his place among the associates, bringing his testimonials of learning, loyalty, good moral character, and public principle, in his hand; suppose these latter to be what the society may approve, how would they elect Mr. ——, whose ideas as " to the promotion of truth, of social order, and loyalty,—loyalty in its genuine sense, not only of personal attachment to the sovereign, but of attachment to the laws and institu-

tions of the country," may be very widely different from those of the
founder of Pantisocracy? Both of these writers would be most desirable
members of such a body; but how can both be elected and the society
preserve a unity of design, and amalgamate individuals so diametrically
opposite in principle?

But, allowing the society to be at present unconnected with politics,
it cannot long remain so; and shall we not, by and by, see it exert the
same sort of influence that we have seen rule similar institutions, both
in this and other countries—we certainly shall. It may safely be
averred, that at no very distant period writers of the greatest learning
and the most brilliant genius would fail of success, were they to be
candidates for admission, not being of the political state party
governing at the time. The experience of the past has uniformly
shewn this to be the case, and it is natural it should be so where bishops
and judges direct. But what have objects purely literary, to which
such societies should be confined, to do with political opinions? Neither
Milton, nor Marvel, nor Sidney, could be members of such a body; but
Cibber and Settle might. What then becomes of the integrity of an
institution, that, under the mask of supporting literature, is the concealed prop of a political party, and excludes from its advantages for
causes which have no connexion with the ostensible object of its establishment. This having been uniformly the case in bodies similarly constituted, there must indeed be saving virtue, in the present society, if
it be exempt from such mischief in a country where party runs so high.
Other academies have been founded with as fair professions as the present, by those who have well understood the advantage of maintaining
an ascendancy over literary men, of arranging them on their side of a
question, and of using them as a shield in contests totally unconnected
with literary matters. The very laws and rules of such societies have
been generally pernicious to genius; being grounded on the theory of
the schoolmen of past times and the pedantry of monkish colleges, they
have proved uncongenial to that portion of literature which is truly
generous, and would now only tend to retard that freedom of thought
which is increasing from the wider diffusion of knowledge, rendered
permanent by the art of printing. A literary society, properly so
called, should hold forth no qualification or disqualification as to members, but what was purely literary; yet the spirit of societies both of
literature and art have never exhibited this consistency. Raphael himself would suffer to-morrow the fate of Barry in the English Academy of
Painting, were he a living member and equally imprudent in the use
of an hasty expression;—but what mischief would such an exclusion do
to Raphael in his art? his pencil would be as graceful as ever, and his
Paintings as much admired. It is precisely the same in an Academy of
Literature, that forgets its genuine object to display its impotent resentment for offences unconnected with its control. But the strenuous
advocates of the society have said that the great object in view is to
" render the pursuit of literature honourable in itself and beneficial in
its results to society." And this it proposes to achieve by giving a
hundred a year to twenty writers whom the society may judge entitled
to the same! Men cannot be rendered more honourable by being made
more dependent; this is not the way to attain the object, nor will any

society in this country, however respectable in rank, render the pursuit of literature more honourable than it is at present or more beneficial in its results. Our literature is formed; our writers that are worthy of it are well supported, and stand high in the public esteem. The society may have a high opinion of the merits of one production, not a dozen copies of which may be sold; while another quite heterodox according to its perspicuous decisions, may be returning wealth and fame to the author. How in such a case can the society help itself, or talk of its foresight and infallibility in literary affairs amid a frequent recurrence of such instances,—and what will the world think of them? As to any thing it can effect for the national literature, we are equally in the dark. The literature of England cannot stand on higher ground than it occupies at present; the works of the society in this respect will be works of supererogation. It cannot compile a better Dictionary than Johnson's, or Todd's Johnson; still less can it improve our lexicography; it must first take high ground in the opinion of the nation, and establish itself at the summit of British literature *de facto*, before it can become an example to be copied. It cannot engross all the genius of the country, nor adequately reward it; this must still be left to the public. It cannot fix a standard of taste in language; the best authors must always be the efficient guides in this respect; and a free nation will not suffer improvement to be at a stand. It cannot mark out new subjects for the higher class of writers; this must be left to individual fancy and feeling. In short, its honorary donations can only act as incitements to young writers, who have still to learn that their most valuable reward, as regards reputation, is to be obtained through the public, and the highest pecuniary advantage through their bookseller.

But the society is not to be supported entirely by government, but also by private subscription. Subscribers are to be considered Fellows, so at least it appears from the proceedings published. From these fellows the officers and council are chosen, and by them will every matter of importance ultimately be decided. Numbers who may become subscribers will be eager to get their money's worth of interference in the transactions of the society. Sir Wm. Curtis, for example, laying aside the study of Mrs. Rundle for that of a less palatable, but somewhat higher, order of reading, may, with the Bishop of —— on one hand, and Mr. Deputy Kilderkin on the other, *assiste*, as the French say, at the deliberations on the merits of the candidates for the medals. Even the Lord Chancellor himself may be seated *vis à vis* with Liston, and shaking his ambrosial curls in the terrors of judicial procrastination over a work of doubtful merit, postpone the consideration of the unhappy author's doom to another meeting. Can such be a state of things to which writers of celebrity will submit, when the tribunal of the nation is open to them, and may it not be boldly pronounced that the road to reputation will be still found to lie that way? The establishment of the society tends also to the contraction and narrowness of every thing connected with literary pursuits. Till now, an English author had "the world before him where to choose" his guides and supporters; yet soon, if the society can become paramount, he must not look beyond its pale. The spirit of our literature must be subdued and reined in; it must proceed only by measured steps; no noble action and graceful curvetting must be tolerated; but the laws of the *manège* must restrain every grace " beyond the reach of art," every motion of which the rusty curb of the College forbids the use.

In a Royal Academy of Literature all the members should be literary men of some celebrity, to be qualified for the business for which they are embodied. Fortunately, the society's influence over the public mind, to any great extent, is not very likely to happen, and therefore much evil need not be dreaded from its anathemas by writers independent of it, should they still continue "neutral, or adverse to the service of the country." Even our Royal Academy of Painting consists of artists; but that of Literature will be essentially composed of subscribers. A Lord Chief Justice out of his place in court is generally but a negative sort of a personage, as a literary umpire more especially. The spirit of lawyers and literary men is as opposite as the poles. Perhaps it is thought a sufficient qualification for a member to have had a certain quantum of Greek and Latin flogged into him in his school-days, and to have kept terms at College. If so, we may congratulate ourselves on our hereditary literati, as a German academy did once on its hereditary mathematicians; thus we have, at last, a royal road to literature. This absurdity is self-evident; but if we must have such a society, let it be openly formed on the principle of absolute power, now so much in vogue in Europe, and well calculated to fetter the mind and make it subservient to its dictates. It is better that Government should at once nominate forty individuals (the Bourbon complement for a literary academy,) and consign over to them the exclusive practice of literary affairs, as it has consigned physic to the academy in Warwick Lane. None should publish a book without a diploma from the legitimate forty; fixed rules should be acted upon in writing tragedy, comedy, history, &c. Then, by rigidly enforcing the execution of this law, letters would speedily descend to so low a level that they would cease to occupy public attention, and no longer excite the apprehensions of our Holy Allies. There is a very un-English feeling abroad, that, instead of showing liberality and expansion of mind, seeks to circumscribe every thing by arbitary control. Our literary renown owes nothing to dogmas or academicians; though occasionally coloured at times too much by a reigning fashion, it was ever free as air—its coruscations had an unbounded space in which to radiate, and owed their splendours to nature, not to the pyrotechnical displays of the laboratory. The support of an academy to our literature in its present state, is that of a reed propping a flourishing oak. The French had scarcely any literature before the foundation of their academy, and therefore there is no similarity in the two cases, nor is it desirable there should be any. We shall soon discover that if this institution do not fall to pieces of itself, it will become a mere thing of party, and that the best introduction to it will be through the minister's closet—it will become the rallying point of his supporters, and will enlarge the sphere of meanness, corruption, and intrigue. We have many writers at present, and there will then be a rapid accumulation of them, that will use the pen on any side and for any party, or for all, if they find it conducive to their private interests, however opposite it may be to the dictates of their consciences. By such the honours and emoluments of the institution will be engrossed, when those who have at present contributed to establish it with pure views and intentions shall have passed away.

It is evident that the means such a society must first adopt, to give it a chance of obtaining influence over the public mind, are, to place itself at the head of the literature of the country, and to unite the best and most popular authors in its support. Mere labourers in the Classical Journal, plodding students, and commentators on ancient text for the thousandth time, no, not even a dozen profound scholars, with the Bishop of Peterborough, and his hundred inquisitorial questions at their head, will make the society succeed without effecting this. The popular authors must unite with the society, or it will never be looked up to. Mere University Grecians will do little for it with the world at large. It must exhibit on its rolls the nobler intellects and higher spirits of the age, or it will remain a secondary thing—a body without a soul—an inefficient name, laborious in microcosmic exertion, and imbecile in the midst of swelling profession. But it is not to be expected that these great names will be recorded on the books of the society. Each feels conscious of his strength, and sees no necessity, nor useful object, in compromising himself with any set of individuals, whose intentions, however good, are characterised by utter destitution of the means which can insure any beneficial consequences to literature from their union. Minds of great power are too independent, and are seldom social enough for such an object; nor will they sacrifice the enjoyment of feeling themselves unrestrained, and descend from their higher studies and flights of fancy to the circumscribed and petty regulations, useless detail, and unmeaning formalities, that give the proceedings of such institutions the appearance of downright frivolity. Medals and prizes may do for scholars and students, but they are of no estimation in the eyes of him who is desirous of earning lasting fame, and whose powers are put forth in vigorous exercise in contending for a far higher reward. The new Royal Society is even objectionable if it contribute to make a portion only of our literature dependent upon it. Its twenty authors must be governed and guided by the fellows, and if they possess sufficient merit in the public eye to be noticed, they will be instrumental, as far as they go, in cramping independence. Our literature is a "chartered libertine," and the attempt to subjugate any part of it to the control of an incorporated body of men may have had its origin simply in a misguided zeal for the benefit of literature, or it may have arisen from the concealed desire to subject it to a species of control which may check its present incorrigible repugnance to be the creature of courtiers, and the instrument of that submissive and debasing spirit which is so rife in the world at present, and which, whether denominated the cause of social order or of the Holy Alliance, is equally unworthy the present times, and degrading to beings gifted with the faculty of reason. From whichever of these causes the Society dates its beginning, it would naturally bear the same aspect of good intention, but it cannot eventually effect good, or promote, in any material degree, the welfare of mankind. The enlightened state of the public mind will, in our day, however, be one of the best antidotes to any evils that may be caused by such an institution. The number of those who reflect, and of those who will watch with jealousy its proceedings and scrutinize them minutely, is very great. A British Academy of Literature, to have succeeded, should have been formed two centuries ago; it is now too late for it to grasp the control of our literature; and yet how fortunate for the Nation that it escaped without possessing such an institution!                                            Y.

---

### THE RETROSPECT.

* * * Di riposo e di pace alberghi veri
O quanto volentieri
A rivedervi io torpo.                            GUARINI.

As turns the pausing traveller back,
  At close of evening, to survey
The windings of the weary track
  Through which the day's long journey lay—
And sees, by that departing light
  That wanes so fast on field and meadow,
How *distant* objects still are bright
  When *nearer* things have sunk in shadow.—

Even so the mind's inquiring eye
  Looks backward through the mist of years,
Where, in its vast variety,
  The chequer'd map of life appears;
And even where Hope's declining rays
  Have ceased to paint the path before her,
The sunshine of her youthful days
  Still casts a cheering influence o'er her.

Oh! youthful days, for ever past,
  That saw my pilgrimage begun,
When clouds of evil scarce could cast
  A passing shadow o'er my sun,
Come, that the wounded spirit may
  Even from your recollection borrow
Thoughts that may cheer the gloom to-day,
  And brighter prospects for the morrow.

Scenes of my youth! ye stand array'd
  In thought before my longing eye—
In all the change of sun and shade
  I see the vision'd landscape lie;
The verdure of the ancient grove—
  The quiet old paternal hall—
The hoary oaks that stoop above
  The dim secluded waterfall.

Once more, ye native vales and hills!
  I do revisit you;—I hear
The waters of my native rills
  That murmur music in mine ear—
I taste the coolness of the bowers
  That oft my youthful feet have haunted—
I scent the fragrance of the flowers
  That erst my youthful hands have planted—

I see the venerable trees
   That round the humble mansion grew—
I breathe the very summer breeze
   That o'er my infant slumbers blew—
I see the very forms that oft
   In other years have hover'd by,
And hear those voices murmuring soft,
   To which my heart hath beat reply.

Oh! magic of the mind! whose might
   Can make the desert heavenly fair,
And fill with forms divinely bright
   The dreary vacancy of air,
And speed the soul from clime to clime,
   Though stormy Oceans roar in vain,
And bid the restless wheels of Time
   Roll backward to the goal again.

The riches that the mind bestows
   Outshine the purple's proudest dye,
And pale the brightest gold that glows
   Beneath the Indian's burning sky:
The mind can dull the deepest smart,
   And smooth the bed of suffering,
And, 'midst the Winter of the heart,
   Can renovate a second Spring.

Then let me joy, whate'er betide
   In that uncounted treasury,
Nor grieve to see the step of Pride
   In purple trappings sweeping by;
Nor murmur if my fate shut out
   The gaudy world's tumultuous din:
He recks not of the world *without*,
   Who feels he bears his world *within*.
                      M.

---

## GRIMM'S GHOST.

### LETTER XIII.

*The Amateur Actor.*

ACTING is like the small-pox. Garrick, and a chosen few besides, took it in the natural way; others, trained to it from childhood, or associating with those who were, are innoculated with it. Captain Augustus Thackeray has lately exhibited symptoms of the disease. He sickened at Woolwich, became feverish in Tottenham-street, and took to his bed upon the regular boards. I thought his clipping the portraits out of Oxberry's edition of the acting drama, and his sticking them round his dressing-room, would come to no good. But the fountain-head of the slaughter was his knowing a man who was intimate with a family who had half a box at Covent-garden Theatre. In his access to this, he frequently found a-jar " the ivory gate" that leads behind the scenes. Man has a natural appetite for the side-scenes of a theatre. Thither our military hero occasionally adjourned, cautiously keeping to the side opposite the prompter, lest that ringer of many bells should be so rude as to inquire his business. It is a hazardous affair to get near actors. We are apt to make comparisons which always redound to our own exaltation. " Macready is great in Virginius," said Augustus Thackeray to himself, " but I think I could do the part better: my voice is to the full as loud as his. Charles Kemble's Mark Antony is a finished performance : but, thank Heaven ! he has no exclusive patent for playing the part, whatever his privileges may be as one of the proprietors of the establishment. I'll go home and study. ' See what an envious rent hath Casca made :' I knew it quite perfect at Harrow, so I shall soon recover it." Those light clouds of self-conceit which float occasionally around the heads of unfledged ensigns and beardless barristers-at-law, shewing to them in shadowy perspective the Field Marshal's baton and the Lord Chancellor's mace, soon enveloped the upper regions of Captain Thackeray. To complete the obumbration, his brother officers at Woolwich gave him the part of Colonel Briton, in the "Wonder." That garrison has for some years been . famous for " cleaving the general ear with horrid speech." William Congreve wrote comedies, and a baronet of the same name invented rockets. They are both clever men in their way : but Love for Love is a pleasanter concern to witness in its progress, than an elliptical cannon-ball. So, at Woolwich, comedies are at present all the vogue, and the rockets are despatched to do duty at Vauxhall Gardens.

Augustus Thackeray was highly complimented for his performance of Colonel Briton. Old Culpepper (who went down by the Southend steam-boat on purpose to witness it) said that in some scenes it run Charles Holland rather hard ; and Mrs. General Macgorget only wished that her nephew Tom Tankerville had played it half as well : he would not then have been laughed at as he was: but he was always a headstrong lad, and for her part she was quite sick of giving him advice. All this was oil to the flame, and Augustus got himself introduced to Charles Kemble the very next evening. The dilettanti performances of the preceding night were of course the subject of conversation. " We at Woolwich," said Thackeray, " have one great advantage over you at the regular theatre—a very great advantage"— " May I ask what it is ?"—" Why, among you there are two or three very good, and all the rest are sticks; but with us at Woolwich we have no *bad* actors." The manager, who plays the part of a perfect gentleman (a character of which he would find it difficult to divest himself, either on the stage or off), answered only with a bow. He might have replied, " No good ones, you would say." Even as a house in the Regent's Park, is a subject upon which it is difficult to agree : the friends of the edifice maintaining that it unites the advantages of town and country, and its enemies maintaining that it absorbs the disadvantages of each. Be that as it may, on the Wednesday following, Thackeray was " at it again."

There is a theatre in Tottenham-street which is noted for enticing slender cornets from Hounslow-barracks, and indentured linendrapers from Oxford-street. Our Captain of course took refuge beneath its portico. He opened there in the Duke Aranza, in the Honey Moon, and was in the highest possible spirits upon the occasion. His grace has to dress three times during the five acts. This, according to Augustus, was a high feather in the cap of the character. " It is a capital part," he observed to Lord Robert Ranter, who was cast for Rolando; " I don't know a better part. First, there's the Duke's private dress: puce-coloured velvet, a beaver hat, a slouched feather, and sugar-loaf buttons—oh! it's a great part! Then there's the cottage dress: drab kerseymere with blue silk facings, high-topped gloves, and russet boots—oh! it's an excellent part! Then there's the Duke's state dress in the last scene : a white plume and diamond button, crimson velvet cloak, and white sattin tronks—oh! it's a delightful part! I quite forgot the white shoes and red rosettes—I don't think there's a better part on the stage !"

The Honey Moon, as honey moons are wont to do, went off extremely well. Audiences are very indulgent when there is nothing to pay. Few things sour a critic more than pulling three shillings and sixpence from his breeches pocket. "Pray, my lord," said Old Culpepper to Lord Robert, "what was the name of the gentleman who played Lopez? He had not much to do: nothing, indeed, but to invite the Duke and Juliana to the village dance; but, I must confess, he threw all the rest of you into the back-ground. Pray what is his name?" " His name!" answered Lord Robert,—" oh, that was Billy Bawl the call-boy from Covent-garden."—"The call-boy? Impossible!"—"Oh, no! it's very true: we paid him thirty shillings." " What a shame!" exclaimed the old slopseller : " only a call-boy? why don't the Covent-garden proprietors put him into Macbeth, or young Mirabel, or Artaxerxes, or something of that sort?" " Why, the fact is, Sir," said the noble amateur, " at Covent-garden poor Billy never gets beyond ' Your ladyship's carriage ;' or at farthest, ' This way, if you please, Sir.' Because the poor fellow is cowed by the regular actors : sad overbearing dogs : but here he is among gentlemen, who put him quite at his ease in a moment."

Lord Robert Ranter has interest with the proprietors. He generally palms some "stick" of an actor upon them once in every season. These would twine "like ivy round a sapling" establishment, but the two old oaks weather it out. Lord Robert spoke to the proprietors about Augustus Thackeray. He might be mistaken: we are all liable to error : but for his part, he had never seen a more promising *début* than his Duke Aranza: his style seemed to be something between John Kemble's and Kean's; free, however, from the stateliness of the one, and the familiarity of the other: he should recommend the proprietors by all means to jump at him: he knew that Elliston would give any money for him, &c. &c. &c. The result was, that the redoubtable Captain got an engagement at Covent-garden Theatre. The terms were neither thirty, no, nor even twenty-five pounds a week. " No matter: money was not his precise object; and there was no doubt that the public voice would force the proprietors to cancel his present articles, and treat him with greater liberality. The cases of Kean and Miss O'Neil were precisely in point. He was determined, for his part, to show the town what gentlemanly acting was. Garrick was a gentleman: he had driven his tilbury last week down to Hampton to see his effects on sale, and he must say, that a more gentlemanly turn out he had seldom witnessed. Not that he meant to patronize the drawing-room chairs ; they were decidedly too short in the elbow : and the Hogarths were vulgar: no elegance in the subjects, and no delicacy in the manner of treating them. But still, Garrick himself was a gentleman, and the view he had from his drawing-room window across the dwarf wall upon the Thames was in capital taste. Garrick shewed them how a gentleman could act, and he was determined to do the same."

"Now heavily in clouds came on the day" when Thackeray, as the Prince of Denmark, was to slouch the accustomed left stocking upon the boards of Covent-garden Theatre. All his friends were mustered upon the occasion : but what are all any man's friends in a Winter Theatre? According to the calculation of Socrates, they might be stuffed into one box, without incommoding each other. In the stage box, on the Prince's side, sat Lord Robert Ranter with his cousin Sir Hans Dabs Oliphant, a great admirer of Shakspeare, every line of whose works he professes thoroughly to understand in spite of his commentators. Sir Hans Dabs brought with him a printed copy of the Hamlet of the immortal bard (upon whom he is himself a commentator in manuscript) bound up with other plays. It is his invariable custom thus to check the actors : and woe be to the wight who misplaces a syllable! Sir Hans has his eye on his book and invariably sets the offender down for a ninny. Should any thing happen to the prompter, there is no baronet in all Marybone parish so well fitted to supply his place. But to return to the hero of the night. The first discovery of him was greeted by the audience with a round of applause. This compliment the Danish Youth returned with a bow, as Princes are accustomed to do. I omitted to mention in its proper place, that Thackeray, while dressing for the part, drew on his jacket rather too hastily, so as to cause a slight starting of the seam under his left arm. This in any other drama would, perhaps, not have been very material : but when the indignant youth in the first scene exclaimed, "I know not *seems,*" he happened to raise his left hand to a height rather above the level of his head. This exhibited a white fissure, which contrasted strongly with the black velvet and bugles around it, and raised such a ludicrous paronomasial association in the minds of some of the audience, that a pretty general titter ensued. The court of Denmark now broke up, and left the son of the late monarch to tell the pit how shamefully he had been used. "O! that this too too solid flesh would melt!" groaned Thackeray, and again raised his left arm. His too solid flesh had by this time, and by this action, increased the aperture. The former titter threatened to mount into a horse-laugh. "It will never do," whispered Sir Hans Dabs Oliphant to Lord Robert. "O! yes, it will," answered his lordship, "the house tailor will set all that to rights in the twinkling of a needle." "My dear Lord Robert," rejoined the critical baronet, "you mistake the matter: they are not laughing at that." "No! at what then?" "Why at the misapprehension of the actor. He has left out three 'ands' and one 'or.' Then, too, when he said

> ' Or that the Everlasting had not fix'd
> His canon 'gainst self-slaughter,'

he raised his arm as if it were charged with a nine-pounder in front of the Woolwich barracks. I don't blame the young man for this : every one according to his own trade : but the true reading is not cannon, a great gun, but canon with a single N, quasi canonical law ; that is to say, spiritual law. Hamlet means to express his regret that religion should stand in the way of his meditated suicide." " Oh, I understand you," said the other, " it was certainly wrong : in uttering the word ' canon' he should merely have pointed towards Doctors Commons." " Exactly so," said the commentator.

Things now went on pretty tolerably until the closet-scene between Hamlet and his mother. " Now for the tug of war," said Lord Robert to his companion. " This is *my* great scene. At Richmond I always get three rounds of applause in it. I admit, my cloak is made of real Genoa velvet : there was a great deal in that : but still in justice to myself I must confess, that my Hamlet is as fine a piece of acting as has been seen since John Kemble : I speak out : egad ! I give it to my mother in the true Nero style !" Whether the audience objected to such treatment of a mother, or whether the elevated elbow once more gave tokens of the separation of sleeve and body, I know not. Certain, however, it is, that coughing now became the order of the night. " I never knew colds more general," said the unconscious amateur as he quitted the stage. " Lord love you, Sir !" said Billy Bawl (who was now reinstated in his proper station behind the regular scenes), " they have no more colds than that kettle-drum : it is you they are coughing at." " Me !" exclaimed Thackeray, " if I thought the public meant to affront me, damme, if I would not pull its nose." " The public has no nose," said a little dapper farce-writer at his elbow. " How do you know that, Sir ?" fiercely demanded the captain. " Because," answered the author, " I have found by experience, that it has no bowels : I therefore infer by parity of anatomy that it has no nose."

" The beautified Ophelia," as Shakspeare, foreseeing that Miss Foote would play the character, has aptly denominated her, was by this time dead and buried. Laertes had attended the funeral, and had jumped upon the coffin. " That is an act which I could never reconcile with decorum," said Lord Robert to the critical Baronet. " Is it customary in Denmark to jump upon the coffin of the defunct?" " Yes, when a brother attends a funeral," valiantly rejoined Sir Hans Dabs Oliphant. Critics do not stand upon trifles. Lord Robert was silenced.

The spectacle of " a great man struggling with the storms of fate" was a most agreeable pastime to the gods of Greece. It still continues so to those of the upper gallery of our winter theatres. Thackeray was quizzed and tormented by those avenging deities, until the green curtain dropped upon the fifth act. " There is a very noisy fellow in the upper gallery," said the amateur, as he rose from his fall, aided by two scene-shifters. " There is," answered the same little dapper damned author; " and he is like the late French Republic, the whole house—one and indivisible."

The friends of the new actor, in front, behaved as new actors' friends usually do. Old Culpepper heartily wished the young man had turned his hand to some other trade. Lady Newbiggin and her plump daughter ascribed it all to those horrid radicals in the galleries : they knew who set them on : there was a man in a red night-cap, very like T——, that was particularly noisy : for their parts, they never could see the use of the water tank upon the roof, if it was not opened to duck discontent : but, upon the whole, they must say that they thought the performance but so so.

This, too, was the opinion of Thackeray's bosom friend, Captain
Ironsides, who pronounced it a decided Daggerwood affair: adding
that Romeo Coates was a fool to him.   Lord Robert Ranter and Sir
Hans Dabs Oliphant slunk from their box as though they had been
detected in probing the pockets of their neighbours.   They made their
exit through the Bow-street door, but were stopped on the upper step
by a sudden shower.   " This is an elegant façade," cried Lord
Robert, stepping back to avoid the wet.   " Very," answered Sir Hans,
imitating the process.   " It is modelled from a temple at Athens,"
continued Lord Robert, with his back by this time in contact with the
outward wall of the building.   " So they say," resumed the Baronet,
clinging to the stucco as perpendicularly as a recruit at the word
" Attention."   It was all to no purpose : the shower still pattered on
their shoes : Scamander did not cling closer to Achilles.   " It is a
pity," said Lord Robert, " that the architect in conveying over the
model, forgot to bring the climate with him."   " A great pity,"
echoed Sir Hans ; " but there is a capital fruit-shed in Broad-court,
over the way.   I always run thither when it rains—that shed and this
portico constantly remind me of my wife's drawing-room grate.   The
polished bars, outside, serve for show, but the black ones, inside, prop
the hot coals."   " That blockhead George has, no doubt, driven
round to the Piazza door," said Lord Robert: " any thing is better
than wet feet—lead on to the fruit-shed."   When the two friends were
safe under deal-board shelter, and both were comfortably seated upon
inverted baskets, with a large assortment of pea-shells crackling
beneath their feet, like autumnal leaves, they resumed their conversation upon the subject of the recent representation.   " I had no
notion," said Lord Robert, " that poor Thackeray would have turned
out such a decided stick : at one moment I had some hopes of him.
Did you observe his ' Frailty, thy name is woman'?"   " No, I was
busy turning over my leaf."   " Well, then, you must have noticed his
' Be buried quick with her'?"   " No," answered Sir Hans, " at that
time I had lost my place."   " Lost your place? Why you never stirred
from the box."   " No, I mean the place in my book : my Hamlet
is bound up with four other plays ; and I got smack into the middle of
the Recruiting Officer, before I knew where I was."

The subject of all this criticism, in the mean time, had retreated to his
lodgings in Hart-street, Bloomsbury, where he slept soundly, unconscious of his failure.   It is the case in all the arts : there is not a hump-
backed man, in all London and Westminster, who does not fancy himself an Adonis.   Not that Thackeray was unaware of the discord in ·
the house, but he ascribed it to every cause but the true one.   Colds
and hoarseness were never more common.   Besides, there was evidently a party sent in : probably by Young or Macready : jealousy is
proverbially a green-room failing : for his part, he thought the proper
reading was not " Beware of jealousy, it is a green-eyed monster."
No ! Shakspeare evidently wrote it " Green-room monster !" and so he
would deliver it, when he should be put up for Iago.   With this valiant
determination, out sallied Thackeray, and in passing through Newport-
market, saw, skewered upon the back of a dead sheep, a large play-
bill, upon which " Theatre Royal Covent-garden—Macbeth," was imprinted in legible characters.   The poor animal, even in death, seemed

conscious of " the bloody business" of which it was the herald, its
nose having marked the pavement below with a sympathetic crimson
tint. " Oh! Macbeth!" ejaculated Thackeray, " that is my next part,
is it? Well, I have no objection: it is not a bad part; but I wish
they would not expect me to play upon opera-nights. Macbeth was a
thorough gentleman; it is true, he killed his friend Banquo, and did
not behave quite hospitably to King Duncan; but still, he was a thorough
gentleman: John Kemble was always too frigid in it, and Garrick
wanted height: yes, Garrick was a punchy little fellow, and dressed the
character in scarlet breeches: Macbeth is nothing without figure." By
this time, the Thespian Captain had entered Portugal-street, where an
old mirror, suspended in a broker's shop, " reflected him back to the
skies," as the Reverend Bate Dudley has it. Thackeray was well
pleased with the exhibition, and walked on, repeating " Macbeth is
nothing without figure." On his return home, he found that the
messenger, whose duty it is to distribute the parts of the play next in
representation, had been at his residence, and had left a manuscript for
his perusal. It lay upon his breakfast-table, and the word " Macbeth" was written in a fair legible hand upon the outside cover.
" Oh, here it is," cried he, carelessly.

> " A happy prologue to the swelling act
> Of this imperial theme."

So saying, he opened the fly leaf, and read " Mr. Thackeray—Macbeth—*the Bleeding Captain.*" " What!" exclaimed the astonished
débutant, when he was able to resume his breath. " Me—expect me
to act the bleeding Captain? expect a perfect gentleman to stagger
on with two cuts on his forehead, and one on his cheek, to tell that
stupid old fool Duncan what a number of men his two generals had
knocked on the head? I won't do it—there must be some mistake."
—" Drive to Soho-square," cried the new actor, jumping into a hackney
cabriolet. The manager received him *suaviter in modo:* but, as touching the bleeding Captain, *fortiter in re:* he was cast for the part and
must perform it. " Never," ejaculated Thackeray: " when I engaged
as an actor, it was under an idea that I should act what I pleased and
when I pleased." " Add thereto, and at what salary you pleased,"
said the manager, " and you would make our profession ' a bed of
roses.' As affairs now stand, however, I am afraid that you are under
articles to play what and when the proprietors please, under a penalty
of thirty pounds." This reminiscence staggered the tragedian.
" Have you any objection to give me up my articles," inquired he.
" None, whatever," answered the other, delivering them up to him.
" Cancel and tear in pieces this great bond," continued Thackeray,
scattering the fragments of the document to the winds ;—" and as for
you, Sir," turning to the proprietor of the mansion, " allow me to say,
that if I ever act again upon your boards, and you don't keep your
audience in better order, damme if I don't call them *out.*"—" Do but
contrive to call them *in,*" answered the manager, " and I will undertake
to re-engage you, for three years, at a rising salary."

MODERN PILGRIMAGES.—NO. X.

*Lausanne.*

To visit Lausanne was one of my oldest and most cherished day-dreams. To see Rome, or Italy, indeed, was a wish too lofty, too impracticable for my youthful thoughts; but Lausanne, thought I, ten years since, on first perusing Gibbon's Memoirs, might be managed, if but some kind hand would put an end to that fellow Bonaparte. The pleasures which I deemed nearest my grasp at that early period, have ever and for ever irrecoverably fled, while those which seemed beyond my wildest wishes I have enjoyed even to satiety. I have swam and floated on the lovely Leman, climbed over the snowy Alps, and threaded their defiles — shot in a gondola beneath the Rialto, and wandered through the empty palace of the Doges—the galleries of Florence have satiated my curious eyes—my step has a thousand and a thousand times overrun the Capitol, and sunk through the begilt and mouldering vaults of the Palatine Hill—Naples has spread forth before me her bay and shores, unrivalled in the interest of name and scenic beauty;—but associations southward, and northward of the Alps, are somehow or other very different sentiments. In Italy or Greece, such sympathy for the by-gone is aggregate, universal—it is for nations, for ages—it is inspired by the memory of a people, and, as it were, by the sum of their greatness. North of the Alps, the associations which pilgrims seek and sing of are individual, excited by a single name, independent of nation or country,—they are warm, domestic feelings, and come more home to our egotistic bosoms, than the high-wrought and often factitious sympathies with Roman or with Grecian greatness.

Englishmen, if they have *more sentiment* in love and private affection than other nations, have undoubtedly much *less* in politics. The romance of public affairs we do not understand. And after the classic essence, with which we become impregnated at college, evaporates, we generally sink into very matter-of-fact honest politicians. It is owing to this, perhaps, that we seem such Goths in Italy. At Clarens, or Ferney, our countrymen are to be seen sentimental; but I never once met an Englishman at Rome with an air or consciousness at all different from that with which he trod Pall Mall or the Strand. Now the French grow heroic in the immortal city, and the Germans mad. But your Englishman is the same stiff, impassive, well-dressed gentleman on Primrose Hill, or the Capitol. At Tasso's dungeon, 'tis true, he looks with interest and indignation; but chains and prisons would move him any where. And such, as a spot of personal and individual association south of the Alps, forms an exception to our division—'tis, however, but an exception, it is Morat, north of the boundary, where the pilgrim views, with a national and patriotic feeling, the bones of the Burgundian invaders.

Once upon the Italian soil, for any one personage, poet, or hero, to claim our undivided interest is impertinence. I remember, the first sight of a helmet on an Italian, or rather an Austrian soldier, at Milan, striking me with more melancholy than would the tombs of an hundred Etruscan bards. I cannot, with Childe Harold, forget the Latin in the Lombard glories—mourn over Venice and Ferrara, and approach the Capitol itself with exhausted sympathics. Once at Domo, or at Susa, the big, collective feeling should come over one, which, as Wordsworth says,

> "Moveth altogether, if it move at all."

But for lovely little spots of circumscribed association, wedded, as it were, to a single name, Switzerland is the country. And the traveller need not diverge from the high Simplon road, in order to visit and enjoy the greater number. Ferney, Coppet, Lausanne, Clarens, will each furnish their supply of pensive food to the sentimentalist. The first I reserve for some gay, satirical mood, so ill according with the scene.—Strange! that a being, that had chosen its resting-place on the banks of the Leman, between the Jura and the Savoy Alps, and with the monarch of mountains ever towering in his view, should there have so dwarfed his powers, so concentrated and narrowed them in the microscope of satire, merely to destroy some petty insect of a rival. To be at Ferney, to look round, and say, here wrote the author of the "Pucelle," is one of those most unpleasant contradictions that *the fact* so often gives to the *probability*.

If nature ever imitated a picture, it was in forming the Leman: beauty and sublimity in all the gradations and variety of each are crowded upon and around it. You drive along the Swiss side of the lake, through meadows and hedges of English luxuriance, trimly kept and divided too, after our country fashion, while the vine, the Swiss cottage, and Swiss costume, add foreign charms to what reminds us so strongly of home. The Jura rises above, the lake spreads beneath, with many a "quiet sail" upon its surface, that look as nothing while they glide over the reflection of the towering Alp upon the lake. The eye, on one side, follows up the curve of the sandy margin to Vevay and Chillon, and on the other side marks the huge masses of Alp that overhang the lake, with a town here and there upon the brink, which, from their comparative size might be almost taken for so many napkins spread out to dry. The approach to the modern republic of Lausanne is worthy of forming the avenue to the most ancient and feudal of castles : it rises and winds in the midst of majestic chesnut-groves, through whose waving foliage is seen at every step, here the bright surface of the lake and its opposite mountain border, and there the subtle spires and lofty brick buildings of the city. Lausanne itself, when entered, does not answer the promise of such an approach ; the traveller is annoyed at its steepness and its straightness, but one glance from almost any window of the town is sufficient to drive away his spleen.

The house of Gibbon was the first object of my search at Lausanne. It belonged to the banker, I was told. The lower part and garden, however, seem to appertain to another tenant, an old lady, into whose apartments I descended from the street, and was straight ushered into the garden to behold what the maiden called "La Gibbon"—an old shattered tool-house.

"It was on the day, or rather night, of the 27th of June, 1787," says Gibbon, "between the hours of eleven and twelve, that I wrote the last lines of the last page, in a summer-house in my garden. After laying down my pen, I took several turns in a *berceau*, or covered walk of acacias, which commands a prospect of the country, the lake, and the mountains. The air was temperate, the sky was serene, the silver orb of the moon was reflected from the waters, and all nature was silent. I will not dissemble the first emotions of joy on the recovery of my freedom, and, perhaps, the establishment of my fame. But my pride was soon humbled, and a sober melancholy was spread over my mind, by the idea that I had taken an everlasting leave of an old and agreeable companion, and that whatever might be the future date of my history, the life of the historian must be short and precarious."

The acacias still flourish, as does the weeping willow which he planted, and I need not add, that the scene remains the same. It had changed, however, more than once for Gibbon. When he first visited, or rather was exiled to Lausanne, " he exchanged his elegant apartment in Magdalen College for a narrow, gloomy street, the most unfrequented of an unhandsome town, for an old, inconvenient house, and for a small chamber ill-contrived and ill-furnished, which, on the approach of winter, instead of a companionable fire, must be warmed by the dull, invisible heat of a stove." When he returned again from London, the contrast was quite in favour of this " unhandsome town." " Instead of a small house between a street and a stable-yard, I began to occupy a spacious and convenient mansion, connected on the north side with the city, and open on the south to a beautiful and boundless horizon. A garden of four acres had been laid out by the taste of M. Deyverdun: from the garden a rich scenery of meadows and vineyards descends to the Leman Lake, and the prospect far beyond the lake is crowned by the stupendous mountains of Savoy."

The French revolution, and the occupation of Savoy by the republican troops under General Montesquiou, once more changed the aspect of the scene for Gibbon : what he admired as the kingdom of Savoy, he did not relish as the department of Mont Blanc.—" My noble scenery," writes he, " is clouded by the democratical aspect of twelve leagues of the opposite coast, which every morning obtrude themselves on my view."

The biography of those days, or the history of men's private opinions during this time, forms a most humiliating study—to observe how idly formed, how stubbornly held and perniciously advanced were the principles of men of the first intellect, yet how easily the political half was overturned by alarm, and, as it were, by very bodily fear, while they kept the religious half firm, merely to preserve some show of consistency. I remember being much pleased with a paragraph in the Edinburgh Review, which sought to prove the necessary union of Toryism and infidelity. The argument, though weak in reasoning, was strong in example; and I wondered at not seeing the name of Gibbon adduced by the side of those of Bolingbroke and Hume. The fact is, that we were imitators of France in those days, and that our historians took their tone servilely from the imposing cant of Parisian society. That the *beaux esprits* of that circle were deists, we are aware ; and that they were, with the exception of Rousseau, (the only man amongst them who possessed *intellectual honesty*,) aristocrats, is not clear, but equally true. There is no despotic act, that will not find itself abetted in the writings of the liberal Voltaire ;—see for example, how the ultras of late quoted his History in support of the invasion of Spain.

He thought the partition of Poland a just act of self-preservation on the part of the surrounding powers, and he seems to have made freedom ignominious, merely with a hatred to the *soutane*. Hume and Gibbon were the gossips and followers of this man and his school; and a more ridiculous, contradictory, tesselated set of principles than theirs, was never stuck together by hazard and imitation—cold and curious in those spiritual and imaginative questions where they should have been generous and confiding, yet unseasonably soft-hearted in those plain passages of life where severe and rational justice was the duty of the moralist and the historian!

The above-mentioned arguer of the necessary connexion between Toryism and infidelity, might have found in Gibbon's Memoirs a most curious proof of his doctrine; as in one passage the historian confesses that his hatred and opposition to Christianity was founded on that most Tory of all Tory principles,—an hatred to innovation.

" Burke's book," writes he to Lord Sheffield, " is a most admirable medicine against the French disease, which has made too much progress even in this happy country. I admire his eloquence, I approve his politics, I adore his chivalry, and I can forgive even his superstition. *The primitive Church, which I have treated with some freedom, was itself at that time an innovation, and I was attacked at the time to the old Pagan establishment."*

Let but two words be altered in this notable exposition of creed, and it will serve precisely any Tory of the present day to oppose Reform withal. So far did this *eleutherophobia* carry Gibbon, that we find this hater of Christianity as an innovation, upholding one of its most detestable consequences—the Inquisition : " I recollect," says Lord Sheffield, " in a circle where French affairs were the topic, and some Portuguese present, he seemingly, with seriousness, argued in favour of the Inquisition at Lisbon, and said, he would not, at the present moment, give up even that old *establishment."*

---

## MYSTIFICATION—THE WHITE PATIENT.

" There 's a knot, a gang, a pack, a conspiracy against me."

" Well, if I be served such another trick, I'll have my brains taken out and buttered, and give them to a dog for a new-year's gift."--*Merry Wives of Windsor.*

THOUGH the word " mystification" is somewhat of the newest in our language, and not very old in the French, from which we have borrowed it, yet the *thing* it represents is by no means an affair of yesterday. Mystification is as old as idleness, and idleness as old as civilization, and civilization as old as Triptolemus and his plough. From the remotest tradition, before History began to write, we hear of mystifications and mystifiers. Was not Saturn finely mystified when he swallowed, what the Irish would call, a lump of a stone, for a young sucking god? Mystification is indeed of all ages, being an integral portion of human nature. Ulysses, the great mystifier of antiquity, was seldom without some practical joke at his fingers' ends; and was never so happy as when he was " selling a bargain." He was so far, however, lucky, that he lived in an age when folks were not " up to snuff," and he had rarely to deal with "the knowing ones." Thus. the old Cyclops had brains as hard as his own anvil, or he never would have been "done" by the "rigmarol" tale of Nobody. Achilles also, or we are much mistaken, proved himself as dull as any modern "great captain" of them all, not to "understand trap," when Ulysses shewed him the armour in the court of the King of Scyros,—and the young rascal in love too, which never fails to sharpen a man's wits, provided he have any to sharpen. The manner in which the wily Greek " *did-dled*" the Syrens, was more knowing; and the way in which he " *bam-boozled*" his wife's suitors, "*flogged the world*," and was "*as rum a touch*" as need be. Yet even Ulysses was mystified by Palamedes, in his young days; and some think that Penelope with her cock-and-bull story of a web, was, in his older and riper experience, "*one too many for him.*"

The ascent of Romulus to heaven, under the nick-name of Quirinus, was a flat mystification of the Romans, who, it must be confessed, were ready-made dupes to the hands of their church and state operators, and swallowed Quintus Curtius's leap, and Menenius Agrippa's sophis-tical fable with equal facility. Brutus's shamming mad was a "*go*" of the first order, though rather too jacobinical for our pure times; and Cæsar's conduct to Cato, in the senate, when he gave him his sister's love-letter to read, was a "*dead take-in.*" In the dark ages, mystifica-tion was universal. The donations to the Papal See were not bad spe-cimens of the art of humming, and the false decretals are allowed to have been an admirable joke. In our own history, Oliver Cromwell shines the prince of mystifiers. His "seeking the Lord" in the shape of a corkscrew was quite "*prime.*" Monk, and Anthony Ashley Cooper were both "*good in their way;*" and Churchill, the great Duke of Marlborough, "*ran his rigs*" on the Stuarts in a superior style. The glorious revo......; but it's as well to stop where we are, lest we break the invisible line, which divides the demesne of history, from that of the attorney-general.

Crossing therefore the water, we proceed at once to remark that the French are the "*mystificateurs par excellence ;*" at least that part of the nation which "lives at home at ease" in Paris, and upon whose hands time and talent are often observed to hang rather heavily. But here we beg to be understood as not alluding in the slightest degree to the government of that country; or, more especially, as insinuating aught against the king's pacific speech, on the eve of the Spanish war. The Bourbons, to do them justice, are all "fair and above board ;" and they speak their intentions with a plainness which none but an ideot can mistake. No, we confine our remarks exclusively to those happy wights, who have no earthly occupation but "*faire le bel esprit,*" and to shew the contempt they feel for that wretched *canaille* by whose labour and industry they are supported, comforted, and *amused.*

In this class flourished "*n'aguères,*" a certain Duc de Caudale, who divided his superabundant talent for mystification between two pur-suits—the cheating his tradesmen, and the seduction of that order of females known in Paris by the name of "*grisettes.*" The former he contrived to effect by holding out the bait of extraordinary and usurious gains ; the latter he was wont to accomplish by an artifice, now suffi-ciently common-place,—a promise of marriage. With this worthy gentleman a promise of marriage was a mere *bagatelle ;* and he gave it with the same indifferent facility that a dashing speculator in London "flies his kites," when on the verge of bankruptcy. By the persevering use of these arts, the Duke acquired for himself a reputation, which, if it was not splendid, was at least wide-spreading; but *reputations are not made for nothing*; and his Grace, accordingly found himself one day under the necessity of leaving Paris, and of returning, for the benefit of his—*character*, to his estates in a remote province.

On the eve of departure, this important event got wind; and the Duke's hotel was besieged by a whole army of creditors. A day later with them, and it would have been the "day after the fair;" but as it was, Caudale was caught on his form, and no doubling could enable him to put off the interview. The horses therefore being at the door, and every thing in readiness for flight, the duns, "horrible monsters," were admitted. The Duke's reception of them was polite; he heard their story with patience, lamented their loss of time, leaned heavily on his "*homme d'affaires,*" whose irregularities, he said, were the cause of their disappointments, and finally, calling for pen, ink, and paper, he asked for their accounts. Running his eye over the numerous bills, with the air of an hasty examination, he noted and signed each separate document, and then, turning to his *intendant,* delivered him a bundle of papers, and desired him to give every creditor his order for payment; which, he observed, was the more easily done, as each paper was endorsed with its owner's name. So saying, he took his leave, mounted his horse and set off. The creditors, eager for their long-looked-for money, scarcely suffered him to leave the room, when they crowded round the man of figures to receive the expected order; but their astonishment may be readily conceived, when, instead of "Please to pay the bearer," each man read in his own billet "I Duc de Caudale, &c. &c. hereby promise to marry Mr. So and So." The intendant, who was perhaps aware of the cheat, endeavoured to excuse his master to the best of his power, saying "It was an unlucky mistake." "It arose entirely from absence of mind and the inveterate habit of writing such promises." "He had no doubt that as soon as his master was aware of the error he would hasten to rectify it;" and in this way he dismissed the enraged dupes, about as well satisfied with their morning's work, as the Jew creditors of the elder Baron de Felsheim with Brandt's mode of "equitable adjustment" in Pigault Le Brun's whimsical novel.

A mystifier in a lower rank in society was Turpin, celebrated by his countrymen and neighbours for a wicked wit. Turpin seems to have been born for the express purpose of humbugging all the world, and to have been what we call a first-rate wag. Happening to sit one day at church next to a jolly fat-faced lady, whose nose was the least prominent feature in her platter-formed visage, he began to fidget and grunt, and make such horrible contortions as induced his good-natured neighbour to ask what ailed him. "Alas! my good lady," cried Turpin, with the utmost gravity of voice and demeanour, "I am a poor paralytic, who cannot use my hands; and here I have been sitting this full quarter of an hour without any one to blow my nose, of which I am in urgent necessity." The answer, as may be anticipated—for women are ever compassionate—was a proposition to assist the sick man in his need. Turpin readily expressed his assent, and the fat lady, seeking his handkerchief in his pocket, lent herself to the operation, which he performed with all the simplicity imaginable, returning to the charge three several times, and making the church ring again with the crowing of his nostrils. Then, turning to the woman, and preserving the hypocritical tranquillity of his countenance and voice undisturbed, he asked her, " *n'est il pas vrai ma bonne dame, qu'il y a bien plus de plaisir à moucher un bon gros nez comme le mien, qu'un villain chien de nez camard comme le votre ?*"—" and now tell me, my good charitable lady, is it not a much greater pleasure to blow such an handsome nose as mine, than to be fumbling at a miserable snub like your own ?"

Turpin, among his other mystifications, for a long time assumed the garb of an hermit. Entering one day into an inn-yard, with another rogue of his own complexion, they found an ass attached to the door. To see it unguarded and to covet it were simultaneous impressions. Stripping off, therefore, the harness from the animal, he crept into it himself, and while his companion drove the beast away, he waited quietly the arrival of the owner. The master of the ass was not a little surprised on his return to find his animal gone and a hermit standing harnessed in his gear. Still more was he astonished when he heard Turpin reverently thanking God for the recovery of his human shape. " At length," cried the mystifier in seeming soliloquy, " my sins are forgiven me, and the time of my penance is expired. I sinned and was changed to an ass ; but Heaven is merciful, and its anger does not endure for ever." So saying, Turpin threw down the harness, and went his way. But, as ill-luck would have it, the ass was soon sent to be sold ; and who should come into the market but its former proprietor. The *anagnorisis* was instant. " Out alas !" exclaimed the good man, " has the wretch sinned again already ! and has he again been turned to an ass ! For the love of God, neighbours, have nothing to say to that animal ; he has deceived me once, but I am not to be taken a second time in the same trap : for, lookye, whoever buys that beast, will find him some day or other, as I did, turned into a hermit."

From these specimens we may see how much superior the upper classes of society are to their humbler fellow-subjects in the refinements of mystification. An odd, grotesque humour is the highest flight of a vulgar mind, whereas in the Duc de Caudale's adventure we perceive not only a moral object and end in his humbugging (the getting rid of his creditors), but also a delicate stroke of satire on his own character and conduct, which shews him deep in the philosophy of " *nosce teipsum.*" The mystification of the lower orders rarely looks farther than to the " fun" which it is calculated to afford, and it is still seldomer absolutely ill-natured. But your thorough-paced mystifiers of the *bonton* for the most part contrive to put forward their perfect indifference to the feelings of their victim. Their mystifications have more of cold " *persiflage,*" and less of the mere animal impulse to laughter in them. They are more recondite, studied, and malicious ; which proves them to depend upon the highest and most intellectual of the human faculties, and evinces in the mystifiers that innate superiority, which in all things distinguishes the genuine China ware, from the Wedgewood and the crockery of God's creation. Every one knows the mystification played off on the unhappy *curé*, who, smit with the love of sacred poesy, was induced to read his tragedy to the Holbachian knot,—a

mystification which threw Jean Jaques into such an uncompromising passion*: The malice of this " good joke" was its predominant
feature, for its wit was not very conspicuous. And what is more, there
was not one of the mystifiers who did not in some degree share
the poor poet's " *mentis gratissimus error*" of thinking better of his
own verses than they deserved. How infinitely superior then is such
a practical jest to the cold conceit of Turpin's nose, and yet how
below the *piquant* mixture of fraud and fun of the Duke's promi-
sory billets. Nothing indeed can more satisfactorily prove the invincible rusticity of Rousseau's bearish character, than his incapacity
for relishing this piece of drollery.

The leading mystifier of Paris immediately before the Revolution,
was La Reyniere, the facetious author of the *Almanac des Gourmands*.
His humour, however, partook largely of the peculiarities of his birth
and education, being essentially *roturier*. His famous supper, which
Grimm describes with such effect, though an expensive joke, exhibited
rather the ostentation of the financier, than the refined thoughtlessness
of expense, which accompanies a determination of paying no debts;
as a mystification, it had no elevation or nobleness of character, and
was indeed a mere *platitude*. Still worse was his joke of putting a
cork hand on the hot stove of the opera, in order to seduce his neighbours into burning their fingers. These observations apply with great
force to the cockney attempts at mystification annually played off on
the first of April;—of which, as a correspondent in the New Monthly
Magazine has already spoken at large, I shall only remark by the
way, that pigeon's milk, one of the favourite engines of April foolery,
is as old as Aristophanes.†

To this train of reflection we were led by a mystification related in
the letters of Mademoiselle Aissé, which is the very sublime of the
art, and " *marqué au bon coin*," by costliness to the mystifier, cruelty
to the patient, and the total absence of all vulgar jocularity and humour.
The story is as follows :—

In the reign of Louis XV. Isissé was the fashionable surgeon of
Paris. One morning he received a note inviting him to attend in the
*Rue Pot' de fer*, near the Luxembourg, at six o'clock in the evening.
This professional *rendesvous* he of course failed not to keep, when he
was encountered by a man who brought him to the door of a house, at
which the guide knocked. The door, as is usual in Paris, opened by
a spring, moved from within the porter's lodge; and Isissé, when it
again closed upon him, was surprised to find himself alone, and his
conductor gone. After a short interval, however, the porter appeared,
and desired him to mount " *au premier.*" Obeying this order, he
opened the door of an antechamber, which he found completely lined
with white. A very handsomely dressed and well-appointed *lacquais*,
white from head to foot, well powdered and frizzed, with a white bag
to his hair, held two napkins, with which he insisted on wiping Isisse's
shoes. The surgeon in vain observed, that having just left his carriage, his shoes were not dirty; the lacquais persisted, remarking that
the house was too clean to allow of this operation being omitted.
From the antechamber Isissé was shewn into a saloon hung like the

---

* See Grimm.  † Γαλατ' ὀρνίθων—aves.

antechamber with white, where a second *lacquais* repeated the ceremony of wiping the shoes, and passed him into a third apartment, in
which the walls, floor, bed, tables, chairs, and every article of furniture were white. A tall figure, in a white nightcap and white morning
gown, and covered with a white mask, was seated near the fire: As
soon as this phantom perceived the surgeon, he cried in an hollow
voice, " I have the devil in my body,"—and relapsed immediately into
a profound silence, which he continued to observe during more than
half an hour, that he amused himself in pulling on and off six pair of
white gloves, which lay on a table beside him. Isissé was greatly
alarmed at this extraordinary spectacle, and at his own reception ; and
his apprehension was not diminished on perceiving that fire arms were
placed within the reach of the white spectre. His fears became at
length so excessive that he was compelled to sit down. By degrees,
however, he gained sufficient courage to ask in a trembling voice, " what
were Monsieur's commands," remarking that " his time was not his
own, but the public's, and that he had many appointments to keep."
To this the white man only replied, in a dry cold tone, " As long as
you are well paid, what does that signify to you ?" Another quarter of
an hour's silence then ensued, when at last the spectre pulled a white
bell-rope, and two white servants entered the room. He then called for
bandages, and desired Isissé to draw from him five pounds of blood.
The surgeon, frightened still more by the enormous bloodletting thus
enjoined him, asked in an anxious tone who had ordered the remedy ?
" Myself," was the short answer. In too great a trepidation to venture
on the veins of the arm, Isissé begged to bleed from the foot, and warm
water was ordered for the operation. Meantime the phantom took off a
pair of the finest white silk stockings, and then another, and then a third,
and so on to the sixth pair, which discovered the most beautiful foot and
ancle imaginable; and almost convinced Isissé that his patient was a
woman. The vein was opened; and at the second cup the phantom
fainted. Isissé therefore was proceeding to take off the mask, but he
was eagerly prevented by the servants. The foot was bound up, and
the white figure having recovered his senses, was put to bed ; after
which, the servants again left the room. Isissé slowly advanced towards the fire, while he wiped his lancets ; making many reflections
within himself upon this strange adventure. All of a sudden, on
raising his eyes, he perceived in the mirror over the chimney-piece,
that the white figure was advancing towards him on tiptoes. His
alarm became still more violent, when, with a single spring, the terrific
spectre came close to his side. Instead, however, of offering violence,
as his movement seemed to indicate, he merely took from the chimney five
crowns and gave them to the surgeon, asking at the same time if he was
satisfied. Isissé, who would have made the same answer had he received
but three farthings, said that he was. " Well, then," said the spectre,
" begone about your business." The poor surgeon did not wait for a
second order, but retreated, or rather flew, as fast as his legs could
carry him, from the room. The two servants who attended to light
him out could not conceal their smiles ; and Isissé, unable longer to
endure his situation, asked what was the meaning of this pleasantry?
But their only reply was, " Are you not well paid ? have you suffered
any injury ?" and so saying, they bowed him to his carriage. Isissé

was at first determined to say nothing of this adventure; but he found on the ensuing morning, that it was already the amusement of the court and city; and he no longer made any mystery of the matter. The "*mot d'enigme,*" however, was never discovered, nor could any motive be imagined for the mystification, beyond the caprice and idleness of its unknown perpetrator.

It is somewhat remarkable that this adventure should, in its leading feature, bear a great resemblance to one that happened to a casual acquaintance of our own, and which, without being a mystification, had all the effect of one.   This gentleman, a surgeon of much practice, residing in a sea-port village in Hampshire, was, one dark winter's night, about the "celebrated hour of twelve o'clock" (to borrow a phrase from a popular novel), called from his bed to visit a patient suddenly taken ill.  "*Linquenda domus et placens uxor*" never reads worse than in the middle of a cold frosty night; but the surgeon (like all other surgeons) comforted himself with the thought of the double *honorarium* "in that case provided;" and, huddling on his clothes as fast as he could, he descended in the dark to open the street-door. On again closing it behind him, and proceeding a few paces down the street, he felt himself suddenly seized by a vigorous grasp, while the muzzle of a pistol pressed hard against his breast.   His interlocutor, wrapped in an immense cloak, in no very silver tones desired him to follow, and, as he valued his life, to proceed in silence.   At the turning of the street a second man started forth from a projecting doorway, and in a low anxious whisper asked, "Have you got him?"   "Got him," was the laconic reply, and the three passed on without farther speaking.   Farther on another confederate joined them, and "Have you got him?" was repeated in the same way, and produced the same brief half-suppressed "Got him" as before.   Thus they proceeded to the outskirts of the village, where they met other men mounted, and holding led horses.   "Have you got him?" cried the horsemen under less restraint, and therefore in a louder key.   "Got him," more freely breathed the inflexible conductor; and placing the terrified surgeon on the saddle of one of the led steeds, he got up behind him, and the whole company scoured away over fields, heaths, and bogs, occasionally reconnoitred and joined by scrutinising védettes, after the accustomed "Have you got him?" had assured them that they *had* "got him," and that all was right.   The poor man's anxiety, increasing at every step that led him farther from the "haunts of man," through ways which, though he perfectly knew the country, were still new to him, was now wound up to absolute despair; when suddenly the horsemen paused, and alighted at the door of a lone cottage, in which lay a wounded man stretched on a bed.   The surgeon was dismounted and ordered to examine and dress the wound, and to prescribe directions for its management: which being done, the escort took to their horses again, and, replacing the surgeon behind old "Got him," returned in the same order and with the same precautions as before. Towards break of day they arrived at the town's end, where, "Got him" having first paid the surgeon handsomely for his night's work, and threatened him with the severest vengeance if he spoke of this adventure, these "ugly customers" took their leave and departed.   In this manner he was, afterwards, several times carried to visit his patient, till the convalescence of the sick man made his visits no longer necessary. It is scarcely necessary to add that the parties were smugglers, who had had an engagement with the custom-house officers; and that the secresy of their proceeding arose from the fear of the man's situation leading to detection.

It would be difficult for the malice of the most practised mystifier to have given more pain than was inflicted on our friend the surgeon by this combination of events, arising out of the " social system" of our sea-coasts; but, after all, nature and chance afford the outlines of our brightest inventions, and we are not to be surprised if they should sometimes succeed better than art in advancing them towards perfection.

Of all the mystifications with which man is acquainted, Voltaire thought life itself the greatest. " *Pourquoi*," he asks, " *existons-nous? pourquoi y a-t-il quelque chose?*" But whatever may be thought of life, the remark is just, as applied to society, which, from first to last, is one entire humbug. Lawyers, physicians, and divines, are mystificators of the first order, and nothing can be a more thorough *mauvaise plaisanterie*, than the persuading men that there is honour in being shot at for sixpence per day. Virtual representation and the sinking fund every one gives up as humbugs, who has three grains of common sense. The Arts are altogether a mass of humbug, theatricals are gross humbugs, churchwardens are humbugs, county petitions are " farces" and humbugs, Whigs are humbugs, Tories are humbugs, and the Radicals themselves are humbugs also. Nay, is not love, divine love, too often a hoax? and woman, the bright oasis in the desert of life, (to make use of an *original* image) a tormenting mystifier? Pleasure is a mystification that leads us on from scrape to scrape, and vanishes from our sight at the moment when it seems just within our grasp. Cards and dice mystify us out of our money, wine does the same by our senses, and the tax-gatherer does both. Poetry is professedly a mystification, and friendship scarce a degree better. In short, whichever way we turn, all is one general mystification; and " nothing is but what is not." The shortest way, then, is to give in to the dupery with the best grace you can. " *Carpe diem*," eat, drink, read the New Monthly Magazine, and be merry. In all circumstances, whether of difficulty or of pleasure, take the thing for what it is worth; remembering that life does not come, like Christmas, " once a year," but only " once in a way;"—and if the joke be a bad one, crying will not mend it. So, with this piece of comfort, which is, after all, as mere a mystification as the rest, for this time I have done; and in plain sincerity bid the reader heartily farewell!                        C. M.

---

LONDON LYRICS.

*Sir Dunder O'Kelly.*

———— Pete regna per undas.                        Virg.

Old Mother O'Kelly the scold,
   Who lived in a county of blunder,
Called great Tipperary, I'm told,
   Thus spoke to her little boy Dunder—
" I've only got you and a cow,
   And, since I can't keep all the three,
I'd better keep her, you'll allow,
   Because the kind creature keeps me."

So Dunder O'Kelly set sail
  From Ireland to better himself,
And climb'd up the Holyhead mail
  To ease Johnny Bull of his pelf.
To follow of glory the path
  And put British beef in his belly,
At Margate, at Brighton, at Bath,
  He sported Sir Dunder O'Kelly.

Sir Dunder in dancing was skill'd,
  And look'd very neat in his clothes,
But indeed all his beauty was kill'd
  By a terrible wen on his nose.
This double appendage, alas!
  He thought neither pretty nor proper,
Nature gave him one visage of brass,
  And Bacchus two noses of copper.

He dived into Bath for a bride,
  The ladies all check'd his advances,
And vow'd they could never abide
  Loose manners, and straiten'd finances.
One lady alone met his flame,
  With a hop, and a jig, and a nod,
I ask'd a blind fidler her name,
  And he answer'd me—" *Moll in the Wad.*"

His looking-glass set the poor knight
  Oft times in his bed-chamber raving,
His ugliness shewing at night,
  And eke in the morning when shaving.
He flung himself down on the floor,—
  Was ever unfortunate elf
So terribly haunted before
  By a ghost in the shape of himself?

Resolved Charon's eddy to pass,
  His pistol he primed, but—oh blunder!
He thought, if he shot at the glass,
  'Twould blow out the brains of Sir Dunder.
So bang went the slugs at his head,
  At once from this life to dissever;
He shot all the quicksilver dead,
  But himself was as lively as ever.

Amazed at the hubbub was he,
  And began, in the midst of the clatter,
All over to *felo de se*,
  But found there was nothing the matter.
So, glad Charon's eddy to shun,
  His sentiments thus he discloses—
" Since two heads are better than one,
  Perhaps 'tis the same with two noses."

To his own Tipperary poor Dun
  From scenes of disturbance and bother,
Trudged back, like the Prodigal Son,
  And fell on the neck of his mother.
At home he now follows the plough,
  And, whilst in his rustical courses
He walks at their tails, you 'll allow
  He never can frighten his horses.

## ON MUSIC.

*No. 5.—With reference to the principles of the Beautiful in that Art.*

THE principles of the Beautiful in Music, so far as they apply to rhythm and *Melody*, have hitherto formed the exclusive object of our investigation. We now propose to direct our attention to Musical *Harmony*, and to ascertain how far that branch of the art is referable to the like principles, in what those principles consist, and how they are brought into action.

Harmony is the simultaneous exhibition of musical sounds, differing in pitch, but bearing a certain relation to each other. When such sounds are heard at the same time that a melody is proceeding, the melody is said to be accompanied by harmony.

The question whether harmony, in this sense, was known to the ancient Greeks, has long been a subject of the most animated discussions; and although these seem to have at length nearly subsided, persons are occasionally met with who, seduced by a few obscure passages in two or three Greek and Roman authors, maintain boldly that the ancients knew and practised harmony. But the arguments which may be brought forward against such an assertion are numerous and unanswerable. The reader, who wishes to form his own judgment, may consult Dr. Burney or Dr. Forkel's Histories of Music, in which, and above all in the latter, the question is fairly and amply discussed, and, we conceive, fully set at rest.

The proofs which Dr. Forkel has accumulated leave no doubt of the utter ignorance of the Greeks as to harmony. And if they were supposed to have been acquainted with it, it certainly is not to them that we are indebted for even a hint on the subject of that branch of the science. We owe them much in melody, but nothing on the score of harmony; the discovery of which, by Western Europe—by England, in all probability—can progressively be traced, from documentary evidence, up to its rude origin in the 10th century.

The word " discovery," after all, is perhaps too high-sounding a term to be applied to the slight and rude traces of the beginnings of a practice, which, during the progress of many centuries, expanded itself, gradually and slowly, into an extended science, resting upon fixed rules, and the successive developement of which affords matter of interest, even in a philosophical point of view. In this respect, and in many others, as we shall hereafter have occasion to remark, harmony may be compared to the art of colouring, which emerged from the uncouth attempts of adorning a simple outline with a daub of *one* pigment, rudely and whimsically applied. Between such a *monochrome* and the Venus of Titian, the distance is as immense, as between the "Descant" of Franco and the harmony in the finale of " Il Don Giovanni." Innumerable and arduous were the intermediate steps which led both the arts to the summit of their perfection. But there was this difference in favour of colouring—and the distinction holds good between painting and music altogether—that in the long career towards that perfection, man had the prototype of imitation, Nature, constantly before him; whereas the laws of harmony, although certainly founded in Nature, lay deeply hidden, and required long and strenuous efforts of the human intellect, to be explored and reduced into a system. Indeed so laborious was the search, so uncertain and irregular its march, that harmony existed as a science, and was subjected to rule, before the fundamental and simple principle upon which it rests was discovered; a principle which shed light over the whole doctrine, and totally changed its aspect.

It would be foreign to our purpose to give a regular historical sketch, however concise, of the origin and progress of the science of harmony. We shall, therefore, content ourselves with observing, that, if the simultaneous exhibition of a melody in a lower and upper octave deserved the name of singing in parts, it not only existed with the Greeks in their antiphony, but must necessarily have prevailed with any nation that sang at all. Whenever a man and woman, or an adult and boy, intend singing in unison, their pitch will be found to be an octave asunder. In this there is no harmony, nor is it likely that such a circumstance would ever have led to it. Its first dawn is to be traced in the organ; an instrument which existed in a rude state, and rather as a rarity, among the Greeks and Romans at the beginning of the Christian era, was improved at Constantinople under the Greek Emperors, from thence found its way into Italy as early as the seventh or eighth century, and can be traced in a more perfect state in various cities of Western Europe in the time of Charlemagne. At that early period, already, the discovery had been made that the sound of the lower notes is rendered deeper, fuller, and stronger, by uniting with them their fifths and octaves. This triple sound, particularly the fifth, is distinctly heard in all bells of a deep note. Hence the organs in the ninth century were constructed upon that principle, which is still in force, with improvements, at the present day; and the simple sound *g*, for instance, was produced by the simultaneous intonation of three distinct pipes *g*, *d*, *g*, by means of *one* key*, and so the others. This contrivance upon the instrument was soon imitated by the voice, and it is asserted that St. Dunstan, the Archbishop of Canterbury, who died towards the end of the tenth century, introduced such a mode of singing in parts. At all events, the practice was common in the eleventh and twelfth centuries, when a strain like the following:—

at which the modern ear and eye revolts, was deemed orthodox and *beautiful*. This was called " organizing," *organizare*.

The bag-pipe and hurdy-gurdy, both instruments of very ancient origin, present similar indications of rude harmony. In the latter, one string, tuned in the tonic note, constantly covibrates with the melody; and in the bag-pipe, the tonic note *and its fifth* keep going in like manner while the melody is proceeding.

Thirds were subsequently introduced; and another mode of singing, called *discantare*, consisted in singing in unison, except at the conclusion of a period, or in some intermediate places, where the second singer fell in with a few thirds, according to certain rules; and much

* By "key," we here, of course, mean the French *touche*. It is to be regretted our Musical terminology does not furnish a less ambiguous word.

at the same time, or a little later, it was ventured to throw in now and then a dissonance.

· In the period between the twelfth and fourteenth centuries, the laws for the progression of chords were investigated and brought under some system, and the artifices of double counterpoint and the fugue were invented. These discoveries, and the whole science of harmony, were so much perfected in the fourteenth and fifteenth centuries, that composers made pieces of four and even more parts. The sixteenth and seventeenth centuries are conspicuous for the numerous compositions of a multiplied number of parts and of great ingenuity and artifice. Fugues with two and even three subjects were carried to great perfection; and Ludovico Viadana invented the rules of thorough-bass and the figuring of chords. Hitherto, however, artifice and scientific contrivances were more studied than melody. The head laboured more than the heart. It was only in the eighteenth century, that the paramount importance of melody was fully felt, that melody was zealously cultivated and brought into intimate union with harmony, and that the latter received new charms by variety of treatment and diversified accompaniment. Into this epoch likewise—just one hundred years ago—falls the important discovery of the musical system of Rameau, which, deducing the doctrine of chords from one simple and general principle, threw, as has already been stated, a great and unexpected light over the theory of harmony.

Great as was the advantage which musical science derived from Rameau's discovery, the benefit would have been incalculably increased, and the study of harmony infinitely simplified and facilitated, if, instead of retaining Viadana's awkward, complex, and perplexing doctrine of thorough-bass, and amalgamating it with his own simple and lucid system of harmony, Rameau had gone one step farther, and devised a new system and notation of chords founded upon his own theory of harmony and fundamental bass. Various attempts have since been made to supply this desideratum, but they have failed of success, and the study of harmony, up to the present day, remains clogged *and retarded* by the obscure, ambiguous, and inadequate figuring of Viadana's uncouth and unsystematic doctrine of thorough-bass. Although this doctrine, in consequence of the great improvements in instrumental accompaniment, is hastening towards a natural dissolution, and the great composers of modern times would probably dispense with any other as readily as with Viadana's, a more philosophic system of chords might still be of great service in simplifying and facilitating the study of harmony. The elements of such a system, free from all figures, we have had in view for some time; but this is not the place for entering upon the subject.

On directing our thoughts to the subject of harmony, the following questions obtrude themselves :—

1st. Is it necessary, that a melody should be supported by other sounds heard at the same time?

2d. If not necessary, is it desirable, and upon what grounds?

The first question admits of no doubt, in our opinion. We should answer it by a direct negative. The Greeks, whose music was highly cultivated, sang in unison; the same is the case with most of our congregations, even when unsupported by the chords of the organist,

Melodies in unison are not unfrequently resorted to by the greatest modern composers, in chorusses and on other occasions, with admirable effect; and the most philharmonic ear is at times deeply affected by a simple air, without any accompaniment, when sung with feeling and *with correct* intonation. The number of singers capable of producing such an effect is very limited. The late Mrs. Jordan and Mr. Incledon often enraptured an audience in this way, and Miss Stephens, likewise, is sometimes very impressive in unaccompanied songs. But there are other singers—and singers of celebrity—(we need not name them) who are by no means successful in such solos. Want of strong feeling is of course one of the causes, and false intonation another. Few singers are quite true in this respect, and what is more, when the incorrectness is slight, few auditors are sensible of it. But although they do not perceive it, it is this minute deviation from the true pitch, which, without their knowing it, diminishes the gratification of the ear. Singers of this description derive great assistance from accompaniment, which tends to set right their intonation, or at all events cloaks the imperfection.

The question whether harmony be a desirable resource of music is one of greater moment, as it has excited doubts with men of cultivated intellect, and even with musical characters of some note, Rousseau among the rest. On the other hand, some have maintained that harmony is as desirable an aid to melody, as colouring is to a drawing in outline. Without going to the full length of the latter assertion, we cannot deny that the comparison is applicable in many respects; and were it not that we feared to exceed our limits, we could wish to draw the parallel in its various bearings. As it is, we consign the task to the reader's hands.

Harmony, in our opinion, constitutes a desirable and very important *accessary* to melody; but we are far from considering it as a principal, and melody only secondary, although it was generally held in that estimation up to the close of the seventeenth century, and there are persons at this time who give it precedence. The advantages derived from harmony are indisputable: it tends to fix definitively the musical sense of a melody, and presents an inexhaustible means of imparting variety, and additional force of expression. We may, without hesitation, assert, that harmony has been the principal means of raising music to a rank among the fine arts.

Whoever should doubt this, let him for a moment imagine an opera, such as " Il Don Giovanni," set to the best possible, *but merely melodic* music. No orchestra, except perhaps a few instruments, to follow the songs in constant unison, or to intervene episodically; no duetts, unless by two persons singing precisely the same tune; no terzetts, no finale, except with the same restriction. Who could endure long such a *monotonous* performance? But we feel aware that we are addressing readers fully convinced, and therefore proceed to the actual and direct effects of harmony.

In order to give an instance of the office of harmony in fixing the musical import of a melody, let us take the following simple phrase,

and see what a different sense and expression it derives from a mere difference of harmony;

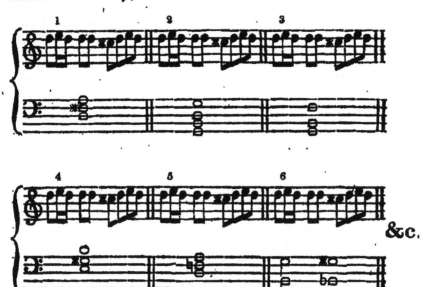

&c.

The above are but a few variations in the expression of the same melody to be obtained from a difference of harmony; we might add many more, might further increase the number by inverting the chords, and finally render the variations infinite by breaking the chords into diversified accompaniment.

What an engine of powerful and varied expression is the aggregate labour of a whole orchestra! How admirably is the character of every instrument made to contribute to the general effect! Koch justly refers to the finale of the first act of " Il Don Giovanni," as a convincing proof of the power and effect of harmony. Another curious instance of the powers of harmony might be quoted from the same opera. It is the warning voice of the statue addressed to the libertine. As the words of the spectre are all set to the self-same note for several successive bars, there is of course no melody whatever; harmony does all, and how awfully mysterious, how heart-thrilling, are those sepulchral sounds!

The above musical phrase of the same melody with varied harmony, clearly shows how readily and positively harmony establishes the import of a melody, otherwise frequently equivocal. In the first example, the chord in the bass at once proclaims the melody to be in D major. In the second, the same melody is, by similar means, assigned to the key of G major. The chord of G 7, in the third example, betrays the tonic C. In No. 4 the chord of E 7 conducts to A major; in No. 5 it is D minor, and the extreme sixth upon B flat in No. 6 leads to A major.

It is on these grounds that harmony presents the most effective means for modulating from one tonic to another, which melody alone

-accomplishes in a much more dubious and inefficient manner. To resort once more to our comparison with the sister art, it is in a manner somewhat analogous that mere outline proves inadequate in expressing foreshortening or perspective, without the aid of colouring, the proper employment of which removes all ambiguity attendant on mere linear indication.

Hitherto we have considered the effect and advantages of harmony, when applied in its most simple form—that of mere plain chords. In this manner it was almost exclusively employed for a length of time, and nearly until the beginning of the last century. For such a confined use of harmony it was sufficient to indicate what chord the composer intended for the support of his melody; and for such a purpose Viadana's Notation of Thorough bass, still in use, (however awkward and complex,) was adequate enough. To resort again to our comparison with colouring,—harmony was then something like painting in its early stages, or like some of the paintings of the Chinese. When the outline was drawn, the face received one coating of flesh-colour all over.; if the garment was to be red, a brush dipped in cinnabar accomplished the intention; the foliage of a tree was dispatched by an even coating of some green pigment; and for a rock, a goodly patch of brown ochre was deemed sufficient. There was no light or shade, no variation of tints. Such was harmony in its more primitive forms. But in process of time great changes were effected in the mode of harmonizing melodies; and it is only from the beginning of the last century that these changes assume a decisive character, and present themselves as additional and powerful means of the Beautiful in the Art. We certainly owe them to the previous study and cultivation of the canon and fugue. Pieces constructed with such artful contrivance, that several parts could, in succession, take up the same subject, and proceed in harmony with parts which had previously begun with that subject, could not do otherwise than advance greatly the science of accompaniment, and lead to the state of perfection in which we find it at this time. The fugue may be considered as the scaffolding employed in the edifice of this branch of the art, which, on the completion of the structure, has been laid aside; and, although almost entirely dispensed with at this day, its study ought, on the same grounds, to be made to form an essential part of the tuition of an incipient composer.

It would greatly exceed the limits and object of our paper, if we were to give a sketch of the gradual improvements in the science of accompaniment, or attempt a systematic enumeration of the many means from which modern accompaniment derives its charms. A cursory glance at some of these is all we can permit ourselves to take.

One of the first steps in the advancement of accompaniment was probably that of breaking the chords into their elements, *i. e.* the exhibiting the sounds of accompaniment in succession, instead of striking them at once,—

When the voice has to sustain a long note, the former method is eligible, for obvious reasons; whereas, when the voice is more active, the accompaniment should be more tranquil.

The modes of breaking chords are very numerous, and thus a pleasing and great variety in the accompaniment is produced. But this variety is farther augmented by distributing the elements of the chord among different instruments, and diversifying the figure under which the instruments, especially the high-toned, such as the violins, flutes, hautboys, &c. are to exhibit their portion of these elements. The Italian composers are inexhaustible in their variety of these kinds of resources, of which the works of Paesiello, Cimarosa, and Rossini, offer endless instances.

The employment of inverted instead of fundamental chords, or a mere change of position in either, presents, on many occasions, farther important advantages to the composer. In the first place, it is productive of great variety; moreover, as any inversion carries less repose to the ear than its fundamental, the sense of the melody may, by this means, be rendered more suspended, or less decisive—a circumstance which greatly influences the doctrine of cadences; and lastly, by a judicious employment of inverted chords, the accompaniment is rendered more soft, flowing, and connected.

Another means of producing the last-mentioned effect is, the employment of what is commonly called a "Pedal Bass," which consists in a continuation, on the part of the bass, of the tonic note of the air along with other chords properly belonging to the melody, instead of using those chords in their direct and natural form. Thus, instead of

we should write, per pedal bass,

Here, the continual sounding of the C in the bass throws an uncommon charm of softness over the melody, which it blends with, and melts as it were into the harmony. The Italians, again, who probably first resorted to this practice, use it with great success for the accompaniment of pastoral and other tender *motivos*; and for those, in fact, it is only eligible. These mellow combinations would little suit marches, airs of forcible expression, strong chorusses, or dance-tunes; and, like every thing else in Music, they must not, by frequent use, be rendered too common, even in cases where they might be deemed applicable.

In vocal pieces, we sometimes observe considerable portions in which the singer acts as it were a subordinate part, the principal melody is consigned to the orchestra, and the voice performs a secondary sort of melody, or sometimes no absolute melody, but rather a part of what might properly be deemed mere accompaniment; nay, sometimes but a continued repetition of the same sound, while the orchestra fills up the musical picture. The effect of all this, when in its proper place, is excellent. Of this kind are the airs of the military hero of the piece, who sings a half sort of melody, while the orchestra plays a regular march, or the chorus performs a similar independent duty. This practice, invented by Paesiello, met with such decided approbation, that airs of this description are to be found in most Italian operas. A fine duett in Rossini's " Mosè nell' Egitto" is of that class, also a song of Douglas in " La Donna del Lago." An instance where the orchestra has the principal, and the singer a secondary melody, occurs in the picture song of Braham's " Devil's Bridge;" and examples where the voice repeats for some time the same note, while the orchestra goes its train, are to be found in most of the Italian comic songs. The vocal accompaniments of chorusses by means of subdued *staccato*-notes, so interesting and effective, may also be mentioned under this head.

Episodic purely instrumental phrases betwixt vocal portions, afford another great resource to the composer, and a relief to the singer. As they occur more or less extensively in almost every song of any pretension, we forbear quotation. In the *recitativo*, these instrumental intercalations are of admirable effect, and almost indispensable. It is here that the composer displays the fertility and luxuriance of his imagination by a constant succession of short instrumental phrases, novel in conception, suitable to the expression of the text, and of the most unfettered freedom of thought. A magnificent specimen of this kind presents itself in Donna Anna's sublime *recitativo*, " Ma qual mai s'offre spettacolo funesto," in Il Don Giovanni. Without referring to any other example, the above *recitativo* affords the strongest possible instance of the power of accompaniment in assisting and heightening the impression which the text and its melody are intended to excite. Without its masterly instrumental support, that *recitativo* would lose its greatest charm, would almost appear insipid. , This power is still more evident in a species of composition introduced upon the German stage, about forty or fifty years ago, under the appellation of *Melodrama*, but which is widely different from the dramatic trash under the same name that has of late taken possession of the English boards. The German melodrama consisted of a scenic representation, consigned to few performers, simple in its plot and action, and highly poetical as to diction. The whole of the text was spoken, not sung, but frequently interrupted by instrumental periods of longer or shorter duration analogous with the import of the text. Benda, the German composer, excelled in these; his " Ariadne in Naxos" and " Medea," scarcely known in England, are masterpieces of composition, replete with the finest thoughts and deepest feeling.

In the present state of the science, indeed, the effect of every melody depends, in a great degree, upon its accompaniment. The latter not only heightens the interest of the former, by fixing more strongly its meaning, and imparting to it the charms of variety, but it operates in a direct manner in aiding and strengthening the melodic expression. The mental agitation produced by fear or despair, the ebullitions of anger, the peaceful sensations of a serene innocent mind, the impassioned accents of love, in short, almost every condition of the human frame, may, independently of melodic means, receive an adequate and forcible colouring from mere accompaniment. Of all this it would, we are sure, be a waste of time to adduce examples. Almost every classic vocal composition may serve as a voucher.

Such, then, are the effects, the advantages, of harmony and accompaniment. Without harmony, Music, as has already been said, would never, probably, have attained the high state of cultivation, the elevated rank among the fine arts, of which she justly boasts at the present day, but which she was far from enjoying even under the fostering care of the tasteful and ingenious Greeks. Notwithstanding the marvellous accounts *they* have handed us of the excellence of their Music, we should not, were the experiment possible, hesitate to risk a comparison between the best Greek *melodic* concert, and the *melharmonic* strains and combinations of a modern performance. The former, we are convinced from their own accounts, must have been simple, monotonous, and meagre in effect, while the combined exertions of a modern band are calculated to excite admiration, even in a philosophical point of view. What a grand, what a wonderful spectacle is the orchestra at the King's Theatre in the finale of "Il Don Giovanni!" In a narrow space we behold some fifty skilful players upon numerous different instruments, collected from every part of Europe. In Greece, these fifty would have all played the same melody; here, more than a dozen parts or melodies are distributed among them, to be played at once, all essentially distinct and different, yet blending into one beautiful whole. Were it not from custom, we should never cease wondering by what spell such a number of individuals can be brought to observe the strictest time: every one knows precisely when to fall in, when to be silent: at one time, all join in one combined effort; at another, one instrument takes the lead, and rivets our attention by the most delicate and fascinating solo: now a singer interposes the soft and heavenly sounds of the human voice, and again a full chorus, with its powerful strains, sets the whole of our frame in vibration. This, this is the work of Harmony—this the triumph of modern Art!

G. L. E.

### AN ATTIC STORY.

In a close garret, six feet square
And full as high, there stood a pair,
'Midst must and dust and fumes mephitic—
A Poet one, and t'other a Critic.
Strange that extremes so wide as these—
The World-of-Wit's antipodes—
Should thus be found to join together;
Birds both—but of what different feather!—

*This* dull and dark, a thing of prey;
*That* brilliant, fluttering, and gay.
When *such* extremes *se touchent*, 'tis worse
For wonder than Kehama's curse.
When Angels come to sport with woman,
We look for something more than common—
Prosing in rhyme, or rhyming history,
Cain, or some other sort of mystery, }
Work for Love's Court, or Court Consistory. }
But when an author and reviewer
Are snugly garreted, be sure
That (whether by flattery or bribe,
The fancied badges of each tribe,)
There's something working in the wind—
A *puff* before, or *blast* behind,
To curl the wave of expectation,
Tickle the gulls, and gull the nation.
Their general junctions such I trow,
But different far their purpose now.
No embryo of the poet's brain
Now wants the critic's venal strain—
No bantling illegitimate,
Begot by Sin on mother Wit,
With bastard claims would seek to wage
War 'gainst dull Sense's heritage—
No satire comes, to wrest the crown
From soberer dunces about town—
No unfledged madrigal is panting
Within its nest, false plumage wanting
To urge it on its primal flight—
No puling Pastoral seeks the light—
No dreary Drama, from the throes
Of a forced birth, whines forth its woes—
No spurious Comedy appears,
With grins for smiles—for satire jeers—
The Poet seeks, in short, to find, }
From the man-midwife of the mind, }
Deliverance of another kind. }

'Twas sometime gone this Poet's Muse
Loosely attired—perhaps *en Blouse*—
Held in fair Italy's warm clime
Flirtation with the Son of Rhyme.
Whether it was the warmth of sky
That lit the Heaven-born damsel's eye,
Or whether 'twas the Poet's tongue
That lured the maid, I leave unsung;
And simply say this amorous bout
"Of linked sweetness long drawn out,"
Going all fair lengths, short of marriage,
Ended, *proh pudor!* in miscarriage.
To cut a naughty story short,
The wanton Muse in this resort
(I mean the garret) hid her shame, }
And left full many a child of Fame— }
The Poet's *title*, not his name— }
(For she'd a litter quite, the strumpet!)
But robb'd them of their father's trumpet.
The young abortions, thus forsaken,
Might for a common man's be taken;

For ev'n Fame's offspring, if unfather'd,
Like chaff is by the blind world gather'd,
Which proves, in spite of gibing mimics,
The moral want of patronymics,
And plainly shows that merit needs
Hereditary title-deeds.

I take 't for fact, each reader knows
The *forms* of youngsters such as those.
'Tis certain quite as Irish May rents,
(When Bards and Muses are the parents)
That children come in other shapes
Than kings', or peers' or fashion's apes ;
And those whose fate I now rehearse
Were little limbless things in verse,
Without a single *foot* to walk on ;
Like old maids without tales to talk on,
Or prudes without some flirt to randle,
Or tea-table undeck'd with scandal,
Or roast pig without ears for garnish,
Or demirep without her varnish.

High up were piled, unstitch'd, unbound,
Unedited, unnamed, unown'd,
Huge printed packages—whole pages
Destined, if born, to live for ages,
But strangled ere they drew their breath—
A species of Hibernian death.
Full many a quire was there bespread
Of fiery thoughts loose scattered,
With many a wild and wicked joke
Uncrack'd, and many a pun unspoke,
And beauties crush'd, and smother'd sweets,
Like Desdemona, *in their sheets.*
The bard, a slave of the whole sex,
Rush'd merciless upon the wrecks,
Like waves on shatter'd masts and decks.
One thought alone his brain imbues,
The *reputation* of his Muse ;
For though her character 's a gay one,
Her fame is more than European,
And the whole world (except her lover)
Thought all her young *penchants* were over.
'Tis therefore that in her behoof
He now would blot each damning *proof,*
And stand in dire resolve—a pattern
For sculptors of a second Saturn.

The only puzzle that appear'd,
Was how to get the garret clear'd.
His progeny in deathlike slumbers
Lay—how unlike those breathing *numbers,*
Their full-grown sisters and their brothers,
The sire the same, but different mothers !
Could he but hope they 'd slumber here
Eternally, he 'd nought to fear ;
When he thought upon the throng
grave rooters-out of song,
temperate resurrection-men
ture, who wield the pen,

Just as a sexton plies the spade,
Who, in the practice of their trade,
Grub up the dark sepulchre's gloom,
Search *subjects* in oblivion's tomb,
And with their glutton maws becramm'd,
Feed on all authors—dead or damn'd—
Our poet swore, and justly too,
He'd snatch his babes from the foul crew;
Therefore the critic's counsel craved
How his young implings might be *saved.*
Quick as the quere was pronounced
The critic on the quarry pounced,
And cried, with a most natural tone,
" *Cut them in pieces*—one by one !"

The poet, shock'd, an instant stood
To mark his friend's imp'rative mood.
He, in accordance with the fire
Of Genius, long'd to have a pyre
Whereon the bodies might be burn'd;
But this the critic overturn'd,
Lest the young offspring of old Fame
Might spring from the consuming flame,
And each a chattering phœnix rise
Up through the chimney to the skies.
To work they went, then, nail and tooth
(Pardon th' inversion), nothing loath.
As for the critic, 'twas his trade
To mar the jokes another made,
And cut (like all his tribe, 'tis said)
The writings he had never read:
*He* plunged *in medias res*—the story
Hack'd, slash'd, and scatter'd, *con amore;*
Quotations flung abroad by chance;
Spoil'd English epigrams in France;
Made puns upon each rumpled fair sheet,
Swore he was brother to Doll Tearsheet;
And glow'd 'midst the *disjecta membra,*
Although the day was quite Novembry.
Aud then the unnatural father, too,
Upon his mangled offspring flew;
And seem'd resolved *d'avance* to try
How he might rob posterity.

Here ends the tale.   The moral is,
That Fame, which wise ones call a quiz,
But which most authors think a treasure,
*One* can forego with honest pleasure,
When he must pay for 't at the price
Of one right feeling's sacrifice.
And also, that though Bards there be
All greatly penitent as he,
Who can, in moments of compunction,
Keep from their souls Fame's flattering unction,—
CRITICS ne'er flinch from their foul function !

## THE ISLAND.*

THE eccentric spirit to whom we are indebted for a new poem under the above title, has returned, in this instance, to that style, or rather that class of work which he seemed to have finally abandoned for something, certainly less generally interesting and attractive, however elevated in rank and ambitious in pretension. It is to his narrative poems—his Giaours, his Corsairs, his Laras, &c. that Lord Byron owes his *popularity* at least, if not his reputation. If it were not for these, and the intense interest that they had excited towards any thing he might offer to the world, his Manfreds, his Cains, and even the noblest of all his productions, his " Heaven and Earth," might have remained *mysteries*, in more senses than one. The latter were a kind of " *Caviare*," that nothing could have rendered palatable " to the multitude," unless their appetite had been previously excited in a degree that prevented them from judging exactly what it was of which they were partaking If even the "Heaven and Earth" had appeared anonymously, and had not included any internal evidence of the source from whence it came, it would have fallen still-born from the press. As it was, people read it without relishing it, praised it without appreciating it, and laid it by without ever intending or desiring to take it up again. Whereas, of all the numerous fragments which this extraordinary writer has put forth, if there is one which indicates the true nature of the poetical structure he is capable of raising, and (we are determined to hope and expect) he some day or other *will* raise, to the glory of his art and the immortal honour of his name—it is this.

The Island, as we have hinted above, is a narrative poem, like those by which the author first became celebrated ; with this difference, however, against it—that it is " founded on facts." We say " against it," for this reason,—that facts are not only such " stubborn," but such stirring things in their individual selves, that any suspected, much more any avowed alteration or embellishment of them, never fails to weaken the effect of a narration in which *they* are to form a distinguishing feature. Abstract truth will very well bear to be " in fairy fiction dress'd ;" that which merely *may have been*, may be described to have been in any manner that the fancy or the feelings of the narrator may suggest, consistently with the object in view. But that which *has been* cannot be safely treated in this way, if the person who treats of it places any dependence on the fact of its having actually happened. To tell us, in the plain and intelligible prose of an eye-witness, that certain events took place thus and thus ; and then to tell us, over again, the same story in substance, but after a different fashion, and one that is intended to be *more poetical ;*—this is something worse than a work of supererogation. If Lord Byron had a mind to tell a story of the mutiny of a ship's company and its consequences—well and good ; the subject would immediately strike us as being well adapted to his powers, and susceptible of the most poetical treatment. But why hamper himself with an actual narration of a mutiny, only to alter or abandon it, just as he might think fit at the moment ;—re-

* The Island ; or, Christian and his Companions. A Poem, by the Right Honourable Lord Byron.

taining the actual names, places, &c. but mixing them up with other names and places, and adapting them to other and fancied events? This is the only general fault we have to find with the interesting work before us. For the rest, it includes several admirable descriptive passages, some fine touches of character and passion, and a few clear, distinct, and highly interesting pictures. It consists of four cantos, the first of which is by many degrees the most inferior: indeed it is inferior to any other piece of writing of the same length that we remember of this author. It merely gives a slight sketch of the completion of the mutiny on board Captain Bligh's ship, and of the captain and part of the crew being set adrift; and then accompanies the mutineers (Christian and his companions) in their adventures in one of the Otaheitan Islands. The second canto introduces us to the two persons who make the principal figures in the poem.—Torquil, a young mountaineer, who formed one of the mutinous crew, and Neuha, an island girl, who attaches herself to him as a lover. The descriptions of each of these are among the best parts of the poem.

> " There sat the gentle savage of the wild,
> In growth a woman, but in years a child,
> As childhood dates within our colder clime,
> Where nought is ripen'd rapidly save crime;
> The infant of an infant world, as pure
> From nature—lovely, warm, and premature;
> Dusky like night, but night with all her stars;
> Or cavern sparkling with its native spars;
> With eyes that were a language and a spell;
> A form like Aphrodite's in her shell,
> With all her loves around her on the deep;
> Voluptuous as the first approach of sleep;
> Yet full of life—for through her tropic cheek
> The blush would make its way, and all but speak;
> The sun-born blood suffused her neck, and threw
> O'er her clear nut-brown skin a lucid hue,
> Like coral reddening through the darken'd wave,
> Which draws the diver to the crimson cave.
> Such was the daughter of the Southern Seas."

The description of the English, or rather Scotch lover, if not so distinct and picturesque, is equally spirited.

> " And who is he?—the blue-eyed northern child
> Of isles more known to man, but scarce less wild;
> The fair-hair'd offspring of the Hebrides,
> Where roars the Pentland, with its whirling seas;
> Rock'd in his cradle by the roaring wind,
> The tempest-born in body and in mind,
> His young eyes opening on the ocean-foam,
> Had from that moment deem'd the deep his home;
> The giant comrade of his pensive moods;
> The sharer of his craggy solitudes;
> The only Mentor of his youth,—where'er
> His bark was borne, the sport of wave and air;—
> A careless thing, who placed his choice in chance;
> Nursed by the legends of his land's romance;
> Eager to hope, but not less firm to bear;
> Acquainted with all feelings, save despair.
> Placed in the Arab's clime, he would have been
> As bold a rover as the sands have seen,

> And braved their thirst with as enduring lip
> As Ishmael, wafted in his desert-ship;
> Fix'd upon Chili's shore, a proud cacique;
> On Hellas' mountains, a rebellious Greek;
> Born in a tent, perhaps a Tamerlane;
> Bred to a throne, perhaps unfit to reign.
> *For the same soul that rends its path to sway,*
> *If rear'd to such, can find no further prey*
> *Beyond itself, and must retrace its way,*
> *Plunging for pleasure into pain;* the same
> Spirit which made a Nero, Rome's worst shame,
> A humbler state and discipline of heart
> Had form'd his glorious namesake's counterpart:*
> But grant his vices—grant them all his own—
> How small their theatre without a throne!"

The remainder of this canto is chiefly occupied with sketches of the island scenery, and reflections arising out of the situations of the "half-savage and the whole." The following grand piece of invective is finely characteristic of the noble writer's style, both of thought, feeling, and expression.

> " Had Cæsar known but Cleopatra's kiss,
> Rome had been free—the world had not been his.
> And what have Cæsar's deeds and Cæsar's fame
> Done for the earth? We feel them in our shame:
> The gory sanction of *his* glory stains
> The rust which tyrants cherish in our chains.
> Though Glory, Nature, Reason, Freedom, bid
> Roused millions do what single Brutus did,—
> Sweep these mere mock-birds of the despot's song
> From the tall bough where they have perch'd so long,—
> Still are we hawk'd at by such mousing owls,
> And take for falcons those ignoble fowls,
> When but a word of freedom would dispel
> These bugbears—as their terrors show too well."

We must counteract the effect of the above not very soothing passage, by the delightful one which follows it, and which is no less characteristic of the author's other style.

> " Rapt in the fond forgetfulness of life,
> Neuha, the South-sea girl, was all a wife;
> With no distracting world to call her off
> From love; with no society to scoff
> At the new transient flame; no babbling crowd
> Of coxcombry, in admiration loud,
> Or with adulterous whisper to alloy
> Her duty, and her glory, and her joy;
> With faith and feelings naked as her form,
> She stood as stands the rainbow in the storm,
> Changing its hues with bright variety,
> But still expanding lovelier o'er the sky,
> Howe'er its arch may swell, its colours move,
> The cloud-compelling harbinger of Love."

Towards the end of the second canto we are introduced to another personage, whose appearance and character contrast somewhat strangely,

---

* The Consul Nero.

but yet very naturally, and with great spirit, with the two above
described. This is a thorough-bred Wapping jack tar, with a pipe and
an oath constantly in his mouth, who comes to announce that a strange
sail is in sight, and that Christian (whom we now hear of on the
island for the first time) has " piped all hands"—anticipating the
nature of its errand. The remainder of the poem is occupied in alluding to the general battle which takes place between the mutineers
and those who have come in pursuit of them, and in describing the
events which follow on the result of that battle; which events are
fatal to all the mutineers, with the exception of Torquil—who is saved
by his mistress plunging with him into the ocean, and taking him, by
a submarine entrance, into a rocky cave, which she has previously
prepared for his reception. Here they remain till the strange ship—
believing them to be drowned—leaves the island; and we are left to
suppose that they live happy for the time to come.

This is the whole substance of the story—if story that can be called,
which is, in fact, little more than a collection of sketches—pieces of
pure execution—scarcely at all bound together by any plot, and
scarcely needing it.

The description of the remnant who escape from the first general
skirmish, and take temporary shelter among the rocks and crags, is
excellent. We have space but for one or two short portions of it.
The following shews us the leader of the desperate band :

> " Stern, and aloof a little from the rest,
> Stood Christian, with his arms across his chest.
> The ruddy, reckless, dauntless hue once spread
> Along his cheek, was livid now as lead.
> His light brown locks so graceful in their flow,
> Now rose like startled vipers o'er his brow.
> Still as a statue, with his lips compress'd,
> To stifle ev'n the breath within his breast,
> Fast by the rock,—all menacing, but mute,—
> He stood ; and save a slight beat of his foot,
> Which deepened now and then the sandy dint
> Beneath his heel, his form seem'd turn'd to flint."

It will be observed, in perusing this part of the poem, that the
manner in which Ben Bunting, the jolly jack tar, is occasionally introduced, (always with his pipe in his mouth) not only gives a fine contrast to the grouping of the pictures (for this part is a series of pictures)
but it communicates an extraordinary reality and naturalness to the
effect.

The death of the last three desperadoes—particularly that of Christian—is finely given. So is the following preparatory passage to it,
which seems to place them before us in a kind of monumental gloom
and stillness, as if they were already changed into their own funeral
effigies.

> " They landed on a wild but narrow scene,
> Where few but Nature's footsteps yet had been ;
> Prepared their arms, and with that gloomy eye,
> Stern and sustained, of man's extremity,—
> When Hope is gone, nor Glory's self remains,
> To cheer resistance against death or chains,—
> They stood, the three, as the three hundred stood
> Who dyed Thermopylæ with holy blood.

But ah! how different! 'tis the cause makes all,
Degrades or hallows courage in its fall.
O'er *them* no fame, eternal and intense,
Blazed through the clouds of death, and beckon'd hence;
No grateful country, smiling through her tears,
Begun the praises of a thousand years;
No nations' eyes would on their tomb be bent,
No heroes envy them their monument;
However boldly their warm blood was spilt,
Their life was shame, their epitaph was guilt.
And this they knew and felt; at least the one,
The leader of the band he had undone;
Who, born perchance for better things, had set
His life upon a cast which lingered yet:
But now the die was to be thrown, and all
The chances were in favour of his fall.
And such a fall!—But still he faced the shock,
Obdurate as a portion of the rock
Whereon he stood, and fix'd his levell'd gun,
Dark as a sullen cloud before the sun."

Christian's death is drawn with a vigorous and spirited hand, but somewhat rude and careless withal:

" Christian died last—twice wounded; and once more
Mercy was offer'd when they saw his gore.
    *    *    *    *    *    *
A limb was broken, and he droop'd along
The crag, as doth a falcon reft of young.
The sound revived him, or appear'd to wake
Some passion which a weakly gesture spake.
He beckon'd to the foremost who drew nigh,
But, as they near'd, he rear'd his weapon high—
His last ball had been aim'd, but from his breast
He tore the topmost button of his vest—
Down the tube dash'd it—levell'd—fired—and smiled,
As his foe fell; then, like a serpent, coil'd
His wounded, weary form, to where the steep
Look'd desperate as himself along the deep;
Cast one glance back, and clench'd his hand, and shook
His last rage 'geinst the earth which he forsook;
Then plunged—"

The poem closes by the return of the lovers from their temporary sanctuary, and the triumphant reception of them by the kind and happy islanders; and the tale of blood and crime ends without leaving that painful impression on the reader which most of this author's serious narrative poems have hitherto done. The following is the concluding passage, which produces an effect similar to that of looking at some of the pictures in Captain Cook's voyages.

" Again their own shore rises on the view,
No more polluted with a hostile hue;
No sullen ship lay bristling o'er the foam,
A floating dungeon:—all was hope and home!
A thousand proas darted o'er the bay,
With sounding shells, and heralded their way;
The chiefs came down, around the people pour'd,
And welcomed Torquil as a son restored;

The women throng'd, embracing and embraced
By Neuha,—asking where they had been chaced,
And how escaped? The tale was told, and then
One acclamation rent the sky again.
And from that hour a new tradition gave
Their sanctuary the name of 'Neuha's Cave.'
An hundred fires, far flickering from the height,
Blazed o'er the general revel of the night,
The feast in honour of the guest, return'd
To peace and pleasure, perilously earn'd;
A night succeeded by such happy days
As only the yet infant world displays."

---

THE BOURSE AT PARIS.—ENGLAND AND FRANCE.—BUYING
A BONNET.

> *Plant.* Tut, tut, here is a mannerly forbearance;
> The truth appears so naked on my side,
> That any purblind eye may find it out.
> *Somer.* And on my side it is so well apparell'd,
> So clear, so shining, and so evident,
> That it will glimmer through a blind man's eye.    *Henry VIth.*

ENTERING lately the temporary enclosure that runs round the new
Exchange at Paris, I stood before the noble front on which the words
"Tribunal de Commerce" have lately been inscribed, deeply penetrated with the simple, I had almost said sublime, grandeur of the
building, musing on the past time when the Parthenon was not less
fresh and perfect, and throwing my thoughts forward into the future,
when the majestic and stupendous temple before me (for such, indeed,
it seems) should be ruinous and dilapidated as that which is now mouldering away upon the Athenian Acropolis, when a brown-visaged
keen-eyed Parisian, of that shabby genteel class which abounds in this
capital, having a ragged hat, long surtout, and the ribbon of the Legion
d'Honneur in his button-hole, walked up to me with an easy courtesy,
took off his superannuated hat, presented his snuff-box, and on the
strength of this unceremonious introduction exclaimed—"Eh bien!
Monsieur, vous conviendrez qu'il n'y a rien de si magnifique à Lon-
dres." Now, as I saw that this unexpected acquaintance meant to
compliment his own sagacity by his instant discovery that I was an
Englishman, and his nationality by vaunting the superiority of his
building, I retorted in the usual way, that is to say, by exhibiting the
same feeling in myself which I condemned in him; so I replied, with
something like a sneer—"O yes, it must be confessed that Paris has a
fine Exchange and no trade: we have nothing at London but the
wealth and the commerce." So far from being hurt at this division,
my colloquist received it as a compliment, made me a smiling bow,
and exclaimed complacently, "Oui, c'est ça!" and, as I really felt
somewhat ashamed of my speech, I determined to listen to him patiently in the future remarks with which he threatened to favour me.
"It is not altogether Corinthian, nor yet Ionic," continued he, looking
up at the capitals of the pillars, and then, with a conclusive nod of
his head, he pronounced—"in fact it is in the very best French style."
This reminded me of the worthy Friar who, being asked, after having

vaunted the architecture of his monastery, in what order it was built, replied—"In the order of St. Dominic:" but I seemed to assent to the position of my informant, who proceeded to declare that the ancient statuary and painting assembled in the Louvre in the time of the Emperor was the finest collection that the world had ever witnessed, and did more honour than all his victories to the name of that—— (here he looked round, and observing that no one was near, concluded) ——to the name of that truly great man.

"And yet," I observed, "though you retained all these masterpieces of art for so many years, not the smallest traces of their influence are perceptible in the modern French school either of sculpture or painting."

"That may very well be, for, though they were invaluable as specimens of what antiquity could do, you will certainly admit" (this is the invariable phrase of a Frenchman when he is making a monstrous assertion) "that we already possessed, among our own artists, modern works of an infinitely superior standard;" and then he twanged through his nose a long list of the illustrious obscure among his compatriots; recapitulated a catalogue of sprawling, theatrical, operatical figures, which, in his estimation, eclipsed the Venus, Apollo, and Laocoon; and triumphantly referred to David's pictures in the Luxembourg as the *ne plus ultra* of the art. O! said I to myself, if this man is to be taken as a sample of his nation, I see clearly enough why their spirit has never been imbued with one single emanation from the fountains of ancient light; enveloped in a cloud of national vanity. through which nothing can penetrate, they talk perpetually of the fine age of Louis the Fourteenth; and though their whole literature and art be but a succession of imitations from the models of that period, each balder and more vapid than the last, they imagine that they are advancing upon all the world, when in fact they are even receding from themselves. Instead of crossing and invigorating the race by an admission from any classical or foreign stock, they have been breeding *in and in*, as the farmers say, and the consequences are the same in the world of Art as in that of Nature,—exhaustion, deterioration, and decay.

Mistaking my silence for acquiescence, my loquacious friend continued, with a nod of still greater satisfaction—"In fact, you must admit that all the recent discoveries, whether useful or ornamental, all that contributes to the instruction, health, comfort, or civilization of mankind, has originated in France." This was somewhat too swingeing a mouthful to be gulped down. "We too," said I, "may claim some little merit of this sort in the last few years; and though I cannot, thus suddenly, recollect a tithe of the benefits we have conferred upon the world, I do remember that, during a war of unexampled extent and severity, we translated the Scriptures, at an immense expense, into almost all the languages of the earth, distributing annually many millions of copies (some thousands of which were bestowed upon France herself), as the most effectual means of promoting human happiness and civilization." Hereupon my auditor arched up his eye-brows until his forehead became thickly engraved with consecutive wrinkles, raised the corners of his nose in bitter scorn, gave a loud tap upon his snuff-box, and delivered himself of a most contemptuous "Bah!"

"Perhaps I should have previously mentioned," continued I, "that by the system of our countrymen Bell and Lancaster, for the explanation and adoption of which we dispersed emissaries throughout Europe, the blessings of education have been almost universally diffused; and we may flatter ourselves to have done more, by this single discovery, towards the amelioration of human destiny, than has been hitherto achieved by all the philanthropists that ever existed."

"Ah, oui, sans doute!—C'est l'enseignment mutuel; mais nous autres, nous avons çela aussi; vous en verrez des écoles partout."

"Very likely, but you borrowed them all from us. Then, without minutely adverting to our innumerable discoveries and improvements in mechanics, particularly in the steam-engine, by which the painful employment of human and animal muscles, as a means of power, promises to be almost superseded, and by whose superior economy the comforts and even luxuries of life are placed within the reach and enjoyment of the humblest classes, I would submit that the highest combinations of science were never blended with more practical and beneficial results than by Sir Humphrey Davy in the invention of the safety-lamp."

"A la bonne heure! Parbleu!" exclaimed my companion; "if we had had as many mines and as much bad air as you, we should have invented this long ago."

"Having noticed," said I, "one or two of the benefits we have conferred upon European society, let me not omit to mention that whatever may have been the motives for extending our empire in Asia, its result has brought sixty millions of natives under a mild and equitable system of government, that forms a striking contrast to the barbarous and ferocious dynasties of its predecessors, and is rapidly advancing the civilization of its subjects:—while in Africa we have, as far as our power extended, blessed, pacified, and humanized the whole country by the suppression of the slave-trade—a voluntary sacrifice which can only be duly appreciated by recollecting that we were the greatest Colonial power in the world. Nay, we even purchased or negotiated its abolition by other governments, though I have understood, Sir, that your countrymen have not yet entirely relinquished the traffic."

"The Emperor, on his return from Elba, pledged himself to its suppression, but as to these"——here my companion again looked suspiciously round, and observing a *marchand de coco* at a little distance, he shrugged up his shoulders, gave me a significant look, and took a pinch of snuff.

"It may be doubted," I resumed, "whether we have done more for the minds or bodies, for the intellectual or physical health of our contemporaries, for while we have been widely diffusing moral improvement, we have, by the introduction of vaccination, laid a basis for speedily extirpating the greatest foe to beauty and life with which humanity was ever afflicted. This discovery, too, with an indefatigable philanthropy, we gratuitously disseminated through the world, without distinction of friend or foe; and the striking diminution of mortality among children, wherever it has been practised, is the best proof of its importance."

"Pour moi, Monsieur, je vous avouerai franchement que je préfère l'inoculation. Que diable! qu'avons nous à faire avec les vaches?"

" These," continued I, without noticing his philosophical question, " are such of the benefits, bestowed upon mankind of late years as more immediately occur to me. I might mention our literature, which, by its unexampled fertility and excellence, supplies sources of gratification to all Europe, and to France in even a greater proportion than her native founts; but your country has doubtless many claims of the kind I have been enumerating, and as they have really escaped my notice, I shall feel sincerely obliged by your enabling me to recall them.".

" Parbleu! Monsieur," replied my confabulist, buttoning up his coat with an air of ruffled majesty, " Ce n'est pas la peine, car vous conviendrez," (here I expected a bouncer)—" you will admit that in the greatest of all arts, that of war, we have conquered all Europe."—" Even if this were quite accurate," said I, " so far from its affording any proof of the benefits you have conferred, I should rather adduce it as a striking evidence of the contrary; but unless we have been grievously deceived, you were somewhat discomfited in Russia."

" Ah! oui—c'est clair : mais c'etoit le froid, le climat; on ne fait pas la guerre aux élémens."——" And if my faith is to be given to public documents," I pursued, " you do not reckon among your victories many triumphs over the British arms. By sea you do not, probably, claim any, and I believe the result was not very dissimilar upon *terra firma*, from St. Jean d'Acre to Maida, and Egypt, and all through the peninsular war down to Waterloo."

" Eh, Dieu! que voulez-vous? perhaps we are not invincible; but whenever we have been beaten, it has been by superior numbers or treachery."——" It would be but fair to grant the same excuse to the adversaries of France," said I ; " in which case her triumphs would reduce themselves to numerical superiority, or more extensive seduction."

" Allez, Monsieur, je vous convaincrai en deux mots que la France ——mais, voyez-vous, il va tomber de l'eau—excusez—j'ai l'honneur de vous saluer." So saying, he raised his venerable hat perpendicularly from his head, replaced it, made me a bow, and shuffled away at a dog-trot. The rain in fact beginning to fall, I removed to the corner of the Passage Feydeau, beside the *marchand de coco* aforementioned, at whose back was suspended a tin cylinder, decorated so as to resemble a little tower, from the three divisions of which, respective tubes, brought round to his front, and furnished with syphons, enabled him to draw off into a polished cup, beer, lemonade, or liquorice-water, according to the taste, or rather the want of it, in his customers. This figure, who was in conversation with a shoeblack in a cocked hat and monstrous plaited pigtail, on the subject of the new bronze figure lately set up in the Place des Victoires, occasionally broke off to bawl out, " Qu'est-ce qui désire à boire—à boire—à boire?" and then earnestly resumed his discussion upon the work of art, which was shortly interrupted by the approach of a small party apparently not long imported from the banks of the Thames. It consisted of three persons; a lady who, besides the evidence of a fair and flushed face, presented a legitimate specimen of what the French term " *la tournure Hollandaise des Anglaises;*" her husband, dressed in a frock coat, and those two rare articles in Paris—a pair of clean yellow gloves and a smooth, well-brushed hat, seemingly very unhappy lest he should lose a spaniel that was following them; and a little girl of twelve or thirteen, who was devouring, with laudable diligence, a huge *brioche* which she had just bought. The second of these personages, addressing himself to the shoeblack and coco-merchant, exclaimed, " I say—quel est le cheming à Vivienne Street?" In answer to which they severally interjected " Comment?" and " Plait-il, Monsieur?" looking up to him with a vacant astonishment, when I came forward and informed him that he was then at the beginning of the Rue Vivienne. A loud whistle, and the cry of " Carlo! Carlo!" were my thanks: the party, after proceeding a little way down the street, turned into a milliner's shop, and, as the rain began to increase to a smart shower, I followed them in, well knowing the courtesy of the Parisian shopkeepers upon these occasions.

Taking a chair by the door, I overheard my countryfolks at the other end proceeding to purchase a bonnet, in which treaty the young lady, on the strength of having learnt French for several years at a Chelsea boarding-school, was put forward as principal negotiator. Of the poor girl's accent I can only say that it was worthy the French, which she began as follows :—" Nous besoinons, s'il vous plait, un bonnet."—This word unfortunately signifies a cap, several of which the *marchande des modes* proceeded to place before them, ejaculating at the same time—" Comme elle parle bien François! c'est étonnant! Mais, voyez donc Zoe, Celestine, Hippolyte, voyez comme elle a bonne mine !" and " Comme elle est gentille!" was echoed by the smiling demoiselles aforesaid. By pointing to some bonnets in the window, the young lady, whose name I found was Harriet explained the object of their visit, observing at the same time that it was excessively stupid of the woman, for of course " *bonnet*" must mean bonnet; and declaring that, in her opinion, the Parisians in general spoke very bad French, not at all like Mrs. Harrison at Chelsea. Carlo, meanwhile, was whisking about among the young ladies, who in various tones and attitudes of mincing terror exclaimed, " Est-il sage?" " They want to know if he is wise, Papa," said the daughter.—" Wise! no; what the deuce, do they take him for Munito?" Miss Harriet gave them a negative reply, when their consternation expressed itself by simultaneous exclamations of " Eh Dieu! il n'est pas sage!—va-t-en!—Ôtestoi de-là!—O Ciel!" and " Méchante bête!" until a whistle from his master brought him crouching to his feet, and relieved them from their apprehensions. The young interpreter now returned a bonnet which had been pressed upon their acceptance, with the observation— " Maman dit que çeçi n'est pas un bon un," and would have added that she wanted one lined with pink, but declared her ignorance of the French for " lined" and " pink;" whereat her father expressed some indignation, observing that it was a dead take-in of Mrs. Harrison to make him pay so much for French, and he always paid her bills regularly, when the child knew no more of it than the Pope of Rome. Signs—that cheap and convenient language which one may learn without Mrs. Harrison—supplied the defect, and the *marchande* produced a bonnet " doublé en couleur de rose," exclaiming, " Ah! celui-çi vous siéra bien," and pretending to be in raptures as she tried it on, she ejaculated, " Voyez, donc, Anastasie, Cassandre, Flavie, Hortense, comme ça va bien à Madame;" when the demoiselles respectively interjected, "C'est gentil—c'est joli—c'est charmant—c'est distingué !" This was decisive, the bonnet was selected, the husband put his purse upon the counter, and at the same moment Carlo, rising on his hind legs, as if to overlook the settlement, deposited his front paws on two pieces of white satin, leaving upon each a large sample of the black liquid mud collected in the kennels of the Rue Vivienne.

Fresh exclamations were occasioned by this accident, and Miss Harriet was made to understand, with some difficulty, that it was necessary to take a yard of each piece. "Combien l'aune?" enquired the father, who had accomplished that extent of French. "Monsieur, cette pièce se vend à sept francs, et celle-ci à neuf," which words she pronounced, as customary, *se* and *neu'*. "How much is that, Harriet?" "I'm sure I don't know, Papa; she says one piece is new."— "Well, well, we all know that, but how much is *se'*?"—"Indeed, Papa, there is no such a number in Chambaud, nor Wanostrocht's Grammar, and they've no right to invent words in that way." Papa shook his head, and began a new abuse of Mrs. Harrison; the *marchande* explained the price by uplifted fingers; the former objected to taking more than half an *aune;* Harriet exclaimed—"Vous faut couper une demi';" and, as I was in momentary apprehension of being appealed to by one or other of the parties, which I knew would entail a colloquy for which I had no time to spare, I made my bow of thanks, and hurried out of the shop, leaving the *marchande des modes*, Papa, Mamma, Miss Harriet, and Carlo, to settle the dispute in the best manner they could. H.

---

### SONNET FROM BENEDETTO DALL' UVA.

#### *On the Siege of Cyprus, in 1571.*

##### In cui Cipro confide, in cui più spera ?

In whom shall Cyprus hope, in whom confide,
   After her wantonness and crimes abhorr'd ?—
  Not in her nymphs and lovers, saith the Lord,
Nor her first Goddess—falsely deified.
Behold, the day is come, when far and wide
   Her cry of desolation shall be pour'd,
   And led in chains before the Scythian horde
Virgins and youths move sadly, side by side.
Now let not him that buys rejoice—nor he
   Who sells be sorrowful—one equal fate,
As equal was their guilt, involves them both.
In vain her walls and bulwarks to the sea
   Does Famagusta rear—against her gate
And towers God's arm is stronger than the Goth.

## MEMOIRS OF HAYLEY.*

In the general rush, which, within the last twenty years has been
made into the literary market, by persons of every age, rank, and
condition, men, women, and children, octogenarians and infants,
lords and day-labourers, all eagerly exposing their wares to sale, the
name of William Hayley, a great trader in his day, and whose credit
stood exceedingly high, has been in considerable danger of being forgotten. The fashion of his goods is, indeed, that of the last century,
and the public, always intent upon novelties, have of late years preferred manufactures from more modern hands. However, as Hayley
was considered one of the most skilful workmen of his own times, this
last specimen of his craft now before us may be regarded as a matter
of interest and curiosity.

To those persons who are attached to literary biography, and more
especially to literary *auto*-biography, these volumes will afford much
amusement. Education, habit, inclination, and fortune, all conspired
to render Hayley a complete author. His existence was one round of
reading and writing; he breathed in an atmosphere of books. He
had no hopes, no wishes, no wants beyond literary eminence and
literary ease. So deeply was he imbued with the quintessence of
authorship, that every thing around him was tinctured with the same
spirit. That his son should have repeated Pindar at the age of five,
and should have become a poet before he was six, is not to be marvelled at; but that an ancient nurse should criticize the " Decline and
Fall of the Roman Empire," would seem somewhat extraordinary, did
we not remember that she resided under the roof of Hayley. The
present Memoirs, then, are the faithful chronicle of an author's life, and
as such are certainly highly curious. They contain no romantic adventures, no brilliant achievements, no wonderful accidents by land or
sea, no surprising relation of political intrigues, and by some persons
they may therefore be thought destitute of interest; but this is a mistake. Incidents like these would be strangely misplaced in the annals
of an author. The only contest in which he engages, is " the battle of
the books." His only travels are round his library. He mingles,
it must be confessed, in politics, but they are those of Rome and of
Athens. His biography is a history of his mind,—of his progress in
his studies,—of his connexion and friendship with men of similar
habits and pursuits, and of his advancement and success in literary
reputation. There is surely something better, and there ought to be
something more interesting in this than in the hair-breadth escapes of
the soldier or the traveller. Then we are admitted in some degree to
inspect the mighty mysteries of author-craft; we see the mode (to be
figurative once more) in which the commodities are prepared for the
literary market, and we become acquainted with the bibliopolistic art.
Moreover, by our familiarity with the corporeal man, we divest ourselves of a portion of that veneration and awe with which we are apt to

* Memoirs of the Life and Writings of William Hayley, Esq., the friend and
biographer of Cowper, written by Himself; with extracts from his private Correspondence and unpublished Poetry; and Memoirs of his Son, Thomas Alphonso
Hayley, the Young Sculptor. Edited by John Johnson, LL. D., Rector of Yaxham
with Welborne in Norfolk. 2 vols. 4to.

regard the abstract author;—but were we to enumerate the various pleasures and advantages of literary biography, we should consume all our ink, and, it may be, with it, our readers' patience.

Hayley flourished at a period which some of our modern illuminati are apt to regard too lightly. In poetry, it is true, the standard of public taste is now considerably higher; but in almost every other branch of literature, there lived at that period many men whose names will be well and long remembered. Johnson and Garrick were passing away, but there was Gibbon as an historian, Warton as a critic, and Watson as a biblical scholar, who may certainly challenge a comparison with any succeeding names. Nay, in poetry itself, there was Cowper, whose excellences, notwithstanding the denunciation of my Lord Byron, are alone sufficient to rescue the age from the charge of poetical barrenness. With these, and with all the other "foremost men" of his time, Hayley was in habits of intimacy, and, in many cases, of correspondence. Of his friendship with Cowper, it is unnecessary to speak. To that friendship, the public owe their acquaintance with the character of that most amiable and admirable man; and to the same source Hayley is principally indebted for the additional share of reputation which he at present enjoys.

For the information of such of our readers, who, inverting the rule observed at the Ancient Concerts, never open a book which has not been published within the present century, we shall trace a slight sketch of the Life of Hayley, which may serve to give some idea of his "Memoirs." He was born in 1745, and of his childhood he has left an account a little too minute and circumstantial. His poetical propensities displayed themselves very early, and one of his first compositions was "A voluntary Epistle to a young Lady, in Latin couplets." At the age of twelve, he was sent to Eton, where he remained six years—imbibed more than the usual share of Greek and Latin—wrote an Ode to Ingratitude, and received "a most severe whipping" for secretly visiting one of the London theatres. On leaving school, he paid a visit to his mother at Chichester, and here we would notice the very feeling and amiable manner in which the biographer expresses himself whenever he has occasion to mention this excellent parent, whose virtues indeed seem to have rendered her worthy of all filial love and reverence. It was now high time for Hayley to fall in love, which he accordingly did on the first opportunity. The object of his adoration was a young lady whom he denominates "the fair Frances of Watergate," and with whom there happened to him the following romantic "love-passage." "When the young Frances and William had been a few days together, it happened that a thunder-storm surprised them in the groves mentioned above. The lady was constitutionally affected by the turbulent elements, and she actually fainted in the arms of William, an incident alluded to in the following impromptu of the young poet." Will the reader pardon the *non-sequitur?* We apprehend that this thunder-storm was ominous, for after a profusion of promises and poetry, vows and verses, the match was broken off in a very inexplicable manner. The worthy Divine, who has edited these Memoirs, has omitted a whole parcel of letters relating to this *embroglio.* We confess we thought this an *hiatus valde deflendus.*

The occupations which employed the time of Hayley during his residence at college, and the friendships which he there formed, were such as might be expected from a person of his studious character and elegant taste. He devoted a portion of his time to improving himself in the art of drawing, read Demosthenes until one o'clock in the morning, and "indulged his fancy on the probable occupations of the distant nymph" to whom he was attached. He appears at this time to have exercised his pen in poetical compositions with considerable assiduity. On leaving Cambridge, Hayley visited Scotland, and resided for a little time in Edinburgh. On his return to Chichester, the love-affair with the gentle Fanny terminated as we have mentioned above.

He now began to think seriously of his prospects in life, for his fortune was by no means ample. At one period he had determined to pursue the law as a profession, and had even become a member of the Middle Temple; but the Muses triumphed over Themis, and Hayley became an author about the same time that he became a husband. His union with the Muse seems to have been more productive of happiness to him than his marriage with his mortal mistress, whose health and spirits were the victims of a nervous disorder.

Determined to push his fortune in the literary world with vigour, Hayley visited the metropolis in the year 1769, and diligently applied himself to dramatic composition. His tragedy of *The Afflicted Father* was offered to Garrick, who appears to have been unwilling to refuse it, but more unwilling to accept it. All the manœuvres of the manager were exerted to extricate him from this difficulty, which was not, however, effected without highly offending the dramatist, and more especially his young bride. *The Syrian Queen* met with no better fortune from Colman; and Hayley, tired of London and the theatres, returned to his paternal retreat at Eartham. Here he employed himself in various studies; composing poetical epistles to many of his friends, and throwing off copies of verses whenever he could find a fair occasion. In 1777, he produced his *Epistle on Painting*. So prolific was the poet's muse, that there was scarcely a single celebrated individual to whom he did not address some stanzas, which were frequently the means of his forming new intimacies and friendships. In this manner he became acquainted with the philanthropic Howard; and the *Epistles on History*, addressed to Gibbon, procured for their author the friendship of that illustrious historian. In 1781, *The Triumphs of Temper*, the most successful of all Hayley's works, made its appearance, and produced a most favourable impression upon the public. He became the popular poet of the day, and even the rough Chancellor Lord Thurlow sought his society. With Gibbon, who appears to have admired his poetry, he became very familiar. Encouraged by his new success, Hayley brought forward another tragedy in 1789, which was represented at Drury-lane and Covent-garden on the same evening. At the former it failed, but was received with tolerable favour at the latter theatre. *Eudora*, another tragedy, was withdrawn after the first night's representation. Hayley's talents were certainly any thing but dramatic. In 1792, he became acquainted with Cowper; but the public are sufficiently informed upon this part of his history. About this period he wrote his *Life of Milton*. Mrs. Hayley, who had been for some time separated from her husband in consequence of her peculiar state of health, died in 1797; and a few years afterwards the poet lost his beloved son, of whom a copious memoir is given in the present volumes. From this period, until his death in 1820, Hayley lived very much in retirement. He was, however, tempted, in the year 1808, to adventure once more upon the perilous sea of matrimony; but the speculation was unfortunate, and in a few years after their union the parties separated. Nothing in Hayley's temper, which was very mild and cheerful, seems to have occasioned either this or his former separation, but his studious habits were, probably, not very agreeable to his companions. He produced several works in addition to those which have been mentioned: an *Essay on Old Maids*, in 3 volumes—a work full of gay amusement, and evincing a considerable extent of reading; several comedies in rhyme; a Life of Romney the Painter, and many other minor compositions.

The Memoirs contain many original letters, some of which possess considerable interest, and also several unpublished poetical pieces, which do not rise above the ordinary level of Hayley's genius. As a short specimen, we shall select a copy of verses addressed to Miss Hannah More, which, from the tone of them, must certainly have been written in the last century. There is something peculiarly *piquant* in the idea of the excellent author of "Cœlebs" and "Moral Sketches" being addressed in the following strain :—

### To Miss Hannah More.

THY verse, sweet sister of the lyre!
  A hapless poet found,
His brain oppress'd with feverish fire,
  His eyes in darkness drown'd :

But with a magical control
  Thy spirit-soothing strain
Dispels the languor of his soul,
  Annihilating pain.

If to relieve the sickly hour,
  Thy distant hand can frame
A tuneful charm of such high power
  To kindle pleasure's flame;

How may he scorn all human charms!
  How blissful his condition!
*Who shall encircle in his arms*
  *So lovely a magician!*

One of Hayley's critical friends imagined the conclusion of these verses "rather too warm," but the poet himself conceived them to be "perfect water-gruel," and thought that the fair object of them must be "very prudish indeed" if they offended her. In fact, Hayley's pen never trespassed beyond the bounds of delicacy, and yet it is singular enough that a comedy which he had written in French, and which was offered to one of the Parisian theatres, was rejected on account of an alleged impropriety in the introduction of a lady upon the stage whose character was not altogether unblemished. Upon the appearance of the Essay on Old Maids, also, the nice sense of propriety in some of the sisterhood was scandalized at several passages in that work, which were not in truth at all calculated to offend decorum.

A very useful lesson upon the unsubstantial nature of literary popularity may be gleaned from these volumes, which furnish abundant instances calculated to make many of our living authors tremble for their posthumous reputation. Several individuals are mentioned by Hayley in glowing terms of praise, whose very names have long since faded from the public ear. Who, for example, in the present generation ever heard of " the immortal Mundy ?" In the same manner Miss Seward is eulogised so warmly as to justify, in some degree, Porson's satirical verses. ". The celebrated Miss Seward," and " the sublime Muse of Lichfield," sound rather amusingly to modern ears. Hayley appears to have measured the reputation of this long-forgotten lady by her own standard; and a more fallacious mode of estimation could not have been adopted. We may here notice the very extraordinary habit in which " the Poet of Eartham," as he styles himself, indulged, of describing his friends by some strange periphrasis, a practice which deteriorates much from his otherwise pleasing style. He appears to have felt an unconquerable aversion to sirnames, for after having once mentioned them, he avoids the repetition of them with the most amusing ingenuity. In his letters he frequently denominates himself " William of the Turret," from a cottage residence to which he had given that name; or, " the Hermit ;" or, in the earlier part of the Memoirs, " the young Poet of Sussex." Gibbon is " the Roman Eagle." Helen Maria Williams " the young Muse," and Mrs. Opie " the excellent Amelia of Norwich." The reader is occasionally at a loss to determine the identity of the personages thus described, and is puzzled between " the amiable Physician of St. Alban's" and " the admirable Physician of Derby."

Nothing is more remarkable in the literary character of Hayley than the strong propensity he displayed for writing epitaphs. No tombstone was too haughty or too humble for this exertion of his talents. He was unfortunate in losing many of his early friends by death, but the mournful pleasure which he enjoyed in celebrating their virtues in an epitaph appears always to have afforded some consolation to his grief. Cowper—his nurse—his footman—Bishop Watson—and a parish clerk (who was lucky enough to die during the Poet's residence within the parish), were all commemorated in very smooth verse. Upon one occasion Dr. Johnson happened to have composed an epitaph upon a lady, to whose manes our Poet had already rendered the same service. Johnson, on seeing the rival lines, without being informed of the author's name, exclaimed, " It is unequal, but the man has much poetry in his mind." " If," adds Mr. Hayley, with great simplicity, " he is the very envious being he is generally supposed to be, he will detest me most cordially."

That portion of the work which has fallen to the lot of the present editor matches exceedingly well with the prior part of the volumes. It contains some details of the last years of the Poet's life, and a summary of his character, upon the whole, fair and candid. We have only space to add, that the " Memoirs of Thomas Alphonso Hayley" present an account of a very amiable and clever boy, who was well entitled to fill a place in Klefekerus's *Bibliotheca Eruditorum præcocium.* An affectionate father, who lost a child like this, in the very bloom of his promise, may be pardoned in consecrating to his memory so copious a memoir as the present.

## BABYLON.

RESPLENDENT the morn of her last day shone
On the cloud-capp'd tower of Babylon ;
And her lofty walls rose in proud array,
And her terraced gardens look'd green and gay,
And the stream of the river of Paradise
Flash'd a flood of light to her clear blue skies ;
She stood in the strength of her haughty sway,
The pride of the turretted Cybele.
Yet the sentinel sees from her battlements high
The Medes and the Persians before her lie,
And their steel helms blaze in the full sun-beam,
Far, far as his vision can catch their gleam :
And long by her hundred gates they had sate,
While she laugh'd in contempt at their battle-state,
And trusting to bulwark and massy wall,
Gave her days to pleasure and festival.
But her time is come—the last sun hath shone
On the tower of magnific Babylon—
The day that shall see her the spoil of the foe,
And trample the strength of the mighty low.

'Tis midnight, and the feast is done,
The revellers wrapp'd in sleep ;
The long-drawn streets of Babylon
Are hush'd in silence deep ;
And her palace floors are floating in wine,
And purple and gold in the pale moonshine
Bestrew them in many a heap :—
The guards are stretch'd drunk in the marble hall,
That no more shall wake at the trumpet's call ;
And glozing courtiers lie tranquil there,
That no more in the crimes of a court shall share ;
And fair girls repose in the harem's bound,
That no more shall dance to the timbrel's sound.
The monarch alone on his golden bed
Tosses sleepless, and fever'd, and hurried.
He had seen at the revel a phantom hand,
Unearthly in hue, and of outline grand,
On the banquet-wall trace in letters of light
The doom of his kingdom, and fall of his might.
But wherefore?—was not every gate
Of brass, and guarded well ?—
And if his trusty guards were beat,
Their shouts and cries must tell—
He had thousands to aid them as brave as their foe,
Then why should danger be threatening him now,
And fear unloose her spell ?—
He starts, then he listens—no sound—not a breath !
Up, king ! 'tis the silence that harbingers death.

They have turn'd the Euphrates, its channel is dry,
And the arm'd host is entering privily ;
The soldiers of Cyrus, the lord of the East,
Are entering the chambers of revel and feast,
And pouring forth blood mix'd with wine on the floors,
Ere the inmates awake or the battle-din roars.
Now the tumult begins, and lock, bolt, and bar,
Give way to the conqueror's cimeter,

And cries, and shrieks, and groans of despair,
Ascend to the skies with the flame's red glare ;
And Belshazzar prepares like a satrap to die,
Rolling fierce in rage his fiery eye,
And grasping his sword (for he knows no retreat),
The victors assail him————

————— The dream of his state—
The glory of Babel the proud, is no more !—
She hath perish'd as lesser things perish'd before ;
She is desolate now and the dragon crawls
O'er the muddy heaps of her ruin'd walls ;
And the serpents creep and wild beasts stray
Where her chambers of state and her proud halls lay—
And nothing is left, save a tale of her fame,
The dream of her glory and wreck of her name !

---

## THE PHYSICIAN.—NO. IX.

### *Of the Instincts of Nature in Diseases.*

NATURE has implanted in man, as well as in all other animals, a certain medical instinct, which is by no means to be disregarded. It laid the foundation of the whole practice of physic, and preceded the discovery of that science. There existed very skilful physicians before doctors were created, and these physicians were indiscriminately men and brutes. Nature, knowing the weakness of her creatures, could not possibly abandon them thus to their fate, for in that case they must soon have perished. The instinct of self-preservation, with which she endowed them when she gave them life, was combined with a certain discrimination, which causes them to select and delight in things tending to promote their well-being, and to avoid and reject such as threaten them with danger and destruction. So deeply has Nature interwoven this secret feeling with the whole mechanism of the animal powers that they can scarcely ever develope themselves in their operations in any other manner than is consistent with our preservation. Too vivid a light, which would injure the eyes if suffered to shine into them, produces from its nature such an effect upon them that they must of necessity contract and thus exclude the redundant rays, without our having occasion to form previously any resolution on the subject, nay, even without our being able to avoid it if we would. When we inhale acrimonious vapours, which, if they were to remain in the lungs, would corrode their delicate texture, we are compelled, by the laws of the animal mechanism, to set in immediate motion all the machinery of respiration, in order to expel these vapours from the chest by an incessant coughing, and this effect takes place absolutely and even against our will. When there is in any of our vessels an obstruction of viscid humours, which by their rapid putrefaction might infect the whole frame, the sensitive machine is enjoined by the laws of Nature to inclose this dangerous spot with an inflammation, which prevents the putrefaction of the obstructed humour, by converting it into a mild and innocent pus. If we attempt to perform an action that would do a dangerous violence to our limbs, pain is commissioned to warn us to desist, and in spite of our firmest resolution we are obliged

to submit. When any of our passions exhausts by its vehemence the
energies of our nature, that very exhaustion has the effect of reducing,
cooling, and moderating it. If we carry the instinct of self-preservation to excess by means of artificial excitements; and are induced, for
example, by the smell of savoury viands to overload the stomach, this
very gratification of the instinct produces a disgust, a loathing of
more food; and if that cannot correct the fault, the stomach is forced
to employ its own powers in a way contrary to its original destination,
and to discharge the superfluous food by a vomiting, in which our resolution has no share. In short, all our actions and movements, as
far as they are animal, are governed by this law of animal nature, and
all tend to our preservation. All imaginations, conceptions, and
desires, in as much as they are felt, excite in the machine peculiar
movements, proportionate to their vivacity; and I know not whether
it be more absurd to infer thence that the body of animals is actuated
by an essence which obeys the law of their preservation, or that it accomplishes all this by the very same mechanical laws by which those
machines move that are not animated by feelings. Of the two notions, that of Stahl is incontestably more rational and more consonant
to nature than that of Des Cartes. Still both are erroneous; for I have
shewn in the above instances, that the effects which by so wise an arrangement take place in the animal economy, though they tend to its
preservation, still do not proceed from the considerations of a rational
essence which governs it, but that they in general either precede such
considerations, or happen in opposition to our own resolutions. In
short, they take place according to the laws of animal mechanism,
which are totally different from other known mechanical laws; and instead of explaining them by numberless errors, philosophers ought to
have been content to have first made themselves acquainted with them.
Thus the natural philosopher is not ashamed first to study the laws of
physical phenomena, or the mechanic to observe the laws of mechanical
effects, and then to explain such as he is capable of explaining, and to
leave those which are incomprehensible to him where he found them.

   As, then, it appears from the preceding observations, that all animal
machines receive the various impressions, which are either serviceable
or detrimental to their preservation, in so decided a manner that they
themselves labour for their well-being and against their destruction;
so we thence deduce this incontestable inference, that, according to the
laws of animal mechanism, every animal body must take in what is
beneficial in a very different manner from what may be pernicious to
it, and this is the foundation of the natural dietetic and medical instinct
innate in all animals. The impression made by a poisonous vegetable
on the senses of an animal excites, even in the most hungry, an instantaneous nausea, on which account it loathes and rejects that vegetable.
If its senses be impaired, and it should by mistake eat any poisonous
food, no sooner has it reached the stomach than it compels that organ
to exert its powers in a manner totally the reverse of its natural functions,
in order to get rid of it by the shortest way; but, should its efforts fail,
the effects of this poison on the animal body produce such movements
as direct the senses and imagination to other things which are antidotes
to it. In like manner the overloading of the stomach takes away the
appetite from all animals, and if they then force themselves to take

food, the most agreeable seems nauseous to them. This natural fasting is the cure of excessive repletion; and there is not a more certain sign that the stomach is relieved of its burden, than the restoration of the regular appetite. The matter of fever, which heats the blood and approaches to putrefaction, has such an effect on the animal economy, that a violent thirst and a desire for acids, and a loathing of flesh and other aliments which have a tendency to putrefaction, take place. Are not all these real maxims implanted by nature in animals for the regulation of their diet and the cure of their diseases?

Greater respect ought to be paid to this instinct in patients than is generally done, because it is the voice and an immediate effect of the wise providence of Nature. It is far from my intention to censure the subtle deductions of a well-directed ingenuity; but still I will take the liberty to observe, that our theories in general cannot be put together in the laboratory itself of Nature, but only behind the curtain, and that we ought to follow them if they stand the test; but that they certainly do not always stand the test, because we follow them whether right or wrong. How often have physicians had occasion to find fault with their predecessors for having kept their seat so pertinaciously in the saddle of their favourite theory as frequently to ride over Nature with their hobby! It is not long since patients afflicted with fever were not allowed a drop of drink, or persons in small-pox a breath of air, though the former were perishing of drought, and the latter by suffocation. In the sequel, physicians became convinced of the extreme absurdity of such excessive caution, and of the violence offered by it to Nature. A change in theories was the consequence, and we are now so unwilling to relinquish the modern ones and to admit the confutation of them by Nature, that we, on the contrary, oppose other instincts with as much obstinacy as our forefathers. Even when our theories are correct, they are inapplicable to particular cases; and were they to be correctly applied, yet the force of habit, and the sensibility of individuals, may sometimes counsel us against their application, when it is directly opposite to some powerful and permanent instinct of the patient. To such patients we ought to sacrifice the best theory, even when they desire pernicious things, that they may not entirely exhaust, in the conflict with the errors of habit, the feeble remains of their powers, which are nearly sinking under the disease. Solenander relates a fact which strikingly illustrates this subject. A peasant was seized with a violent fever, and every one was convinced that it was impossible for him to recover. The physician who attended him asked, if there was any thing that he had been particularly fond of which he should like to have. " Sir," replied he, " I have a mortal dislike to the food and the physic prescribed for me, as well as to the soft bed on which I am laid. For nineteen years I have lain upon straw in the open air, and eaten nothing better than black bread, cheese, and onions." The physician, considering this as the last will and testament of his patient, caused it to be duly executed. He was laid at night upon straw, had cold water given him to drink, and bread and cheese to eat; and next morning he was up by the fire-side. Another physician of my acquaintance prescribed slops for a patient, who grew so much worse, that he directed him to take the strong beer to which he had been accustomed, and which invigorated and restored him. I could relate a thousand instances of this kind. The common man is well acquainted with them from repeated experience, and usually founds upon them his secret contempt of medicine. At the same time he judges inconsiderately. What does he know of the conditions and limitations that we must take such pains to discover before we dare either to sanction or to oppose the instincts of Nature in our patients? We are, indeed, obliged to do both; for either Nature and the physician are not infallible, or the most skilful physician is frequently incapable of distinguishing the desires originating in subtlety of understanding or obstinacy, from those dictated by the genuine animal instinct—the secret minister of Nature. There is no subject more deserving of close investigation than this.

Addison considered nothing as more mysterious than the natural instinct of animals, which sometimes rises far above reason, and at others falls infinitely short of it. He could not venture to pronounce it a property of matter, neither could he, on account of its extraordinary effects, regard it as an attribute of an intelligence. He therefore looked upon it, like gravity in bodies, as an immediate impression of the First Mover, and as the Divine Power operating in its creatures.

There cannot be a more judicious comparison than this. As gravity imparts to a body the skill to pursue invariably the shortest way to the centre of the earth, without having the least consciousness of this action; so instinct directs animal bodies to their natural destinations, as though Nature herself had thoroughly instructed them in the secrets of her views; and thus they perform actions which are consonant with the laws of wisdom without knowing any thing of the matter. As Nature has endued physical bodies with peculiar properties, such as gravity, attraction, and the like, so has she bestowed others on animal bodies; and, if I may be allowed the expression, incorporated the most essential maxims of her wisdom into living machines, just as an artist makes an automaton that performs certain human actions, but in other respects can do no more than any other machine. The whole animal kingdom is full of instances of this sort. It is not out of respect, as every reader will easily believe, that a certain beetle described by naturalists, buries the dead moles and toads which it finds, but the instinct which teaches it to subsist upon those animals, and to deposit its eggs in them, impels it to this action. The pigeons which are trained to carry letters to distant places are not more sensible than other pigeons: nothing but the blind instinct to return to their young governs them in this proceeding. It is requisite that they should have left young at the place to which they are to fly; and lest they should take a fancy to stop by the way to drink or to wash themselves, their feet are dipped at their departure in vinegar. The Soland geese in St. Kilda steal, as Martin informs us, the grass out of one another's nests, not for the sake of stealing, but because they pick up grass wherever they find it, to form a soft depository for their eggs: and as these geese live together in flocks of many thousands, they find it every where in the nests of their companions. Highly as Ulloa extols the almost human caution and intelligence manifested by the mules in America in descending the lofty mountains, yet a closer examination will show that it is nothing but the fear of falling at the sight of the precipices, which occasions all their caution, without any farther consideration. If at Lima they stand with their legs wide apart when they hear a subterraneous rumbling, this proves nothing more than an habitual mechanical action acquired by frequent repetition; because when the earth shakes, they are obliged to assume a firmer position with their burdens, and they take the noise and the earthquake for one and the same thing, since the one invariably accompanies the other. Such is the real history of the supposed intelligence and cunning of animals. Nature must have known how far it was necessary for the skill which she conferred on animal bodies to extend, in order to the attainment of the purposes of self-preservation, self-defence, and the propagation of their kind. So much is certain, that all these instincts have their appointed limits, beyond which no animal can go; and hence it is, that the animals, so long as they follow their instincts, perform actions of apparently astonishing intelligence, but in other respects are so stupid as not to manifest the slightest trace of cunning in their operations. A hen, whose providence and perseverance we admire, when she lays her eggs in some sequestered spot, where she sits on and turns them, and almost sacrifices herself in her attention to them, bestows the same pains on a lump of chalk which is put under her. She leads her chickens about that they may learn to scratch up the ground and to seek worms and insects. At the same time she will tread upon one of them, and affrighted at the cries which the pain extorts from it, she clucks to warn and to soothe it; but yet she has not the sense to raise her foot and to set it at liberty. A lobster will, with inconceivable dexterity snap off his leg when one of his fellows seizes it with his claw: but if you put one of his legs between his own claw, he will not have the sense to open his claw and to remove his leg, but breaks it off, as if there were no other method of releasing himself. The ostrich hatches her eggs, as it would appear, for the purpose of having young ostriches; she nevertheless quits them for every trifle, and leaves them to perish; nay, she will even break most of them herself, for the purpose of feeding with them the young ones which she already has. This bird has, moreover, the silly instinct to swallow every thing that comes in its way, without discriminating, like other animals, whether it is hurtful to it or not. An ostrich swallowed, in Shaw's presence, several leaden bullets hot from the mould. It will greedily devour its own excrements and those of other birds, and of course manifests not the least choice in obeying the instinct of appetite. The crocodile would multiply with dangerous rapidity, were it not so stupid as to devour its own young, according to the testimony of Ulloa. Thus, too, the male tiger destroys its own species in its young; and it is observed of one of the bug family, that the female is obliged to use the greatest precaution to defend her eggs and her young from the male. The ascent and descent of larks are the result of an instinct implanted in those birds, which they follow without any consideration; for they do the very same over the sea as upon land, and hence frequently perish in the water. A thousand other examples of this kind might be adduced. They prove that these actions, which seem to manifest so much intelligence, are but the actions of a machine, adapted to certain particular purposes, and that to those purposes alone this apparent intelligence extends.

What can be inferred from all this, but that in the complicated relations in which an animal becomes involved during the whole course of its life, cases must sometimes occur, in which the natural instinct, that is not guided by reason, but merely developed mechanically, operates very improperly and quite the contrary way to what it ought to do, or in which, at least, it fails of completely effecting the object of nature? Every thing in nature has its limits, its deficiencies, and its exceptions: how, then, should the instincts of animals alone be exempt from them? Traces of these deficiencies, and of this perverse application, are but too frequently met with in the animal kingdom. Though most animals follow a natural instinct in the selection of their food, and readily distinguish and reject such substances as are pernicious; still naturalists demonstrate, that they frequently choose the wrong and greedily eat poisonous vegetables which kill them. Many animals cannot distinguish food that has been most manifestly impregnated with poison, from any other; though they immediately recognize those aliments which they need for their subsistence by much less perceptible signs. A horse, which is so dainty in his food, when left to himself cannot resist the inclination to drink when he is overheated, and this error costs him his life. He wounds himself with great stupidity when a sprig of thorn is fastened beneath his tail, by pressing it violently against his haunches; whereas he need but raise it to spare himself the pain. The extreme difficulty, also, of removing a horse from a stable which is on fire, is a well-known fact; and, in consequence of this obstinacy, he is consumed with it. In the rutting season, many animals exhaust themselves to such a degree that it is a long time before they recover their strength. In short, it must be admitted that, in many cases, the instincts of Nature precisely counteract their objects, and that nothing is farther from truth than that they are infallible.

Man, who in one point of view is an animal, just as every animal is in one point of view a machine, has his appropriate animal appetites, as other animals have theirs. So little difference is there, in this respect, between him and the brutes, that on this side he can claim no superiority over them. For his preservation he has, in common with them all, hunger and thirst, the dread of pain, and concern for his life; he defends himself like them, and like them he propagates his kind. Moralists must testify the ill-success of their lessons, when they tend to bring the actions which men perform by means of their animal instincts under the control of prudence and reason.

Such instincts, then, we have also in our diseases; and it is as clear as the sun that they are but consequences of the unusual sensations which we experience in a state of disease. The craving for drink in fever, the impulse to counteract putrefaction of the humours by acids, to alleviate pain by rubbing and chafing the contracted nerves, to perform all sorts of violent motions, &c. are but the effects of feelings according to which the machine changes, and, with its new excitements, aims, as it were, at new objects, of which the soul, however, neither comprehends nor knows any thing.

Much as it behoves us to respect these instincts of the sick as the almost immediate impulses of Nature, still we should go too far were we to believe that these instincts, in the human animal at least, were infallible, and ought absolutely to be followed. Far from it!—our appetites, considered by themselves, have the same defects as those of all other animals ; and as they are not, any more than the latter, effects of our reason, but mere operations of the animal machine, they are not to be more highly regarded in us than in the brutes. We should drink cold water, when overheated, with the same avidity as the horse, did not reflection or experience forbid us. The instinct of propagation impairs our constitutions much more than those of animals. Our urinary vessels hold a stone that is passing through them as firmly as the stupid lobster holds his leg in his claw; and, to afford relief, the physician must correct this perversion of the maxim, which is so applicable to an infinity of other cases, in order to save us from destruction. It is frequently the case, that, when the stomach is overcharged, we have the same appetite for food as if it were empty, and we should injure our health were we blindly to obey this impulse. Ebn Athir, an Arabian writer, relates, that the Caliph Abdalmelek was attacked by a disease which, according to the physicians, could not fail to prove mortal in case of his drinking any thing. His thirst, however, became so violent, that, unable to endure it any longer, he ordered his son Valid to give him some drink. Valid, who loved his father, would not gratify him in violation of the express prohibition of the physicians. The Caliph then applied to his daughter, Fatime, and Valid still opposed the fulfilment of his wish; when Abdalmelek became angry, and threatened to disinherit his son if he persisted in his disobedience. He was therefore obliged to comply; and no sooner had the Caliph swallowed the fatal draught of water, than he swooned, and shortly afterwards expired. If this example be liable to suspicion, still the natural antipathies in diseases are instincts of nature as well as the appetites; and yet persons in hydrophobia, who have such a horror of water, are tormented with thirst. In short, were it necessary, I could adduce a great number of facts to prove that the instincts of Nature, both in health and in disease, are frequently as fallible and as perverse as in the irrational animals.

The animal instincts of man lose, moreover, much of their weight with physicians, because reason and sophistry interfere too much in this business of Nature, though it is above their comprehension. There is no end to our refinement upon our appetites, and this renders a matter already sufficiently ticklish and intricate, so uncertain, that the instances of men who have benefited themselves by obeying their animal instincts are very rare. It is almost impossible for us to leave these instincts, even if we would, in their natural purity; because, in all our animal actions, and in our very feelings, reason always interferes, and we cannot impose silence on the soul. Hence our patients often deem *that* an impulse of Nature, which is a mere suggestion of their reason or imagination; and even if they really feel such an impulse, their sophistry does not fail immediately to pervert it. This bungling of the soul in the laboratory of Nature justly renders the animal instincts of man so problematical to physicians, that they are always extremely cautious how they gratify them. Nor does it appear that we shall ever gain a much better insight into this matter than we have yet done; for the instincts of animals are a work out of the most secret cabinet of Nature, into which we never shall penetrate.

It is, therefore, my duty to exhort my readers in the most serious manner, neither to give way too confidently to their natural instincts, nor entirely to oppose them.   Each of their appetites is a dangerous temptation for them.   Nature will not suffer us to keep them in absolute subjection; neither will she bear us harmless if we blindly give ourselves up to their control.   Where, in this case, is the middle way? I cannot tell: and if I could, of what benefit would it be?   Middle ways are difficult to keep; they are ways upon which neither physicians nor patients are commonly found.

---

### THE TREASURES OF THE DEEP.

WHAT hid'st thou in thy treasure-caves and cells?
Thou hollow-sounding and mysterious Main!
—Pale glistening pearls, and rainbow-colour'd shells,
Bright things which gleam unreck'd of, and in vain.
—Keep, keep thy riches, melancholy sea!
      We ask not such from thee.

Yet more, the Depths have more!—What wealth untold
Far down, and shining through their stillness lies!
Thou hast the starry gems, the burning gold,
Won from ten thousand royal Argosies.
—Sweep o'er thy spoils, thou wild and wrathful Main!
      Earth claims not these again!

Yet more, the Depths have more!—Thy waves have roll'd
Above the cities of a world gone by!
Sand hath fill'd up the palaces of old,
Sea-weed o'ergrown the halls of revelry!
—Dash o'er them, Ocean! in thy scornful play,
      Man yields them to decay!

Yet more! the Billows and the Depths have more!
High hearts and brave are gather'd to thy breast!
They hear not now the booming waters roar,
The battle-thunders will not break their rest.
—Keep thy red gold and gems, thou stormy grave—
      Give back the true and brave!

Give back the lost and lovely!—those for whom
The place was kept at board and hearth so long;
The prayer went up through midnight's breathless gloom,
And the vain yearning woke 'midst festal song!
Hold fast thy buried isles, thy towers o'erthrown,
      —But all is not thine own!

To thee the love of woman hath gone down,
Dark flow thy tides o'er manhood's noble head,
O'er youth's bright locks and beauty's flowery crown;
—Yet must thou hear a voice—Restore the dead!
Earth shall reclaim her precious things from thee,
      —Restore the Dead, thou Sea!

---

THE WINDS.—A DIALOGUE.

*Spirit* 1. Hark !—what trampling sound is nigh;—
'Tis above us,—in the sky !—

*Sp.* 2. The howling winds are in the air:
Shall we call them, Master fair?

*Sp.* 3. How they sigh, and how they rave !—
One is sweeping o'er the wave
Loaden like a thunder-cloud :
On his breast his head is bow'd—

*Sp.* 1. Ha! I see his hideous stare
Piercing through his stormy hair :
Lightnings round his loins are flung,
Forked like the serpent's tongue !

*Sp.* 2. Shall we call them, Master dear?
Give thy word!

*Magic.*             Appear ! appear—
Will ye not speak?—My ears are stunn'd by noises,
Which rush against them, and my soul is toss'd
As in a whirlwind of tempestuous dreams.
Where do ye loiter?—Oh ! blow on, blow on :
I *live* in this abundant harmony.
Now would I float upon the riotous storm,
Zephyr-like,—leaf-like, and be borne far off
To giant islands,—to bright jutting crags,
Cold as December, or where mountains lift
Their gleaming shoulders in the Boreal light.
Now let me roll on clouds or sleep in air,
Or from Atlantic billows touch the moon—
Cradle me—rock me—and ye, brooding Winds !
Mutter your spells from shore to echoing shore.—
Oh ! my soul 's wilder than the music.—Hark !—
Look, where that bright-wing'd snake the Lightning comes,
Tearing the sky !—Fain would I cling unto him,
And dart from cloud to cloud,—from earth to air,—
From air to heaven, and in that topmost road
Whence Phaeton tumbled with his blazing car
And scorch'd the Padus, move like a Sun.—Hark ! hark !
The sounds are nearer : once more, Spirits, appear !

*Winds.* (*above*)—We are here :—we are here.

1st *W.*   *I* have come on the ice-blast.

2nd *W.*  And *I* on the hot Simoom.

3rd *W.*  And *I* have brought blight from a Tartar night.

4th *W.*  And *I* am sick from the tomb :
For I was bred
On a fainting morn,
Where the Ague and yellow Plague are born,
Where the panther springs,
And the vampire stings,
And the serpent rattles his scaly rings.

1st *W.*  Look !—This is a bolt which Hecla threw,
When her white heart crack'd in the burning blue :
The Spirits that lay on her blazing snows
Were shook from their ages of cold repose,
And awoke with their mother's shrieking throes.

2nd *W.*  And, see, what *I* gather'd when Nile was bare !
It lay on a crocodile's forehead square,
Like a soul near the jaws of the gaping Hell,
But I saw it, and liked its lustre well,

And I swore by the power.
Of that dark hour
That I'd bring it to thee in thy Paduan bower.

3rd *W.*   I have a rose,
But its red blood flows
No longer,—no longer its bosom glows;
The morning's rain
Shall sparkle in vain,
For nothing can raise its life again.

*Spirit.*   It *seems* to live.

3rd *W.*   But it hath died,
In its first fresh crimson pride.—
Like the starry light that streams,
On the poet's figured dreams,
It but *seems* :—
Like the beauty that betrays
Trusting passion with its gaze,—
Like the meteor eyes that lie
On the forehead of the sky,—
Like the madman's phantom crown,—
Like the flushing virgin's frown,—
It but *seems.*

*Magic.*   Thou art the best of all—and worst ;
For never since the clay was cursed
With knowledge, and an ample scope
To grieve in, has the masquer Hope
Been match'd, when in his fair false way
He strives to lure a soul away.

                                           ÆOLICUS.

---

BRITISH GALLERIES OF ART.—NO. VII.

## Lord Egremont's Gallery at Petworth.

To those who possess the happy skill of extracting delight from that which, as yet, is but an imagination to them—who have faith enough to believe before they see, as well as after—there are few things more pleasant than to travel through the whole length of a long summer's day,—

" From morn to morn, from noon to dewy eve,"

with the certainty constantly present to them, of seeing, at the end of their journey, some object, or set of objects, the sight of which they have been looking forward to and reckoning upon as one of the ends for which they were living in the past, and which, when they have thus appropriated it, is to become one of the means by which they are to live in the future. A feeling of this kind turns every thing we see into beauty,—like the imagination of the youth who is journeying towards his mistress—in Mr. Crabbe's tale of " The Lover's Journey ;" and that which it *finds* beautiful, it contributes not only to heighten and multiply, but to impress upon the senses, and through them on the memory, in a way that nothing else can—not even the most strenuous and predetermined efforts of the will. To those who have not already seen the princely domain of the Earl of Egremont at Petworth, I would fain convey such a notion of it, that till they set out to visit it for themselves, it may thus dwell in the distance before them, like a bright spot in the land of promise ; secure that, when they do visit it, I shall not, in so doing, have anticipated the impressions they will receive from it, but only have prepared the way for those impressions, and thus rendered their effect more certain and more lasting. And yet it is presumptuous in me to reckon on being able to accomplish this. The utmost I can hope to do is to furnish another " Yarrow unvisited" to those who will never see Petworth but in hope and intention;—that is to say, those who hope to see it, without intending; and those who intend to see it every summer, till the winter comes, when it is too late.

And here let me premise, that, as the beauties of Nature more than divide the palm of admiration with those of Art, on this enchanting spot, it is but fair that they should meet with their due share of notice in this description. The truth is, that the latter have as much fallen short of the expectation I had previously formed respecting them, as the former have surpassed it; and I propose to let the one make up for the deficiency of the other, to the reader, as it has done to me.

In an obscure part of Sussex, on the Chichester road, about fifty miles distant from London, stands the most uncouth and unsightly of villages, named Petworth; consisting of dwellings *(houses,* the inhabitants probably call them)—seeming to have been constructed in every age since the invention of the art, except the civilized ones; and apparently adapted to every purpose but the one they are intended for; the largest looking like prisons for the confinement of malefactors— the smallest like sheds for the shelter of animals—and all seeming to have been contrived and arranged for the express purpose of shutting out or destroying all ideas connected with and dependent on the beauties of external nature and " the country"—all closely and confusedly huddled together, as if to prevent the intrusion of any thing in the shape of a tree or a patch of grass, and barely room enough left between them for the passers-by to wind their way along.

Let the reader fancy himself placed over-night in the midst of this barbarous and outlandish spot—at the Swan Inn, perchance—having arrived there too late to judge of the kind of place he is in, and fancying that, as he has been travelling all day *from* London, he must by this time be *in the country.* When he wakes in the morning, and finds himself in the kind of spot I have described, his first impulse, of course, will be to wander forth in search of something different from what he sees about him; and, nothing natural or pleasant presenting itself to him spontaneously as if to court his admiration, he will probably at once enquire " the way to the Park Gate?" It is a chance if he finds any one to answer his question civilly or intelligibly; for the inhabitants of a village like this are generally as rude and uncouth as their houses, and imagine that any one who does not know " the way to the Park Gate," (which *they* know so well) must be little better than a natural. But when he does find the object of his search, let him pause for a moment before he enters, and recall to his mind the different objects that he has just been winding his way among, and the general scene that he is leaving—thus turning them to the only good they are susceptible of, by unconsciously making them serve as a foil and a contrast to what he is presently to behold. On entering the gate nearest to the back of the Swan Inn, I need not call upon him to dismiss from his mind all memory of that which has just been occupying it; for the scene of enchantment and beauty that will now

burst upon his delighted senses is not of a nature to permit any thing
else to interfere with it ;—like a lovely and beloved bride on her bridal
day, it must and will hold and fix, not only his feelings and affections,
but his fancy—his imagination—his whole soul undividedly. Oh!
there *is* a set of chords in the human mind which cannot choose but
vibrate and respond to the impressions which come to them from external nature—which cannot choose but do this independently of all previous knowledge, of all habit, of all association! Take a savage from
his native spot—who has never seen any thing but his own cabin, the
glen in which it stands, the mountain stream where he slakes his
thirst, and the eternal woods through which he pursues his prey ; and
place him in the presence of such a scene as that which will greet the
spectator when he has entered a few paces within the walls of Petworth
Park ; and if he be not moved, rapt, and inspired with feelings of delight, almost equivalent to in degree, and resembling in kind, those
instinctive ones which would come upon him at the first sight of a
beautiful female of his own species, then there is no truth in the knowledge which comes to us by impulse, and nothing but experience can
be trusted and believed. I speak, however, of a *natural* savage, not
one who has been made such by society and custom. I can easily
conceive, for example, that half the boors and clowns in Petworth
itself pass daily through the scene I am about to describe, without
ever discovering that it differs in any thing from the ploughed field
where they are going to work, or the dusty road that runs through a
corner of their village.

Let the spectator enter the park from the gate I have mentioned
above, and turning to his right hand on entering, and passing under a
few limes irregularly planted, he will emerge (still keeping to his right
hand) in front of the mansion-house belonging to this beautiful domain.
It is a building of great extent, perfectly uniform, and of singular
plainness,—without portico, columns, wings, ballustrades, towers,
spires, domes, or any thing that can be supposed to have been placed
about it for mere ornament—nothing that makes any pretension to
vie in attraction with the scene of beauty in the midst of which it
stands. On the contrary, it seems placed there, not to rival, still less
to overlook or command that scene—but merely to complete and form a
consistent part of it. Or, perhaps, it is still better adapted to convey to one
the idea of a perpetual spectator fixed for ever to the spot, in silent admiration of a scene that, but for some one thus to admire it, would not
be quite complete. Without going into a particular description of this
nobly simple structure, but merely adding that its general character,
and the appearances it has borrowed from time and the elements,
bespeak it to be neither ancient nor modern, but holding a station
exactly between the two,—without the unwieldy grandeur of the one,
or the fantastical common-place of the other,—let us turn at once to
the lovely scene on which it looks forth. Standing immediately in
front of the mansion, a level lawn extends before you to a very considerable distance in the centre, and bounded there by a bright water
stretching irregularly all across ; and on the right, by a rich sweep of
rising ground, reaching nearly to the mansion itself, and crowned by a
dark grove of beeches and chesnut-trees. From the edges of this
water on either side, and from small islands within it, rise groups of
trees, in twos, threes, and fours, and here and there a single one—all

so disposed as to bear a half-conscious, half-unconscious reference to each other, and all possessing a relative beauty, both of form, situation, &c. which heightens and is heightened by the positive one. Leaving for a moment out of view the left side of this scene, let the eye now pass across this narrow break of water, and rest on what extends beyond it. Immediately from the opposite bank the ground rises,—not abruptly, as it does on the right hand on *this* side,—but softly, and in a way that is perceptible only from its effect on the objects which rest upon it. It rises in this way for a considerable distance again, in a rich semi-circular sweep of lawn, with only one clump of firs and larches placed at about the middle of it, surrounded by a regular white fence, and looking like a single jewelled brooch placed on the forehead or the breast of a rural beauty. This sweep is also crowned by a dark diadem of trees, and forms the first *distance* of the view—above and behind which rise, and intersect each other, two more distances of bright green hills, the furthermost of which is also crowned with rich trees, of that peculiar kind of growth which gives them the form of clouds rolling and clustering over each other— dark green clouds clustering over and embowering open spaces of light green sky. From a point of this distance towards the left, where the trees seem to open for a space to admit it through, rises a lovely Gothic spire; and at another point considerably higher, and on the right, a grey antique turret looks forth from out the dark foliage. The reader has now before him the whole of this delicious view, with the exception of the left side; all the distant part of which, however, he must consider as just within that distance which "lends enchantment to the view," without in the least degree impairing the distinctness of it, or even taking away its home look—that look which gives it a connexion with the more immediate parts. When he has given life and finish to all this portion of the scene, by peopling the turf on *this* side of the water with herds of deer, dark, dappled, and white; the water itself with swans and wild-fowl; and the rising hills on the other side with flocks and cattle; he may pass his eye onward, across the whole left side of the scene, and let it rest on an expanse,—evidently beyond the precincts of the domain itself, yet seeming virtually to form a part of it,—than which nothing was ever seen more perfectly adapted to give the needful crown and finish to the whole, by inviting the imagination to wander sufficiently far to give it exercise and employment, and yet not leading it far enough away to dissipate the unity of effect which is the chief charm in sights of this kind. This expanse consists of an extensive rising plain, terminated by the range of hills which form the boundary to the sea on this coast; the whole brought into that kind of cultivation which gives an appearance quite peculiar to English scenery—an appearance as of a natural garden, no spot of which is without the most perfect cultivation, and yet on no spot of which can the actual marks of the cultivator be distinguished;— an appearance which gives the best notion we can possibly gain of the distant views our first parents might be supposed to contemplate in Paradise.

Such is the picture which presents itself to the spectator from the principal windows of Petworth. From various other points of view in this magnificent domain (the enclosing wall of which extends for four miles along the high road) others offer themselves to the sight, scarcely less complete in their detail, and all of the same elegant and graceful character. But I must content myself with offering this one to the reader's notice, as an example of what he will meet with among the natural objects which claim his attention here,—and turn at once to my more immediate subject—the Works of Art.

The interior of Petworth is on a scale of grandeur and magnificence commensurate with its external character; being scarcely inferior in extent and splendour to many royal palaces. Indeed the grand hall and staircase a good deal resemble those of Hampton Court; the walls, ceiling, &c. being ornamented in a similar manner, with allegorical paintings on an immense scale, by Sir James Thornhill. These we shall pass by at once, as not coming among the objects of our search; and proceed to name a few of the principal works of the old painters: premising, however, that the chief riches of this collection consist in portraits, and those chiefly by Vandyke.

The room you first enter at the right-hand corner of the Hall, called the Square Dining-room, is among the richest and most interesting. Here is what may undoubtedly be considered as one among Vandyke's choicest masterpieces in the way of portraiture—*The Earl of Strafford.* There is a sober solemnity in the colouring of this admirable work, which he did not always duly attend to where it was needed; in the air and attitude there is a mixture of conventional nobility, and of conscious natural power, which is finely characteristic; and the head is inimitably forcible and consistent with the rest of the figure. This is truly an *historical* picture, and may be perused and studied with as much reliance on its authenticity as any written portrait that we possess in history. Vandyke's and Titian's portraits of known historical characters are in this respect not less interesting and less worthy of study than those of Tacitus or Lord Clarendon—if indeed they are not more so, in proportion as men can hide and disguise their characters more easily in their words and actions than they can in their looks. A fool never *looked like* a wise man yet—though many a score have passed for such; and a knave can no more put on the personal appearance of an honest man, than he can *be* one.

The portrait of *Henry, Earl of Northumberland,* when confined in the Tower, by the same artist, is scarcely inferior to the foregoing in character and importance; and there is also a nobly rich, yet sombre tone of colour spread over it, which gives it a most impressive effect. There are several other portraits in this room, by Vandyke also, worthy of the highest admiration and the most careful perusal and study, but which cannot be described in detail with any good effect. I will mention in particular an exquisite one of Lady Rich, another of the Earl of Newport, and one containing three persons, one of whom is another Earl of Northumberland.

The other works in this room that call for particular mention are a curious portrait of Oliver Cromwell, in which the bent brow and compressed lips finely bespeak the character of the close and determined usurper; two very pretty rural Hobbimas; and an execrable picture of Macbeth in the Witches' cave, by Sir Joshua Reynolds—which seems to me to evince a total want of sentiment, imagination, taste, and even execution. If Sir Joshua had discoursed no better about historical painting than he practised it, his lectures would have enjoyed a somewhat less degree of reputation than they do; and they enjoy too much as. it is. In fact, a permanent and adequate treatise on this Art is still a desideratum in our literature; and it is but too likely to remain so: for where shall we look for a union of that knowledge, practical skill, and ability to develope these, which such a task requires? There is but one person among us in any degree qualified for the office; and he has neither the industry nor the will to undertake it.

In another dining-room, which I think adjoins to the above-named, will be found a most curious and elaborate work, apparently by Breughel, of a Turkish Battle; and also one or two excellent sea-pieces by Vandervelde. But we must pass on from these, through a room containing some of Charles's Beauties—*all-alike*—by Kneller and Lely; and fix our attention to incomparably the richest and most charming room in the gallery. It contains five more of the Beauties of Charles's court, painted by Vandyke,—which, for a certain courtly and exclusive air, added to a perfect simplicity, naturalness, and truth of expression, surpass any thing of the kind I have ever seen. The colouring, too, is delicacy itself—mixed with a clearness and richness, the effect of which is perfectly magical. Nothing can be more striking than the difference between these pictures, and those professing to represent the same class of persons by Lely and Kneller, in the preceding room, and indeed wherever else they are to be found. The latter painters had but little, if any perception of the peculiar characteristics which the habits of a court life cast over the external appearance of those who constantly partake in them—or rather, which they *did* cast over it in those days; and Vandyke had a more perfect and intense perception of this than he had of any thing else in nature or art. And, accordingly, the one represents his persons as they never were seen but in a court, and the others as they never were or could be seen in any court in existence. The one knew that a court beauty, while she remains innocent, is likely to be, and in fact *is*, one of the purest and most innocent of human beings; and he has represented them as such accordingly; witness the divine portrait of the Countess of Devonshire, in this room. The others knew of no difference between a court-beauty and a courtesan, and represented them accordingly;— witness almost every picture they ever painted. Pass backwards and forwards from one of these rooms (which are adjoining) to the other, and you will at every glance perceive, that, though each set of portraits profess to represent precisely the same class of persons, there is as much difference between them, generally, as well as in every particular, as there is between Polly Peachum and Suky Tawdry in the Beggars' Opera.

The ladies whose presence (for it is like their actual presence) beautifies this room, must allow their names to grace my page also, in order that the immortality they owe to Vandyke—or rather, which he repaid them in return for that which *they* bestowed on *him*—may not be entirely confined to the frames which contain their pictures. Incomparably the loveliest of them—for a certain natural innocence, sweetness, and purity, added to an inimitable court air and grace—is the one which I have named above—the Countess of Devonshire. The others are the Countesses of Bedford, Leicester, Sunderland, and Carlisle.

There is another picture in this room, which, notwithstanding the total dissimilarity of its subject, will bear to be characterized by exactly the same phrases as I have applied to the above lovely portrait. It is a landscape by *Cuyp*—next to the principal one at Dulwich, beyond comparison the most exquisite I have ever seen. I have said that I was disappointed in this gallery. I was so—but not dissatisfied. I should have been content to have gone all the way from London to see it, if it had consisted of *this* picture alone. It represents a perfectly open country, without either dwellings, human figures, or even foliage—except a few trees that rise at the extremity of the right-hand side. The only actual objects on which the eye is called upon to rest in particular, are two cows lying side by side on the right—one drinking on the left— one looking forth from the middle distance, and apparently lowing— and three others in the second distance standing close together. How is it possible to extract an effect as of enchantment, from a scene like this—where there is a total absence of the interest arising from either beauty of form, association of ideas, variety of object or of action, contrast of colour, or any of those adventitious aids on which so much usually depends, even in the finest efforts of Art ? I know not—but so it is, that, from the most unpractised to the most cultivated and fastidious eye, none can look upon this picture without feeling riveted to it, by a charm, the nature of which few of them will pretend to expound. Not I, for one. Thus much I will say, however—that there must be something in it more than a mere reflection, even the most perfect, of mere nature. The scene itself here represented, could under no circumstances call forth the feelings that this representation of it calls forth. Not but every point of its detail is absolutely true to nature, and will bear the minutest examination in this respect. But there is a something infused into every part of it, and spread over it as a whole, which can neither be described nor seen, but only *felt ;* and which, if it is not nature, is true and responsive to it, as the needle is to the Pole —we know not why. It is, in fact, nature seen through the halo that is cast about it from the mind of genius ; and like many a piece of pure description from the pen of a poet, it affects us more vividly, and touches us more nearly, than the actual scene described could do under any circumstances. The splendid vision of natural beauty, in all its richness and variety, that presents itself to the eye on looking from the windows of the room where this picture hangs, does not affect the mind more, and will not dwell upon the memory longer, and be recurred to oftener, than this simple representation of a bare open space of ground, with a few cows feeding, a group of trees, and a sunshiny sky. A volume might be written on the causes of this, and the reader of it no nearer to a solution of the problem at the end. The shorter and the better way is, to admit at once the miraculous power of genius, and bow down before it in token of a confiding and admiring love.

From the delightful room containing the above pictures, we pass into the library, which offers nothing of sufficient importance to be particularly described ; though it is perhaps the most merely entertaining portion of the collection,—from the number of small cabinet gems it includes. Among these there is a sweet Magdalen, by *Carlo Dolce,* an interesting portrait of Anna Boleyn, and several very pleasing pieces of the Dutch school.

In an anti-room adjoining to this, we meet with two very interesting portraits : one of Sir Isaac Newton, by Kneller, and another of Edward VI. by Holbein ; and in the large state dining-room which follows this, we have a most capital one of Harry VIII. by the same extraordinary artist,—who could produce—and in fact has produced in the instance before us—the most admirable force and spiritedness of general effect, not only in spite of, but by means of, an infinite minuteness of particular detail. The bluff, bold-faced, impudent, and swaggering tyrant was never represented in a more characteristic manner than in this picture of him.

Besides the pictures in this Gallery, there are many pieces of ancient sculpture ; but I cannot think them of a character to merit a particular and detailed examination. They consist chiefly of single figures, most of which have been greatly mutilated, and restored by modern hands ; and when this is the case, the whole of that interest which arises from their antiquity is lost. To attempt to restore the missing parts of a fine Greek statue, is worse than idle—it is impertinent. The merest fragment is more valuable in itself than any restoration of this kind can render it : for, however cleverly the work may be performed, so far from feeling satisfied that we see the object in the state in which the original artist left it, we feel certain that nothing can ever place it in that state. But if it cannot be in the same state, it may be in a better ?—So much the worse ! For we want to see, not what Phidias and Praxiteles did *not* produce, but what they *did*. Let us see the fragments as you find them, and we have this wish gratified to a certain extent ; but, add to them, and you *must* alter them, at all events. It is on this principle that the Elgin Marbles, and the Venus Victrix, are the most interesting and affecting pieces of sculpture in the world. If another Phidias were to arise among us, and attempt to restore them to what even he should deem their pristine state, he would utterly destroy their value. Let him try to rival them, if he pleased ; (which he could not do, however, in *our* days, though he were twenty Phidiases :) but let him not touch and tamper with them.

There is one piece of sculpture in the collection at Petworth that struck me as being exceedingly valuable and fine. It is a group of Pan and a young Apollo ; the latter with a set of pipes in his hand, as if learning to play. This group, in some respects, resembles Annibal Caracci's noble picture, on a similar subject, called Silenus and Apollo. The *graceful awkwardness* of the youthful god is very happily conceived, and executed with great truth and spirit.

---

## LINES TO SPAIN.

Fair Land, of whose romantic bowers
　The Arab in his desert dreams,
Where chiefless halls and Moorish towers
　Hang mouldering o'er thy silent streams ;
By them seen rolling to the sea
　In many a bright and varied maze,
　As they have view'd the tide of days
　　Lapse down into eternity !
No more upon their summits hoar
　War's standard towers sublime ;
Where battle's pennon stream'd of yore,
　Waves thy green banner, Time !
Of thraldom banish'd from the land,
　Proud monuments—those voiceless domes,
And later wrecks like rivals stand,
　Oppression's graves, and Freedom's homes.

There Ebro's waters as they flow
Steal on the ear like voice of woe,
As if the scenes that tinged its flood
So silvery bright with hues of blood
   Dwelt there for evermore !—
As if the shades of perish'd hosts,
   That imaged in its bosom lay,
Like the pale forms of Stygian ghosts,
   When Zaragoza pass'd away—
When round her shatter'd walls sat down
The legions of the Iron Crown,
   Still haunted its sweet shore.
Few years have pass'd with years that be
Beyond the hills—beyond the sea,
   The earth and ocean o'er,
Since her pale ruins told too well,
How long she fought—how late she fell ;
When the last thunders peal'd her knell,
And thrice ten thousand souls' farewell
   Her passing breezes bore.
Her's is a tale that cannot die,
   Eternal as the day and night ;
It shall be heard when men shall sigh
   In hopelessness to guess her site.

Vain would this feeble strain essay
Thy forms of beauty to pourtray ;
To speak of eyes beneath whose light
The bosom heaves, as heaves the breast
Of ocean to the Queen of Night,
   When winds have wander'd to their rest,—
Beneath whose beams the heart doth beat
   Offering the incense of its sighs,
In days of old as music sweet
From Memnon's statue rose to greet
   The day-star in the skies.

Go—with thy pencil try to trace
   In hues of earth the light of Heaven,
   But deem not to thine art is given
The gleams of soul on beauty's face
With brightest tints of earth to paint—
   Those lights of feeling undefined,
So softly—beautifully blent
   Into a rainbow of the mind.
Oh! may thy foes be as the rack
   Before the rising tempest's sway !
Thy sons—the whirlwind at their back
   To scourge them from thy clime away !
Be silent, vale and orange-grove,
Long, long the peaceful haunts of love !
When day is in its ocean grave,
   And fast the pale-grey twilight fades,
And starlight trembles on the wave,
   Be heard thy pensive serenades
That steal on beauty's bower of rest,
   Soft as the melody that flow'd
Down Eden's steeps—when in the West
   Love's star in lonely brightness flow'd,
   And man held converse with his God !     G. M.

## TABLE TALK.  NO. VII.

### On Londoners and Country People.

I do not agree with Mr. Blackwood in his definition of the word *Cockney*. He means by it a person who has happened at any time to live in London, and who is not a Tory—I mean by it, a person who has never lived out of London, and who has got all his ideas from it.

The true Cockney has never travelled beyond the purlieus of the Metropolis, either in the body or the spirit. Primrose-hill is the Ultima Thule of his most romantic desires; Greenwich Park stands him in stead of the Vales of Arcady. Time and space are lost to him. He is confined to one spot, and to the present moment. He sees every thing near, superficial, little, in hasty succession. The world turns round, and his head with it, like a roundabout at a fair, till he becomes stunned and giddy with the motion. Figures glide by as in a *camera obscura*. There is a glare, a perpetual hubbub, a noise, a crowd about him; he sees and hears a vast number of things, and knows nothing. He is pert, raw, ignorant, conceited, ridiculous, shallow, contemptible. His senses keep him alive; and he knows, inquires, and cares for nothing farther. He meets the Lord Mayor's coach, and without ceremony treats himself to an imaginary ride in it. He notices the people going to court or to a city-feast, and is quite satisfied with the show. He takes the wall of a Lord, and fancies himself as good as he. He sees an infinite quantity of people pass along the street, and thinks there is no such thing as life or a knowledge of character to be found out of London. " Beyond Hyde Park all is a desert to him." He despises the country, because he is ignorant of it, and the town, because he is familiar with it. He is as well acquainted with St. Paul's as if he had built it, and talks of Westminster Abbey and Poets' Corner with great indifference. The King, the House of Lords and Commons are his very good friends. He knows the members for Westminster or the City by sight, and bows to the Sheriffs or the Sheriffs' men. He is hand and glove with the Chairman of some Committee. He is, in short, a great man by proxy, and comes so often in contact with fine persons and things, that he rubs off a little of the gilding, and is surcharged with a sort of second-hand, vapid, tingling, troublesome self-importance. His personal vanity is thus continually flattered and perked up into ridiculous self-complacency, while his imagination is jaded and impaired by daily misuse. Every thing is vulgarised in his mind. Nothing dwells long enough on it to produce an interest; nothing is contemplated sufficiently at a distance to excite curiosity or wonder. *Your true Cockney is your only true leveller.* Let him be as low as he will, he fancies he is as good as any body else. He has no respect for himself, and still less (if possible) for you. He cares little about his own advantages, if he can only make a jest at yours. Every feeling comes to him through a medium of levity and impertinence; nor does he like to have this habit of mind disturbed by being brought into collision with any thing serious or respectable. He despairs (in such a crowd of competitors) of distinguishing himself, but laughs heartily at the idea of being able to trip up the heels of other people's pretensions. A Cockney feels no gratitude. This is a first principle with him. He regards any obligation you confer upon him as a species of imposition, a ludicrous assumption of fancied superiority. He talks about every thing, for he has heard something about it; and understanding nothing of the matter, concludes he has as good a right as you. He is a politician; for he has seen the Parliament House: he is a critic; because he knows the principal actors by sight—has a taste for music, because he belongs to a glee-club at the West End; and is gallant, in virtue of sometimes frequenting the lobbies at half-price. A mere Londoner, in fact, from the opportunities he has of knowing something of a number of objects (and those striking ones) fancies himself a sort of privileged person; remains satisfied with the assumption of merits, so much the more unquestionable as they are not his own; and from being dazzled with noise, show, and appearances, is less capable of giving a real opinion, or entering into any subject than the meanest peasant. There are greater lawyers, orators, painters, philosophers, players in London, than in any other part of the United Kingdom: he is a Londoner, and therefore it would be strange if he did not know more of law, eloquence, art, philosophy, acting, than any one without his local advantages, and who is merely from the country. This is a *non sequitur;* and it constantly appears so when put to the test.

A real Cockney is the poorest creature in the world, the most literal, the most mechanical, and yet he too lives in a world of romance—a fairy-land of his own. He is a citizen of London; and this abstraction leads his imagination the finest dance in the world. London is the first city on the habitable globe; and therefore he must be superior to every one who lives out of it. There are more people in London than any where else; and though a dwarf in stature, his person swells out and expands into *ideal* importance and borrowed magnitude. He resides in a garret or in a two pair of stairs' back room; yet he talks of the magnificence of London, and gives himself airs of consequence upon it, as if all the houses in Portman or in Grosvenor Square were his by right or in reversion. " He is owner of all he surveys." The Monument, the Tower of London, St. James's Palace, the Mansion House, White-Hall, are part and parcel of his being. Let us suppose him to be a lawyer's clerk at half-a-guinea a week: but he knows the Inns of Court, the Temple Gardens, and Gray's-Inn Passage, sees the lawyers in their wigs walking up and down Chancery Lane, and has advanced within half-a-dozen yards of the Chancellor's chair:—who can doubt that he understands (by implication) every point of law (however intricate) better than the most expert country practitioner? He is a shopman, and nailed all day behind the counter: but he sees hundreds and thousands of gay, well-dressed people pass—an endless phantasmagoria—and enjoys their liberty and gaudy fluttering pride. He is a footman—but he rides behind beauty, through a crowd of carriages, and visits a thousand shops. Is he a tailor? The stigma on his profession is lost in the elegance of the patterns he provides, and of the persons he adorns; and he is something very different from a mere country botcher. Nay, the very scavenger and nightman thinks the dirt in the street has something precious in it, and his employment is solemn, silent, sacred, peculiar to London! A *barker* in Monmouth Street, a slop-seller in Ratcliffe-Highway, a tapster at a night cellar, a beggar in St.

Giles's, a drab in Fleet-Ditch, live in the eyes of millions, and eke out a dreary, wretched, scanty, or loathsome existence from the gorgeous, busy, glowing scene around them.   It is a common saying among such persons that "they had rather be hanged in London than die a natural death out of it any where else"—Such is the force of habit and imagination.   Even the eye of childhood is dazzled and delighted with the polished splendour of the jewellers' shops, the neatness of the turnery ware, the festoons of artificial flowers, the confectionery, the chemists' shops, the lamps, the horses, the carriages, the sedan-chairs : to this was formerly added a set of traditional associations—Whittington and his Cat, Guy Faux and the Gunpowder Treason, the Fire and the Plague of London, and the Heads of the Scotch Rebels that were stuck on Temple Bar in 1745.   These have vanished, and in their stead the curious and romantic eye must be content to pore in Pennant for the scite of old London-Wall, or to peruse the sentimental mile-stone that marks the distance to the place " where Hicks's Hall formerly stood!"

The *Cockney* lives in a go-cart of local prejudices and positive illusions ; and when he is turned out of it, he hardly knows how to stand or move.   He ventures through Hyde Park Corner, as a cat crosses a gutter.   The trees pass by the coach very oddly.   The country has a strange blank appearance.   It is not lined with houses all the way, like London.   He comes to places he never saw or heard of.   He finds the world is bigger than he thought it.   He might have dropped from the moon, for any thing he knows of the matter.   He is mightily disposed to laugh, but is half afraid of making some blunder.   Between sheepishness and conceit, he is in a very ludicrous situation.   He finds that the people walk on two legs, and wonders to hear them talk a dialect so different from his own.   He perceives London fashions have got down into the country before him, and that some of the better sort are dressed as well as he is.   A drove of pigs or cattle stopping the road is a very troublesome interruption.   A crow in a field, a magpie in a hedge, are to him very odd animals—he can't tell what to make of them, or how they live.   He does not altogether like the accommodations at the inns—it is not what he has been used to in town.   He begins to be communicative—says he was " born within the sound of Bow-bell," and attempts some jokes, at which nobody laughs.   He asks the coachman a question, to which he receives no answer.   All this is to him very unaccountable and unexpected.   He arrives at his journey's end; and instead of being the great man he anticipated among his friends and country relations, finds that they are barely civil to him, or make a butt of him ; have topics of their own which he is as completely ignorant of as they are indifferent to what he says, so that he is glad to get back to London again, where he meets with his favourite indulgences and associates, and fancies the whole world is occupied with what he hears and sees.

A Cockney loves a tea-garden in summer, as he loves the play or the Cider-Cellar in winter—where he sweetens the air with the fumes of tobacco, and makes it echo to the sound of his own voice.   This kind of suburban retreat is a most agreeable relief to the close and confined air of a city life.   The imagination, long pent up behind a counter or between brick walls, with noisome smells, and dingy objects, cannot bear at once to launch into the boundless expanse of the country, but "shorter excursions tries," coveting something between the two, and finding it at White-conduit House, or the Rosemary Branch, or Bagnigge Wells. The landlady is seen at a bow-window in near perspective, with punch-bowls and lemons disposed orderly around—the lime-trees or poplars wave overhead to "catch the breezy air," through which, typical of the huge dense cloud that hangs over the metropolis, curls up the thin, blue, odoriferous vapour of Virginia or Oronooko—the benches are ranged in rows, the fields and hedge-rows spread out their verdure; Hampstead and Highgate are seen in the back-ground, and contain the imagination within gentle limits—here the holiday people are playing ball; here they are playing bowls—here they are quaffing ale, there sipping tea—here the loud wager is heard, there the political debate. In a sequestered nook a slender youth with purple face and drooping head, nodding over a glass of gin toddy, breathes in tender accents—"There's nought so sweet on earth as Love's young dream;" while "Rosy Ann" takes its turn, and "Scots wha hae wi' Wallace bled" is thundered forth in accents that might wake the dead. In another part sit carpers and critics, who dispute the score of the reckoning or the game, or cavil at the taste and execution of the *would-be* Brahams and Durusets. Of this latter class was Dr. Goodman, a man of other times—I mean of those of Smollett and Defoe—who was curious in opinion, obstinate in the wrong, great in little things, and inveterate in petty warfare. I vow he held me an argument once "an hour by St. Dunstan's clock," while I held an umbrella over his head (the friendly protection of which he was unwilling to quit to walk in the rain to Camberwell) to prove to me that Richard Pinch was neither a fives-player nor a pleasing singer. "Sir," said he, "I deny that Mr. Pinch plays the game. He is a cunning player, but not a good one. I grant his tricks, his little mean dirty ways, but he is not a manly antagonist. He has no hit, and no left-hand. How then can he set up for a superior player? And then as to his always striking the ball against the side-wings at Copenhagen-house, Cavanagh, sir, used to say, ' The wall was made to hit at!' I have no patience with such pitiful shifts and advantages. They are an insult upon so fine and athletic a game! And as to his setting up for a singer, it's quite ridiculous. You know, Mr. H———, that to be a really excellent singer, a man must lay claim to one of two things; in the first place, sir, he must have a naturally fine ear for music, or secondly, an early education, exclusively devoted to that study. But no one ever suspected Mr. Pinch of refined sensibility; and his education, as we all know, has been a little at large. Then again, why should he of all other things be always singing "Rosy Ann," and "Scots wha hae wi' Wallace bled," till one is sick of hearing them? It's preposterous, and I mean to tell him so. You know, I'm sure, without my hinting it, that in the first of these admired songs, the sentiment is voluptuous and tender, and in the last patriotic. Now Pinch's romance never wandered from behind his counter, and his patriotism lies in his breeches' pocket. Sir, the utmost he should aspire to would be to play upon the Jews' harp!" This story of the Jews' harp tickled some of Pinch's friends, who gave him various hints of it, which nearly drove him mad, till he discovered what it was;

for though no jest or sarcasm ever had the least effect upon him, yet he cannot bear to think that there should be any joke of this kind about him, and he not in the secret: it makes against that *knowing* character which he so much affects. Pinch is in one respect a complete specimen of a *Cockney*. He never has any thing to say, and yet is never at a loss for an answer. That is, his pertness keeps exact pace with his dulness. His friend, the Doctor, used to complain of this in good set terms.—" You can never make any thing of Mr. Pinch," he would say. " Apply the most cutting remark to him, and his only answer is, ' *The same to you, sir.*' If Shakspeare were to rise from the dead to confute him, I firmly believe it would be to no purpose. I assure you, I have found it so. I once thought indeed I had him at a disadvantage, but I was mistaken. You shall hear, sir. I had been reading the following sentiment in a modern play—' The Road to Ruin,' by the late Mr. Holcroft—' For how should the soul of Socrates inhabit the body of a stocking-weaver?' This was pat to the point (you know our friend is a hosier and haberdasher). I came full with it to keep an appointment I had with Pinch, began a game, quarrelled with him in the middle of it on purpose, went upstairs to dress, and as I was washing my hands in the slop-basin (watching my opportunity) turned coolly round and said, ' It's impossible there should be any sympathy between you and me, Mr. Pinch : for as the poet says, how should the soul of Socrates inhabit the body of a stocking-weaver?' ' Ay,' says he, ' does the poet say so? *then the same to you, sir*!' I was confounded, I gave up the attempt to conquer him in wit or argument. He would pose the Devil, sir, by his ' *The same to you, sir.*' "

We had another joke against Richard Pinch, to which the Doctor was not a party, which was, that being asked after the respectability of the *Hole in the Wall*, at the time that Randall took it, he answered quite unconsciously, " Oh! it's a very genteel place, I go there myself sometimes!" Dr. Goodman was descended by the mother's side from the poet Jago, was a private gentleman in town, and a medical dilettanti in the country, dividing his time equally between business and pleasure; had an inexhaustible flow of words, and an imperturbable vanity, and held " stout notions on the metaphysical score." He maintained the free agency of man, with the spirit of a martyr and the gaiety of a man of wit and pleasure about town—told me he had a curious tract on that subject by A. C. (Anthony Collins) which he carefully locked up in his box, lest any one should see it but himself, to the detriment of their character and morals, and put it to me whether it was not hard, on the principles of *philosophical necessity*, for a man to come to be hanged? To which I replied, " I thought it hard on any terms!" A knavish *marker*, who had listened to the dispute, laughed at this retort, and seemed to assent to the truth of it, supposing it might one day be his own case.

Mr. Smith and the Brangtons, in " Evelina," are the finest possible examples of the spirit of *Cockneyism*. I once knew a linen-draper in the City, who owned to me he did not quite like this part of Miss Burney's novel. He said, " I myself lodge in a first floor, where there are young ladies in the house : they sometimes have company, and if I am out, they ask me to lend them the use of my apartment, which I readily do out of politeness, or if it is an agreeable party, I perhaps join them. All this is so like what passes in the novel, that I fancy myself a sort of second Mr. Smith, and am not quite easy at it!" This was mentioned to the fair Authoress, and she was delighted to find that her characters were so true, that an actual person fancied himself to be one of them. The resemblance, however, was only in the externals ; and the real modesty of the individual stumbled on the likeness to a city coxcomb!

It is curious to what a degree persons, brought up in certain occupations in a great city, are shut up from a knowledge of the world, and carry their simplicity to a pitch of unheard-of extravagance. London is the only place in which the child grows completely up into the man. I have known characters of this kind, which, in the way of childish ignorance and self-pleasing delusion, exceeded any thing to be met with in Shakspeare or Ben Jonson, or the old comedy. For instance, the following may be taken as a true sketch. Imagine a person with a florid, shining complexion like a plough-boy, large staring teeth, a merry eye, his hair stuck into the fashion with curling-irons and pomatum, a slender figure, and a decent suit of black—add to which the thoughtlessness of the school-boy, the forwardness of the thriving tradesman, and the plenary consciousness of the citizen of London—and you have Mr. Dunster before you, the fishmonger in the Poultry. You shall hear how he chirps over his cups, and exults in his private opinions. " I'll play no more with you," I said, " Mr. Dunster—you are five points in the game better than I am." I had just lost three half-crown rubbers at cribbage to him, which loss of mine he presently thrust into a canvass pouch (not a silk purse) out of which he had produced just before, first a few halfpence, then half a dozen pieces of silver, then a handful of guineas, and lastly, lying *perdu* at the bottom, a fifty pound bank-note. " I'll tell you what," I said, " I should like to play you a game at marbles"—this was at a sort of Christmas party or Twelfth Night merry-making. " Marbles!" said Dunster, catching up the sound, and his eye brightening with childish glee, " What! you mean *ring-taw?*" " Yes." " I should beat you at it, to a certainty. I was one of the best in our school (it was at Clapham, Sir, the Rev. Mr. Denman's, at Clapham, was the place where I was brought up)—though there were two others there better than me. They were the best that ever were. I'll tell you, Sir, I'll give you an idea. There was a water-butt or cistern, Sir, at our school, that turned with a cock. Now suppose that brass ring that the window-curtain is fastened to, to be the cock, and that these boys were standing where we are, about twenty feet off—well, Sir, I'll tell you what I have seen them do. One of them had a favourite taw (or *alley* we used to call them)—he'd take aim at the cock of the cistern with this marble, as I may do now. Well, Sir, will you believe it ? such was his strength of knuckle and certainty of aim, he'd hit it, turn it, let the water out, and then, Sir, when the water had run out as much as it was wanted, the other boy (he'd just the same strength of knuckle, and the same certainty of eye) he'd aim at it too, be sure to hit it, turn it round, and stop the water from running out. Yes, what I tell you is very remarkable, but it's true. One of these boys was named Cock, and t'other Butler." " They might have been named Spigot and Fawcett, my dear Sir, from your account of them." " I should not mind playing you at fives neither, though I'm out of practice. I think I should beat you in a week: I was a real good one at that. A pretty game, Sir! I had the finest ball, that I suppose ever was seen. Made it myself,—I'll tell you how, Sir. You see, I put a piece of cork at the bottom, then I wound some fine worsted yarn round it, then I had to bind it round with some packthread, and then sew the case on. You'd hardly believe it, but I was the envy of the whole school for that ball. They all wanted to get it from me, but lord, Sir, I would let none of them come near it. I kept it in my waistcoat pocket all day, and at night I used to take it to bed with me and put it under my pillow. I couldn't sleep easy without it."

The same idle vein might be found in the country, but I doubt whether it would find a tongue to give it utterance. Cockneyism is a ground of native shallowness mounted with pertness and conceit. Yet with all this simplicity and extravagance in dilating on his favourite topics, Dunster is a man of spirit, of attention to business, knows how to make out and get in his bills, and is far from being henpecked. One thing is certain, that such a man must be a true Englishman and a loyal subject. He has a slight tinge of letters, with shame I confess it—has in his possession a volume of the European Magazine for the year 1761, and is an humble admirer of Tristram Shandy (particularly the story of the King of Bohemia and his Seven Castles, which is something in his own endless manner) and of Gil Blas of Santillane. Over these (the last thing before he goes to bed at night) he smokes a pipe, and meditates for an hour. After all, what is there in these harmless half-lies, these fantastic exaggerations, but a literal, prosaic, *Cockney* translation of the admired lines in Gray's Ode to Eton College :—

> "What idle progeny succeed
> To chase the rolling circle's speed
> Or urge the flying ball?"

A man shut up all his life in his shop, without any thing to interest him from one year's end to another but the cares and details of business, with scarcely any intercourse with books or opportunities for society, distracted with the buzz and glare and noise about him, turns for relief to the retrospect of his childish years; and there, through the long vista, at one bright loop-hole, leading out of the thorny mazes of the world into the clear morning light, he sees the idle fancies and gay amusements of his boyhood dancing like motes in the sunshine. Shall we blame, or should we laugh at him, if his eye glistens, and his tongue grows wanton in their praise?

None but a Scotchman would—that pragmatical sort of personage, who thinks it a folly ever to have been young, and who, instead of dallying with the frail past, bends his brows upon the future, and looks only to the *mainchance.* Forgive me, dear Dunster, if I have drawn a sketch of some of thy venial foibles, and delivered thee into the hands of these Cockneys of the North, who will fall upon thee and devour thee, like so many cannibals without a grain of salt!

If familiarity in cities breeds contempt, ignorance in the country breeds aversion and dislike. People come too much in contact in town; in other places they live too much apart, to unite cordially and easily. Our feelings, in the former case, are dissipated and exhausted by being called into constant and vain activity; in the latter, they rust and grow dead for want of use. If there is an air of levity and indifference in London manners, there is a harshness, a moroseness, and disagreeable restraint, in those of the country. We have little disposition to sympathy, when we have few persons to sympathise with : we lose the relish and capacity for social enjoyment, the seldomer we meet. A habit of sullenness, coldness, and misanthropy, grows upon us. If we look for hospitality and a cheerful welcome in country places, it must be in those where the arrival of a stranger is an event, the recurrence of which need not be greatly apprehended, or it must be on rare occasions, on " some high festival of once a year." Then indeed the stream of hospitality, so long dammed up, may flow without stint for a short season; or a stranger may be expected with the same sort of eager impatience as a caravan of wild beasts, or any other natural curiosity, that excites our wonder and fills up the craving of the mind after novelty. By degrees, however, even this last principle loses its effect : books, newspapers, whatever carries us out of ourselves into a world of which we see and know nothing, becomes distasteful, repulsive ; and we turn away with indifference or disgust from every thing that disturbs our lethargic animal existence, or takes off our attention from our petty local interests and pursuits. Man, left long to himself, is no better than a mere clod ; or his activity, for want of some other vent, preys upon himself, or is directed to splenetic, peevish dislikes, or vexatious, harassing persecution of others. I once drew a picture of a country life : it was a portrait of a particular place, a caricature if you will, but, with certain allowances, I fear it was too like in the individual instance, and that it would hold too generally true. *See* ROUND TABLE, vol. ii. p. 116.

If these, then, are the faults and vices of the inhabitants of town or of the country, where should a man go to live, so as to escape from them ? I answer, that in the country we have the society of the groves, the fields, the brooks, and in London a man may keep to himself, or choose his company as he pleases.

It appears to me that there is an amiable mixture of these two opposite characters in a person who chances to have passed his youth in London, and who has retired into the country for the rest of his life. We may find in such a one a social polish, a pastoral simplicity. He rusticates agreeably, and vegetates with a degree of sentiment. He comes to the next post-town to see for letters, watches the coaches as they pass, and eyes the passengers with a look of familiar curiosity, thinking that he too was a gay fellow in his time. He turns his horse's head down the narrow lane that leads homewards, puts on an old coat to save his wardrobe, and fills his glass nearer to the brim. As he lifts the purple juice to his lips and to his eye, and in the dim solitude that hems him round, thinks of the glowing line—

" This bottle's the sun of our table "—

another sun rises upon his imagination ; the sun of his youth, the blaze of vanity, the glitter of the metropolis, " glares round his soul, and mocks his closing eye-lids." The distant roar of coaches is in his ears—the pit stare upon him with a thousand eyes—Mrs. Siddons, Bannister, King, are before him—he starts as from a dream, and swears he will to London ; but the expense, the length of way, deters him, and he rises the next morning to trace the footsteps of the hare that has brushed the dew-drops from the lawn, or to attend a meeting of Magistrates! Mr. Justice Shallow answered in some sort to this description of a retired Cockney and indigenous country-gentleman. He "knew the Inns of Court, where they would talk of mad Shallow yet, and where the bona robas were, and had them at commandment: ay, and had heard the chimes at midnight!"

It is a strange state of society (such as that in London) where a man does not know his next-door neighbour, and where the feelings (one would think) must recoil upon themselves, and either fester or become obtuse. Mr. Wordsworth, in the preface to his poem of the "Excursion," represents men in cities as so many wild beasts or evil spirits, shut up in cells of ignorance, without natural affections, and barricadoed down in sensuality and selfishness. The nerve of humanity is bound up, according to him: the circulation of the blood stagnates. And it would be so, if men were merely cut off from intercourse with their immediate neighbours, and did not meet together generally and more at large. But man in London becomes, as Mr. Burke has it, a sort of "public creature." He lives in the eye of the world, and the world in his. If he witnesses less of the details of private life, he has better opportunities of observing its larger masses and varied movements. He sees the stream of human life pouring along the streets—its comforts and embellishments piled up in the shops—the houses are proofs of the industry, the public buildings of the art and magnificence of man; while the public amusements and places of resort are a centre and support for social feeling. A playhouse alone is a school of humanity, where all eyes are fixed on the same gay or solemn scene, where smiles or tears are spread from face to face, and where a thousand hearts beat in unison! Look at the company in a country theatre (in comparison), and see the coldness, the sullenness, the want of sympathy, and the way in which they turn round to scan and scrutinize one another. In London there is a *public;* and each man is part of it. We are gregarious, and affect the kind. We have a sort of abstract existence; and a community of ideas and knowledge (rather than local proximity) is the bond of society and good-fellowship. This is one great cause of the tone of political feeling in large and populous cities. There is here a visible body-politic, a type and image of that huge Leviathan the State. We comprehend that vast denomination, the *People,* of which we see a tenth part daily moving before us; and by having our imaginations emancipated from petty interests and personal dependence, we learn to venerate ourselves as men, and to respect the rights of human nature. Therefore it is that the citizens and freemen of London and Westminster are patriots by prescription, philosophers and politicians by the right of their birth-place. In the country, men are no better than a herd of cattle or scattered deer. They have no idea but of individuals, none of rights or principles—and a king, as the greatest individual, is the highest idea they can form. He is "a species alone," and as superior to any single peasant, as the latter is to the peasant's dog, or to a crow flying over his head. In London the king is but as one to a million (numerically speaking), is seldom seen, and then distinguished only from others by the superior graces of his person. A country 'squire or a lord of the manor is a greater man in his village or hundred!

### THE NAPOLEON MEMOIRS.[*]

In a former number, in taking a review of "Las Cases' Journal," we slightly glanced at the first part of these Memoirs, of which important production four parts are now published—two dictated to General Gourgaud, and more immediately and strictly historical—two more dictated to the Count de Montholon, entitled "Historical Miscellanies," containing notes and observations upon several modern French publications which reached Napoleon at St. Helena, and gave false or imperfect views of his personal conduct, or of the political and military events of his reign.

When Napoleon, having ceased in 1814 to be Emperor of France, was about to depart for the Island of Elba, his farewell promise to the remnant of his old companions in arms who witnessed that extremity of his fortune, was, that he would prepare a record of the great transactions they had achieved together. The events that so rapidly ensued interfered with the design,—but the final and not inglorious struggle to be once again the foremost man of the world having failed, and he himself doomed to a sentence that extinguished every hope, he no longer deferred its execution. On the passage to St. Helena he commenced the present work, and was constantly occupied upon it during the six years that he continued to hold out against the miseries of exile, and the climate, and the governor of St. Helena. The quantity of matter condensed in these volumes is so great, and the subjects so various, that it would be quite impossible, in such a notice as the present, to give any thing like a perfect analysis of their contents. A large space is dedicated to accounts of battles, with minute and elaborate critical remarks upon military evolutions, which we profess our incompetency to appreciate, or at all times to follow—though, doubtless, this portion of the work will be deemed by many to be the most interesting and instructive ; we shall therefore confine our extracts and observations to such passages as serve to illustrate the character and policy of this extraordinary man, who, by the force of his genius and ambition, raised himself (*he* repeatedly asserts " without a crime") from the station of a military adventurer to be the imperial chief, the creator and director of the most formidable combination of political resources that modern Europe has seen confederated against the stability of hostile thrones and institutions.

One of the first great events recorded in these volumes is the Revolution which placed Napoleon at the head of the French government—the celebrated scene of the 18th and 19th Brumaire. It is given in that minute detail which always imparts so much light and interest to the narrative of a great transaction.

He was in Egypt when information of the increasing inefficiency and unpopularity of the existing government reached him. The men whom the accidents of the Revolution had called to rule the affairs of France were distrustful of each other, and had lost all public confidence and respect. The French people felt that they were misgoverned, and were prepared by that impression, and by their recent familiarity with innovations, for any change that should promise a more effectual consolidation and management of the national resources. Under these

---

[*] Memoirs of the History of France during the Reign of Napoleon, dictated by the Emperor at St. Helena, &c. 2 Livraisons, consisting of 4 volumes.

circumstances Napoleon, confiding in his talents and in the influence of his fame, formed the hardy project of crushing the factions that agitated the country, and of raising himself upon their ruins to the summit of his ambition. He consigned the command of the Egyptian expedition to Kleber, and repaired to France. His unexpected arrival was hailed with demonstrations of general joy. By the time he had reached the capital, he had seen enough to satisfy him that what he projected might be achieved.

" The nature of past events had informed him of the general condition of France, and the intelligence that he had procured on the road (from Frejus to Paris) had made him intimately acquainted with all that he required to know. His resolution was taken. What he had not even wished to attempt upon his return from Italy, he was now determined to effect. His contempt for the government of the Directory, and for the political intriguers of the day, was extreme. Resolved to assume the chief control in the state, and to restore to France her days of glory, by giving an energetic impulse to public measures, it was for the execution of this project that he had come from Egypt ; and all that he had just witnessed in the interior of France had only served to confirm his determination."

In the prosecution of this bold design he proceeded with caution. He went rarely into public—he admitted the visits of none but a few select friends, with whom he conferred upon the relative strength of the different parties, and the respective proposals that were tendered to him by each. Bernadotte, Augereau, and other leaders of the Ja-cobins, offered, on certain conditions, to place him at the head of a military dictatorship ;—a more moderate party, consisting of Regnier, Boulay, &c. were for committing to him the direction of the govern-ment as it then stood. The Directory was divided—Siéyes was for abolishing the present Constitution (La Constitution de l'an III.) and substituting one that he had framed. His views were supported by the Director Roger-Ducos and the majority of the Council of Ancients. The remaining three Directors, Barras, Moulins, and Gohier, proposed that Bonaparte should resume the command of the army of Italy. The two latter were sincere ; but Barras, who was then intriguing for the restoration of the Bourbons, thought of nothing but retaining his present ascendancy. After deliberating over these several proposals, Napoleon was finally hesitating between those of Siéyes and Barras, when the following occurrence betrayed the duplicity of the latter :—

" On the 8th Brumaire (October 30th) Napoleon dined with Barras. The company was small. In the course of conversation after dinner, ' The Re-public,' said the Director, ' is going to ruin—the present system will never do, —the government is without energy—we must have a change, and appoint Hedouville President of the Republic. With regard to you, General, your intention is to repair to the army ; and as for myself, sick, desponding, and exhausted as I am, I am good for nothing but to retire to a private station.' Napoleon looked at him intently, without uttering a word—Barras sunk his eyes and was confounded :—the conversation ended there. General Hedou-ville was a man of extreme mediocrity. Barras said not what he thought ; his countenance betrayed his secret.

" This conversation was decisive. A few moments after, Napoleon went to Siéyes. He informed him that for ten days past the several parties had been addressing themselves to him—that he had resolved to proceed in concert with him (Siéyes) and the majority of the Council of Ancients, and that he now came to give him a positive assurance of this intention. It was agreed that the change could be effected between the 15th and 20th Brumaire."

The sequel is equally curious and characteristic of the men and the times :—

" When Napoleon returned home, Talleyrand, Fouché, Rœderer, and Réal, were there. He told them with entire simplicity, and without any movement of countenance that could betray his own opinion, of what Barras had just been saying. Réal and Fouché, who were attached to that director, felt at once all the impolicy of his dissimulation, and repaired to his house to remonstrate with him. About eight o'clock on the following morning, Barras came to Napoleon, who had not yet risen—he insisted upon seeing him, entered, and said that he feared his meaning had been misunderstood the night before—that Napoleon alone could save the Republic—that he came to place himself at his disposal—to do whatever Napoleon should desire, and act any part that should be assigned him—and earnestly entreated to have an assurance that if he had any project in view, he would count upon Barras. But Napoleon had already taken his part: he answered that he desired nothing—that he was fatigued and indisposed—that after the arid climate of Arabia, he found his frame affected by the moist atmosphere of Paris, and by similar common-places he put an end to the interview."

. Such were some of the petty matters that preceded and accelerated the momentous crisis that was at hand. The remaining particulars are given with the minute fidelity of an historian relating what he had actually witnessed ;*—but we must refer our readers to the work itself. The final result was, that the plans which Napoleon, in concert with Siéyes, adopted, completely succeeded. The Directory was abolished. Napoleon, Siéyes, and Roger-Ducos were named provisional Consuls until a new Constitution should be framed. The new Constitution, from which however the subtleties contained in the portfolio of Siéyes were as much as possible excluded, was proclaimed on the 24th of the following December ; and Napoleon, as first Consul of the French Republic, took his place among the sovereigns of Europe.—As such, his character and actions now form one of the most interesting topics in the range of historical investigation.

When a deputation from the town of Capua waited upon Terentius Varro, with an address of condolence upon the defeat at Cannæ, the beaten Consul, in his reply, implored them to be firm in their fidelity to Rome, and among other arguments, did not omit to assure them that Hannibal was altogether a most fiendlike personage—that he was in the habit of building bridges and mounds of human bodies, and had actually initiated his savage troops in the practice of feeding upon human flesh. During the fourteen years of Napoleon's formidable ascendancy, it was a standing point of policy to cheer the efforts of his enemies by similar calumnies: in proportion as we became alarmed, we became abusive ; every new victory, or master-stroke of policy on

---

. * The day before the final blow was struck at St. Cloud, to which the sitting of the Legislative Chambers had been transferred by a decree of the 18th Brumaire, Augereau, who was secretly opposed to Napoleon, presented himself at the Tuileries where the troops were passing in review ; Napoleon advised him to absent himself from St. Cloud on the following day—to keep quiet, and not cancel the services he had already rendered his country, for that no effort could counteract the intended movement. Augereau assured him of his entire devotion, and his desire to march under his orders. " Eh bien, General," said he, " est-ce que vous ne comptez pas toujours sur votre petit Augereau !" Next day, however, when a rumour reached Paris of the proceedings at St. Cloud, le petit Augereau posted thither, and imagining from the tumultuary scene there that Napoleon was lost, approached him and observed, " Eh bien ! vous voici dans une jolie position !"

his part, was the signal for fresh levies of libels upon ours; and to such an extreme of contumely had we arrived, and so popular had this mode of carrying on the war become, that ten years ago every man who wished to be considered a friend to his king and country, felt bound to admit that Bonaparte was a monster in human shape—that he poisoned his soldiers, murdered his prisoners, betrayed his friends, was brutally insulting to subjugated kings and queens—in a word, that he was so irretrievably and inordinately vicious, that, for example-sake, no well-conducted person should ever mention his name without a thrill of execration. But he has since fallen, and is now in his grave, and his character and actions may at length be spoken of with something like the impartiality which the future historian will not refuse the most extraordinary being of the modern world.

Napoleon's talents have been seldom questioned. They were of so high and rare an order, that finding no one of his own age with whom to compare him, we must resort to the few great names of the human race—Hannibal, Alexander, Cæsar, Charlemagne—conquerors, legislators, founders of empire—men of universal renown. The conspicuous qualities of his mind were energy and sagacity—intellectual hardihood to conceive vast designs, and boundless fertility in creating and applying the means to attain them. He was equally eminent in war and policy; and his achievements in both were marked by far less of accident and adventurous experiment than was once imagined. He went into battle with an assurance of success founded upon previous, and for the most part unerring calculations. This was the secret of his confidence in his fortune. He compared, as if it were an abstract scientific question, the physical and moral forces of his troops with those arrayed against him, and where he found the former preponderate, gave the word to march and conquer. The most unskilled in military science may collect this from the general tenor of the volumes before us. Throughout, when discussing the various battles he had won, he appears to claim credit, not so much for having been actually victorious when once the conflict had begun, as for having by previous arrangements and combinations brought the certain means of victory to the field. He was persuaded, and could not afterwards divest himself of the conviction, that he had done this at Waterloo; and hence his expression, so much ridiculed by those who mistake its real import, that he, and not Wellington, *ought* to have gained the day.

. The same qualities of mind, the same preparatory forethought in speculation, and energy in action, and for a long time the same success, distinguished him as a statesman. His boldness here, as in the field, was the result of profound calculations, through which none but the most penetrating and combining intellect could have passed. His saying was, that in all his great measures, "he marched at the head of large masses of opinion." This military allusion illustrates the genius of his civil policy. In all his projects, whether foreign or domestic, he marshalled the passions and opinions that sided with him, computed their numerical and moral force, and where he found they must prevail, advanced at the charge-step to his object. In a word, he manoeuvred the national mind as he would a great army; and having had the art of persuading the citizen, as well as the soldier, that he was leading him on to glory, he exacted alike from both, and met with the same measure of discipline and subordination.

Under Napoleon's government there was a suspension of political liberty in France. His maxim was that the few should plan, and the many acquiesce and execute. He established and encouraged free discussion in the cabinet, but he discountenanced all popular interference in state measures, as he would a spirit of mutinous dictation in the camp. We are no advocates for this mode of rule; but in speaking of the despotism of Napoleon as a personal crime, we should in fairness remember that he was accountable for it to his subjects and not his enemies, and that they were content to overlook its rigour for the many benefits it imparted. He asserts that his government was "eminently popular." He surely did much to make it so. He rescued France from the sway of the demagogue. He consolidated the national energies, and forced them into channels that led to national objects. He made talent the surest road to distinction. He was the patrón of unbounded religious toleration. Under his reign no Frenchman could be molested and degraded upon the fantastic doctrine, that certain dogmas had certain remote and influential tendencies which should disqualify for the enjoyment of civil rights. He framed a comprehensive and intelligible code of laws (the greatest want of modern nations), in which he justly gloried as a lasting monument of his concern for the public good. These and his other great acts of general utility attached the French to his government, despotic as it was, and rendered them the willing instruments of his schemes of aggrandizement, in the products of which they were themselves to share.

We have stopped to offer these remarks, because we feel that it is not to the glory of England to depreciate this extraordinary man. Her real glory consists in having withstood the shock of his genius—in having so long resisted his imperial pretensions and asserted her own against a confederacy of hostile powers, such as no people uninspired by the pride and energy of freedom could have braved.

We proceed to extract some farther specimens of these Memoirs. The general contents, independently of the martial details, embrace the multiplied objects of his ambitious policy, which may be summarily described to have been, to render France the arbitress, and Paris the capital of the world; to consolidate Italy into a separate kingdom; to transfer the seat of the Papal power to the metropolis of France; to subjugate the several Continental states into obedience, or terrify them into an alliance; and, above all, to break the naval and commercial, and thereby the political influence of England in the affairs of Europe. Upon the subject of these vast designs, the present work supplies invaluable materials for the future historian; but their very importance precludes our entering upon them. Any one of even the subordinate topics connected with them would more than exhaust our limits. We shall, therefore, go on according to our original intention (and without any attempt at regular order) to take up such passages as have interested us by their novelty, and are capable of being compressed into our remaining space.

The following may be adduced as a characteristic example of Napoleon's originality and skill as a political intriguer. In 1800 it was the great object of France to detach the Emperor Paul from the alliance of England and Austria. He was at that time known to be deeply chagrined by the losses his army had sustained in Switzerland, and to be greatly dissatisfied with the conduct of his allies. Napoleon seized the occasion of turning those feelings to account, and, knowing his vulnerable point to be on the side of his heroical pretensions, he directed his operations against that quarter. A little after the battle of Marengo he had flattered the vanity of Paul by sending him the sword which Leo the Tenth had presented to Ile-Adam, as the reward of his bravery in defending Rhodes against the Infidels; but an opportunity now offered of making a more brilliant and substantial present. Ten thousand Russian soldiers were prisoners of France. Napoleon proposed to England and Austria to exchange them for an equal number of Frenchmen. The offer, as no doubt expected, was refused. Napoleon exclaimed against the refusal as an act of narrow-minded injustice, and declared that, as a proof of the high estimation in which he held such brave soldiers, he would restore them without ransom to the Czar. The Russian officers accordingly received their swords, and all the prisoners were collected at Aix-la-Chapelle, where they were newly clothed and equipped in the most splendid style that the manufactures of France could effect. A Russian general was appointed to organize them into battalions and regiments. The ardent and impetuous Paul could not hold out against this. He forthwith despatched a courier to Napoleon with the following singular letter :—

"Citizen First Consul,—I do not write to you in order to enter into discussions upon the rights of men or of citizens. Every country governs itself according to its own discretion. Wherever I see at the head of a country a man who knows how to govern and fight, my heart yearns towards him. I write to make you acquainted with my dissatisfaction towards England, who violates every right of nations, and is never guided but by her selfishness and interest. I wish to unite with you for the purpose of putting an end to the injustice of that government."

Shortly after the proposed treaty of alliance was formally executed.

In the account of Egypt, a portion of the work that will probably have most attractions for general readers, we have a short digression upon polygamy, and a proposed explanation of that institution different from those of preceding speculators.

"These countries (Africa and Asia) being inhabited by men of various colours, polygamy is the sole means of preventing mutual persecution. In order that the blacks should not be at war with the whites, and the whites with the blacks, and the copper-coloured with both, their legislators have judged it expedient to make them all members of one family, and thus to counteract that tendency in man to hate whatever is not himself. Mahomet considered that four wives were sufficient to attain this object, inasmuch as each man could have one white, one black, one copper-coloured, and one of some other colour. Doubtless it was also in the spirit of a sensual creed to favour the passions of its votaries ; and in this respect policy and the Prophet have been able to act in concord."

The doctrine of Montesquieu is more obvious and satisfactory. In warm climates where this usage has almost exclusively prevailed, female attractions pass rapidly away. A Nourmahaul or Fatima of those regions, however adorable in her teens, becomes to outward appearance, quite elderly at the age of twenty, and a wrinkled matron at twenty-five. But Selim, who is only three or four years older at the period of this catastrophe, is still in the prime of youth and Oriental sensibility, and in spite of his eternal vows, finds his affections wandering from the object of his first attachment. He is once more *devoré du besoin d'aimer*, and if the laws were so unreasonable as to denounce his second dream of connubial felicity, the danger, or rather the certainty would be, that like the fashionable husband of every clime and age, he would defy the law and set up a separate establishment, to the great scandal of the neighbourhood, the inextinguishable indignation of his neglected partner, and followed in due course by everlasting appeals to the Cadi on the subject of their domestic jars. The legislators of the East, therefore, perceiving the consequences of prohibiting an usage originally founded upon the caducity of female charms, and which would inevitably continue in one form or another, whether they sanctioned it or not, have permitted polygamy; under the restriction, perhaps, in the first instance, of not allowing a second wife until the first was on the wane;—but as laws made for the convenience of the rich are liberally construed, the transition was easy from an old and a young wife to two simultaneous young ones, and so on to as many as the husband could afford to support. But although we take Napoleon's conjectures on this subject to be incorrect, there is no want of his accustomed sagacity and boldness in the application that he would make of his doctrine. Speaking in another place of the condition of St. Domingo, he says,

"The question of the liberty of the Blacks is one full of complication and difficulty. In Africa and Asia it has been resolved, but by the means of polygamy. There the blacks and whites form part of the same family—the head of the family having wives of various colours, all the children are brothers, are reared in the same cradle, bear the same name, and sit at the same table. Would it then be impossible to authorize polygamy in our islands, restricting the number of wives to two, a white and a black? The First Consul had some conferences with theologians, in order to prepare the way for this important measure. Polygamy prevailed among the patriarchs in the first ages of Christianity—the Church tolerated a species of concubinage, of which the effect was the same. The Pope, the council have the means of authorising a similar institution, since its object would be to conciliate and produce social harmony, and not to extend the indulgence of the senses. The effects of these marriages would have been limited to the colonies, and suitable measures would have been taken to prevent their producing any disorder in the present state of our society."

Some of our female readers who, probably know little of Napoleon's style of thinking and writing except from his bulletins and other public documents, may wish to see how he treats subjects of a lighter kind:—and as one of the crimes imputed to him during the war, was a barbarous contempt of all gallant feeling and observance towards the sex, we shall select a passage, in which he recalls, after a lapse of many years, the impressions made upon him by the ladies of Egypt. The description is very much in the minute and caressing manner of Rousseau.

"The General-in-chief had numerous occasions of observing some of the most distinguished women of the country to whom he granted audiences. They were either the widows of Beys or Katchefs, or their wives who came during their absence, to implore his protection. The richness of their dress, their elevated deportment, their little soft hands, their fine eyes, their noble and graceful carriage, and their extremely elegant manners, denoted that they were of a class and an education above the vulgar. They always commenced by kissing the hand of the Sultan Kebir*, which they afterwards raised to their forehead, and then to their breast; many of them expressed their wishes with the most perfect grace, and in an enchanting tone of voice, and displayed all the talent and the softness of the most accomplished Europeans.

* The Great Sultan—the title by which Napoleon was designated by the Arabs.

The propriety of their demeanour and the modesty of their attire added to their attractions, and the imagination took pleasure in forming conjectures respecting the charms of which they would not allow so much as a glimpse."

A little farther on he gives an instance of their propensity to assert the rights of women, even to petitioning himself for a redress of connubial grievances ; and considering what a frightful despot he was, he appears from his manner of relating the anecdote, to have regarded the stirrings of natural ambition in the bosoms of these aspiring gipsies with singular indulgence.

"The women have their privileges :—there are some things which their husbands cannot refuse them without being considered barbarians, monsters, without causing a general outcry against them ; such, for example, is the right of going to the bath. It is at the vapour-baths that the women assemble ; it is there that all sorts of intrigues, political and other, are planned ; it is there that marriages are settled. General Menou, who had married a female of Rosetta, treated her after the French manner : he led her by the hand into the dinner-room—the best place at table—the most delicate morsels were for her ; if her handkerchief chanced to drop, he was on the alert to pick it up. As soon as she related these particulars in the bath of Rosetta, all the others began to entertain hopes of a general change of manners, and signed a petition to the Sultan Kebir, that their husbands should be made to treat them in the same way†."

While we are upon the subject of Napoleon's demeanour to women, we cannot refrain from inserting an example that we have met for the first time in these volumes, and which, upon higher grounds than those of courtesy, must be considered as most creditable to his memory. His public despatch from Cairo, (August 19, 1798,) announces to the Executive Directory the defeat of the French fleet at Aboukir—a disaster which he attributes to Admiral Brueys, who, in violation of repeated orders, neglected to remove his squadron from that exposed situation. On the same day he writes as follows to the widow of Brueys.

"Cairo, 3d Fructidor, year VI. (19 Aug. 1798.)

"Your husband has been killed by a cannon-ball while he was fighting

---

* We throw together two or three shorter anecdotes that occur in this portion of the work.

Napoleon gave frequent dinners to the Sheiks. Athough our customs were so different from theirs, they found chairs, and knives and forks extremely convenient. At the conclusion of one of these dinners, he one day asked the Sheik El-Mondi, " For the six months that I have been among you, what is the most useful thing I have taught you ?" " The most useful thing you have taught me," replied the Sheik, half-serious, half-laughing, " is to drink at dinner."—The custom of the Arabs is not to drink until the repast is over.

At a dinner given to the General-in-chief by the Sheik El-Fayoum, the subject of conversation was the Koran. " It comprises all human knowledge," said the Sheiks.—Napoleon asked, " Does it contain the art of casting cannons, and making gunpowder ?" " Yes," they replied, " but you must know how to read it ;" a scholastic distinction that has been more or less employed by every religion.

One day that Napoleon was surrounded by the Divan of the great Sheiks, information was brought that the Arabs of the tribe of the Osnadis had killed a Fellah and carried off the cattle. He manifested his indignation, and in an animated tone ordered a staff-officer to repair forthwith to Baireh with 200 dromedaries and 300 horsemen to obtain restitution and punish the offenders. The Sheik El-Modi, who was present at this order, and observed the emotion of the General-in-chief, said to him with a smile, " Is that Fellah your cousin, that his death should put you in such a passion ?" " Yes," replied Napoleon, " all that I command are my children." " Taib†," said the Sheik, " you speak there like the Prophet."

† An Arab word expressing great satisfaction.

on board his vessel. He died without suffering, and a death the mildest and the most desired by military men.

I deeply sympathise with your sorrow. The moment that separates us from the object we love is terrible: it severs us from the world—it affects the frame with convulsions of agony. The faculties of the mind are annihilated—it retains no relations with the world, except through the medium of an incubus which alters every thing. Mankind appear more cold and selfish than they really are. In such a situation we feel, that if nothing obliged us to live, it would be far better to die; but when, after that first impression, we press our children to our heart, tears and sentiments of tenderness reanimate nature, and we live for our children. Yes, Madam, let yours from that first moment open your heart to melancholy. You will weep with them, you will watch over their infancy, you will instruct them in their youth—you will talk to them of their father, of your grief, of the loss which they and the Republic have suffered. After having re-attached yourself to the world through the influence of filial and maternal love, appreciate for something the friendship and the lively interest that I shall ever entertain for the widow of my friend. Be persuaded that there are some men, though small in number, who deserve to be the hope of the afflicted, because they feel acutely for mental suffering. (Signed) BONAPARTE."

There is a little of the mannerism of the period in the above, but every British woman, whose husband or brother has fallen for his country, will appreciate its value and the motives of the writer. A single authentic document like this refutes and outlives a thousand calumnies.

There are fewer symptoms in this publication of Napoleon's tendency to a belief in predestination than we expected to have found. The feeling, however, now and then breaks out — pretty strongly in his despatch from Egypt announcing the naval defeat at Aboukir; and also in the account of his marriage with Marie-Louise. Upon that occasion Prince Schwartzenberg, the Austrian ambassador at Paris, gave a splendid fête at Paris, to which Napoleon and the new Empress were invited. In the midst of the festivities, a temporary ball-room, which had been constructed in the garden of the Ambassador's hotel, took fire. Many persons perished. Among them the Ambassador's sister-in-law, who was suffocated in the attempt to rescue one of her children. The writer proceeds—

" In 1770, during the fête given by the city of Paris to celebrate the marriage of Louis the Sixteenth with Marie-Antoinette, two thousand persons were overturned in the fosses of the Champs-Elysées, and perished. Afterwards, when Louis and Marie-Antoinette met their death upon the scaffold, this terrible accident was recollected and converted into a presage of what followed—for it is to the insurrection of that great metropolis that the Revolution must be immediately attributed. The unfortunate issue of a fête given by an Austrian ambassador, under similar circumstances, to celebrate the alliance of two houses in the persons of Napoleon and Marie-Louise, appeared an inauspicious omen. The misfortunes of France have been solely caused by the change of policy on the part of Austria. Napoleon was not superstitious, yet upon that occasion he had a painful presentiment. The day after the battle of Dresden, when, during the pursuit of the Austrian army, he learned from a prisoner that Prince Schwartzenberg was rumoured to have been killed, he observed—' He was a brave man; but his death is so far consoling, that it was evidently he who was threatened by the unhappy omen at his ball.' Two hours after it was ascertained at head-quarters that it was Moreau, and not Prince Schwartzenberg, that had been killed the day before."

There are numerous other personal traits dispersed through the work, and which, independently of their intrinsic interest, greatly relieve the severity of the historical and military details. If any credit be due to his statements here, and in his recorded conversations at St. Helena, both of which agree with the reports of the best informed Frenchmen, who have no motives to traduce him, his moral character must be taken to have been grossly misrepresented before his fall. In his public capacity he exhibited the feelings, or let us rather call them the crimes, inseparable from ambitious men and ambitious governments. Like other warriors, he was indifferent enough to the effusion of human blood, provided the victory was secured. Like other persons and states aspiring to empire, he made light of the rights and institutions that were opposed to his plans of dominion. But apart from these, the almost universal vices of nations and rulers, he seems as an individual to have been tainted by very few of the noxious passions and caprices of exalted station. His personal habits were laborious and temperate. In private intercourse, if any intercourse with such a man can be called so, he usually succeeded in fixing the unbounded admiration and attachment of those who approached him. In his distribution of favours, there was little of the petty perfidy and mystery of Courts. The system which he directed demanded talent in every department, and wherever he found it, he appropriated it, promptly and even abruptly, but in general so judiciously that he had seldom cause to repent of his selection. From the tone in which he speaks of public men, it may be collected that he was very far from entertaining a contempt for virtue. He asserts, that personal probity formed one of the highest recommendations to his favour—although it was a melancholy fact, that in France during his day, moral worth was, for the purposes of her government, not the most valuable qualification. Even his ambition, culpable and destructive as it was, was not untinged by magnanimity. His abdication at Fontainebleau, the severest trial of human pride, was not so involuntary and sudden as was at the time supposed. In a despatch to Caulaincourt (4th Jan. 1814) appended to this publication, he announces his intention, if called upon, to make that sacrifice.

"Would they (the Allies) reduce France to her ancient limits? It would be to degrade her. They deceive themselves if they imagine that the reverses of war can make the nation desire peace upon such terms. There is not a French heart that would not in six months' time feel the scandal of such a peace, and that would not reproach the government that could be base enough to sign it. If the nation seconds me, the enemy marches to his destruction. If fortune betrays me, my resolution is taken—I do not cling to the throne—I shall never disgrace the nation, or myself, by subscribing such shameful conditions."

The style of these volumes is simple, perspicuous, and animated. The notes, as we are informed by the editors, are more exclusively his own composition—and, even though we had been ignorant of that fact, would have struck us as among the most original parts of the work, both in matter and execution. There are frequent sketches more or less in detail of contemporary characters. To give an idea of their general manner, we shall conclude our extracts and the present subject with his notice of two of his favourite generals who fell in the battle of Essling—

" On this day perished two generals, the Duke of Montebello and St. Hilaire—both of them heroes, and the best of Napoleon's friends. He wept for their loss. They would never have deserted him in his adversity; they would never have been faithless to the glory of the French people. The Duke of Montebello was a native of Lectoure. When a *chef de bataillon* he distinguished himself during the campaigns of 1796 in Italy. As a general he covered himself with glory in Egypt, at Montebello, at Marengo, at Austerlitz, at Jéna, at Pultusk, at Friedland, at Tudella, at Saragossa, at Eckmül and at Essling, where he found a glorious death. He was cautious, sagacious, and daring; before an enemy his presence of mind was not to be shaken. He owed little to education—Nature had done every thing for him. Napoleon, who had witnessed the progress of his mind, often remarked it with astonishment. For manœuvring five and twenty thousand infantry on the field of battle, he was superior to all the generals of the French army. He was still young, and would have become more perfect; perhaps he might even have reached to a proficiency in the highest branch of tactics *(le grande tactique)* which as yet he had not understood.—St. Hilaire was a general at Castiglione in 1796. He was remarkable for the chivalry of his character. He had excellent dispositions, was a kind companion, a kind brother, a kind relative. He was covered with wounds. His attachment to Napoleon commenced at the siege of Toulon. They called him, alluding to Bayard, ' *le Chevalier sans peur, et sans reproche.*' "

---

### THE SWORD OF THE TOMB.[*]

#### *A Northern Legend.*

" Voice of the gifted elder Time!
Voice of the charm and the Runic rhyme!
Speak! from the shades and the depths disclose,
How Sigurd may vanquish his mortal foes—
    Voice of the buried past!
" Voice of the grave! 'tis the mighty hour
When Night with her stars and dreams hath power,
And my step hath been soundless on the snows,
And the spell I have sung hath laid repose
    On the billow and the blast."
        Then the torrents of the North
        And the forest pines were still,
        When a hollow chaunt came forth
        From the dark sepulchral hill.

" There shines no sun through the land of dead,
But where the day looks not the brave may tread;
There is heard no song, and no mead is pour'd,
But the warrior may come to the silent board
    In the shadow of the night.
" There is laid a sword in thy father's tomb,
And its edge is fraught with thy foeman's doom;
But soft be thy step through the silence deep,
And move not the urn in the house of sleep,
    For the viewless have fearful might."
        Then died the solemn lay,
        As a trumpet's music dies,
        By the night-wind borne away
        Through the wild and stormy skies.

---

[*] The idea of this ballad is taken from a scene in " Starkother," a tragedy by the Danish Poet, Oehlenschlager.

The fir-trees rock'd to the wailing blast,
As on through the forest the warrior past
Through the forest of Odin, the dim and old,
The dark place of visions and legends told
　　　By the fires of northern pine.
The fir-trees rock'd, and the frozen ground
Gave back to his footstep a hollow sound,
And it seem'd that the depths of those mystic shades
From the dreamy gloom of their long arcades
　　　　Gave warning with voice and sign.
　　　　　But the wind strange magic knows
　　　　　To call wild shape and tone
　　　　　From the grey wood's tossing boughs,
　　　　　When Night is on her throne.

The pines closed o'er him with deeper gloom,
As he took the path to the monarch's tomb,
The pole-star shone, and the heavens were bright
With the arrowy streams of the northern light,
　　　　But his road through dimness lay !
He pass'd, in the heart of that ancient wood,
The dark shrine stain'd with the victim's blood,
Nor paused, till the rock, where a vaulted bed
Had been hewn of old for the kingly dead,
　　　　　Arose on his midnight way.
　　　　　Then first a moment's chill
　　　　　Went shuddering through his breast,
　　　　　And the steel-clad man stood still
　　　　　Before that place of rest.

But he cross'd at length, with a deep-drawn breath,
The threshold-floor of the hall of death,
And look'd on the pale mysterious fire,
Which gleam'd from the urn of his warrior-sire
　　　　With a strange and a solemn light.*
Then darkly the words of the boding strain,
Like an omen, rose on his soul again,
—" Soft be thy tread through the silence deep,
And move not the urn in the house of sleep,
　　　　For the viewless have fearful might !"
　　　　　But the magic sword and shield
　　　　　Of many a battle-day
　　　　　Hung o'er that urn reveal'd
　　　　　By the tomb-fire's waveless ray.

With a faded wreath of oak-leaves bound,
They hung o'er the dust of the far-renown'd,
Whom the bright Valkyriur's glorious voice
Had call'd to the banquet where gods rejoice,
　　　　And the rich mead flows in light.
With a beating heart his son drew near,
And still rung the verse in his thrilling ear,
—" Soft be thy tread through the silence deep,
And move not the urn in the house of sleep,
　　　　For the viewless have fearful might !"
　　　　　And many a Saga's rhyme,
　　　　　And legend of the grave,
　　　　　That shadowy scene and time
　　　　　Call'd back to daunt the brave.

---

* The sepulchral fire, supposed to guard the ashes of departed heroes, is frequently alluded to in the Northern Sagas.

But he raised his arm—and the flame grew dim,
And the sword in its light seem'd to wave and swim,
And his faltering hand could not grasp it well—
From the pale oak-wreath with a clash it fell
    Through the chamber of the dead.
The deep tomb rung with the heavy sound,
And the urn lay shiver'd in fragments round,
And a rush, as of tempests, quench'd the fire,
And the scatter'd dust of his warlike sire
    Was strewn on the champion's head.
      One moment—and all was still
      In the slumberer's ancient hall,
      When the rock had ceased to thrill
      With the mighty weapon's fall.

The stars were just fading, one by one,
The clouds were just tinged by the early sun,
When there stream'd through the cavern a torch's flame,
And the brother of Sigurd the valiant came
    To seek him in the tomb.
Stretch'd on his shield, like the steel-girt slain
By moonlight seen on the battle-plain,
In a speechless trance lay the warrior there,
But he wildly woke when the torch's glare
    Burst on him through the gloom.
    "The morning-wind blows free,
      And the hour of chace is near;
      Come forth, come forth with me;
      What dost thou, Sigurd, here?"

"I have put out the holy sepulchral fire,
I have scatter'd the dust of my warrior-sire!
It burns on my head, and it weighs down my heart,
But the winds shall not wander without their part
    To strew o'er the restless deep!
"In the mantle of Death he was here with me now,
There was wrath in his eye, there was gloom on his brow,
And his cold still glance on my spirit fell
With an icy ray and a withering spell—
    Oh! chill is the house of sleep!"
    "The morning wind blows free
      And the reddening sun shines clear,
      Come forth, come forth with me,
      It is dark and fearful here!"

"He is there, he is there, with his shadowy frown,
But gone from his head is the kingly crown,
The crown from his head, and the spear from his hand—
They have chased him far from the glorious land
    Where the feast of the gods is spread!*
"He must go forth alone on his phantom-steed,
He must ride o'er the grave-hills with stormy speed,
His place is no longer at Odin's board,
He is driven from Valhalla without his sword!
    But the slayer shall avenge the dead!"
      That sword its fame had won
      By the fall of many a crest,
      But its fiercest work was done
      In the tomb, on Sigurd's breast.
                  F. H.

---

* Severe sufferings to the departed spirit were supposed by the Northern Mythologists to be the consequence of any profanation of the sepulchre.

## MR. IRVING.

WE would recommend to Mr. Washington Irving, in whatever quarter of Germany he may be, to post back to England without delay, and look after his particular celebrity; for here is a synonimous gentleman, who has started during his absence, and is not only in the full enjoyment of a slap-dash renown of his own, but from a natural puzzle occasioned by identity of name, is coming in, among certain classes of his admirers, for supplemental honours which of right belong to the author of the Sketch-book.

We have been to "the Caledonian," the cant appellation by which the scene of Mr. Irving's oratory is now familiarly known, in the neighbourhood of Hatton Garden. We would not willingly exaggerate—still less would we indulge in any thing verging upon irreverent levity—but the exhibition was so new in a place of Christian worship, and so much bustle and curiosity have been excited regarding the principal performer, that, as mere reporters of passing novelties, we consider ourselves fully justified in giving a faithful summary of what we felt and saw.

The whole concern has a theatrical air. You must have a ticket of admission. When, installed in your seat, you cast your eyes upon the scene, you at once perceive that the persons around you are strangers to the place and to the sentiment that should prevail there—that they have come, not to say their prayers, but to have it to say that they have heard Mr. Irving. You look in vain for the keen and homely countenances, and the composed demeanour of a Scotch congregation; in their stead you have a miscellaneous assemblage of tittering misses, corpulent citizens, single gentlemen "from the West end" with their silk umbrellas, members of Parliament, and, "the flowers of the flock," a gallery full of the choicest specimens of the fair population of chariots and landaulets. The service begins at eleven; for the preceding half-hour, on the morning of our attendance, the passages leading to the gallery were the scene of tremendous rushing and confusion—all memory of the day and place was obliterated—there was nothing but the most unsightly working of shoulders and elbows, producing combinations of attitude, and varieties of ludicrous endurance, which no gravity could resist. We cannot stop to specify many examples; but the public sympathy is justly due to the young lady with the pink-lined bonnet who was so mercilessly jammed in by a column of dowagers and dandies and never thought of fainting away; and to the apoplectic-looking gentleman in blue, who by one heroic plunge emerged from his wedge, and, losing an arm of his coat in the effort, clambered up the gallery-stairs with this portion of his raiment dangling askant from his back like an hussar's supernumerary jacket.

This extraordinary scene would have astonished us, if we had been less familiar with the fury of a great capital for every thing in the way of sights and novelties. The bare announcement, in our fashionable circles, of the arrival of a Caledonian preacher, whose eloquence opened upon his congregation with the force of a galvanic battery, was quite sufficient to collect around him all the high-born and the loveliest sinners in the land, impatient to partake in the delicious horrors of a shock. Then the whisper ran that the personage in question was neither more nor less than one of Sir Walter's Covenanters—a palpable, living and authentic illustration of the Scotch Novels—so superior to any of Westall's, that the artist was thinking of applying for an injunction. Here was a sight indeed! and as potent a stimulus for all this bustling and rushing for priority, as if Diana Vernon, or Meg Merrilies, or Old Mortality himself had come to town. There was another ground of attraction, and also of rather a worldly kind—Mr. Irving had announced his intention of " passing the limits of pulpit theology and pulpit exhortation." He determined upon employing weapons not heretofore wielded at the altar, and directing them against the most influential classes in the country. He came " to teach imaginative men, and political men, and legal men, and scientific men, who bear the world in hand, and having got the key to their several chambers of delusion and resistance, to enter in and debate the matter with their souls, that they might be left without excuse;" and the published example (the work now before us*) of " this new method of handling religious truth" had apprised the community, that a part of his plan was to level the boldest, and were he not a holy man, we should say, the most bitter personalities against some of the most eminent writers of the day. But, suspending our opinion for the present upon the merits of such a mode of exhortation, was more wanting to secure to the inventor a brilliant auditory? What food for male and female curiosity! What a relief to the ordinary dulness of Sabbath occupation! What woman, with a woman's nature, could resist the prospect of seeing " the heartless Childe" dragged by a spiritual critic to the altar, and made to undergo a salutary smarting for the petulance and wanderings of his heroes; or of beholding Moore, with all his crimes and Melodies upon his head, soundly belaboured in the pulpit by a Calvinistic chastiser of Anacreontics? What scene of Sheridan's could compare with a debate between Mr. Irving and Mr. Canning's soul, upon the honourable member's Parliamentary ways? Lord Eldon, too, with his own and a more illustrious conscience to answer for; and Mr. Robinson, with the enormities of his budget; and the Broughams and Scarletts; and Sir Humphrey, in spite of his safety-lamp; and Mr. Jeffrey, so carnally insensible to the strains of the water-poets;—all of these 'might be summoned by name and roughly communed with (as some of them have already been) to the inexpressible edification of a fashionable and overflowing congregation.

But to return from this not altogether irrelevant digression. Mr. Irving ascended the pulpit at eleven o'clock. The first effect of his appearance is extremely startling. He is considerably more than six feet high. He has a pallid face—the outline rather triangular than oval—the features regular and manly. The most striking circumstance about his head is a profusion of coarse, jet-black hair, which is carefully divided in the centre and combed down on either side, after the Italian fashion in the middle ages. The eye-brows and whiskers are in equal abundance. Upon the whole, we thought the entire countenance much more Italian than Scotch, and imagined that we could discover in the softness and regularity about the mouth and chin some resemblance to the Bonaparte family. There is a strongly marked

* The Oracles of God; Four Orations. Judgement to come, an argument in Nine Parts, pp. 548.

organical defect in the eyes: when upturned, they convey the idea of absolute blindness. The forehead is high and handsome, and far too anxiously displayed. We were sorry to see Mr. Irving's fingers so frequently at work in that quarter to keep the hair in its upturned position. The petty care bestowed upon this point, and the toilet-associations connected with bleached shirt-wrists, starched collar, and cherished whiskers, greatly detracted from his dignity of aspect, and reduced what might have been really imposing into an air of mere terrific dandyism. His age, we understand, is about forty years. If any one should ask us, take him all in all, what he looked most like, we should say, that when he first glided into view, his towering figure, sable habiliments, pallid visage, and the theatrical adjustment of his black and bushy hair, reminded us of the entry of a wonder-working magician upon the boards of a real theatre.

The style of the discourse we heard was so similar to that of his publication, upon which we shall observe hereafter, that for the present we shall confine ourselves to Mr. Irving's pulpit manner. His voice is naturally good: it is sweet, sonorous, and flexible, but he miserably mismanages it. His delivery is a tissue of extravagance and incorrectness. There is no privity between his sentiments and accents. There is no want of variety of intonation, but it is so capriciously introduced, that in one half of the emphatic passages his tongue seems to be utterly ignorant of the sense and bearing of what it is commissioned to articulate. The tones are at one moment unmeaningly measured and sepulchral—the next as inappropriately raised to the highest pitch of ecstatic fervour. His discourse took a review of the wonders of the animal and vegetable creation; and he was as enwrapt and vehement upon the budding of a flower, or the growth of an insect, as if he were throwing off the most appalling thoughts that can agitate the human frame. This want of conformity between the matter and the manner was painfully apparent throughout. Let any one imagine the Battle of Prague, or any other piece of descriptive music, with the marks for expression transposed or dispersed at random, and the leading passages executed accordingly. We should then have *pianissimo* volleys of cannon, *sotto voce* trumpet-calls, and *maestoso* wailings of the faint and expiring. The effect would not be more fantastic and provoking than Mr. Irvings incessant misappropriation of his tones to his topics.

His gesture is equally defective in dignity and propriety. It is angular, irregular, and violent. In many passages intended to be argumentative or persuasive, his hands were going through petty and vulgar evolutions, as if he were attempting to explain by signs the method of effecting some common mechanical operation. More than once he abruptly grasped with both hands the edge of the pulpit on the right, and reclining his body in that direction, like one seized with a sudden pain in the side, declaimed over his left shoulder to the auditors in the farther gallery. The movements of his countenance were to the full as infelicitous as his attitudes and gesture. Instead of a natural play of features, instead of " looks commercing with the skies," we had forced, anomalous, and at times, quite terrific contortions. In some passages where the subject would have demanded composure or elevation of feature, the preacher stooped over the pulpit, so as to bring one ear almost into contact with the cushion, knit his brow, assumed a sort of smile or leer, and when the period was closed, returned to his position with a kind of triumphant jerk, precisely like a man who felt that he had just made a good satirical hit. There was one circumstance in Mr. Irving's method that would alone have destroyed the effect of any eloquence. He read his discourse, and it so happened that throughout he read it incorrectly. After taking up the commencing clauses of a period, he drew back from the book, and recited them with all the fervour of extemporaneous creation, but suddenly, in the very midst of the sentence, he had to break off and refer to the manuscript again, and here he perpetually failed to catch at once the point from which he was to continue. Five or six times his eye lighted upon the matter he had just delivered, and the congregation had it over again with a clumsy " I say," to give it the air of an intended repetition. This, and frequent mistakings of particular words, and a good many false quantities, (for Mr. Irving seems to be no prosodian), gave altogether a slovenly and bungling character to the entire exhibition. During a discourse of an hour and forty minutes, there was but one short passage that we can except from these remarks. It was a description of Paradise; and he delivered it well. There was no extravagance of posture or gesticulation, and his tones had sweetness, sincerity, and elevation. With this single exception, he made little impression. As far as we could judge from the demeanour of those around us, they were utterly unmoved. There were now and then some unseemly, though not unnatural titterings among the younger females, at the warmth of the metaphors and personifications introduced into a description of the effects of Spring upon the animal and vegetable worlds.

We had almost omitted to state, that Mr. Irving used a regular white handkerchief, with which he had frequent occasion to remove the starting drops from his brow. We are afraid that the colour was chosen for effect. On retiring from the chapel, when we cast a last look to catch the character of his countenance in repose, we observed him, as he reclined in the back of the pulpit, performing the same operation with an honest Belcher pattern.

We have read Mr. Irving's book. It was no slight task, but we positively have read it through. It now and then evinces some power; more however in the way of phrase, and in the accumulation of forcible common-places, than in original conception : but on the whole, we regard it as an imprudent publication, and considered with reference to its main object, which has been very pompously announced, the conversion or exposure of the intellectual classes, as an utter failure. The author appears to us to be a man of a capacity a little above mediocrity. He is, we doubt not, thoroughly versed in the theological doctrines of his church ; for this is a matter upon which we do not presume to pronounce. His reading among popular English authors seems to have been tolerably extensive. We also give him credit for the most genuine zeal, notwithstanding the unnecessary tone of exaggeration and defiance with which it is accompanied—but here our commendations must cease. His taste is vicious in the extreme. His style is at once coarse and flashy. It is, in truth, the strangest jumble we have ever encountered. There is no single term by which it can be described. He announces his preference for the models in the days of

Milton, but he writes the language of no age. The phraseology of different centuries is often pressed into the service of a single period. We have some quaint turn from the times of Sir Thomas More, puritanical compounds that flourished under Cromwell, followed by a cavalcade of gaudy epithets, bringing down the diction to the day of publication. His affectation of antiquated words is excessive, and quite beneath the dignity of a Christian preacher. Mr. Irving should recollect that *wot* and *wis* and *ween*, and *do* and *doth* and *hath*, upon the latter of which he so delights to ring the changes, are all miserable matters of convention, having nothing in life to do with the objects of his ministry—that there is no charity in giving refuge to a discarded expletive—no glory in raising a departed monosyllable from the dead. His style has another great defect. It is grievously incorrect. When he comes to imagery, his mind is in a mist. He talks of " *abolishing* pulses," " *evacuating* the uses of a law," the " *quietus* of torment," " erecting the *platform* of our being upon a new *condition* of probation." Some of his sentences are models of " metaphorical confusion." We seldom met with a more perfect adept in the art of " torturing one poor thought a thousand ways." He contrives that a leading idea shall change its dress and character with a pantomimic rapidity of execution. The Bible is with him, at one moment, a star, the very next a pavilion. Again, " the rich and mellow word, with God's own wisdom mellow, and rich with all mortal and immortal attractions, is a better *net* to catch childhood, to catch manhood withal, than these pieces of man's wording." We could multiply examples without number ; they occur in every page.

Apart from these defects, which might have been overlooked in a work of less pretension, but which, wherever they prevail, are unequivocal proofs of slovenly habits of thinking, we may generally say of Mr. Irving's composition, that in the unadorned passages, where he prefaces or sums up a topic, it resembles the version of a Papal document, cumbrous, verbose, and authoritatively meek ; that in his scriptural imitations, he sometimes succeeds in bringing together masses of awful imagery, the complete effect of which, however, is too often counteracted by the intrusion of some petty quaintness ; and that his Platonic personifications of the soul, and the descriptions of its final beatitude, have a good deal of the pastoral manner and gorgeous colouring which render certain parts of the Pilgrim's Progress so delicious a treat to the imagination of the unlettered Christian.

In justice to Mr. Irving we shall select one or two of the most faultless of his impressive passages that we can find. His death-bed scenes are perhaps among the best :—

" And another of a more dark and dauntless mood, who hath braved a thousand terrors, will also make a stand against terror's grisly king—and he will seek his ancient intrepidity, and search for his wonted indifference ; and light smiles upon his ghastly visage, and affect levity with his palsied tongue; and parry his rising fears, and wear smoothness on his outward heart, while there is nothing but tossing and uproar beneath. He may expire in the terrible struggle—nature may fail under the unnatural contest ; then he dies with desperation imprinted on his clay !

" But if he succeed in keeping the first onset down, then mark how a second and a third comes on as he waxeth feebler. Nature no longer enduring so much, strange and incoherent words burst forth, with now and then a sentence of stern and loud defiance. This escape perceiving, he will gather up his strength, and laugh it off as reverie. And then remark him in his sleep—how his countenance suffereth change, and his breast swelleth like the deep; and *his hands grasp for a hold, as if his soul were drowning;* and his lips tremble and mutter, and his breath comes in sighs, or stays with long suppression, like the gusts which precede the bursting storm; and his frame shudders, and shakes the couch on which this awful scene of death is transacted. Ah! these are the ebbings and flowings of strong resolve and strong remorse. That might have been a noble man; but he rejected all, and chose wickedness, in the face of visitings of God, and therefore he is now so severely holden of death.

"And reason doth often resign her seat at the latter end of these God-despisers. Then the eye looks forth from its naked socket, ghastly and wild—terror sits enthroned upon the pale brow—he starts—he thinks that the fiends of hell are already upon him—his disordered brain gives them form and fearful shape—he speaks to them—he craves their mercy. His tender relatives beseech him to be silent, and with words of comfort assuage his terror, and recall him from his paroxysm of remorse. A calm succeeds, until disordered imagination hath recruited strength for a fresh creation of terror; and he dies with a fearful looking-for of judgment, and of fiery indignation to consume him."

This is undoubtedly striking; but is it original vigour, or a mere collection of appalling circumstances, which it required little skill to assemble? We have marked in italics the single idea that we did not recognise as common-place.

We like the following much better. The prevailing sentiment has little novelty, but it is natural and affecting, and is given in better taste. Describing the lukewarmness of modern Christians, and their addiction to worldly enjoyments and pursuits, he proceeds—

"They carry on commerce with all lands, the bustle and noise of their traffic fill the whole earth—they go to and fro, and knowledge is increased—but how few in the hasting crowd are hasting after the kingdom of God! Meanwhile, death sweepeth on with his chilling blast, freezing up the life of generations, catching their spirits unblessed with any preparation of peace, quenching hope, and binding destiny for evermore. Their graves are dressed, and their tombs are adorned; but their spirits, where are they? How oft hath this city, where I now write these lamentations over a thoughtless age, been filled and emptied of her people since first she reared her imperial head! How many generations of her revellers have gone to another kind of revelry!—how many generations of her gay courtiers to a royal residence where courtier-arts are not!—how many generations of her toilsome tradesmen to the place of silence, where no gain can follow them! How time hath swept over her, age after age, with its consuming wave, swallowing every living thing, and bearing it away unto the shores of eternity! The sight and thought of all which is my assurance that I have not in the heat of my feelings surpassed the merit of the case. The theme is fitter for an indignant prophet, than an uninspired sinful man."

We cannot forbear extracting one more passage for the singularity, if not the excellence of the style. It is quite in the manner of an ancient Covenanter—

"I would try these flush and flashy spirits with their own weapons, and play a little with them at their own game. They do but prate about their exploits at fighting, drinking, and death-despising. I can tell them of those who fought with savage beasts; yea, of maidens who durst enter as coolly as a modern bully into the ring, to take their chance with infuriated beasts of prey; and I can tell them of those who drank the molten lead as cheerfully as they do the juice of the grape, and handled the red fire and played with the bickering flames as gaily as they do with love's dimples or woman's amorous tresses. And what do they talk of war? Have they forgot Cromwell's iron hand, who made their chivalry to skip? or the Scots Cameronians, who seven times, with their Christian chief, received the thanks of Marlborough, that first of English captains? or Gustavus of the North, whose camp sung psalms in every tent? It is not so long that they should forget Nelson's Methodists, who were the most trusted of that hero's crew. Poor men! they know nothing who do not know out of their country's history, who it was that set at nought the wilfulness of Henry VIII. and the sharp rage of the virgin Queen, against liberty, and bore the black cruelty of her Popish sister; and presented the petition of rights, and the bill of rights, and the claim of rights. Was it chivalry? was it blind bravery? No—these second-rate qualities may do for a pitched field, or a fenced ring; but, when it comes to death or liberty, death or virtue, death or religion, they wax dubious, generally bend their necks under hardship, or turn their backs for a bait of honour, or a mess of solid and substantial meat. This chivalry and brutal bravery can fight if you feed them well and bribe them well, or set them well on edge; but in the midst of hunger, and nakedness, and want, and persecution, in the day of a country's direst need, they are cowardly, treacherous, and of no avail.—Oh! these topers, these gamesters, these idle revellers, these hardened death-despisers!—they are a nation's disgrace, a nation's downfall."

It would be beside our province to engage in any discussions upon the purely theological parts of Mr. Irving's work; but there are other matters rather hastily introduced, as it strikes us, and intemperately handled, and indeed in some degree affecting *ourselves*, upon which we cannot refrain from offering a few remarks. We allude to his vehement and sweeping denunciations against the literature of the day—

" Our zeal towards God, (he says) and the public good, hath been stung almost to madness by the writings of reproachable men, *who give the tone to the sentimental and political world*. Their poems, their criticisms, and their blasphemous pamphlets, have been like gall and wormwood to my spirit, and I have longed to summon into the field some arm of strength, which might evaporate their vile and filthy speculation, into the limbo of vanity, whence it came."

This must not be taken to apply solely to those publications that have been recently under prosecution, and which we, profane as Mr. Irving may think us, reprobate as sincerely as himself; neither is it an incidental ebullition, but one of the ever-recurring anathemas in which he has indulged against his intellectual contemporaries, with their ungodly recreations, " their Magazines of wit and fashion," their " death-despising" Reviews of the latest publications. Poor Mr. Colburn, he little dreamt, some few months back, of what was brewing for him at the other side of the Tweed; he little expected that one of these Sundays he might be summoned, with a *duces tecum* of the New Monthly and its contributors, to the bar of this spiritual police-office in Hatton Garden, to answer for their dark and Anti-Calvinistic ways. But there we are—and without cavilling upon points of jurisdiction, we would simply ask our judge to examine us before he condemns us, and then candidly to say whether, in point of fact, we are to be classed among the sinister signs of the times. Is it unholy to indulge once a month in a little unwounding pleasantry? Is a letter from the Alps a deed of darkness? A description of St. Peter's, or Notre Dame, a lurking attack upon the kirk of Scotland? Had our Parthian Glance at a departed year any tendency to shake the public confidence in a future state? Is the Ghost of Grimm as graceless and vicious as the embodied Baron himself was? We would respectfully put it to · Mr. Irving's conscience, in his uninspired moments, whether these are matters that can endanger the souls of the readers or the writers? and whether, as a Christian censor of the age, he may not be risking his dignity and influence in exaggerating, like an ostentatious sophist in want of topics, the innocent pastimes of, on the whole, a tolerably well-conducted generation, into abominations that will surely be visited with never-ending wrath?

But there is another and a more important question which this gentleman has been indiscreet enough to raise. He has crossed the Tweed with the avowed design of calling out, as it were, the intellect of the age for the supposed affronts it has offered to his notions of religion. We say nothing of the self-possession of any single person undertaking so adventurous a project; but, as the sincere friends of religion, we deprecate it as an ill-considered and dangerous proceeding. With regard to the main point, the malignant influence against which his zeal is directed, we consider Mr. Irving's assertions on the subject to be full of his characteristic exaggeration. There are now, as there at most times have been, many men of talent among the influential classes, who, unfortunately for themselves, are cut off by their peculiar habits of thinking from the consolations of Christianity, but perhaps there never was a period when such persons so cautiously abstained from the promulgation of their particular opinions. There may be one or two exceptions, but the great mass of the persons to whom we refer feel too deeply the importance of religious sanctions to the well-being of society to think of substituting in their place the cold and unavailing dogmas of a philosophical creed. Feelings of decorum, of good taste, and even of personal respectability, come in aid, and confirm those habits of salutary forbearance. The question then is, whether any service can be rendered to religion by the tone and manner which Mr. Irving has assumed towards this class. Will defiance and abuse convert them? Will offensive personalities even against those who have declared their opinions, conciliate the rest? Is it wise, by unfairly confounding poetry and criticism with blasphemy, to alarm the self-love of many, who are already, tacitly it may be, but virtually upon his side? And lastly, is there no danger in impressing upon the other orders of the community that among the high and educated all sense of religion is extinguished? These are matters upon which we cannot undertake to dwell, but it really does occur to us that they deserve Mr. Irving's most serious consideration. It would be a miserable ending of his mission to discover too late that his zeal had produced mischiefs beyond the powers of his oratory to heal.

Mr. Irving is a man of warm feelings, and can eulogise as exorbitantly as he censures. It may be interesting to know that one of the schools of modern poetry has escaped his condemnation. In the midst of his treatise upon "Judgement to come," we have the following burst of rhetorical criticism. The subject is Mr. Wordsworth—

"There is one man in these realms who hath addressed himself to such a godly life, and dwelt alone amidst the grand and lovely scenes of nature, and the deep unfathomable secrecies of human thought:—would to Heaven it were allowed to others to do likewise! And he hath been rewarded with many new cogitations of nature and of nature's God; and he hath heard, in the stillness of his retreat, many new voices of his conscious spirit—all which he hath sung in harmonious numbers. But mark the Epicurean soul of this degraded age! They have frowned on him; they have spit on him; they have grossly abused him. The masters of this critical generation (like generation, like masters) have raised the hue and cry against him; the literary and sentimental world, which is their sounding-board, hath reverberated it; and every reptile, who can retail an opinion in print, hath spread it, and given his reputation a shock, from which it is slowly but surely recovering. All for what? For making nature and his own bosom his home, and daring to sing of the simple but sublime truths which were revealed to him—for daring to be free in his manner of uttering genuine feeling, and depicting natural beauty, and grafting thereon devout and solemn contemplations of God. Had he sent his Cottage Wanderer forth upon an 'Excursion' amongst courts and palaces, battle-fields, and scenes of faithless gallantry, his musings would have been more welcome, being far deeper and more tender than those of 'the heartless Childe;' but because the man hath valued virtue, and retiring modesty, and common household truth, over these the ephemeral decorations or excessive depravities of our condition, therefore he is hated and abused."

Now all this, which was intended to be very fine, appears to us to be the merest puerile declamation; and it is, besides, (what is quite out of all rule in a Christian teacher) an attempt to domineer over the free expression of public opinion, in matters purely temporal, by spiritual threats and denunciations. If Mr. Wordsworth had been an extraordinarily gifted being, who had brought tidings of immortal truths in morals or science, and had been scurvily used by his age, it might have been pardonable, if not appropriate, in one of his friends to slide him into a theological treatise in the character of a dishonoured prophet. But the plain matter of fact is, that this gentleman's career has not been peculiarly sacred or supernatural; neither has it, as far as we can discover, been visited with that precise degree of martyrdom that could warrant so vehement an episode in his behalf. As to worldly matters, Mr. W. has long held a lucrative appointment under the Crown. We glance at this, not surely for the purpose of casting any imputation upon him or his patrons, but simply to shew that so far he has not been a neglected man. He has, on the contrary, been a fortunate and a favoured man. Mr. Irving should have recollected this, and have given the age of Wordsworth a little credit for so material an item in its dealings with him. But Mr. Wordsworth has been a poet, and the wrongs his genius has encountered from this " reptile" age, have been, it would appear, of so transcendant a cast, as to be made a fit subject of ghostly sympathy and indignation in a discourse upon doomsday and the doctrine of final retribution. Now these mighty and unprecedented indignities, which Mr. Irving would thus preposterously exalt into an affair of the skies, consist of two or three, not unfrequent, and with deference we say it, altogether earthy circumstances. Mr. Wordsworth is a clever man, and has the pardonable ambition of being thought so. Living at his ease—happily for himself, undistracted by the cares and bustle of active life, he has indulged a good deal in imaginative reveries, and has submitted numerous specimens of his musings to the decision of the

public.  The public, not a very unusual proceeding, have differed upon
their merits.  They suited the taste of some, and these persons have
been as ardent in their eulogies, as Mr. Irving or Mr. Wordsworth
himself could desire.  Others, however, took the " reptile" side of the
question, and explained their reasons.  They admitted, and warmly
commended his occasional tenderness and sublimity, but they also saw
much to condemn and deplore.  They denied that they could understand him, where in point of fact he was unintelligible.  They reprobated his propensity to form fantastic conjunctions between what was
elevated in sentiment and mean and repulsive in real life.  Adopting the
principle, that verisimilitude was a prime essential in every work of
art, they did not expect to be rated from the pulpit for suggesting that
a pedlar, with a poetical pair of wings, was an innovation upon good
taste—that a sentimental leech-catcher was not at all adapted to catch
the public—that a metaphysical vagrant could never be rendered an
appropriate expounder of the mysterious movements of the soul of
man.  Mr. Irving may like all this, and we shall never make any un-
mannerly attack upon him for differing from us, but in the name of fair-
dealing, let him not overwhelm us with his holy vituperation for presuming in matters of criticism to judge for ourselves.

To conclude our remarks upon Mr. Irving and his oratory, we do
not hesitate to assert, that he has altogether mistaken the extent of his
powers, and the taste and spirit of the age before which it has been his
lot to display them.  He might have done in the days of Knox—
proffers of martyrdom and flaming invectives were in those times provoked, and were therefore natural and laudable—now, they are unnecessary, and for that reason ridiculous.  But it is Mr. Irving's fate,
when he gets upon a favourite topic, to throw aside the important fact
that he is living and exhorting in the year 1823, and in the metropolis
of England.  He, is far fitter to be a missionary among semibarbarous
tribes, than an enforcer of doctrines that are already familiar to his
hearers ; or he would do excellently well as a reclaimer of a horde of
banditti in some alpine scene.  There, amidst the waving of pines, and
rustling of foliage, with rocks and hills and cataracts, and a wilder
audience around him, his towering stature, vehement action, and
clanging tones, would be in perfect keeping.  His terrific descriptions
of a sinner's doom would touch the stubborn consciences of his lawless
flock.  His copious tautology and gaudy imagery would be welcomed
by their rude fancies as the most captivating eloquence.  To them,
his exaggeration would be energy—his fury, the majesty of an inspired
intellect—but in these countries his coming has been a couple of centuries too late.  We understand that he has been called " an eloquent
barbarian :" it would have been more correct to say that his was barbarous oratory.

## THE TRANCE OF LOVE.

### FROM THE ITALIAN.

Love in a drowsy mood one day
Reclined with all his nymphs around him,
His feather'd darts neglected lay,
And faded were the flowers that crown'd him;
Young Hope, with eyes of light, in vain
Led smiling Beauty to implore him,
While Genius pour'd her sweetest strain,
And Pleasure shook her roses o'er him.

At length a stranger sought the grove,
And fiery Vengeance seem'd to guide him,
He rudely tore the wreaths of Love,
And broke the darts that lay beside him;
The little god now wakeful grew,
And angry at the bold endeavour:
He rose, and wove his wreaths anew,
And strung his bow more firm than ever.

When lo! th' invader cried, "Farewell,
"My skill, bright nymphs, this lesson teaches,
"While Love is sprightly, bind him well
"With songs and smiles and honey'd speeches;
"But should dull languor seize the god,
"Recall me on my friendly mission,
"For know when Love begins to nod,
"His surest spur is OPPOSITION!"          M. A.

---

## THE LADIES *versus* THE GENTLEMEN.

Mr. Editor,—I hope I shall not be accused of an "ignorant impatience," if at the end of seven years from the battle of Waterloo, I complain that matrimony is not yet reduced in these kingdoms to a peace-establishment. Our ears have been dinned with the outcries of starving manufacturers; and the men in our family have been for ever occupied in getting up and attending meetings on agricultural distress; but not one word have you heard of complaint from the fair sex, not one remonstrance, not one petition lies on the table of the House from the "distressed spinsters;" though our bachelors continue to "caper nimbly in a lady's chamber" without a notion of wedlock, and, when our mothers hint an inquiring innuendo, as to their "intentions," coolly parry the attack by quoting a chapter from Malthus. During the continuance of a war, by which the female world was threatened with the fulfilment of Mother Shipton's ill-omened prophecy of but one husband among six wives, it was nothing very extraordinary that mothers should encounter some little difficulty in getting off "a set" of daughters; and as I am one of a rather numerous family, my expectations, notwithstanding my being "brought out" by a very marrying *chaperon*, were not exalted. But now, when

"Grim-visaged war has smooth'd his wrinkled front;"

and all the professions are overstocked,—when men are "as plenty as blackberries,"—and Captains and Colonels have nothing better to do with themselves than to "marry and settle in the country,"—

"I lose my patience, and I own it too,"

at finding our difficulties rather increase than diminish; and at observing the Lady Aucherleys as much embarrassed as ever with their " nine Miss Simmons's."*

Individually, Sir, I have as yet no reason for despair: my charms are not yet faded; nor do I receive any broad hints from the men that I am singled out for singleness. On the contrary, I have no lack of " cut-mutton majors" and sauntering cornets, to spoil our sofas with their boots, and to waste precious time in a gossipry that like the passages in Gray's Long Story, " lead to nothing." Our house, indeed, is constantly beset with these idlers, ever ready to " bestow their tediousness on whoever will listen to them," and always in marching order, to " breakfast, dine, or sup, with Nong-tong-paw,"—to ride away mornings and flirt away nights. But they have no more idea of marrying than of settling their debts; and should a girl be weak enough to listen to them, would as soon think of repaying the father's dinners as returning the daughter's passion. No, Sir, the young men of the present day may " court an amorous looking-glass," but if they court any thing else, it is with no settled purpose: for the only " *tie*" which does not fill them with horror, is the tie of their cravat.

It was not, then, without considerable indignation that I perused your animadversions upon female speculations in matrimony, in a recent article on " Select Society;" which accuses our mothers of their mercenary attentions to young men, and of going out of their way to marry their daughters; and which treats us as little better than common swindlers and takers of husbands upon false pretences. Really, Mr. Editor, this is most unreasonable! for, if the mountain will not come to Mahomet, surely Mahomet must go to the mountain. Besides, the statement is altogether *exparte*, and " like an ill-roasted egg, all on one side." For if the attack of an experienced matron is often closely calculated and well-combined, the beaux are on their side perfect Vaubans, and conduct the defence with a skill and pertinacity at least equal to that of the besiegers. There is nothing on earth so impenetrable as a genuine dangler, nothing so *rusé* as a trading lady's man. If he finds himself left out of a party, and neglected, as one from whom nothing is to be expected, he immediately takes the alarm, grows warm in his manner, constant in his attentions, and does " *l'impossible*," to induce an inference that he is about " to pop the question." Nothing, however, is farther from his intention; and no sooner does he perceive that he has excited an interest, and that mamma begins to have her eye on him, than he draws in his horns like a snail, entrenches himself in generalities, avoids all openings to an *éclaircissement*, and " backs out" (to use a phrase of his own) with a dexterity, which leaves neither the consolation of being affronted, nor the advantage of disengagement. In this way he alternately blows hot and cold, as the occasion may require, tantalizing mother and daughter with an endless succession of hopes, which he never means to realize, and of fears which he takes good care shall never be reduced to certainty. Years pass, seasons succeed to seasons, " whole summer suns roll unperceived away," and we are " surprised to hear that we grow old," without, at the same time, hearing any thing of a ring and a licence.

---

* " Sketches of Character."

Upon creatures such as these "cupboard lovers," feeling and affection would be flung away. The cold, the heartless, and the speculating, are alone safe in their society; and if in a game of "diamond cut diamond," a rich young egoist is now and then "brought down at a long shot," or enticed by a scientific combination of female wit, matronly cunning, and fraternal *surveillance*, into committing matrimony, where is the mighty harm? According to all codes, murder in self-defence is justifiable. Then, in the name of mercy, leave us poor girls to be "killing" in our own way, and do not insist upon a candour and sensibility, which, meeting no return, is at least as idiotical as it is innocent. It is scarcely possible to conceive a situation more pitiable, than that of an amiable, frank, and warm-hearted girl, who listens unsuspectingly to the blandishments of one of these mock sentimentalists, believing a man merely because he tells a lie with a grave face, and suffering herself to be entrapped into a real passion, for a wretch fit only to associate with St. Augustine's snow lady.

"Once, and but once, my heedless youth was bit;"

when, finding a good deal of apparent good-nature, and some really good conversation, with a more than usual warmth and sincerity of manner, I really thought that at last I had met "my match." Abandoning myself to all those sentiments which are natural to our sex on the presumption of a solid engagement, and indulging in all those illusions

"Che gusta un cor amato riamando,"

I cherished during an entire winter the flattering error. I mistook assiduity for affection, and an *air empressé* for a genuine attachment. *Mais hélas!* "*airs empressés, vous n'êtes pas l'amour!*" At the proper season for leaving town we went to a fashionable watering-place, in order to avoid the inconvenience of a direct invitation of the swain, on a visit to our own house in the country; and he—did not follow us, but set off to Paris, in search, as we were informed, of fresh game, leaving me to drink the spa-water, and experience——

"Quel che puo sdegno in cor di donna amante."

I cannot express to you how deeply I was (not mortified, no, that feeling was quite absorbed in a more painful sentiment, but) wounded. Shame at being so egregiously duped, and humiliation at the advantage I had afforded to a heartless puppy, in suffering him to read and play upon my affections, remained dormant for months, while I was absorbed by the more tender emotions I had so imprudently allowed to grow up in my bosom. But as I have some firmness of mind and natural spirit, indignation at length took the lead, and I was no longer unhappy.

In the good old times, we women had only to be on our guard against the men who had designs on our persons. A reasonable portion of prudence and propriety sufficed to ensure a girl a triumph over her would-be seducer, and seldom failed to conduct the wincing, reluctant Lovelace into the bands of holy matrimony—a striking example of the superiority of virtue over vice, and of the force of beauty armed by modesty and discretion. But now these dangers exist only in novels. A girl of real flesh and blood has nothing to encounter half so formidable as the Adonises who have no designs at all. Actions for love-damages, with their attendant consequences, awards and attorneys' bills, are worth all the duennas and maiden aunts in the world, keeping those few *beaux restes* of the old school, who find either time or energy to be mischievous, at a respectful distance; and instead of dreading the passions of the other sex, our greatest dangers arise from those who know not what passion is. Against these enemies, selfishness must be opposed by selfishness, and cunning met by finesse; for art, and a regular system of tactics, can alone avail; and after all, though the victory may be brilliant, it is not in one case in a thousand that we can boast of its being profitable.

The truth is, I more than half suspect the self-satisfied gentleman, who is the hero of your article on "Select Society *," and who, by the by, from his own confession, seems totally unqualified for good company in any *genre*, writes under the influence of personal pique; and being disappointed in some reasonable expectation of winning youth, beauty, and a large fortune, upon the small outlay of his own personal accomplishments, takes this method of venting his spleen, and discharging his anger against the whole sex. I have known many of these difficult gentlemen, who, after thinking nothing too good for them, and passing the summer of life in vain attempts upon handsome heiresses and buxom rich widows, sat down at last, on the turn of their age, with some dowdy, neither remarkable for sense, beauty, nor spirit, and without even the charms of the pocket, to compensate for the total absence of those of the person and the mind. But, be this as it may, the malapert censor might have remembered, that in matrimony, we girls are necessarily influenced by our parents, to whose guidance we are compelled to submit ourselves; and that, if we seem cunning and rapacious, it is most frequently the fault of a too anxious mother. But the men in indulging their selfish views, in sedulously avoiding a *poor* girl, whatever may be her merit, or in trifling with the feelings and engrossing the time of an unmarried female, without the most distant idea of making her a wife, act for themselves, and have no one upon whom they can shift the blame. Besides, if girls really do look too sharp after a husband, it must not be forgotten, that matrimony, a mere episode in men's fortunes, is every thing to a female. To remain single is, with a woman, inevitably to lose caste; while your old bachelor is only the more courted and feasted for his celibacy. In the order of nature, men are destined to labour for the support of their families, and it is but just that a female, in seeking a partner for life, should look out for protection and support. But your modern Benedicts, your heroes who complain of the artifices of the sex, seek only, in their efforts to marry, the wife whose means must support their idleness and supply their extravagance.

Under all these circumstances the men have little reason to complain; and the less when it is considered that, being confined to defensive operations, we can play off no arts but upon those who wilfully place themselves within the sphere of our fascinations, while the men are at liberty to engage, or not engage, when and where they please. There is however another sort of dangler, whose faults I shall plead in farther

---

* Page 91.

abatement of the "select" gentleman's charge; and this is the man, who, being perhaps under circumstances which render marriage not altogether prudent, cannot decide between love and ambition. Such a man, without scruple, will master a girl's affections, and indeed would be happy to marry the object of his preference; but then he would at the same time retain all the luxuries and superfluities, which, as a single man, he has been used to enjoy. Placed like the metaphysical donkey between two identical bundles of hay, and without strength of mind to form a decided volition and either give up the world or his mistress, he would fain eat his cake and have it too: thus he professes honourable intentions, compromises the character and the repose of the lady by incessant assiduities in public, and by the warmest protestations of endless devotion in private; and by binding her in a pledge to be his, whenever he may find it convenient to demand her hand, he effectually excludes all access of more independent or more *marrying* lovers. In the mean time, at best, life slips away unenjoyed; nine times out of ten the passion cools; but the gentleman does not break off—he dare not do that. His attentions however slacken, and the wretched woman becomes the victim of the most torturing suspense, of the cruelest heart-burnings, without power to cut the man she begins to despise, or to force his oscillating thoughts to a determination. Oh! Mr. Editor, you know something of the "pleasures of hope," but you know also that hope deferred maketh the heart sick; and you will feel for the fate of a human being whose life and love have been blighted by such a sickly admirer.

> "Quante vedove notti,
> Quante dì solitarj,
> *Ha* consumato indarno."

I must not, however, grow grave, though this is a case which, as my careless brother Tom is wont to say, would indeed make a person swear. All I ask of you is, privately to give me up the name of the flippant youth who has indited the precious farrago of which I complain; and to throw him for a season in my way; and if I do not play the fish up the stream and down the stream, ay, and bring him to the shore, too, with the single hair of his own egregious vanity, never say again that there's faith in a woman's word. Pardon this immeasurable letter, which *en revanche,* shall, in contradistinction to all feminine epistles, have no postscript; and consider me as

Your humble servant, and constant reader,      Delia

---

## LONDON LYRICS.

### Five Hundred a Year.

That gilt middle-path, which the poet of Rome
Extoll'd as the only safe highway to bliss:
That "haven" which many a poet at home
Assures us all Guinea-bound merchantmen miss:
    That bless'd middle line,
    Which bard and divine
In sonnet and sermon so sigh for, is mine;—
My uncle, a plain honest fat auctioneer,
Walk'd off, and bequeath'd me Five Hundred a-year.

I ne'er, if I live to the age of Old Parr,
  Can fail to remember how stared brother Bill,
Jack bullied, and Tom, who is now at the Bar,
  Drove post to a Proctor to knock up the will.
      They never could trace
      What beauty or grace
      Sir Christopher Catalogue saw in my face,
  To cut off three youths, to his bosom so dear,
  And deluge a fourth with Five Hundred a-year!

The will, though law-beaten, stood firm as a rock,
  The probate was properly lodged at the Bank;
Transferr'd to my name stood the spleen-moving stock,
  And I, in the West, bearded people of rank.
      No longer a clerk,
      I rode in the Park,
      Or lounged in Pall Mall till an hour after dark.
  I enter'd, what seem'd then, a happy career,
  Possess'd of a gig and Five Hundred a-year.

Ere long, I began to be bored by a guest,
  A strange sort of harpy, who poison'd my feast:
He visits, in London, the folks who dwell West,
  But seldom cohabits with those who live East.
      Bar, door-chain, or key,—
      Could not keep me free,—
      As brisk as a bailiff in bolted *Ennui.*
  " I 'm come," he still cried, " to partake of your cheer,
  I 'm partial to folks of Five Hundred a-year."

Meanwhile my three brothers, by prudence and care,
  Got onward in life, while I stuck by the wall;
Bill open'd a tea-shop in Bridgewater Square,
  And Jack, as a writer, grew rich in Bengal.
      Tom made his impressions
      Through Newgate transgressions,
      And got half the business at Clerkenwell Sessions.
  They march'd in the van, while I lagg'd in the rear,
  Condemn'd to *Ennui* and Five Hundred a-year.

Too little encouraged to feel self-assured,
  Too dull for retorts, and too timid for taunts;
By daughters and nieces I 'm barely endured,
  And mortally hated by mothers and aunts.
      If e'er I entangle
      A girl in an angle,
      Up steps some Duenna, love's serpent to strangle;
  "Come hither! dont talk to that fellow, my dear,
  His income is only Five Hundred a-year."

Without tact or talents to get into ton,
  No calling to stick to, no trade to pursue:
Thus London, hard stepmother, leaves me alone,
  With little to live on and nothing to do.
      Could I row a life-boat,
      Make a boot, or a coat,
      Or serve in a silversmith's shop, and devote
  My days to employment, my evenings to cheer,
  I 'd gladly give up my Five Hundred a-year.

## WHY DO WE LOVE?

I often think each tottering form,
  That limps along in life's decline,
Once bore a heart as young, as warm,
  As full of idle thoughts as mine—

And each has had his dream of joy,
  His own unequall'd pure romance ;
Commencing, when the blushing boy
  First thrills at lovely woman's glance :

And each could tell his tale of youth,
  And think its scenes of love evince
More passion, more unearthly truth,
  Than any tale before, or since.

Yes—they could tell of tender lays,
  At midnight penn'd in classic shades ;
—Of days more bright than modern days ;
  —Of maids more fair than living maids.

Of whispers in a willing ear,
  Of kisses on a blushing cheek ;
(—Each kiss—each whisper far too dear
  For modern lips to give, or speak.)

Of prospects too, untimely cross'd,
  Of passion slighted or betray'd ;
Of kindred spirits early lost,
  And buds that blossom'd but to fade.

Of beaming eyes, and tresses gay,
  —Elastic form, and noble brow ;
And charms—that all have pass'd away,
  And left them—*what we see them now !*

And is it so !—*Is* human love
  So *very* light and frail a thing ?
And must youth's brightest visions move,
  For ever on Time's restless wing ?

Must all the eyes that still are bright,
  And all the lips that talk of bliss,
And all the forms so fair to-night,
  Hereafter—only come to this ?

Then what are Love's best visions worth,
  If we at length must lose them thus ?
If all we value most on earth,
  Ere long must fade away from us ?

If that *one* being whom we take
  From all the world, and still recur
To all *she* said—and for her sake
  Feel far from *joy,* when far from her—

If that one form which we adore
  From youth to age, in bliss or pain,
Soon withers—and is seen no more,
  —Why do we love—*if love be vain ?*

## TABLE TALK.—NO. VIII.

### On the Old Age of Artists.

Mr. Nollekens died the other day at the age of eighty, and left 240,000 pounds behind him, and the name of one of our best English sculptors. There was a great scramble among the legatees, a codicil to a will with large bequests unsigned, and that last triumph of the dead or dying over those who survive—hopes raised and defeated without a possibility of retaliation, or the smallest use in complaint. The king was at first said to be left residuary legatee. This would have been a fine instance of romantic and gratuitous homage to Majesty, in a man who all his life-time could never be made to comprehend the abstract idea of the distinction of ranks or even of persons, He would go up to the Duke of York, or Prince of Wales (in spite of warning), take them familiarly by the button like common acquaintance, ask them *how their father did ;* and express pleasure at hearing he was well, saying, " when he was gone, we should never get such another." He once, when the old king was sitting to him for his bust, fairly stuck a pair of compasses into his nose to measure the distance from the upper lip to the forehead, as if he had been measuring a block of marble. His late Majesty laughed heartily at this, and was amused to find that there was a person in the world, ignorant of that vast interval which separated him from every other man. Nollekens, with all his loyalty, merely liked the man, and cared nothing about the king (which was one of those *mixed modes*, as Mr. Locke calls them, of which he had no more idea than if he had been one of the cream-coloured horses) —handled him like so much common clay, and had no other notion of the matter, but that it was his business to make the best bust of him he possibly could, and to set about it in the regular way. There was something in this plainness and simplicity that savoured perhaps of the hardness and dryness of his art, and of his own peculiar severity of manner. He conceived that one man's head differed from another's only as it was a better or worse subject for modelling, that a bad bust was not made into a good one by being stuck upon a pedestal, or by any painting or varnishing, and that by whatever name he was called, *" a man's a man for a' that."* A sculptor's ideas must, I should guess, be somewhat rigid and inflexible, like the materials in which he works. Besides, Nollekens's style was comparatively hard and edgy. He had as much truth and character, but none of the polished graces or transparent softness of Chantry. He had more of the rough, plain, downright honesty of his art. It seemed to be his character. Mr. Northcote was once complimenting him on his acknowledged superiority— " Ay, you made the best busts of any body!" " I don't know about that," said the other, his eyes (though their orbs were quenched) smiling with a gleam of smothered delight—" I only know I always tried to make them as like as I could !"

I saw this eminent and singular person one morning in Mr. Northcote's painting-room. He had then been for some time blind, and had been obliged to lay aside the exercise of his profession ; but he still took a pleasure in designing groups, and in giving directions to others for executing them. He and Northcote made a remarkable pair. He sat down on a low stool (from being rather fatigued), rested with both hands on a stick, as if he clung to the solid and tangible, had an habitual twitch in his limbs and motions, as if catching himself in the act of going too far in chiselling a lip or a dimple in a chin ; was *bolt*-upright, with features hard and square, but finely cut, a hooked nose, thin lips, an indented forehead ; and the defect in his sight completed his resemblance to one of his own masterly busts. He seemed, by time and labour, to " have *wrought* himself to stone." Northcote stood by his side—all air and spirit, stooping down to speak to him. The painter was in a loose morning-gown, with his back to the light ; his face was like a pale fine piece of colouring ; and his eye came out and glanced through the twilight of the past, like an old eagle looking from its eyrie in the clouds. In a moment they had lighted from the top of Mount Cenis in the Vatican—

> " As when a vulture on Imaus bred
>   Flies tow'rds the springs
>   Of Ganges and Hydaspes, Indian streams,"

these two fine old men lighted with winged thoughts on the banks of the Tiber, and there bathed and drank of the spirit of their youth. They talked of Titian and Bernini ; and Northcote mentioned, that when Roubilliac came back from Rome, after seeing the works of the latter, and went to look at his own in Westminster Abbey, he said—" By G——d, they looked like tobacco-pipes."

They then recalled a number of anecdotes of Day (a fellow-student of theirs), of Barry and Fuseli. Sir Joshua, and Burke, and Johnson were talked of. The names of these great sons of memory were in the room, and they almost seemed to answer to them—Genius and Fame flung a spell into the air,

> " And by the force of blear illusion,
>     Had drawn me on to my confusion,"

had I not been long ere this *siren-proof!* It is delightful, though painful, to hear two veterans in art thus talking over the adventures and studies of their youth, when one feels that they are not quite mortal, that they have one imperishable part about them, and that they are conscious, as they approach the farthest verge of humanity in friendly intercourse and tranquil decay, that they have done something that will live after them. The consolations of religion apart, this is perhaps the only salve that takes out the sting of that sore evil, Death ; and by lessening the impatience and alarm at his approach, often tempts him to prolong the term of his delay.

It has been remarked that artists, or at least academicians, live long. It is but a short while ago that Northcote, Nollekens, West, Flaxman, Cosway, and Fuseli were all living at the same time, in good health and spirits, without any diminution of faculties, all of them having long passed their grand climacteric, and attained to the highest reputation in their several departments. From these striking examples, the diploma of a Royal Academician seems to be a grant of a longer lease of life, among its other advantages. In fact, it is tantamount to the conferring a certain reputation in his profession and a competence on any man ; and thus supplies the wants of the body and sets his mind at ease. Artists in general, (poor devils!) I am afraid, are not a long-lived race.

They break up commonly about forty, their spirits giving way with the disappointment of their hopes of excellence, or the want of encouragement for that which they have attained, their plans disconcerted, and their affairs irretrievable; and in this state of mortification and embarrassment (more or less prolonged and aggravated) they are either starved or else drink themselves to death. But your Academician is quite a different sort of person. He "bears a charmed life, that must not yield" to duns, or critics, or patrons. He is free of Parnassus, and claims all the immunities of fame in his life-time. He has but to paint (as the sun has but to shine), to baffle envious maligners. He has but to send his pictures to the Exhibition at Somerset-House, in order to have them hung up: he has but to dine once a year with the Academy, the Nobility, the Cabinet-Minister, and the Members of the Royal Family, in order not to want a dinner all the rest of the year. Shall hunger come near the man that has feasted with princes?—shall a bailiff tap the shoulder on which a Marquis has familiarly leaned, 'that has been dubbed with knighthood? No, even the fell Serjeant Death stands as it were aloof, and he enjoys a kind of premature immortality in recorded honours and endless labours. Oh! what golden hours are his! In the short days of winter he husbands time; the long evenings of summer still find him employed! He paints on, and takes no thought for to-morrow. All is right in that respect. His bills are regularly paid, his drafts are duly honoured. He has exercise for his body, employment for his mind in his profession, and without ever stirring out of his painting-room. He studies as much of other things as he pleases. He goes into the best company, or talks with his sitters—attends at the Academy Meetings, and enters into their intrigues and cabals, or stays at home, and enjoys the *otium cum dignitate.* If he is fond of reputation, Fame watches him at work, and weaves a woof, like Iris, over his head—if he is fond of money, Plutus digs a mine under his feet. Whatever he touches becomes gold. He is paid half-price before he begins; and commissions pour in upon commissions. His portraits are like, and his historical pieces fine: for to question the talents or success of a Royal Academician is to betray your own want of taste. Or if his pictures are not quite approved, he is an agreeable man, and converses well. Or he is a person of elegant accomplishments, dresses well, and is an ornament to a private circle. A man is not an Academician for nothing. "His life spins round on its soft axle;" and in a round of satisfied desires and pleasing avocations, without any of the *wear and tear* of thought or business, there seems no reason why it should not run smoothly on to its last sand!

Of all the Academicians, the painters, or persons I have ever known, Mr. Northcote is the most to my taste. It may be said of him truly,

> "Age cannot wither, nor custom stale
> His infinite variety."

Indeed, it is not possible he should become tedious, since, even if he repeats the same thing, it appears quite new from his manner, that breathes new life into it, and from his eye, that is as fresh as the morning. How you hate any one who tells the same story or anticipates a remark of his—it seems so coarse and vulgar, so dry and inanimate! There is something like injustice in this preference—but no! it is a tribute to the spirit that is in the man. Mr. Northcote's manner is completely *extempore*. It is just the reverse of Mr. Canning's oratory. All his thoughts come upon him unawares, and for this reason they surprise and delight you, because they have evidently the same effect upon his mind. There is the same unconsciousness in his conversation that has been pointed out in Shakspeare's dialogues; or you are startled with one observation after another, as when the mist gradually withdraws from a landscape and unfolds objects one by one. His figure is small, shadowy, emaciated; but you think only of his face, which is fine and expressive. His body is out of the question. It is impossible to convey an adequate idea of the *naiveté*, and unaffected, but delightful ease of the way in which he goes on—now touching upon a picture—now looking for his snuff-box—now alluding to some book he has been reading—now returning to his favourite art. He seems just as if he was by himself or in the company of his own thoughts, and makes you feel quite at home. If it is a Member of Parliament, or a beautiful woman, or a child, or a young artist that drops in, it makes no difference; he enters into conversation with them in the same unconstrained manner, as if they were inmates in his family. Sometimes you find him sitting on the floor, like a school-boy at play, turning over a set of old prints; and I was pleased to hear him say the other day, coming to one of some men putting off in a boat from a shipwreck—" *That is the grandest and most original thing I ever did!*" This was not ego-tism, but had all the beauty of truth and sincerity. The print was indeed a noble and spirited design. The circumstance from which it was taken happened to Sir Harry Englefield and his crew. He told Northcote the story, sat for his own head, and brought the men from Wapping to sit for theirs; and these he had arranged into a formal composition, till one Jeffrey, a conceited but clever artist of that day, called in upon him, and said, " Oh! that common-place thing will never do, it is like West; you should throw them into an action something like this."—Accordingly, the head of the boat was reared up like a sea-horse riding the waves, and the elements put into commotion, and when the painter looked at it the last thing as he went out of his room in the dusk of the evening, he said that "*it frightened him.*" He retained the expression in the faces of the men nearly as they sat to him. It is very fine, and truly English; and being natural, it was easily made into history. There is a portrait of a young gentleman striving to get into the boat, while the crew are pushing him off with their oars; but at last he prevailed with them by his perseverance and entreaties to take him in. They had only time to throw a bag of biscuits into the boat before the ship went down; which they divided into a biscuit a day for each man, dipping them into water which they collected by holding up their handkerchiefs in the rain and squeezing it into a bottle. They were out sixteen days in the Atlantic, and got ashore at some place in Spain, where the great difficulty was to prevent them from eating too much at once, so as to recover gradually. Sir Harry Englefield observed that he suffered more afterwards than at the time—that he had horrid dreams of falling down precipices for a long while after—that in the boat they told merry stories, and kept up one another's spirits as well as they could, and on some complaint being made of their distressed situation, the young gentleman who had been

admitted into their crew, remarked, " Nay, we are not so badly off
neither, we are not come to eating one another yet !"—Thus, whatever
is the subject of discourse, the scene is revived in his mind, and every
circumstance brought before you without affectation or effort, just as it
happened. It might be called *picture-talking.* He has always some
pat allusion or anecdote. A young engraver came into his room the
other day, with a print which he had put into the crown of his hat, in
order not to crumple it, and he said it had been nearly blown away
several times in passing along the street. " You put me in mind,"
said Northcote, " of a bird-catcher at Plymouth, who used to put the
birds he had caught into his hat to bring them home, and one day
meeting my father in the road, he pulled off his hat to make him a low
bow, and all the birds flew away !" Sometimes Mr. Northcote gets to
the top of a ladder to paint a palm-tree or to finish a sky in one of his
pictures ; and in this situation he listens very attentively to any thing
you tell him. I was once mentioning some strange inconsistencies of our
modern poets ; and on coming to one that exceeded the rest, he descended the steps of the ladder one by one, laid his pallet and brushes
deliberately on the ground, and coming up to me, said—" You don't
say so ; it's the very thing I should have supposed of them : yet these
are the men that speak against Pope and Dryden." Never any sar-
casms were so fine, so cutting, so careless as his. The grossest things
from his lips seem an essence of refinement : the most refined become
more so than ever. Hear him talk of Pope's Epistle to Jervas, and
repeat the lines—

> " Yet should the Graces all thy figures place,
> And breathe an air divine on every face ;
> Yet should the Muses bid my numbers roll
> Strong as their charms, and gentle as their soul,
> With Zeuxis' Helen thy Bridgewater vie,
> And these be sung till Granville's Myra die :
> Alas ! how little from the grave we claim ;
> Thou but preserv'st a face, and I a name."

Or let him speak of Boccacio and his story of Isabella and her pot of
basil, in which she kept her lover's head and watered it with her tears,
" and how it grew, and it grew, and it grew," and you see his own eyes
glisten, and the leaves of the basil-tree tremble to his faltering accents !

Mr. Fuseli's conversation is more striking and extravagant, but less
pleasing and natural than Mr. Northcote's. He deals in paradoxes and
caricatures. He talks allegories and personifications, as he paints
them. You are sensible of effort without any repose—no careless
pleasantry—no traits of character or touches from nature—every thing
is laboured or overdone. His ideas are gnarled, hard, and distorted,
like his features—his theories stalking and straddle-legged, like his
gait—his projects aspiring and gigantic, like his gestures—his performance uncouth and dwarfish, like his person. His pictures are also
like himself, with eye-balls of stone stuck in rims of tin, and muscles
twisted together like ropes or wires. Yet Fuseli is undoubtedly a man
of genius, and capable of the most wild and grotesque combinations of
fancy. It is a pity that he ever applied himself to painting, which must
always be reduced to the test of the senses. He is a little like Dante

or Ariosto, perhaps; but no more like Michael Angelo, Raphael, or Correggio, than I am. Nature, he complains, puts him out. Yet he can laugh at artists who "paint ladies with iron lap-dogs;" and he describes the great masters of old in words or lines full of truth, and glancing from a pen or tongue of fire. I conceive any person would be more struck with Mr. Fuseli at first sight, but would wish to visit Mr. Northcote oftener. There is a bold and startling outline in his style of talking, but not the delicate finishing or bland tone that there is in that of the latter. Whatever there is harsh or repulsive about him is, however, in a great degree carried off by his animated foreign accent and broken English, which give character where there is none, and soften its asperities where it is too abrupt and violent.

Compared to either of these artists, West, the late President of the Royal Academy, was a thoroughly mechanical and common-place person—a man "of no mark or likelihood." He, too, was small, thin, but with regular, well-formed features, and a precise, sedate, self-satisfied air. This, in part, arose from the conviction in his own mind that he was the greatest painter, and consequently the greatest man, in the world. Kings and nobles were common every-day folks, but there was but one West in the many-peopled globe. If there was any one individual with whom he was inclined to share the palm of undivided superiority, it was with Bonaparte. When Mr. West had painted a picture, he thought it was perfect. He had no idea of any thing in the art but rules, and these he exactly conformed to; so that, according to his theory, what he did was quite right. He conceived of painting as a mechanical or scientific process, and had no more doubt of a face or a group in one of his high ideal compositions being what it ought to be, than a carpenter has that he has drawn a line straight with a ruler and a piece of chalk, or than a mathematician has that the three angles of a triangle are equal to two right ones.

When Mr. West walked through his gallery, the result of fifty years' labour, he saw nothing, either on the right or the left, to be added or taken away. The account he gave of his own pictures, which might seem like ostentation or rhodomontade, had a sincere and infantine simplicity in it. When some one spoke of his *St. Paul shaking off the serpent from his arm*, (at Greenwich Hospital, I believe,) he said, " A little burst of genius, Sir !" West was one of those happy mortals who had not an idea of any thing beyond himself or his own actual powers and knowledge. I once heard him say in a public room, that he thought he had quite as good an idea of Athens from reading the Travelling Catalogues of the place, as if he lived there for years. I believe this was strictly true, and that he would have come away with the same slender, literal, unenriched idea of it as he went. Looking at a picture of Rubens, which he had in his possession, he said with great indifference, " What a pity that this man wanted expression !" This natural self-complacency might be strengthened by collateral circumstances of birth and religion: West, as a native of America, might be supposed to own no superior in the Commonwealth of art : as a Quaker, he smiled with sectarian self-sufficiency at the objections that were made to his theory or practice in painting. He lived long in the firm persuasion of being one of the elect among the sons of Fame, and went to his final rest in the arms of Immortality! Happy error! Enviable old man!

Flaxman is another living and eminent artist, who is distinguished by success in his profession, and by a prolonged and active old-age. He is diminutive in person, like the others. I know little of him, but that he is an elegant sculptor, and a profound mystic. This last is a character common to many other artists in our days—Loutherbourg, Cosway, Blake, Sharp, Varley, &c.—who seem to relieve the literalness of their professional studies by voluntary excursions into the regions of the preternatural, pass their time between sleeping and waking, and whose ideas are like a stormy night; with the clouds driven rapidly across, and the blue sky and stars gleaming between!

Cosway is the last of these I shall mention. At that name I pause, and must be excused if I consecrate to him a *petit souvenir* in my best manner; for he was Fancy's child. What a fairy palace was his of specimens of art, antiquarianism, and *virtà*, jumbled all together in the richest disorder, dusty, shadowy, obscure, with much left to the imagination, (how different from the finical, polished, petty, modernised air of some Collections we have seen!) and with copies of the old masters, cracked and damaged, which he touched and retouched with his own hand, and yet swore they were the genuine, the pure originals. All other collectors are fools to him: they go about with painful anxiety to find out the realities:—he *said* he had them—and in a moment made them of the breath of his nostrils and of the fumes of a lively imagination. His was the crucifix that Abelard prayed to—a lock of Eloïsa's hair—the dagger with which Felton stabbed the Duke of Buckingham —the first finished sketch of the Jocunda—Titian's large colossal profile of Peter Aretine—a mummy of an Egyptian king—a feather of a phoenix—a piece of Noah's Ark. Were the articles authentic? What matter?—his faith in them was true. He was gifted with a *second-sight* in such matters: he believed whatever was incredible. Fancy bore sway in him; and so vivid were his impressions, that they included the substances of things in them. The agreeable and the true with him were one. He believed in Swedenborgianism—he believed in animal magnetism—he had conversed with more than one person of the Trinity—he could talk with his lady at Mantua through some fine vehicle of sense, as we speak to a servant down-stairs through a conduit-pipe. Richard Cosway was not the man to flinch from an *ideal* proposition. Once, at an Academy dinner, when some question was made whether the story of Lambert's Leap was true, he started up, and said it was; for he was the person that performed it:—he once assured me that the knee-pan of King James I. in the ceiling at Whitehall was nine feet across (he had measured it in concert with Mr. Cipriani, who was repairing the figures)—he could read in the Book of the Revelations without spectacles, and foretold the return of Bonaparte from Elba—and from St. Helena! His wife, the most lady-like of Englishwomen, being asked in Paris what sort of a man her husband was, made answer—" *Toujours riant, toujours gai.*" This was his character. He must have been of French extraction. His soul appeared to possess the life of a bird; and such was the jauntiness of his air and manner, that to see him sit to have his half-boots laced on, you would fancy (by the help of a figure) that, instead of a little withered elderly gentleman, it was Venus attired by the Graces. His miniatures and whole-length drawings were not merely fashionable—they were fashion itself. His imitations of Michael Angelo were not the thing. When more than ninety, he retired from his profession, and used to hold up the palsied hand that had painted lords and ladies for upwards of sixty years, and smiled, with unabated good-humour, at the vanity of human wishes. Take him with all his faults and follies, we scarce " shall look upon his like again!"

Why should such persons ever die? It seems hard upon them and us! Care fixes no sting in their hearts, and their persons " present no mark to the foe-man." Death in them seizes upon living shadows. They scarce consume vital air : their gross functions are long at an end—they live but to paint, to talk or think. Is it that the vice of age, the miser's fault, gnaws them? Many of them are not afraid of death, but of coming to want ; and having begun in poverty, are haunted with the idea that they shall end in it, and so die—*to save charges.* Otherwise, they might linger on for ever, and " defy augury !"

---

## MRS. DOBBS AT HOME.

" The common chat of gossips when they meet."  DRYDEN.

WHAT! shall the Morning Post proclaim
For every rich or high-born dame,
From Portman Square to Cleveland Row,
Each item—no one cares to know ;
Print her minutest whereabouts,
Describe her concerts, balls, and routs,
Enumerate the lamps and lustres,
Shew where the roses hung in clusters,
Tell how the floor was chalk'd—reveal
The partners in the first quadrille—
How long they danced, till, sharp as hunters,
They sat down to the feast from Gunter's ;
How much a quart was paid for peas,
How much for pines and strawberries,
Taking especial care to fix
The hour of parting—half past six ?—
And shall no bard make proclamation
Of routs enjoy'd in humbler station?
Rise, honest Muse, to Hackney roam,
And sing of——" Mrs. Dobbs at Home."

He who knows Hackney, needs must know
That spot enchanting—Prospect Row,
So call'd because a view it shows
Of Shoreditch Road, and when there blows
No dust, the folks may one and all get
A peep—almost to Norton Falgate.
Here Mrs. Dobbs at Number Three
Invited all her friends to tea.
The Row had never heard before
Such double knocks at any door,
And heads were popp'd from every casement,
Counting the comers with amazement.

Some magnified them to eleven,
While others swore there were but seven,
A point that's keenly mooted still,
But certain 'tis that Mrs. Gill
Told Mrs. Grub she reckoned ten :—
Fat Mrs. Hobbs came second—then
Came Mesdames Jinkins, Dump, and Spriggins,
Tapps, Jacks, Briggs, Hoggins, Crump, and Wiggins.

Dizen'd in all her best array,
Our melting hostess said her say,
    As the Souchong repast proceeded,
And curtsying and bobbing press'd
By turns each gormandizing guest,
    To stuff as heartily as she did.
Dear Mrs. Hoggins, what!—your cup
Turn'd in your saucer, bottom up !—
    Dear me, how soon you're had your fill,
Let me persuade you—one more sup,
    'Twill do you good, indeed it will :—
Psha now, you're only making game,
Or else you *tea'd* afore you came.

Stop Mrs. Jinkins, let me stir it,
    Before I pour out any more.—
No, Ma'am, that's just as I prefer it.—
    O then I'll make it as before.

Lauk! Mrs. Dump, that toast seems dry,
    Do take and eat this middle bit,
The butter's fresh, you may rely,
    And a fine price I paid for it.—
No doubt, Ma'am,—what a shame it is !
And Cambridge too again has ris !
You don't deal now with Mrs. Keats?
No, she's a bad one :—Ma'am, she cheats.—
Hush ! Mrs. Crump's her aunt.—Good lack !
How lucky she just turn'd her back !

Don't spare the toast, Ma'am, don't say no,
I've got another round below,
I give folks plenty when I ax 'em,
For cut and come again's my maxim,
Nor should I deem it a misfort'n,
If you demolish'd the whole quart'n,
Though bread is now a shameful price,—
Why did they 'bolish the assize?

A charming garden, Mrs. Dobbs,
For drying.—Ain't it, Mrs. Hobbs ?
But though our water-tub runs o'er,
A heavy wash is such a bore,
Our smalls is all that we hang out.—
Well, that's a luxury, no doubt.

La ! Mrs. Tapps, do only look,
Those grouts can never be mistook ;
Well, *such* a cup ! it can't be worse,
See, here's six horses in a hearse,
And there's the church and burying-place,
Plain as the nose upon your face :
Next dish may dissipate your doubts,
And give you less unlucky grouts :

One more—you must—the pot has stood,
I warrant me it's strong and good.

There's Mrs. Spriggins in the garden;
What a fine gown!—but, begging pardon,
It seems to me amazing dingy—
Do you think her shawl, Ma'am,'s real *Injy?*—'
Lord love you! no :—well, give me clo'es
That's plain and good, Ma'am, not like those.
Though not so tawdry, Mrs. Jacks,
We do put *clean* things on our backs.

Meat, Ma'am, is scand'lous dear.—Perhaps
You deal, Ma'am, still with Mrs. Tapps.—
Not I;—we know who's got to pay,
When butchers drive their one-horse chay,—
Well, I pay nine for rumps.—At most
We pay but eight for boil'd and roast,
And get our rumps from Leadenhall
At seven, taking shins and all.
Yes, meat is monstrous dear all round;
But dripping brings a groat a pound.

Thus on swift wing the moments flew,
Until 'twas time to say adieu,
When each prepared to waddle back,
Warm'd with a sip of Cogniac,
Which was with Mrs. Dobbs a law,
Whene'er the night was cold and raw.
Umbrellas, pattens, lanterns, clogs,
Were sought—away the party jogs,
And silent solitude again
O'er Prospect Row resumed its reign,
Just as the Watchman crawl'd in sight,
To cry—"Past ten—a cloudy night!"

---

## MEMOIRS OF A HAUNCH OF MUTTON.

" I, in this kind of merry fooling, am nothing to you; so you may continue and
laugh at nothing still."—*The Tempest.*

THIS is the age for memoirs, particularly of royalty. Napoleon is
making almost as much noise after his death as he did in his life-time;
Marie Antoinette, by the assistance of Madame de Campan, has obtained a revival of her notoriety; and Louis Dix-huit has effected his
escape to Coblentz only to fall into the claws of the critics, by proving
that every king is not a Solomon. This epidemic is understood to be
spreading among the rulers of the earth, and several of the London
booksellers have already started for different capitals of Europe for the
purpose, it is said, of treating with crowned authors. Fortunately
there is no royal road to biography any more than to geometry; the
right divine does not include all the good writing, nor has legitimacy
any exclusive alliance with Priscian. Men who have brains inside may
scribble as well as those who have crowns outside; beggars and thieves
have given their own lives to the public; nay, even things inanimate—
a wonderful lamp, a splendid shilling, a guinea, have found historians;

why then should the lords of the creation have all the memoirs to
themselves?

> "All our praises why should Lords engross?
> Rise, honest Muse, and sing"——

"The Haunch of Mutton," which, for aught that appears to the contrary, may claim a rectilinear descent from the Royal Ram eternized
by Mother Bunch, and so be entitled to rank with the best imperial or
kingly records that are now issuing from the Row. Into this investigation, curious as it would be, it is not my purpose to enter; it would
be irrelevant to my title, which has only reference to sheep after they
are dead, and designated as mutton; but I cannot refrain from noticing
that even in this point of view the subject I have chosen is poetical, for
a poet, like a Merino or South Down, is annually fleeced and sheared,
and at last cut up by the critical dissectors; but he is no sooner dead
than he acquires a new name, we sit down to his perusal with great
satisfaction, make repeated extracts which we find entirely to our taste,
and talk complacently of his rich vein, ready flow, his sweetness, tenderness, and so forth.

Suffice it to say, that the sheep from which our hero, *i. e.* our haunch
was cut, drew breath in the pastures of Farmer Blewett, of Sussex,
whose brother, Mr. William Blewett, (commonly called Billy,) of Great
St. Helen's, in the city of London, is one of the most eminent Indigo
brokers in the Metropolis. The farmer having a son fourteen years of
age whom he was anxious to place in the counting-house of the said
Billy, very prudently began by filling his brother's mouth before he
opened his own, and had accordingly sent him an enormous turkey at
Christmas, a side of fat bacon at Easter, and at Midsummer the identical haunch of South Down mutton, whose dissection and demolition
we have undertaken to immortalize. Ever attentive to the main chance,
the broker began to calculate that if he asked three or four friends to
dine with him he could only eat mutton for one, while he would have to
find wine for the whole party; whereas, if he presented it to Alderman
Sir Peter Pumpkin, of Broad-street, who was a dear lover of good
mutton, and had besides lately received a consignment of Indigo, of
which he was anxious to propitiate the brokerage, he might not only
succeed in that object, but be probably asked to dinner, get his full
share of the haunch, and drink that wine which he preferred to all
others—*videlicet*, that which he tippled at other people's expense.
Whether or not he succeeded in the former aim, our documents do not
testify, but certain it is that he was invited to partake of the haunch in
Broad-street, (not being deemed a presentable personage at the baronet's
establishment in Devonshire-place); Mr. Robert Rule, Sir Peter's book-
keeper and head clerk, who presided over the city household, was asked
to meet him, as well as his nephew, Mr. Henry Pumpkin, a young col-
legian, whose affection for his uncle induced him to run up to London
whenever his purse became attenuated, and who in his progress towards
qualifying himself for the church, had already learnt to tie a cravat,
drive a tandem, drink claret, and make bad puns. Four persons, as
the baronet observed, were quite enough for a haunch of mutton, and
too many for one of venison.

"I shouldn't have waited for you, Harry," exclaimed the baronet,

as his nephew entered. " No occasion, Sir; I am always punctual—
Boileau says, that the time a man makes a company wait for him is always
spent in discovering his faults."—" Does he? then he's a sensible
fellow; and if he's a friend of yours you might have brought him to
dinner with you.—But you needn't have made yourself such a dandy,
Harry, merely to dine at the counting-house."—" Why, Sir, as I expected the dinner to be well dressed for me, I thought I could not do
less than return the compliment."—" Ha, ha, ha! do you hear that
Billy?—not a bad one, was it? Egad, Harry doesn't go to College for
nothing. But there's the 'Change clock chiming for five, and we ought
to have dinner. Ay, I remember when four was the hour, and a very
good hour too."—" I lately tumbled upon a letter of Addison's to Swift,"
interrupted Henry, " dated 29th Feb. 1707, inviting him to meet
Steele and Frowde at the George in Pall-mall, at two o'clock, which
was then the fashionable hour. And apropos of haunches, I remember
reading, that in 1720, the year of the South Sea bubble, owing to the
fancied riches suddenly flowing in upon the citizens, a haunch of venison rose to the then unexampled value of five guineas, so that deer
were dear indeed for one season."—" A fine thing to have been owner of
a herd that year," said Mr. Blewett.—" Capital!" observed Mr. Rule,
with an emphatic jerk of the head.—" In the mean time where is our
haunch of mutton?" inquired the Alderman:—" do, pray, Mr. Rule, see
about it—the cook used to be punctual, and it is now two minutes and
a half past five." Mr. Rule bowed and disappeared, but presently returned, announcing that dinner was served.

Sir Peter sat at the head of the table, and as Philip the servant was
about to remove the cover, laid his hand upon his arm to stop him,
until he was provided with a hot plate, vegetables, and sweet sauce, so
as to be all ready for the attack when the trenches were opened.
" Beautiful!" he exclaimed, as the joint was revealed to him; " done
to a turn—admirably frothed up!" so exclaiming, he helped himself
plenteously to the best part, and pushing away the dish said " he had
no doubt the others would rather help themselves." Mr. Rule, who
had not yet achieved independence enough to be clownish, volunteered
to supply his neighbours, which he did so clumsily, that Harry declared he should never be his joint executor; and Mr. Blewett applied
his more experienced hand to the task. For the first ten minutes
so much went into the baronet's mouth that there was no room for a
single word to come out; but, as his voracity became gratified, he found
leisure to ask his guests to drink wine, and to cackle at intervals what
he termed some of his good stories.—" Clever fellow, King Charles:
they called him the mutton-eating King, didn't they?—cut off his head
though for all that—stopped his mutton-eating; egad!—I say, Billy,
did I tell you what I said t'other day to Tommy Daw, the bill-broker.
Tommy's a Bristol man, you know: well, I went down to Bristol about
our ship the Fanny that got ashore there."—"The Fanny, Capt. Tyson,
was in Dock at the time," interrupted Rule; " it was the Adventure,
Capt. Hacklestone, that got ashore."—" Well, well, never mind—
where was I?—O, ay;—so says Tommy to me when I came back, Is
Betsy Bayley as handsome as ever?—who bears the bell now at
Bristol?—Why, says I—the bellman, to be sure! Ha! ha! ha! ha!—
Egad, I thought Tommy would have burst his sides with laughing—

Who bears the bell at Bristol? says he—"Why the bellman, says I?
Capital, wasn't it?"—"Capital," ejaculated Mr. Rule, with a most
decisive energy.

"It's a pity this stewed beefsteak at the bottom should be wasted,"
said Blewett, "nobody tastes it."—"It won't be wasted," replied Harry,
"it economizes our dinner."—"How so?"—"Because it serves to
make both ends *meet*."—"Aha! Billy," roared the Baronet; "he had
you there. I told you Harry didn't go to college for nothing."—"By
the by, sir," continued the nephew, "did you ever hear of Shakspeare's
receipt for dressing a beefsteak?"—"Shakspeare's!—no—the best I ever
eat were at Dolly's;—but what is it?"—"Why, sir, he puts it into the
mouth of Macbeth, where he makes him exclaim—'If it were done
when 'tis done, then it were well 'twere done quickly.'"—"Good,
good," cackled the Baronet, "but I said a better thing than Shakspeare last week. You know Jack Foster the common council man,
ugly as Buckhorse—gives famous wine though;—well, we were talking
about the best tavern, (I'll thank you for some sweet sauce, Mr. Rule);
and so says I—(and a little of the brown fat if you please)—and so
says I—Jack, I never see your face without thinking of a good dinner.
'Why so?' says Jack. Because it's ordinary every day at two o'clock,'
says I." Here the Baronet was seized with such a violent fit of laughter
that it brought on an alarming attack of coughing and expectoration; but
he no sooner recovered breath enough than he valiantly repeated—"Why,
so, Jack?—Because it's ordinary every day at two o'clock, says I"—
which he followed up with a new cackle, while Mr. Rule delivered
himself most dogmatically of another "Capital!" and relapsed into
his usual solemnity.

"The greatest compliment ever offered to this joint," resumed the
nephew, "proceeded from a popular actor now living, who deemed it
the *ne plus ultra* of epicurism. Having been a long time in London
without seeing Richmond Hill, he was taken by some friends to enjoy
that noble view, then in the perfection of its summer beauty. The day
was fine—every thing propitious:—they led him up the hill and along
the dead wall till he reached the Terrace, where the whole glorious
vision burst upon him with such an overpowering effect, that he could
only exclaim, in the intensity of his ecstasy,—'A perfect Haunch, by
Heaven!'"

"You will be at Kemble's sale to-morrow, Sir Peter?" inquired
Blewett.—"What!" replied the nephew, "are poor John Philip's books
to be sold? I shall attend certainly. I understand he possessed the
first edition of Piers Plowman—The Maid's Tragedy—Gammer Gur-
ton's Needle, and——" "Hoity toity!" interrupted Sir Peter; "what
the deuce is the lad chattering about?"—"Bless me, Mr. Henry,"
cried Rule, "you have surely seen the catalogue of the great sale in
Mincing Lane—1714 bales of Pernambuco cotton, 419 of Maranham,
96 hogsheads and 14 tierces of Jamaica sugar, 311 bags of coffee, and
66 casks of Demerara cocoa. I believe I can favour you with a perusal of the catalogue with all the best lots marked."—"Infinitely
obliged to you," replied Harry, "but I had rather undergo the lot of
being knocked down myself."

"Aha!" exclaimed the Baronet, with a look of gloating delight;
"now we shall get on again. Here comes the Argyle with some hot
gravy;—that was a famous invention."—"Nothing like it," replied

Harry, "in the Marquis of Worcester's whole Century. A distinguished writer desires one of our noble families to consider the name of Spenser the poet, as the fairest jewel in their coronet. May we not extend the same remark to the ducal race, whose name will, by this discovery, be constantly in our mouths?"—"Ay, and whose celebrity will thus be kept up, hot and hot," added Sir Peter. "Egad, I'll drink their healths in a bumper, and take another slice upon the strength of it. One ought to encourage such ingenious improvements."

"I am afraid, Sir Peter, that the best side's all gone," said Mr. Blewett, with a whine of pretended regret, which had a prospective reference to the brokerage on the indigo. "That I beg leave to deny," retorted Harry, "for it is one of the Peptic precepts, that in politics and gastronomy, the best side is that where there is most to be got, and there are still a few slices left under the bone."—"If we had a good stimulating sauce now," said the Alderman, "I could still go on." "But there," continued the nephew, "we are still nearly as deficient as we were in the time of Louis Quatorze, whose ambassador at London complained that he had been sent among a set of barbarians who had twenty religions and only three fish-sauces."—"Why, Billy," cried the Alderman to Blewett, "you seem as down in the mouth as the root of my tongue;—blue as your own Indigo."—"That's a famous lot of Guatimola you have just received, Sir Peter, by the Two Sisters, Capt. Framlingham: may I call to take samples?"—"We'll talk of that by and by, Billy: meantime take a sample of port: help yourself."—"He can't help himself, poor fellow," said Harry, "for the bottle's empty." The Baronet nodded to Rule, who instantly betook himself to a basket in the corner of the room, and began decanting another with mathematical precision. "Take care, Rule, it won't bear shaking—I have had it fourteen years in bottle."—"And port wine," observed Harry, "is like mankind—the older it gets, the more crusty it becomes, and the less will it bear being disturbed."—"A little tawney!" said the uncle, smacking his lips; "I doubt whether this is out of the right bin."—"No, sir," replied the nephew; "this seems to be out of the *has been*. *Troja fuit*:—but you have got some prime claret."—"Ay, ay, we'll have a touch at that after the cloth's cleared; but will nobody take another mouthful of the haunch? the meat was short, crisp, and tender, just as it ought to be." "Capital!" ejaculated Rule, with a momentary animation, succeeded by his habitual look of formality. "Then the table may be cleared," continued the Alderman, "but zooks! Harry, how comes it you never said grace before dinner?" "You were in such a hurry, sir, that you forgot to ask me: it was but last week you called me a scapegrace, and I may now retort the epithet." "Say grace now then, saucebox." "I have not yet taken orders, Sir Peter." "Yes you have, you have taken mine, so out with it." Harry compressed the benediction into five words—the cloth was removed—a bottle of Chateau Margaud was placed upon the table to his infinite consolation—the talk quickened with the circulation of the wine, and many good things were uttered which we regret that we cannot commemorate without travelling out of the record, as our subject ceased with the dinner, being expressly confined to the "Memoirs of a Haunch of Mutton."     H.

## THE MOORISH BRIDAL SONG. *

THE Citron groves their fruit and flowers were strewing
Around a Moorish palace, and the sigh
Of summer's gentlest wind, the branches wooing,
With music through their twilight-bowers went by;
Music and voices from the marble halls,
Through the leaves gleaming, midst the fountain-falls.

A song of joy, a bridal song came swelling
To blend with fragrance in those southern shades,
And told of feasts within the stately dwelling,
And lights, and dancing steps, and gem-crown'd maids;
And thus it flow'd;—yet something in the lay
Belong'd to sadness as it died away.

" The Bride comes forth! her tears no more are falling
To leave the chamber of her infant years,
Kind voices from another home are calling,
She comes like day-spring—she hath done with tears!
Now·must her dark eye shine on other flowers,
Her bright smile gladden other hearts than ours!
         —Pour the rich odours round!

" We haste! the chosen and the lovely bringing,
Love still goes with her from her place of birth,
Deep silent joy within her heart is springing,
For this alone her glance hath less of mirth!
Her beauty leaves us in its rosy years,
Her sisters weep—but she hath done with tears!
         Now may the timbrel sound !"

Know'st thou for whom they sang the bridal numbers ?
—One, whose rich tresses were to wave no more!
One whose pale cheek soft winds, nor gentle slumbers,
Nor Love's own sigh to rose-tints might restore!
Her graceful ringlets o'er a bier were spread—
—Weep for the young, the beautiful, the dead!          F. H.

---

## SONNET FROM THE ITALIAN.

YE warbling birds, that thus, from bough to bough,
    Pour forth, at eve, your melting melodies !
    Ye free and happy people of the skies,
    Whose loves no stain of sordid avarice know!—
Far other feelings in your bosoms glow—
    Ye reck not of man's vain and empty ties,
    Nor dream of broken vows, nor faith that flies
As swift as rivers run, or breezes blow.
O happy ye! whose soft emotions own
    No deity but Love—condemn'd to flee
    With us before a sullen father's frown.
Alike in age, in beauty, and in love,
    The God of Love himself hath mated ye,
    Who never links the raven with the dove.

---

* It is a custom among the Moors to sing the bridal song when the funeral of an
unmarried woman is borne from her home.

## WINCHESTER.

" ————Great Arthur's seat ould Winchester prefers,
Whose ould Round Table yet she vaunteth to be her's."

MICHAEL DRAYTON.

WINCHESTER is certainly the most quiet, unobtrusive, and unpretending place I ever entered. There is a religious solemnity in its high way and very market-house; a dim and shadowy gloom over its most frequented thoroughfares;—indeed, one part of the High-street itself is but a monkish cloister, with disproportioned and swollen columns, and flat heavy architrave, instead of slender and reeded shafts, with flowering tracery above them. The by-streets have the same relation to the High-street that the cloisters have to a cathedral:—they are of the same age and character, only more silent and gloomy, more deep and broad in their shadows—so deep, indeed, that having taken up my quarters with " mine host" of the Fleur de Lis, who resides in one of them, I am writing by candle-light an hour before sun-set. All this falls well enough in with my humour; or my humour, cameleon-bred, has taken its colouring from surrounding things. How the gay trappings and rich " harnessing," with the " drums and trumpets," and parading of two thousand military, might have destroyed its quiet during the war, I know not; but I am grateful that at my visitation the sole inhabitant of these splendid barracks was an unobtrusive serjeant, with enough of the citizen about him, in half a dozen civil children, to leave the illusion perfect. But even in those worst of times—at least we poor speculators may be allowed so to speak of them without offence, for our " calling," as Falstaff would say, is then secondary to a posting messenger, and our brain labours to the lying nonsense, or hasty nothing, of a third edition—even then, the appearance of this city was never disfigured with the temporary, black, dull-looking, boarded hovels, that in most other places are called barracks. Here it would be no excess to say our soldiers are lodged like princes; for they are quartered in the very palace, and the exterior remains perfect and unchanged, erected by Charles II. and designed and executed by Sir Christopher Wren. It is, on the whole, a fine building, though much inferior to many of his other works. It stands on an elevation immediately above the town, and from all the surrounding country has a good though not a grand effect. It is built principally of brick, with a regular front, which never can have a grand effect, be the magnitude of the edifice what it may. There is a poverty in the material which in an uniform building can never be kept out of mind; and the only instances in which I have seen brick used on a large scale where this feeling has not predominated, have been in the few old bay-windowed, turreted, half-castellated, deep-courted, and close-wooded houses of the nobility of the Tudors; where you have no long and open approach, but enter direct, from the deep shadows of old trees, into the deeper shadows of the court-yard and the mansion—

" Chamberis and parlers of a sorte,
With bay windows goodlie as may be thought,
The galleries right wele y wrought,
As for dauncinge and otherwise disporte."

Most nations are fond of originality, and believe many ridiculous

things that flatter this humour; but, if the English were to put in a
claim to this fine old mansion of our ancestors, I question if their pretensions would not be admitted. Your cognoscenti, and professional gentlemen might gibe us with our humility, but a little indifferent originality
is worth the Parthenon on the Calton-hill and the newly christened
Achilles together. "Well, Sir, but of what order is it—Tuscan, Doric,
Ionic, Composite, or Corinthian?" I answer, not one of them; for if it
were, how could it be original? But I say it has all the characteristics
that distinguish originality, and are its highest pretensions—adaptation,
and use. It is well, admirably well, suited to this varying, ever-shift-
ing climate of ours:—instead of looking out for six months together
from a "commanding eminence" into the raw air, and over a vast map
of indistinguishable melancholy, you look into a warm court-yard
against a high ivied tower, with the little sun that may be reflected from
it, and with a swarm of birds chattering and joying themselves, or out
under the thick branching oaks upon the herd of fat deer sheltered and
browsing at the very threshold:—instead of the thin frame-work, and
bald poverty of your Italian window, which neither does nor was intended to shut out the bitter cold of our December, or the cutting
winds of March, you have the mullions and tracery of the magnificent
old bay-window, with its three feet of solid pannelling below, and its
deep-stained glass above, the very shadow of which is warmth and positive enjoyment.

On the site of the present barracks stood the old Castle, the history
of which is closely interwoven with the early records of our country:
indeed, whoever shall visit Winchester has need of some antiquarian
lore, or a spirit of research that bids defiance to hard names and many
centuries: and close adjoining is the County-hall, originally the chapel
of the Castle, and enclosed within its walls. Here is preserved the
"ould round table" which for so many centuries has been the boast of
Winchester. That this table was ever King Arthur's, I need not add,
is a fable; but if seven or eight centuries are old enough to gratify
curiosity, it is probably of no less age, and if not the festive board
when "Arthur held high feast at Pentecost, was that of "King Stephen
and his worthy Peers." It is made of thick oak plank, painted over,
and portioned into different compartments, each division being labelled,
in old English characters, with the name of a knight; except that in
one of them, instead of the name, is the full-length portrait of Arthur
himself, looking like the knave of clubs on a Pope Joan board. It
was possibly to this very hall, that Markham and the gallant young
Lord Grey were removed while King James's farce of execution and
pardon were going on. They had been both confined in the Castle,
and the place of execution was within the Castle-yard, and in sight of
Raleigh, who was still confined there; and Sir Dudley Carleton, in the
minute and interesting description of this scene, to be found in the
Hardwicke state papers, says, that when Markham was on the scaffold the sheriff was secretly withdrawn by one of the grooms of the
bedchamber, and on his return told the prisoner that as he was so ill
prepared "he should yet have two hours respite, so led him from the
scaffold, without giving him any more comfort, and locked him into
*the great hall to walk with Prince Arthur.*" The same ceremony having
been gone through with Grey, the same mystery was observed in his
removal, "and he was likewise led to *Prince Arthur's* hall."

But, after all, the College and the Cathedral are the real glory of Winchester. The former, according to the hints and insinuations of her affectionate children and historians, might claim a higher antiquity then the "auld round table" itself ever pretended to; they run back, with an occasional halt in its history, of an odd century or two, to the very Romans themselves. But without credulity enough to pin our faith on such speculations, it will yet be admitted that Winchester is the parent both of Eton and Westminster, and has undoubted antiquity enough to satisfy any ordinary appetite; and, which is much more to its honour, it has not grown old with passing centuries; it is still full of vigour, and is now, as from the first, distinguished for the reputation of its scholars. The Education Committee, it is true, reported against some abuses; and some abuses, which they did not report against, flourish here, such as fagging and flogging; but these are barbarities sanctioned by so many ages, so interwoven with early habits and prejudices, so sanctified by all that makes bull-baiting pleasurable and cock-fighting Christian entertainment, that they excite no astonishment; yet surely it is ridiculous to see the legislature itself, goaded on by the humanity of the age, push beyond the bounds of a wise legislation, to protect animals from the tyranny of power and the brutality of passion, while the age itself surrenders up its youth a victim to both.

But forgetting these things, in which Winchester college is unfortunately not singular, it is a delightful place. Seen from a little below the falls of the mill, it is all that I had hoped it might be. Its seclusion, and the quiet of its immediate neighbourhood—its own venerable buildings, the still more venerable ruins of Wolvesey adjoining—the clear stream in front—the city houses, backed by the Cathedral on one side—and on the other, the open fields, stretching out to, and bounded, in the distance, by the towers of St. Cross, half hidden in noble trees, are all that imagination ever pictured a college when dreaming of collegiate ages, and what it could not have continued, but that the town has gradually decreased from its original splendour, and instead of extending beyond and eventually enclosing this fine building, has progressively shrunk from it. The approach, also, from the High-street, at least as I came to it, is just what it should be—first, through an avenue of elms, to the Cathedral itself—then the Prebendal houses—then the close, with some most majestic trees scattered about, that seem of little less antiquity than the buildings themselves—then the old Priory gateway, and immediately after, Kingsgate, with its druidical remains, which leads directly to the College. You now enter through a noble gateway into an outer court; and it is much to be regretted that its uniformity is destroyed by a modern building occupying one side of the square, and destroying the unity of design and appearance, which, but for this and the school-room, would be perfect throughout the whole range. Thence we pass into the inner-court under an arch and tower, ornamented with three canopied niches, containing statues of the Virgin, the angel Gabriel, and of Wykeham himself, in an attitude of adoration: and it is pleasant to observe, that the statues, the loss of which is so much to be regretted in all Gothic buildings, have here, even in the outer gateway, escaped the iconoclastic rage of the puritans. This inner-court is all that can be desired, and the hall, the chapel, the dormitories, and the surrounding offices, have a perfect conformity. The first feeling on entering here is of admiration. There is not a line or an ornament that is not consistent and in harmony with the rest of the building; and the bold buttresses of the hall, the rich windows, the superlatively light and beautiful tower of the Chapel, with the entrance gateway, are the most elegant assemblage of gothic ornaments, without break or offence from modern incongruities, that I ever witnessed. Hence we pass, either into the Chapel, or by a flight of stone steps into the Hall. The Chapel is now undergoing extensive repairs, and the general effect is lost by the necessary scaffolding; but when this is cleared away, it must be singularly imposing. The windows are all, or nearly all, filled with stained glass, which, like the statues, are wanting in most other Gothic buildings — its proportions are more than commonly grand—the roof is at an unusual elevation, and the groining of the roof is rich and bold without being oppressed or encumbered with ornament.

The Refectory, or College Hall, as it is called, is a handsome lofty room open to the rafters, which are ornamented in consequence. Here are many things worth observation, as illustrative of the manners of our ancestors, and now to be met with in few but collegiate places. Just before we enter, are three impenetrable old oak doors, with an outer half-door and ledge on the top; these are the hatches from which the tables are served, and so often mentioned by the old writers. Maria alludes to it in her jest on Sir Andrew's dry palm, " bring your hand to the buttery-bar, and let it drink." Immediately on entering there is a large covered basket fixed in the flooring to receive the broken victuals, a portion of which, if not the whole, are regularly sent to the poor prisoners in the gaol. These are customs that bear evidence of the considerate humanity of our ancestors, and it is to be regretted that our age hath let such practices die away—" Did our charity," says Lady Frugal, in her bitter revilings of Luke, " redeem thee out of prison,

> When the Sheriff's basket, and his broken meat,
> Were your festival exceedings."

In advancing farther into the room, it will be observed that the flooring at the upper end is raised some inches. This is, no doubt, the dais, about which commentators have often written, and which is mentioned in the description of the feast in Cedric's Hall in Ivanhoe.

Proceeding on from the Chapel Hall, we enter the cloisters, which are also open to the roofing, and much inferior to what I had expected. In the area of these is a very elegant little chapel in the highest preservation, originally built and endowed for a charity, where masses were to be performed for the dead. Its revenues, however, are gone, and it is now well filled with books, and converted into a library, where is preserved, a curious record of patience and folly, the genealogical table of Wykeham, uninterruptedly brought down from Adam. Of all things it requires most time to judge correctly of a library—mine was very limited :—it bears no proportion in magnitude, nor should I think in worth to Eton; yet there were many choice and some valuable works in it.

The School-room fortunately forms no part of this pile of building, but is concealed behind it. The strange perversity of the age in which it was built, seems to have defied all circumstance; for what else can account for the introduction here of any other order but Gothic? In itself it is finely proportioned, and every way noble. Over the entrance is a metal statue of the founder, presented by old Cibber, which, to make the whole consistently ridiculous, has been painted and gilt. Another of the absurdities is a monstrous representation of what is called a Trusty Servant, shewn in a small room adjoining the college hall. The humour of the thing, if it have any, is in giving reality to what were considered the moral excellences of such a character—in fact, such a pictorial representation as Mad Tom has given a poetical one, " hog in sloth, fox in stealth, wolf in greediness, dog in madness, lion in prey." Of course the worthy represented here is the reverse of all this, and the qualities and excellences which are presumed to be com- mon to both beasts, for such a servant would deserve no better men- tion, are represented by the four-footed ones—thus the trusty servant is not dainty in his diet, therefore the figure has the snout of a hog instead of the " human face divine," the feet of a deer, the ears of an ass, and is altogether a monstrous and most ridiculous compound. The figure has evidently been repainted ; and this is acknowledged, but the design and colouring of the original have al·,ays, it is said, been strictly followed. I much question this. It is habited in the regular " blue coat" of· the servants of the sixteenth century ; but it is proba- bly as old as that ; for early in the seventeenth, when most of the pe- culiarities of dress were fast wearing out, this was giving way. " I may well call 'em companions," says Lucie, in Middleton's comedy of A Trick to Catch the Old One, " for since *blue coats* have been turned into cloaks, we can scarce know the man from the master."

Having been delighted beyond measure with my visit here, I stretched out to St. Cross, which I have before mentioned as visible in the dis- tance. I could not hope for any equal gratification; yet St. Cross can disappoint no one, come after it what will, or be the visitor's imagina- tion what it may. The walk to it is through some luxuriant meadows, on the banks of the Itchin, and at the foot of St. Catherine's-hill ; and the whole surrounding neighbourhood is full of recollections. A Roman encampment is yet distinctly visible on the hill itself, which is the summer play-ground of the boys at the College, and the fabled scene of their *dulce domum*, which, though all may have heard, none know the full force of but a Wykehamist. Unless you have made one in a St. Catherine's pilgrimage, and joined in the chorus there, or have learnt it while yet a child, with something of mysterious reverence, in the immediate neighbourhood, you are shut out from its deep feeling for ever. The song, however, it will be admitted by all, is beautiful— it is a triumphant burst of exultation at the approach of holidays, with a passionate anticipation of home, its welcome and its joys. The real age and author are unknown. The occasion, as I heard many years ago, when the song was to me a sealed book, for I could scarcely arti- culate its language, from one who found equal difficulties from the in- firmities of age, but who connected with it some of the pleasantest recollections of an innocent life, is told in a few words.—An only son, whose father died while he was yet an infant, had been brought up by his mother with more than usual tenderness, but, while he was at school here, she too died. At the approach of the holidays he received a notice from his guardians that he must spend them at the College. The sudden change—the loneliness of his situation—the universal blank that the world presented to him, took a strong hold on his ardent imagination, As the holidays approached, the gloom seemed to thicken: the holidays came, and he was alone :—he used then to visit this hill,

> "Without acquaintance of more sweet companions
> Than the old inmates to his love—his thoughts,"

and sit there, in contemplative melancholy, whole hours together :—home, home, the memory of it was for ever present: he feasted on the joys he had known, and in some moment of agonising remembrance he wrote this song ;—but before his companions returned he had died of a broken heart. It was sorrow feeding itself joyously on the passion that must destroy her. It is in the same spirit that Constance dwells with such fearful minuteness on all that was most lovely in young Arthur—

> "For since the birth of Cain, the first male child,
> To him that did but yesterday suspire,
> There was not such a gracious creature born.
>
> *K.Phil.*  You are as fond of grief as of your child.
> *Cons.*  Grief fills the room up of my absent child,
> Lies in his bed, walks up and down with me,
> Puts on his pretty looks, repeats his words,
> Remembers me of all his gracious parts,
> Stuffs out his vacant garments with his form ;
> Then, have I reason to be fond of grief."

The story is possibly a fable, but it is worth remembering.

St. Cross, which we now approach through lines of "hedge-row elms," is situated in a rich bottom, at the foot of this hill, with the rapid Itchin running between them. It is difficult to know how best to describe this place, or to do it justice. At the same time that it bears evidence to the influence and extraordinary wealth possessed by the Romish church, its very existence is one of ten thousand proofs, that its influence was often exerted, and its wealth often directed, to good. If it accumulated vast riches, it supported extensive charities ; it endowed hospitals, it founded colleges, it relieved the sick, the poor, the helpless, and the friendless, all over the kingdom ;—it was a channel through which men's charities were dispensed, and not a sink that engulphed them. If it remind us of the celibacy of its clergy, yet is it an evidence that a churchman without a needy family of his own, may provide for many and through many generations :—if of the indolence of its cloisters, yet of their quiet and seclusion—of a poor dwelling for learning and literature to be at rest in. In brief, if it remind us of its errors, so does it of those virtues from which its errors sprang.

St. Cross is a noble institution! It does honour to human nature. A man will think the better of himself that hath eaten of its hospitality as I have done, and every stranger may do. The world hath forgotten what charity means,—it knows not how to give,—it is all vile, paltry, self-flattery,—it is "the picture in little:"—we throw half-pence to a beggar as we give a kick to a dog, to rid us of an annoyance;—we do not stoop to raise up the fallen, but bend towards them ;—we are eaten up with orders and degrees, and know nothing of the simple dignity of human nature. The universal stamp of fellowship and brotherhood, is left out of the new coinage. The Romish religion taught us better by humbling itself; it was lip-honour, if you please, but it was honour. A churchman was then noble above all nobility; yet had the church its Carmelites, and mendicant friars, its brothers of St. Dominic, and St. Augustine, and by its constitution the proudest of its dignitaries must, on occasion, perform the meanest offices, especially to the poor. When a man was worn out with age, or sunk with poverty and misfortune, they did not put a brand of shame on his forehead—they did not put a bell round his neck, nor send him to a workhouse, or to break stones upon the road, but to "the Alms-house of Noble Poverty"—Domus elemosynaria nobilis paupertatis, &c. as this place was named by Beaufort. The very words have honour in them! Poverty was then no shame. We hold the same doctrine, but our conduct gives the lie to it. It is now a shame! a corroding, cankerous shame; that eats the heart! It is the very worst offence in the whole calendar :—"veray poverte," that is poverty of spirit, "is sinne properly," says the Wife of Bath ;—we make no distinctions; the age is not critical in such matters; it is not only an offence, but offence without apology, for it hath not one way to bribe opinion.

"There is not," says the historian of Winchester, "within the island any remnant of ancient piety and charity of the same kind, which has been so little changed in its institution and appearance as this, The lofty tower, with the grated door and porter's lodge beneath it, the retired ambulatory, the separate cells, the common refectory, the venerable church, the black flowing dress and the silver cross worn by the members, the conventual appellation of *brother*, with which they salute each other ; in short, the silence, the order, and the neatness, that here reign, serve to recall the idea of a monastery to those who have seen one, and will give no imperfect idea of such an establishment to those who have not had that advantage." This is a very admirable description; and yet weak and imperfect, when I remember the full and unmixed feeling of delight and astonishment with which I first entered the place itself. I had "bid good-morrow" to the sun that morning, and been stirring before the plough was in the furrow. I had wandered over the dewy fields, watching the trout in the river, and beguiled onwards by the fresh beauties of the scene, and the joyous songs of birds, that came floating "upon the wings of silence ;" and had thus passed some hours in quiet indolence, when, directing my course, with the instinct of appetite, to the village, I turned suddenly and entered St. Cross. The first gateway and the outer court were passed in a humour between curiosity and indifference, when the whole burst upon me with the suddenness and indistinctness of a vision. It seemed unreal—it was a picture of imagination, that had left nothing imperfect. The picturesque and beautiful cells of the brothers on the one side—the ambulatory on the other—the church, such a church ! before me—the archway and tower beneath which I stood—the noble refectory with its arched staircase, overrun with the finest creeper I had ever seen, in its most luxuriant foliage, when its leaves were just embrowned with Autumn—such a scene may be imagined, but cannot be described. But the brothers, in their long black robes, and the silver cross on their breast, where could an *Englishman's* imagination have found them? The sun was shining as strong as it ever does in September, directly on the front of the brothers' cells, and in a seat before one of them, was a venerable grey-headed old man, taking his frugal meal, attended on, with all the patience of virtue, by a young and beautiful girl, whose service seemed to anticipate his wants—he was little short of a hundred years old, as I afterwards learnt. From the hall-door others of the brethren were passing with their daily allowance; and, pacing backwards and forwards, under the shelter of the cells, and in the warm sunshine, quite unconscious that she was observed, was a lady reading, who paused as every brother passed, as if to make an affectionate inquiry, and receive his blessing—this was the chaplain's daughter. It was the most bewildering scene I had ever witnessed. I stood for some minutes in silent admiration, with something of painful astonishment, and was not sorry to see a brother approaching the gateway, with two large "jacks" of beer, and doles of bread;—this was the porter, or

> Rather one that smiles, and still invites
> All that pass by ;—

and his burthen was for indiscriminate distribution to wayfaring travellers. Whoever shall think this picture overwrought, let him visit St. Cross as I did,—not with a throng of companions in mid-day, but alone, and before the dew is off; and let him then tell how infinitely short I have fallen of his own feeling.

The entire buildings of this place, the whole establishment indeed, are grand and imposing. In the few charitable endowments of the last century, there is too much of calculation—we seem to do good grudgingly—it may be right, but let us admit there is something noble in the magnificent disregard of our ancestors. Here is a church worthy such an institution—not a hall, not an overgrown room, but a church that could receive half a dozen country parishes. Every place has its ornament, and more ornament than was wanting, if we calculate by the square and rule. Why a double-arched entrance? Why two towers? Why an ambulatory? Why a portico to the refectory? Why such a church? Or why a church at all when the refectory would serve its purpose? Because it was " the Alms-house of Noble Poverty."

This charity, after all, is but a remnant of what it once was. It was originally founded by King Stephen's brother, and subsequently enlarged by Cardinal Beaufort. It was at first "to provide thirteen poor men, who were otherwise unable to maintain themselves, with every necessary. They were required to reside in the house, and they were allowed each of them daily a loaf of good wheat bread, of three pounds four ounces weight, and a gallon and a half of good small beer. They had also a pottage called mortrel, made of milk and wastelbred, a dish of flesh or fish, as the day should require, and a pittance for their dinner, likewise one dish for their supper. Besides these thirteen resident poor men, the foundation required that one hundred others, the most indigent that could be found in the city, but of good characters, should be provided every day with a loaf of bread, three quarts of small beer, and two messes for their dinner, in a hall appointed for this purpose, called, from this circumstance, Hundred-mennes hall; and as this was a very ample allowance, they were permitted to carry home with them whatever they did not consume on the spot. There was also a foundation for a master, with the salary of from seven to eight pounds annually, together with a steward, four chaplains, thirteen clerks, and seven choristers, the latter of whom were kept at school in the hospital, besides servants." "And on the anniversary of the founder, instead of one hundred poor men, three hundred were fed; and other extraordinary charities were bestowed on the chief festivals of the year." To this, Cardinal Beaufort "made an endowment for the maintenance of two more priests, thirty-five additional poor men, residents in the house, and of three women, being hospital nuns, to attend upon the sick brethren." Alas! how is it now fallen! "Instead of seventy residents, as well clergy as laity, who were here entirely supported, besides a hundred out-members who daily received their meat and drink, the charity consists at present but of thirteen resident brethren, exclusive of one chaplain and the master. It is true, however, that certain doles of bread continue to be distributed to the poor of the neighbourhood; and what is perhaps the only vestige left in the kingdom of the simplicity and hospitality of ancient times, the porter is daily furnished with a certain quantity of good bread and beer, of which every traveller or other person whosoever, that knocks at the lodge and calls for relief, is entitled to partake gratis." Of this bread have I eaten, and of this beer have I drunk, and, though neither hungry nor thirsty, with a delight and enjoyment I had never known before. It was a kindness done me by strangers—men whose very existence was almost forgotten,—a hand stretched out in fellowship and courtesy, from the darkness of many passed ages—it was a fine commentary on that humanity which teaches us to judge charitably of the errors and opinions of our fellow-men, for we now hold that these men erred grievously—to extend our good wishes and kind offices to the utmost bounds of the habitable world:—it was a real honour done to God, because it was unconditional charity to his creature, for it was here only to ask and to receive.

I have but little more to add, and that I do with infinite regret. It is impossible, I think, to inquire into the origin, and the present condition of this noble endowment, without a firm conviction that it is abused. While the number of its poor brotherhood is reduced to thirteen, the mastership is a fitting office for the son of a bishop, and that bishop was the controller and administrator of the charity. It signifies not that from the earliest times the master has been some person of distinguished consequence—that William of Wykeham appointed his intimate friend—that it has been held by many men who were removed hence to bishopricks;—the question is, in what spirit was it held? That an important charity of this nature should be under the special government of some distinguished person, is easily enough understood; but there were offices of honour as well as profit, and when we know the master's salary was from 7*l.* to 8*l.* annually, we cannot doubt that this was one of the former; and the more readily do I believe it abused, from knowing the original extent of the charity, its reduced numbers, and that the master's income alone is supposed to exceed the whole expense of the establishment. It is indifferent how long the charity has been abused; we know indeed that the mastership has been for many years considered of great pecuniary value; but so it was probably before Wykeham by patient exertion and "long prosecuted suits, both in the ecclesiastical and temporal courts," brought back its revenues to their original destination. Neither will it be denied that the property of this charity was cruelly despoiled by Henry VIII.; but how happens it that the spoliation has fallen altogether on the institution, and is only known by the reduced numbers of the brethren, and the abolition of the charitable donations—by leaving one side of the great quadrangle to be pulled down as tenantless, and in converting the " hundred-mennes' hall" into a brewery?

But I must here take a farewell of St. Cross, and return to Winchester. I am unfortunately no antiquary, having no pretensions to the character—my enjoyment is confined to the memorable and the beautiful, to what excites or recalls delightful feeling. I am insensible therefore, cold as death, to one half the excellence of this city; and yet never was a stranger change than the place wrought in me. The very air is infectious: we read of, hear of, see nothing of a much later age than " our Henry:" my common talk is now about John de Pontissara, Bishop de Blois, and Bishop de Rupibus; I am quite reconciled to Roger de Inkpen, and Saint Rombaldi—indeed saints and martyrs are my familiars. It is well my first visit was paid to the palace, for I should never have gone afterwards. Sir Christopher was born but yesterday—my choice architects are Walkelin and De Lucy, William of Wykeham, Bishop Edyngton, and Warden Thruibren. That the divisions and subdivisions for captains and subalterns have not left a room distinguishable in the palace, ought to have been no subject of regret; for though hardly a wall is in existence of the old Priory of St. Swithin that adjoined the Cathedral, I am, thanks to Mr. Milner, as familiar with its whole architectural economy, as " the hostel" where I kennel. Here were the dormitories—there the refectory—a little farther to the north, the cellarer's store-house and the buttery—that one was the apartment for the novitiates—this the Prior's quarters—and as the whole is a fine smooth level, like a bowling-green, there is nothing to obstruct one's passing familiarly through the whole suite of apartments. But, reader, it is probable you never were at Winchester, or only passed through it in your way to Hampton, " since the Conquest," as we say here, called Southampton; you have, therefore, no sympathy with me. With all your respect for the immortal Alfred, you would not be content to hear me dwell with enthusiasm on all that remains of Hyde Abbey, his own foundation, and the burial-place of himself and family. Of St. Mary's Abbey, founded by Ethelswitha, his queen, not one stone remains upon another. There are no less, I believe, than forty or fifty churches here in much the same situation; and as I despair of giving sufficient variety to this catalogue of nothings, I will pass at once to the Cathedral.

There is a solemnity, a mysterious intermingling of the shadows of old trees with its own deeper shade, that makes the approach to it strangely impressive. The common church-yard in which it is situated, much as it detracts from its general appearance, adds something to this feeling. Its magnitude, its beauty, its bold and severe simplicity, all concur to tame down the passions and to humble the heart; and no man can have spent an hour in gazing on it, but he came away the wiser and the better.

Of its exterior, hardly an opinion can be given, that must not, to be just, be limited to the very spot on which we may imagine ourselves standing. The nave, the transepts, and the choir, are all of widely different ages, and even the north and south sides of the nave, differ from one another. The line of noble windows, the solid grandeur of the buttresses, and the uniform simplicity of the whole northern exterior of the nave, leave it, in my judgment, almost without a rival, in ecclesiastical architecture; but, from the south side, the cloisters have been swept away, the buttresses, if it ever had them, are gone with the cloisters, and this barbarous mutilation has not only destroyed the beauty of that part, but the security of the building itself. I think, as a whole, the finest view of the exterior is from the north-east. There is a dignity in the massy proportions of Anglo-Norman architecture, that, on a large scale, approaches the sublime, and the range of building from the chapel of the Virgin at the east end, to the north transept, including the tower, though but a portion of the cathedral, is amply sufficient to prove it. The east end of the choir, indeed, does, by the multitude of its ornaments, injure the general effect, and detract something from its uniform simplicity, nor can I agree to the commendation which better judgments have passed on the choir itself. I speak from feeling, and without any pretensions to critical accuracy; but it seemed to me too much broken into parts, and those parts were uniform and tasteless;—the flying buttresses, though light, I do *not* think "elegant"—the dome canopies, which crown the turrets, I do *not* think "gorgeous;" and *I do* think that a dome canopy, though to be met with elsewhere, is directly opposed to every principle from which Gothic architecture takes its sublime character; and as to the "profusion of elegant carved work that covers the whole east front," I can only say there seemed to me an astonishing dearth of invention in the multitudinous repetition of the same ornament, and that ornament poor and common.

Upon entering the great west door of this cathedral, I felt it was inferior to Westminster. The almost painful sense of sublime astonishment was wanting. The pillars are heavy—the roofing low—the general proportions are inferior; I speak comparatively, of course. It wants the magic lightness that distinguishes the other. It is grand, but it takes its grandeur from its vastness—its length is great, but the transepts break the connexion between the east and west ends; and it is enough that the connexion actually exists in stone walls; there must be a continuity of feeling in the heart of the spectator, which is impossible when the nave is of one age, the transepts much older, and the east end, to which they lead the eye, of a much later date. Still it is a noble building, and the magnificent east window is a beauty, and a great beauty, wanting in the other. But the greatest enjoyment here, and whence we obtain the most accurate knowledge of its magnitude and architectural riches, is in a patient examination of the separate parts of the cathedral, and of the chapels and shrines contained in it. In the latter, Winchester is without a rival—those of Wykeham, Waynflete, Beaufort, and Fox, are a constellation superior to any in the kingdom that fall within my knowledge; and let me here do justice to the latter in that commendation of the interior of the choir, which I could not, with sincerity, give to the exterior. These shrines, or chantries, are what such erections ought to be, consistent and in harmony with all surrounding objects, and a splendid ornament to the building that encloses them.

The chantry of Wykeham is simple and elegant, and its high preservation does honour to his children, here and at New College. It is superior, I think, to all, in the delicacy of its proportions, the simplicity of its ornaments, and the general lightness of its appearance. The chantry of Fox is, in taste, its direct opposite. It is oppressed with ornament, and frittered away into minute parts, till the general design is indistinguishable. It is an enigma—a sort of mysterious confusion of columns, arches, pedestals, niches, groining, and sculpture, that, till the eye is familiar with, the mind cannot reduce to order. That great man seems to have had the taste of a carver, or an upholsterer, rather than a sculptor or an architect. Yet the chantry of Fox is not without beauty; there is something exquisite in the finishing of the ornaments, and the relative proportion of such a multitude of parts, when we can bring ourselves to the consideration of these things.

Waynflete and Beaufort's chantries stand immediately opposite, in equal and admirable condition, and have, both from size and situation, a vague general resemblance, although broad distinctions are visible to. an accustomed eye. The cardinal's tomb is generally admitted the more elegant; but are not the columns that support the canopy too light for the incumbent weight? Do they not want something of proportionate richness? This judgment may seem hypercritical, for without the objection the work would be perfect; but it originates in a comparison with Waynflete's, which in this particular I prefer. The gorgeous canopies, and pendents, the rich fan-work, and the clustering pinnacles above, are beyond all description, and beyond the graver itself. There is a fine figure of the Cardinal—as, I omitted to observe, there is of Wykeham—in all the splendid trappings of his high office, beneath this canopy. The parts of the Cathedral itself that deserve special attention are without number, and it is a fine illustration of the rise and progress of Gothic architecture, from the dignified simplicity of the Anglo-Norman, to the delicacy and refinement of the age of Henry VII.

---

## TO A JASMINE FALLEN FROM LELIA'S BOSOM.

FAIR flowret! ere thy evanescent dream
  On Lelia's bosom fled, I saw thee shine
With virgin freshness there, and stainless seem
  As Purity within her holiest shrine.
But now thou'st lost her ever-varying heart,
  Her lover's fate was thine, and thou wast riven
From thence to seem—pale, drooping as thou art—
  Like some fallen spirit weeping its lost Heaven.
Sweet flower! thy perfume caused thee joy and death,
  For woman's bosom can delight and slay;
And thou wast chosen for thy perfumed breath,
  To feel its bliss, and sigh thy life away.
Yet, withering flower! thy blight was ecstasy,
And I would welcome death to only die like thee!

C. L.

---

CIVIC SPORTS.—NO. I.

Extracted from the Journal of Simon Swandown.

*Shooting.*

"The boy thus, when his sparrow's flown,
The bird in silence eyes."      GAY.

MONDAY, Sept. 1. 9 A. M.—Took down from back attic my legacy gun, so called because it became mine under the will of Sir Diggory Drysalt, my maternal uncle. Used by him, with tremendous effect, when a grenadier in Colonel Birch's first Loyal London, in the battles of Shad Thames and Primrose-hill. Thought it prudent to ascertain the death of this Gunpowder Percy: drew out the ramrod and thrust it down the barrel; felt a soft substance at bottom, and trembled; screwed up my courage and the soft substance, and found the latter to be a doll's pin-cushion, probably pushed in by little Sally. Borrowed Bob's duster and Molly's scowering-paper, and rubbed off the rust. Looked about for a game-bag, and luckily alighted upon my uncle's havresack, in which I moreover found seventeen old cartridges. Put on my shoot-ing-dress, viz.—my white hat, my stone-blue coat and black velvet collar, my white Marcella waistcoat, my India dimity under ditto, my nankeen trowsers, and my ditto gaiters, not forgetting my military boots and brass spurs. Jammed down ramrod till it rang again, to the great terror of Mrs. Swandown, of whom I took leave, singing—

"Adieu, adieu, my only life,
My honour calls me from thee."

Set off, in high spirits, to meet Jack Juniper, Kit Cursitor, and Tom Tiffany, by appointment, at half-past nine, at the Cumberland Arms, opposite St. Luke's Hospital, in the City Road. Saw a poll-parrot at a window in Carpenter's Buildings: longed for a shot, but housemaid too sharp. Terrier puppy barked at a bedstead in Broker's Row: looked round, and found that she had made a point at a bulfinch—cocked and levelled, but broker kept walking to and fro. Arrived at place of appointment without seeing any more game. Found Jack Juniper and Kit Cursitor discussing a plate of biscuits and a couple of glasses of brandy and water. Waited twenty minutes for Tom Tiffany; Jack in the mean while, to pass the time, said he would play "Water parted" with his finger upon the rim of the rummer: could not catch the tune, probably because it was all in one note. Examined our pieces: Kit's wanted a flint, and Jack's lock too rusty to go, though he pulled till he nearly sprained his fore-finger. Borrowed some oil, with three wasps in it, of the barmaid, and got a flint from a bald pavier in the road. Rang the bell to pay, when who should turn up but Tom Tiffany, in high dudgeon: back up, like the half-moon at Lower Holloway. Told us his brother Sam had walked off with the family fowling-piece across Shoulder of Mutton Fields, to slaughter snipes in Hackney brook. Asked landlord if he could lend us a gun, but he had nothing but a horse-pistol. Hobson's choice, so Tom had nothing to do but to take it. Too short to bring down pheasants, but quite long enough to do for the little birds.

10 A. M.—Marched up the City Road singing—
   " By dawn to the downs we repair."

Looked sharp to the right and left, and saw a hen and two chickens pecking under a wheelbarrow on the road-side. Jack Juniper seized the three dogs by the collar that they might not run in and frighten the game. Kit and Tom stole upon tip-toe to within six yards of the barrow, when the Tally-ho Paddington coach sent hen and chickens scampering into a front garden in Pleasant Row. Swore that Tally-ho should never see another eighteen-pence of my money. Halted to rest ourselves upon the bridge on the Regent's Canal. Looked over the parapet and pointed our guns downward to nab the sea-gulls as they came through the arch. Saw something red steal out: took it for a pheasant, and cocked: proved to be a bargeman's cap: grounded arms again, and saw him steer his vessel into a sort of water pound. Asked baker's boy about it: boy said it was in the lock, and that the bank on the other side was the key. Threatened to shoot him if he gave me any more of his sauce. Kept an eye on barge, and saw it begin to sink. Wondered at the coolness of the Father Red-cap, who walked from stem to stern, smoking his pipe as if nothing was the matter. Kit Cursitor said they had scuttled it on purpose to chouse the underwriters, and that he had known the captain of a Dutch schooner hanged for similar practices. Kit talked of advising the underwriters to defend the action, and pay the premium into court: when lo and behold the barge took a lower level and slid off through the farther water-gate. Strolled on to Sadler's Wells, and halted at a lamp post to read play-bills. Betted Jack Juniper a shilling that he would not hit the words " Water fiend" at ten yards off:—fired, and lodged two shots in the W. Stood for ten minutes looking into the New River, and counting the straws that floated down it, with now and then a child's paper-boat by way of a change. Tom Tiffany chucked a boy's hoop-stick into the stream—black poodle jumped in after it, and brought it out, wagging his tail—shook his coat and splashed my nankeens:—thought of calling Tom to account for it, but did not like the looks of his horse pistol.

 11 A. M.—Pushed our guns under an old woman's wheelbarrow, and started a Tom cat—game made for Pentonville, we following—fired my piece, and brought him down in the chapel-yard—looked about for churchwarden to borrow keys—luckily, Deputy Dewlap's funeral just then entered at South gate: followed in the wake of mourners, picked up cat and popped him into Cursitor's blue bag. Trotted on to Islington, swerved to the right, and entered fields at the back of Canonbury-house: saw five strange-looking birds trying to hide themselves in a glass case. All four fired: Tom's pistol flashed in the pan, but the guns went off: down went the birds, and up ran a tall fellow in a blue apron, swearing that we should pay for shooting his stuffed birds. Found to our surprise that they were dead before we came near them. Man in blue apron asked for our license, but Lawyer Kit gave it as his opinion that none was legally requisite to shoot a dead bird. Subscribed for a purse of nine and sixpence, to quiet the proprietor, and resolved to be more cautious in future.

 12 M.—Strolled up Highbury-place, wondering at the beauty of the

gentlemen's seats on our right, which lay so thick that you could not push a brick between: charmingly contiguous to the city: nothing wanting but a speaking-trumpet to ask the news at Batson's. Heard a rumbling in our rear: looked round, and beheld the Highbury coach, which stopped alongside of us, and let loose a woman from the inside and a boy from the box. Woman with luggage enough to stock the Barnet van. Saw her give a canary-bird in charge to the housemaid: loitered about premises, and in about two minutes saw the cage stowed on the dresser of the kitchen: peeped down area: half-cocked uncle's legacy, but could not get rid of confounded cook chopping parsley in the window. Scrambled over five-barred gate to join my companions, who had made a short cut for Holloway: obstructed by a dry ditch; took a run to leap it; forgot my spurs, which caught in each other and sent me on my hands and knees on the opposite side of the gap. Piece went off in my fall, and killed a duck. Crammed the defunct into my havresack, and came up with my cronies close to the turnpike. They took the pathway, but I followed the Bedford coach through the gate. Stopped by gate-keeper, who demanded three half-pence: would not pay, and referred it to Lawyer Kit, who gave it in favour of gate-keeper, pointing to the board upon which rate of tolls was printed, viz. " For every horse, mule, or ass, three half-pence " Tossed down the coppers and walked on. Halted at corner of Duval's Lane: drove of geese: called a council of war: Jack Juniper offered the driver two shillings to let him fire among the flock: bargain made: Jack let fly, and missed: geese set up a general hiss, and Kit advised us to discontinue the action.

1 P. M.—Turned down a green lane on our left, thinking that the game on the high road might be too wild. Drove a gander before us, holding out our guns in a slanting direction, while Tom Tiffany with his horse pistol kept the dogs at bay. Looked over our shoulders, and, when we found ourselves out of view from the road, fired a volley. All missed: gander screamed, and was making past us back to the highway, when, with admirable presence of mind, I knocked him on the head with the butt end of my piece. Gave him a thump each to secure ourselves of his demise, and crammed him into Kit's blue bag, which he filled choke full, like a bill in Chancery.

2 P. M.—Steered on towards Pancras, wondering at the romantic beauties that met us at every turning: caught a peep at the Small-pox Hospital, and longed for a pop at a patient. Put up a couple of gipsies and a donkey: recovered arms just in time: had my fortune told, viz. that I should stand upon some boards that would slip from under me: walked back to Kit for a solution: could make neither head nor tail of it: resolved to ask the exciseman at the club: determined to make a knot in my handkerchief as a memorandum, and found gipsies had eased me of my yellow Barcelona. Walked back to shoot them for the larceny, but found, as Kit expressed it, the writ returned *non est inventus.* Arrived at Holywell Mount: read printed notice, " It is lawful to shoot rubbish here:" took the hint, fired, and blew Jerry Bentham off a book-stall.

3 P. M.—Dinner at the Adam and Eve, Camden Town. Pigeon-pie at top, and lamb-chops at bottom. Tom Tiffany in the chair,

and I deputy. Asked Tom for a piece of the pie: carving-knife slipped, and in went his fist through the top crust, penetrated the pigeon, and stuck in the beefsteak sod at the base. " Now *your hand's in,*" said Jack Juniper, " I 'll thank you for some of that pie." Tom wiped the gravy from his wristband, and did not seem to relish the joke, but all the rest of us laughed ready to kill ourselves. Asked the waiter if he had any ginger beer: answered " Yes, Sir," and rushed out, returning instantly with a stone bottle. Began to loosen wire: bottle hissed and spit like a roasting apple: all looked on in awful silence: at length out bounced the cork and hit Tom Tiffany on the bridge of his nose: Tom cocked his pistol to return his adversary's fire: but the other bawling " Coming, Sir," bolted through the door like lightning: poured out foaming liquor in a glass, meaning to take a delicious draught, and found that I had swallowed a concern in which vinegar, brickdust, and soapsuds, were the working partners.

4 P. M.—Prowled round the brick-fields near the Newington-road, to start birds that love a warm climate. Saw a hopping raven with its left wing clipped: went up within a yard of it and brought it down: clapped the black game into my havresack, and told a milk-maid that the brood came over from Norway every autumn. Eyed Deputy Firkin's apple-tree that hung over the New River: felt very desirous of bringing down a leash of pippins, but saw a little man in black on the watch. Jack Juniper shut both his eyes and pulled his trigger: down dropt the man: all took to our heels, with our heads full of the new drop. At length says Lawyer Kit, " Let's go back and get him an apothecary ; if he dies after that, it will be only felo de se." Back we stole, in sad tribulation, and found to our great relief that Jack had shot a scarecrow. Tom changed trowsers with the deceased, his own being a little the worse for wear : Canonbury clock began to toll, and we made the best of our way towards the Shepherd and Shepherdess, firing in the air to take the chance of whatever might be flying that way. Saw a fine turkey under a wicker enclosure : rammed down cartridge : presented and pulled trigger : no effects : remembered Gargle's prescription as to pills—

" If one won't do,
Why, then, take two :"

and rammed down another cartridge ; still no effects : ditto with four more: at last bang off went my musquet : thought there was an end of the world : fell senseless upon my back, and when I opened my eyes found Tom Turpentine smacking my palms with an old shoe, taken from an adjoining dust-heap, and Jack Juniper pouring water into my mouth taken from an adjoining ditch.

5 P. M.—Felt much soreness about my left shoulder, and determined to poach no more upon Finsbury Manor. Climbed up an Islington coach : took a seat upon the box, and put my fire-arms between my legs and my bag in the boot. Descended at the back of the 'Change, crossed into Lombard-street, and, having arrived safe and sound in Bush-lane, gave Molly the game to dress for supper, and walked up-stairs to drink a comfortable dish of tea with Mrs. Swandown.

### VISIT TO THE MUSEUMS OF SEVILLE IN 1822.

SPAIN has furnished a brilliant epoch in the history of painting, and amongst the various schools that flourished in that country none occupied a more deservedly distinguished rank than that of Seville. But the glory of Spain, with regard to the Fine Arts, has been long on the wane, and, instead of witnessing the creation of new *chefs-d'œuvre* in painting, she has for some time back been fated to deplore the loss of those left her by her gifted children of former days. The long-protracted ravages of the destructive war into which she was goaded by Napoleon have occasioned her greatest losses in this way. An immense number of pictures fell, either by fair or foul means, into the hands of the French marshals and generals, and other *powerful amateurs*, who, through motives of curiosity or profit, followed the head-quarters of the French armies. A not inconsiderable number has been purchased by English travellers, which are now dispersed over England, and serve to add another charm to the splendid country mansions of Great Britain; where it is to be hoped they are secure from such rapacious wholesale collectors as those who despoiled Spain, at least until the Holy *(lucus à non lucendo)* Alliance shall have more fully matured its philanthropic plans.

However, notwithstanding these multiplied losses, Seville is, of all the cities in Spain (not excepting Madrid), the one which still possesses the richest pictorial treasures. God and the French army only know if she will long have this remnant of her glory to boast of! If the magnanimous leader of the French deliverers should, in the intoxication of unaccustomed triumph, remember that the walls of the *Louvre* are but scantily and scurvily covered, poor Seville may be forced to furnish the necessary canvass, and this in the course of events may lead to a second stripping of that long gallery; and so the eternal wheel goes round.

In the possibility of such an event, let us here record the most remarkable paintings, which were to be seen at Seville in 1822 and the commencement of 1823. This unpretending list may enable those of our readers who may visit Seville in 1824 to denounce the robbery. Let our first visit be, as Christians, if not good Catholics, to the Cathedral, where are assembled the productions of the principal masters of the Sevilian school. A short time back there was placed in the sacristy one of the most remarkable works of *Pedro de Campagna*—a Descent from the Cross, which formerly adorned the church of Santa Clara. Campagna was born at Brussels in the commencement of the sixteenth century, and came to reside at Seville in 1548. His style appears to have been partly modelled upon the works of Michael Angelo; but in the simplicity of his composition, his colouring, and the stiffness of his figures, he resembles the painters of the old German school. On each side of the crucifix, which occupies the middle of the picture, Joseph of Arimathea and another person are mounted upon ladders, and employed in gently lowering down the body of our Saviour, whilst Mary Magdalen and Saint John are at the foot of the Cross endeavouring to console the Virgin Mary, who is in a half-kneeling posture,* with the

---

* This is a very common attitude with the Irish female peasantry during the celebration of mass, or at the graves of their relatives, by which they endeavour to recon-

body inclined backwards. It is on tradition that the celebrated Murillo used to remain for whole hours absorbed in admiration of this picture; and that on one occasion, the sacristan, having lost all patience, roughly demanded of him what kept him from quitting the church? To which the enthusiastic artist replied—" I am waiting till these holy men have lowered the body of our Saviour." Murillo is buried in the church of Santa Clara, under the very spot where he was accustomed to stand whilst contemplating this picture. This is a glorious instance of the " ruling passion strong in death," and a fine practical illustration of the line—" even in our ashes live their wonted fires." It was an act of sacrilege against the divinity of genius to have removed this picture from the church of Santa Clara. The Cathedral contains also several fine pictures of *Louis de Vargas,* who was born and died at Seville, but who during a sojourn in Italy studied under the great masters of the time. Raphael appears to have been amongst the number, for traces of his instruction are sometimes discernible in the beautiful colouring and expression of Vargas's pictures, which also exhibit something of the grand and severe style of Michael Angelo. There is in a little side-chapel an Adoration of the Shepherds by Vargas. The Virgin is clothed in white, with her face towards the spectator; she is pointing out the child in the crib to the shepherds, some of whom are on their knees offering presents, and others behind them bending forward in an attitude of respectful curiosity. Another of his pictures is known under the name of *La Gamba* (the leg), from a very beautiful leg which the painter has conferred upon Adam, and of which Perez de Alesio said, when finishing his Saint Christopher, that this leg was infinitely more precious than the whole body and limbs of his Saint. The defect of this picture consists in there not being enough of light thrown upon the principal group. Another subject treated by Vargas is the Presentation in the Temple. The Virgin in this picture is represented with the same celestial expression of countenance as that which characterises the Virgin of the first-mentioned picture. It is evident that both have the honour of no very remote degree of relationship with the Madonnas of Raphael. The Saint Christopher of Pedro de Alesio, of which we have just spoken, is a colossal figure forty feet high, so that the compliment paid to Adam's handsome leg was by no means a trifling one. This enormous Saint was painted in *fresco,* but the colours being now altogether faded, it is only with the eye of faith that we can form any opinion of its merit. Pedro de Alesio studied under Buonarotti; he died at Rome in 1600. Another pupil of Buonarotti's, Ferdinand Sturm, furnished the pictures which decorate the chapel *de los Santillanos.* Amongst them is a Resurrection, and several Saints. But the tints have become as brown and swarthy as the holy originals would have become, had they lived ever since under the burning sun of Andalusia. A minor altar in this chapel

cile their devotional respect with their love of ease; being apparently kneeling, while at the same time the weight of the body rests upon the upturned heels. It is also this attitude that Canova has chosen for his celebrated statue of the Magdalen, now in the possession of the Marquis de Sommariva, at Paris. This the finical *petit-maître* posture-master Parisian critics call ungraceful and ignoble. They cannot see that it is finely and simply indicative of utter prostration of strength, and faintness from extreme anguish. They had never seen an opera-dancer kneel thus; therefore it was *hors les règles du beau.*

contains some works of Zurbaran ; the principal of which is Saint Peter
seated on a throne and clothed in pontifical robes. The good Saint
must feel not a little surprised at being thus exhibited to posterity as a
Pope. There are several little pictures surrounding this large one ; representing various passages in the life of the Saint. Zurbaran displays
but little imagination ; he seems, however, to have been skilful in the
technical part of his art. There is in the same church a picture by his
master, Juan de las Roclas, representing Santiago or Saint Jaques
mounted upon a huge white horse, equipped as a knight, and busily
employed in belabouring and overthrowing the Moors in the battle of
Clavijo. It is evident from this picture that the Spanish painters took
as great liberties with *costuming* their Saints, as the priests of that
country did and do with accoutring their images. Terror, rage, and
despair, are depicted with great force and truth in the features and gestures of the prostrate Moors. Amongst them is a young Saracen who
painfully endeavours to raise up his dying head and brave, at least with
looks, the aspect and flaming sword of the Saint. This is a fine idea,
and perfectly well realised by the painter. Pedro de Alesio has treated
the same subject for the church of Saint Jaques, where it figures over
the grand altar.

One of the finest pictures in the Cathedral is the Vision of
Saint Antony, by Murillo. It is placed in the Chapel of the Bap-
tistery. The Saint, in a moment of mystical ecstasy, stretches forth
his arms and raises his noble countenance towards the infant Jesus,
who is smiling on him from a couch of transparent clouds, which are
painted with infinite art. Through the entrance of the cell is seen a
Gothic cloister, the light of which is not the same as that of the cell.
All the objects in this fine composition are executed with admirable
truth and beauty.

To see the other *chefs-d'œuvre* of Murillo (whose merit can be justly
appreciated only by those who have been at Seville), we must visit the
Church of the Hospital *de la Caridad*, where his finest productions are,
or rather were to be seen ; for one of his four great pictures, after
having been stolen by the French, was restored at the Peace of 1815,
and has since remained at Madrid, where it forms one of the principal
ornaments of the Gallery of *San Fernanda*. The subject is Saint Isabella, Queen of Portugal, who devoted herself to the care of the poor,
the sick, and the mutilated. Here Murillo sported in his own element ;
for, as it is well known, there never was a painter who shewed so strong
a predilection for imitating the disgusting casualties and diseases of
afflicted human nature. His beggars covered with filth, vermin,
and ulcers, excite horror and loathing from the very fidelity and excellence of their execution. It is almost impossible to conceive how the
artist could have so far conquered the natural repugnance excited by
such hideous nastiness, as to enable him to copy with minute accuracy
such objects. One is almost forced to think that to his ardent love of
painting, must have been joined a mind inaccessible to human suffering.
It is however much to be deplored that Murillo did not exercise his
extraordinary talent for the imitation of nature upon more attractive
objects : for, having given it this direction, his excellence " served him
but as an enemy," and became " a sanctified and holy traitor to him,"

inasmuch as, the better he succeeded, the greater was the disgust excited. One of the other three pictures that are still to be seen in the Hospital *de la Caridad,* represents a *San Juan de Dios,* who is carrying on his back a sick man to the hospital, in which charitable office he is assisted by an angel. The second is our Saviour, in the midst of a beautiful country, feeding the multitude, who are skilfully disposed in groups. The third is Moses striking the rock and causing a living stream to spring from it, to which a crowd of men and animals are hurrying to slake their thirst. In the principal figures of the two last pictures there is a want of character observable. They seem even to have been executed with a feeble pencil. Indeed the same may be said of the first picture, in which *San Juan de Dios* and the angel have nothing of the *ideal* about them. On the contrary, their features are rather harsh and vulgar. One is inclined to suppose that Murillo had blunted the fine tact of genius, by a too continued attention to the grosser and ruder models of nature, if the celestial features of his Saint Isabella did not triumphantly prove that he was complete master of the *beau idéal,* when he took the pains to seek it, or the subject inspired him.

The Capuchin Church *de la Porta Macarera* formerly possessed some of Murillo's paintings, but they are now dispersed. Since the suppression of the convents and other religious communities equally useless, if not hurtful, an excellent idea has been put in execution, that of depositing in one of the reformed churches a great number of the pictures that belonged to the ancient communities. The selection might have been more judicious; but even as it is, it has served to rescue from destruction or dispersion several masterpieces of the Spanish school. This collection is destined to remain stationary and serve as a provincial museum, if our Lady and the Duke d'Angoulême be not of a different opinion. Over the space formerly occupied by the grand altar of the church in which the pictures are exhibited, is placed a large painting by Zurbaran, taken from the College of Saint Thomas Aquinas, and representing his saintship, who occupies the middle of the piece. Over his head are seen the Saviour and the Virgin Mary, attended by angels and Saints Paul and Dominick. In the foreground is Charles V. in complete armour, and on his knees, and around him are several other personages. For the expression of the features, the *chiaroscuro* and the draperies, this is a *chef-d'œuvre.* The composition has nothing remarkable in it, but this is too often the case in those pictures which have been executed in Italy and Spain according to orders which had more of superstition than sound taste in them. Over this is a charming *Madonna* by Juan de Castello, remarkable for its colouring and purity of style, qualities which this artist seems to have borrowed from his brother Augustin de Castello. There are also in this new Museum several productions more or less remarkable of Valdes, Murillo, and Ribera. It possesses, moreover, a fine piece of statuary in *terra cotta* representing Saint Jerome. This is the work of Torregiano, an excellent Italian sculptor. It was executed for the Convent of *Buenavista,* near the city. Fortunately the artist did not behave so ungallantly to this Saint Jerome in *terra cotta,* as he did to a *Madonna* of the same fragile materials, which he had modelled for the Duke d'Arcos; for in a dispute with this *Senore,* the irritated artist dashed the unoffending lady, instead of the insolent lord, to pieces. " The hand that made her, marr'd her." Such a burst of passion and sacrilegious destruction, in the presence of a grandee of Spain, was a crime not to be forgiven; and the sculptor was immured, without examination or trial, in a prison at Seville, where he died in 1522.

Besides this collection of the Museum, there is not a church in Seville which does not possess one or more specimens of the first-rate Spanish masters—such as Campagna, Villegas, Vargas, &c. At *Santa Maria la Blanca*, there is a Virgin supporting the body of Christ, by *Vargas*—on the borders of this picture are painted the figures of saints. The Hospital of *San Lazaro*, beyond the walls, possesses a Saint Lazarus robed as a bishop, by *Villegas Marmotego.* Thus to *episcopalize* Saint Lazarus is quite as *anachronismatical* a sin as clapping the tiara upon the unconscious head of Saint Peter : but we are inclined to pardon the painter's *extemporal* error, for the admirable manner in which he has painted the episcopal costume. Villegas is buried in the Church of San Lorenzo, at the foot of another of his pictures, representing a *Madonna.* It is a pity that the Last Judgement, painted on *fresco*, in the court of the *Casa de la Misericordia*, is in such a ruinous state, that in a short time it will be impossible to criticise it. The parochial church of Saint Isidore possesses a picture of the death of this saint, by Roclas. It is one of his best productions. The scene is a Gothic cathedral, in which the holy bishop is seen upon his knees, his head inclined, his hands joined, and his whole air and attitude indicating the flight of his soul to another and a better world. The expression of his countenance is extremely touching : he is supported by some attendant ecclesiastics ; in the air are seen the Saviour, the Virgin, and a company of angels, hailing the departure of the Saint with voices and musical instruments : towards this bright choir, the dying bishop, though with head reclined in the languor of approaching death, directs a look of love and hope. The colouring of this picture approaches very near that of the Venetian school, upon which, in fact, Roclas had formed himself. The same resemblance may be traced in the Martyrdom of Saint Andrew, a large picture containing thirty figures as large as life.

A cloth-merchant of Seville has had spirit and taste enough to form a collection of paintings nearly as numerous as that of the provincial Museum. He has covered with pictures the walls, not only of his apartments, but of his staircase, his court, and even his shop. In this distribution, a very strict attention has not been paid to the *lucidus ordo;* but however there is much, and of what is valuable, to be discovered in this *belle confusion.* Amongst the Italian pictures, one is agreeably surprised to find an Adoration of the Shepherds, by Michael Angelo ; it is of small dimensions, but of the most exquisite finish : also a Penitent Magdalen in a Grotto, by Titian, opposite to which is a picture by Murillo, representing the same subject. There is a Marriage of Saint Catherine, by Corregio, so exactly similar in all respects to a picture of the same master in the gallery of the *Louvre*, that it must puzzle the most acute connoisseur to determine which of the two is the original. Near this is a Dying Saint Agnes covering her bruised and wounded bosom with a part of her garments, by Guido Reni. In specimens of the Spanish schools, this collection is still richer, or at least contains a greater number. There are about twenty pictures by Murillo, the most remarkable of which is Christ and Saint John. The forms and faces of these two figures are given with the most striking truth and excellence. The back-ground represents a verdant and flowery plain, through which the Jordan is seen winding. There is also another remarkable picture of a Dead Christ, supported by two Angels, by Loes de Morales, a master whose works are very rare. There are four pictures indicative of the Life of Christ, by Juan de Valdes Leal; some scenes from the Old Testament, by Pedro de Orrente, &c. In a word, to go minutely through the collection of this spirited and tasteful merchant would furnish forth a volume, for he seems to have neglected none of the great schools, national or foreign. He has, amongst others, some fine pictures of Wouvermans and other French masters. We cannot conclude this brief notice without expressing our respect for the character of a man who devotes the profits of his industry to so elegant and intellectual a gratification; and we most sincerely wish him and his pictures a safe delivery from the magnanimous Angoulême and his band of *deliverers*. His morning and evening prayer should be—From such *liberators, libera nos, Domine.*               D. S.

## ANCIENT SONG OF A GREEK EXILE.

Where is the Summer, with her golden sun?
—That festal glory hath not pass'd from earth!
For me alone the laughing day is done;
—Where is the Summer, with her voice of mirth?
    —Far in my own bright land!

Where are the Fauns, whose flute-notes breathe and die
On the green hills? the founts, from sparry caves,
Through the wild places bearing melody?
The soft reeds whispering o'er the river-waves?
    —Far in my own bright land!

Where are the temples, through the dim wood shining,
The virgin-dances, and the choral strains?
Where the sweet sisters of my youth, entwining
The fresh rose-garlands for their sylvan fanes?
    —Far in my own bright land!

Where are the vineyards, with their joyous throngs,
The red grapes pressing when the foliage fades?
The lyres, the wreaths, the lovely Dorian songs,
And the pine-forests, and the olive-shades?
    —Far in my own bright land!

Where are the haunted grots, the laurel-bowers,
The Dryad's footsteps, and the minstrel's dreams?
—Oh! that my life were as a southern flower's!
I might not languish then by these chill streams,
    —Far from my own bright land!               H.

### EARLY RECOLLECTIONS.

WHEN we begin to feel the influence of age, when the boasted era of experience arrives, and we have a "moist eye, a dry hand, and a yellow cheek," it is wonderful with what pretension of contempt we are wont to treat the younger part of the community. We assume airs of severity before it, and seem to take a pride in gibing it. We put on the mantle of wisdom because we have no other left in our wardrobe fitting to our circumstances; and with as much importance and more selfishness than we ever before experienced, we assume the functions of legislators on the strength of our vicinity to second childishness. There is a little art in acting thus. Time has taken away every thing by which we can exercise an influence, save this reputation of wisdom; and to do ourselves justice, we know how to make the most of it. We thus contrive to keep up a degree of respect when our grey hairs would otherwise excite pity. We see that age is a state of neglect unless an impression of sageness accompanies it, and we cling to our last anchor to avoid shipwreck on the shoals of forgetfulness. Without "heat, affection, limb, or bounty," we cannot brook neglect. Some, but comparatively a very few, have stored their minds with intellectual wealth, and improved them by the observations of years—

> " Till old experience do attain
> To something like prophetic strain."

To venerate such is just and proper; it was to an old person of this character, no doubt, that the feeling of the Spartans was directed when they stood up in the theatre at Athens. But that those who have never profited by experience should put on the appearance of having done so to gain a respect to which they are not entitled, instead of the sympathy due to incapacity and decay, is rather hard upon the rising generation. The majority, too, of aged people assume the stoic, and pretend a scorn for the warm temper, sanguine feelings, intrepid integrity, and open manners of youth. They snub, and wound, and stifle, its generous emotions, often preaching the vanities of life only because they can no longer share in them. They seldom reflect on their own youth, but imagine that age and imbecility form the only state of existence in which man is to be imitated and admired. But it is perhaps wrong to cavil with erroneous notions where error is consolatory—where there are no vivid pleasures to be enjoyed, and the future prospect offers nothing but increase of decay and greater enfeeblement of the senses. Still it becomes those to reflect, who preserve the power of reflection, that early recollections are a source of the purest pleasure, and that they who live upon the memory of the past should not undervalue the brightest part of it.

I knew one aged person who loved youth for the pleasure he derived in his old age from the remembrance of his own youthful sensations. Seventy years had passed over his head, and, unlike Justice Shallow, he had little gratification in recounting the mere frolics of boyhood: if he alluded to them at all it was when he had cheered his old veins with a glass of claret, and a youthy impulse shone forth from a loophole of the grey tenement that enclosed it. He would now and then talk at such times of the "bona robas," and the "midnight chimes," and the "wildness of his youth;" but it was rather from the love he bore to

the recollection of the vivid sensations of that day-spring of life, than to
the frolics themselves. At other times, in his hours of loneliness amid
the isolation of age, he mentioned only his sensations, and would talk
with delight of the smell of a flower when he was young, and the remembrance of the lively affection of the senses which he never experienced afterwards. These reminiscences of early life would have
made him unhappy, had not his philosophy resigned him to the inevitable laws of our common nature. His years were green to the last.
He was beloved by the young, in whom he would find mementos of
emotions which he had forgotten, and watch impressions, once his own,
that the lapse of years had obliterated from his mind. He was no
cynic—no obtuse preacher of the folly of every state of life except age
—no cruel damper of youthful hope, because he could not partake in
its expectations—no severe censurer of its aberrations, under the assumed garb of wisdom, chilling the warm glow of generous hearts, and
extinguishing, with a hard time-worn brow knit into a frown, the sparkles
of lively and joyous spirits,—peace to his manes!

It is delightful to fling a glance back to our early years, and recall
our boyish actions glittering with the light of hope and the sanguine
expectations of incipient being. But the remembrance of our sensations when we were full of elasticity, when life was new and every
sense and relish keen, when the eye saw nothing but a world of beauty
and glory around, every object glittering in golden resplendency—is the
most agreeable thing of all. The recollection of boyish actions gives
small gratification to persons of mature years, except for what may,
perchance, be associated with them. But youthful sensations experienced when the age of enjoyment was most keen, and the senses exquisitely susceptible, furnish delightful recollections, that cling around
some of us in the last stage of life like the principle of being itself.
How do we recollect the exquisite taste of a particular fruit or dish to
have been then—how delicious a cool draught from the running
stream! A landscape, a particular tree, a field, how much better defined and delightfully coloured then than they ever appeared afterwards. Objects, too, were then of greater magnitude and consequence
to us. We examined every thing more narrowly and in detail. As
we advanced farther in life, we regarded them more in collective numbers. Single objects which afforded us pleasure, had the power of at-
taching the heart not possessed by a multiplicity. To the youth a little
comparative space is a universe. The parental house is an edifice of
magnitude, however small its superficies may be in reality; the garden
is vast, and the meadow seems of unbounded extent; a mile is the
measure of an immense distance, and the blue hills at the boundary of
the horizon appear the limits of a world. Having had no opportunity
of making a comparison with objects really extended, the present visible is his universe, and his perceptions, readily including even the minutest that he sees, impress them clearly on the memory. When the
world becomes known, it is looked at in larger portions, and cannot be
grasped in detail. We only see and retain masses, and consequently a
less vivid but more general picture of things; and we rarely again feel
that interest in insignificant objects which we felt in boyhood, unless
they are connected with some contingent circumstance that gives them
importance. It is not the common regret we feel in retrospection, that

alone attaches us so strongly to the scenes and sensations of youth; there is the superior attachment we naturally have for individuality— we cannot love a multitude as we love one, and our affection is divided and confused on mingling in the great world. There was a single tree opposite the door of my father's house: I remember even now how every limb branched off, and that I thought no tree could be finer or larger. I loved its shade—I played under it for years; but when I visited it after my first absence for a few months from home, though I recognised it with intense interest, it appeared lessened in size; it was an object I loved, but as a tree it no longer attracted wonder at its di- mensions; during my absence I had travelled in a forest of much larger trees, and the pleasure and well-defined image in my mind's eye which I owed to the singleness of this object I never again experienced in observing another.

Can I ever forget the sunny side of the wood, where I used to linger away my holidays among the falling leaves of the trees in autumn! I can recall the very smell of the sear foliage to recollection, and the sound of the dashing water is even now in my ear. The rustling of the boughs, the sparkling of the stream, the gnarled trunks of the old oaks around, long since levelled by the axe, left impressions only to be obliterated by death. The pleasure I then felt was undefinable, but I was satisfied to enjoy without caring whence my enjoyment arose. The old church-yard and its yew-trees, where I sacrilegiously enjoyed my pastimes among the dead, and the ivied tower, the belfry of which I frequently ascended, and wondered at the skill which could form such ponderous masses as the bells and lift them so high,—these were objects that, on Sundays particularly, often filled my mind, upon viewing them, with a sensation that cannot be put into language. It was not joy, but a soothing tranquil delight, that made me forget for an instant I had any desire in the world unsatisfied. I have often thought since, that this state of mind must have approached pretty closely to happiness. As we passed the church-way path to the old Gothic porch on Sundays, I used to spell the inscriptions on the tombs, and wonder at the length of a life that exceeded sixty or seventy years, for days then passed slower than weeks pass now. I visited, the other day, the school-room where I had been once the drudge of a system of learning, the end of which I could not understand, and where, as was then the fashion, every method taken seemed intended to disgust the scholar with those studies he should be taught to love. I saw my name cut in the desk, I looked again on my old seat; but my youthful recollections of the worse than eastern slavery I there endured, made me regard what I saw with a feeling of peculiar distaste. If one thing more than another prevent my desiring the days of my youth to return, it is the horror I feel for the despotism of the pedagogue. For years after I left school I looked at the classics with disgust. I remembered the heart-burnings, the tears, and the pains, the monkish method of teaching, now almost wholly confined to our public schools, had caused me. It was long before I could take up a Horace, much less enjoy its perusal. It was not thus with the places I visited during the short space of cessation from task and toil that the week allowed. The meadow, where in true joviality of heart I had leaped, and raced, and played—this recalled the contentedness of mind, and the overflowing tide of delight I once experienced, when, climbing the stile which led into it, I left behind me the book and the task. How the sunshine of the youthful breast burst forth upon me, and the gushing spirit of unreined and innocent exhilaration braced every fibre, and rushed through every vein. The sun has never shone so brilliantly since. How fragrant were the flowers. How deep the azure of the sky! How vivid were the hues of nature! How intense the short-lived sensations of pain and pleasure! How generous were all impulses! How confiding, open, and upright all actions! "Inhumanity to the distressed, and insolence to the fallen," those besetting sins of manhood, how utterly strangers to the heart! How little of sordid interest, and how much of intrepid honesty, was then displayed! These sensations experienced in youth, and recalled in after-life, if deemed the fruit of inexperience, and inimical to the perfidious courtesies of society, should at least make us concede that we have exhausted some part of our stock of virtue and principle since—that we have been losers in some points by the lapse of time, if we have been gainers in others, more in harmony with conventional interests and views, and, we may add, with conventional vices.

The sensations peculiar to youth, being the result of impulse rather than reflection, have the advantage over those of manhood, however the pride of reason may give the latter the superiority. In manhood there is always a burden of thought bearing on the wheels of enjoyment. In manhood, too, we have the misfortune of seeing the wrecks of early associations scattered every where around us. Youth can see nothing of this. It can take no review of antecedent pleasures or pains that become such a source of melancholy emotion in mature years. It has never sauntered through the rooms of a building, and recalled early days spent under its roof. I remember my feelings on an occasion of this sort, when I was like a traveller on the plain of Babylon, wondering where all that had once been to me so great and mighty, then was—in what gulph the sounds of merriment that once reverberated from the walls, the master, the domestic, the aged, and the young, had disappeared. Our early recollections are pleasing to us because they look not on the morrow. Alas! what did that morrow leave when it became merged in the past! I have lately traversed the village in which I was born, without discovering a 'face that I knew. Houses have been demolished, fronts altered, tenements built, trees rooted up, and alterations effected, that made me feel a stranger amid the home of my fathers. The old-fashioned and roomy house where my infant years had been watched by parental affection, had been long uninhabited, it was in decay—the storm beat through its fractured windows, and it was partly roofless. The garden and its old elms, and the cherished feelings of many a happy hour, lay a weedy waste—

> Amid thy desert walks the lapwing flies,
> And tires their echoes with unvaried cries;
> Sunk are thy bowers in shapeless ruin all,
> And the long grass o'ertops the mould'ring wall!

But the picture it presented in my youth, exhibits it as true and vivid as ever. It is hung up in memory in all its freshness, and time cannot dilapidate its image. It is now become an essence that defies the mutability of material things. It is fixed in ethereal colours on the tablets of the mind, and lives within the domain of spirit, within the circumference of which the universal spoiler possesses no sovereignty.

I lately entered the church-yard of my native parish before-mentioned, and visited the tombs of those who in my youth were its busy inhabitants. The old Squire with his patrician monument, surrounded by an iron-railing to distinguish him in death from the plebeian dust around—he who used to halloo to the hounds with a cry like the war-whoop of the savage, dole forth rustic justice, or what he imagined to be justice, for it was sometimes, when poachers were concerned, naturally a little twisted from the true meaning of the word, by reason of his worship's venatorious prejudices. In these prejudices, however, he was outdone by the Vicar, who reposes within the great aile in the bosom of mother-church, not far from his fellow-sportsman. In fact, the Squire was, after all, the better practical Christian of the two. The Parson held the temporal as well as spiritual weapons, and advocated the preservation of game in the pulpit, out of which he would suffer no one to labour for its destruction that was not qualified like himself. How often I remember the return of both these defunct worthies from the chase, jaded and muddy, yet awful personages in the eyes of the cottagers, who gazed upon them and the bespattered horses from their doors as if they had been monarchs. Near the Squire reposed old Robin the huntsman, and not far off, around, a score of more ignoble personages, of whom I had numberless early recollections of character and circumstance. How busily memory employed itself at that moment! How I found the shadows of the past move in long array before me, following time into oblivion! I asked myself to what end they had lived, toiled, and mouldered away into dusty forgetfulness? I contrasted the feelings I once had when treading the same spot, with those that then came over me: then all the future was promised happiness, the past left no regretful feelings, and the present was pretty evenly balanced between pleasure and pain. But now the past is loaded with melancholy recollections, and the future with apprehension, and even these mournful recollections of past time are ranked among the gratifications of the present. I remember, when a boy, the landlady of the Full Moon Inn, the hotel of the village—she was even then styled an 'old woman,' who still survives, and looks strong and well:—she is an isthmus connecting two generations, having borne nearly the same aspect to both. After a certain period at the commencement of old age, the personal appearance in hale individuals changes very slowly: from sixty-five to seventy-five there is less alteration in some robust frames than might be naturally expected. This venerable remnant of other times had not changed her habits and manners. Like all who live in subservience to the law of custom rather than reason, she was a stern enemy to innovation of every kind. I entered her sanded parlour, and found the same pictures on the walls, and the same pieces of grotesque china, I had seen when a boy. Here, thought I, I can fling myself back again into the past. Here I can cogitate upon "lang syne," and practise an innocent deception on the senses. The locality was, in truth, no illusion, and while sipping a glass of the old lady's sherry, I hailed the shades of former years, and "toasted lips that bloomed no more." I forgot the long interval of chequered existence that had intervened since I beheld the same scene with the eyes of youth. I conversed with other years, and held solemn communion with the images of the departed. Meditation brought out of the storehouse of memory many a forgotten incident that lay piled under the lumber of more recent impressions. The window of the room where I sat was open, and the fragrant blossom of an old white-thorn tree without came into the room, and brought with it a killing remembrance of the smell it bore long ago, as if no other could have exhaled so sweet an odour. The meadows beyond it looked the greenest I had ever seen, and the distant hills, aërially tinted, were to me for a short space more beautiful than my eyes had lighted upon before : all wore the colouring it was clothed with in my youth. The illusion was short, but delightful, and was dispelled by the painful reflection, that it was but an illusion, and only a minute portion of what was remaining, like an oasis in a tide of sand that had overwhelmed all beside of a beautiful landscape, or like a flowery eminence seen above a rising flood, and not yet buried beneath its waste of waters.

What must have been the feelings of the Emperor of France, when, after a battle with the Allies in 1814, he found himself under the very tree at Brienne, where he had read " Jerusalem Delivered" in his youth. He would no doubt have exchanged all the splendours of his turbid existence to recall those times again. How delighted was Johnson on visiting, just before the close of existence, the same willow-tree at Lichfield which he had known in his boyhood. Waller, in his old age, bought a small house and a little land at Coleshill, that he might return again to the place of his early recollections, and " die like a stag where he had been roused." How many similar instances might be quoted of attachment to the times of youth. We revert to them in the last period of existence, as if we would fain run our course of years over again; and yet this is really the case with very few of us---we love them perhaps because the innocence and artlessness of youth give us more satisfaction upon reflection than the artifice and selfishness of our intervening years.　　　　　　　　　　　　　　　　　　　　　　　　　　　　　Y. I.

---

### ' TO ANNA.

MAY thy lot in life be happy, undisturb'd by thoughts of me!  
The God who shelters innocence, thy guard and guide will be ;  
Thy heart will lose the chilling sense of hopeless love at last,  
And the sunshine of the future chase the shadows of the past.

I never wish to meet thee more—though I am still thy friend,  
I never wish to meet thee more, since dearer ties must end ;  
With worldly smiles, and worldly words, I could not pass thee by,  
Nor turn from thee unfeelingly with cold averted eye.

I could not bear to meet thee 'midst the thoughtless and the gay,  
I could not bear to win thee deck'd in fashion's bright array ;  
And less could I endure to meet thee pensive and alone,  
When through the trees the evening breeze breathes forth its cheerless moan.

For I have met thee 'midst the gay—and thought of none but *thee*,  
And I have seen thy bright array—when it was worn for *me* ;  
And often near the sunny waves I've wander'd by thy side,  
With joy—that pass'd away as fast as sunshine from the tide.

I never wish to meet thee more—yet think not I've been taught  
By smiling foes to injure thee by one unworthy thought ;  
No—blest with some beloved one—from care and sorrow free,  
May thy lot in life be happy, undisturb'd by thoughts of me!

## LA VAUDERIE.

" J'ay veu grant *Vauderie*
En Arras pulluler,
Gens plein de rederie
Par jugement brusler."    JOH. MOLINET.

I WOULD lay a trifle, gentle reader (any thing you please under a crown) that you do not *recollect** what Vauderie is ; and therein, some will say, " your state is the more gracious." For, exclusive of that, the thing is in itself, like the Knight's pancakes, " naught."—What, I pray you, is all knowledge, whether of good or of evil, but " the fruit of that forbidden tree, whose mortal taste" brought into the world the censorship, the law of libel, and the Constitutional Society,—a fruit of which the Emperor of Austria sayeth to his subjects, " the less you eat, the better." But, granting,—what cannot be disputed with a worse argument than three hundred thousand bayonets,—that the Emperor of Austria knows what's best for his own subjects (and his worst enemies cannot say that he dispraises the dish in order to have it all to himself), yet you and I, " my public," are not, I thank Heaven for it, of his parish ; and therefore, all new international law notwithstanding, under no necessity of crying at his sermons. I shall, then,—let the said Emperor take it as he pleases,—proceed to give you my notions on the subject of " Vauderie ;" and it is the more necessary to know something of the matter, inasmuch as it is a relick of those good old times, which *read* so well in novels and in manifestoes, and for the revival of which, so much of the best blood in Christendom, ay, and what's more, of the best gold in Threadneedle-street, has been shed without stint or forbearance. Besides, I do not absolutely despair of hearing a belief in Vauderie once more declared, as it was of old, " part and parcel of the common law of the land."

To define Vauderie after the manner of lexicographers and encyclopedists, it is—in political economy a branch of finance,—in theology, an heresy,—in the arts, a method of aërial vectitation,—and in commerce, a species of barter, that is, or has been contraband, by all the laws of the civilized world. Now the practice of Vauderie is in this wise :—

He, or she (for in this affair, the gender makes little difference), who would " *Aller en Vauderie,*" must first make provision of a certain ointment, with which the palms of the hands must be anointed, as must also a small switch, which is then to be placed between the legs ; when, forthwith the party is carried through the air, and brought to a vast assembly, where there stand tables loaded with good cheer, — but where,—saving your presence—the " evil one" presides " *en vrai Amphitryon,*" in the form of a goat, with a monkey's (prehensile ?) tail. To this feast, however, you are not invited *gratis*. The price of admission is an act of homage (you cannot get into Almack's under a dozen at least, and plenty of *antichambering* to boot) which is paid to his

---

* Observe, I do not say " don't *know* ;" for none but your political critic has a right to presume on the ignorance of his reader, and to hector and rhodomontade, as if nobody ever read a book but himself. *I* observe the decencies of literature ; and if you will do me justice, so ; if not, have the goodness to write the next article yourself.

black highness under a form so extraordinary that I must give it you in the quaint old French of my author. " *Puis baisoient le diable en forme de boucq au derriere avec candeilles ardentes.*" This the country gentlemen must not expect me to translate; or to explain farther than by saying, that it is a *middle term* between doing homage to the Pope, and saluting one's grandmother. After this act of reverence to "old horney," the candidate for admission marks his disrespect for "all good angels," by an attitude * which at Eton is considered as the last proof of canonical obedience to the powers that be. Here let me *obiter* remark, that the devil acts more fairly by his servants than the government of France; which when it purchases of the people an act of homage in the form of *Vive le Roi*, by a donative of tongues and sausages, bribes the poor dupes with money taken out of their own pockets; whereas what the Devil gives for supper is beyond dispute his *peculium*, or private property, and a real largesse to his admirers.

These trifling ceremonies performed, you go to supper, " with what appetite you may," and then—but I think I may as well translate no farther, " *pour doubte que les oreilles innocentes ne fussent averties de si villaines choses.*" By this time, reader, you will have formed a shrewd guess that *Vauderie* is nothing more nor less than that *rather darkcoloured* art, of which Sir Matthew Hale avers there is no doubting the reality, seeing that divers acts of parliament have been passed to punish its practice :—a species of *non sequitur* by the way, in the use of which that great lawyer is by no means singular : *Credo quia impossibile est*, being at least as much a maxim of law as of theology. The fact is, that the same fooleries and indecencies of which the royal hero of " Nigel" was wont to accuse the victims of his " doings" against witchcraft, had in France, some century or more before, been imputed by an excess of malignity to a religious sect, known by the name of *Vaudois*, whose members were the precursors of Calvin and Luther. Barbarous as were the times, yet the humanity of the people revolted against persecution for conscience sake ; and it was thought expedient by the supporters of establishments in that day to calumniate those innovators they hated and feared, before they ventured to destroy them.

Le Clercq, in his Mémoires, gives a curious account of a crusade against the Vaudois which took place in Arras in the year 1459, in which the bigotry and superstition of the inquisitors seem to have degenerated into a mere thirst for plunder. The principles adopted in the trial of those accused of this crime were the same which are known to have directed the ordinary proceedings of the Inquisition. The rack was employed, not only to extort confession of his own offences from the accused, but to force from him testimony for inculpating others. No one was permitted to succour an individual when once arrested ; and not even father, brother, mother, or sister, could interfere in the process, without subjecting themselves to be included in the accusation. The most insidious solicitations and false promises were held out to seduce those to confess, whom pain and fear could not overcome: and the confession once made was inevitably turned against the accused, and read to the people assembled at the execution, as a

---

* " Puis monstroient le cul devers le ciel et le firmament, en despit de Dieu."

justification of the procedure, and a bar to sympathy or assistance. Thus every fresh victim became the instrument for putting on their trial all the individuals within the range of his personal knowledge; for as long as torture was applied, men were forced to give utterance to whatever passed through their minds; and the rack was continued till memory and imagination were exhausted; and nothing new, either of truth or falsehood, remained to be extorted.

Thus the fanaticism of the people was preserved at its boiling point, and the suffragan Bishop of Arras, one of the most zealous in the conduct of these infamies, even lost his senses from the exaltation of his bigotry; unless, indeed, he became insane through the goading of a conscience ulcerated by reiterated murders. So heated was his imagination, that he continually declared in all assemblies that many bishops and cardinals were "*en Vauderie;*" and that so numerous were those who thus allied themselves with the Devil, that they wanted but a sovereign prince to join them in order to overthrow the whole Christian world.

The horror excited in the public mind by these events, rendered Arras the scandal of all France. A citizen of that time could scarcely obtain a lodging in a public inn; and such was the dread of the daily confiscations which in these cases followed conviction, that all who had lent money to an Arras merchant, hastened to call it in before the bishop and the feudal chief could seize on the debtor's effects, and divide the property between them.

Encouraged by their success, the inquisitors proceeded to attack persons of greater consequence; and amongst others they fixed upon a certain Seigneur de Beauffort, who, escaping from their search, appealed to the Duke of Burgundy. The duke, in consequence, assembled a council of the most learned men in his dominions to consult upon the case. Of these, some denied *in toto* the possibility of the offence; others credited the accusation, but attributed the phenomena to mental illusion, or to deceits practised on the credulous; while some held it "blasphemous" to deny that supernatural agency, which was a direct corollary from the established religion. After this consultation a deputation was forwarded from these "sad and learned" personages, to examine into the matter on the spot, and to superintend the processes going on before the Bishop at Arras. They were, by the Duke's order, accompanied by his herald "*Toison d'or;*" because, says the chronicle, it was asserted that "only the rich were accused, for the sake of confiscation, at which the Duke was greatly troubled."

What private instructions these men received, does not appear; but that they were hostile to the procedure, may be collected, from the more favourable treatment of the prisoners, and from the fact that no new processes were commenced after this time. Notwithstanding, however, the presence of the deputation, Beauffort and three other persons were condemned. Beauffort was sentenced to be scourged, to be confined for seven years, and to pay enormous fines to different churches and monasteries: two others were sentenced to similar punishments; and the fourth, who had resisted the rack with the greatest firmness, was burned alive. After a lapse of two years, Beauffort's family appealed to the Parliament of Paris; and, armed with their warrant, and a good troop of horse, they forced the Bishop's prison, and liberated the accused. But, notwithstanding all their interest and the right of their case, they never succeeded in reversing the sentence, or bringing the matter to a final decision. How many persons were burned under this infamous process is not stated; but from the context it should appear that the number was very great. According to Le Clercq's account, almost all the accused were brought to acknowledge their guilt, either by the torture, or the false promises of their persecutors, that, if they confessed, they would be let off with a short penance, whereas (it was intimated) they would certainly be burned if they persisted in a denial. When brought to the stake, many made loud complaints of this treachery, and publicly accused the prosecutors of their falsehood: but this declaration of innocence was, by the malice of the torturers, construed into a fresh obedience to the Devil, " de quelles choses," says our author, " *je m'attens à Dieu.*"

Such then, gentle reader, was " *La Vauderie,*" which in its day was, no doubt, regarded as a useful prop to authority; and which, considering the tendency of events, may, as I have said, again become fashionable with the " *Eteignoirs*" of the Holy Alliance. It is true that the judges of the land have recently declared against the reality of witchcraft in a very edifying manner; but I should like to hear Mr. Justice *this*, or My Lord Chief *that*, persist in such heresy, if a quintuple alliance should agree that *La Vauderie* is a valuable part of the social system, and one of the best pieces in the *marqueterie* of their religious mosaics. The revival of the penal laws against the black art in Europe might in various ways be turned to a good account; and the measure might the more safely be adopted by the οἱ ἐν τέλει, the successors of Napoleon, as there is little apprehension that the weapon would be turned against themselves, common report and notoriety, amply testifying that they are " no conjurors." The Carbonari,[*] for instance, those night-mares of despotism, might thus very conveniently be rendered formidable to *all other* old women, and put down without fear or hesitation. Their profession would give some colour to the charge; and no one could doubt that they were at least "bewitched," since their infatuation extends to offering offence to such rulers, and that, spurning at the numerous comforts provided by their paternal government, they presume to look for a *gratior libertas* than that which Italy enjoys under the *pious* sway of the father-in-law of the Ex-Emperor of France. But not to travel from home, are we not pestered with reprobates, who, in order " to raise the wind," would not hesitate to go twenty times to the Devil? which seems to come very nearly within the definition of the black art; and would, in the eye of the law, render the offenders amenable to a more summary justice than is to be had under the insolvent act. The penal laws against witchcraft might likewise become supplementary to the libel laws, inasmuch as they would evidently embrace the case of those who sell themselves to the (printer's) devil.

They might farther be turned to good account in keeping down a superfluous population. For if poverty be *primâ facie* evidence against those suspected of other crimes, why not in the case of witchcraft also? Too many, indeed, of our countrymen are known to be driven on the

---

[*] Literally, *Colliers.*

practice of various black arts by the pressure of the times; and nothing
is more reasonable to suppose than that they who have not a guinea
*on the face of the earth*, should be desirous to change their element, and
mount into the air, if it were only to escape from their creditors. The
very circumstance of their having the " Devil in their pocket," would
tell against them.

Not the smallest advantage derivable from this project would be
the facility with which his Majesty's ministers might get rid of Mr.
H— by burning him for a witch. For they might most conscientiously
swear that he is consuming them night after night by a slow fire. This
much, indeed, is certain, that more than one of them has shewn himself
eager to draw blood from that gentleman, which could only proceed
from their apprehension of his *casting figures* and preventing the butter
from coming when they churn.

The revival of these laws would also operate against a certain institution for the subjugation of literature; for assuredly " the Devil was
in" the parties who first hit on such a wild-goose scheme: and it is farther to be remarked, that the powers of casting their readers into a
deep sleep, which are evinced by some of its members, exceed all that
we read of the myrtle sprig which the Devil gave to Lewis's Monk, and
can only be attributed to the same infernal agency. Another race of
evil-doers, whose operations would be restrained by these laws, is that
of the porter-brewers, whose cauldrons " bubble bubble, toil and
trouble," with ingredients, than which the witches in Macbeth could produce nothing more deleterious. I need say nothing to the opponents
of Catholic emancipation. The alliance of the Pope and the Devil
is of ancient standing; and to deal with the one is plainly to deal
with the other.

An attorney, they say, is " a match for the Devil;" and his bill of
costs, the Devil *in propria persona*. These sable-suited gentry may
therefore be safely trusted to the operations of the revived law, by
which their bills and themselves will be committed to the same fire.

From these numerous advantages there are, to be sure, some drawbacks. The New Monthly Magazine, for instance, must forego all commerce with several " comical Devils," who are wont to set their readers
in a roar. Grimm's Ghost must no more be evoked; and " the devilish
good fun" of Peter Pindaric must thenceforward slumber in oblivion.
Our readers will likewise no longer be " enchanted" by divine poesy.

Another important consideration is, that the Corinthians and Tom
and Jerry boys will no more be permitted to " play the Devil;" which
will be a heavy loss to society, " eclipsing the gaiety of nations," and
diminishing the " harmless amusement" of the worthiest members of
the community.

All things, however, considered, the balance is decidedly in favour
of the project; and as soon as Louis " of the large-stomach" shall have
brought back the Inquisition into Spain, there is little room for doubt
that a rider will be tacked to his next decree for abolishing the
English Parliament, which shall enjoin all good Christians to believe in witchcraft, and condemn to the flames all that are " en
Vauderie" with the dæmon of Liberty, possessed of a (reasoning) devil,
or dare to utter the cabalistical word—Constitution.                M.

## THE "THREE MIGHTY."

WATCH-fires are blazing on hill and plain
Till noon-day light is restored again,
There are shining arms in Raphaim's vale,
And bright is the glitter of clanging mail.

The Philistine hath fix'd his encampment here—
Afar stretch his lines of banner and spear—
And his chariots of brass are ranged side by side,
And his war-steeds neigh loud in their trappings of pride.

His tents are placed where the waters flow,
The sun hath dried up the springs below,
And Israel hath neither well nor pool,
The rage of her soldiers' thirst to cool.

In the cave of Adullam king David lies,
Overcome with the glare of the burning skies;
And his lip is parch'd, and his tongue is dry,
But none can the grateful draft supply.

Though a crowned king, in that painful hour
One flowing cup might have bought his power—
What worth in the fire of thirst could be
The purple pomp of his sovereignty!

But no cooling cup from river or spring
To relieve his want can his servants bring,
And he cries, "Are there none in my train or state,
Will fetch me the water of Bethlehem gate?"

Then three of his warriors, the "mighty three,"
The boast of the monarch's chivalry,
Uprose in their strength, and their bucklers rung,
As with eyes of flame on their steeds they sprung.

On their steeds they sprung, and with spurs of speed
Rush'd forth in the strength of a noble deed,
And dash'd on the foe like a torrent-flood,
Till he floated away in a tide of blood.

To the right—to the left—where their blue swords shine
Like autumn-corn falls the Philistine;
And sweeping along with the vengeance of fate,
The "mighty" rush onward to Bethlehem gate.

Through a bloody gap in his shatter'd array,
To Bethlehem's well they have hewn their way,
Then backward they turn on the corse-cover'd plain,
And charge through the foe to their monarch again.

The king looks at the cup, but the crystal draught
At a price too high for his want hath been bought;
They urge him to drink, but he wets not his lip,
Though great is his need, he refuses to sip.

But he pours it forth to Heaven's Majesty—
He pours it forth to the Lord of the sky;
'Tis a draught of death—'tis a cup blood-stain'd—
'Tis a prize from man's suffering and agony gain'd.

Should he taste of a cup that his "mighty three"
Had obtain'd by their peril and jeopardy?
Should he drink of their life?—'Twas the thought of a king!,
And again he return'd to his suffering.

I.

## WRITERS OF IMAGINATION.

Do we not owe much more to writers of imagination than is generally acknowledged? This is a query which I think must be answered affirmatively. Literature has mainly contributed to the present advanced state of civilization; and in enquiring what branches of it have more particularly tended to those refinements which spring from generous and noble feelings, it must be conceded to our poets and romance-writers. Much was gained from the ancients that produced an influence upon the character of modern nations; but perhaps their writings operated most beneficially by exciting a love of research, and arousing genius to exertion. This idea gathers strength from the fact that the study of the ancients did little in awaking the flame of civil liberty.* They were long the inmates of cloisters and of courts, but they effected no direct change in favour of liberal feelings. Inquisitors tortured, Popes duped, Monks cheated, and Princes trampled on mankind, but no spontaneous spirit of resistance was aroused among the people by the free circulation of the classics. They were, no doubt, an indirect cause of original thinking and the uncontroeled operations of genius, by propagating a taste for study and feeding the flame of emulation; but, directly, they were harmless enough to be tolerated by the present Czar of Muscovy, or the feudal sovereign of Hungary himself. It will be found that their present state of literature, or at least that state in which there is the most extensively diffused taste for letters, is a pretty good criterion of the grades of the different nations of Europe in refinement. Whatever each separate class of authors may have contributed to this end, the diffusion of high and generous feelings is principally owing to writers of imagination. To them we are largely indebted for the better sentiments of the age, and for all that by exciting the passions leads to eminence and renown. This is mainly owing to their prominent principle of keeping the mind dissatisfied with common-place things, their power of creating images superior in every respect to reality, which we admire and would fain imitate; and the admiration they infuse for what is good and excellent, or sublime and daring. Writers on science have ameliorated the physical condition of man, enlarged his stock of information, and increased his luxuries. In devoting themselves to their own peculiar studies, they were urged on by the desire of improvement, which very desire, the moving spring of all, is increased by the dislike of standing still; and the spirit of ambition which imaginative writers greatly assist nature in sustaining. Like the trophies of Miltiades that would not let Themistocles rest, the visions and day-dreams that haunt the mind and fill the soul with things better than the world and society afford it, by making us discontented spur us to pursue those beyond our reach, and keep us in progression.

What can some branches of literature effect towards the refinements of social life—writers on law, for example? They may enable the lawyer to improve his practice, and arrive at the end for which he

---

* The Editor begs leave to say, that he thinks his correspondent utterly at fault in his opinion respecting the influence of classical learning on the progress of liberty in the modern world.

labours—his private profit; /for in spite of cant this is the sole object
of the profession.   For this the members drudge and dispute on both
sides of a question, or on either side, just as they are hired, and their
efforts, in plain fact, are alone directed to their individual advantage.
There is no enthusiasm in the pursuit beyond what springs from the
love of gain; and inasmuch as it is for the public good that intricate
and contradictory laws should be made clear when they can be made
so at all, writers on law may be merely styled useful, and nothing more.
A pure legislation must depend on civilization; but this is not the
lawyer's, but the statesman's calling, and emanates from public opinion
expressed by its representatives, and its spirit must be governed by the
variations of time and circumstances.   Writers on grammar, medicine,
and technical, and limited arts, contribute indirectly and remotely to
refinement.   The Bentleys of their age, who devote volumes to the
correction of a comma, or the supposed use of an obsolete letter, are
but abstractedly beneficial, inasmuch as they smooth the way to learning
for the great spirits that are destined to operate good through the
medium of the passions.   Those writers who appeal to reason make
very slow progress in imposing conviction, compared with those who
operate the other way.   By the alchemy of association and the power
of appeal to the heart through its vivid pictures, more impression is
made on mankind by one writer of imagination, than by twenty reason-
ers.   Reason will never be any other than a regulator.   The writer of
imagination leads us to better objects and desires than the world exhibits to our senses, and thereby keeps alive a perpetual wish of improvement by the contemplation of what ought to exist, and the dissa-
tisfying us with what really does.

   Let us examine facts.   Writers of imagination, far above all others,
have been in advance of the time in which they lived.   Gifted with a
species of intellectual foresight, they have appeared to pour forth their
effusions as if in the midst of times they were never destined to see,
but in the more refined spirit of which they were fully qualified to partake.   They breathed a different intellectual atmosphere from contemporaries, and were acknowledged by those of the highest refinement in
their day with a respect that could only have arisen from a sense of
discriminating admiration.   Monarchs and courts, till late times, associated with poets and romance-writers: the court formerly being the
most enlightened and refined circle in the state, the centre of knowledge and fine feeling, there was a natural affinity between them.   As
a portion of the people attained a higher state of mental culture, they
approached the court itself, and at last equalled, and a numerous body
of them surpassed, most of the individuals composing it, in cultivated
intellect.   Writers then naturally felt the tone of a considerable portion of the popular feeling to be most in unison with their own, and the
latter became to writers of imagination what courts had been in earlier
times.   Part of the people having become as discerning as the individuals
whom chance, interest, or caprice, may have elevated to carry on affairs
of state for the monarch, where talent and intellect should have constituted the qualification—talent that, discarding prejudice, would have
assimilated things to the light of the age—is one great cause of
the present feverish feeling of some European nations.   In Russia, for
instance, where the court is among a dark people, it is still the centre
of the intellectual refinement of the empire.   Writers of imagination,

born with more vivid conceptions than other men, have lived in an ideal world, which the nature of human desires led them to pourtray more perfect and noble than the world of reality. This gave them more independent spirits, more lofty and romantic ideas, and also enabled them to reason; for Locke allows that it is not necessary for men to devote their lives to the study of logic to reason well. Pure thoughts and lofty principles influenced by genius, that do not suffer common prejudices to affect them, will weigh things with the greatest impartiality, and come to the most rational conclusions. In past and even in present days, how much that the world sanctions appears absurd and barbarous in the eye of genius. The judges would have burnt all the old women in England without compunction, if evidence had been tendered that they were witches, in the days of John Milton, and even for fifty years afterwards; the poet, we may answer for it, would not have condemned one. Dante would never have made a hell for many great men of his time deemed by the multitude among the mighty and noble, had he looked upon them with the eyes of his own age. He contemplated them as not of his own time, and with the impartiality of a future and wiser generation. Vulgar minds cannot comprehend the ideas of men of genius; they think them audacities or chimerical innovations; but they who contribute to the improvement of mankind belong but a small part of them to present time—they are the heritage of unborn ages. Honest and good men may labour in their world of realities in a circle of minute duration, be useful, industrious, and virtuous followers in a beaten track, content with what they see, and thinking the world precisely as it should be in every respect. They, however, are but the wheels of society, not the moving causes. Sir Thomas More is a remarkable instance among imaginative writers, and seems at first to constitute an exception to the foresight, if it may be so denominated, of that class. But he was bred a lawyer, and suffered the pernicious leaven of the profession to neutralize the effect of the divine spirit with which he wrote. More condemned persecution · in his works as not fit for his Utopian state of society; but he practised it, from his inveterate obedience to custom, when he should have nobly resisted it from principle.

Writers of imagination, by what is wrongly called deception, more properly fiction, send us in search of better things than we already possess. Present and limited use is not so much their object as to delight and allure. From the spirit of correction and improvement, which originates in the desire of possessing better things than we see around us, old and bad laws are repealed; the legislative body bows to public opinion, and changes old and absurd usages for those that are more rational and useful; the commercial restrictions of past times are removed; a more liberal toleration is sanctioned, and a system consistent with the state of mental culture is introduced. Fixed things are injurious to that eternal desire of perfection, with which the better order of minds is imbued. We must not stand still, but we shall infallibly do so if we have no longing after idealities. Our line of action may be uniform, but, notwithstanding, we must pursue it from the expectation of overtaking what is better than we have yet come up with. Genius is, most of it, that eternal hope ever alive in the mind, of something better than present good—the quenchless vestal fire, the soul of every thing great and noble in the world. Imaginative writers' dwell in a world of spirit, glorious in beauty and boundless in extent. Let the tale be a deception—let the poem be a fiction—let the metaphysician show his teeth at it, and the mathematician snarl and sneer, because he cannot lay down its length and breadth ; it is from this very cause its beneficial effects arise, and that it is so useful to mankind. It is because it keeps alive better things than their philosophy can teach, that its elements are so valuable: A touching ballad shall make a million friends to a virtuous object; a hundred sermons shall not procure one. A " lilibullero" shall uncrown a tyrant before a mathematician can construct a fort in which to shelter himself from his fury. The direct effects of works of the imagination sometimes seem irresistible ; and if any chance to be impugnable on the score of principles—for all writers will have their imperfections, more or less—there is a property mysteriously attached to the mass of public opinion, that makes it reject what is erroneous, as it were, by the subtlest intuition, and profit by the purer portion.

Let us examine the earliest writers of imagination, and compare them with mere schoolmen,—how liberal are their views—how refined their sentiments ! Matter-of-fact men, who deal only in the tangible, are of the earth earthy : the natural is their sphere—they deal in cubes and blocks—they must see and touch, to believe. They ever gravitate to the centre: their looks are always " downward bent," and they enjoy no " visions beatific." Their grovelling and heavy imaginations are unequal to mounting with the " sightless couriers of the air." They see only with " leaden eyes that love the ground ;" and if they dream, they dream by rule and compass. The eye that " doth glance from heaven to earth, from earth to heaven," is to them the organ of a distempered brain. Where should we arrive if we considered human nature only in the mere matter-of-fact way it exhibits itself in the world—a thing of petty interests, selfish, overreaching, deceitful, infirm, and perishable ?—if we always kept to the reality of the picture, and contemplated it in its naked truth ?—if we could not mark out nobler destinies for it than its realities show, and fill up the defects of what is, with the images and desires of what would render existence more delightful? What a glorious light flashes on the offspring of imagination, the herald of a more perfect state of things existing somewhere ! How they seem imbued with qualities of the most redeeming character ! Even in the darker times, how they sparkled with native radiance ! what a contrast they formed to the bigotry, prejudice, and ignorance of ecclesiastical writers, and the plodders after the dogmas of blind scholastics ! Before philosophy glimmered, and Galileo was incarcerated by churchmen for promulgating sublime truths, too vast for the understandings of monks and cardinals, writers of imagination had forced their way for ages and satirised the crimes of consistories and the knavery of the Apostolic Church—thus insensibly undermining the Vatican. Fiction triumphed in the cause of truth, and, opening the eyes of mankind, innovated on established order, preparing Europe for the Reformation. Boccaccio, by exposing the licentiousness of the clergy in his Decameron, contributed to this good end nearly two hundred years before Luther appeared. There seemed to be such an innate love in remote times for writers of imagination, that they flourished in spite of secular and ecclesiastical opposition, secretly applauded by the enlightened among the great, at a time when works of science that interfered with superstition would have been strangled in their birth, and their authors burned at the stake by a council of churchmen from pure *l'amour de Dieu.*

Poetry, being the first step among barbarous nations towards refinement, made way for civilization; while in later times princes and courts loved and encouraged poets, and writers of romance were deemed almost divine. But the regard for literature is now more strong among the people. Modern princes have not kept pace with the advancement of their people, because taste and knowledge cannot increase hereditarily; they must therefore be content to follow, with their courts, the current of public opinion, and be in this respect on a level with the rest of the nation. Few modern princes will wish to show an isolated condition of mind, pretending to despise that which they cannot comprehend. Nor will they, because their subjects are become more refined, affect the vulgar feeling of Louis XIV. when he said to the Duke de Vivonne, who was a healthy ruddy-looking personage, " Mais à quoi sert de lire ?" and got the following reply, " Sire, la lecture fait à l'esprit ce que vos perdrix font à mes joues." There seems to be no affectation, however, in the Emperor of Austria on this head; his intellects, indeed, are naturally weak, and his notions feudal. Else, while he trampled upon Italy, he would not have doomed Pellico, the young, the charming poet of that country, to wear out life in chains and in a dungeon, merely on suspicion of being a friend to his native land. Pellico, to his misfortune, was not slave enough in spirit. Had he been a slave, he had breathed the pure air of Heaven—he had now seen the sun that will probably never again shed its beams upon him!

The direct communication of dry facts would not improve mankind unless all were able to reason impartially and well—alas, how few can! The best relation of the life of a virtuous man, accurately given in cold narrative, would not do half as much in the cause of virtue as a fictitious character of suffering goodness, worked up with the graces of style and the embellishments of eloquence, and written to touch the passions. Every-day examples would not move us towards what is excellent. There is something more than bare truth by which men are to be affected. A stimulant must be applied to the mind as well as the body. We must contemplate ideal goodness, if we would avoid retrograding. We must follow a route trackless as the eagle's, and, rising above a real, keep hope alive by contemplating an invisible creation. The reign of poetry and romance is one of spirit engendering enthusiasm and inspiration, the quality that makes a hero of a soldier, an artist of a mechanic, and a martyr of a saint. It cannot be enjoyed without a temporary abstraction from what is around us, but must rise above the impure tainted atmosphere of common life. The air-woven delicate visions of poetical inspiration will not appear in the clouded, foggy, dense climate of every-day routine; they must float in " gaily gilded trim" beneath unclouded skies, and in the full glory of the sunbeam, in fields of ether, and amid the rich hues of the rainbow. But for scenes of imagination, those cities of refuge to which the mind may fly now and then from the toil, dulness, and weary repetitions of morning, noon and night, and night, noon and morning, what careworn wretches should we be ! So far from valuing works of fancy less as we advance in civilization, we shall love them more, because we fly to them with more enjoyment from the fatigue of professional pursuits and the right-angled formalities of daily avocations, which multiply around us, as luxury increases our wants.   No; let the author of Waverley write on ; let poets pour forth their strains; let the Radcliffes of the time lead us into the horrors of romance, and let the empire of imagination live for ever !  Let the plodding lawyer worship his fee, confound right and wrong, and entangle his clients as he may, scoffing at the splendours of fiction.   Let the physician look wise and considerate, and shake his head, while his patient suffers nothing but " consumption of purse."   Let the merchant traffic, and the tradesman truck : let the Jew cheat, and the attorney inveigle : let earthquake and plague devastate : let man be cruel and oppressive to fellow-man, sell his blood and muscle, or butcher him in war for the sake of a hogshead of sugar, a roll of tobacco, or the dreamy right of some king divine to " govern wrong :" let dulness and impudence prosper, and merit remain in obscurity : let ignorance and incapacity fill the seat of justice, while common sense is pilloried : let all these things be daily, and go their roundabout as matters-of-course:—whither can we turn from them ? where can we go aside from observing them with repulsion and disgust, but to the empire of imagination ?  Sickened with such objects as constitute the greater part of our realities, we may meditate on forms of female beauty like the Juliet of Shakspeare, or the Rebecca of Ivanhoe—we may solace ourselves with " mask and antique pageantry," and

> " Such sights as youthful poets dream
>   On summer eves by haunted stream :"—

with the deeds of Roncesvalles, or of British Arthur ; or

> " Call up him that left half told
>   The story of Cambuscan bold,
>   Of Camball and of Algarsife,
>   And who had Canace to wife :"—

we may visit scenes and beings of a purer world than our own ; and when forced to return to every-day things, return to them with renovated spirits, and the hope that the delightful creations in which we have been revelling, may at some future time be realized to our senses, if not in this world, in another.                                        Y.

---

### SONG.—SILENT GLANCES.

Oh ! there are moments dear and bright,
  When Love's delicious spring is dawning,
Soft as the ray of quivering light,
  That wakes the early smile of morning ;
'Tis when warm blushes paint the cheek,
  When doubt the thrill of bliss enhances ;
And trembling lovers fear to speak,
  Yet tell their hopes by silent glances.

And when young Love rewards their pain,
  The heart to rosy joys beguiling,
When Pleasure wreathes their myrtle chain,
  And Life's gay scene is fair and smiling ;
Oft shall they fondly trace the days,
  When wrapt in Fancy's waking trances,
They wish'd, and sigh'd, and loved to gaze,
  And told their hopes by silent glances.            M. A.

*Knowle Park, the seat of the Duchess of Dorset.*

IF the searcher after the riches of Art expects to find, in every British Gallery, a storehouse like some of those which we have had occasion to explore in several of our previous papers under the above title, he will be grievously disappointed;—and moreover his *being* disappointed will prove that he deserves to be so. The votarist who is not content to make a pilgrimage to the shrine of *one* saint, but must have a whole calendar to attract him, has mistaken his calling, and may turn critic as soon as he pleases—for he has no true love for that about which he professes to concern himself. Those who are accustomed to lament that the Battle of Waterloo ever took place, either forget, or do not attach a proper value to, the fact, that it caused to be dispersed all over the civilized world those miracles of Art which were collected within the walls of the Louvre : and if it did no other good but this, it was worth all that it cost. It is not in human nature duly to appreciate that which it obtains with ease, or can have by asking for ; or that which it cannot help seeing if it would. This is one reason why the French artists and critics have not made one progressive step in Art during the last five-and-twenty years. Not that they did not sufficiently *admire* the works of the old masters that were collected in the Louvre ; for they thought many of them nearly equal to their own David's ! They admired, without being able to *appreciate* them. Another reason for this, and one which makes the French artists and critics more excusable, is that, in point of fact, beauty, of whatever kind it may be, does in a great degree counteract itself, when it is present in several different objects in nearly the same degree of perfection. As two perfect negatives in our language destroy the effect of each other, so do two perfect beauties. Two such sights under the same roof as the Venus and the Transfiguration, is what "no mortal can bear," to any good effect ; not because their influence is too much, but because it is none at all. They *kill* each other, like ill-assorted colours. And this is not a matter of taste, of habit, or even of feeling—as far as consciousness is concerned ; it is a matter of nature, and therefore of necessity. True lovers of nature love the sun, the moon, and the stars, each with a perfect love. But if all were to appear together, they could love neither, except as a part of the whole. And thus it was with the Louvre. As a convocation of all beauty and power in Art, it was duly appreciated, even by the French. It was adequately admired as THE LOUVRE. But in this general admiration all detail was merged and lost ; and of consequence, all the effect of detail was lost too : for it is not *galleries* that make artists—but *pictures*. Individual efforts alone can produce individual efforts—like can alone engender like. Great national collections of pictures may produce good, on the same principle,—by engendering *their* like, and thus collaterally aiding high art, by giving it that encouragement without which it cannot extend itself and flourish. But it is greatly to be feared that, even in this point of view, they are upon the whole mischievous rather than beneficial ; since they are more calculated to diffuse than concentrate the efforts which they may call forth, and thus lose in quality more than

they gain in quantity. It is to private collections alone that the lover of
Art should perhaps look for the true encouragement which Art needs,
and without which it cannot support its due claims to the attention and
admiration of mankind: and *these* can never, like the late collection
at the Louvre, counteract their natural and proper effect, by growing
to an inordinate and unnatural size, and (like Aaron's rod), swallowing
up all the rest.

But this brings me home to my subject; from which I was led away
by the consideration that, if the interesting spot I am now about
to describe does not possess such distinguished objects of attraction, in
the way of mere excellence in art, as many of its rivals do, it is not on
that account unworthy to be included in these desultory and informal
notices; since it does possess several objects well worthy of attention, and has in the way of portraits an attraction peculiar to itself;
besides being one of the oldest collections of the kind, and therefore
very probably the origin of many of its more youthful and ambitious
competitors. In choosing the subjects of these papers, I must also not
forget that they are intended to be popular and amusing, rather than
didactic, and must therefore occasionally fix on one in which natural
objects and associated circumstances claim at least an equal degree of
attention with mere works of art; and in this respect Knowle Park is
well fitted to my purpose.

At the extremity of the pleasant town of Seven Oaks, in Kent, exactly
opposite to the nice old church, stands a plain unpretending gate, which
opens at the touch of every comer, and leads out of the public road
into a thickly-set plantation of young trees, rising on each side the
carriage way, and thus forming a dark overshadowed grove even in
the fullest sunshine. This way leads down windingly to two neat stone-
built lodges, joined to each other by another set of gates; and on passing these second gates you emerge upon the park itself. Immediately
you pass the lodges, there rises before you, at a distance of about a
hundred yards, a noble mass of foliage, consisting of oaks, beeches,
and chesnut trees, finely blended and contrasted together in point of
shade and colour, but wearing the appearance of a solid impenetrable
body, rising like a green wall, to shut out all intruders from the imaginary scene beyond. The bright gravel-road,—which intersects the
rich turf between this mass of trees and the spot where you enter the
park,—branches into two, just as it reaches the trees, and pierces into
the thick of them in opposite directions. In passing along this road
the visitor will do well to pay " homage due" to a beautiful company
of beeches, eight in number, that stand on the right, detached from any
others, and seem to form, as they rise on their solid pillar-like stems,
one happy family,—having so perfectly adapted themselves to each
other that they seem to bend but as one form to the breeze, sigh but
with one voice, or smile but with one happy face in the sunshine. The
manner in which trees thus conform themselves to each other, and to
the circumstances about them, offers one of the most beautiful analo-
gies to our moral nature that I am acquainted with; and one that is
too little observed and attended to.—Nearly opposite to the point where
this beautiful family of beeches stands, a lovely glade stretches away
into the distant part of the domain, bounded on either side by other
forest-trees of almost equal height and beauty. Immediately on pass-

ing this glade on the one side, and stately company of beeches on the other, you take the right branch of the road where it separates, and, winding through the dark solemn grove formed by the great mass of trees I have before mentioned, in the space of about another hundred yards you again emerge upon another part of the park, and the venerable front of the mansion rises before you, beautiful in the unadorned dignity of its grey old age. Approaching it, across the thick elastic turf which clothes the whole park, the visitor should seat himself for a moment beneath the handsome sycamore that stands opposite to the gate of entrance, and contemplate this finely preserved monument of grey antiquity. This principal front, looking on the park, consists of a high gate of entrance, flanked by two square embattled towers, rising considerably above the rest of the building, and wings of equal extent and similar appearance stretching out on each side. These wings consist of a plain wall of grey stone, rising, at it were, immediately out of the turf, pierced with three stories of triple-arched windows, and embattled at top in the ogee manner. This front, though in a state of perfect preservation, presents not the slightest appearance of ornament—not even in the form of a tree or shrub to take off the bare nakedness of its aspect. And I believe it may be regarded as one of the purest as well as best-preserved pieces of antiquity that can be seen; being apparently of the same age with the front of University College, Oxford, and greatly resembling that reputed eldest daughter of Alma Mater, in style and general appearance—the manner in which it is embattled, the form of the windows, &c. being nearly the same. On entering the gate, too, (which we will now do) we find ourselves in a plain quadrangle exactly like many of the University ones, with the apartments ranged at the four sides of it in like manner; and, opposite to the entrance, another gate leading to a second court, of similar form and dimensions with the first.

On reaching the interior of the building, the first apartment in which we find ourselves is the old baronial hall; and before turning for good to the works of art which we are now to seek for, it will be well to direct the visitor's attention to the admirable taste, or rather feeling, with which every thing he has hitherto seen, and will see throughout the place, (and particularly in this hall) is preserved in its pristine state—for to preserve all things in the state that they were four hundred years ago, seems to have been the sole object of its possessors in the *alterations* they have from time to time been compelled to make. They have altered things always with a retrospective eye—never with a prospective one. Accordingly, with the exception of Warwick Castle, I know not where can be found so pure and unfaded a picture of the olden time, as it respects architecture, internal arrangement, furniture, and the habits and customs which these illustrate and recall.

The first object of Art that strikes the observer, on entering this fine old Hall, is a noble antique statue of some Greek orator or philosopher—said to be Demosthenes, and not unworthy to represent that splendid example of Greek genius. It is a whole-length figure, as large as life, elevated on a pedestal; and is among the finest and most perfect remains of antiquity. It represents an aged man, of commanding aspect and deportment, holding a scroll in his hand, which he is contemplating with a calm, cool, and self-involved look.' But the chief merit of the work is one that is peculiar to the Greek statues of the best time of the Art—namely, a purity, simplicity, and natural truth of expression, which has never been approached by later artists, and scarcely attempted :—so much easier is it, and as a general principle so much more effective, to depict that which is not, than that which is—and so many more admirers are there to be found for pretence and affectation, than for the bare simplicities of Nature. It may be doubted whether this statue represents Demosthenes ; and at all events it includes nothing peculiarly characteristic of that sublime declaimer. It is more likely to be one of the philosophers ; and perhaps the best use the spectator can make of it is to regard it as a personification of what Philosophy itself *ought to be*, and of what it approached to in those days more nearly than it had done before, or has since.—Of the pictures in this hall the principal are three by Rubens, Jordaens, and Snyders. The Rubens is, for richness and force of expression, one of the artist's finest works ; and for colouring inferior to few. It is a kind of triumph of Silenus ; in which the god is represented as reeling ripe with wine, and attended by a train who are administering to his pleasures in various ways. The face of Silenus I will compare, for the *quantity* of expression it includes, to that of the child in Wilkie's " Cut Finger." With the exception of that, I have seen no expression which so " o'eriaforms its tenement of clay." The flesh seems literally melting away with the meaning that is flowing in upon it, and is ready to burst with over-much excitement. The excitement, however, and the expression which it gives rise to, are purely animal ; and are perhaps on that very account more difficult to depict in the perfection that they appear in here, from the circumstance of mere animal expressions being much less frequently observable in the human countenance than intellectual ones. Accordingly, I am disposed to believe that it required a more vivid and realizing imagination in Rubens to paint this picture, and such as this, than it did in many of the Italian artists to give us those divine symbols of intellectual beauty which we are accustomed to look upon as higher efforts of the art. And, in fact, as far as regards the efforts themselves, they unquestionably are of an infinitely higher character ; but with respect to the artists who produced them, I can scarcely think that this is the case. It is on this principle I should say, of the Apollo Belvidere and the Venus de' Medici, that the former is the finest work in the world, as it respects the art and the spectator, and the latter the finest as it respects the artist—that the former is calculated to do most good in the world now it is produced, and is therefore the most valuable ; but that the latter required, not only greater natural genius in the artist who produced it, but greater knowledge, taste, and practical skill. There is another face in the above picture which is almost equal to the one I have mentioned. It is that of the Satyr who stands behind Silenus, leering over his shoulder, and blowing two pipes. Without having any thing in it strictly *human*, there is an imaginative truth of expression that is wonderful.

To the right of the above picture hangs one by Jordaens, on the Finding of Moses, which exhibits a grace and chastity of style seldom to be met with in this rich and vigorous but unpoetical delineator of natural truth. The principle female figure, in particular, has a courtly ease and elegance about it not unlike some of Vandyke's best figures of this kind.

The other picture which I have named, by Snyders, is one of those admirably spirited representations of animals, in which this artist has remained unrivalled, and even unapproached, till the present day,—when we have one among us who, notwithstanding his extreme youth, is already worthy to be named in the same page. It is to be hoped, however, that Edwin Landseer will not confine his exquisite talent to so very limited a sphere as that in which his predecessor moved. He who could paint such a picture as the one before us, or as many of those by the young artist I have just named, must be qualified to excel in any department of the art which requires bold and vigorous handling, and a quick sense of natural truth; for in this line of art, imagination can have little if any thing to do, except in the mere *mechanical* arrangement of the objects : a human face or form such as was never actually seen by the eye, may yet produce a very fine effect, and an effect of *truth*, on the spectator ; because in these we permit the imagination to judge of what the imagination has created. But in the animal world it is different. There, we can only recognize that as true which we *remember* to be true ; there the memory is the only judge, and the only admirer. In the mere mechanical arrangement, however, of Snyders's pictures, and of the one before us as an example, the imagination has much to do, and it is done with infinite skill and to very admirable effect. The different figures are so arranged with reference to each other, that every one of them produces its own individual effect, at the same time that it forms a necessary part of the whole group, and increases the effect of that. Each forms a whole of itself, and produces its effect accordingly; and each constitutes an essential part of the united whole, and cannot be separated from that without destroying its consistency and continuity. There is a convolution and an involution of parts in Snyders's best pictures, which is not the less effective for not being always obvious or obtrusive. There is, however, an occasional affectation and exaggeration in the attitudes and actions of his animals which is never to be met with in the works of his young rival; while there is a force, spirit, and boldness which the latter occasionally want.

On leaving the great hall, you ascend to the upper apartments by a staircase, the ornamental parts of which are worth a glance, notwithstanding their extreme rudeness—or rather, on that very account, as finely consistent with the primitive character of the whole building. They have evidently been restored ; but it is equally evident that they have been *only* restored—not substituted in the place of others. I allude to the fresco paintings which cover the walls of the staircase, galleries, &c. and which may be looked upon as fair specimens of the state of ornamental art in this country, at a time when in others it had reached a pitch of comparative perfection.

I shall name the rooms in the order in which they are shewn to the casual visitor,—lingering in them, or not, as their contents may seem to demand. The first is called "The Brown Gallery," and contains a collection of portraits that would be invaluable, if they were but authentic; but, as it is, they are not without great interest, as affording at least glimpses and imaginations of the distinguished people whose names they bear. It would be endless to name these portraits, as the Gallery is of considerable length, and the walls are entirely covered with them. They chiefly represent persons of the time of Holbein, and are almost all copies, and very indifferent ones, of that singular artist.

The next room is "Lady Betty Germain's Bed-room." The very names of these places, even without the sight of them, carry one back half a score of generations. This room, and "The Spangled Bed-room," which follows, contain nothing worthy of remark, except some curious old faded tapestry, and a noble ebony wardrobe that seems to tell of fine old silk dresses that, in default of a wearer, could stand alone and go to court by themselves,—so stiff, stately, rustling, and alive does the very imagination of them seem.

In a dressing-room adjoining to the last-named bed-room there are two clever candlelight scenes by Schalken; but their light is nearly extinguished, in consequence of the scrupulous care with which the modern impertinencies of cleaning and renewing are avoided.—In "The Billiard Room," which we arrive at next, there is an excellent portrait of Sir Kenelm Digby, by Vandyke; and two copies of Titian's wonderful pictures, the Diana and Acteon, and Diana and Calisto—remarkable only for the extraordinary manner in which the painter has avoided all traces of a resemblance to his great originals.

We next reach "The Venetian Bed-room," said to be in the state in which it was used by James the Second when he visited this mansion. In the dressing-room adjoining to this there is a very excellent and interesting portrait of Mistress Margaret Woffington, as she undoubtedly claims to be called while looking at her here—for she is as demure as a boarding-school miss that has just been *produced*, and as little realizes one's ideal of *Peg* Woffington. In this room there is also a fine sketch by Rubens, of Meleager and the Boar, replete with that spirit of motion which he gave in such an unrivalled manner. The whole scene seems as if it were *passing* before your eyes, and would presently disappear. In "The Bow-room," which succeeds the above, there are some good family portraits by Reynolds, Hoppner, &c. but none striking enough to attract one's attention from the delightful air of youthful antiquity which pervades this fine apartment. Observe, in particular, the noble fire-place, with its marble columns reaching almost to the ceiling; the brazen *dogs*, chafing-dish, &c.

In "The Chapel Room," which you are next shewn into, there is nothing worth naming connected with Art, except a very curious and admirable carving, said to be cut out of one piece of wood, of the Saviour bearing the Cross, &c. It consists of a great variety of figures, the expressions and attitudes of which are extremely well preserved. They tell you that this curious old relic belonged to Mary Queen of Scots.—The next room is called "The Organ Room," on account of its containing the first organ that ever was constructed. This, too, is a most curious relic. It has the appearance of a large square box, with a few rudely cut finger-keys placed at the top outside; and presents altogether a singular contrast to the elegant and elaborate instruments of which it claims the merit of being the venerable parent.—In this room there is also a portrait of Sir John Suckling. It is, as a work of Art, a wretched performance; as indeed the majority of those are which we meet with in this state part of the Castle. But this would be no matter —or but little in many instances—if we could depend on their likeness to the originals. But I am afraid they will not bear us out in this. The above, at all events, is entirely different from two or three old engravings that are extant of that accomplished scholar, courtier, wit, poet, and gentleman.

Passing through the chapel, we reach "The Crimson Drawing-room," in which there are several pictures of various degrees of merit; but none first-rate. Some of them which bear first-rate names are evidently copies; and others have been greatly injured by time and accident. Upon the whole, the pictures in this room, though they are more numerous (with the exception of portraits) than those collected in any other apartment, do not call for particular mention.

The only other works of art necessary to be named in this part of the Castle are a set of copies, by Mytens, of the Cartoons of Raffaelle. These are capable of giving a *general* notion of those sublime works to such as do not choose to seek the originals; but to such as are acquainted with the latter, or ever intend to be so, they had better be passed over with a mere cursory look. It is scarcely possible to copy the general grouping and arrangement of those works without producing a certain grandeur and solemnity of effect; but the detail (in which more than half their power consists) must be contemplated in the originals alone: and those who do not see these, had, in fact, better not see any imitations or *hints* of them, but keep the mere *name* of "The Cartoons of Raffaelle" to produce their own impression on the imagination. The above-named copies occupy an apartment called "The Cartoon Gallery." The only other apartment belonging to the state or show part of the Castle is "The King's Bed-room." It does not contain any of those objects of which we are immediately in search; but as we are to pass through it, it may be worth while to mention what many will consider as more than an equivalent for their absence. Here is the bed of gold and silver tissue, made *exprès*, at a cost of eight thousand pounds, for the monarch (James I.) to pass a night in—here are tables and looking-glass frames formed entirely of that fine rich old chased silver which gives such a splendid antique effect to some of the rooms in Windsor Castle—and above all, here is the identical key used by Charles Earl of Dorset, when Lord Chamberlain to William the Third; and that used by Edward Earl of Dorset, when holding the same post in the court of Charles the First. I have always thought it childish enough to feel any interest in the mere sight of relics of this kind. The name has always seemed to me quite as good as the thing. The *idea* of more tangible objects of this kind answers all the purpose that the sight of them can be made to do, by calling up all the associations connected with them just as effectually. And yet I question whether the most determined philosophiser on such subjects as these ever entered the room containing the above objects without not only looking at them with a feeling of interest and curiosity, but without taking them up and handling them—so much, by another species of association, does the sight and touch *seem* to bring home to one, ideas, images, and feelings, that can be compassèd in no other way. And, in fact, the *seeming* is in this case every thing: so that it is but a spurious philosophy after all, and what is worse, an affected one, to endeavour or pretend to do without any of those aids which nature (or habit, which is the same thing) has placed in our way in cases of this kind. Let every visitor, then, to this curious old apartment—young or old, gentle or simple,—rich or poor,—take up these keys, and make them, if he can, serve as the " Open sesame !" to the doors of by-gone times ; and while he turns them in his hand, and hears in imagination the bolts fly back which answered to them, let him, if he pleases, fancy himself in the actual presence of those in whose presence *they* have frequently been.

The remaining apartments in this fine old monument of antiquity, are those which the family occupy. They are only remarkable generally for the delightful air of *comfort* which breathes through them, arising from the total absence of all pretensions at modern ornamental splendour,—which cannot by any art be made to blend consistently with the real results of antique taste. The only objects of fine art to which I shall refer in this part of the Castle, are those which I alluded to in the commencement of this paper ; namely, a collection of portraits, which, in point of extent at least, is perhaps unique. In order to avoid a mere enumeration of these (which their extent will not admit of in my limited space), it may be said that there is scarcely a celebrated name belonging to the last three hundred years, connected with literature, science, and the fine arts, whose effigy may not be found in this most interesting collection. I will add, that if the mansion of Knowle Park had contained no other objects of art than these portraits, they alone would have entitled it to be noticed among our British Galleries.

---

### THE LAST MAN.

#### WRITTEN BY T. CAMPBELL.

ALL worldly shapes shall melt in gloom,
  The Sun himself must die,
Before this mortal shall assume
  Its Immortality !
I saw a vision in my sleep,
That gave my spirit strength to sweep
  Adown the gulf of Time !
I saw the last of human mould,
That shall Creation's death behold,
  As Adam saw her prime !

The Sun's eye had a sickly glare,
  The Earth with age was wan,
The skeletons of nations were
  Around that lonely man !
Some had expir'd in fight,—the brands
Still rusted in their bony hands ;
  In plague and famine some !
Earth's cities had no sound nor tread ;
And ships were drifting with the dead
  To shores where all was dumb !

Yet, prophet like, that lone one stood,
  With dauntless words and high,
That shook the sere leaves from the wood
  As if a storm pass'd by,

Saying, we are twins in death, proud Sun,
Thy face is cold, thy race is run,
   'Tis Mercy bids thee go.
For thou ten thousand thousand years
Hast seen the tide of human tears,
   That shall no longer flow.

What though beneath thee man put forth
   His pomp, his pride, his skill;
And arts that made fire, flood, and earth,
   The vassals of his will ;—
Yet mourn I not thy parted sway,
Thou dim discrowned king of day:
   For all those trophied arts
And triumphs that beneath thee sprang,
Heal'd not a passion or a pang
   Entail'd on human hearts.

Go, let oblivion's curtain fall
   Upon the stage of men,
Nor with thy rising beams recall
   Life's tragedy again.
Its piteous pageants bring not back,
Nor waken flesh, upon the rack
   Of pain anew to writhe ;
Stretch'd in disease's shapes abhorr'd,
Or mown in battle by the sword,
   Like grass beneath the scythe.

Ev'n I am weary in yon skies
   To watch thy fading fire ;
Test of all sumless agonies,
   Behold not me expire.
My lips that speak thy dirge of death—
Their rounded gasp and gurgling breath
   To see thou shalt not boast.
The eclipse of Nature spreads my pall,—
The majesty of Darkness shall
   Receive my parting ghost!

This spirit shall return to Him
   That gave its heavenly spark ;
Yet think not, Sun, it shall be dim
   When thou thyself art dark !
No ! it shall live again, and shine
In bliss unknown to beams of thine,
   By Him recall'd to breath,
Who captive led captivity,
Who robb'd the grave of Victory,—
   And took the sting from Death !

Go, Sun, while Mercy holds me up
   On Nature's awful waste
To drink this last and bitter cup
   Of grief that man shall taste—
Go, tell the night that hides thy face,
Thou saw'st the last of Adam's race,
   On Earth's sepulchral clod,
The dark'ning universe defy
To quench his Immortality,
   Or shake his trust in God !

## ON THE ART OF SINGING SONGS.

GOLDSMITH, I think, says, that he seldom heard a young man attempt to sing in company without exposing himself; and it is too true that, owing to various causes, few people of any age can sing a song without grieving their friends. Yet, songs are the delight of mankind. Among ruder nations they are employed to animate heroism or to express sentiments for which common language is too poor ; and among people of the greatest refinement they often make an important part, or, as it were, the completion and consummation, of social enjoyment. Old gentlemen, who used to sing, are always delighted to find that vocal music is not yet extinct ; old ladies, who used to be sung to, at, or of, are reminded by a skilful voice of the days when they and the world were young and happy ; middle-aged people of the smallest pretensions to feeling, both men and women, love a song ; and the young, who like pleasure in every shape, never object to it in this its most harmonious and seductive shape of all. There is no part of the country in which singing is not held in estimation. In the southern counties of this island, from the moisture of the air and the fatness of the soil, singers are not abundant, but singing is, perhaps, prized the more on that account. In the central parts, and generally on what is called by geologists *London gravel,* a voice is more common, but scarcely less admired. In the eastern parts, among marsh-water, reeds, willows, wolds, and rabbit-warrens, singing is a patent of nobility ; whilst in Yorkshire and other wild parts of the country it is considered a very exalted proof of gentle breeding ;—but among the mountains of Wales, in the glens and by the river sides in Scotland, in the depths and passes of the Highlands to the very remotest parts, and in every nook and corner of Ireland, singing is valued to a degree which less romantic people, and those who live in the plains, must strain their faculties to understand. The Welsh themselves sing tolerably, but with a certain monotony peculiar, I think, to mountaineers, and which haunts you too in Scotland, and is painfully recognised in the long-drawn and twanging close of an Irish ditty. The natives of Scotland, to speak without partiality, do in general sing in a manner unutterably frightful; but then you occasionally meet some fair-haired lovely woman in that country, one who might personate the loveliest heroine of Scottish poetry or the Scottish novels, who sings you into the third heaven. The Irish, strange to say, though exquisitely endowed with taste, and excelling on instruments of all kinds, and passionate to excess in all their feelings, are very deficient in vocal music ; insomuch that it was acknowledged, in all the four provinces of that kingdom, that one great advantage of the exchange of militias was the importation of singers and songs from England. The French have some of the prettiest songs in the world, if they knew how to sing them ; their street-singing is exquisite ; and it is a fine thing to hear a whole regiment of their dragoons— officers, sergeants, corporals, privates, " pioneers and all," singing, as they are wont on a march, some grand national air; but on ordinary occasions their nasality is absolutely alarming, and they sing, as Rousseau used to say, as if grievously afflicted with the cholic. As this is not intended to be a treatise on music, it is unnecessary to go on to Italian singing. My present object is to treat especially and particularly of domestic, festival, and after-supper singing,—an art little known on the Continent, but much cultivated in many parts of this country.

I suppose no man who has ears to hear will deny that singing is a great advantage to any man. People are often supported through all the formalities of reception at an evening party, and endure all the meagre hospitalities of the occasion, and the arrangement of the card-tables, and the intense heat, and the abortive attempts at sprightly and continuous conversation, and all that must be undergone on these occasions, for hours, in the hope of hearing some vocal gentleman sing a favourite song at last: and as singers are every where scarce, the singing gentleman is feasted, flattered, coaxed, seduced from the whist-table, and, above all, entreated by all the lovely voices and faces in the room to sing *that sweet song* which he sung at Mrs. So and So's. Blushing, and delighted, and palpitating, he seems averse to begin, when, in fact, his heart pants for that breathless silence of sweet tongues, without which no man of any vanity can venture, in cold blood, to begin a cherished and valued song. At last the general pause takes place, and that sun-flower conversion of all eyes upon the singer, during which even those who hate him must force their faces into an expression of delighted expectation. This is a moment fatal to the inexperienced, but to a practised and familiarised singer worth six weeks of common existence. Dinner companies also are occasion-ally collected together, of which, unfortunately, ladies form no part; and after a certain hour in the evening, there being no summons to the drawing-room, a good song is worth its weight in gold. How de-lightful it is in such circumstances to find that a man who has been sitting next to you, and who ate heartily and drank freely, but was withal heavy, mute, and unimaginative, starts at once into a delightful companion, and, whilst he sings at least, is as good as the rest of the company! To say the truth, however, this seldom happens : the true singer, the man with a voice of various power, and with well-chosen songs, is a man of soul and feeling, and talks as much or more than the other guests : every thing interests him, every thing animates him ; a thousand things rouse him into vinous eloquence, a thousand things affect him ; and what an advantage has such a man, at an hour when the party feels little interest in any thing, and can scarcely be roused by any thing, when eloquence itself is powerless, when wit is exhausted, all activity of mind at an end, and all the softer affections in a state of lethargy, who, by the simple power of his voice and by the aid of song, can call up from the depths of sleepiness all the lively feelings of his hearers, and can kindle them into enthusiasm or soften them into sen-timent as he chooses. This the singer can do with ease ; for he is mas-ter of a divine art which can throw enchantment over much that would be otherwise mean and insignificant. With what complacent and re-viving countenances do the people turn to him ! with what re-animated and glistening eyes regard him ! acknowledging the mighty supremacy of his harmonious and irresistible accomplishment. There are, be-sides, such things as supper-parties, *petits soupers* of agreeable people, nearly exploded, it is true, in the economical rage for those unsocial and lower-extremity-fatiguing things called Stand-up suppers, but still in existence, after which a song is always desired, often requested, and ever received as a favour of the highest value. And what a reward it

is for a singer to behold the glowing faces round the table, all their
bloom called forth by good eating and drinking, and all eyes fixed upon
him, proving that there is still an ungratified desire of pure and celestial harmony, a longing after that minstrelsy, which is one of the things
in which we excel the beasts that perish! How pleasant is it to see
the gentlemen drinking the delight of singing and their wine at once,
and still more to see the females, who refuse the wine, actually intoxicated with a song! Other occasions there are, particularly in mountainous and romantic countries,—long nights of revelry, in which every
man sings who can, and every man who cannot sing makes a noise.
There are moments of earthly existence yet more precious, in which a
song may sway or soften a heart, and bless the singer beyond the power
of words or even of songs to express.

Enough has been said to prove the value of a voice. It remains to
be told what are the requisites for a domestic, festival, or after-supper
singer; what kind of songs he should sing on different occasions and
at different hours; and in what manner he should sing them: subjects
involving many particulars and of the highest interest.

He who aspires to the character of a social singer, and would sing
with comfort and credit in private parties, must possess, 1st. A voice.
2d. A considerable share of modest assurance and presence of mind.
3d. Excellent wind. 4th. Good taste in the selection of his songs.
5th. Good understanding, that he may know what he sings. 6th. Imagination and passion, that he may feel what he sings. A public singer
may be destitute of all these qualifications except the first and second,
and yet, by the direction of others, by management and by imitation,
may pass very well; but no man can be a good private singer without
them all. His voice must be powerful, that it may be heard, that it
may affect, that it may move, that it may overpower; yet not too
loud, lest it should annoy, and torture, and distress, and deafen. He
should be able to sing boldly and freely, but no less able to sing faintly,
sweetly, and as it were dyingly. By an excellent *wind*, it is not meant
that he should merely be able to sing "voce magna et bonis lateribus,"
for every carpenter can do as much; but that he should have that
power, that compass and variety, that height, and breadth, and depth
of voice, which may no less express every pathetic feeling than every
manly sentiment, avoiding the boisterous extreme on one hand and
contemptible whining on the other. There is great art in commencing
a song in the proper key; yet cleverness in that particular is indispensable, otherwise the singer seems to be running a race or paying a
penalty, rather than singing for amusement. Time should be ordered
not by *beating* it, for that is unpardonable, but by favouring the expression in such a manner as to excuse any liberties that may be taken
in this particular. The singer must cunningly profit by every sentimental pause to collect his scattered breath; yet this should be done
without gasping as the tragedians do, without that perpetual winking
of both eyes, so commonly affected among public singers, and without
any ungentlemanly effort or straining. Nothing hurts a singer so much
as not thinking well enough of himself. He should know his own
value, and sing upon it; without overrating either his efforts or his
merit. If he fancies his sounds are never to be forgotten, he is mistaken; and he may be assured, let him sing as well or as ill as he

chooses, his song will soon be thought of no more. But it behoves him to cast out all fear and trembling, to begin calmly, collectedly, courageously; let him be spirited where he ought, and insinuating where he may, but let all be done coolly and with something of dignity, so as to seem to say that, however delightfully he may sing, singing is rather the result of his other accomplishments than his only excellence.

The selection of songs is a very important point, for which no intelligible rules can be given which do not pre-suppose taste, judgment, and discrimination. I do not mean merely the selection according to the composition of the audience, for that is a matter in which the common sense of men will commonly guide them safely; but the disposition and arrangement, especially where, as will frequently happen, there is only one singer in the company. Let the singer beware of that fault, ever committed by ladies who perform, albeit superlatively, on the pianoforte, who, to the destruction of ears and the ruin of the fine mechanism of the nerves, will go on playing one piece after another in the same style and time until men who hate music have an opportunity of rejoicing over the tortures of those who presume to think they admire it. Let him rather consider the disciplined art of bands of military music, which ever intersperse airs of different measure and expression; now a solemn march, and now a spirited and enlivening strain. This is the great secret of making a musical-party productive of pleasure; and the neglect of it the true and only cause of all the trouble of the entertainers being generally productive of weariness and pain to their visitors as well as themselves. This rule being kept in mind as regards singing, it is only necessary to avoid singing such songs as, for private or public reasons, nobody present can sympathize in. I remember the officers of a marching regiment being invited, when at Yarmouth, to dine on board the admiral's ship, on which occasion the gentlemen of the navy were much distressed by the incredible length and monotony of some old fighting songs of some persevering old captains, and the officers of the land-service were exceedingly disturbed by a succession of sea-songs retorted upon them by their most vociferous entertainers. In general, in a mixed company, there are some who sympathize with songs of both these descriptions, but a succession of either is a proof of the worst possible taste. In the same way, four or five love-songs, or four or five Scotch songs, or four or five Irish melodies, are very afflicting; besides that the style of songs ought to depend, not on professional feelings or personal attachments, but on the style of the voice; a matter in which many singers grievously offend. There are men of great gravity who have the misfortune to think themselves pleasant in a comic song: I know a country gentleman, with a most effeminate throat, who is sadly addicted to hunting-songs; and another, whose voice would command attention at the Westminster-hustings, who is never so happy as when he is demolishing some simple ballad or soft and plaintive ditty. Men of this mistaken taste have a great aversion to *solos:* whatever they hear well sung, they fancy they could sing well; and to prove it, they make choruses where none are intended, and, with the best intentions in the world, drive a sensitive singer to the brink of insanity.

It is the custom of some singers always to put forth their best song first; but these, if they go on, please less and less as they proceed :

others too cautiously husband their best song so long that it is never asked for at all. The best song, and every man who sings has his best, should be sung not ,the first nor yet the last in the evening : it may more properly be placed second ; always remembering that the first song, which it is my advice be a short one, be of so sweet and enticing a character that it may become the sure cause of the second being asked for : *then* the singer may give full scope to his genius, then

> " With wanton heed, and giddy cunning,
> The melting voice through mazes running,"

he may *extasiate* his audience, and then, if he has any power, that power will assuredly be deeply felt.

I must be allowed to add a few words on eating and drinking, in that particular point of view in which they affect singing. No prudent man should sing on an empty stomach ; for that is a laborious and a gainless occupation. Singers should live well : the best singers I have known in my time were all remarkably alert with a knife and fork ; and I could indeed give very scientific reasons for the action of the lungs being thereby facilitated. Let the singer breakfast without fear ; and if time seems to pass but heavily, let him afterwards divert his leisure with a kind of rehearsal, for the memory is often most capricious on the subject of songs, and nothing has a more miserable effect than a song, like

> " Th' adventure of the bear and fiddle,
> Begun and broke off in the middle."

In this pleasing occupation the hours will glide smoothly on till dinnertime. Let the singer make a valiant dinner, but let him never forget, that if eating be vitally essential to singing, drinking drowns the voice altogether. Let him not listen to the advice of men who, secure in the notorious discordance of their own sounds, would tempt him on and on by their example, with hollow assurances that " he will sing the better for it." Let him believe me and confide in me when I assure him, that any thing beyond a very few glasses of wine is fatal to all the softer notes of the voice, and productive of a hoarseness and untunableness which will be death to his ambition : I mean after dinner, with a prospective view to singing in the drawing-room : for as regards the time intervening between supper and that oblivion which a good companion wishes to avoid, no rules are required. Let him remember also that tea may be as overwhelming to his voice as wine : I recommend one cup of coffee, but no tea : your great tea-drinkers have a nervous tremulousness in their voices which I can detect through the whole of the first song. It is unfeeling to ask a gentleman to sing at an evening-party before the entrance of the refreshments, and yet more cruel to ask him to begin before their complete departure from the circle. Those who, with voices " unconscious of a song," wish their company to perform, should consider these things ; they should regulate the heat of their rooms by Fahrenheit's thermometer ; they should invite neither too many nor too few to give sound every advantage which the di-. mensions of the apartment are calculated to allow ; they should have the instrument well tuned, carefully observing that it is not too loud, for nothing gives a singer more sincere distress than to find himself engaged in an unworthy competition with keys and wires.

Considerable difference of opinion has long existed respecting the superior agreeableness of singing with music or without; it is a question which will probably long continue to divide, not the hearers only, but singers themselves. Music helps and shields even an indifferent voice, and one great advantage of singing to music is the necessity it involves for the singer to stand; for, although a sitting posture is insuperably depressing to the voice, and utterly destructive of expression, except where the singer accompanies himself; yet to stand up voluntarily, without music, is what few dare attempt. Altogether, I cannot bring myself to advise it: it has reason and sense on its side, but what are reason and sense in a matter wherein the foolish, who are ever the felicitous majority, may find subject for empty laughter the following morning! To sing well indeed without music requires a master; there must be no tricks in such a performance; no dropping of notes; no smothering of sounds; no evasion of difficult parts: all must be clear, fair, audible, and dexterous. On the whole, perhaps the most equitable conclusion we can come to is, that a good singer should be able to sing either with or without an accompaniment. In this department there is much yet to be done. I have often thought that if I could be taught the mere mechanical part of composition, I could devise such spirit-stirring accompaniments to some of my favourite songs, particularly to those of an heroic or patriotic cast, as would be productive of an effect altogether unknown to modern times. But this speculation, as well as directions concerning the management of particular songs, I must defer.                                     C.

---

PEREGRINATIONS OF THOMAS TRYATALL.—NO. II.

PLEASURE is certainly the polar star of a Frenchman. He is the needle which points to it most faithfully—but one that has no variations. North, South, East, or West, (for though his magnet shifts, it always preserves its attraction,) is quite the same to him. Other men make pleasure a recreation or an enjoyment. It is a Frenchman's business and happiness. His national exaggeration cannot, in this instance, go too far, nor far enough. Words have no power to express the sensation excited in the breast of a Parisian by the announcement of a fête, a procession, the spectacle, the Carnival, or *Longchamps*. He looks at the almanac, watches the weather, counts the days, and pants through the moments in indescribable agonies of enjoyment. It is astonishing with what acuteness he catches up every flying report, and ascertains every fact, connected with the *summum bonum* of the month or the minute, as the case may be. Exhibitions, which take many weeks and amazing wisdom for their arrangement, are often suspended or stopped by a sudden caprice, of which the public gets a few hours notice. English travellers, or even those who may be residents in Paris, often cut a foolish figure, hoaxed and mystified by the undesigning frivolity of ministers, mistresses, managers, or—censors. An announced airing of the king, or the playing of the water-works at Versailles or St. Cloud, or the representation of a tragedy at the Français, or a ballet at the Opera, is frequently put off at the very time that the English part of the population are swallowing their early dinner, in danger of choking from fear of being late, stepping into their carriages, or half way gone to the place of exhibition. I have known several of my haughty countrymen, who would not confess to being hoaxed, even by the whole cabinet council, assert that they saw the king driving out, and comment upon his looks, on a day that I knew him to be suffering in his bed from an indigestion; and a particularly sensitive baronet once gave me a detailed critique on a tragedy, for which I had seen him take places for himself and family—but which was changed for one of Molière's comedies, by a sudden freak of the censorship, an hour before the rising of the curtain. In this case my friend might, to be sure, have been honestly deceived; for I sat in the pit, and saw him sound asleep, from the first music to the end of the fifth act.

The weather, too, frequently takes in the English. I have seen them of an evening a little misty or threatening, but a fine Vauxhall atmosphere, crowding up to Tivoli or Beaujon, though the *fête extraordinaire*, fireworks, rope-dancing, balloon, elephant, &c. had been all decidedly adjourned, and placarded all over Paris a full hour before. The fact is, as I said before, or meant to say, we do not make so much of these things. We hear of an intended entertainment, and we resolve to go to it. We think no more of it till the time comes. We employ the interval in other rational ways—reading, writing, drinking, or what not. Not so the Frenchman. He has his mind's eye always on the one object. He is abstracted from every thing else, but all alive to that. He keeps on the fidget eternally; and looks for every shifting of the minister's will as closely as he watches every change of the wind—for in proportion to a Frenchman's delight at a show is his dread of a shower. Punch and Judy are not more necessary to his happiness, than an umbrella to his security. Amusement rules supreme as " the god of his idolatry;" but rain divides with ridicule the empire over his apprehensions—I ask a thousand pardons, his *sensibilité*. All this being matter-of-fact, it was quite a matter-of-course that my friend Monsieur le Vicomte Vaurien should present himself, according to appointment, at my lodgings the morning of Longchamps; and, the morning being threatening, it was just as natural that he should appear with a brown silk parapluie under his arm.

" My Got, how unfortunate!" exclaimed he as he came in, " de vind is veering vesterly." " Yes, a little unlucky, no doubt," said I, " but not enough to be vexed at, Monsieur le Vicomte. It may clear up yet." He shook his head despondingly. " I am quite ready," continued I: " is your carriage at the door?" " Vat door? Got bless my soul, 'tis at de *Magasin de Voitures à louer*." " And how the deuce are we to get to it this raw morning?" " *Diable!* ve must walk" —and we did walk accordingly. I may here mention, that this appeared as odd as it was uncomfortable. The spirit of our contract was, that I should go with the Vicomte in his carriage; and I therefore (being at the time a downright invalid) thought it a curious circumstance that, instead of driving up to my door, he told me coolly I should walk to the carriage, instead of the carriage rolling towards me. But I thought of Mahomet and the mountain, and—we set out.

A dreadful half-hour's promenade through the wretchedest part of

Paris brought us at length to a sort of bazaar for carriages; and such a collection as presented itself—

Barouche and Buggy, Tandem, Random,
Jarvey, Gig, and Whiskey—

would have made the fortune of a showman in England. We entered the yard, the Vicomte first in due order of precedence and propriety. I recollected the good old family-coach that first caught my attention at Maurice's lodgings, and I pleased myself into the notion of my approaching drive in that rumbling representation of worn-out nobility, heraldic distinctions, and privileges gone by. No absolute suzerain of the good old times, demanding *le droit de cuissage*, could have stepped out more boldly to put his spurred and booted leg into the bed of his new-married vassal, than did I prepare the strut which was to lead to my entrance into the family-coach of the Vauriens; but I looked round in vain for this anticipated depository of my pride. I observed, indeed, ready for immediate use, a miserable calèche, furnished with the degenerate remains of a truly aristocratical set of harness to a pair of animals that seemed modelled from the Rosinante of Don Quixote; while a scowling and surly-looking driver, miserably dressed, stood beside, and threw a look at us as if he did not like his company. All this was rather strange; nor did the aspect of things look much brighter from my observing my friend the Vicomte in ardent conversation with a broad-set boisterous woman, who was evidently mistress of the place. He seemed eloquent, and she decided; and in fact, to let my readers into the secret at once, she was insisting on the Vicomte's offering some security for the hire of the calèche, which was to serve as our conveyance to the delights of Longchamps. A word or two explained this to me clearly; and with the vivacity which men sometimes muster up, when they start from a fit of castle- (or carriage) building, I jumped into the vehicle, calling out hastily, *"Allons, Monsieur le Vicomte! Allons, Cocher! Partons, Partons!" "Grand merci!"* cried the woman: *"si Monsieur l'Anglais l'a choisi, c'est bien lui qui est responsable. Montez, François; montez, M. Maurice! C'est une affaire finie."* The coachman and the Vicomte got up at the word, and away we drove; my friend endeavouring to smother his mortification, and I doing my best to conceal my observation of his embarrassment. He went muttering on, however; every jolt over the pavement giving an energetic vibration to such expressions as "Dam beast! Canaille! Hosh-posh! Affront a nobleman!" I let him go on uninterrupted, and listened patiently to his cooler confession, that the carriage I had set my heart on not being his, he was obliged to hire one for the day, and having forgotten the little formality of entering into a written engagement, the wretched woman had refused to suffer him to get into the calèche, on his remonstrance at her exorbitant demand; but that my being an Englishman was security, she being protected without papers in her transactions with a foreigner. This seemed all so plausible that I swallowed it most credulously, and we drove on; but after-circumstances made me rather anxious to hear the point mooted by some legitimate propounder of international law.

The rain did not fall, luckily for the Vicomte, but most unfortunately for me, for the dust rose in whirlwinds, by which I was nearly blinded, but to which he seemed quite insensible—as if "*jetter le poudre eux yeux*" was an operation as natural for him to suffer as to perform. While driven along towards the Bois de Boulogne he gradually recovered his composure. The world began to be on the move. A few early equipages came straggling forward; and the sun darted down his glaring rays upon us, enough to raise a smile under any French mustachio, maugre the piercing North-east wind, on which the edge of every sunbeam seemed sharpened, they cut so keenly. We had nearly reached the term of our first *course* (the site of the ancient Abbey, from which, and the pious processions of its tenants, the degenerate pilgrimage of our day derives its name) when I was struck by a change of countenance in the Vicomte beside me, and by some convulsive twitches and contortions in his limbs, that seemed to announce a severe nervous attack. "My dear friend, you are unwell, I fear," cried I.— "Oh, no, no—'tis noting, noting at all," replied he, with a dignified complacency;—but he kept fumbling at his watch-pocket, as if its neighbourhood was the seat of his malady. "What is the matter, my dear Vicomte?" asked I, impatiently. "Have you lost any thing?" —"Oh, noting, noting at all," returned he gaily, "a mere bagatelle— only my vatch, but 'tis no matter."—"Shall we return and look for it?" said I.—"Got bless my soul, no," replied he, with emphasis, "'tis not vorth the while. If 'tis lost 'tis lost—dere's end of it, you know; and a Frenchman is too mosh philosopher to care for sosh hosh-posh trifle like dat." A laugh closed the sentence, and I pondered silently upon it.

The sharp wind, and the jolting of our "infernal machine," began now to produce their natural effects—for a considerable inclination to eat is the legitimate consequence of air and exercise. The Vicomte, too, was in want of something consolatory, and readily agreed to my proposal that we should stop at one of the tent-like constructions scattered by the road-side, and refresh ourselves with some of the *à la fourchette* temptations of its larder. We were quickly seated, and as quickly served. A capital fricandeau, an unimpeachable omelette, a plate of cold *haricots blancs*, with oil and vinegar, for the Vicomte, and a portion of *épinards au naturel*, for myself, were the chief ingredients of our repast. For our sour and surly cocher, I ordered a bottle of vin de Surenne, celebrated for its acidity, hoping that it would bring him to good humour, on the principle that two negatives make an affirmative. He sipped it growlingly, like a cur picking a bare bone, (if I may be allowed the Irishism,) and I should have moralised deeply, no doubt, on his invincible savageness, had not my attention being excited by the waiter flinging our bill (for which I had called) upon the table, and by the exhibition of some symptoms in my friend and boon companion precisely similar to those which had betrayed his anxiety in the carriage. "What now, Vicomte?" asked I, less anxiously than before, "what has got possession of you?"—"By Got, 'tis de very deevil!" was the reply, accompanied by a most abstracted air and rapid gesticulation. "Indeed!" said I, "we must drive him out then. Fill a bumper, Vicomte." As he took no notice of my summons, I did the service for him, and his left-hand,

——— "raised
By quick instinctive motion,"

poured the contents of the glass into their proper reservoir, but his right kept unceasingly rubbing about the lower extremities of his waist-coat; and had such friction only followed the swallowing of the wine it would have been natural enough—for the *boisson* was most execrable, though announced to us as "*Beaune, première qualité.*" "Speak out, my dear Vicomte," said I once more, "unburthen yourself."—"By Got, I am unburden already," replied he: "I have lost my purse—my money—*vingt-deux Napoléons—trois pièces de cent sous—sept ou huit francs—et quelques petites pièces!*" The appalling solemnity of this enumeration, and the prodigiousness of the sum, in comparison with the circumstances of the loser, filled me with sympathetic alarm. I started up, and swore that I suspected the ill-looking cocher of having picked his pocket as he stepped in and out of the carriage. He scouted this idea as impossible. I then turned the battery of my accusations upon a couple of "scurvy mechanics," who were regaling themselves at a table beside us, and proposed calling in the police for a general search. This the Vicomte would not listen to for a moment, saying aloud, with great feeling, and his hand placed on his breast—"*Monsieur, non! Je connois trop l'honneur Français; je n'accuse personne; si le sort m'a fait perdre cette somme inconsidérable, c'est perdu: voilà le total!* But, my dear Sir," added he in English, and in a subdued tone, "have de goodness to pay de bill, if you please." On these words he stalked towards the calèche with a very imposing and rather awful demeanour, leaving me to explain to the waiter and the other listeners the cause of his magnanimous expressions. I paid the bill, and re-joined the representative of the noble race of the Vauriens, with very elevated notions of his philosophy, and profound respect for himself and his whole family to the remotest generation.

We soon re-entered the line of carriages, and proceeded at the regu-lation snail's-pace adopted on these occasions. My contemplation of the Vicomte, who was in a moment as lively, as chatty, and as much at his ease, as if he had found, instead of losing, twenty guineas and a gold watch, prevented me from paying much attention to the unmean-ing and uninteresting procession in which I made one, and which an-nually sets all Paris in a flutter, and may be called *la fête par excellence* of milliners, mantua-makers, and hackney-coachmen. This spectacle of Longchamps is, of all others, the most stupid and the most devoutly worshipped of the periodical frivolities of Paris. No one of any fashion could presume to hold up his or her head for the rest of the year, if they did not, on this all-fools'-day, occupy a seat in some kind of vehicle, and sit up for hours to be stared at in the open air by the walking population of the capital. On the particular occasion which I describe, the crowd of carriages was inconceivable. But the day was not kindly. The sun was hot and the air raw. The year and the season did not pull to-gether. The first was advanced, but the other backward—just like the ludicrous imitation of an English equipage which figured before me—a monstrous blue and gilded caricature of the Lord Mayor's coach, dragged by four old white horses, the leaders and wheelers pull-ing most obstinately in different directions, to the great amusement of the crowd, and the horrible discomfiture of the old aristocratical couple within, their clumsy postilions, with cocked-hats and huge jack-boots, and the two footmen, in their scarlet coats and yellow plush breeches of the true cut and pattern of the *siècle de Louis XIV.* This was the most barefaced revival of the *ancienne régime;* but there were many minor attempts, and much laughable absurdity of our own day. The train of king's pages, for instance, on their piebald horses, and in a most quizzical costume; with various laughter-moving efforts to look English on the part of the other equestrians, both masters and grooms. The whole thing had the air of a forced production. The white dresses of the ladies were out of all keeping with the coldness of the weather; and the profusion of artificial flowers in their bonnets looked quite preposterous, when compared with the leafless branches of the trees that stretched their skeleton arms across the Boulevards. I was out of patience at the whole display; yet not so much annoyed by the folly of the multitude, as indignant at the meanness with which they submitted to be swore at, and rode over, and shoved, and jostled, and commanded, and abused, by some dozens of mounted gensdarmes— those military masters of the ceremonies, whose wand of office is the bare blade of a sabre—who give curses instead of courtesy—and put fears of despotism and tyranny into the hearts that should be filled with associations of joy. What hope can there be for such a people? thought I. But hold! I am afraid I have got to the length of my letter; and if I give myself more rope I may get hanged, or guillotined, or something of that sort, one fine morning.

I sat it out till six o'clock. Less would not satisfy the Vicomte; and the coachman repelled my effort to quit the calèche. He insisted on my remaining until it was delivered safe and sound into "the place from whence it came." I was, therefore, obliged to suffer half-a-day's martyrdom, which may partly account for my disapproval of the show; and having paid the woman forty francs (being double the common price, on account of the fête), I parted with the Vicomte—for ever, I do believe. He gave me a squeeze of the hand, which was forebodingly forcible, and an assurance that he would come the next morning to settle his share of our day's expenses—a promise which he most faithfully remembered to forget; and it may be well to add, that when I called on him two days afterwards, the old portress told me he had gone into the country for some weeks; and to my enquiry if he had recovered his watch and money, she replied by a turn on her heel, slamming the door in my face, and the emphatical utterance of the interjection "Bah!"

---

## WHAT LIFE TO CHOOSE.

     " Not to know at large of things remote
     From use, obscure and subtle; but to know
     That which before us lies in daily life,
     Is the prime wisdom."
                         *Paradise Lost.*

" WHEN I look round upon the material world," says a Pagan writer, " and observe the ineffable beauty and harmony of all its arrangements, the magnificent machinery of the heavenly bodies, the unerring precision with which they perform their majestic evolutions, as well as the regular succession of seasons and interchange of elements, by which the earth is maintained in undiminished splendour and fertility, I recognise on all sides the power and the presence of a benignant Deity; but when I direct my observation towards the moral world, and reflect that the creation, the object, and the final conclusion of all this glorious pageant have been hitherto unrevealed to us, and threaten to remain involved in impenetrable obscurity; when I observe the confusion of principles, with the disorder, uncertainty, and darkness, that perpetually surround the destiny of man; when I see vice and irreligion triumphant and rewarded, piety and virtue oppressed and wretched, the mental and bodily anguish of innocent individuals, the perpetual struggle of nations to torment one another, with the general predominance of human and animal suffering in the endless alternations of destroyer and victim, I am lost in astonishment at the contrast of the physical and moral systems; and in spite of myself relapse into scepticism and doubt." Authority that *he* possessed not has removed part of the difficulty by revealing to us that the present is but a probationary existence—the prelude to another, in which all the inconsistencies and imperfections of which he complained will be finally adjusted and atoned upon immutable principles of right; but it must be confessed, that enough remains unexplained to harass and perplex the prying spirit. The origin and existence of vice and pain, the unmerited sufferings of animals, for whom we are not warranted in admitting a future state of retribution,—these, and many other insolvable points, which, like so many *ignes fatui*, are as sure to elude our grasp as to lead us into pitfalls and difficulties, will be altogether avoided by the wise man, who, fixing his attention upon the consolatory perfectness of the material world, and confiding in the benignity which pervades it, will patiently await the fulness of time when the same spirit of goodness shall give a similar unity and completeness to the moral scheme of creation.

Down to the minutest divisions of human occupation it will be found that the men whose pursuits bring them in contact with inanimate nature, enjoy their avocations much more than those who are conversant with humanity, and all the modifications of the social and moral system. *Chamfort* observes, that the writers on physics, natural history, physiology, chemistry, have been generally men of a mild, even, and happy temperament; while, on the contrary, the writers on politics, legislation, and even morals, commonly exhibited a melancholy and fretful spirit. Nothing more simple: the former studied nature, the others society. One class contemplates the work of the great Being, the other fixes its observation upon the work of man: the results must be different. The nymphs of Calypso, as they caressed and fondled the infant Cupid, became unconsciously penetrated with his flame, and if the power of love be thus subtle, that of hatred is, unfortunately, not less pervading. We cannot handle human passions, even to play with them, without imbibing some portion of their acrimony, any more than we can gather flowers amid the nettles without being stung. Into every thing human a spirit of party becomes insinuated, and self-love is perpetually forcing us to taste of its bitterness; but there is no rivalry with nature; our pride does not revolt at her superiority, nay, we find a pure and holy calm in contemplating her majesty, before which we bow down with mingled feelings of delight and reverence. Contrast this with the effects produced upon us by human grandeur and elevation. Hence the charm of solitude; it places us in communion with things, whereas society fixes our regards upon man.

The age of Ascetics and Hermits is, however, passed away; intercourse with our kind is not to be interdicted, but regulated. "These things," as Milton says in his Areopagitica, "will be, and must be; but how they shall be least hurtful, how least enticing, herein consists the grave and governing wisdom. To sequester out of the world, into Atlantic and Eutopian politics, which never can be drawn into use, will not mend our condition, but to ordain wisely in this world of evil, in the midst whereof God has placed us unavoidably." Love of the country, and even of a partial seclusion, is not by any means misanthropy. "I love not man the less, but Nature more," when I recommend all those who have the privilege of a choice, to fly from the fermenting passions of crowds and capitals, whose acrid influence gnaws into the heart, and to appeal to the peaceful balmy ministerings of rural life. Farming, the primitive natural business of man, is probably the most healthful, both for body and mind; it places us, as it were, in daily contact with the Deity, by our unceasing experience of his superintending love, connects earth with heaven, and brings religion home to our business and bosoms. Cincinnatus felt this when he made such haste to beat the Volscians, that he might hurry back to his plough. I envy him the turning up of the first furrow; and I may say, in imitation of Alexander's speech to Diogenes, that if I were not a writer for the New Monthly Magazine, I should wish to be a farmer!!

Gardening, which exalts man into a species of creator, is another recreation fraught with all soothing and sweet delights; and it is pleasing to reflect, that some of the most eminent persons of antiquity are associated with its cultivation. Appius gave his name to a particular apple, Lucullus to a cherry, and Manlius to a pear. When Diocletian was pressed to resume the supreme authority, which he had abdicated, he exclaimed—"Ah! if Maximian could see the plants which I cultivate in my garden, at Salona, he would speak to me no more of empire." Cicero, in his defence of Amerinus, alleges his rural pursuits as a proof that he could not be guilty of his father's murder. "Vita autem hæc rustica, quam tu agrestem vocas, parsimoniæ, diligentiæ, justiciæ magistra est." Fabius and Scipio might both have gained prizes at the Horticultural Society, had it fortunately been of earlier institution; and we are told of Mæcenas that he might have realised a more aspiring destiny, but that

> "Maluit umbrosum quercum, Nymphasque canoras,
> Paucaque pomosi jugera culta soli,
> Pieridas, Phœbumque colens in mollibus hortis."

Many of the arts elicit sensations not less pure and unalloyed. Sculpture is also a species of creation, and one can hardly imagine any thing more delightful than the life of an ancient statuary, whose business it was, in the formation of his deities, to exalt the pleasure derived from contemplating the most rare and exquisite specimens of human symmetry into devotional rapture, and taste, as it were, the religion of beauty. He dedicated to the divinities the finest and most faultless forms of real existence, devoting himself to their production with the combined enthusiasm of the senses and of the spirit. This is the whole secret of the *beau idéal*, about which so much has been written: there is no rising above nature without going out of nature, which is deformity, not beauty. The phrase is an invention of modern sculptors, who can never reach the perfection of the ancient artists, because they are unimbued by the same stimulating feelings. Chiselling out men and monuments, human virtues and vices, their sensations as well as their works, are of a lower order. In Roman Catholic countries, where pictures are dedicated to religion, the finest painters have been produced: they have felt the same animation as the ancients, and have probably surpassed them. Portrait-painters, gazing more frequently upon stupid and repulsive countenances than upon those that are attractive or intelligent, and brought into perpetual collision with human foibles and vanities, can have no very ardent impulse or lofty sensations: but the landscape-painter's is probably the most delicious pursuit to which human talent can be devoted. Perpetually looking out upon a face of eternal youth and beauty, whose smiles and frowns, in their inexhaustible variety, form but so many alternations of loveliness, he derives from every minute form, from every tint of earth, rock, or leaf, from every passing variety of cloud or sky, a charm that has reference to his art over and above the natural one that addresses itself to his sense;—looking through nature up to nature's God, he feels the placid influence of the scene he paints; and in his solitary rambles,

> " Exempt from public haunt,
> Finds tongues in trees, books in the running brooks,
> Sermons in stones, and good in every thing."

He who draws out the hidden harmonies of Nature into new combinations, possesses a fountain of pure and inexhaustible gratification. The musician has a perpetual resource against ennui; he can soothe the heart, while he delights the ear; his art, like charity, is twice blessed—" it blesseth him that gives, and him that takes;"—he is generally a happy man.

We have considered some of those avocations that associate us with Nature and the physical world; let us now briefly notice some of those that place us in relation with man and morals, beginning with the professions. Nothing so strikingly illustrates the total nullity and blindness to which human reason may be reduced by the force of long-continued habit, titular honours, and external pomp, as the fact, that men of even good sense and humanity can become enamoured of a military life. As a matter of necessity, I arraign not its existence; but that it should be ever embraced as an affair of preference, is somewhat astounding. Strip it of its externals, view it abstractedly, analyse its nature and object, and if the word glory cannot alter the immutable truth of principles, nor a gold epaulette metamorphose every action of its wearer, we cannot cease to wonder that men should be so infatuated as to worship a painted devil for an angel. That it is the road to wealth, honours, rank, may be very true; but does it conduce to happiness? That is an enquiry which may be left to its professors to solve.

Medicine and surgery will hold out few attractions to those who are not prepared to sear their hearts as a preliminary qualification for their practice. Painful and distressing profession! that turns to us perpetually the darkest side of human nature, subjects us to the harrowing repetition of mental woe and bodily anguish, to sickness, decay, death: while it exposes to us moral as well as physical deformity, by bringing to our cognisance the selfishness of friends, the hollowness of relatives, the hypocrisy of heirs. It has been observed, that as we become acquainted with physical evils we despise death, and as we are familiarised with the evils of society we despise life. Medical men are liable to both impressions, and the result is not unfrequently manifest in their sentiment and temperament, which are rarely enviable. There may be some, who, in the lofty consciousness of dispensing health or allaying pain, of preserving domestic ties unsevered, and the link of friendship unbroken, enjoy an exquisite gratification, that atones to them for manifold annoyances and miseries. Let such men be venerated; for what are the momentary sufferings of the martyr, who gives his body to the flames, compared to his who offers up his mind as a perpetual and living sacrifice for the good of others?

The Law is nothing but a vast arena of the vices and evil passions of mankind, where its professors, stripping off their moral clothing, appear as gladiators to fight for victory, not for justice! To stand in the midst of a wrangling crowd, and constitute a focus for all its hateful feelings, to be made the confident of " wretched rogues forlorn," to be the depositary of their offences, to witness perjury, to advocate wrong, and oppose truth and justice, when hired to do it by a client; and finally, to be promoted to the bench that you may listen all day long to the evidence of repulsive crimes, and condemn their miserable perpetrators to the prison or the gallows. This, too, is a course which, as society is constituted, must be run by some, and may be run by many with public applause and the rewards of dignity and riches; but is it a career to be selected by him who is balancing as to what course of life to choose? I submit questions without presuming to supply an answer.

But the Church——ay, here, indeed, we cannot be at a loss; and he who feels within himself that he can faithfully, conscientiously, and holily discharge the duties of a minister of the Gospel, may be assured that he is embracing the happiest and most dignified of all professions. But if he be actuated by the spirit of a church rather than of a religion—if the *odium theologicum* can find a place in his bosom, and he seek to establish or oppose a sect rather than a principle—above all, if he be capable of desecrating the office by associating it with political feeling and interested motives—let him pause upon the threshold, for he cannot possibly step forward with advantage to others, and certainly not with benefit to himself.

The career of Politics will find few advocates among those who are more solicitous for mental peace than for worldly advancement. The field is narrow, the combatants fierce; cupidity and shame embitter their exertions; triumph is exposed to acerbity and perpetual irritation; failure adds the stings of envy to the mortification of defeat. Such are the trials to which the actors are exposed, and even the writers upon politics cannot altogether escape the contagion of their hatefulness. Machiavel could not have been a happy man, any more than the kings, ministers, and diplomatists, who were eager to avail themselves of his crooked, unprincipled, and heartless subtlety.

This analysis might easily be extended; but if I have not said enough to determine " What Life to choose," I have at least indicated what to avoid; so that if the reader be wise in his wishes, I may safely ejaculate, in bidding him adieu--" Dii tibi dent quæ velis !"

H.

## LAS CASES' JOURNAL.*

This interesting work is now brought to a close. *The two concluding parts, which we proceed to notice, record the conversations of
Napoleon from the 25th of October 1816, to the 25th of the following
month, the day upon which Las Cases was separated from his master.
The interest is sustained to the last. The matter, to be sure, as in the
preceding portions, is extremely desultory. The mind is hurried
away, without preparation, from the petty anecdotes of the Tuileries,
and the Emperor's contempt for physic, to his instructive reflections
upon his ancient grandeur, and his comprehensive designs for the consolidation of states and institutions; but in the midst of these violent
transitions we have the great interlocutor himself before us, sustaining
a paramount unity of action. There is no wandering of the mind from
him—but we follow him through every variety of mood and topic,
intensely arrested by the resistless interest of every thing, whether trivial or important, that may drop from his lips, and yielding, we hope
not unpardonably, to the many affecting associations connected with
his past and present fortune.

During the last month of Las Cases' intercourse with him, Napoleon's
health continued to decline. The several symptoms are minutely stated,
and, although so duly ridiculed at the period in our public offices,
appear to have been the sure forerunners of the malady that laid him
in his grave. But it was an established point of our political creed, to
believe in the impossibility of Bonaparte's dying of disease or of a
broken heart. Now that the question of his mortality is at rest, it may
be mentioned as not utterly incredible, that in his desponding moments
he seemed to regard his possible vitality as among the calamities of
his condition. Las Cases being sent for one day, found him in his
chamber with a handkerchief rolled round his head. He was seated in
an arm-chair, beside a great fire, which he had ordered to be kindled.

" What," said he, " is the severest disorder, the most acute pain to which
human nature is subject?" I replied that the pain of the present moment
always appeared to be the most severe. " Then it is the tooth-ache," said
he. He had a violent secretion of saliva, and his right cheek was much
swelled and inflamed. He was also affected by a severe nervous cough, and
occasional yawning and shivering, which denoted approaching fever. " What
a miserable thing is man!" said he, " the smallest fibre of his body assailed
by disease is sufficient to derange his whole system. On the other hand, in
spite of all the maladies to which he is subject, it is sometimes necessary to
employ the executioner, to put an end to him. What a curious machine is
this earthly clothing! and perhaps I may be confined in it for thirty years
longer?"

A day or two after, the signs of a sinking spirit broke out in a sim-
pler and more affecting manner.

The Emperor observing on his drawers some confectionary or sweetmeats
which had been accidentally left there, he desired me to bring them to him ;
and seeing that I hesitated and felt embarrassed, as to how I should present
them, he said, " Take them in your hand ; there is no need of ceremony or
form between us now. We must henceforth be messmates."

---

* Journal of the Private Life and Conversations of the Emperor Napoleon at St.
Helena, by the Count de Las Cases. Parts VII. and VIII.

But we leave these details to turn to matters of a higher and more permanent interest, with which the present portion of this work pre-eminently abounds.

In one of their conversations, Napoleon, adverting to his return from Elba and his second fall at Waterloo, confessed to Las Cases, that in that first struggle he was no longer sustained by his former confidence in his fortune. He mentioned as a remarkable circumstance, that every advantage he obtained at this period, was immediately followed by some reverse. He had marched through France, and arrived in the capital amidst the universal enthusiasm and acclamations of the people; but no sooner had he reached Paris, than by a sort of magic, and without any adequate motive, all around retracted and grew cold. He despatched agents to Austria, and had every hope of effecting a reconciliation with that power; but Murat with his fatal enterprise, of which Napoleon was suspected to have been the mover, started up and baffled all his attempts at negotiation. Then came the first successes of the campaign of 1815, so quickly followed by his final overthrow at Waterloo.

"Yet," he continued, "I must confess that all these strokes of fate distressed me more than they surprised me. I felt the sentiment of an unfortunate result—not that this in any way influenced my determination and measures, but the foreboding certainty haunted my mind."

As a proof that such was Napoleon's state of feeling at this period, Las Cases has inserted the following anecdote:—

When on the banks of the Sambre, the Emperor early one morning approached a bivouac fire, accompanied only by his aide-de-camp on duty (General C——). Some potatoes were boiling on the fire, and the Emperor asked for one, and began to eat it. Then, with a meditative and somewhat melancholy expression, he uttered the following broken sentences:—"After all, it is endurable. Man may live in any place and in any ways. The moment, perhaps, is not far remote.....Themistocles!"

In the preceding year (1814) when he was quitting the Tuileries to enter upon the short and unfortunate, but brilliant campaign which followed, his mind was visited by forebodings, in which some dream of him shaped, that if he fell, it would be by the Bourbons. The few of his particular friends to whom he communicated his apprehensions, vainly endeavoured to remove them by representing, that the Bourbons were forgotten—that they were wholly unknown to the present generation." "There is the real danger," was his invariable reply, an expression full of meaning, and of which the French can by this time comprehend the entire import. This presentiment explains a remarkable passage in his parting address to the officers of the National Guard. "You elected me—I am your work, and it is for you to defend me." After which, presenting to them the Empress and the King of Rome, he added, "I go to oppose the enemy, and I consign to your care all that I hold most dear." We are informed by Las Cases that at this decisive moment, Napoleon foresaw that he should be betrayed, and had resolved, before quitting Paris, to secure the person of him (Talleyrand, we presume) who proved to be the main-spring of the plot by which his overthrow was effected. He was prevented from executing his intention only by representations, and it may even be said offers of personal responsibility, on the part of some of his ministers, who assured him, that the individual suspected had more reason than any one else to dread the return of the Bourbons. Napoleon yielded; at the same time emphatically expressing fears that he might have cause to regret his forbearance.

A little farther on we have, upon the same subject, a still more striking and characteristic passage. After the check sustained at Brienne, the evacuation of Troyes, the forced retreat on the Seine, and the degrading conditions which were transmitted from Chatillon, but which were so generously rejected, the Emperor, who was closetted with one of his friends, overpowered at the sight of the miseries that were impending on France, suddenly rose from his chair, exclaiming with warmth—

" Perhaps I still possess the means of saving France..... What if I were myself to recall the Bourbons ! The Allies would then be compelled to arrest their course, under pain of being overwhelmed with disgrace and detected in their duplicity—under pain of being forced to acknowledge that their designs were directed against our territory rather than against my person. I should sacrifice all to the Country. I should become the mediator between the French people and the Bourbons. I should oblige the latter to accede to the national laws, and to swear fidelity to the existing compact. My glory and name would be a guarantee to the French people. As to me, I have reigned long enough; my career is filled with acts of glory, and this last will not be esteemed the least; I shall rise the higher by descending thus far...." Then after a pause of some moments he added, " But can a repulsed dynasty ever forgive ? Can it ever forget ? Can the Bourbons be trusted ? May not Fox be right in his famous maxim respecting restorations ?" Overcome by grief and anxiety, he threw himself on his couch, and was shortly after roused to be made acquainted with the march of the flank of Blucher's corps, on which he had for some time been secretly keeping watch. He rose to put into action that new spring of resources, energy, and glory, which will for ever consecrate the names of Champ-Aubert, Montmirail, Chateau-Thierry, Vauchamps, &c. &c.

In the present, as in the preceding volumes, several of Napoleon's conversations turn upon his various plans for the aggrandizement of France, and the stability of the new institutions upon which his government was founded. We have observed in a former number upon his ineffectual efforts to create a naval power capable of contesting the dominion of the seas with England. We here find him returning to the same subject, and explaining the difficulties he encountered. The name of Suffren, who died in 1789, being casually mentioned, Napoleon made enquiries respecting him, saying, " that although, upon the report of his having rendered important services to France, he had been very liberal to his family, he had never had an opportunity of forming a correct opinion of his character." Las Cases proceeded to describe him, and it is a little curious to observe the class of qualities that would, it appears, have recommended the possessor to the highest favour of Napoleon :—

" Suffren possessed genius, invention, ardour, ambition, and inflexible steadiness. He was harsh, capricious, egotistical, a most unpleasant messmate, was loved by no one, though valued and admired by all. He was a man with whom no one could live on good terms. He was impatient of control, fond of condemning every thing, and, while he incessantly declaimed against the utility of tactics, he proved himself to be a perfect tactician. In short, he evinced all the irritability and restlessness of genius and ambition deprived of elbow-room. On obtaining the command of the Indian squadron, he went to take leave of the King, and one of the officers of the palace could with difficulty open a passage for him through the crowd. 'I thank you,' said he to the usher, grunting and snorting in his usual way, 'but when I come out, Sir, you shall see that I know how to clear the way for myself,' and he kept his word."

Las Cases continuing to mention his successes in India, which were mainly attributable to his contempt for the established routine of naval technicalities:—

" Oh," exclaimed the Emperor, " why did not Suffren live till my time? or why did I not light upon a man of this stamp? I would have made him our Nelson. I was constantly seeking for a man qualified to raise the character of the French navy, but I could never find one. There is, in the navy, a peculiarity, a technicality that impeded all my conceptions. If I proposed a new idea, immediately Ganthaume and the whole marine department were up against me. 'Sire, that cannot be.' Why not? 'Sire, the winds do not admit of it.' Then objections were started respecting calms and currents, and I was obliged to stop short. How is it possible to maintain a discussion with those whose language we do not comprehend? How often in the Council of State have I reproached naval officers with taking an undue advantage of this circumstance. To hear them talk, one might have been led to suppose that it was necessary to be born in the navy to know any thing about it. Yet I often told them, that had it been in my power to have performed a voyage to India with them, I should, on my return, have been as familiar with their profession as with the field of battle. But they could not credit this." Napoleon went on to observe upon a plan, which after long hesitation he had been prevailed on to adopt, the enrolment of several thousands of children from six to eight years of age. The result was clamour and discontent on the part of the public, who turned the whole affair into ridicule, styling it 'the massacre of the innocents.' Subsequently he had been assured, he said, by De Winter, Verhuel, all the great naval commanders of the North and others, that from 18 to 20 (the age for the Conscription) was early enough to begin to learn the duties of a sailor. Alluding to the Swedes and Danes, who employ their soldiers in the navy, and to the Russians, with whom the fleet is but a portion of the army, he added that in creating crews for his men-of-war he had planned something of the same kind, but that at every step he had been encountered by obstacles and prejudices. It required all his perseverance to succeed in clothing the sailors in uniform, forming them into regiments, and drilling them by military exercise. Yet the men thus disciplined were not worse sailors than the rest, and made the very best soldiers. " If," he repeated, " instead of being thus opposed by obstacles, I had found in the navy a man capable of entering into my views and promoting my ideas, what importance might we not have obtained! But during my reign, I never found a naval officer who could depart from the old routine and strike out a new course."

In another conversation he went over his system of interior policy, the necessity upon which it was founded, and the gradual improvements he had projected. Among these, the abolition of lucrative offices was one of the changes that he most anxiously contemplated. The necessity of conciliating individuals had compelled him to annex liberal salaries, absolute fortunes, to offices of trust; but he had hoped in process of time to render the performance of all high public duties gratuitous.

" I would have discarded those needy individuals, who cannot be their own masters, and whose urgent wants engender political immorality. I would have wrought such a change in opinion, that public posts should have been sought after for the mere honour of filling them.....The love of place is the greatest check to public morals. A man who solicits a public post, feels ~~dependence~~ sold beforehand. In England the greatest families, the ~~rage~~, disdain not to hunt after places. Their excuse is, that the enormous burdens of taxation deprive them of the means of living without additions to their income. Pitiful pretence! It is because their principles are more decayed than their fortunes. When people of a certain rank stoop to solicit public posts for the sake of emolument, there is an end to all independence and dignity of national character. In France the shocks and commotions of our Revolution might have afforded an apology for such conduct. All had been unsettled, and all felt the necessity of re-establishing themselves. To promote' this object with the least possible offence to delicacy of feeling, I was induced to attach considerable emolument and high honour to all public posts. But in course of time, I intended to work a change by the mere force of opinion. And this was by no means impossible. Every thing must yield to the influence of power, when it is directed to objects truly just, honourable, and great."

These were, we fear, chimeras. We question the possibility of effecting such a revolution in any country, where a taste for ease and refinement has once taken root; and we greatly apprehend, that, among all the nations of Europe, modern France is the very one where the necessary simplicity of character, and practical exaltation of sentiment, would be most difficultly produced, and the least likely to be permanent. Still there is something consolatory in finding, that such a man as Napoleon, experienced as he was in the vices and selfishness of public men, should have clung to the hope, that a system of government founded upon a virtuous preference of the general good was not, after all, so visionary as to forbid the experiment. What follows is more in his character as a keen and severe appreciater of the morals and opinions of his time. After he had developed the preceding views, Las Cases expressed his surprise that he should never have thrown out a hint of the important objects he had in contemplation.

" What would have been the use of promulgating my intentions ?" said he, " I should have been styled a quack, accused of insinuation and subtilty, and have fallen into discredit. Situated as I was, deprived of hereditary authority, and of the illusion called legitimacy, I was compelled to avoid entering the lists with my opponents. I was obliged to be bold, imperious, and decisive. You have told me that in your Faubourg they used to say, ' *Why is he not legitimate ?*' If I had been so, I certainly should not have done more than I did; but my conduct might have appeared more amiable."

Two or three days after, we find him revealing, at considerable length, and with his accustomed animation, some of the principal objects of his general policy. One of his great plans, he said, was the concentration of France, Spain, Germany, and Italy, each into a separate nation, but bound together by a federal compact, and, if possible, by a unity of codes, principles, opinions, and interests. The concentration of France was perfected—that of Italy far advanced. In Spain, he asserts, it would have been accomplished, had it not been for the reverses he sustained at distant points, and the error he committed in transferring his whole forces to the distance of a thousand leagues from that country. Had it not been for this, he expected in the course of three or four years to have effected such a prosperous revolution in the condition of the Spaniards, as would have well entitled him to their gratitude. This hope might have been reasonable, or it may have been only the sophistry of an ambitious mind, seizing upon any pretext for open and unprovoked aggression ; but he was at least prophetic in one point of his concluding observations upon this topic : " I should have saved them from the tyranny by which they are now oppressed, and *the terrible agitations that await them.*" His remarks upon Germany, though few, have a prospective interest, that gives them no small importance.

". The concentration of the Germans must have been effected more gradually, and therefore I had done no more than simplify their monstrous complication. Not that they were unprepared for concentralization. On the contrary, they were too well prepared for it, and they might have blindly risen in reaction against us, before they had comprehended our designs. How happens it that no German prince has yet formed a just notion of the spirit of his nation, and turned it to good account? Certainly if Heaven had made me a prince of Germany, amidst the many critical events of our times, I should, infallibly, have governed the 30,000,000 of Germans combined ; and from what I know of them, I think I may venture to affirm, that if they had once elected and proclaimed me, they would not have forsaken me, and I should never have been at St. Helena."

Then after some melancholy details and comparisons, resuming the previous subject, he said,

". At all events this concentration will be brought about sooner or later by the very force of events. The impulse is given, and I think that, since my fall, and the destruction of my system, no grand equilibrium can possibly be established in Europe, except by the concentration and confederation of the principal nations. The sovereign who, in the first great conflict, shall sincerely embrace the cause of the people, will find himself at the head of all Europe, and may attempt whatever he pleases."

Here again he returns to his motives for withholding all disclosures upon the subject of these and his other adventurous projects. The passage is remarkable, and one of the most explanatory that we recollect him to have given, of that air of incomprehensibility with which, in the fulness of his power, he was pleased to envelope his proceedings.

"It will perhaps be asked," he says, "why I did not suffer these ideas to transpire? why I did not submit them to public discussion; since they would doubtless have become popular, and popularity would have been an immense reinforcement to me? My answer is, that malevolence is ever more active than good intention ; that at the present day, the power of wit overrules good sense, and obscures the clearest points at will ; and that to have submitted these important subjects to public discussion would have been to consign them to the mercy of party-spirit, passion, intrigue, and gossiping, while the infallible result would have been discredit and opposition. I conceived, therefore, that secrecy was the most advisable course. I surrounded myself with that halo of mystery, which pleases and interests the multitude, —gives birth to speculations which occupy the public mind, and finally, affords opportunities for those sudden and brilliant disclosures which exercise such important influence. It was this very principle that accelerated my unfortunate march to Moscow. Had I been more deliberate, I might have averted every evil; but I could not delay, and afford time for comment. With my career already traced out, with my ideas formed for the future, it was necessary that my movement and my success should seem, as it were, supernatural."

While we are upon this subject we may in passing observe, that these and similar disclosures contained in other parts of the present work, have been received in a somewhat singular spirit by certain persons among the French, who shared in Napoleon's power, and still profess a devotion to his fame. To some of these, who had constant access to his person, and were considered to have been admitted to his confidence, it has not been a little mortifying to find their old master proclaiming that, after all, they had been as ignorant as the multitude of his secret motives and intentions upon the most important occasions of his career.

They accordingly assert pretty roundly and confidently, that the Emperor has been mystifying the Count Las Cases and Europe; that these elaborate explanations of his uncommunicated views and objects are all a juggle, invented for the sole purpose of his individual justification, and therefore to be treated by all sagacious readers, as neither more nor less than a brilliant imposture. We cannot stop to adjust the conflicting probabilities between the Exile's veracity and the splendid incredulity of his former servants. We simply give as not an incurious circumstance, the feeling which we have recently discovered to exist upon this portion of the conversations at St. Helena.

There are, we doubt not, many excellent persons among us, who still think that the penance of Napoleon's latter years was but a poor expiation of his manifold exploits. To these it may be a gratification to know, that, in the plenitude of his glory, he was not exempt from the petty vexations of domestic life. It is not surprising that such a man should have had an expensive wife, but it is at once ludicrous and lamentable to think that her rage for caps and bonnets should have compelled him to employ an imperial *coup-de-main* upon such an object as a refractory Parisian milliner. Such however, appears to have been the necessity of his situation.

"Speaking of the Empress Josephine, he says, "Her extravagance vexed me beyond measure. Calculator as I am, I would, of course, rather have given away a million of francs than have seen 100,000 squandered away." He informed us, that having one day unexpectedly broken in upon Josephine's morning circle, he found a celebrated milliner, whom he had expressly forbidden to go near the Empress, as 'she was ruining her by extravagant demands.' My unlooked-for entrance occasioned great dismay in the academic study. I gave some orders unperceived to the individuals who were in attendance, and on the lady's departure she was seized, and conducted to the Bicêtre. A great outcry was raised among the higher circles in Paris; it was said that my conduct was disgraceful. It soon became the fashion to visit the milliner in her confinement, and there was daily a file of carriages at the gate of the prison. The police informed me of these facts. 'All the better,' said I; 'that I hope she is not treated with severity; not confined in a dungeon.' 'No, Sire, she has a suite of apartments, and a drawing-room.' 'Oh, well!' let then be. If this measure is pronounced to be tyrannical, so much the better; it will be a diapason stroke for a great many others. Very little will serve to shew that I can do more.'"

But what follows was still more provoking.

He also mentioned a celebrated man-milliner who, he remarked, was the most insolent fellow he had ever met with in the whole course of his life. "I was one day," said the Emperor, "speaking to him respecting a *trousseau* that he had furnished, when he had the presumption to call my conduct in question. He did what no man in France except himself would have ventured to do; he began with great volubility to prove to me that I did not grant a sufficient allowance to the Empress Josephine, and that it was impossible she could pay for her clothes out of such a sum. I soon put an end to his impertinent eloquence; I stopped him short with a look, and left him unnoticed."

The present, like the former volumes, brings us acquainted with many personal traits which would deserve to be recorded, although Napoleon had never been a monarch. We have already noticed the rapidity and precision of his judgments upon literary topics; we give one farther example.

"At first he expressed his surprise that the Romans should have had no tragedies; but then again he observed, that tragedy, in dramatic represpotation, would have been ill-calculated to rouse the feelings of the Romans, since they performed real tragedy in their circuses. The combats of the gladiators," said he, " the sight of men consigned to the fury of wild beasts, were far more terrible than all our dramatic horrors put together. These, in fact, were the only tragedies suited to the iron nerves of the Romans."

There are many scattered sayings which mark the man.

Speaking of the elements of society, he said, " Democracy may be furious—but it has some heart—it may be moved. As to Aristocracy, it is always cold and unforgiving."

One day, when the Emperor was reproaching an individual for not correcting the vices which he knew he possessed, " Sir," said he, " when a man knows his moral infirmity, he may cure his mind, just as he would cure his arm or his leg."

It was asked in his presence, how it happened that misfortunes which were yet uncertain often distressed us more than miseries that had already been suffered : " Because," observed the Emperor, " in the imagination, as in calculation, the power of what is unknown is incommensurable."

The same promptness of scientific analysis will be recognised in the following anecdote.—The Count Las Cases, who, by the way, is singularly prone to exalt every casual coincidence into a miraculous interference, related an instance of the kind, as reported to him by Charette, the hero of La Vendée. Charette, in his youth, was off Brest in a small cutter, when a furious gale of wind came on. The mast was carried away ; the vessel became unmanageable, and certain destruction seemed inevitable. At the moment of extreme danger, the whole crew, by a spontaneous impulse, made a vow of a taper to Our Lady of Rocouvrance at Brest, if she would vouchsafe to ensure their safety. The wind instantly abated. It was in the month of December, and the night was long and dark. The vessel, which had got entangled among ridges, drifted along at hazard, and the crew had resigned themselves to the will of fate, when they unexpectedly heard the ringing of a bell. They sounded, and finding but little depth of water, they cast anchor. At daybreak they found that they were at the mouth of the river of Landernau. The bell they had heard was that of the neighbouring parish church.

" The cutter," continued the Count, " had miraculously escaped the numerous sand-banks that are dispersed about the entrance of Brest. She had been carried through the narrow inlet of the port, had passed three or four hundred ships that were lying in the roads, and had at length found a calm station at the mouth of the river."—" This," said the Emperor, " shews the difference between the blindfold efforts of man, and the certain course of nature. That, at which you express so much surprise, *must necessarily have happened.* It is very probable, that with the full power of exerting the utmost skill, the confusion and errors of the moment would have occasioned the wreck of the vessel ; whereas, in spite of so many adverse chances, Nature saved her : she was borne onward by the tide ; the force of the current carried her *precisely through the middle of each channel,* so that she could not possibly be lost."

We would recommend this explanation to our Irish friends as a formula of reasoning that may be occasionally applied to the course of miracles which Prince Hohenlohe has undertaken for the benefit of the tongue-tied ladies of their country.

Among the numerous historical details that are scattered throughout the present publication, there is a full account of the affair of the unfortunate Duke d'Enghien, and of the manner in which Napoleon recurred to it. In the presence of strangers he adopted a line of argument founded almost exclusively on the law of nature and state politics. With those whom he admitted to the intimacy of private conversation, he descended into the following particulars:—

"I was one day alone, I recollect it well; I was taking my coffee, half-seated on the table on which I had just dined, when sudden information is brought to me that a new conspiracy has been discovered. I am warmly urged to put an end to these enormities. They represent to me that it is time, at last, to give a lesson to those who have been day after day conspiring against my life; that this end can only be attained by shedding the blood of one of them; and that the Duke d'Enghien, who might now be convicted of forming part of this new conspiracy, and taken in the very act, should be that one. It was added, that he had been seen at Strasburg; that it was even believed that he had been in Paris; and that the plan was, that he should enter France by the East, at the moment of the explosion, whilst the Duke of Berry was disembarking in the West. I should tell you (observed the Emperor) that I did not even know precisely who the Duke d'Enghien was (the Revolution having taken place when I was yet a very young man, and I having never been at Court); and that I was quite in the dark as to where he was at that moment. Having been informed on those points, I exclaimed, that if such were the case, the Duke ought to be arrested; and that orders should be given to that effect. Every thing had been foreseen, and prepared—the different orders were already drawn up—nothing remained to be done but to sign them; and the fate of the young Prince was, thus, decided. He had been residing for some time past at a distance of about three leagues from the Rhine, in the States of Baden. Had I been sooner aware of this fact, and of its importance, I should have taken umbrage at it, and should not have suffered the Prince to remain so near the frontiers of France; and that circumstance, as it happened, would have saved his life. As for the assertions that were advanced at the time, that I had been strenuously opposed in this affair, and that numerous solicitations had been made to me, they are utterly false, and were only invented to make me appear in a more odious light. The same thing may, be said of the various motives that have been ascribed to me. These motives may have existed in the bosoms of those who acted an inferior part on the occasion, and may have guided them in their private views; but my conduct was influenced only by the nature of the fact itself, and the energy of my disposition. Undoubtedly, if I had been informed in time of certain circumstances respecting the opinions of the Prince, and his disposition—if, above all, I had seen the letter which he wrote to me, and which, God knows for what reason, was only delivered to me after his death, I should certainly have forgiven him."

We had noted several other striking passages for insertion; but we are reminded by our limits that it is time we take a final leave of this interesting work—the most attractive and important, in numerous points of view, that has appeared in modern times. To the extraordinary person of whom it treats, we foresee that we shall have many future occasions to recur. His character and conduct have raised questions of vital interest that will long be remembered and discussed. Among these (and it is one of not the least singular circumstances of his history) the question of his personal merits has met with rather a curious destiny in this country. He is detested and decried for his despotism and aggression by that class of politicians among us who would abridge, if they could, both at home and abroad, the privileges of thought and action—by the admirers of the Holy Alliance—the

apologists of
tripes, if not
England to a
Napoleon's da

enabl'
have
have
ness
great                  unrelieved by any
acts of public vi            the principles of
their school, be           nd every friend of
human happiness would blush to be his apologist.*

## THE ISLE OF FOUNTS,

### An Indian Tradition.

Son of the Stranger! wouldst thou take
  O'er yon blue hills thy lonely way,
To reach the still and shining Lake,
  Along whose banks the West-winds play ?
—Let no vain dreams thy heart beguile,
Oh ! seek thou not the Fountain-Isle !

Lift but the mighty Serpent-King,†
  Midst the great Rocks, his old domain,
Ward but the Cougar's deadly spring,
  —Thy step that Lake's green shore may gain ;
And the bright Isle, when all is past,
Shall vainly meet thine eye at last !

---

* We have not room to speak of the Eighth and last Part of this publication.—
It comprises a variety of interesting correspondence undertaken with the view of
alleviating the situation of the captive, and also the adventures and sufferings of the
Count Las Cases after his separation from Napoleon. With regard to the removal
of Las Cases from St. Helena, he unquestionably violated the conditions upon
which he had himself consented to remain. The innocent or unimportant nature
of the documents which he attempted to transmit through a secret channel to
Europe, did not render him the less amenable to the consequences of a breach of
his own agreement. But in other respects (with the honourable exception of his
treatment by Lord Charles Somerset at the Cape of Good Hope), he seems to have
been miserably buffeted about. The account of his journey from Gravesend to
Francfort, where at last he found an asylum, is more like a chapter of Caleb Williams than a detail of probable occurrences, and affords a very edifying picture of
the prevailing horror at the idea of allowing any authentic intelligence of Napoleon's condition and sentiments to transpire.

† The Cherokees believe that the recesses of their mountains, overgrown with
lofty pines and cedars, and covered with old mossy rocks, are inhabited by the
Kings or Chiefs of the Rattlesnakes, whom they denominate the " bright old inhabitants." They represent them as snakes of an enormous size, and which possess
the power of drawing to them every living creature that comes within the reach of
their eyes. Their heads are crowned with a large carbuncle of dazzling brightness.
See Notes to Leyden's " Scenes of Infancy."

Yes! there, with all its rainbow-dreams,
Clear as within thine eyes-o's flight,
The Isle of founts, the Isle of dreams,
Floats on the wave in golden light,
And lovely will the shadows be
Of groves whose fruit is not for thee!
And breathings from their sunny flowers,
Which are not of the things that die,
And singing voices from their bowers,
Shall greet thee in the purple sky:
Soft voices, even like those that dwell
Far in the green seed's hollow cell.
Or hast thou heard the sounds that rise
From the deep chambers of the Earth?
The wild and wondrous melodies,
To which the ancient Rocks give birth?*
—Like that sweet song of hidden caves,
Shall swell those Isle-notes o'er the waves.

The emerald waves!—they take their hue
And image from that summer-shore,
But wouldst thou launch thy light canoe,
And wouldst thou ply thy rapid oar,
Before thee, hadst thou morning's speed,
The sunbright land should still recede!

Yet on the breeze thou still shalt hear
The music of its flowering shades;
And ever shall the sound be near
Of founts that ripple through its glades!
The sound, and sight, and flashing ray,
Of joyous waters in their play.

But woe for him who sees them burst
With their bright spray-showers to the Lake!
Earth has no spring to quench the thirst
That semblance in his soul shall wake,
For ever pouring through his dreams,
The gush of those untasted streams!

Bright, bright in many a rocky urn,
The waters of our deserts lie,
Yet at their source his lip shall burn,
Parch'd with the fever's agony!
From the blue mountains to the main,
Our thousand floods may roll in vain.

E'en thus our Hunters came of yore
Back from their vain and weary quest;
—Had they not seen th' untrodden shore,
And could they midst our wilds find rest?
The lightning of their glance was fled,
They dwelt amongst us as the dead!

They lay beside our glancing rills,
With visions in their darken'd eye,
Their joy was not amidst the hills,
Where elk and deer before us fly;
Their spears upon the cedar hung,
Their javelins to the wind were flung.

* The Stones called by the South American Missionaries *Laxas de Musica*, from which travellers on the Oroonoco have occasionally heard, towards sun-rise, subterranean sounds, resembling those of the organ.—*Humboldt's Travels.*

They bent no more the forest-bow,
  They arm'd not with the warrior-band,
The moons waned o'er them dim and blow—
  —They left us for the Spirit's land!
Beneath our pines yon greensward heap
Shows where the Restless found their sleep.

Son of the Stranger! if at eve
  Silence be midst us in thy place,
Yet go not where the mighty leave
  The strength of battle and of chase!
Let no vain dreams thy heart beguile,
—Oh! seek thou not the Fountain-Isle!          F. H.

---

### PERANZÚLES,

#### *A Spanish Historical Fragment.*

Thᴇ same age that produced the *Cid*† gave birth to Pedro, Lord of Valladolid, whose surname Anzúres, or Anzúles, was by the soft pronunciation of the Castilians blended with his baptismal appellation, into *Peranzúles.* He must have known the former hero at the height of his glory, and heard, probably with a pang of generous emulation, of the conquest of Valencia; that noble city, whose possession crowned the Spanish hero's career of glory, and which, with every title to be distinguished from two smaller towns of the same name, by calling herself the *Great*, or taking the addition of any of the Spanish monarchs, has preferred the badge of her ancient lord, and is still known as Valencia of *the Cid.*

The memory of Peranzúles is, however, preserved with veneration in the early annals of Spain, not so much for his achievements in the field, as for his being the model of that firmness of mind, which, fixed on justice and honour as upon a rock, leads its possessor through life, unshaken by the storms which make the very sands boil in the surface of those boisterous gulfs, the courts of nascent and half-civilized states. Peranzúles stands, in Spanish history, as the original of the genuine national honour,—not the ruffian spirit of revenge, which, under the reign of Spanish despotism, concealed the knife under the same cloak that hid the face—but that intrepid fear of just blame, which steels the heart against every other fear in the universe.

Hardly any thing but his loyalty could mark the distance which separated the Lord of Valladolid from those to whom he paid allegiance. By descent and connexions he was almost a peer of the independent princes who reigned in different parts of Spain. His knightly accomplishments, and probably some mental cultivation above the rude champions who surrounded the throne of Alphonso VI. induced the Castilian monarch to intrust the education of his daughter, Urraca, to Peranzúles. Whether the probability of her succeeding to the throne made the acquisition of something above feminine softness desirable, in the opinion of a warlike monarch; or that, the Castilian females being deemed too deficient in all but the arts of pleasing, tutors were pre-

---

* See Mariana's History of Spain, Book X. Chap. 8.; and Zurita, Annals of Aragon, Book I. Chap. 28.

† The year of the *Cid's* death is not well known. It is supposed to be 1098.

ferred to governesses in that age and country, we are not able to decide.

Where the difference of age secured both master and pupil from the secret growth of a dangerous passion, nothing seems more apt to create a pure and lasting attachment than the duties performed by the noble Castilian to the daughter of his sovereign. But that princess had none of the noble qualities which adorned her father; and, if we may be allowed to conjecture from the scanty notice which history gives of her mother, Urraca had derived from that source a selfish, turbulent spirit, which, even without her peculiar and grosser failings, would stand in the way of gratitude to the virtuous instructor of her youth.

Prince Sancho, the only son of Alphonso VI. being slain near Uclés, in a battle against the Moors, Urraca became heiress to the throne of Castile. She was at that time * the widow of Raimund, Lord of Galicia, a son of William I. Count of Burgundy, whom the Castilian king had chosen, out of the noble adventurers that joined his standard from France, to share the throne with his daughter in the event of her accession. Alphonso, now far advanced in years, saw with increasing concern, that within a short time the sceptre he had wielded with glory, would glide into the feeble grasp of a young volatile woman, who appeared alike intemperate in the enjoyment of power and of pleasure. Anxious for the glory of a kingdom which, under his sway, had given the first signs of a settled ascendancy over the Moors, he feared that the infant son of Urraca, if allowed to grow under the exclusive influence of his mother, might disgrace the name of Alphonso, which, in the fond hope of imparting his own spirit, the old king had given his grandchild. The fate of his family and kingdom hung upon the choice of a husband for the heiress, whose hand was already a subject of contention among the grandees. To obviate, therefore, the feuds and divisions with which Gomez, Count of Candespina, and Peter, Count of Lara, the two chief suitors, threatened the state, Alphonso announced his fixed determination of giving Urraca to the Prince of Aragon. Not long after the marriage, the two crowns became vacant; and Alphonso of Aragon, who, by his numerous victories against the Moors, obtained the addition of *Conqueror*, assumed, in right of his wife, the title of Emperor of Spain, which the kings of Leon and Castile claimed, at that time, as due to the extent and importance of their dominions.

The last illness of Alphonso VI. though it had obliged him for a whole year to abandon the cares of government, had not been perceived in the weakness of delegated power, for that power was in the hands of Peranzúles. Upon the death of the king his master, Alphonso of Aragon, well acquainted with the worth of that noble Castilian, confirmed his powers to govern the kingdom; and when the Queen's impatience to appear at her court of Toledo prevailed upon him to send her to Castile some time before he could follow her, it was upon condition that she would strictly adhere to the advice of her former tutor.

Urraca's spirit, now emboldened with power, and become ungovernable with the love of pleasure, could ill brook the control of a virtuous man, who fearlessly opposed her misrule and jealously watched her conduct. Lara and Candespina, who formerly sued for her hand, were now

* A. D. 1109.

rivals for the intimacy to which the Queen's levity seemed to encourage them equally. Peranzúles, finding his efforts unequal to preserve the honour of the Spanish throne, urged the necessity of the King's presence at Toledo. It seems that one of his despatches was intercepted by the Queen, who having already set up pretensions to absolute and independent sway over her portion of the kingdom, enforced a sentence of banishment on Peranzúles, for addressing the King by the title of Emperor of Castile and Leon.

The party which encouraged the Queen in her attempts towards independence, though strong enough to deprive Peranzúles of his Castilian states, and oblige him to take refuge in Aragon, had not yet acquired the nerve and consistency which were necessary to make head against the King; who, aware of his wife's misconduct, hastened from Aragon to Toledo, and confined her in the fortress of Castellar, on the banks of the Ebro. Alphonso's military renown, and the decision of his character, struck awe into the restless and aspiring nobles; while the justice of his administration, and the benefits he conferred on the commonalty by rebuilding the towns of Billorádo, Berlánga, Séria, and Almasán, which lay dismantled by the Moors, attached the nation to his person, and cemented his power in the kingdom. His right in fact to the throne was, in those times, considered by many as equal to that of his wife; for both were great grandchildren of Sancho the Great; and the order of succession by representation was still unsettled in Europe.

Prince Alphonso, Urraca's son, was in the mean time in Galicia, under the care of Peter, Count of Trava, his tutor. This nobleman, assisted by the Bishop of Santiago, formed a plan for liberating the Queen; which being carried into execution, put the power of the state into the hands of the Galician party. Alphonso of Aragon, whose distance from Castile had favoured the views of his enemies, penetrated with an armed force into the revolted provinces, and carrying every thing before him, overran in a short time Galicia, Castile, and Estremadura, reducing fortresses, and laying waste the lands of his opponents.

It was not, however, Alphonso's power and military prowess which the united barons had solely to fear. The Queen's natural levity, combined with her unruly ambition, disconcerted at once the well-laid plans which were at work to expel the Aragonese from the Castilian throne.

Consanguinity, even in the third remove, was deemed, in that age, to invalidate marriage; yet this supposed impediment was constantly overlooked in the negotiation of every royal match, as if both parties were glad to leave a flaw in the contract, which might, at their option, free them from its obligations. In the present instance, the Galicians having possessed themselves of the Queen's person, lost no time in pleading the nullity of a marriage, which was the most plausible of Alphonso's claims to the government of Castile and Leon. A petition was accordingly addressed to the Pope, who appointed the Bishop of Santiago, and some other prelates of the Galician party, to examine the merits of the case, and pronounce the sentence of divorce according to Canon Law. While the Bishops were intent on the execution of their commission, the Queen, jealous of the power which her protectors assumed, and aware that Treva, her sole tutor, had no object but that of governing the kingdom in his pupil's name, fled secretly to her husband, whom she was artful enough to appease by her tears.

The Queen's reconciliation with Alphonso brought fresh troubles on the Galician party. Treva's rivals for power could not endure the thoughts of his reigning in the name of the young prince. A force was raised to take the royal pupil out of his hands, and both were besieged in a castle, which, from its strength, seemed only to be reduced by famine. Unwilling to carry dissension to extremities, and thinking that the presence of the Queen, whom they knew too well to suppose she would long continue quiet with her husband, might reconcile their bending interests, a secret interview was procured, where Urraca concerted a second escape to Galicia. The plot, however, coming to Alphonso's knowledge, he, with a degree of forbearance which could hardly be expected in that rude age, conveyed his wife to Soria, then on the limits of the two kingdoms, and, having obtained a divorce, in an Ecclesiastical Court, allowed her to depart in perfect liberty.

The divisions of Spain, to which we here give the name of kingdoms, were, in those days, far from exhibiting an organised society, existing under a regular government, and forming the compact bodies to which we are accustomed at present. A number of fortified towns and castles stood at considerable distances, without other ties but those of religion, language, and an almost nominal allegiance to the same monarch. Hence the surprising facility with which they changed masters, not only as fortune or intrigue favoured, by turns, some of the more powerful chiefs among the Spaniards, but even as the strength or imbecility of their princes pushed or withdrew the limits between the Moors and the Christians. Under this imperfect system of policy, we must not be surprised to find Alphonso committing the principal fortresses of Castile into the charge of some of his noblemen, and expecting that they would continue in his allegiance, notwithstanding his separation from Urraca.

On none did he repose more confidence than Peranzules, whom, during the imprisonment of the Queen, he had recalled to be the main support of the Castilian crown, and to help him in the work of improving that kingdom. The most important towns and castles of the country were accordingly, in that nobleman's keeping; while, during the frequent expeditions of the King, either against the Aragonese Moors, or to quell the rebellions which broke out in Galicia, Peranzules appeared at the helm of the state by a kind of natural right.

Alphonso's feelings of surprise and indignation on receiving intelligence that Peranzules had surrendered all the towns and castles into the hands of the Queen, without resistance or delay, and merely upon a simple summons, cannot be easily described. Burning with thoughts of revenge, that Aragonese was collecting an army to repossess himself of what he had meant to preserve, probably, as a compensation for the claims to the throne which he had resigned, when, upon a muster-day, as he was surrounded by the flower of his warriors, a knight, in bright armour, and mounted upon a spirited war-horse, was seen to approach the splendid group, which formed the King's court, in the open field. Unable to guess who the stranger could be, the eyes of all were rivetted on his person, while he drew up to within a short distance. Here, alighting from the horse, and letting down his beaver, Peranzúles was recognized with a suppressed emotion—the first note of an indignant shout from the crowd of warriors. This sudden ebullition was changed into suspense, when they saw the ancient knight take off his helmet, and exchange it for something which he took from the hands of his attendant.

The thin white locks which, freed from the casque, fell over a countenance where neither fear nor shame had ever impressed a line, though furrowed, and that deeply, by thought and age, seemed to dazzle at once the multitude of proud eyes which had been raised to look down on the Castilian. Their aim was changed, their eyelids were relaxed, and none looked straight before him but Peranzúles. He advanced with humble dignity to the King's presence, where, bending one knee to the ground, and holding up a halter in his right hand: "My Liege (he said)—I have addressed your Highness by that word which I cannot utter without myself sealing the doom which you have already passed against my life. With that life, indeed, I swore to answer for the places which you intrusted to my loyalty, and here I come to lay it down at your feet. Yet think not that, with life, you will take away my honour, nor sully the name of Peranzúles with the odious reproach of treachery. It has pleased Heaven, indeed, to try me on the brink of the grave by the conflicting claims of the most opposite duties. But I appeal to all who know the laws of Castile and the rules of Spanish knighthood, whether I swerved from the path of honour by delivering up the towns to their and my *natural* queen, whose crown you gave back when you put her away. Alas! that I should have to blush for my country!—As for myself, though the affront which you have put on the blood of our kings might be supposed to cancel all former obligations, I will have no traitor in future times screen himself behind the name of Peranzúles. Let those whom Fortune may compel to decide between the rights of contending sovereigns—those who, to be just, must be faithless—learn the only price at which they can save both conscience and honour. I have delivered my trust to the right owner, and now give up my life to whom I pledged it."

The King beckoned his knights under a wide-spread oak, whose shade had often been cast over his ancestors while debating the interests of their infant kingdom. Resentment was still stirring in his bosom: but the unanimous voice of his nobles, in favour of Peranzúles, restored the complete ascendancy of his generous mind. They all declared that, by the laws of knightly honour in Spain, the Castilian was guiltless. The King might take his life as a forfeiture; but could not blame, nor reproach him as a criminal.

Alphonso, opening a way through the circle of knights within which he had held his council, came to where the Lord of Valladolid stood alone, holding the rope with as firm a grasp, as if he clung to it over the stormy sea. It was, indeed, the only stay which, in his view, could keep him from sinking into shame. The King did not speak till he had clasped the venerable warrior in his arms. "Peranzúles, (he said) thou hast been a judge between contending crowns, and judged honourably and truly. Let none, however, assume that proud office, who cannot, like yourself, face him whom he has cast in judgment!"

### THE LIVING FRENCH POETS.—NO. I.

#### *De Béranger.*

PIERRE Jean de Béranger is one of those geniuses which are rare in the poetical literature of every nation, but most rare in that of France. The rules of French versification have seldom allowed its followers to display originality of thought or manner ; and while we see the prose writers of that country developing the most poetical sentiments in their unrhymed sentences, the poets, in the everlasting monotony of their verse, are prosaic to the last degree. Many reasons conspire to produce these paradoxical effects ; and the most evident are to be found in the national character. That love of finery, and exaggerated notion of grandeur and grandiloquence, so undeniable in Frenchmen, lead the great majority of their poets, of their best ones too, to follow the beaten track of their predecessors. Then the vanity of upholding the fancied dignity of the Muse ; the pride of being enrolled among the train of "faultless monsters" to which French poetry has given birth ; and the imperfect conception of the art in a country which boasts of practising it on the narrowest existing scale ;—all this unites to make French poets the willing slaves of an unexampled system of constraint. But a few of them have, from time to time, sent forth sweet notes of wildness through the bars of their cage—and De Béranger dances in his chains.

This writer is only known to the world under the humble designation of "Chansonnier." Song-writing is the line which he has wisely selected, for the display of powers fitted for the very highest walks of poetry. He thus has not only made choice of the style to which his language is best adapted, but has completely limited the attacks of national criticism. Had he chosen the tragic or the epic line, he would have at once thrown himself into the cross-fire and sharp-shooting, in which the little wits of his country are so expert. The grand labour of French criticism has ever been to give words a supremacy over thoughts ; to make refinements of idiom superior to bursts of feeling ; and to place language on the pedestal where Nature ought to be worshipped. In the spirit of this principle they have put the most ridiculous restrictions on every branch of poetical composition within their reach ; they have bowed down to an idol of imaginary perfection ; and one of the high priests of this false worship, La Harpe, has acknowledged, with an air of boasting rather than repentance, "Parmi nous le Poëte ne jouit pas du tiers de l'idiome national ; le reste lui est interdit comme indigne de lui. Il n'y a guère pour lui qu'un certain nombre de mots convenus." But the volatile spirit of song-writing rises above the atmosphere of these contemptible constraints. It admits of the whole range of the language. Few words are too low, and none too lofty, for its usage. The poet may in that line attain the liberty, which the same La Harpe imagines to have been confined to the Greek and Latin writers, of being by turns "natural without fearing to appear mean, and sublime without dreading to be thought bombastic." The songs of De Béranger are the proofs that the canons of criticism are mere nullities when genius will oppose them ; and the success of his efforts has cleared at least one path for the vigorous exercise of intellect that seeks its developement in poetry. In this point of view he has done more for the literature of France, in the space of seven or eight years, than the host of dull critics of the Academy have effected against it for above a century.

The importance in France of this apparently most humble line of poetry must be well understood, to make us comprehend the amazing popularity of De Béranger. To come to such an understanding, we must divest ourselves of all our own national notions on the subject; for with us the thing is not felt. Music bears away from poetry (with few exceptions) the whole interest of this species of composition, as may be clearly accounted for by the perusal of the doggrel words which disgrace our best English melodies. The author who exclaimed, "Give to any one the making of a nation's laws, so I have the writing of its songs," must have had, as well as a high notion of his own poetical powers, some particular views not expressed in his so-often-quoted sentence; for, if it referred to any country but France, we see no profound wisdom in its application. But there the song is indeed a powerful weapon. The ancient government of that country has been wisely and wittily called "une monarchie absolue, tempérée par des chansons;" and their influence in the present state of the constitution (tempered by circumstances of a different nature) may be best learned in the consideration of the individual case before us.

Voltaire says, that, in order to succeed in song-writing, "Il faut avoir dans l'esprit de la finesse et du sentiment, avoir de l'harmonie dans le tête, ne point trop s'élever, ne point trop s'abaisser, et savoir n'être point trop long." De Béranger probably unites all these qualities in a degree superior to any of his predecessors; but if he has sometimes gone beyond the limits here prescribed, if occasionally he has raised himself above the level here laid down, if his modesty has induced him to give the name of songs to strains of bolder flight, it would be a rigorous critic indeed who would turn into a reproach the character given of such productions in these words of Benjamin Constant, "Béranger fait des odes sublimes, quand il ne croit faire que des simples chansons." It is universally allowed in France that this writer has surpassed all his rivals. That, independent of the elevation of thought and style, of the generous philanthropy and pure patriotism which are properly his own, he combines the ease of Blot, the joyous tone of Collé, and the flowing naiveté of Panard. It is difficult to find any parallel for him in his own country. He resembles, perhaps, La Fontaine more than any other of the French poets, but that chiefly in the ease and gracefulness of his diction; for there are many distinctive points in their separate styles, in which it would be impossible to trace any analogy. Nor should we be more successful in attempting a comparison between De Béranger and foreign writers. We might trace a resemblance in some particular poems to those rapid transitions of Horace, from the loftiest flights to the graceful utterance of some moral or familiar sentiment. Like Tibullus, who pauses in the midst of his amorous transports to sing of his death, Béranger in one of his songs, "Le Bon Vieillard," has outstripped Time, to anticipate the advance of age, and to bring before us, in a manner at once tender and striking, the recollections and regrets which, for the sake of literature and his friends, we rejoice to see in such a distant perspective. Similitudes may be sought for him in our own country. We have remarked some shallow efforts of this kind. That which compares him to Moore has been certainly the most unhappy, for of all writers he resembles him the least. De Béranger has nothing whatever of the voluptuous tenderness and elegant versification of the author of Lalla Rookh. We never find his songs depending on the grace of a metaphor or the *tournure* of a phrase. He has something infinitely more natural and manly, if less finished and seductive. There is a reason and a philosophy in his style, that savours more of sense than sentiment—more of the mind than the heart—a distinction which physiologists who give *all* the honour to the head will scarcely comprehend, unless they make broad allowance for a fanciful illustration of a poetical subject. But lest what we have said might be construed into a denial of tenderness to De Béranger, we express our full coincidence in the following summary given by a French critic of the qualities of his poetry. "Every true-born affection, every generous sentiment, benevolence, toleration, philosophy, respect for the laws, belief in a Supreme Being, sublimity of mind, are as evident in the verses of Béranger as they are deep-rooted in his heart; but patriotism is the ardent passion which appears to govern it supremely."

Vivacity of expression, joined to considerable force of thought, are the chief characteristics of De Béranger's songs. His weightiest ideas are presented to us with a surprising elasticity of language. When he is satisfied to trifle with a frivolous subject, some word or phrase of mingled vivacity and shrewdness is sure to be found, as if involuntarily, in its natural place; but in many of his more serious pieces, when some deep thought lies hidden under a surface of gaiety, the expression has invariably a suitable elevation. But even when indulging in the boldest images, he rarely loses that familiar air which renders his bitterest satires so palatable, which has gained him the merit of bringing the ode within the comprehension of the vulgar, and secured for him the title of " the Poet of the People." He has, moreover, the uncommon merit of putting nothing useless into a style which we might think forced, from its very nature, to have recourse to superfluities. Every verse seems to contain some thought or image; and, what is little common to song-writers, he has the art of convincing without making use of any of the usual forms of argument. There is at once a precision and a picturesqueness in the terms which he employs, and an amazing aptness in their application—an animation and piquancy, which harmonize well with the originality of his thoughts, and gracefully adapt themselves to all the varieties of his subject. And in remarking the faults of this writer, we find them, with few exceptions, those of his subjects, not of his mind. These being, for the most part, chosen for their familiarity, seem naturally to lead to occasional negligence. In the freedom of his diction, he sometimes falls from *naïveté* to triviality, a distance no greater than from the sublime to the ridiculous; and he occasionally appears to write less for the people than the populace; or, to express my meaning by a phrase of Mercier, when speaking of one of the leading orators of the Convention, " En voulant être populaire, il est quelquefois *populacier*."

With regard to the graver charges which have been advanced against De Béranger, and which apply to his opinions as a man, rather than his qualities as a poet, we wish to leave them untouched. In an examination of his writings, we do not conceive it necessary to enter into an inquisition on his principles; and we think that a just notion of his literary merit may be obtained, without an analysis of his religious and political creed. The intolerant spirit of party may delight to peer into the recesses of men's minds, and drag forth the secret of their abstract opinions. But we hold this utterly unjustifiable in candid literary enquiry. The private conduct of a public writer has rarely much connexion with his works; and even if it has, even when we may trace the analogy between his life and opinions, it is of little importance to the world, which is rarely benefited by isolated examples of good or ill, although sensibly affected by the writings of the man, whose personal influence is as nothing. But should our opinion be ineffectual to stop this evil of modern criticism; should the desire, so natural to mankind, of scrutinizing the conduct of our neighbours, prevail over the suggestions of a considerate reserve, we believe there does not exist an individual who might more fearlessly court the scrutiny than the subject of our present notice. He is a man of exemplary conduct in the limited sphere to which he has voluntarily circumscribed himself. Of simple manners and most frugal habits, he possesses at once a generous, philosophic, and highly independent mind, as exemplified in his frequent refusal of the proffered benefits of a numerous circle of friends, as well as in other points of conduct which will be noticed hereafter.

It is not, however, our purpose to hold up the songs of De Béranger as invulnerable to the censures of moral, any more than literary, criticism. We consider them, on the contrary, to contain occasional passages highly offensive to the rigorous notions of a large portion of society; and some few songs, which the most tolerant reader would willingly erase from the book. To specify these, is an easy task. "La Bacchante," "Ma Grand'mère," "Margot," "Le Soir des Noces," "Le Bon Dieu." These five songs, deducted from the one hundred and sixty-three which compose the two published volumes, and occasional purifications in a few of those which remain, would remove every cause of censure, and render the republication of the work in this country highly desirable. But even for the fault of publishing these pieces, excuses may be fairly found in the consideration of the author's situation in life. A man like Béranger, self-educated, thrown in his tenderest years upon the world, and that the world of revolutionary disorganization, may well find absolution for those scanty offences, for which he had ample precedents in the compositions of many a noble and cassocked author of his own country, from the Duke de Nivernais to Cardinal Bernis. It must also be recollected, that the song in France has always been a licensed vehicle for the utterance of sentiments which might be thought to pass the bounds of strict decorum; a "chartered libertine," for which no latitude was held excessive, and no subject sacred. De Béranger was the first author in this line, whose uncommon powers brought its privileges into hazard; and it will be seen, from the following short biographical sketch, that the trial in his person was less an individual attack, than a serious question discussed between the crown and the nation.

It is not often that the composition of a poet offers in a couple of short stanzas, the most leading details of his birth, parentage, and education. An unpublished song of De Béranger, highly admired in Paris for its modesty and its poetical merit, commences thus; and our readers need not fear its being spurious, for we copy it from the author's manuscript.

Dans ce Paris, plein d'or et de misère,
En l'an du Christ mil-sept-cent-quatre vingt,
Chez un tailleur, mon pauvre et vieux grand-père,
Moi, nouveau né, sachez ce qu'il m'advint.
Rien ne prédit la gloire d'un Orphée
A mon berceau, qui n'etait pas de fleurs ;
Mais mon grand-père, accourant à mes pleurs,
Me trouve un jour dans les bras d'une fée.
Et cette fée, avec de gais refrains,
Calmait le cri de mes premiers chagrins.

Le bon vieillard lui dit, l'âme inquiete,
" A cet enfant quel destin est promis ?"
Elle repond. "Vois le sous ma baguette,
Garçon d'auberge, imprimeur, et commis.
Un coup de foudre ajoute à mes presages :
Ton fils atteint, va perir consumé ;
Dieu le regarde, et l'oiseau ranimé.
Vole, en chantant, braver d'autres orages."
Et puis la fée, avec de gais refrains,
Calmait le cri de mes premiers chagrins.

To this information, that he was born in Paris in the year 1780, that his grandfather was a tailor, he himself an attendant in an inn, (kept, we believe, by his mother,) struck by lightning in his youth, apprenticed to a printer, and subsequently a clerk in a public office, little is to be added of De Béranger's early life. He has been heard to say that he learned to read he scarcely remembers how ; but that the first books he studied were the Bible, and a translation of Homer. In these volumes consisted the whole library of the "Auberge," and it may be conceived how powerfully such studies must have aided to fix the bias of so poetical a mind. In the printing-office he had a wider field for improvement. He there learned the rules of his mother tongue, its orthography and versification—and beyond these, his knowledge of language does not extend. Neither is there any thing apparent in his songs to make us suppose him a man of extensive reading, beyond the volume of the human mind. *That* he has deeply studied ; and for his admirable commentaries upon it, we cheerfully dispense with a display of learning,—for pedantry would be, to poetry such as his, a gloomy shadow thrown across the face of a bright portrait of life and manners.

In his humble station of clerk in the office of public instruction, he found leisure for the composition of some of those songs which have since become so celebrated. He was in the habit of singing these productions in the society of his friends, and they soon got abroad. " Le Senateur" and " Le Roi d'Yvetot"—the first, a bitter satire against the corruption and subserviency of senators—the latter, a not less keen attack upon the Emperor,—were particularly popular ; and it is said, that Napoleon laughed at the wit of the lesson, by which he failed to profit. Lucien Bonaparte, the great patron of letters of his day, had heard of De Béranger, and became his protector. Upon the voluntary exile of Lucien, the poet was desirous of proving his gratitude by the dedication of a volume of pastoral poetry. The censors suppressed the dedication, which contained expressions little palatable to the Imperial taste. De Béranger on this abandoned his intention, and his Idyls remain to this day unpublished. When Napoleon lost his empire for the first time, the noise of his fall was not echoed by the muse of De Béranger. He scorned to libel, when in misfortune, him whom he had satirized in the fulness of his power. Quietly fulfilling the duties of his station, he saw the return of the Emperor, but he did not profit by his temporary success. He was offered during the hundred days the office of censor, a place of considerable emolument and influence, but little suited to the free and liberal turn of his mind. He unhesitatingly refused it. In the year 1815, during the occupation of France by the Allies, he was prevailed on to publish a small volume of songs. Its success was prodigious; and although it contained several of those afterwards selected for prosecution, they did not then attract the vengeance of the ministers. With his celebrity came its natural consequence—improvement. He wrote new songs, each one better than the other. Subjects of the most inviting nature presented themselves in the political tergiversation, and the revival of religious excess, which every day became more evident. De Béranger seized on such topics, and made the chastisement of the offenders his peculiar province. The government became indignant, and the "Chansonnier" was deprived of his place. But there never was a more perfect triumph prepared for a literary man, than this *destitution* procured for its intended victim. His cause was at once espoused as national, and he, pronounced a martyr. His private friends, a numerous party, rallied round him, and the public joined in circles of increasing extent, till the whole surface of society was ruffled by the wide-spreading eddies of discontent, emanating from him who floated buoyantly on the troubled waters. A new edition of his songs was announced, with an additional volume. Ten thousand copies were printed, and instantly sold. The prosecution of the author was resolved on; the suppression of the work commanded; and the discovery of *four* copies rewarded the zeal of the police. De Béranger was brought to trial on four separate charges, namely, for having outraged morality, insulted religion, offended the King's person, and excited the public to sedition. Fourteen songs were selected to bear out these charges. [*] The interest created was quite unparalleled. The court was crowded to an excess scarcely before witnessed; and the powers of the counsel employed in the prosecution and defence were exerted to the utmost. The result was, the acquittal of the accused on the first and third charges, and his conviction on the second and fourth, by a majority of the jurors (conformably to the French law) of seven to five; but it was discovered by the judges, after the jury returned their verdict, that the fourth charge (which was literally " d'avoir provoqué au port public d'un signe extérieur de ralliement non autorisé par le Roi") was not qualified as an offence by the

---

[*] La Bacchante; Ma Grand'mère; Margot; Deo gratias d'un Epicuréen; La descente aux Enfers; Les Capucins; Les Chantres de Paroisse; Les Missionnaires; Le Bon Dieu; La Mort du Roi Christophe; Le Prince de Navarre; La Cocarde blanche; L'Enrhumé; Le Vieux Drapeau.

criminal code. De Béranger then stood only liable to punishment on the second charge, " d'avoir commis le délit d'outrage à la morale public et religieuse ;" and his sentence for this offence was, three months' imprisonment, a fine of 500 francs, (20*l.*), and the suppression of his work.

The announcement of so slight a penalty on charges so serious, the small majority of the jury by which he was convicted, and the general feeling that the attack was prompted much less by respect for religion and "bonnes mœurs" than by political malice, left De Béranger and his friends no triumph to desire. He enjoyed his imprisonment and paid his fine; for the first was a continued fête, and his wealthy friends showered offers upon him, which, if accepted, would have repaid his forfeited francs a thousand-fold. But he declined all assistance. The profits of his publication produced a sum which gives him an annual income of about 80*l.*, and on this he lives independent, respectable, and content. He has written but little since his trial. An occasional Song escapes him, as it were, without effort; and if he does not court, he has too much gallantry to decline, the visits of the willing Muse.

In the spirit of this independence De Béranger passes his days. The soundness of his judgment causes him to be consulted in almost every important question, by several of the leading members of the *Coté Gauche;* and he is not more valued in public as a poet, than in his private circle as a politician. Literary friends continually urge him to write, and we may safely say that all parties look anxiously for the publication of those Idyls already alluded to, and which are pronounced to be admirable by many competent judges to whom they have been shewn. It is natural to suppose that a man, who possesses so much conversational talent, and who is so intently listened to, has had many of his sayings recorded. We shall content ourselves with citing one of these. When urged to compose a song against a celebrated statesman then in disgrace, he replied, "à la bonne heure, quand il sera ministre." We should be glad to see this reply reprinted in as many multiplications as the copies of his songs, which are altogether, including the editions of Bruxelles and Geneva, 35,000.

In conclusion we have only to say, that though we could wish to give the reader an idea of De Béranger in an English translation, we feel the difficulty of the task, and the probability of our failure if we should attempt it. But we shall give one specimen in the original:—

### Le Vieux Drapeau.

De mes vieux compagnons de gloire,
   Je viens de me voir entouré.
Nos souvenirs m'ont enivré;
   Le vin m'a rendu la mémoire.
Fiers de mes exploits et de leurs,
   J'ai mon drapeau dans ma chaumière.
Quand secoûrai-je la poussière
Qui ternit ses nobles couleurs ?

Il est caché sous l'humble paille
   Où je dors pauvre et mutilé;
Lui qui, sûr de vaincre, a volé
   Vingt ans de bataille en bataille !

Chargé de lauriers et de fleurs,
　Il brilla sur l'Europe entière.
Quand secoûrai-je la poussière, &c.

Ce drapeau payait à la France
　Tout le sang qu'il nous a coûté.
Sur le sein de la liberté
　Nos fils jouaient avec sa lance.
Qu'il preuve encore aux oppresseurs
　Combien la gloire est roturière.
　　　　　　　　Quand, &c.

Son aigle est resté dans la poudre,
　Fatigué de lointains exploits:
Rendons-lui le coq des Gaulois,
　Il sut aussi lancer la foudre.
La France, oubliant ses douleurs,
　Le rebénira libre et fière.
　　　　　　　　Quand, &c.

Las d'errer avec la victoire,
　Des lois il deviendra l'appui.
Chaque soldat fut, grâce à lui,
　Citoyen au bord de la Loire.
Seul il peut voiler nos malheurs,
　Déployons-le sur la Frontière!
　　　　　　　　Quand, &c.

Mais il est là près de mes armes:
　Un instant osons l'entrevoir.
Viens, mon Drapeau! Viens, mon espoir!
　C'est à toi d'essuyer mes larmes.
D'un guerrier qui verse des pleurs,
　Le Ciel entendra la prière.
Oui, je secoûrai la poussière
Qui ternit tes nobles couleurs!

G

---

## ACCOUNT OF AN APPARITION,

*Seen at Star-Cross, in Devonshire, the 23d July, 1823.*

" 'Tis true, 'tis certain, man, though dead, retains
Part of himself; th' immortal mind remains:
The form subsists without the body's aid,
Aërial semblance and an empty shade."
　　　　　　　　　　　　　　　　Pope.

I am perfectly aware of the predicament in which I am placing myself, when in the present age of incredulity I venture to commit to paper, in all sincerity of spirit and fulness of conviction, a deliberate and circumstantial account of an Apparition. Impostor and visionary, knave and fool, these are the alternate horns of the dilemma on which I shall be tossed with sneers of contempt, or smiles of derision; every delusion practised by fraud or credulity, from the Cock-lane Ghost, down to the Reverend Mr. Colton, and the Sampford Spectre, will be faithfully registered against me, and I shall be finally dismissed, according to the temperament of the reader, either with a petulant rebuke for attempting to impose such exploded superstition upon an enlightened public; or with a sober and friendly recommendation to get my head shaved, and betake myself to some place of safe custody with as little delay as may be. In the arrogance of my supposed wisdom, I should myself, only a few weeks ago, have probably adopted one of these courses towards any other similar delinquent, which will secure me from any splenetic feeling, however boisterous may be the mirth, or bitter the irony, with which I may be twitted and taunted for the following narration. I have no sinister purposes to answer, no particular creed to advocate, no theory to establish; and writing with the perfect conviction of truth, and the full possession of my faculties, I am determined not to suppress what I conscientiously believe to be facts, merely because they may militate against received opinions, or happen to be inconsistent with the ordinary course of human experience.

The author of the Essay on the Nature and Immutability of Truth, represents Berkeley as teaching us, " that external objects are nothing but ideas in our minds; that matter exists not but in our minds; and that, independent of us and our faculties, the earth, the sun, and the starry heavens have no existence at all; that a lighted candle is not white, nor luminous, nor round, nor divisible, nor extended; but that for any thing we know, or can ever know to the contrary, it may be an Egyptian pyramid, the King of Prussia, a mad dog, the island of Madagascar, Saturn's ring, one of the Pleiades, or nothing at all." If this be a faithful representation of Berkeley's theory, it may be adduced as a striking illustration of the perversity of human reason, that such a man shall be deemed a philosopher, and persuade bishops and divines, in spite of the evidence of their senses, to adopt his notions, and deny the existence of matter; while the poor wight, who, in conformity to the evidence of *his* senses, maintains the existence of disembodied spirit, is hooted and run down as a driveller and a dotard. Dr. Johnson's argument, that the universal belief in ghosts, in all ages and among all nations, confirms the fact of their apparition, is futile and inconclusive; for the same reasoning would establish the truth of necromancy, witchcraft, idolatry, and other superstitions; but the opposers of this belief not only brand as impostors all those who relate their own experiences of its confirmation; they not only repudiate the Agatho-dæmon of Socrates, and slight the averment of Scripture, that Saul desired the Witch of Endor to raise up the spirits of those whom he should name; but they deny even the possibility of the fact. To admit a posthumous existence in the next world, and reject the competency of nature to accomplish a similar mystery in *this*, is surely an unwarranted limitation of her powers. Who shall circumscribe the metamorphoses of our being? When we start from the ante-natal void into existence, the change is certainly wonderful; but it is still more strange, startling, and incomprehensible, when we quit life in the fulness of intellect, and return into the invisible world. In the first case, we advance from nonentity to a very confined state of consciousness, to an animal existence, for an infant has no mind. That celestial portion of our system is evolved by the painful elaboration of time and of our own efforts; it requires a series of years to perfect its inscrutable developement; and is this sublime image and emanation of the Deity to be suddenly, instantly, degraded into a clod of earth, an inert lump of matter, without undergoing any intermediate state of existence between death and final resurrection? Abstract theory sanctions the supposition of Ghosts; and by what authority do we gainsay those who solemnly declare that they have beheld them? They never appear, it is urged, to more than one person at a time, which is a strong presumption of individual falsehood or delusion. How so?—this may be the law of their manifestation. If I press the corners of my eyes, I see consecutive circles of light, like a rainbow; nobody else can discern them—but will it be therefore maintained that I do not? It is notorious, that in dreams objects are presented to us with even a more vivid distinctness than they assume to the visual organ; but it would be idle to assert that those configurations were not presented to us, because they were invisible to others. Our waking eyes may indeed be made the "fools of our other senses, or else worth all the rest;"—granted; but still you may give us credit for the sincerity of our relation, for we pretend not to describe apparitions that other men have seen, but those which we ourselves have witnessed.

It may not be unimportant to remark, that so far from my being subject to the blue devils and vapours with which hypochondriacs and invalids are haunted, I possess that happy physical organization, which ensures almost uninterrupted health of body and mind, and which, in the elasticity and buoyancy of my spirit, renders the sensation of mere existence an enjoyment. Though I reside in the country, winter has for me no gloom; nature has prepared herself for its rigours; they are customary; and every thing seems to harmonise with their infliction; but for the same reason that the solitude of a town is desolating and oppressive, while the loneliness of the country is soothing and grateful, I do feel the sadness of perpetual fogs and rains in July, although they excite no melancholy feeling at the season of their natural occurrence. To see one's favourite flowers laying down their heads to die; one's plantation strewed with leaves not shaken off in the fulness of age, but beaten to earth in the bloom of youth: here a noble tree laid prostrate; and there a valuable field of corn lodged in the swampy soil (which were familiar objects in July last), is sufficient to excite melancholy associations in the most cheerful temperament. Confessing that mine was not altogether proof against their influence, and leaving to the caviller and the sceptic the full benefit of this admission, I proceed to a simple statement of the fact which has elicited these preliminary observations.

Actuated by the disheartening dulness of the scene to which I have alluded, I had written to my friend Mr. George Staples, of Exeter, requesting him to walk over some day and dine with me, as I well knew his presence was an instant antidote to mental depression, not so much from the possession of any wit or humour, as from his unaffected kindness and amiability, the exuberance of his animal spirits, the inexhaustible fund of his laughter, which was perpetually waiting for the smallest excuse to burst out of his heart, and the contagion of his hilarity, which had an instant faculty of communicating itself to others. On the day following the transmission of this letter, as I was sitting in an alcove to indulge my afternoon meditation, I found myself disturbed by what I imagined to be the ticking of my repeater; but, recollecting that I had left it in the house, I discovered the noise proceeded from that little insect of inauspicious augury, the death-watch. Despising the puerile superstitions connected with this pulsation, I gave it no farther notice, and proceeded towards the house, when, as I passed an umbrageous plantation, I was startled by a loud wailing shriek, and presently a screech-owl flew out immediately before me. It was the first time one of those ill-omened birds had ever crossed my path; I combined it with the *memento-mori* I had just heard, although I blushed at my own weakness in thinking them worthy of an association; and, as I walked forward, I encountered my servant, who put a letter into my hand, which I observed to be sealed with black wax. It was from the clerk of my poor friend, informing me that he had been that morning struck by an apoplectic fit, which had occasioned his almost instantaneous death! The reader may spare the sneer that is flickering upon his features: I draw no inference whatever from the omens that preceded this intelligence: I am willing to consider them as curious coincidences, totally unconnected with the startling apparition which shortly afterwards assailed me.

Indifferent as to death myself, I am little affected by it in others. The doom is so inevitable; it is so doubtful whether the parties be not generally gainers by the change; it is so certain that we enter not at all into this calculation, but bewail our deprivation, whether of society, protection, or emolument, with a grief purely selfish, that I run no risk of placing myself in the predicament of the inconsolable widow, who was reproached by Franklin with not having yet forgiven God Almighty. Still, however, there was something so awful in the manner of my friend's death, the hilarity I had anticipated from his presence formed so appalling a contrast with his actual condition, that my mind naturally sunk into a mood of deep sadness and solemnity. Reaching the house in this frame of thought, I closed the library window-shutters as I passed, and entering the room by a glass-door, seated myself in a chair that fronted the garden. Scarcely a minute had elapsed, when I was thrilled by the strange wailful howl of my favourite spaniel, who had followed me into the apartment, and came trembling and crouching to my feet, occasionally turning his eyes to the back of the chamber, and again instantly reverting them with every demonstration of terror and agony. Mine instinctively took the same direction, when, notwithstanding the dimness of the light, I plainly and indisputably recognised the apparition of my friend sitting motionless in the great arm-chair!! It is easy to be courageous in theory, not difficult to be bold in practice, when the mind has time to collect its energies; but taken as I was by surprise, I confess, that astonishment and terror so far mastered all my faculties, that, without daring to cast a second glance towards the vision, I walked rapidly back into the garden, followed by the dog, who still testified the same agitation and alarm.

Here I had leisure to recover from my first perturbation; and as my thoughts rallied, I endeavoured to persuade myself that I had been deluded by some conjuration of the mind, or some spectral deception of the visual organ. But in either case, how account for the terror of the dog? *He* could neither be influenced by superstition, nor could his unerring sight betray him into groundless alarm, yet it was incontestable that we had both been appalled by the same object. Soon recovering my natural fortitude of spirit, I resolved, whatever might be the consequences, to return and address the apparition. I even began to fear it might have vanished; for Glanville, who has written largely on ghosts, expressly says—"that it is a very hard and painful thing for them to force their thin and tenuous bodies into a visible consistence; that their bodies must needs be exceedingly compressed, and that therefore they must be in haste to be delivered from their unnatural pressure." I returned, therefore, with some rapidity towards the library; and although the dog stood immovably still at some distance, in spite of my solicitations, and kept earnestly gazing upon me, as if in apprehension of an approaching catastrophe, I proceeded onward, and turned back the shutters which I had closed, determined not to be imposed upon by any dubiousness of the light. Thus fortified against deception, I re-entered the room with a firm step, and there in the full glare of day did I again clearly and vividly behold the identical apparition, sitting in the same posture as before, and having its eyes closed !!

My heart somewhat failed me under this sensible confirmation of the vision, but, summoning all my courage, I walked up to the chair, exclaiming with a desperate energy—"In the name of heaven and of all its angels, what dost thou seek here!"—when the figure, slowly rising up, opening its eyes, and stretching out its arms, replied—"A leg of mutton and caper-sauce, with a bottle of prime old port, for such is the dinner you promised me." "Good God!" I ejaculated, "what can this mean? Are you not really dead?" "No more than you are," replied the figure. "Some open-mouthed fool told my clerk that I was, and he instantly wrote to tell you of it; but it was my namesake, George Staples, of Castle-street, not me, nor even one of my relations, so let us have dinner as soon as you please, for I am as hungry as a hunter."

The promised dinner being soon upon the table, my friend informed me, in the intervals of his ever-ready laughter, that as soon as he had undeceived his clerk, he walked over to Star Cross to do me the same favour; that he had fallen asleep in the arm-chair while waiting my return from the grounds; and as to the dog, he reminded me that he had severely punished him at his last visit for killing a chicken, which explained his terror, and his crouching to me for protection, when he recognised his chastiser.　　　　　　　　　　　　　H.

---

## SONNET.—THE INFANT.

I saw an infant—health, and joy, and light
　　Bloom'd on its cheek, and sparkled in its eye;
　　And its fond mother stood delighted by
To see its morn of being dawn so bright.
Again I saw it, when the withering blight
　　Of pale disease had fallen, moaning lie
　　On that sad mother's breast—stern Death was nigh,
And Life's young wings were fluttering for their flight.
　　Last, I beheld it stretch'd upon the bier,
Like a fair flower untimely snatch'd away,
　　Calm, and unconscious of its mother's tear,
Which on its placid cheek unheeded lay—
　　But on its lip the unearthly smile express'd,
　　"Oh! happy child, untried, and early bless'd!"

*Reydon, Suffolk.*　　　　　　　　　　　　　　　　　　A. S.

## ADA REIS : A TALE.

Notwithstanding the very able and philosophical reasoning of the
Edinburgh Reviewers concerning the unruly tendencies towards criticism of " the age we write in," we cannot quite bring ourselves to believe that authors exist in the great scale of nature for the sole purpose of
being set up, or set down by the critics, like so many nine-pins, which stand
or fall, as the bowler goes wide of his mark, or "tips all nine" in one furious
sweeping article. We cannot indeed deny that the taste of the times should
be respected, and are fully aware that " those who live to please, must
please to live;" still less are we disposed to question the " great moral
lesson" which the " article on the press" displays ; or to doubt the sharp-
sightedness of our brethren in the North on the subject of " utility;"
but we do think it advisable in a reviewer not to make too free with
the Cayenne and mustard of vituperation, if it be only to avoid ex-
hausting the gustatory nerves of the reader, and so spoiling the market ;
and we for the most part endeavour to " do our spiriting gently," and
bear in mind that live authors have " eyes, hands, organs, dimensions,
senses, affections, and passions ;" that they "laugh when they are tickled,
and die when they are poisoned," and are " warmed and cooled by the
same winter and summer as a Christian is."

It has been said that there are very few books wholly bad ; and literary faults are scarcely to be computed as crimes against society (the
case of libel, of course, being duly excepted): although, therefore, it
may be necessary that reviews should now and then have " a severe
article," and give some unlucky scribbler " a good cutting up," in
order to retain the ear of the public ; yet is it neither policy nor humanity to run a muck against all author-kind, and treat every one as an
enemy who has written a book.

Having premised thus much, the reader will doubtless be prepared
to find us in a merciful mood ; and we frankly own that the production
now under consideration is one that has some claims to our lenity. First,
whatever may be thought of the matter, because its author is a woman ;
and next, because she does not write from mercenary motives ; but is
actuated, in thus publishing her labours, by a mere good-natured wish
of multiplying innocent amusement. We are no advocates for giving
the great exclusive privileges in literature, for permitting them to
abuse argument and lay down the law, on the strength of their aristocracy. To spare designing malice or tolerate dulness and pretension
in the " nobiles et tanquam nobiles" of the earth, for the sake of their
gold tassels, is a base dereliction of duty to the public ; but when all
is fair and above board, a reviewer is bound in courtesy to practise
some forbearance to those who are much better employed in writing
even a bad book, than in setting society a bad example of idleness and
dissipation ; and a critic may be permitted to consider a noble author,
as one who is anxious to make some return to the community for all
those accumulated advantages which its institutions have heaped on his
favoured head.

There is one very considerable advantage to the public attendant
upon the literary propensities of the great, which still farther tempts
us to a lenient estimate of their " doings;" and this lies in the insight

such works afford unto the character and peculiarities of high-born intellects. Very few of us are suffered to pass the magic circle within which the exclusively upper classes congregate; and the most favoured of us have but rare occasions for knowing what a great man's brains are made of. The points of view from which these favourites of fortune look down upon men and things, engender conclusions very different from those which ordinary people form on the same subjects; and as these persons exercise so wide an influence on the destinies of the species, it is good to have some means for analysing their conceptions. Shut up among themselves, or coming into contact with general society, without either giving or receiving much impulse, transacting little or no business personally, and having their most ordinary wants anticipated, those among them who take not a leading part in politics, live in a world of their own, which bears as little resemblance to this "work-a-day world" of ours, as the French Institute does to the Dom Daniel. The works, therefore, of a noble author, whether they be wise or silly, amusing or dull, good for something or for nothing (in themselves), are at least interesting as part and parcel of their author's mind, as reflections of intellects with which we must otherwise remain unacquainted, and as it were anatomic preparations of that singular variety of the human animal, which is at once so important, and so difficult to examine in the recent subject.

The fair authoress of Ada Reis, if we may judge from her writings, possesses a mind powerfully modified by the circumstances of her caste and position, and in itself not unworthy of some consideration by the philosopher. Acute, ingenious, imaginative, capable of quick and shrewd observation, with feelings as exalted as her fancy, she has yet, by the force of circumstances been so far removed from the flat realities of life, that she scarcely sees any thing as it really is. Her acquaintance with literature, though more general than her knowledge of the world, having been equally independent of necessity and business, has likewise exempted her from that mental discipline which is essential to regular composition. Her sagest pages have, therefore, a wildness or an oddity about them; and there is an inequality in her steadiest march, which betrays feelings under little command, and ideas which flow quite independently of volition.

Taking her works as a faithful index of her mind, nothing can be more *bizarre* than the nature and composition of her notions. In all that concerns the fashionable world,—that world of which the Editor of the Morning Post is the geographer,—its follies, its dissipations, its heartless inanity, and its freezing apathy, she is perfectly at home; and what she has seen, she paints with considerable fidelity, and a force occasionally approaching to that of our best novelists. Hence it is, that of all her works, Graham Hamilton will the most universally please. But beyond this sphere, her notions are the result of a miscellaneous and not very judicious reading, coloured by an imagination whose activity has found food for passions, which wealth, rank, and the peculiarities of the social epoch, would otherwise have kept in an insipid abeyance. Of the real world, of the cares, anxieties, and difficulties through which men pass in their daily efforts for subsistence, she knows nothing. Of their duties and relations she has but vague and confused conceptions, partly the fruit of that sort of early instruction which the children of the great receive, but more the creation of a heart disposed to be affectionate, and of sensibilities too prone to exaggeration; the whole perhaps a little tinctured by the philosophy of the Hannah More school. Her pages exhibit in curious and sometimes in droll points of contrast, this strange mixture of simplicity and shrewdness, of domesticity and dissipation, of wild ideality, and satirical touches of real characters and passing follies. In perusing her works, we seem to accompany her in those her rapid and frequent journeys which the daily papers daily commemorate, between Whitehall and her country villa. In the exercise of her "*modò Thebis, modò posuit Athenis*" faculty, she uses no discretion, and she passes from the fairy creations of her imagination to the impertinences and insipidities of the saloon and the ball-room, with an abruptness which to some may appear to require a clue. Her style, as unsettled as her subject, changes from grave to gay, from sentimental to satirical, according to the state of her temperament at the moment of composition. Her books, therefore, are not formed for those sage and *à plomb* persons who demand a "*cui bono?*" at every step, and require a mathematical and moral precision in all they read. In Ada Reis, indeed, the authoress has laboured hard to extract a moral; but she alone perhaps could conceive that any thing bearing upon actual life could be abstracted from personages and adventures so wild and fantastic. Those readers, however, who are less fastidious, and who pause not to inquire, "Is this probable?" "Is that in nature?" and who, without judging a work as a whole, are contented with a quick succession of melo-dramatic scenery and events, interspersed with some passages of great descriptive force, will not be disappointed in the perusal.

The story is Asiatic, and is coloured with the *diablerie* of an Arabian tale. The adventures turn on a compact with the evil powers, or at least with their magic-gifted servants; for it is not very clear which is intended. The events succeed each other with the rapidity, and with something of the wildness of a dream. They have, consequently, but little sustained interest; but amidst the most unreined extravagance of the story, there are perceptible glimpses of the human heart, which are not the less interesting because they are somewhat out of place and proportion. But the author's *fort* is evidently description. In this she occasionally exhibits powers that might be turned to a better account. In giving, therefore, a specimen of the work, we shall make our selection with a view to the illustration of this talent. The following passages are from the 10th chapter and 2d vol. and relate to the earthquake at Lima.

"Ada Reis entered, his air wild and terrified. 'Didst hear nothing?' he cried. 'Hast seen nothing?' he said, darting by her (Fiormonda.) 'Hark! again! Look, look from the casement.'

"A lurid beam burst from the dense clouds; a noise loud and terrible aroused every inhabitant of the house. Condalmar returned calm, and with a smile. The heat was intense; the forked lightning flashed along the skies; screams rent the air; the terrified slaves and menials rushed into the presence of their master kneeling and quaking. The howling of dogs was then heard; strange and dismal sounds filled the air: a sulphureous smell infected the streets: the beasts of burden, as they passed along, seemed scarcely able to sustain themselves under the loads they bore. In the market-place, in the grand square, the gardens and plains adjoining the town, the terrified inhabitants had assembled together, lamenting aloud, and saying the last day was at hand. The churches were suddenly filled; and, of whatever religion, Catholics, Protestants, Heretics, and Pagans, prostrated themselves before the altars, fearful of they knew not what danger.

"Condalmar addressed himself to Ada Reis, and proposed that before it was too late they should fly from this state of horror and alarm, and remove as quickly as possible to Callao. . . . .

"Arrived at Callao, they found the scene there, if possible, more terrific than at Lima. Never had the sun risen upon greater calamity. The whole population of the place were assembled on the beach; parents clasping their children, and husbands their wives; and all invoking Heaven for mercy and compassion.

"The night proved more sultry than the day had been; cattle and dogs traversed the country alone in wild affright. Children wept, they knew not why. Strangers inquired of each other the meaning of these terrible portents; many fled from the city and fort of Callao and betook themselves to the sea; but Ada Reis was of opinion that to attempt the sea in its present state were more dangerous than to remain on land; for the whole sky was of a purple tint, and the waves, with a still swell, seemed rising above the level of the shore. Subterraneous noises were heard the whole of the day, sometimes resembling the bellowing of oxen, and at others the discharge of artillery, or thunder rattling at a distance.

"In a short time Ada Reis joined them; and even at such a moment they could not abstain from impious raillery and profane jesting. 'Should the earth quake, I will not,' said Ada Reis. At that moment a tremendous shock threw Fiormonda forward, and in the next a concussion so violent ensued, that the building broke asunder into ruins.".... "The concussion was repeated; sulphurous flames broke forth from the bosom of the earth: then at once were heard on all sides the screams of the dying, the roaring of thunder, the wild howling of animals, the crash of churches, palaces, buildings toppling one upon another; all in a moment destroyed, and burying under them their miserable inhabitants."

In the last volume, which is in many respects inferior to the others, the authoress drops on a sudden the elevated and sustained tone of writing; and bringing her personages into a species of hell or purgatory of her own imagining, becomes at once familiar and satirical. After the manner of Dante, or rather of Quevedo, she proceeds to dispose of classes and predicaments, and in her wilfulness spares neither herself nor her friends. It is in this part of her work that she exhibits most especially a nervous sensibility to injury, that vents itself in traits and anecdotes of those with whom she is displeased. Through the whole work, indeed, we are grieved to find that the writer is evidently ill at ease. Gracious Heaven! how little is every worldly prosperity to happiness! High birth, wealth, ease, distinction, the confluence of all physical goods, with friends, relations, and admirers—are all insufficient to fill that aching void, the human heart? When every thing, which in prospect seems most desirable, conspires to render a mortal happy, there is still a waking busy devil within, to conjure up imaginary woes, to create constructive miseries, to subtilize and sophisticate, to magnify and to distort, to exaggerate expectation, and to manufacture disappointment. Let not the cold moralist, triumphant in his own composure, say that this is madness, ingratitude, fretfulness unworthy of sympathy, or folly beneath compassion. Man does not desire to be miserable, he does not seek to suffer. Ideal miseries (if those in question be ideal) are not the less miseries because they proceed from within: nor is hypochondriasis a less painful disease, because it creates its own symptoms, or holds them more remotely from external causation. Perhaps it is utterly impossible for beings of exalted sensibility to carry on to the grave the delusions of life, and to avoid a conviction of the worthlessness of the mass of mankind and of the insipidity of the bulk of existence. A contented disposition is the gift of Nature; and it should seem that it is a boon often bestowed as a compensation for the absence of splendid talents and a creative genius. It occurs at least too frequently, that where the imaginative faculties take the lead, fancy delights to dip her pencil in the gloomiest colours.    C.

---

### MIND AND BODY.

#### Veluti in Speculum.

Says Mind to Body t'other day,
  As on my chin I plied my razor,
Pray tell me—does that glass pourtray
  Your real phiz, or cheat the gazer?

That youthful face, which bloom'd as sleek
  As Hebe's, Ganymede's, Apollo's,
Has lost its roses, and your cheek
  Is falling into fearful hollows.

The crow's fell foot hath set its sign
  Beside that eye which dimly twinkles;
And look! what means this ugly line?
  Gadzooks, my friend, you're getting wrinkles!

That form which ladies once could praise,
  Would now inspire them with a panic;
Get Byron's belt, or Worcester's stays,
  Or else you'll soon be Aldermanic.

At sight of that dismantled top,
  My very heart, I must confess, aches:
Once famous as a Brutus crop,
  You now are balder than Lord Essex.

Since Wayte's decease your teeth decline:—
  Finding no beautifier near 'em,
Time's tooth has mumbled two of thine,
  Well may they call him—"*edax rerum.*"

Behold! your cheeks are quite bereft
  Of their two laughter-nursing dimples,
And pretty substitutes they've left—
  (Between ourselves) a brace of pimples!

The fashions which you used to lead,
  So careless are you, or so thrifty,
You most neglect when most you need,
  A sad mistake when nearing Fifty.—

Stop, stop, cries Body—let us pause
  Before you reckon more offences,
Since you yourself may be the cause
  Of all these dismal consequences.

The sword, you know, wears out the sheath,
  By steam are brazen vessels scatter'd;
And when volcanoes rage beneath,
  The surface must be torn and shatter'd.

Have not your passions, hopes, and fears,
    Their tegument of clay outwearing,
Done infinitely more than years,
    To cause the ravage you're declaring?

If you yourself no symptoms show
    Of age,—no wrinkles of the spirit:
If still for friends your heart can glow,
    Your purse be shared with starving merit:

If yet to sordid sins unknown,
    No avarice in your breast has started:
If you have not suspicious grown,
    Sour, garrulous, or narrow-hearted:

You still are young, and o'er my face
    (Howe'er its features may be shaded)
Shall throw the sunshine of your grace,
    And keep the moral part unfaded.

Expression is the face's soul,
    The head and heart's joint emanation;
Insensible to Time's controul,
    Free from the body's devastation.

If *you*'re still twenty, I'm no more :—
    Counting by years how folks have blunder'd!
Voltaire was young at eighty-four,
    And Fontenelle at near a hundred!        H.

---

## BOND-STREET IN SEPTEMBER.

ROUSSEAU says, that all great cities are alike; as far as my own observation extends I can confirm the remark, and yet the portrait which they exhibit is one which our first parents could hardly have been brought to comprehend. Even if that primitive pair could have contemplated the many myriads that were to descend from them, and spread over the face of the earth, they could never have imagined that in various parts of its surface a million of beings would be huddled together in one narrow voluntary prison of stone and brick, so confined that they were born and died, lived, fed, and slept, in successive layers or stories from the cellar to the garret, obtaining that accommodation for the functions of existence by mounting above one another's heads, which could never have been afforded by the superficial extent of the ground they occupied. Thousands of hecatombs of animals, brought weekly from the surrounding country for the support of this multitude, and the whole condensed population, with all the animal remains, plunged into the earth within the straitened enclosure of the walls, age upon age, generation upon generation, laid over one another until the entire mass upon which the city stands becomes a putrescent abyss of corruption and *adipocire*, like that extracted from the cemetery of the Innocents at Paris! Such are the prominent features in which all great cities resemble one another; and they are quite sufficient to make me thank Heaven that I live not immured within any such pestiferous enclosure, where the very complexion of the inhabitants seems a reflection from the pale flag of Death which is perpetually shaking before their eyes.

Notwithstanding the family likeness perceptible in all those enormous mounds and accumulations of brick and bones, flesh and furniture, men and mortar, beasts and buildings, which constitute a city; and the similarity of habits and appearances, generated by all such multitudinous congregations, there is a sufficient diversity in the appearance of each individual capital when viewed under different circumstances and seasons. Perhaps no place in the world offers so striking a contrast to itself as London in and out of the season. When I speak of London, I put entirely out of view those industrious and useful classes who, living in the *terra incognita* eastward of the Bar, labour unintermittingly for the gratification of the westward population, and of course present a monotonous activity all the year round: but who that has ever seen Bond-street in all its gaiety and glitter, in its days of clattering hoofs and sparkling equipages, when its centre forms an endless line of moving magnificence, and its gorgeous shops on either side reflect an ever-changing galaxy of belles and exquisites, would recognise the same place in the latter end of September, deserted, silent, spiritless, " so dull, so dead in look, so woe-begone," that it makes one "as melancholy as a gib-cat, or a lugged bear," to take the same walk for five minutes, which a few months before would in less space of time have evaporated the densest spleen, and possessed us with all bright, joyous, and spiritual fancies ? The ghost-looking house-painters whom one encounters here and there with their poisoned visages; the scaffoldings under which one is so often obliged to pass at the risk of lime in your eyes, and the certainty of it upon your clothes, if you are so fortunate as to escape a brickbat upon the head; the dismantled shops, and the hot, dusty, empty street, as if they were not sufficiently miserable objects in themselves, complete the prostration of our spirits by recalling their past cheerfulness, and so aggravate their present gloom. Innumerable associations connected with Bond-street lift it, in its time of glory, so completely out of its materiality that we never think of it as a mere street, and in the season of its thick throngs we have no time to compare the ideal with the real, by subjecting its buildings to the matter-of-fact judgment of the eye. One might, indeed, lose that useful organ in the process, for those members of the Pococurante society—the porters, reck not if with the sharp angles of their humeral freightage they reduce us all to a Cyclopean community : and, moreover, one's optics are kept in such perpetual activity in catching the salutations of the smiling beauties who whisk by in their vehicles, in nodding to Lord A—— and Sir Harry B——, or in cutting old General C——, or any other established bore, that he who should be caught gazing upwards at the houses would infallibly be set down for a rustic star-gazer, if he were not knocked down for a London somnambulist.

Last month, however, in the solitude and vacancy of the footpath, I thought I might safely venture to look upwards and contemplate the street in its architectural character, when, O Heavens! what a bright web of association, what a tissue of Corinthian imaginations was instantly dissolved and frittered away. It was as if I gazed upon the corpse of one whom I had known in all the bloom and beauty of vitality. An ugly, irregular, desolate, dingy, beggarly, old-fashioned succession of brown-brick tenements, stretched before me, like Falstaff's ragged regiment, forming a mean and pitiful contrast with the swaggering looks and undue pomposity of the shops. As there was at that moment no delusion of fashion to redeem the inconsistency, I amused myself with calculating how the real features of this celebrated street would affect the novel-reading misses and bonnet-buying spinsters of the country, who from the frequent reference to this scene of action, in newspapers and romances have been accustomed to invest it with something of a romantic and magnificent character. To add to my annoyance, it was one of those close, damp, sultry days, expressively termed *muggy* by the Londoners, and as my lungs panted under the hot moisture of the atmosphere, I echoed the ejaculation of the worthy farmer dying of an asthma—" If once I can get this plaguy breath fairly out of my body I'll take deuced good care it shall never get in again." As I thought of the buoyant and elastic breezes which I ought at that moment to have been enjoying in Gloucestershire, under my favourite clump of aspens, whose ever-fluttering leaves at once shaded me from the sun, and supplied me with the music of a perpetual waterfall, I felt in all its intensity the sentiment of Dante—

> " Nessun maggior dolore
> Che ricordarsi del tempo felice
> Nella miseria."

But perhaps the most pitiable and lugubrious of all the spectacles encountered at the West end in this season of emigration, are the disconsolate wights who being unable to procure an invitation to the country, and without money to get conveyed thither condemn themselves to a daily imprisonment, and steal forth in the dusk like the light-shunning bat, or the bird of Minerva, or rather, like ghosts of themselves, to haunt the spots which they loved in their days of fashion. A man must have a character to lose before he will thus submit to realise the Heautontimorumenos of Terence; but it is so easy to acquire the reputation of being " an idle fellow about town, visiting in all the genteel circles," that few West-endians and Bond-street loungers think themselves exempt from the observances which this state imposes. No condition is more sternly, more inexorably exacted by Fashion, than an absence from London in September, and it must be confessed that the wretches who are unable to comply with this mandate have at least grace enough to feel the full infamy of the stigma that attaches to their delinquency. No pickpocket has a quicker eye for a Bow-street officer, no spendthrift dandy has a keener perception of an approaching bailiff, than these victims of fashion have of an advancing acquaintance, if they are compelled to run the gauntlet of recognition beneath the garish eye of day. Reading him as far off as if he were a telegraph, they prepare all their wiles, doubles, and escapes, sometimes stealing into a shop, or bolting down a street or even a blind alley, or facing right about, so that if the enemy can even swear to their backs, he may not be able to aver that he has seen their faces in London, when its purlieus are under the ban and interdict of Fashion.

With a malicious pleasure I have occasionally amused myself in counteracting all these manoeuvres and devices by running down a side street, getting a-head of the game, and encountering him in front when he thought I was far behind; or by managing to run plump up against him at a corner, that I might observe the various degrees of

self-possession and impudence with which the different culprits carried
the thing off. Some were overwhelmed with instant shame, gave me a
confused nod, and hurried on to avoid all interrogation; but the generality adopted the approved method of conscious guilt by becoming
the attacking parties, and starting off into exclamations and surprises.
"What, Harry Seven Oaks in London? Credat Judaeus Apella!"—
then the eyes are rubbed, and after an incredulous stare the party continues—"It is Harry, by Heaven!—why, my dear fellow, have you
forgotten that this is September?—what would they say were I to mention this at H—— House, or Lord S——'s, or the Marchionets of
D——'s?" Now it is clear, that a man who attacks you in this way,
and even hints at betraying you to your noble friends, cannot himself
be in the same predicament. He must be a mere accidental traveller
over the forbidden ground; at all events, he wishes you to infer it; but
for fear you should not have ingenuity enough to draw that conclusion,
he takes care to add, that he is a mere bird of passage, having only arrived that morning from Cheltenham or Harrogate, and intending to .
set off next day for Dawlish or Sidmouth. Joe Manton, and his fellow-
gunsmith Egg, have as many charges to endure as their own fowling-
pieces, for several of my acquaintance have declared that after writing
repeated letters without effect, they had been obliged to run up
to London to reclaim their guns, which had been left to be repaired; never failing to add, in a tone of indignant reproach—
"and you know pheasant shooting begins in ten days!" One friend
had thrown himself into the London mail upon learning the dangerous
illness of an uncle, from whom he had considerable expectations, and
whom he accused of a scandalous want of consideration for falling sick
at the time of the County races. Another, who was the indisputable
author of some very ingenious charades in rhyme, informed me with
a significant look, that a letter from his quiz of a bookseller had compelled him to run up to make certain preliminary arrangements for the
publishing season. A third poor fellow, who began to walk rather
limpingly as he specified his disaster, was under the necessity of
coming all the way from Scarborough to consult Astley Cooper, respecting the old wound he received at Talavera; and a fourth, after
frankly stating that he had never left London, declared, that he was so
tired of all the bathing-places and the different noblemen's seats of
which he had the run, that he was determined, for once and away, to
pass an autumn in London, out of fun and novelty, and just to see what
the thing was like.

Love of the country is with me a passion which has sprung up as the
others subsided; perhaps a certain age is necessary for its full and
sufficing fruition, before one can feel assured that if we walk out into
the fields, look forth upon the green earth, the blue sky, and the dashing waters, and so put ourselves in communion with Nature and the unseen spirit of the universe, we shall infallibly tranquillize our bosoms,
however agitated, by imparting to them the blandness and serenity of
the surrounding landscape. If we become less social as we advance
in life, we certainly sympathize more with nature, a substitution of
which few will find reason to complain. The coxcombs of whom I
have been writing had none of this feeling; they loved London rather
than the country; yet they hated it so much when it was under the

proscription of fashion that they invented all sorts of ingenious lies to apologize for their presence. Strange inconsistency! that a man should deem it more respectable to be a liar than to be accounted poor; more strange still, that an Englishman who boasts so much of his liberty and resists with so much pertinacity the smallest encroachment upon his free agency, should voluntarily become the slave of the most capricious of all despots—Fashion.

---

### THE PHYSICIAN.—NO. X.

#### On the Power of Habit.

If any one would instruct mankind in the art of preserving health and attaining longevity, without having occasion to submit to the numerous rules laid down by physicians for the regulation of their conduct in regard to these points, let him teach them the secret of habituating themselves to every thing. Custom permits those who place themselves under her protection to live as they please, and bestows health and long life at the cheapest rate. She marches in triumph over the tables inscribed with the laws of physicians, and shows her votaries that they may enjoy health, while pursuing a way of life, which, according to Hippocrates, must speedily and infallibly precipitate them into the grave. Custom, nevertheless, operates agreeably to the principles of medicine, and serves rather to confirm than to invalidate them, as will be manifest to every one who forms correct notions on the subject.

Habit, or custom, for I shall use these terms indiscriminately, is not a property of mere mechanical machines. A watch, for instance, cannot be accustomed to any thing: animal machines alone are susceptible of this quality. These machines are moved by the senses and by perceptions: and herein consists the whole secret of habit. Sense, which resides in the nerves, when communicated to the brain, produces in the soul perceptions or feelings; and both this sensibility of the nerves and these perceptions of the soul cause movements in the machine that are sometimes voluntary, and at others of a different nature. Metaphysicians assert, that perceptions frequently repeated in the soul, gradually become more and more faint, and at length so weak that it is much the same as if they never took place. Often-repeated sensations which the soul feels strongly at first, cease in time to produce any impression upon it; and in this case we say that we are accustomed to such sensations. But though the perceptions of the soul cease to make that impression on the brain which once occasioned the movements that accompany the perceptions, still the sensibility of the nerves alone, without the co-operation of perceptions, is capable of effecting the same movements, agreeably to the laws of sense. In this case, sense alone, without any consciousness and perception of the soul, after it has been very frequently produced in the nerves, gives rise to actions and movements,—which at first never took place without consciousness and without perceptions in the soul. We then say, that we are accustomed to certain actions, to certain movements, that they have become mechanical to us. The nerves themselves may, by frequently-repeated impressions, gradually lose their sensibility, and then we are not only accustomed to the sensations, because such a nerve has ceased to communicate perceptions to the soul; but the actions and movements of the machine, which used to accompany the perceptions and the sensibility excited in this nerve, also cease to take place, because the moving power, sense, is annihilated in the nerve. Thus we are enabled by habit to endure more, and are secured from the effects of certain sensations, which used infallibly to attend those sensations. We thus escape the troubles and dangers, which many sensations would bring in their train, if we were not accustomed to them. Whoever is capable of reflecting a little, will easily be able to deduce the numerous examples of the power of habit recorded in the sequel from these principles, which I shall not do, because it is not my intention to treat the reader with speculations, but with practical remarks on habit, that each may thence learn to determine the application of this animal property to his own particular case.

It is common to use the expression, that a person is accustomed to something, in an improper signification. Of a person, who by degrees learns to see distinctly in the dark, we say, he is accustomed to darkness, while in fact it is only his soul that feels more acutely and discriminates more precisely. As the muscles of the body become stronger by frequent exercise, and capable of moving greater loads; we say of persons who have thus increased their strength, that they are accustomed to hard labour, whereas they have only acquired vigour in a physical manner, as a magnet by degrees becomes capable of supporting a heavier object, and as a young tree that is bent will raise a greater weight the stronger it becomes by its growth. Thus, too, it is the practice to say of the movements which we learn to perform with greater celerity, that we have acquired it by habit, though the real state of the case is, that machines employed in the constant repetition of the same movements, become more supple and pliant, and in time overcome many little obstacles; for it is well known that a machine composed of many wheels goes much more easily and smoothly when it has been worked for some time, than it did at first. This mode of expression, how erroneous soever, we are now compelled to adopt; and as in the sequel of this paper, I shall include all these cases among customs, I would merely remark for the information of my speculative readers, that they must not seek to account for these customs, improperly so called, according to the laws of sense, but on physical principles.

It will now be easy to perceive how far the instances of the power of habit are from invalidating the general doctrines of medicine. Physicians warn every one against exposure of the chest, and threaten those who disregard their admonitions with catarrhs and inflammatory fevers. Such, indeed, are the consequences of that degree of cold which prevents the circulation of the juices and causes obstructions. Nevertheless, a female with open bosom shall brave a cold sufficient to freeze twenty young men, without sustaining any injury. Is this any refutation of us? By no means. The principle remains true, that cold occasions obstructions, catarrhs, and inflammations. But the degree of cold which produces these results in thousands, has not the same power over the lady, because the nerves of her bosom are inured to it, and it has no more effect upon her than a cook-air would have upon the others.

"For this reason I was justified in commencing the present paper by asserting, that the way to endure without inconvenience what physicians consider as dangerous, is to accustom ourselves to every thing. To illustrate this position, I will go through the principal things to which we may habituate ourselves; that I may at the same time have an opportunity of adding some remarks serviceable to such as think fit to choose this convenient way for preserving health and attaining long life, contrary to all the rules of the science.

A few general rules must be premised. Though Celsus has remarked, that people ought to accustom themselves to every thing, that they may not sink under every trivial accident, still he advises a good choice in the things to which they should strive to become habituated. Gardens, fields, the city, the water, the chace, are all praised by him, but he recommends exercise in preference to repose. Thus there are things to which people must not accustom themselves, because it is more beneficial to life and health that they should not acquire this facility. As habit does away with the effects of certain sensations and perceptions, so it can also annihilate such effects as are conducive to health. Indolent repose weakens the animal powers; it is, therefore, better that it should be oppressive to us, that we may avoid it, than that we should learn by habit to endure it. This observation applies to numberless other cases. When we have accustomed ourselves to a hundred things, still a thousand others are left to which we are not accustomed, and which, on account of our being habituated to the former, we cannot bear without the greater danger. Whoever has habituated himself to digest coarse food, is attacked with fever, if he is confined to a light delicate diet. It would, therefore, have been more serviceable to him if he had not accustomed himself solely to hard fare. Well then, you will reply, let people habituate themselves to opposites, to cold and heat, to heavy and light food, &c. But it should be known that this is not always practicable; and it is the more dangerous to accustom ourselves to some things only. Great caution is therefore necessary, in the choice of the things to which people strive to habituate themselves, and they ought, moreover, to consider the whole state of the body, and all the circumstances in which they are at present, or may in future chance to be. Nay, more—habit extends only to the animal nature; all the parts of the mechanism of the human body do not belong to this nature, though they are requisite for health and life. There are, of course, circumstances in human life, which the power of habit cannot control, because they are not within its domain. Blood when obstructed, tends to putrefaction, and habit cannot prevent this, because it is a merely physical, but not an animal effect. It is, therefore, proper to guard against such habits, the consequences of which extend to the physical nature of the human body, where they are no longer under its control. On account of the great complication of the animal with the mechanical and physical changes in animals, the cases, indeed, are rare, in which any thing of this kind could happen. Their bare possibility, however, demonstrates, that he would act very unwisely, who should imagine, that he ought to be able to accustom himself to every thing, or who should be weak enough to suffer himself to be persuaded by the authority of old adages, that there is nothing in nature to which people may not habituate themselves; that, what one has accustomed himself to, another may; and that by habit we may produce a complete revolution in nature. These much too general maxims are as false as it would be to assert, that we ought not to accustom ourselves to any thing; that habit does not enable us to endure more than what nature is capable of enduring without it, since the weakest person, in particular things to which he has accustomed himself, is stronger than the most robust man; that we cannot wean ourselves from any thing that has once become natural; or, that we ought to wean ourselves from such things only as are troublesome.

It is, moreover, to be observed, that no habit is to be acquired suddenly, but only by long practice. We ought not, therefore, to rely upon it too early, and to expose ourselves to dangers which we are not yet capable of enduring. This indiscretion costs many their lives. When they have several times indulged in irregularities or excesses with impunity, they become bold, and venture once more at an unlucky moment to repeat them, under the idea that habit has rendered them harmless.

The safest habits are those which we have acquired, not of ourselves, but through the management of those who had the care of us in our tenderest infancy. Adults find it more difficult, and the aged very rarely succeed, in gaining new habits. For the sick and persons of weak constitutions, it is never advisable to attempt to acquire new habits, or to relinquish old ones, whether in themselves beneficial or pernicious. Paul Jovius says of the physician of Pope Clement VII., named Curtius, that he was considered as being to blame for his death, because he persuaded his Holiness, who, though yet a hearty man, was advanced in years, to adopt a more regular way of living than he had previously been accustomed to. The same animadversion is passed by Onuphrius Panvinius, on the physician of Pope Julius III., who was affected with the gout; though others are of opinion, that he brought upon himself the fever of which he died by feigning indisposition, from reasons of state, and, to save appearances, taking lighter food than he had been used to do. Galen expressly forbids the attempting of any alteration, even in bad habits, during illness, and relates a case in point. A certain Aristotle of Mytilene, had never drank cold water, but was attacked with a disease in which it was thought necessary for him to take it. The patient declared his conviction that it would produce spasms, and appealed to an instance of the kind within his own knowledge; he nevertheless strove, for his benefit, as he thought, to overcome habit. He drank the water, and died. So essential is it, that physicians themselves should be guided by the habits of their patients; and upon this is grounded the maxim of those who assert, that they will not have any physician, who is not acquainted with the nature of their constitution. This nature is made up chiefly of their habits; and that Celsus was perfectly right when he observed, that no physician could be so serviceable to a patient as one who was at the same time his intimate friend.

So much for general rules! Let us now consider the principal and the most common things over which habit can acquire dominion, and we shall be astonished what it is capable of effecting, when it determines to violate all the laws of medicine.

Every one knows what dangers they have to apprehend who live in an unwholesome air. Habit, however, can enable people to endure it. Sanctorius relates, that a man, who had lived twenty years in a close dungeon, became sickly as soon as he was liberated; and that he never could regain his health, though he had the best medical advice, till he furnished occasion for his being once more confined in the same prison. I knew a female myself, who had lived so many years shut up in her apartment, that even in the finest weather she durst not open her window, because the fresh air made her faint away. Birds that have been long confined in close rooms, become sickly and die as soon as they are exposed to the air. There are people who are so habituated to a dry, and others to a damp air, that they cannot endure any other. How many travellers fall sick when they quit their own country and breathe a foreign air! How the unfortunate armies engaged in the crusades were thinned as soon as they reached the distant theatre of operations! Observations of this kind induced Paul Zacchias to advise patients to seek the air of their native country, to which they were accustomed, though it were even bad in comparison with that in which they actually were. Habit enables the hunter, as Cicero says, to pass the night upon the snow, and, in the day-time, to brave the scorching heat of the sun upon the mountains. Soldiers afford instances of the same kind. Vegetius remarks that the most experienced generals have exercised their troops in snow and rain, in consequence of which they have remained healthy while in camp, and been rendered vigorous and persevering in battle. I might also adduce in evidence our stage-coachmen who travel day and night in all weathers: nay, our labourers, our farming-men, and in particular the trampers, some of whom scarcely know what it is to lodge in a house, prove every day by their example, that the most inclement weather has no effect upon them. In their case, however, a few circumstances are to be considered. Most of these persons are the offspring of robust parents, and from their infancy have been exposed to all the vicissitudes of the seasons. Such as have perished in their apprenticeship, if I may so term it, are not taken into the account; and even those who are most inured to hardships are often suddenly attacked by diseases which consign them to the grave. If, therefore, people are to be so brought up as to be rendered extremely hardy, a large proportion of them must be expected to perish in the attempt. The Ostiaks, who rove about in the northern parts of Siberia, and can withstand all weathers, would no doubt be more numerous, if they were not so hardly bred. It is easy to imagine how many of them must perish, if the women, according to Weber's account, bring forth their children during their excursions, in the open air, and immediately after their birth sometimes plunge them into the snow, at others put them into their warm bosoms, and in this manner pursue their route with them. Such as survive this treatment, indeed, are so much the more hardy. A Tartar infant, which has stood the test of being plunged, just after its birth, into water, through a hole made in the ice, an Ostiak, or a Russian, will afterwards experience no inconvenience, when, on arriving at manhood, he runs naked out of the hot bath and leaps into the river which is full of floating ice: on the contrary, this is to him an agreeable refrigerant. All the hardy persons who triumph over Nature, have laid the foundation of their robust constitution in the first years of infancy, when nobody cared whether they lived or died. From being thus hardly brought up, the Laplanders, the Swiss, and the peasantry of almost every country, can defy the vicissitudes of the weather, scarcely feel the severest cold, and are rendered capable of enduring the fatigues of war. Hence it is evident that these people are not fit models for the imitation of persons descended from less hardy progenitors, and who have been more delicately reared.

The most offensive effluvia, which delicate persons cannot endure, are frequently a refreshment to those who are accustomed to them. Vega cured a seaman who was thrown into an almost fatal swoon by the savoury smells of a grand entertainment, by causing him to be laid on the beach and covered with mire and sea-weed, by which means he came to himself again in about four hours. Lemnius relates of a peasant who fainted at the smell of the drugs in an apothecary's shop, that he recovered on being carried to a dunghill. Strabo has remarked that the Sabæans, who swooned at perfumes, were revived by means of burnt rosin and goats' hair. Such persons resemble the Kanaanban, who live in mud, as in their proper element; and yet we find that such hardy people are sometimes suddenly deprived of life by a violent stench.

In regard to food, it is very certain that habit can raise us above the standard of ordinary men. " Meat and drink to which we are accustomed," says Hippocrates, " agree with us, though naturally pernicious ; but not those aliments to which we are unaccustomed, though naturally wholesome :" and hence he concludes, that it is more beneficial to adhere to the same sorts of food than to change them abruptly, even though we substitute better in their stead. Alexander the Great, when in India, found it necessary to forbid his army the use of wholesome food, because it carried off the men, owing to their not being accustomed to it. So true is the observation of Celsus, that " whatever is contrary to our habits, whether it be hard or soft, is prejudicial to health."

Excess in eating and drinking may even become habitual. When Dionysius, the Sicilian tyrant, was prevented by a siege from indulging in this kind of excess, he wasted away till he was enabled to resume his habits of intemperance. Drunkards, in the morning, when sober, can scarcely stand upon their legs ; but when they return home at night intoxicated, they walk with as firm a step as the most sober of us all. Many of them continue to swill till the moment of their death, and even prolong their lives by so doing ; for to deprive them by force of their liquor would, in reality, but accelerate their end. Sanctorius advised a Hungarian nobleman to give up drinking strong wines ; but he was reduced so low by confining himself to lighter sorts, that he was absolutely obliged to return to the strong. Such habits ought not to induce any one to imitate them ; for the very practice by which they are acquired injures the constitution to such a degree, that no sooner have we gained the desired habit than we perceive how near it has brought us to a premature grave. Wepfer saw a person who could swallow melted butter by spoonfuls without injury; and I myself knew an old man, whose veracity I had no reason to doubt, who declared that he had often drunk at once a pint of melted fat without sustaining any inconvenience. Pechlin states, that some one had so accustomed himself to putrid water in Holland, that when, on account of debility of the stomach, he was advised to relinquish that beverage, he found it impossible to dispense with it, at least boiled and mixed with spice. Wine, on the other hand, was so disgusting to him, that he never could take it otherwise than diluted with water. But what person would be so mad as to accustom himself to drink melted fat or putrid water? We ought not to accustom ourselves to any thing to which we cannot become habituated but to the injury of our health and the peril of our lives.

To this class belong particularly medicines and poisons; especially as many seek either fame or benefit in habituating themselves to them. I have frequently condemned the unlucky mania of many healthy persons for taking physic; the very habit which is thus acquired is the strongest reason for desisting from the practice. According to the laws of habit, the more frequently medicines are employed, the weaker is their operation; and to what remedies shall the sick have recourse, when they have already accustomed themselves to their use in health? Experience proves these pernicious effects from all species of medicines and poisons. A cathartic frequently repeated ceases to produce any effect. Theophrastus knew a person who ate black hellebore by handfuls, without vomiting or purging. The common use of mercury renders that remedy inefficacious in the venereal disease. The men who are obliged to work in quicksilver mines are thrown in the first days into a violent salivation; when they are afterwards compelled by blows to use same, this dangerous occupation, that effect ceases, and no sooner has habit enabled them to withstand the influence of the metallic effluvia than death carries them off. Of opium I shall here say nothing, as I intend to make it the subject of a distinct paper.—A woman who had brought a consumption upon herself by the immoderate use of spirits, when reduced to the last extremity, sent for a physician; she was in a hectic fever, quite emaciated, swollen, and completely exhausted. She had been previously accustomed to drink a bottle of French brandy every day, and the physician actually found her intoxicated. He exhorted her to discontinue this practice, and her attendants were strictly forbidden to give her any spirituous liquors. She had scarcely passed a day in this forced abstinence, when all about her prepared for her speedy dissolution. She became delirious; her eyes were fixed; her cough almost choaked her; she could not sleep a wink; excessive perspiration at night, and diarrhœa in the day, exhausted her small remains of strength: she seemed no longer to see, to hear, or to feel. The doctor, who exerted all his skill for her relief, could not prevent her becoming daily worse; and though the patient earnestly solicited the indulgence of brandy, he forbade it for that reason the more strictly. She passed nine days in this state between life and death. At length her maid-servant took pity on her and gave her a bottle of brandy. She drank about a third of it at once, and the remainder in the course of the day. Her evident improvement induced her attendants to supply, before unknown, to the physician, with her usual quantity of spirits. Her delirium subsided; she recovered her senses, and talked rationally as long as she was furnished with the means of intoxication. Her cough became less troublesome; she slept well, and was able to sit up a considerable time. In this attended state she remained about a month, at the expiration of which she became insensible, and expired in two days. There are numerous instances of this kind, from which a physician may learn that, in diseases arising from habit, it is proper to relax a little in the severity of his principles. Some of these facts are related by Monro.—A man-cook, whose nose was nearly cut off, had lost a great deal of blood. He was allowed to take wine in barley-water, or whey, but he remained very weak, frequently fainted, and was troubled with head-ache. He had been accustomed to drink daily a considerable quantity of ale, wine, and spirits. At his request some ale, with a quartern of brandy, was given him, and from that time he began to mend, and continued to improve by the daily repetition of this allowance.—A man had broken his leg, and the physician confined him to milk and water and slops. He slept badly at night; his pulse was weak and quick; and he complained of thirst and head-ache. On the third day, upon a continuance of this diet, he was still sleepless and delirious; got out of bed, tore away the cradle in which the leg was laid, and knew nobody. At the same time his weak pulse intermitted. The physician was informed that this man had been for many years a drunkard: he therefore permitted him to drink ale and brandy. He slept the next night, and his fever and delirium were gone. He had drunk, the preceding day, a Scotch quart of ale and a quarter of a pint of brandy; and continuing to do the same daily, he recovered without farther accident.—A distiller fell into a vat containing hot spirits, and scalded his legs, thighs, and belly, so dreadfully, that the skin of those parts soon turned quite hard and black. As his pulse was very quick, he was let blood; and a strict diet was recommended. Next day he was a great deal weaker, with much anxiety, and a low quick pulse. The third day he was very ill and insensible. His wife begged that she might be allowed to give him some brandy. Her request was complied with, and her husband grew better; the skin of the injured parts began to suppurate, and he completely recovered. His wife then confessed that she had given him a pint of brandy a day. To such a degree can habit weaken the effect of so strong a liquor as brandy.

Liban informs us, that the Ethiopians eat scorpions, and Mercurialis states, that the West Indians eat toads: neither of these facts is without a parallel in Europe. At Padua and Rome, there were two children who ate scorpions, and a girl took great pleasure in eating frogs, lizards, serpents, mice, and all sorts of insects. Another ate live lizards and caterpillars with pepper and vinegar. Of spider-eaters, who grew fat upon those disgusting insects, I could easily collect half a dozen instances from different writers. Galen relates of an old woman, that she had gradually habituated herself to make a meal of hemlock; and Sextus Empiricus assures us, that there have been persons who have taken thirty drams of that poison without injury. A student at Halle accustomed himself on purpose to arsenic, which he took with his food, from a boy; and though it at first occasioned vomiting, yet in time he could bear a considerable quantity. Hence it is evident, how one who habituates himself needlessly to physic, breaks down himself the bridges which, in case of emergency, might carry him in safety over the abysses of disease.

Even the use of our limbs, walking, standing, dancing, riding, speaking, singing, swimming, the ready use of the right or left hand, and a thousand other actions and movements, depend on practice; and this is the foundation of all the corporeal talents which excite the astonishment of mankind. Tulpius makes mention of a woman who could thread a needle, tie firm knots, and write with her tongue. Ropedancers, and people who have grown up in a savage state, display equally extraordinary feats. We may therefore easily infer, that strength also, and capability of enduring fatigue, may be acquired by practice. A robust young fellow, just sent to the galleys, is surprised at the fatigue which his older and much weaker comrades can go through. The ancient physicians were aware of the reason of this. " An infirm old man," says Hippocrates, " can perform hard labour to which he is accustomed, with greater ease than a young man who is ever so strong but unaccustomed to it ;" and Celsus has an observation to the same effect.

The senses, also, are powerfully influenced by habit. By accustoming our eyes to spectacles and glasses, we soon render them incapable of seeing without those auxiliaries. By habit, our ears gradually become insensible to the loudest noise, our nose to the most noisome stench, our palate to the most disgusting taste ; and the Lacedæmonian youths were so accustomed to stripes, that, though beaten to death, they would not make a wry face. Memory, wit, presentiments, passions, may all be introduced by habit into the machine : hence it has been not unaptly remarked by a modern writer, that thought itself is but a habit. Moræus long since conceived the same idea, when he observed, that " we have to ascribe life, and even wisdom itself, to nothing but habit; and that this alone, and not reason, governs our minds." Even study, otherwise so injurious, becomes innocent through habit. Many ancient philosophers, and among the moderns, Mallebranche, Cassini, Newton, Hofmann, Fontenelle, and other studious men, lived to an advanced age.

By way of conclusion, I must not omit to mention the natural evacuations, over which, habit has a very powerful influence. Many people have natural discharges of blood, which must not be stopped. There is an instance of a healthy person, who had such a constipation, as to receive but one call from nature every five weeks. Many perspire naturally very abundantly, others not at all. Whoever should attempt to alter such habits, whether hurtful or beneficial, would bring his patients into great danger, and not accomplish any good purpose. Oh how many useful maxims does this single paper present to my readers and my colleagues! I could not exhaust the subject in as many sheets as I have here devoted pages to it.

## THE POET AMONG THE TREES.

OAK is the noblest tree that grows,
  Its leaves are Freedom's type and herald ;
If we may put our faith in those
  Of Literary-Fund Fitzgerald.

Willow 's a sentimental wood,
  And many Sonneteers, to quicken 'em,
A relic keep of that which stood
  Before Pope's Tusculum at Twickenham.

The Birch-tree with its pendent curves,
  Exciting many a sad reflection,
Not only present praise deserves,
  But our posterior recollection.

The Banyan, though unknown to us,
  Is sacred to the Eastern Magi.
Some like the taste of Tityrus,
  " Recubans sub tegmine fagi."

Some like the Juniper—in gin ;
  Some fancy that its berries droop, as
Knowing a poison lurks within
  More rank than that distill'd from th' Upas.

But he who wants a useful word,
  To tag a line or point a moral,
Will find there 's none to be preferr'd
  To that inspiring tree the Laurel.

The hero-butchers of the sword,
  In Rome and Greece and many a far land,
Like Bravos murder'd for reward,
  The settled price—a laurel-garland.

On bust or coin we mark the wreath,
  Forgetful of its bloody story,
How many myriads writh'd in death,
  That one might bear this type of glory.

Cæsar first wore the badge, 'tis said,
  ' Cause his bald sconce had nothing on it,
Knocking some millions on the head,
  To get his own a leafy bonnet.

Luckily for the Laurel's name,
  Profaned to purposes so frightful,
'Twas worn by nobler heirs of fame,
  All innocent, and some delightful.

With its green leaves were victors crown'd
  In the Olympic games for running,
Who wrestled best, or gallop'd round
  The Circus with most speed and cunning.

Apollo crown'd with Bays gives laws
  To the Parnassian Empyrean ;
And every schoolboy knows the cause,
  Who ever dipp'd in Tooke's Pantheon.

Daphne, like many another fair,
  To whom connubial ties are horrid,
Fled from his arms, but left a rare
  Memento sprouting on his forehead.

For Bays did ancient bards compete,
  Gather'd on Pindus or Parnassus;
They by the leaf were paid, not sheet,
  And that's the reason they surpass us.

One wreath thus twines the heads about,
  Whose brains have brighten'd all our sconces,
And those who others' brains knock'd out,
  'Cause they themselves were royal dunces.

Men fight in these degenerate days
  For crowns of gold, not laurel fillets;
And bards who borrow fire from bays
  Must have them in the grate for billets.

Laureates we have, (for cash and sack,)
  Of all calibres and diameters,
But 'stead of poetry, alack!
  They give us lachrymose Hexameters.

And that illustrious leaf for which
  Folks wrote and wrestled, sung and bluster'd,
Is now boil'd down to give a rich
  And dainty flavour to our custard!

---

### FORTUNE-TELLING.

*" Le présent est gros de l'avenir."*—Leibnitz.

" THOU rascal Beadle, hold thy bloody hand!"—let her escape; I make no charge against that Gipsy, whose eye flashes like lightning through the dark clouds of hair that thou hast shaken over her brow: —if the wenches of the laundry choose to hang my shirts upon a hedge, she is as free to gather them as to pluck

" The lady's smocks all silver white
  That paint the meadows much bedight."

It may be a weakness, but I have had such a sneaking kindness for Gipsies ever since I read, when a boy, the Adventures of Bampfylde Moore Carew, that I have more than once felt a temptation to desert from school and join their encampment as we passed it in our way to the bathing-place. Beneath a few scattered trees, that formed the entrance to a dark grove, their principal tent was usually planted; before it was poised upon three sticks the mysterious cauldron, the blue smoke losing itself amid the trees, and around it were huddled those counterparts of the Jewish miracle, the Arabs of Europe, whose swart looks, shadowy elf-locks, and dark glittering eyes, awakened impressions that combined the romantic and the awful; while the lazy luxury of their wood-wandering life found congenial sympathies in that love of idleness, bird's-nesting, and vagabondage, which, if I may judge by myself, is inherent in all boys. Even the lean Rosinante that was tethered behind them, the panniered donkey browsing thistles a little farther back, the implements of the tinker's trade, that, faintly glimmering amid the foliage, assumed the sublimity of warlike spoil, and the copper-coloured imps of children flitting athwart the umbrageous depths of the grove,—all combined to strike upon that organ of vagrancy which must have been strongly developed upon my juvenile skull, although the vigilance of ushers and schoolmasters fortunately preserved me from following its impulse. But I would not " put into circumscription and confine" any one of these " native burghers of the wood," even though he had subjected me to the imputation of being a perfect Descamisado; he shall not be fain to hug the whipping-post, because he has been too intimate with my hen-roost, nor shall he be made to supply the place of the duck whom he has inveigled from my horse-pond; and if my house-dog chase him undieted from the pantry-door, his canine teeth shall assuredly forget their cunning for the remainder of that day. Civilisation has rendered the surface of society so monotonous and Quaker-like, that it was quite refreshing to stumble upon any thing so original, wild, and picturesque, as a nomadic tribe disavowing the social compact, acknowledging no government, claiming a knowledge of futurity, making a public profession of idleness and of living upon the community, as if they were the nobility of low life, and exhibiting in their fine sunburnt physiognomies decisive evidence of their Oriental origin. It was like encountering a Salvator Rosa after poring over views of Turnham Green and Battersea Rise.

Cleopatra was a Gipsy, and the females of the tribe are generally so beautiful, that one might fancy them to be lineally descended from that king-fascinating brunette; but as to the men, it must be confessed that they marvellously lack the assistance of the turban and the scimitar; for our mean, tame, prosaic vestments do but ill assimilate with the wildness of their looks and the poetical licence of their lives. A hat is a sad extinguisher of the romantic; coats and waistcoats are the types of a well-ordered nation of quiet shopkeepers, rather than of free rovers, chiromancers, and professors of palmistry; while our lower garments, or Ineffables, sit but awkwardly upon—" an outlandish people calling themselves Egyptians, using no craft nor feat of merchandise, who have come into this realm, and gone from shire to shire and place to place in great companies, and used great, subtle, and crafty means to deceive the people,"—for thus are they described in a Statute of Henry the Eighth. In spite, however, of their uncongenial attire, I found so many attractions in their propinquity, so much association connected with their haunts and purlieus, that I once fixed my residence at Norwood, then invested with a moral, or at least an imaginative beauty by their frequent apparition amid its shades; but their descents, like angel-visits, soon became " few and far between;" they were at last routed out, (to use the irreverent phraseology of the journals,) and Norwood being instantly desecrated into a vulgar eminence sprinkled with civic villas and cockney cottages, I struck my tent like the Gipsies, and bade it a long adieu.

" They toil not, neither do they spin;" and why should they, when the ingenious rogues can live upon the future hopes of mankind, if they have not convenient and ready access to their present possessions? Poor human nature, unwilling to submit to that

—" Blindness to the future, wisely given,
That none might know the secrets hid by Heaven,"

is perpetually struggling to " peep through the blanket of the dark," and obtain a glimpse of futurity. Innumerable proofs of the utter impossibility of success, regularly reiterated in every succeeding age, have given a new direction to its developement, without eradicating a delusion that seems to be inherent in the constitution of our minds. Prophecies and predictions are so interwoven with our religion, that we easily fall into the mistake of supposing that they may be made influential upon the ordinary occurrences of life, not perceiving that we are arguing from the exception, instead of the rule which has been laid down for the moral government of the universe. Many of those who lend themselves to this superstition would revolt from the idea of being deemed Fatalists and Necessitarians; yet to this result, or to its own refutation, a belief in any sort of fortune-telling must inevitably tend; for if we cannot, with all our efforts, avoid that future doom of which we have a foreknowledge, we admit the doctrine of Fatalism; and if we can, we prove the fallacy of the prediction. To establish the futility of divination is, however, so much more easy than to abolish its influence, that it may be questioned whether the sturdiest disbeliever in profession be not sometimes a convert in his practice. An event foretold by our own minds when in the irrational state of sleep, or, in other words, a dream, is certainly much less likely to be confirmed than an oracle regularly delivered by the established seers or necromancers; yet which of us ever dreamt that a certain number in the lottery was drawn a capital prize without buying it, or wishing to buy it, or at least noting it down in our pocket-book, that we might compare the result with the mysterious revelation? Hundreds of tickets are purchased every year upon the faith of this somnolent inspiration: if one at last succeeds, it is trumpeted through the town with all the goggle-eyed credulity of gossips and gudgeons; nothing is said of the innumerable failures; and men of otherwise good sense fall into the most fantastical fooleries and chimæras in the hope of discovering the lucky number by which they may enrich themselves in the next rotation of the wheel. By a singular perversion of reason, we use the most preposterous diligence to reduce to a certainty that which is essentially and in its very nature a matter of hazard, as if a game of chance could be otherwise than what it is. Dice, cards, and numbers, being infinitely precarious in their combinations, are precisely the elements from which they would construct a system of regular succession. Montaigne exclaims—" Oh! que celui qui fagoterait habilement un amas de toutes les âneries de l'humaine sapience dirait merveilles!"— Such would be the wonders recorded by him who should collect and publish all the puerile and frivolous superstitions of gamesters.

In the earlier stages of the world it would seem as if nations could not be governed and kept in awe without some quackery of this sort. The Roman commonwealth, founded on a pretended miracle, and regulated by fabricated revelations in the Egerian Cave, was subsequently administered by Sibylline forgeries, and that systematic code of augury which became interwoven with every Pagan establishment. That our fates should be made dependent upon the stars, planets, and constellations, however preposterous a conceit, at least imparts a dignity to our nature by conjoining earth with Heaven; but that the doom of kings, empires, and individuals, should be regulated by the flight of unconrious birds, as expounded by sky-gazing augurs; or by the entrails of victims, as analysed by the butchers of Haruspicy; or by the four elements, as elucidated by holy impostors of various nations, is an evidence of stupid credulity that levels civilised man to the savage, and leaves him very little elevated above the beasts of the field. The practice of Paganism long survived its belief, so has that of Divination, unless we are to suppose that the young persons of the fair sex, and the old women of both, are serious proselytes to its efficacy when they submit the lines of their hand to Gipsy judgment, interpret the cabalistic writing of coffee or tea grounds in a cup, or determine their destiny by the casual upturnings of the cards. O the profound conception, that we should carry about with us in our palm a manual of futurity, have the whole book of fate engraved upon the narrow space between our four fingers and our thumb, and thus literally and truly make our life and destiny the work of our own hands! What is it to cram the Lord's Prayer and Belief into the narrow limits of a sixpence, when we may have the fortunes and adventures of three-score years and ten contracted into the compass of a single palm? He who said that man was an abridgment of the universe, uttered a fine idea, but how much finer to imagine this epitome of the world reduced to a handful, and thrust carelessly into one's breeches-pocket. O the bright conceit, that our horoscope should be revealed to us in a cup, and our fate be prefigured in the hieroglyphical writing of coffee-grounds and tea-leaves, or shuffled out to us in the oracular demonstrations of the four suits! If it has been maintained that speech was given us to conceal our thoughts, it may be predicated, with equal assurance, that man was endowed with a reasoning mind to atone for the irrationality of his actions.

A faith in divination and fatalism can never want converts so long as it affords us a convenient scape-goat for our crimes and follies; and who is there among us that does not lay this flattering unction to his soul whenever his pride or self-conceit are wounded. If we succeed in our undertakings, we very demurely assign the merit to our own talent, prudence, and forethought; if we fail, our bad luck bears all the blame of our bad conduct; we impute our own blindness to Fortune, and even make the heavens responsible if we happen to miss our way upon earth. "This is the excellent foppery of the world, that when we are sick in fortune, often the surfeits of our own behaviour, we make guilty of our disasters the sun, moon, and stars, as if we were villains on necessity, liars by a divine thrusting on, adulterers and drunkards by an enforced obedience of planetary influence." To this extent we are all superstitious alike; we admit the influence of the blind goddess upon one half of human destiny; we believe in her after an event has occurred, while we deride those who imagine that the same event could have been previously subject to her direction. We cheerfully stand sponsors to our virtues and successes, while we affiliate our vices and disasters upon any one that will father them.

There is one sense in which, without the inspiration of prophecy or the charge of imposture, we may reasonably and beneficially venture to indulge in the mystery of Fortune-telling. Knowing that, in the

z 2

established succession of human affairs, certain causes will produce correspondent effects, we may read the future in the past, and boldly predict that the spendthrift will come to want, the debauchee to premature decay, the idler to contempt, the gamester to bitterness of soul, if not to suicide, the profligate to remorse, and the violator of the laws to punishment; while we may as safely augur that the practice of the opposite virtues will be productive of results diametrically contrary. Human passions, the great elements of change, being the same in all ages, and nations being but an aggregate of individuals, we may in like manner ascend from particular cases to mighty empires, and deduce the revolutions that are to be from those that have been. All states have their birth, manhood, and death; their increase, renown, and decay; their morning, noon, and night. Nature ever works in a circle, more or less large according to circumstances and the materials it has to embrace; but she invariably fills up the round of destiny, and then begins afresh, recommencing but to end, and ending but to recommence. Here we may prophesy upon a large scale, though we cannot live to see the fulfilment of our prognostications. He, however, may be confirmed at no very distant day, who predicts that Rome, the immortal city, the mistress of the world, will lay its proud head in the dust with Tyre and Sidon, and Palmyra and Jerusalem, and Nineveh and Babylon. The depopulation of another century will reduce her inhabitants to a handful of men, whom the increasing mal-aria will presently sacrifice or disperse; wolves will, finally, range over the silent waste of the Seven Hills as freely as before the time of Romulus and Remus; the marble temples will sink into the infectious marshes that surround them; and if there be one stone left upon another, it should be that which covers the tomb of the Cardinal de St. Onuphrio, and bears the following inscription, as applicable to the City as the Saint:—" Hic jacet umbra—cinis—nihil!"      ·H.·

---

### SONNET.—THE SUNLESS SUMMER.

Ah! sunless Summer! thou indeed dost seem
  Like my sad youth, o'ercast with clouds and gloom;
  There is no brightness in thee, and my bloom
Is early fading like thy watery beam:
And if at times a faint and sickly gleam
  Of hope shines forth, the prospect to illume—
  'Tis a deceitful promise, for my doom
Is waking grief, that mocks each flattering dream.
  Yes, joyless season! thou like me art cold,
And pale, and cheerless, damp'd with showers and shade:
  My days, like *thine*, in dreary course have roll'd,
*Thy* hopes, like *mine*, have only smiled to fade;
Yet still point forward to that time more bright,
When mortal suns shall set in cloudless light.      A. S

### FRENCH COMIC ACTORS.

THE two most entertaining actors in the world, and in their way the most perfect, are scarcely known at all in England, even by those of our countrymen who pretend to be acquainted with Paris and its theatres, and who talk of Talma as familiarly as if they were in the habit of taking tickets at his benefit. But the theatre these actors perform at is one which it is not *the fashion* for the English to attend; for no other reason, that I could ever discover, but that it is incomparably the most amusing theatre in Paris. Though another reason, why these admirable actors are not so much sought after by foreigners, may be, that they generally perform in pieces the comic effect of which chiefly depends on those local circumstances, or passing events of the day, about which foreigners can be expected to feel but little interest, and the drift of which is also conveyed in dialogue consisting of language almost entirely idiomatical, and filled with allusions and turns of expression that can be known to, and therefore thoroughly relished by, natives alone.

But even this reason is a very indifferent one; for (to say nothing of the witnessing of any one of these pieces being invaluable as a *lesson* in the language, and worth a score of the best that can be got in any other way for love or money) the actors I speak of are—the one so miraculously true to nature, and the other so irresistibly comic in every tone, look, and motion, that it is scarcely necessary to understand what they say, to be infinitely amused and delighted with them. But our countrymen, being all " sage, grave men," choose to pay their eight or ten francs to be permitted to sleep away their evening over a solemn farce, yclept a tragedy, in a *première loge* of the Théâtre Français, or in hearing, without listening to, that still less amusing enormity, a grand opera at the Académie de Musique,—when they might, for thirty sous, be laughing away three or four hours (for I defy them to help laughing, whether they understood or not) in the pit of the prettiest little theatre in Paris, witnessing as many different pieces, each unlike all the rest in character, and yet each as light as a feather, as lively as a jig, and as gay as a May-day garland; and each performed by actors most of whom are admirable in their respective lines, and two of them, in particular, absolutely unique. It is of these two that I am about to speak; and I must mention their names before the reader will know who I mean—which should not be: the names and qualities of Brunet and Potier ought to be known every where, if it were only to place as a set-off against those of another set of French actors, not a tenth part so clever or respectable, with whose performances the stage of Europe is at present ringing from side to side. And to shew the just manner in which each set is appreciated in France, I may add, that the Parisians would scarcely consent to part with the former, even if, by so doing, they could get rid of the latter. Indeed, the farce of Potier and Brunet is almost capable of making them forget, if not forgive, that of Chateaubriand and Louis XVIII.: if it had not, I don't know what would have become of the Bourbons by this time!—Or rather, I *do* know.

Brunet and Potier are as unlike each other as they are unlike all other actors. Each is " himself alone," and dependent on nothing but

himself for support—not even on his character. And yet neither can
be seen to the best advantage except when he is performing with the
other;—which is singular, because there is evidently a spirit of rivalry
between them, and each would, and in fact does, carry away the whole
of the applause and attention at the moment he is speaking, and no
part of the audience seem to feel that there is any other claimant before
them, till he has done. But the moment he *has* done, and it comes to
the other's turn to be heard, *he* (whichever it may be) is all in all, and
his rival nothing. The way in which the ball of fun is thus kept up
between them, for a whole scene, or even a whole piece, is as remarkable as it is amusing. I have gone to the Théâtre des Variétés night
after night, for weeks together—solely to see these two actors perform;
and without pretending to be familiar with half the turns of expression, or to understand half the allusions, on which the joke of the moment has depended, I have never been so much entertained by the performances of any other comic actors whatever—not even the best of
our own: which proves to me that it must depend almost entirely on
the actors themselves, and not on any thing that they may have to deliver. If they happen to be performing a witty or a humorous part,
you laugh at the wit and humour of the part, as well as at their performance of it. But if they have nothing to do, they make as much
out of that as if it were ready made to their hands—provided the character they perform be not directly opposed to their different styles;
—which, indeed, they take care shall never be the case; for they have
the power, in this respect, all in their own hands. As a proof of their
complete self-dependence, one of the pieces in which, when it was in
vogue, they were the most irresistibly amusing, (*Je fais mes Farces,*)
is the most absolute and unmixed nonsense, from beginning to end, that
ever was penned;—if indeed it ever *was* penned; but to see these two
actors perform in it, one would be tempted to suppose that *their* parts,
at least, were left blank, and that they filled them up with any thing
that came into their heads at the moment.

On the other hand, (and this, more than any thing else, proves the
rich and sterling talent they possess,) when by accident they have any
thing to perform that really deserves the name of a *character*, they do
it in the most rich, and yet the most chaste and unexaggerated manner.

Though Potier must, I believe, be considered as the greatest favourite of the two,—if a distinction of this kind must be made,—yet
Brunet deserves the first particular mention, on account of his long
standing, as well as the class of his performances—inasmuch as the ability to give a pure and simple imitation of nature, is a more rare and
valuable talent, than that of originating the most ludicrously extravagant exaggerations—whether of nature or of manners.

Brunet's person, though perfectly well-formed, is diminutive to a remarkable degree; and though he is at present advanced considerably beyond middle age, there is a youthful and even child-like simplicity in his
expression and voice, that is admirably adapted to the rather limited
range of characters he adopts. These are, generally speaking, the
*Jocrisses* of the French comedy and farce—the simple, truth-telling,
untaught, unteachable valets and serving-men—the antitheses of the
*Frontins* of the same race—the cunning, lying, clever, intriguing ones;
or the gentle, bashful, backward, betrayed village lovers—the pro-

tages, of the old folks, and the cloaks and butts of the young ones—in opposition to the bold, handsome, enterprising, and successful suitors—the favourites of the fair; or, lastly, the mild, meek, submissive, milk and water husbands—horned, hen-pecked, and abused by virago wives and intriguing rake-hells.

These are the general lines of characters that Brunet adopts. But many of his principal parts do not rank among any of these; and his most successful ones are perhaps those in which he is made the subject of some ludicrous equivoque, kept up through the whole piece, and the fun of which arises out of his being thrown into circumstances and situations of all others the most unfitted for his mild, simple, and gentle nature. Such, for instance, as *Jocrisse chef des Bands Noirs*—where, simple country youth as he is, travelling through a forest on his affairs, he is mistaken by a band of robbers for their new chief, who is to meet them there about that time, and who has been elected to the office by another part of the band; and he is installed into his new honours whether he will or no—they mistaking his reluctance for modesty, and his protestations to the contrary, for an innocent deceit put in practice to try them. This piece was got up here; but it did not succeed, even though Liston played the part; for no actor at present living has the slightest pretensions to rival Brunet in his own line.

As I have hinted above, the characteristic qualities of Brunet's acting are, its absolute naturalness—its exquisitely unconscious *naïveté*—its perfect simplicity—and, throughout all these, a mildness and kindliness, both of voice, look, and manner, that amount to the pathetic. In fact, to speak after the fashion of the times, paradoxically, Brunet is the most comic of actors, in consequence of having nothing in the slightest degree comic about him, either natural or acquired—either in his person, his voice, his manner, or his mode of dressing his characters. His performances are chaste, and true to nature, in a degree that was perhaps never attained by any other actor; or rather, which no other actor ever had the courage or the taste to keep himself within the limits of. He never "exaggerates his voice" beyond the pitch of common speaking; he never makes a movement or a tone of expression that would attract particular attention in the intercourse of common life; and as for a grimace, or any thing approaching to it, I believe it never enters into his thoughts as a means of heightening the effects he aims at; and if it did, his bland and gentle features are incapable of it. If it should be asked, how is it that, under these circumstances, he succeeds in producing comic effects? I believe it must be answered that, in fact, he does not, *by his acting*, produce any—that all *that* produces is sensations pleasing and delightful in the highest degree, but not such as can truly be called *comic*—and that when these latter arise from his performances, as they perpetually do, it is in consequence of the ludicrous contrasts and associations that are made to take place from character, situation, turns of phrase, &c.; and the effects of which do, in fact, greatly depend on this very absence of any thing laughable or ridiculous in the actor. I believe this to be susceptible of a more lengthened and interesting developement and explanation than my limits permit me to attempt; especially when another person, equally gifted with the above, is waiting to be noticed.

Potier is, I should judge, still a young man—his person exceedingly

spare and thin—his face long, lean, and cadaverous—and his whole appearance indicative of any thing rather than self-enjoyment, or the
faculty of creating it in others. Even his voice is more like the creak
of the bird of evil omen, than one that is come to announce glad tidings
to all who hear it. And yet, you cannot help feeling, every time you
look at and listen to him, that the slightest change in any quality belonging to him must be for the worse—in so extraordinary a manner
does he adapt them all to his purposes, and make them work usefully
together; or rather, so completely does he change their nature, by
making the rich comedy of his mind shine through and blend with them
all. In this respect he performs a miracle similar to that of Cervantes
in creating Don Quixote and Sancho Panza. These *two* persons in
name, are in fact but *one* in the mind of the reader. But for this, they
would never produce any thing like the effect they do. The Knight
of the Woeful Countenance would be a piece of pure pathos, from beginning to end, if he had not been allied, body and soul, with the Squire
of the Comic Countenance. I will venture to say that no reader ever
thought of one without the other. It cannot be. And thus it is with
the mind and person of Potier. They are Sancho and Quixote joined
in one; the qualities of the latter being not merely merged in the
former, but their nature changed to a conformity with that. And, as
I have said that Brunet is exquisitely comic, precisely on account of
there being nothing in the slightest degree comic about him, so it might
be added, in the same paradoxical spirit, that Potier produces the most
comic effect that any actor ever did, not in spite of, but in consequence
of, his personal qualities being emblems of all that is sad and sorrowful. I believe that Potier's style is not to be described—or described
in no other way than by saying that it is perfectly original, unique, and
nondescript. It has nothing natural about it, except in particular instances; and yet it is not in the least degree artificial or constrained.
Every thing flows from him as easily and unconsciously as it does from
Brunet; but it seems to pass through a peculiar medium which changes
it all, whatever it may have been before, into the most rich and extravagant drollery. It is impossible to conceive of any thing, however
serious or however insipid, that would not become droll, in passing
through the lips of Potier. And this takes place without any appearance of effort, without any extravagance or affectation of tone or manner, and without any grimace whatever. You cannot perceive how it
is done, or what constitutes the difference between this actor's performance of a particular character and any other's. And yet, there is
scarcely a character he performs that would not be intolerable in any
other hands afterwards.

I have said that Potier can be as chaste an actor as any, when he
pleases, and when the part he has to perform seems to deserve it. His
" *ci-devant Jeune homme*"—a character resembling our Lord Ogleby—
is the most purely natural as well as the most exquisitely finished performance of the kind I have ever seen; and I have seen all that England has to shew in the same class. Potier, in fact, *can* be chaste;
but it is very seldom his cue to be so: for rare indeed must be the wit,
and rich the character, that should not give way to his own irresistible
*forcing.* When —— is present, nature, wit, character, and every thing
else.                    nsense—nonsense the most extravagant and un-

definable in its character, and yet the most universal and irresistible in its effects. I never knew even a Frenchman that could give any reasonable account of his liking for Potier, and yet I never knew one that did not secretly like him better than any other actor they have: I say secretly, for the *critical* spirit is even more prevalent there than it is here, and I believe very few Frenchmen would dare openly to go so far as I do in my admiration of this actor. His most characteristic and attractive performances are *mere nonsense*, they say—he is a *mere* "farceur:" as if mere nonsense were not, occasionally, better than mere sense, or mere wisdom, or mere any thing else. The truth is, they cant with their lips about his being inferior to some of their actors of the *old school;* but they make amends, both to him and themselves, by going to see him six times where they go once to any of the others: and this is doing him the best kind of justice, and giving him the best of all possible fames. And what fame, after all, is, or can be, like an actor's, as far as regards the personal gratification it brings with it? What effect is the imagination of all the immortality in the world of the Future capable of producing in the human mind, compared with the actual and present enjoyment experienced by a favourite actor before a favouring audience? This indeed "comes home to the bosom" in a way that nothing else can—for under no other circumstances is actual, tangible applause offered in so immediate and so unequivocal a manner—with so little delay—with so lavish a hand—and in connexion with such heightening and inspiring associations.

To be a favourite preacher, must be something—to be a favourite author, not a little—to be a favourite speaker in a popular assembly, much; but to be a favourite actor must be—every thing. In proof of this, nobody runs away from home to turn preacher, or writer, or speaker—or to follow any other pursuit to which his friends may have insurmountable objections. But how many run away from home to turn actors! The very imagination of the thing (for these clandestine ones seldom reach to more than that) is enough to compensate for all the thousand disadvantages attending such a step. I have often wondered why it is that actors are so very solicitous about what the critics will say of them the next day in the newspapers. What should they, whose ears are ringing with the acclaim of a thousand voluntary voices or the thunder of a thousand hands, care for the scribbling of one paid pen? It is a strange instance of the perversity of poor human nature. It is the "splendid shilling" that the miser is *expectant* of possessing, and that, until it becomes his, he looks at with an eye of greater favour, and values more, than all his previous hoard. In fact, what we have, is nothing—what we want, is every thing. Possession had need be "nine points of the law;" for while it almost gives us the right to a thing, it almost takes away the faculty of enjoying it. But, notwithstanding his sensitiveness to criticism, a favourite actor is an enviable person. Whatever we may say or think to the contrary, we would none of us, if we were put to the proof, give up our own identity for that of any other person. But if I were compelled to part with mine—to " change my humanity" with any one—it should certainly be with either France's Potier, or our own Kean: for I had rather be Potier than Talma, or Kean than either.                     Z.

## THE FIRST-BORN OF EGYPT.

WHEN life is forgot, and night hath power,
  And mortals feel no dread;
When silence and slumber rule the hour,
  And dreams are round the head;
God shall smite the first-born of Egypt's race,
The destroyer shall enter each dwelling-place—
  Shall enter and choose his dead.

" To your homes," said the leader of Israel's host,
  " And slaughter a sacrifice;
Let the life-blood be sprinkled on each door-post,
  Nor stir till the morn arise,
And the Angel of Vengeance shall pass you by,
He shall see the red stain, and shall not come nigh
  Where the hope of your household lies."

The people hear, and they bow them low—
  Each to his house hath flown;
The lamb is slain, and with blood they go
  And sprinkle the lintel-stone;
And the doors they close when the sun hath set,
But few in oblivious sleep forget
  The judgement to be done.

'Tis midnight—yet they hear no sound
  Along the lone still street;
No blast of a pestilence sweeps the ground,
  No tramp of unearthly feet
Nor rush as of harpy wing goes by,
But the calm moon floats in the cloudless sky,
  ' Mid her wan light clear and sweet.

Once only, shot like an arrowy ray,
  A pale blue flash was seen,
It pass'd so swift, the eye scarce could say
  That such a thing had been:
Yet the beat of every heart was still,
And the flesh crawl'd fearfully, and chill,
  And back flow'd every vein.

The courage of Israel's bravest quail'd
  At the view of that awful light,
Though knowing the blood of their offering avail'd
  To shield them from its might:
They felt 'twas the Spirit of Death had past,
That the brightness they saw his cold glance had cast
  On Egypt's land that night :—

That his fearful eye had unwarn'd struck down
  In the darkness of the grave,
The hope of that empire, the pride of its crown,
  The first-born of lord and slave :—
The lovely, the tender, the ardent, the gay;
Where were they ?—all wither'd in ashes away,
  At the terrible death-glare it gave.

From the couches of slumber ten thousand cries
  Burst forth 'mid the silence dread—
The youth by his living brother lies
  Sightless, and dumb, and dead !
The infant lies cold at his mother's breast,
She had kiss'd him alive as she sank to rest
  She awakens—his life hath fled !

And shrieks from the palace chambers break—
  Their inmates are steep'd in woe,
And Pharaoh hath found his proud arm too weak
  To arrest the mighty blow:
Wail, King of the Pyramids! Egypt's throne
Cannot lighten thy heart of a single groan,
  For thy kingdom's heir laid low.

Wail, King of the Pyramids! Death hath cast
  His shafts through thine empire wide,
But o'er Israel in bondage his rage hath past,
  No first-born of her's hath died—
Go, Satrap! command that the captive be free,
Lest their God in fierce anger should smite even thee,
  On the crown of thy purple pride.      I.

---

## LITERATURE AND LAW.

WE live in strange times, when narrow prejudice, stale custom, and misty doubt, are arranged in triumphant warfare, against the most rational deductions and the clearest decisions of common sense. It is in vain that we are placed on the proud intellectual eminence of modern times, thrown up by the accumulated labours of gifted spirits for so many ages. It is in vain that we glory, and justly glory, in the progressive emancipation of the mind from the trammels of superstition, and the degrading state of a blind submission to spiritual or temporal authority—if we cannot make our advantages available, and, in yielding homage to rule and law, be satisfied that we submit only to what is just and reasonable. When this is not the case, but, on the contrary, the regulations by which we hold liberty or property are capricious, narrow, and revolting to sense and policy, the evil is not less mischievous to the individual than to the entire community, by making contemptible the very laws towards which all should feel respect as well as obedience. No social compact is worth any thing where there is this variance. Man is not in our times, Heaven be praised for it! the passive instrument he once was; he has put on a character more consistent with his grade in the creation, and the knowledge of those inherent rights which Nature informs him are inalienably his own. The mischief, then, of legal decisions not grounded in reason, must be evident, even if based upon precedent; but how much more so when precedent itself is rational and correct, and novelty and absurdity make their appearance hand-in-hand together to overturn it.

It may be easily conjectured that I refer to the late decisions respecting literary property. The two leading Reviews, the Edinburgh and Quarterly, have both agreed in opinion upon the extraordinary doctrine which has emanated from the Court of Chancery on this subject, —a doctrine subversive of the right of property, contrary to former decisions, pernicious in effect, and absurd in practice. After what has been said in these able publications, it might seem almost superfluous to add any thing more; the Edinburgh, in particular, having shewn that former decrees of the Court of Chancery for the last century were diametrically the reverse of those of the present Chancellor, and that works both libellous and immoral, such as no author would now publish, have been protected, as regards a property in them, in that Court. The Edinburgh, taking up the question in a view strictly legal, has impugned the present practice as a professional writer would do, by quoting former cases, and among them the piracy of the libellous and immoral Miscellanies of Pope, Swift, and others. In this mode I have no intention to second it; but there are two or three important reasons notwithstanding, why the subject should be noticed at present. In the first place, it seems tantamount to a duty that every literary work should, as much as possible, expose the serious evil of the new doctrine, and contribute a modicum to the exposure of its fallacy. In the next place, an instance somewhat different from the former, but of a character equally singular, has occurred in the Vice-Chancellor's Court too recently to have been noticed in the before-mentioned publications; and lastly, it is beneficial to society to second public opinion on such a question, upon grounds which have nothing to do with law, but are derived from universally received principles of justice, within the boundaries of which all law decisions must at no very distant period be circumscribed.

The success of an application to the Court of Chancery for an injunction to restrain a pirate, or, in plainer terms, a thief, who deprives another of his property, and deals openly in the stolen wares, never should depend on the tendency of the writings stolen, because the application to that Court should simply be considered as a temporary protection for a disputed property, the nature of which, and the ownership also, is to be subsequently judged of elsewhere. In the view of the Chancellor, a book ought to be but as so much waste paper of a certain value, more or less, that constituted a property. He is placed in the situation of a trustee of a litigated property, to prevent injury, which he must hold entire until the question at issue between the parties is decided by an arbitrator. Should the work be immoral, it is part of the question for the Court of Law to decide, and for that alone. The final decision may be that the work is of such a nature as that an action cannot be sustained. "You, Mr. Author, or Bookseller, have been robbed, but you have been robbed of contraband goods, as has clearly appeared in evidence, and therefore you can have no satisfaction here, for, that which the law cannot recognise as a property, it cannot secure to you." Such seems to have been the spirit of practice until Lord Eldon, placing himself in the situation of a Judge and Jury of the Law Courts, refused the plaintiff's application, and made himself the censor of literary works—thereby, if bad, according to his notions or doubts, indirectly sanctioning piracy, and aiding the circulation in the cheapest possible form, and in augmented numbers, by the robber. It is true, the plaintiff may still apply to a Law Court; but, in the interim, the pirate sells edition upon edition, and, before the trial can be brought on, he has achieved his object—sold all he might ever be able to sell, if he but used common diligence, and rendered even the expenses of an action at law a useless waste of money. Here, then, is an evil, confessedly of great magnitude, removable by following the former practice of the Court and the simplest dictates of reason—a path, indeed, so plain that a child could not err in it—and the difficulty seems to me how to find an excuse for deviating from the beaten track. If a book be immoral, giving it tenfold circulation, by allowing its piracy, must be infinitely more pernicious than permitting the man who at all events is the rightful owner of the property, to hold it, bad as it may be, till a Court of Law decides against him. In Chancery it seems that the reverse of the maxim " Of two evils choose the least " is to become an established precedent.

Who, in such cases, if the Chancellor is made a judge of literature as well as equity, is to fix the limit when he shall cease to have doubts? The property of the subject is to lie open to plunder, because the caprice, political prejudice, incapacity, or what not, of a Chancellor, may make him refuse it the instant protection of the law. I deny the ability of nine Chancellors out of ten to form correct opinions on literary works. Men bred to the law, who have grown old in the pursuit, toilsome and arduous as it is, are the persons in society the worst constituted of any to form opinions on literary matters: they have all their lives been employed with line and rule, upon case and fact, compressing their energies into one narrow pursuit, and cramped within boundaries over which imagination dares not cast an excursive glance. They are to act only upon facts; and in proportion as they would climb to high eminence in their profession, they must stifle every feeling that would lead them aside into scenes of fancy or fiction; they must be deaf to the voice of the charmer, " charming never so wisely; " the " spoils of time," in the page of any but law history, they must not contemplate; the poetry of life must be a dead letter to them; and they must abhor the pages of romance, and the very book of Nature itself. Is it not likely, therefore, with such, that the visions of the poet, and the lively scenes of the novelist, run but a bad chance of fair and honest interpretation? Twelve men, who have not been indurated by the character of such a pursuit against the impressions of external nature, and who are still governed by the dictates of sober sense, are infinitely to be preferred as judges in such matters. Moreover there is no earthly reason why authors or booksellers should be excluded from the safeguard, as to property, that their fellow-subjects receive, from the first to the last step that the law can afford. If the great names that now reflect so much glory on England had been involved in the doubts of a Chancellor, how would their noblest works have been treated. Let us imagine a pirate of Spenser's Faery Queen brought up to Lincoln's Inn, what justice could the author expect? how many stanzas would be found exceptionable! Milton would be esteemed as worthless as Byron in " Cain;" and Pope would be lost past redemption, were it for his " Eloise" alone—more especially, perhaps, as she was under guardianship at the time she is supposed to have encouraged her lover's passion! But if such would be the fate of works of fancy, what have we not to fear for political publications that may taunt the very Chancellor himself, his friends and supporters? How may the cause of truth be injured, and property in a work of such a nature be deteriorated, under pretence of its being libellous! It is not meant to insinuate that the present Chancellor would so act, but it is possible he or his successors might; and what sort of security for property is that which remains at the mercy of one man's prejudices?

But every work may now be printed that will remunerate the robber; and this brings me to the last most curious decision in the Vice-

Chancellor's court. I say any work may be printed, because it appears that injunctions are only now to be granted after it is shewn by a Court of Law that they are deserving protection; and then, when an injunction is not of the smallest advantage it may be had on being applied for—the Court of Law, be it observed, having previously passed judgement on the pirate for the self-same piracy! All the time, to be sure, the thief sells the stolen property; but he is, if the proceeding in a Law Court be against him, to declare to the Court of Chancery, on an application from the party robbed, the profit he has made by the theft up to that time. A notable shift in justice; thus making the thief disgorge the plunder, or what he may choose to say as the amount of it. Thus, too, the quality of the goods purloined are made to constitute the guilt, or otherwise, of the taker! The persons who pirate books are known to be not worth sixpence; and it is notorious, that a penny can never be obtained from this low class of pilferers, let the future decisions of the Law Courts be what they may. Responsible and respectable booksellers hold such conduct in a just abborrence. Thus sagely, therefore, has the court managed, that the injured can have no real remedy—instead of protecting the property till trial in a Law Court, where, if deemed immoral or libellous, no redress would be given, and a penalty might afterwards attach to the publication. The rightful proprietor may, indeed, marvel at the wisdom of such a decision—but I will state the proceeding itself.

Soon after the three last Cantos of Don Juan issued from the press, a low tradesman immediately printed and circulated a pirated edition; an injunction was applied for and granted by the Court of Chancery, to restrain him from selling the pirated copies. He had the hardihood, however, to come personally into court and apply for the injunction to be set aside, on the ground that the book was of an immoral tendency, and that therefore he had a right to print and circulate as many copies as he pleased. The Court, it is to be presumed, in its great zeal for the public good and its high regard for public morals, granted the prayer of the pirate, with the proviso, that he kept an account of the profits until a Court of Law should decide whether the work was of a nature that entitled it to protection. Now, it being clear that the party who first applied for the injunction was the rightful owner of the work, good or bad as it might be, the line pointed out by reason and common sense indicated, that, until it was found by a verdict in a Law Court not entitled to protection, the real owner had a claim upon the justice of the country. Indeed this can be the only use of an application to Chancery—namely, that a temporary relief may be instantly afforded, until the question is decided elsewhere. The Vice-Chancellor, however, did not let the character of the book rest upon his own doubts of its tendency; but he thought " the Court had no original jurisdiction in such cases, and that it only interfered to prevent an injury." Now, if the work be unimpeachable, a Court of Law gives the remedy, until which, injury is prevented by the interdiction of the work to the pirate; this would seem to be the proper course of proceeding, for it is surely more reasonable that the rightful owner should be secured until the question has been brought to an issue, than that the plunderer should be suffered to circulate a cheap edition, for the copy-right of which the real owner had probably paid a large sum of money. This edition he could not afford to sell for five times the sum of the edition pirated, and consequently could not command for it an equal circulation with the coarse editions, which had cost the plunderers nothing but the expense of printing and paper. It is therefore obvious, that the bookseller, if he be subsequently protected in a Court of Law, must suffer great injury, even were it possible for him to make the pirate refund the exact sum of profit he had made. The Vice-Chancellor observed, that he had refused the protection of the Court lately to a song, because it was " a flippant trifling production;" but what had the nature of the production to do with the matter, when it might have involved a great property? The very act of going into Chancery, by men in the full possession of their faculties, is of itself sufficient evidence that it is for no trivial object in value, when the expences of the Court are considered. It will not be denied, that in a country like England, an article which the Court may regard as very trifling in itself, and which is in fact really so, may involve property to an enormous extent.

This decision of the Vice-Chancellor is still much more consistent than the refusal of his superior in Chancery to interfere because of his own doubts of the tendency of a publication. If a Chancellor's notions of equity are to be made the sole rule of the Court, they must change with every new Chancellor; there is no guessing the extent of the mischief they may produce. Few works that have had a great circulation, and that are stupendous monuments of the Nation's glory, have been free from passages and sentiments in policy, morals, and religion, that some scrupulous Chancellor might not imagine undeserving the protection of his court. Lord Chancellors are as much party-men in politics as others, and they may be to the full as much bigots in religion;—this may be lax in morals; that may be unimpeachable as to morals, but not overnice about religion; and the opinion of each is still to be equally good upon both points, and equally decisive as to the property which may depend upon them. It has been remarked, on the authority of Selden, " that the making the Chancellor's sense of equity a rule for the administration of justice in Chancery, was like making the length of the Chancellor's foot the standard of cloth measure—one Chancellor might have a long foot, another a short one, and so on." If it is to be so, Chancery law will become very unsatisfactory to the public mind. The question of preceding law, in the Edinburgh Review, is so clearly in opposition to the late decisions, that one is wholly at a loss to account for them.

But if we examine the allegations of the defendant, and the grounds which he urged in support of setting aside the injunction, we shall discover matter for the astonishment of the country. Men defending themselves in cases of action, or indictment for libel, when their feelings are warm, often give the rein to vituperation against individuals, and are instantly checked by the judge, who informs them, that one libel is not to be defended by another. In the Court of Chancery, however, there is no resemblance to this sort of proceeding. From a professed regard to public morals, the Court refuses its protection to the comparatively limited circulation of a work of doubtful tendency, in the hands of the rightful owner; but still farther to evince its regard for morals, allows a pirate to circulate without number, in the cheapest

possibly form, that, very property, and security, in Court, the herefore
injurious ground of defence, that he work is immoral, ... Now, in con-
dering Chancellors had made it a rule to refuse their protection to
such property, which it does not appear they have done, the officer
who fills the seat of equity at present, seems bound to take the means
most consistent with reason and justice, to keep the circulating as
limited as possible;—and if the reverse had been the preceding practice,
he should have laboured to effect an alteration. At present, it appears,
as if the Court were determined to annoy the proprietor of the work,
rather than do what was consistent with sound sense, even at the expense of fourfold injury to those morals, of which it alleges itself the
champion. Ought the reason urged by a pirate to secure himself in
the enjoyment of his plunder, ever to be listened to in a British court
of justice, but as an additional charge of criminality against the
speaker? How venial is the offence of the worst libellers, to such an
offender as this! The libeller may have endured repeated and unprovoked provocation from the libelled; the latter may be one high in
office or rank; he may be a landlord who has oppressed his tenant, a
seducer who has robbed the libeller of all he holds dear in the world;
or the latter may have overstepped the bounds of prudence, and in a
moment of the indignant feeling of honest patriotism, he may have
hurled a well-merited but imprudent sarcasm at the head of an authority. Here there is some motive in palliation of the offence—something redeeming even in a breach of the rigid enactments of the law.
But what palliation is there for a vile pander in lucre,—a man careless
of consequences, so that he may put money into his pocket, coming
unblushingly into the sanctuary of justice, and there holding up his
head, the brazen token of avarice and dishonesty, and pleading that the
work before the Court is licentious, wicked, and will corrupt the community, and that, therefore, he is justified in administering a tenfold
dose of its poison for his private advantage? Is not the allowing such
a wretch to reap the fruits of his infamy a greater evil, inflicted on
society, and a more mischievous decision, than securing the rightful
owner until a Law Court has decided the matter? But even were good
sometimes attained by such means, they ought not to be used, being
unworthy the dignity of character, and the pure attributes which should
attend the administration of justice. Though the law may not have
forbidden many practices in its execution, it does not follow that it is
always correct to act upon them. A sheep-stealer was hung at Exeter
a year or two ago, who was convicted solely on the forced evidence of
two of his children; now, though a conviction was legal under such circumstances, it was once nobly observed by a judge in a like horrid
case, that he should not suffer the trial to proceed—he would not punish
one crime by the permission of a greater. It is manifestly a greater
mischief to suffer a pirate to justify himself for a literary robbery, by
alleging that he had committed a robbery of immoral goods, and that
therefore he had a right to spread the mischief infinitely farther than it
would otherwise have reached—it is manifestly a greater evil to allow
this in open Court, than to concede a temporary protection to him who
fairly possesses the right of property.

He who feels a respect for the courts of judicature of his country,
and is well acquainted with the operation of what passes in them upon

society, will have observed with regret that decisions like the present are little calculated to add to that veneration for the law, the existence of which has been for a long time one of the surest safeguards of social order. It requires little expertness in the subtleties of the legal profession, to judge clearly in a case like the present. It is a plain straight-forward question, and will admit of as little subterfuge as any that ever came before a court. Why it is that persons of all parties see it in the same light, and that lawyers alone labour to obscure what is in itself so simple, cannot easily be explained. There is no labyrinth to unravel, no ancient statutes to unroll, no authority but plain sense to consult, and the cause of the preference given to the new practice is altogether a riddle. No one can wish to see the taste of the age corrupted. Let immoral publications be discouraged, let them be put down, if need be, by proper methods; but let their circulation be no longer extended; on the ground of their pernicious effects on public morals, by a British court of justice, nor let the opinion of any single individual, whatever may be his station, consign to plunder those literary works that do not square with his varying notions and capricious views. We see too much adherence to the forms rather than the substance of justice among present lawyers. They are too apt, in their profession, to run into extravagances rather than appear destitute of craft. As the world gets more enlightened, however, we shall find that it will prefer a plain and clear law-practice; and that the circumvolutions, fictions, tautology, anomalies, and inconsistencies of our law administration, must give way to a more simple and lucid developement of the principles of justice, and to the straightening and clearing the intricate by-ways that lead to it.      Y. I.

---

## THE DAUGHTER OF MEATH.

TURGESIUS, the chief of a turbulent band,
Came over from Norway and conquer'd the land;
Rebellion had smooth'd the invader's career,
The natives shrank from him, in hate, or in fear;
While Erin's proud spirit seem'd slumbering in peace,
In secret it panted for death—or release.

The tumult of battle was hush'd for awhile,—
Turgesius was monarch of Erin's fair isle;
The sword of the conqueror slept in its sheath,
His triumphs were honour'd with trophy and wreath;
The princes of Erin despair'd of relief,
And knelt to the lawless Norwegian Chief.

His heart knew the charm of a woman's sweet smile,
But ne'er, till he came to this beautiful Isle,
Did he know with what mild, yet resistless controul,
That sweet smile can conquer a conqueror's soul—
And oh! 'mid the sweet smiles most sure to enthrall,
He soon met with one—he thought sweetest of all.

The brave Prince of Meath had a daughter as fair
As the pearls from Loch Neagh, which encircled her hair;

The Tyrant beheld her, and cried, "She shall come
To reign as the Queen of my gay mountain home;
Ere sunset to-morrow hath crimson'd the sea,
Melachlin, send forth thy young daughter to me!"

Awhile paused the Prince—too indignant to speak,
There burn'd a reply in his glance—on his cheek;
But quickly that hurried expression was gone,
And calm was his manner, and mild was his tone:
He answer'd—"Ere sunset hath crimson'd the sea,
To-morrow—I'll send my young daughter to thee!

"At sunset to-morrow your palace forsake,
With twenty young chiefs seek the Isle on yon lake;
And there, in its coolest and pleasantest shades,
My child shall await you with twenty fair maids:
Yes—bright as my armour the damsels shall be,
I send with my daughter, Turgesius, to thee."

Turgesius return'd to his palace;—to him
The sports of that evening seem'd languid and dim;
And tediously long was the darkness of night,
And slowly the morning unfolded its light;
The sun seem'd to linger—as if it would be
An age ere his setting would crimson the sea.

At length came the moment—the King and his band
With rapture push'd off their light boat from the land;
And bright shone the gems on their armour, and bright
Flash'd their fast-moving oars in the setting sun's light;
And long ere they landed, they saw through the trees,
The maidens' white garments that waved in the breeze.

More strong in the lake was the dash of each oar,
More swift the gay vessel flew on to the shore;
Its keel touch'd the pebbles—but over the surf
The youths in a moment had leap'd to the turf,
And rush'd to a shady retreat in the wood,
Where many veil'd forms mute and motionless stood.

"Say, which is Melachlin's fair daughter?—away
With these veils," cried Turgesius, "no longer delay;
Resistance is vain, we will quickly behold
Which robe hides the loveliest face in its fold;
These clouds shall no longer o'ershadow our bliss,
Let each seize a veil—and *my* trophy be *this*!"

He seized a white veil, and before him appear'd
No fearful weak girl—but a foe to be fear'd!
A youth—who sprang forth from his female disguise,
Like lightning that flashes from calm summer skies;
His hand grasp'd a weapon, and wild was the joy
That shone in the glance of the Warrior-Boy.

And under each white robe a youth was conceal'd,
Who met his opponent with sword, and with shield.
Turgesius was slain—and the maidens were blest,
Melachlin's fair daughter more blithe than the rest;—
And ere the last sunbeam had crimson'd the sea,
They hail'd the Boy-Victors—and Erin was free!

T.

GRIMM'S GHOST.

LETTER XVI.

*Autumnal Leaves.*

WHO has not heard of the Duke of Buckingham, who was driven
from London to Mulgrave Castle, Yorkshire, by the great plague?
On the abatement of that scourge, in the autumn of the same year,
the Duke made preparations for returning to his favourite Mall in
Saint James's Park. His rural tenants waited upon him in a body, to
bewail his departure, and respectfully asked when they might hope to
see him again. " Not till the next plague," answered his Grace. The
same Duke, by the way, thus execrated a dog that had offended him—
" Get along with you for a rascally cur ! Ah, I wish you were married and settled in the country."—The late Duke of Queensberry must
be well remembered by most middle-aged inhabitants of the metropolis. Often has my disembodied shade flitted under Lord William
Gordon's wall, opposite the veteran's Piccadilly residence, to gaze upon
him, with his straw hat, green parasol, and nankeen trowsers bleached
by repeated ablutions. " Does not your Grace find London very
empty ?" bawled a morning visitor in his soundest ear, on the fifteenth
day of a hot September. " Yes," answered the Duke; " but it is
fuller than the country."—These are the only two men of whom I ever
heard who pleaded a justification on being seen, like autumnal leaves,
scattered about the streets of London during the fall of the year.
Many others have pleaded a general justification. Doctor Johnson
said, he who is tired of London is tired of existence. Charles Morris
eulogizes " the sweet shady side of Pall Mall," in strains which, like
his favourite beverage, become the mellower for age; and Doctor
Moseley used to say, " I am half distracted whenever I go into the
country; there is such a noise of nothing." All these were celebrated
men, who could brazen it out. The common herd of mortals invent
excuses: they shuffle like a May-day sweep, and lie like the prospectus of a new Magazine. They never saw the humours of Bartholomew
Fair before: they could not, till last Sunday, get a ticket to hear the
Reverend Edward Irving: they have a particular wish to see " the
Great Unknown" in the Haymarket; or the pavement of St. James's
Square is about to be Mac-adamized, and they are bent upon patron-
izing the process.

Lord Robert Ranter is still sneaking about St. James's Street. I
call it sneaking, because, if his optics start any being near the Palace,
he backs up Bury Street; or, if hard pushed, he is intently eager upon
decyphering the allusions in the caricature-shop. Dean Swift tells us
that two of the brothers in the Tale of a Tub made great circuits to
avoid meeting, whereby it usually happened that they encountered
each other. So it fell out last Wednesday with Lord Robert and Captain Augustus Thackeray. The former saw the dapper farce-writer,
mentioned in my last, skipping down St. James's Street, and the latter
beheld young Culpepper swaggering up it. Both were, of course,
ashamed of being autumnal leaves, and both, at the same moment,
bolted into the pastrycook's-shop on the right side as you walk from
Pall Mall to Piccadilly. Each was of course surprised at meeting the

other in London in September. But the mischief did not end here.
The farce-writer was suddenly arrested in his brisk bobbing career by
an odour of mock-turtle soup; and young Culpepper felt a penchant
for a glass of cherry bounce. The consequence was, that all four
men upon the floor of the confectioner. Now came the moment for
two pair of imaginations to come into play. Lord Robert was quite
on the wing; he merely stayed to see Madame Vestris commence her
re-engagement: Captain Thackeray was never more surprised in his
life than in finding himself in town; but the fact was, that his gun
burst last week at Sir Frank Featherspring's, and he had merely come
to purchase a new one. Young Culpepper had been summoned from
Margate to oppose the discharge of an insolvent debtor; and the dapper
farce-writer had sprained his ankle in stepping out of a box at the
Brighton Theatre, and was come to town for advice.—Four greater
falsehoods were never uttered under the roof of Westminster Hall!

The usual question of—"Who would have thought of meeting you
in town at this time of the year?"—having been reciprocally pro-
pounded, all four of our autumnal leaves grew wondrous loving.
"Misery," says the proverb, "makes a man acquainted with strange
bedfellows." September may be said to generate associations equally
extraordinary. Young Culpepper proposed a dinner at his father's
house in Savage Gardens on the following day. The invitation was
joyfully acceded to. As the party separated, young Culpepper and
the farce-writer issued together up Jermyn Street. "I declare I am
quite pleased with Lord Robert's manner," said the former; "I never
knew him so gracious: what can it be owing to?" "The season,"
answered the dramatist: "People of fashion grow quite warm and
hearty when nobody of any note sees them. If the sun were but half
so hot, it would be a capital thing for the harvest." "Well! that accounts for it," ejaculated the young citizen: "old Mrs. Poppleton
stopped her carriage yesterday in Russell Square, on purpose to ask
me to dine with her. She reproached me quite tenderly for never
coming near her: and lo and behold! I found that the foundation of
the feast was her want of a fourth to make up a rubber. She was beating the highways and hedges, and luckily happened to alight upon me."

Old Culpepper received the party with great civility. He, too, was
an autumnal leaf, and he too had his lie ready for being in town. They
could not get a house at Ramsgate; Broadstairs was too retired; and as
for Margate, Mrs. Culpepper would not hear of it: so they meant next
Saturday, to try Brighton: he was aware that there was a terrible creature there, especially from Saturday to Monday: but the air being
do Mrs. Culpepper's stomach good, and he himself had never seen a
chalk pier.

After dinner, at which "the hot and hurried Jane" administered,
without being the authoress of any material catastrophe, Lord Robert
Ranter expressed to Captain Thackeray his surprise at not having seen
his name in the Covent-garden play-bills, after the performance of
Hamlet. "Why, the fact is," said the Captain, "upon reflection, I
did not think it quite a gentlemanly thing to supersede Kean or
Macready: they enjoy a certain portion of popular favour; and being in,
it would not be quite fair to clamber over their heads. No! I have
lately taken to writing my mind coward writing plays, rather than acting
you and Mr. Tom, they accordingly rapped with their hand.
as much as to say.—Well, well, go on. The music, accordingly,

Before dinner, I was looking over the Life of Hayley, in Mrs. Culpepper's window-seat, yonder. I see that the poet, at his outset in life, speculated upon writing two plays per annum, which, at five hundred pounds each (his estimated rate of profit), would give him a thousand a year—a very gentlemanly addition to any man's income. I rather believe, that in point of fact, Hayley never got a thousand pence from the theatre, which I am rather surprised at, for he was unquestionably a gentleman: indeed, he behaved to both his wives in the highest style of fashion."—"At my dramatic outset," said the dapper farce-writer, "my expectations were not less sanguine than those of the poet of Eartham. My first production was a comedy, and my last one a farce." "I should like to know the history of both of them," said old Culpepper, pushing the bottle to him at the same time. "I had once some taste for the drama myself. I shall never forget poor John Palmer at the Royalty. Ah! he was the man for Don Juan. I am told, Lord Byron has failed lately in the part: and well he may. Nobody will ever come up to John Palmer—there was a leg for you!" "My first comedy," said the dramatist, "was called 'Love in Jeopardy:' it was accepted by the proprietors of Covent-garden Theatre." "I am sorry for it," said the founder of the feast; "John Palmer was the man for comedy, and he was at Drury-lane. There was brown powder! poor fellow! and such a pair of blue silk stockings." "Nothing could equal my joy at seeing it advertised in the red bills of the day," continued the writer of farces. "Except your fear at the drawing up of the curtain," said Thackeray: "Egad! that is an awful moment. I felt it myself the other day in Hamlet. I slew whole squadrons at Waterloo, without a tenth of the trepidation I then felt." "My piece was successful," continued the play-wright; "and at that time authors received their remuneration by taking the profits of the third, sixth, and ninth nights. The celebrated Cumberland shook my hand, and dubbed me the modern Congreve. On the third night, an envious shower of rain fell at six o'clock, insomuch, that the expences did not enter the house." "The rain might have thinned the pit and galleries," observed the honest slopseller, "but that could not have kept the company away from the dress-boxes." "I beg your pardon, sir," retorted the follower of the Muses; "people of fashion, in these days, did not like to expose their horses: coachmen then did not want Mr. Martin of Galway to teach them humanity. Well! the sixth night arrived, and a finer night I never witnessed. I looked out upon the chapel-leads from the window of my lodging in Martlet-court, and they were as dry as a bone. Off I went to the Theatre at a quarter before six, and stationed myself in what was then called the slips. The house was very respectably filled, and I calculated upon at least a hundred pounds beyond the expenses. At the close of the first music, however, to my great annoyance, Lewis, the manager, made his appearance, and informed the house, that Mr. Middleton having been taken suddenly ill, Mr. Toms had kindly undertaken to read the part of Courtly, and hoped for their usual kind indulgence. You might have knocked me down with a feather. Happily, however, the audience did not seem to think there was much to choose between Mr. Middleton and Mr. Toms; they accordingly slightly clapped with their hands, as much as to say—'Well, well! go on.' The music, accordingly, continued, and I was ready to dance to it for joy. The prompter now rang his bell, and the green curtain slowly rising, discovered a genteel drawing-room, with two red chairs, and a sofa of the same material painted in the flats. Lewis, at this juncture, once more issued upon the stage. My heart was in my mouth! 'Ladies and Gentlemen,' said the stage-manager, ' I am extremely sorry to appear again before you, to entreat your farther indulgence; but the fact is, that Mrs. Esten, who was to have played the part of Eugenia, is taken so alarmingly ill, that her life is despaired of: under this awful visitation, Mrs. Twiselden has kindly undertaken—' The audience would hear no more: groans, hisses, catcalls, and sucked oranges, assailed the apologist from every quarter."—" I should like to see the sucked orange that dared fly at John Palmer," said old Culpepper. " Ah! he was the man for an apology—such a white cambric handkerchief."—"Lewis retreated, of course," said the narrator, " and in two minutes re-appeared, with a proposal couched in the following words: 'Ladies and gentlemen, I feel greatly concerned at having excited your displeasure, and have only to add, that I am authorized by the proprietor to inform you, that whoever objects to his arrangement may again receive his money at the door.' ' Oh! very well,' exclaimed at least two hundred voices; and away stalked the utterers to the right and left, carrying away my property in their pockets. Scarcely knowing what I did, I rushed out of the house, and ran, as if the devil drove me, to Mrs. Esten's abode in Orange-street. The drawing-room windows of the lady glittered with lights, and ostrich feathers were waving in every direction. My thundering appeal to the knocker brought to the door Mrs. Bennett, her mother. ' Good heavens! madam,' said I, ' I have left the Theatre in the greatest confusion from the absence of your daughter.' ' Oh, Sir!' whined the matron, 'such an alarming illness'—' Illness, madam! what with all these lamps and ostrich feathers!' ' Oh! only a few particular friends to keep up her spirits,' rejoined the old lady. Finding that nothing was to be gained in that quarter, I returned to Covent-garden, and discovered a ' beggarly account of empty boxes.' ' Really, Sir,' said I to Lewis, ' I think that, under the circumstances, the Theatre should allow me the money that *was* in it.'—' You may try 'em, if you please,' said Lewis, with his accustomed jerk of the head; ' but I think I can venture to say you won't catch them at it.'"—" Fill your glass, Sir," said Culpepper; " I think I can venture to say that poor John Palmer would never have served you so. Ah! there was a leg! and such a pair of silver buckles! I see him now, starting back and making his hair-powder fly over the fiddlers' heads.—Well; but your ninth night?" " Oh! on the ninth night," said the poet, " the play was Fontainville Forest—a stupid ghost thing of Bowden's."—" I wonder you did not call Lewis out," observed Captain Thackeray; " there's nothing like a bullet for making people civil. So much for your first play; and now for your last farce."—" Not till you have tasted this cool bottle," said old Culpepper: " there, try that; you may be a very good poet, but you are a bad hand at passing the bottle. Ah! poor John Palmer! he was the man for passing the bottle: we shall never see the bottle passed again!—But I beg pardon; you were going to tell us about your last farce."—" Why, the history of my last farce," said the bard, " is told in two words: it was neither more nor less than egregiously and unanimously damned. Not a single point told.

They set off dully; and when once the audience are at fault, the very things that would otherwise delight are sure to disgust. In order to imbibe unbiassed opinions, I had stationed myself in the two-shilling gallery. How short-sighted an expedient! The people there were absolutely frantic with rage. The author was a villain: they only wished they had him there; might the devil fetch them if they would not throw him over into the Pit. Alarmed for my personal safety, I followed an orange-woman up the benches, and stole out of that populous pandemonium: awhile I hesitated on the brink of the upper row— ' Shall I stop here?' said I to myself; ' or shall I stop at the stage-door?'" " Stop any thing but the bottle," interrupted the founder of the feast. " Well! at length I slowly paced down stairs, walked into Hart-street, and entered at the stage-door. Afraid to face the pity of the actors in the Green-room, I wandered amid the scenery at the back of the stage, among a motley assemblage of baronial castles, woods, cascades, butchers' shops, and Chinese pagodas; yet still the howls and hisses rang in my ears. While standing there, like Orestes tortured by the Furies, two scene-shifters saw and recognised me. ' Well! never mind, Dick,' said the one of them to the other (affecting not to know me), ' I 'll bet you a pot of beer this farce looks up, after all.' Thus I commenced my dramatic career by being put upon a level with Congreve, and ended it by being pitied by a scene-shifter!"—" But, zounds!" exclaimed the Thespian Captain, " you did not put up with it, did you? Where were your pistols?"—" Put up with it!" said the poet; " to be sure I did: how could I help myself?"—" Very badly," said the slopseller, " if I may judge from your conduct here: the bottle has stood at your right elbow two minutes and a half, and you have not helped yourself yet."

## OUR LADY'S WELL.[*]

Fount of the Woods! thou art hid no more
From Heaven's clear eye, as in time of yore!
For the roof hath sunk from thy mossy walls,
And the Sun's free glance on thy slumber falls,
And the dim tree-shadows across thee pass,
As the boughs are sway'd o'er thy silvery glass,
And the reddening leaves to thy breast are blown,
When the Autumn-wind hath a stormy tone,
And thy bubbles rise to the flashing rain—
Bright Fount! thou art Nature's own again!

Fount of the Vale! thou art sought no more
By the Pilgrim's foot, as in time of yore,
When he came from afar, his beads to tell,
And to chaunt his hymn, at our Lady's well.
There is heard no *Ave* through thy bowers,
Thou art gleaming lone midst thy water-flowers;
But the herd may drink from thy gushing wave,
And there may the reaper his forehead lave,
And the woodman seeks thee not in vain—
Bright Fount! thou art Nature's own again!

[*] A beautiful Spring in North Wales, formerly dedicated to the Virgin, and much frequented by Pilgrims.

Fount of the Virgin's mind shrine
A voice that speaks of the past is thine!
It mingles the tone of a thoughtful sigh
With the notes that ring through the laughing sky;
Midst the mirthful song of the summer-bird,
And the sound of the breeze, it will yet be heard!
Why is it that thus we may look on thee,
To the festal sunshine sparkling free?—
'Tis that all on earth is of Time's domain—
He hath made thee Nature's own again!

Fount of the Chapel with ages grey
Thou art springing freshly amidst decay!
Thy rites are past, and thy Cross lies low,
And the changeful hours breathe o'er thee now!
Yet if at thine altar one holy thought
In man's deep spirit of old hath wrought,
If peace to the mourner hath here been given,
Or prayer from a chasten'd heart to Heaven,
Be the spot still hallow'd while Time shall reign,
Who hath made thee Nature's own again!                F. H.

## MEMOIRS BY BARON FAIN AND GENERAL RAPP.[*]

We have to congratulate the public on the appearance of two more volumes of Memoirs relative to the reign and character of Napoleon, which in their different ways are calculated to throw a strong light upon their subject; to enhance the credibility of many known anecdotes; while they add to the number of facts already accumulated; and to give precision and fixity to the ideas which philosophy shall entertain of the singular being from whom they derive their interest,—his motions, and their ends. It is thus that the present generation is favoured with the possession of knowledge, which in the less stirring ages, ere the press had received the full developement of its powers, was neglected and lost, or at best, left to be recovered by posterity through the purblind labours of antiquarians, the casual good luck of compilers, and the conjectural felicity of historians in tracing causes and their effects. Scarcely three years have elapsed since the decease of Napoleon in his "lonely isle," and already we are in possession of abundant materials for history, reflecting his mind in every point of view from which it could be approached, and illustrating his greatest actions by the minutest traits of manifestation, which have escaped in moments of domestic privacy, of confidential intercourse, or of uncontrollable excitement.

Baron Fain and General Rapp, the authors of the Memoirs now under consideration, present two more instances of that unbounded attachment and affectionate admiration which Napoleon seems to have inspired in all who were placed near his person; and their testimony will doubtless have its weight in removing that fabric of prejudice and of falsehood, which a cowardly and contemptible expediency had

[*] "Memoirs of General Count Rapp, First Aide-de-Camp to Napoleon; written by himself, and published by his family." 1 vol. 8vo.—"The Manuscript of 1814; a History of Events which led to the Abdication of Napoleon. By Baron Fain." 1 vol. 8vo.

erected for the grossest purposes of national deception. "Politicians,"
says a valuable political writer*, "speak to live; and so inveterate is
their malice, that they blast even those whom they patronise." Never,
perhaps, was political malice more ingenious and more active to mis-
represent than against Napoleon Bonaparte; and never did it recoil
with more deadly effect than upon those of his enemies who have not
disdained to belie their victim, that they might the more securely destroy him. To this systematic attack on the character of the Emperor,
and its operation on the natural credulity of our countrymen, allusion
has been already made in a former number; but the evil still exists.
Though Napoleon be dead, the interests connected with his name are
in full and vigorous existence; and there are too many who have (or
fancy they have) an advantage in decrying his memory, and misrepresenting his deeds. The truth is, however, of the last importance to
humanity. The life of this man, and the age in which he moved, form
the most wondrous page which history has yet presented to the contemplation of philosophy; and accordingly as it is read, the future
destinies of society may receive a brighter or more sombre colour. A
great experiment has been made upon human nature; and the welfare
of mankind is deeply involved in the fairness of its exposition.

The reigning dynasties of Europe most egregiously miscalculate in
supposing that *they* profit by the disseminated story of Napoleon's imputed crimes. Legitimacy and usurpation have run a race of error, in
which each has been more anxious to seek in the other an example to
justify its own excesses, than a beacon to preserve it from that mistake
and folly which have forced them both in their turn to abdicate with
disgrace. It is in vain that the powers that be signalize the tyranny
and violence of the powers that are no more; so long as they imitate or
even exceed them; and there is the less danger in leaving the Emperor
in possession of those personal virtues with which nature and circumstance had endowed him, since let them have been what they might, he
has not the less plunged the nation he governed in all but hopeless and
irretrievable ruin. However ennobling and spirit-stirring might be
the genius of his reign, as compared to the lethargic leadenness of
common-place despotism, however great the activity he impressed on
the people he goaded to new exertions, still his influence was tyrannical;
and being so, was inevitably hostile to humanity; and the virtues by
which it was accompanied can rank as little better than splendid faults,
unredeeming in the eye of philosophy, as were the virtues of the Pagan
philosophers in the estimate of Catholic self-sufficiency. Could the
genius and the ardour of a despot suffice to carry a nation forward to
the acmé of prosperity, Napoleon had wherewithal to have succeeded;
but the thing itself was impossible; and the knowledge of this fact is
of no trifling import to mankind. The same infirmity of human nature
which will not suffer the private man to act morally well, when uncontrolled by the will of his fellow-creatures, effectually prevents a king
from doing politically right, when emancipated from all law and judgment of society. Of this truth Napoleon affords the happiest illustration; and it is a capital crime against society to aim at destroying its
effect, by denying the good qualities, or magnifying the faults, of this

singular man, in the hope of sinking him to the level of the tyrants who may figure in the every-day roll of despotism and sottishness.

To cover Napoleon personally with obloquy, to make of him a theatrical Richard the Third, a raw-head-and-bloody-bones of the nursery, in short, to put the *man* in the place of the *emperor*, is to turn the passions of society against a combination that is already passed, and to avert its attention from truths that are eternal, and from interests that are momentarily pressing. The vices of despots are a convenient cover for the original sin of despotism. The life of Napoleon, as it has been read to the people of England, has been made a perpetual apology for absolute monarchy; and the Emperor the scape-goat of his caste. The lesson to be learned from his real character is, on the contrary, an exposition of the value of institutions; a demonstration of the little opportunity which a despotic government affords even the best ruler for *willing* good, and of the invincible obstacles it opposes to his carrying into effect even his few praiseworthy intentions.* On this subject, Rapp has a passage strongly in point, which we shall, therefore, take leave to quote :—

"'Many persons have described Napoleon as a violent, harsh, and passionate man; this is because they have not known him. Absorbed as he was in important business, opposed in his views, and impeded in his plans, it was certainly natural that he should sometimes evince impatience and inequality of temper. His natural kindness and generosity soon subdued his irritation; but it must be observed that, far from seeking to appease him, his confidents never failed to excite his anger. ' Your Majesty is right,' they would say, ' such a one deserves to be shot or broken, dismissed or disgraced: I have long known him to be your enemy. An example must be made; it is necessary for the maintenance of tranquillity.'

"If the 'matter in question had been to levy contributions on the enemy's territory, Napoleon, perhaps, would demand twenty millions; but he would be advised to exact ten millions more. He would be told by those about him, ' It is necessary that your Majesty should spare your treasury, that you should maintain your troops at the expense of foreign countries, or leave them to subsist on the territory of the Confederation.'

"If he entertained the idea of levying 200,000 conscripts, he was persuaded to demand 300,000. If he proposed to pay a creditor whose right was unquestionable, doubts were started respecting the legality of the debt. The amount claimed was perhaps reduced to one half, or one third; and it not unfrequently happened that the debt was denied altogether.

"If he spoke of commencing war, the bold resolution was applauded. It was said war enriched France; that it was necessary to astonish the world, and to astonish it in a way worthy of the great nation.

"Thus, by being excited and urged to enter upon uncertain plans and enterprises, Napoleon was plunged into continual war. Thus it was, that his reign was impressed with an air of violence contrary to his own character and habits, which were perfectly gentle.

---

* Napoleon had a great idea of his own powers of beneficence. He says, " Archimède promettait tout si on lui laissait poser le bout de son levier. Je en casse fait autant par tout où l'on m'eût laissé poser mon énergie, mon persévérance, et mes budjets."—*Las Cases, 5ième Partie.* Napoleon, indeed, did much to advance the physical condition of his people; but not so much as a free people might have effected for themselves with the same means. Then his moral miscalculations overthrew all; and had they not brought the country to a prompt and precipitous ruin, they would have inevitably entailed a chronic decay upon it, equally subversive of all permanent prosperity. Tyranny may have its incidental advantages; but it will not, and it cannot come to good.

'" Never was there a man more inclined to indulgence, or more ready to listen to the voice of humanity: of this I could mention a thousand examples."

We have dwelt once more upon this " sophism of the man for the thing," as Jeremy Bentham would call it, and with the greater emphasis, because it is daily wielded with a mischievous efficacy by the enemies of all liberal institutions, and because it is ostentatiously put forth by those who would wheedle us at once out of liberty and common sense. The " despotism of Napoleon," the " crimes of the Usurper," are the cuckoo notes of *Ultraism ;* as if the service of other tyrants were perfect freedom ; and as if oppression were not equally ruinous and demoralizing in the long-lined descendants of a Rodolf, or a Vitikind, as in the most ephemeral fungus of anarchy and revolution.

The publication of the numerous French memoirs which have appeared within the last eighteen months, is calculated to form an epoch in political discussion; and, in more senses than one, to influence public opinion. The life of Napoleon is, in all its details, a course of political philosophy, a running commentary upon human nature and society. From the dirty, obscure, and mole-like workings of courtly diplomacy, to the zeal and enthusiasm of the common soldier, the nature and potentialities of the human heart in all classes were laid bare to his inspection, and were employed in his calculations. He was likewise personally acquainted with almost every individual who now figures on the stage of Europe. He had fathomed the shallowness, and applied his touchstone to the baseness of those pigmies, who, enveloping themselves in his mantle, now imagine that they have attained to his gigantic proportions : and the details of his conversations, his opinions, and the facts he related to his recording friends, which have become public property through these publications, derive additional importance, from the frequent and strong lights they reflect upon those who at present hold in their hands the destinies of nations. The Memoirs of General Rapp we consider as among the most valuable of the recent additions to our stock of information concerning Napoleon, and " *le grand siècle,*" of which he is the hero. The traits of character and the reflections on events which are given by Las Cases, O'Meara, &c. however estimable they may be for their self-evident veracity, and for the proximity of the narrators' approaches to the great man they paint, are still but portraitures of Napoleon in exile ; and the statements which he makes to them of opinions and facts, are but recollections, for the most part modified by the success or failure of the combinations to which they relate. They are the judgments of a man changed in his fortunes, influenced by experience, and forced, both by circumstances, and his own human nature, to put the best face upon things, and to colour transactions (not fraudulently indeed, but unconsciously,) into an appearance of philosophy and consistency. The sketches of Gen. Rapp, on the contrary, exhibit his master in the heat of action, in the hurry and the bustle of the passing moment. They shew the man as he was at the time—they preserve his ideas in the instant of their formation—they embalm his motive impressions, such as they occurred in the act of volition ; and not such as they appeared to himself to have been on a distant retrospection, through a long vista of years, and a still longer perspective of mighty and overwhelming events.

The character of Rapp, as with great naiveté he paints it himself, and as he is represented by all who knew him, admirably fitted him for recording with fidelity whatever passed under his observation. Frank, loyal, a soldier of fortune, yielding lightly and promptly to the impulses of a generous disposition, and speaking with boldness, and even with abruptness, the first dictates of his heart, he seems frequently to have incurred the transient displeasure of Napoleon, by a forgetfulness of the state and dignity of the Imperial position; and by a hasty resentment at the distance which followed the substitution of a royal court for a military household, and the establishment of a cold etiquette between those who had hitherto enjoyed the free intercourse of a camp. Yet by Napoleon he was liked and esteemed; and the Emperor, notwithstanding an occasional petulant outcry against his aide-de-camp's "mauvaise tête," frequently observed of him, that " it was not easy to find a man of more natural good sense and discernment than Rapp." The style of the memoir corresponds with this eulogium of its author. It shews no elaborate effort to systematize; it neither eulogizes nor depreciates *ex professo*; it paints neither a god nor a dæmon. Grateful for personal kindness and professional advancement; full of admiration for the military talents and the good qualities of his master, Rapp is neither overpowered by a sense of the Imperial greatness, nor blinded to the errors of the man. His anecdotes arise out of the events he relates, as mere matters-of-fact, and are thus totally divested of artificial colouring, and free from all ground of suspicion. There is in them, on the contrary, an open *off-handedness* (to use a significant Irishism), which forces on the reader an irresistible conviction of truth and fair dealing.

To the vile and worthless part of the French nobility—to those who, after betraying Louis XVI. to the scaffold, by their silly flight and fatal intrigues, returned to lay themselves under the feet of Napoleon—Rapp entertained a rooted antipathy; and he had a clear and just view of the Emperor's bad policy as a *novus homo*, and the " child and champion" of the Revolution, in adopting the old nobility into the machinery of his new government. This sharp-sightedness was perhaps increased by a soldier's jealousy on seeing these men step between the army and its General. Notwithstanding this pique, the prevailing fairness of Rapp's narrative warrants our crediting his account of the conduct of the *anciens nobles* towards the Emperor; more especially as it is corroborated by a vast many other authorities.

" Most of these same nobles, however, allege that they had yielded only to compulsion. Nothing can be more false. I know of only two who received Chamberlain's appointments unsolicited. Some few declined advantageous offers; but with these exceptions, all solicited, entreated, and importuned. There was a competition of zeal and devotedness altogether unexampled. The meanest employment, the humblest offices, nothing was rejected. It seemed to be an affair of life and death. Should a treacherous hand ever find its way into the portfolios of MM. Talleyrand, Montesquiou, Segur, Durac, &c., what ardent expressions may be found to enrich the language of attachment. But the individuals who held this language now vie with each other in giving vent to hatred and invective. If they really felt for Napoleon the profound hatred which they now evince, it must be confessed that, in crouching at his feet for fifteen years, they did strange violence to their feelings. And yet all Europe can bear witness, that from their unrestrained manner, their never-varying smile, and their supple marks of obedience, their services seemed to be of their own free choice, and cost them but little sacrifice."

What follows is in page 149, *àpropos* to another subject—

"The Emperor had several long conferences with the Minister of Police. He complained of the Faubourg St. Germain. The contrast of humility and boldness alternately displayed by the old nobility, in the antechambers and saloons, disconcerted him: he could scarcely conceive that these men were so base and perfidious as to destroy with the one hand while they solicited favours with the other. He appeared inclined to severity; but Fouché dissuaded him from that course. 'It is a traditionary remark,' said he, ' that the Seine flows, the Faubourg intrigues, solicits, devours, and calumniates. This is in the order of nature; every thing has its attributes.' Napoleon yielded; he avenged himself only on men. It was proposed that he should make a solemn entry into the capital; but this he declined: the conqueror of the world was superior to the triumphs which transported the Romans. On the following day the court left Fontainebleau. The Emperor rode to Paris without stirrups: he outstripped all his escort; none but a chasseur of the guard was able to keep up with him. In this manner he arrived at the Tuileries."

To the domestic affections of Napoleon, Rapp bears honourable testimony; and we of our personal knowledge can aver, that his mother, habitually spoke of him, with the tears in her eyes, as " being in the height of his power and imperial sway a dutiful and affectionate son." Politically speaking, this strong family feeling was a fault. An unmeasured ambition to enrich and advance his family, betrayed the Emperor into those false calculations concerning Spain which laid the foundation of his ruin. On the other hand, had he attended to his brother Lucien, he might have met a less horrible fate, and what is of still more importance, Europe might have escaped the long chain of calamities under which it now suffers, and of which no mortal can foresee the termination. On what trifles do the dearest interests of man most commonly depend!! Upon one occasion, in some discussion on the imperial plans and policy, Lucien, heated by dispute, dashed his watch with violence to the earth, and exclaimed, " You will destroy yourself, as I now destroy this bauble, and a time will come when your family and your friends will not know where to lay their heads. All the family, says Rapp, except his mother, "*tout abreuve d'amertumes,*" have drenched him with vexations; and numerous stories of domestic *tracasseries* have got wind through other channels. Without, however, crediting every anecdote, in which *rovit* has too probably drawn upon *truth,* we may remark upon the strange nature of volition, whose strength bears so little relation to that of the other mental powers. He, whose nod governed Europe from the Tagus to the Borysthenes, was unable to master the obstinacy or the caprice of a domestic *coterie;* and the lightest fancies of a headstrong woman may have often outweighed the deliberate designs of the world's master. In Chapter V., the testimony of Rapp confirms what Las Cases has related of Napoleon's manner in council, and of his desire to avoid flattery and hear the truth. But the desire to reign, and to be treated with ingenuousness, are incompatibles. Napoleon's petulance alone, his impatience of nonsense, was enough, in such a man, to frighten away candour from his presence. On his return from Russia, he one day

deplored with great emotion the death of his soldiers swept off by
cold, hunger, and the Cossack's lance; when a courtier ventured to put
in his word, and with a rueful countenance to reply, " Yes, we have
suffered a severe loss." " True," rejoined Napoleon, " Madame
Boulli is dead." Who, that is exposed to such treatment, could venture to hazard an opinion, unless perfectly certain beforehand of its
success with the Emperor ?

After the few preliminary chapters dedicated to a sketch of Napoleon, in his several relations of soldier, citizen, governor, and head of a
family, the rest of the volume is occupied with an account of those military and political transactions, in which Rapp himself took a part ;
and more especially the conquest of Prussia, the fatal campaign of
Russia, the siege of Dantzic, and the events of the hundred days. Rapp
was among the number of those who had accepted a commission from
Louis XVIII ; and the dialogue which he records as having passed
between himself and Napoleon, on his return to the Tuileries, is well
worthy of perusal.

The description of the burning of Moscow is written by Rapp with
a vivacity almost dramatic : the reader seems to watch the progress of
the flames as he advances. The ill-fated retreat from Russia is likewise detailed with no less vigour and effect. Throughout the whole
work, indeed, the narrative is rapid and clear. Attention rarely flags,
though the subjects are sometimes treated at great length ; the siege of
Dantzic, more especially, is as protracted on paper as it was in the
field. It was the great military event of the author's life ; and of
course a theme on which he dwells with complacency. To conclude,
the whole work abounds with philosophic reflection; and in the style
and manner of its composition far exceeds what might have been expected from a mere soldier, whose education must have been hasty, if
it was not neglected.

Of Baron Fain's volume, we have scarcely left ourselves space to
speak. It embraces only the events which preceded and occasioned
the Abdication in 1814 ; and it is chiefly occupied with the military
events of that singular campaign ; which, though the least successful,
was the most wonderful in its display of military talent, and the developement of Napoleon's resources. Although thus employed with
marches and countermarches, the work, like all other works which
treat of Bonaparte, abounds in matter interesting to the moralist, the
philosopher, and the hunter after anecdotes.

We cannot, however, in closing this article, pass over in silence the
leading impression we have received from a perusal of the Memoirs of
which it treats : and that is, the conviction of the overwhelming dispa-
rity of means to ends in the great drama of Napoleon's life. What infinite toil and suffering, what carnage, what desolation, what waste of the
products of peaceful industry, were occasioned through a long series
of years to carry the French eagles to Moscow, that they might be
driven back to the capital, and be there trodden under the feet of a barbarian conqueror ;—to raise one man to the summit of Imperial ambition, that he might be dashed from his precipitous height, to dispute
and chicane on the rock of St. Helena, to writhe under an ignoble and
paltry tyranny, and to die obscurely, the victim of petty vexations, and
of hardships that scarcely bear narration! What, on the other hand,

have his enemies attained by the success of their arms? The people, a transfer of masters, and perpetuated slavery!—the combined kings, an uncertain and precarious power, a throne raised with sand over the womb of a volcano!!! Such are the mysterious, yet the whimsical destinies of man, under existing systems. His talents, genius, perseverance, affections, his tears, sweat, and blood, are but as a rattle in the hand of an infant, which is agitated to make the amusement of an idle moment, and is broken to pieces on the first impulse of satiety or caprice.

---

## TRUTH AND YOUNG ROMANCE, A SONG.

Young Romance through roses straying,
　Saw old Truth trudge lamely on;
*One* in pleasure's light was playing,
　The *other* sigh'd for pleasures gone:
Cries Romance, "O rest a minute,
　And discuss our views of Earth:—
*Yours* may have most prudence in it,
　But in *mine* is all the mirth."

"Ah!" says Truth, "this world discloses
　Nought but vain delusive wiles,
Thorns are under all your roses,
　Sadness follows all your smiles:"
—Cries Romance, "Perhaps I often
　Colour life with tints too warm;
Yet *my warmth* a *shade* may soften,
　While *your coldness* chills a charm."

"What is Love?" the sage then asks him—
　"Love—in summer-hours so sweet?
Wintry weather soon unmasks him,
　And your idol proves a cheat!"
"Love!" the youth replies, "O sever
　Real Love from vain deceits;
Constant Love brings hours that never
　Lose their sunshine or their sweets."

"*Friendship* too, you call a treasure,
　But," says Truth, "it is a tie
Loosely worn 'mid scenes of pleasure,
　And when fortune frowns—thrown by."
"Friendship," he replies, "possesses
　Worth which no dark change destroys;
Seeking, soothing our distresses,
　Sharing, doubling all our joys."

"Go," says Truth, "'tis plain we never
　Can such hostile thoughts combine;
Folly is your guide for ever,
　While dull sense must still be mine."
Cries the Boy—"Frown on, no matter,
　Mortals love my merry glance;
E'en in Truth's own path they scatter
　Roses snatch'd from young Romance."

T.

## A DAY AT FONTHILL ABBEY.

THE world may just at present be divided into two classes of persons; those who have seen Fonthill Abbey, and those who have not: and it is the somewhat monopolizing and ambitious desire of this paper to make itself agreeable to both these classes. For the former, it would endeavour to retrace the scenes which they have lately visited, but which the cursory glance they were compelled to take at them can scarcely have permanently fixed on their memory, and which a second view of this kind may perhaps effect; and to the latter it would present the best, because the only substitute they will be able to compass, by the time they are reading this. But to each it can only hope to offer a sketch, an outline, a mere pen-and-ink drawing of the scene in question;—leaving the fillings-up, the colouring, and the light and shade, to be supplied by the memory of the one and the imagination of the other.

The domain of Fonthill is so extensive, and the attractions it offers to the spectator are so numerous and various, that, in order to apply our limited time and resources in the most advantageous manner, we shall adopt the arrangement laid down for the casual visitors to this singular spot; for we can afford but a day to what cannot be duly examined and explored in less than a month;—unless, indeed, the readers of the New Monthly Magazine are disposed to meet in a body, and sign a *Round Robin* to the Editor, insisting on *our* being allowed to exercise "sole sovereign sway and mastery" in these pages during the next or any given month. In which case, on receiving due notice and double pay, we will engage to supply the usual number and variety of articles, including the usual quantity of entertainment, and of course written with the usual, or rather the *unusual* portion of talent,—the subject-matter being all drawn from this fertile source. In the mean time, we must proceed in the routine above-named.

Placing the reader at once before the outer gateway of what is called the Old Park, we will first invite him to admire the grand character of this almost triumphal arch, and then, passing through its noble portal, enter the outward inclosure of the grounds immediately attached to the mansion. On passing this gate we find ourselves on the borders of a noble lake, the banks of which rise majestically on the opposite side, and are clothed with a rich grove of forest trees, of an immense height. The first sight that we have to point out, as not exactly consistent with the true taste that we had expected to find reigning and ruling throughout this spot, is a whole *flock* of swans, congregating together on the lake. There is a saying, that "some people's geese are all swans;" but it is quite as great and as common a mistake to make all our swans into geese. There is nothing enhances the value of a thing like its rarity;—or rather its value chiefly *consists* in its rarity, if it is an object of mere ornament. Even if it be ever so beautiful to the sight, its beauty loses its effect in proportion as it becomes multiplied. The swan that

—— "on still St. Mary's lake
Floats double, swan and shadow,"

is a lovely and highly poetical object; but multiply it to a whole flock, and the charm is broken at once. A swan is an object which depends, for its effects, purely and entirely on the beauty of its form and motion; its appearance as an ornament to natural scenery should therefore be, like those of angels, "few, and far between." The effect of a whole company of *moons* floating through the sky together, would border on the ludicrous; and a whole flock of swans are, upon the same principle, no better than so many geese!

"But how is this?" we hear our companion exclaim; "a Ciceroni turned critic, will never do. We came all this way to see beauties, not defects; and unless we *look for* them, we never *can* see them. Away, then, with the critical spirit, and shew us nothing but what is worth seeing—or rather, worth coming to see; which faults and defects can in no case be, though they were the finest that were ever committed." The reproof is merited, and we bow before it, and stand corrected. Once for all, then, this spot does include many points well worthy of discommendation; and let those who like the task, undertake to supply this desideratum.

This, then, is the portal, behind which has been rising, year by year for a quarter of a century,—"rising like an exhalation"—a scene which was said to surpass the fictions of eastern fancy, and which was created apparently only that it might *not* be seen! And what is the "Open Sesame!" which is at last to dissolve the charm, and lay bare these mysterious inclosures to the rude and vulgar gaze of all comers? Alas! a little bit of gold!—Gold—the only universal picklock—the only veritable *aquà mirabilis*, which can dissolve all things—the only true Talisman of Oromanes,—which no force nor art can withstand, and which, sooner or later, all things must and will give way before—from the *most* accessible and yielding, to the least so—from the conscience of a politician to the pride of a misanthrope—from the impalpable echoes of Saint Stephen's Chapel, to the massive portals of Fonthill Abbey! That which would not hitherto have moved at the mandate of all the Sovereigns of Europe, the Holy Alliance included, now flies open of itself a hundred times a day, at the mere sight of a *half-sovereign*, presented by the, perchance, soiled fingers of a London cockney or a country boor!

Proceeding along the carriage-way through the old park, with the fine lake before mentioned lying all along the view on the left, backed by a lofty grove of trees, and embowered lawns rising and falling on the right, we presently arrive at an elevated spot, where this part of the domain terminates; and passing on for a short distance to the westward, along a public lane, we reach a rusticated lodge, beside a gateway cut in the wall which surrounds the whole inner portion of the grounds.

There is a pleasant story connected with this wall, which may amuse us while we are waiting our turn to be admitted through its mysterious gateway. Two young gentlemen, one of whom has since turned out an enterprising traveller, and whose success may probably be traced to the spirit excited by the romantic termination of this first adventure, contrived to scale this barrier, and make their way into the grounds—attracted by the rumoured wonders of the place. But it so happened, that they were almost immediately met by the owner, who, instead of directing his servants to shew them the gate, received them with a haughty politeness, and, after leading them through the splendours of his solitary dwelling, set them down to a princely entertainment. When night arrived, however, and they proposed to take their leave, (doubtless overjoyed with the success of their adventure, and anticipating the curiosity and envy they should excite among their friends, by the tale they had to tell,) they were conducted to the spot where they had been first met, and informed, that, as they had found their way *in*, they might now find their way *out* again as well as they could! And they were left to themselves! What became of them, it is difficult to guess, and they themselves have probably never disclosed: for the place is a perfect labyrinth even in the day-time, and there is a single pathway through it which measures above twenty miles, without once crossing or retreading a footstep of the same ground. This capital piece of practical wit was not unworthy the author of Vathek, and is in fact, not unlike some of those bitter ones which Vathek himself used occasionally to indulge in.

The avenue we enter on passing through the above-named gate, consists of a narrow carriage-way, with a greensward path on each side of it, bounded and shut in by a thick plantation, chiefly consisting of firs, larches, and pines, the spaces between the pillar-like stems of which are filled by a variety of flowering shrubs, and wild underwoods, so that you cannot judge of its extent, except by the almost impenetrable darkness which pervades it wherever you attempt to look through; with the exception, however, of one point, where a magnificent view of the adjacent country suddenly breaks upon you at an unexpected opening on the left, near the termination of the road. This road is above a mile in length, and winds about perpetually, so that you can never see for a hundred yards before you; and you get no glimpse of any object but the road itself and the bordering plantation, except at the opening I have just noticed.

Before we reach the summit of this road, which ascends nearly the whole length of it, let us examine this delightful carpet on which we are treading: it is worth the trouble; for it is rarer than that which proceeds from the rarest looms of Persia. Nothing but the absolute solitude which has reigned in this spot during so many years, could have completed the formation of such a one. You observe, as your feet cease to press upon it, it springs up from under them, as if it were not made or accustomed to be trod upon. It is composed of a thick elastic body of various kinds of evergreen moss, low ground-fern that is almost like moss, wild thyme, and numerous sweet-smelling ground-flowers; the whole matted and interlaced together by a network of wild strawberries; their innocent little flowers peeping out here and there, as if afraid, yet anxious to be seen. Smile not contemptuously, *gentle* reader, if we now ask you to step off this sweet border, and not to make a common footpath of it. It was made for the eye and the mind, not for the feet; and if we do nothing better than induce you to keep on this gravel road instead, we shall not have accompanied you here in vain, either as it regards ourselves or you. If Mr. Wordsworth's poetry had done nothing better than teach a few lovers of Nature never to tread upon a daisy, the consciousness of this alone might repay him for all the ignorant and heartless vituperation it has called forth!

Having arrived within a few paces of the summit of the above road, now, for the first time, the extraordinary building, which we have chiefly come to see, bursts upon us—first its majestic tower, clothed, as it frequently is, in obscuring mists, which almost give it the appearance of descending from the clouds, instead of ascending to them; then the crowd of *subject* towers, turrets, and spires, which cluster round about it; and lastly, that gigantic wing which projects from the eastern side, and forms the exterior of the great baronial hall—not yet completed. It is not part of our plan to pause here, and examine the details of this unique building, which, on a slight turn of the road, we now stand in the august presence of. Whether viewed from this point, or from any of the numerous others which the grounds afford, we shall find, that the general impression derived from it, is of a complicated nature, but in every respect commensurate with the means which have been lavished to produce it.

Before we proceed farther in our examination of this stupendous building and the external objects connected with it, we had, perhaps, better at once take a cursory glance at its interior; for, otherwise, we may chance to get so imbued with the impressions of its external grandeur, as to be disposed to look at its internal and merely ornamental riches in too critical a taste.

The view which we have now seen of the Abbey must be considered as the back part of it; and it is here that, following the routine laid down for the casual visitors, we will enter,—at a little low portal, latticed, and opening to a small narrow passage. Those who are disposed to exclaim against this unimposing entrance, (and this number includes nearly all that come,) should remember that it belongs to the *offices* alone; and is, under the usual circumstances, intended merely for the servants: the principal entrance itself, looking to the West, being incomparably the grandest portion of the building.

On passing through the Eastern entrance just named, the first room we enter is one which gives a good foretaste of the splendours we are to expect in the rest of the internal arrangements. It is called the Oak Dining-parlour; and though sadly disfigured at present by tables set out with ugly Dresden china, and execrable modern-looking silver *plateaus, epergnes,* and the " *unlike,*" it is a noble apartment, enriched with elaborate oak carvings covering every part of it, except the large pannels, which are filled with tapestry. The rich massive gothic window-frames of this apartment, glazed with immense sheets of plate-glass, and finished at top by small compartments of painted glass, are in admirable taste; and that portion of them which bows out on the South, forming the lower part of the oriel which is thrown out here, produces a fine effect. These windows are hung with curtains of purple damask satin, without draperies, but depending straight down from brass rods. It may here be noticed that this is the fashion of all the curtains throughout the mansion: there is not a single drapery to be seen, or any substitute for it; but merely the curtains themselves running on plain brass rods. If it were not for the extraneous objects which at present disfigure this room, it would be the richest and most characteristic that we shall see among them all. Quitting this room, which is numbered 3, we pass through a passage (4), and ascend a small confined turret (5), and, continuing on through a narrow corridor (6), we reach the Oak Library (7). Here we find a vast variety of splendid works on Art, such as the Florence, Dresden, and Orleans

Galleries, &c., and a charming little sculpture of a reclining Nymph. The room itself calls for no particular remark. Leaving it, we pass on to a little boudoir (8) pannelled entirely with cedar-wood, in which we find the finest work in bronze which this collection contains. It is a reduced copy of the antique statue of a Faun and Child, now at the Louvre. Passing on through two small antechambers, and another corridor looking to the East (9, 10, and 11), we arrive at the Gallery Cabinet (12); a sweet little room hung with crimson and gold, and presenting a splendid look-out from its high narrow windows, each consisting of one piece of plate-glass. It is not uncommon, in passing through these rooms in company with casual visitors, to hear them complain of the want of *comfort* which exists throughout the place. There is no accounting for people's tastes; but they must have strange and most exclusive notions of comfort indeed, who cannot find it in some one or other of the different classes of apartments that they will meet with here. To our thinking (and we are unluckily somewhat fastidious in such matters) this little apartment that we are now in is the very ideal of snugness and comfort; and there are many such.

In order to preserve the routine on which we set out, we will now return through 11 and 10, to the Vaulted Library (13). Admiring, as we pass through it, the sweet and sombre stillness of this little low-roofed gallery, (for such it is), and contrasting it with the lively richness of the little Chintz Boudoir (14) in which it terminates, we now descend another turret staircase (15), and passing through a small but lofty vestibule (16), we suddenly find ourselves in a place perfectly unique in its kind, and magical in its effect on the senses as well as the imagination. This is the Grand Saloon or Octagon (17). The centre portion of Fonthill Abbey consists of an octangular tower, springing up from amidst the surrounding portions of the building, to a height of more than two hundred and sixty feet; and it is within this tower that we now stand. We will place ourselves in the centre, and for a while contemplate the detail around us; for the general impression which this unrivalled apartment produces, it would be idle to attempt to *describe*, because in every spectator it must vary in a thousand different degrees, according to the different associations he may connect with it, and even the mood of mind in which he may visit it. For ourselves, we have experienced its effects under every variety of circumstance; in the stillness of the fresh morning, when the sun was visiting it with his first rays—in the glare of mid-day, when gazing crowds were pacing it, looking upward and around in empty admiration, and not daring to speak, lest they should put to flight the superb silence that seems to be the presiding Genius of the place—in the gloaming of evening, when the receding light seems reluctantly to leave its gorgeous windows, majestic arches, and mysterious recesses—and finally, in the still darkness of midnight, by the guiding ray of one glimmering lamp, we have wandered through its "visible darkness," and explored the dim vestibules and vaulted corridors, and winding turrets, that adjoin to it, till the spirit of old romance became young again within us, and we have yearned to act over again The Mysteries of Udolpho!—We shall, however, not attempt to describe the general impression received from the sight of this superb saloon; but its individual features may be glanced at with advantage. Standing in the centre, then, and looking first on a level with our sight, we see before us, supposing our back to be turned towards the great Western entrance, a lofty arched vestibule and portal (20 and 21) opening into a grand state apartment (22), all that we can discover of which is an immense mirror reflecting the external scenery presented to it through the opposite entrance from the grounds. Turning to the right, through a similar vestibule (16) we look down a superb oak gallery (74) with a rich stone ceiling covered with fan-shaped tracery, and terminating in a gothic oriel window of three compartments. On the left again, through a corresponding arch and vestibule, (31) we discover, first a long gallery (32) somewhat similar to the last named, except that the ceiling is flat, and of brown oak richly carved and ornamented: in continuation of this, ascending one step, is a vaulted corridor (33) dimly lighted by rich painted windows and the ribs of the vaulting richly gilded; in continuation, a smaller apartment called the sanctuary (34), rising another step, hung with crimson satin damask, with a superb fan-shaped and gilded ceiling, and dimly lighted by pierced gothic doors lined with crimson cloth; and last of all, rising another step, the perspective is terminated by a still smaller apartment called the Oratory (35), hung also with crimson satin damask, the mouldings richly gilded, and the ceiling being still more superbly worked than either of the preceding. This apartment consists of five sides of an octagon, and is finished, in the centre compartment, by a large mirror, which repeats the whole opposing scene as far as the oriel window which terminates the other long gallery.

From the centre of the Saloon, where we are now standing, the detail of these apartments cannot be distinguished quite so plainly as would appear by this description: but they have been brought a little forward here, and just looked into, in order that we may avoid passing through them again in performing our regular routine. We have now seen three points of this view. The fourth and last, which presents itself on turning to the West, is infinitely finer than either of the preceding, and is perhaps quite unrivalled by any thing else of the kind that can be seen. Instead of looking along a level, as in the preceding views, the eye, immediately on reaching the extremity of the octagon, or saloon, descends down a spacious staircase, which terminates in a grand entrance-hall, built in the old baronial style (19); which hall opens on the great western Avenue, or lawn, by a pair of arched gothic doors, more than thirty feet in height. Immediately over this great arched doorway is an organ-gallery; over that a high narrow painted window; and then the pointed roof shoots upward to a height of eighty feet, at once supported and ornamented by massive beams of dark brown oak, richly carved and fretted. The effect of the view through this door, up what is called the Great Western Avenue, is highly characteristic and impressive; and it is imagined in fine taste—blending together, as it does, the outer domain with the inner, and forming them into one stately and magnificent whole. This avenue consists of a smooth-cut lawn, extending about half a mile, and about the width of the great saloon itself—bounded on either side by low shrubs, which jut into it somewhat irregularly, so as to take away any stiffness and formality, yet of sufficient uniformity to preserve the general unity of effect. Immediately behind, or rather out of these shrubs, rises a plantation, consisting chiefly of firs and larches, which have not yet attained a sufficient height to give them a character of grandeur; but, from the spot we are now situated on, they produce all the required effect.

Having gazed our fill at the magnificent *coup-d'œil* which presents itself from the centre of this saloon, we must now proceed in our routine. We quitted it at number 17; or rather we have been remaining there all this while, and only making excursions, with our eye, into the adjoining apartments. Passing on, then, through the eastern vestibule and portal (leaving 18 and 19 behind us—as we have looked down them in our last *coup-d'œil*), we enter the Great Dining-room (22), the first of the grand state-apartments. This is of great height, and is hung and carpeted with crimson; and the ceiling is of solid square oak beams, finished with gilded carving at the extremity of each beam. And it is here that we first find ourselves among the ornamental riches of this extraordinary place. Pictures, cabinets, vases, candelabras, and curious objects of various kinds, here crowd upon us in a profusion which so entirely distracts the attention, that we will not pretend to concern ourselves with them at all; for, however rare and valuable many of them may be, they are unquestionably much too numerous to produce any distinct and satisfactory effect; and they are, in fact, altogether unadapted to the situation in which we find them. Once for all, then, we will here take leave of the mere *curiosities* of Fonthill Abbey, as in no way connected with that permanent and characteristic part of it, which it is alone worth while for us to endeavour to *fix* on the visitor's memory: confessing our belief, however, before we finally dismiss them, that they offer to the taste (or want of taste—whichever it may be) which hungers after such matters, the most gorgeous and costly assemblage of the kind that was ever collected together under one roof, in this portion of the globe at least; and that they go near to give one a glimmering and indistinct notion of the treasures of the pre-adamite sultans themselves *! The pictures, however, we would not willingly pass over so lightly, as there are many in this collection which deserve the utmost attention and admiration that can be bestowed upon them. But we must restrain ourselves altogether on this point for the present; or the resolution we had formed, of not encroaching on more than double our allotted limits, will be of no avail; to say nothing of such encroachment including another, which we are still less disposed to make, on the department of our coadjutor, the author of " British Galleries of Art."

From the great dining-room we pass into the Crimson Drawing-room (23)—another noble apartment—square, lofty, with a ceiling of solid beams, and a " great gazing window," occupying nearly the whole side on which it is placed. This is followed by another drawing-room (24), of similar character, but still larger in its dimensions, and more rich in its architectural decorations, as well as those appertaining to art and virtù. This apartment is hung with blue satin damask, and is probably the first time this kind of hanging has been used as a ground for the exhibition of pictures. The effect, however, is extremely good. The unrivalled cabinets, tables, chandeliers, &c. which enrich

---

* *Vide* Vathek.

this and the last room, may be glanced at as we pass on, but must not
be attended to in detail.

Passing out of this grand suite of rooms, through what is called
Becket's Passage (from the great painted window at the extremity of
it representing Thomas à Becket), we again find ourselves among the
small *cabinet* apartments; and here, to say the truth, we feel ourselves
more at home, and would more willingly pause and reflect, than in the
more imposing and gorgeous portions of this vast labyrinth—for such the
visitor will suppose that it has the air of being, when we tell him that
he has not yet passed through one-third of the different parts enumerated in the routine which we are following. But he need not be alarmed
at this information; as we will contrive to hurry him through what
remains, in a manner that shall not fatigue him, in order that we may
have a little time left, before our " day" closes, to look at the external
objects which appertain to this spot.

Pausing, then, for a moment, in the little octagon cabinet (26),—
which is another of those exquisite little apartments that we have noticed before,—it is impossible to avoid looking at a few of the gems of
art which it contains—for we shall find nothing like them in any other
part of our search. But we must *only* look at, not describe them; for
if we once begin to do that, adieu to all hope of completing our circle
to-day.

Quitting this lovely little retreat, we pass on through the Northern
Passage (27), which contains a fine bronze statue of the Venus de'Medici, the size of life; and, peeping into the Crimson Breakfast Parlour
(28) as we pass by, continue our route through (29) the Porcelain
Room—which is only another name for a mere china-shop. This
room is in by far the worst taste of any in the Abbey, and deserves all
the censure that the most carping critic can bestow upon it—as being
altogether out of keeping with any other part of the building. Passing
through, and forgetting it as quickly as we can, we find ourselves again
in the long grand gallery noticed in our *coup-d'œil* from the centre of
the octagon. Passing over, then, this noble suite of apartments, from
number 30, to number 35, we continue our route, by turning up a
narrow staircase (36), which passes out of the sanctuary on the left,
and leads to the upper Lancaster room (37). This is a billiard-room,
and is hung with many pictures. It is followed by the State Bed-
room (38)—a fine and characteristic apartment, containing a superb
bed of crimson damask, with solid ebony pillars and framework, covered
with a quilt of the richest Brussels lace. As our fair companions take
an interest in these matters, it may be well to let them know, that if
rarity alone deserves their admiration, they cannot bestow too much
upon this same coverlid; for they may search all the royal palaces in
Europe, and not find another of the kind. There are various other
articles in the economy of this rich apartment which will attract and
deserve their attention; but we must leave it hastily, and pass on
through the ante-room (39), and the little vaulted gallery adjoining
(40), into what is called the Tribune Room (41.) Here we must stop a
moment to admire the stupendous and truly impressive view from this
room, which opens on to the great saloon, in the form of a parapet or
tribune. The view is, above, to the top of the great tower; around, to
the galleries and vestibules that occupy this part in correspondence

with the room in which we are standing, and between each compartment of which is an immense painted window; and below, to the grand Saloon itself, where the gorgeous shadows from those windows are falling; and, across these, down the stairs of the Great Hall, and through the lofty arched door-way, on to the great western avenue and lawn. In the above we may confidently reckon on looking upon a view altogether unique in its way; and not only so, but conceived in admirable taste, and executed in a manner as nearly as possible faultless; and producing an effect on the spectator which cannot be experienced without emotions of the most rare and valuable kind.

We will now pass on again, and, taking but a glance, as we go, at the series of apartments, &c. from number 41 to number 47—descend the winding staircase of the Lancaster turret, and passing across the grand saloon, arrive at a lobby (48) which leads us to the great staircase of the tower (49). This, though it is rather tiresome work, and will scarcely repay us for our trouble, we must hastily ascend, or we shall be accused of not having seen the chief *lion* of the place. Mounting, then, a tedious number of stairs—which are a little relieved by the looks-out that we now and then get through the loop-hole windows that give them light—we arrive, at last, at a sort of gallery, or arcade, which runs round the upper part of the great tower, and communicates with four small apartments, called Nunneries, which fill as many of its sides. These occupy the numbers from 50 to 57. Having passed through these, in which there is little to admire except the view on to the great saloon below, we again ascend the great staircase, till we reach an open platform (58). As we have mounted thus far, we may as well complete our ascension, from this platform, up through the interior of the central tower (59) and the Gazebo, or star-chamber, (60) to the Tower Gallery itself—which is the highest point to which there is any regular means of ascent. Here we stand, then, on the summit of this far-famed tower, overlooking a spot which, even within the memory of most of us, was a barren heath—an interminable extent of bare *down*, with scarcely a tree upon it; and which now, by the means of one man, and under the inspection of one superintending assistant, has become what we now see it—a magnificent domain, including nearly all the natural beauties that can belong to a spot of the kind, and crowned by a building of unrivalled extent and grandeur.

But it is not for Ciceroni to indulge (themselves) in reflections upon what they see; otherwise here would be a fine opportunity for so doing. Leaving this, then, till we have cast off our present character—(which we must be allowed to do so soon as we have shewn our company fairly through the labyrinthine mazes of this extraordinary building)—we will pass on again,—first commending to their attention the view that presents itself from this tower; chiefly on account of its enabling them to glance, as on a map, at the *plan* which has been pursued in arranging the grounds within the inner circle of the domain: for the surrounding country presents nothing peculiarly entitled to notice, or that may not be equalled, if not surpassed, by most other views taken from an equal height.

Descending now the Grand Staircase (which, by the way, is any thing rather than grand, except as compared with the exceedingly confined ones which lead to every other department of the building, with the undernamed exception) we reach, at the foot of it, the great hall; and again descending the staircase of *that*, which really is a fine one, and correspondent with its situation, we turn to the left at the foot; and crossing the western cloisters (62),—leaving on the left a little court-yard with a small and insignificant fountain in the centre,—we once more, by passing up a narrow staircase leading from the oak dining-parlour, find ourselves entering upon a new suite of internal apartments, as richly arrayed as those which we have already passed through, and as gorgeously ornamented in the way of pictures, cabinets, curiosities, and costly articles of virtù of every denomination. The first of these is called the Western Yellow Drawing-room (72), which is hung with yellow damask, and gilt mouldings; and fitted up in parts with gothic oak bookcases, carved and arranged in admirable taste. This room also contains the grand *show-piece* of the place, in the shape of an enormous ebony cabinet, occupying nearly the whole side of the apartment, and reaching to the ceiling; and which is filled with a nondescript and nameless variety of what, for lack of a better generic title, we are obliged to call, in the language of catalogue-makers, " articles of virtù," but which are, generally speaking, in as vicious a (want of) taste as any thing can well be; being costly merely in virtue of their rarity and remoteness from all pretensions to either beauty or utility: using the term " beauty" to signify a quality founded in some natural principle of taste; and "utility," as that which is, or may be made, in some way or other, subservient to our mental wants and propensities;—in which sense, indeed, the one quality may be said in some degree to merge in the other; since beauty is, in this view of it, the most *useful* thing in the world.

Passing out of this gorgeous apartment, through a little ante-room (64), we find ourselves in another of those sweet little retreats which are the exclusive boast of this spot, and which in some sort redeem the splendours by which they are surrounded, by permitting the latter to be used as contrasts to *them*. But there is no feeling the rich repose and still sweetness of this and similar apartments, unless we could visit them alone; so, glancing round for a moment at the really beautiful works of art which this little cell contains, and looking out upon the flower-crowned terrace on which it opens (71), and, through the loop-hole windows which light it, upon the rich prospect below, we will pass through another yellow drawing-room (73) nearly similar to the one above-named, and across the gallery noticed in our first *coup-d'œil*, and finally close our peregrination by resting our somewhat wearied forms—for there is no denying that, by this time, they are so—on one of the couches which stand before the mysterious curtains that fill the recesses of the great Saloon.

Thus, gentle reader,—for " gentle" we will evermore proclaim you, if you have borne with us, pleased and patiently, all through this long, and (which is not our fault) somewhat monotonous range of splendours—thus have we led you through every open apartment of a building which is, with all its faults, calculated to excite a deeper interest in the spectator than any other of the kind that we could any where point out: and we have endeavoured to indicate to you chiefly the merits of what we have met with. The defects (as we hinted in the outset of our examination) we are ready to expatiate on at equal length, on the con-

ditions there named; which we have little hope (or rather, fear) of
being complied with,—since the world is more than sufficiently supplied
with persons whose chief talent lies in finding fault, and who are so
conscious of the superiority of their claims on this score, and so desirous that others should be equally convinced of that superiority, that,
if they cannot get paid for calling it into action, they are generous
enough to perform the task gratis.

Here, then, beneath this great western arch of the saloon, we slip-off
our character of Cicerone, and having rested a moment to get rid of
the feeling of it, descend the stairs of the Great Hall, and sally forth,
alone, into the scene which has been all along beckoning us to its company from every window that we have passed; and which invitation
we have had much ado to say nay to: for, after all, it is the external
part of Fonthill Abbey, and the natural objects appertaining to it, that
are alone worth serious and particular attention; and it is only when
the spectator is alone, that this attention can be bestowed upon them.

It is, of course, not our intention to give any thing in the shape of a
detailed description of grounds, the inner circle of which extends above
seven miles.   All our already transgressed limits will permit us to attempt is, to notice the general impression they are calculated to produce,
in connexion with the magnificent building which crowns and overlooks
them.   And first of the building itself.   There are various points of
view from which it may be seen; but none towards which it presents
an aspect of more imposing and majestic beauty than that which is
situated at the top of the great avenue on which the western doors
abut.   Standing on this spot, it rises before us with a look of solemn
and stately grandeur, the effect of which has probably never been surpassed; and which effect, if we mistake not, arises in a considerable
degree from the peculiar character of the building, coupled with the
situation in which we meet with it.   It has all the individual as well as
general character of one of those stupendous religious temples which
have come down to us from Gothic times; but, unlike any one of those,
it stands detached from all other of the works of man, on the summit of
an immense fir-clad hill, which it crowns as with a diadem.   Hitherto the
idea of a great cathedral has come to us accompanied by all sorts of
associations connected with cities, societies, and population; but here
we meet with it, utterly silent and solitary: reigning, it is true; but
reigning over the still realm of Nature alone,—like a queen on a desert
island, without a people.

There is still another accidental feeling which contributes to the effect produced by this building.   It is, as far as the memory of a general
impression of mere size will enable us to judge, of greater extent than
any other building of a similar character in Europe; and when we
come to enquire into the history of these latter, we find, when they are
finished at all, that *such* a portion was completed under the direction of
*such* an abbot, in the year so and so; that this wing was added a century or two after, by such a bishop, by the aid of funds collected in
such and such a manner; and so of the rest: that all, in fact, have
demanded the united means, talents, and spirit of several individuals,
or public bodies, and the lives of several architects, to bring them to
the state in which we now see them:—but that *here* is one, equal to
most, if not all of them in extent, grandeur, and beauty, which has

sprung up at the command of *one* private individual and under the direction of *one* architect.

In threading the interminable mazes of the grounds surrounding this majestic mass of architecture, it is probable that something like the same complex and imaginative impression is received. Speaking for ourselves, we are sure that this is the case. The late owner of this place was at once the inventor, the creator, and the *sole* possessor of it. This, however, would have been nothing, if he had been like the usual possessors of such spots. But the author of Vathek is no common person; and the paths which he, and *he alone*, has trodden—where he has pondered his bitter thoughts, and dreamed his fantastic dreams, and mused his lofty imaginations; and whence he is now exiled for ever, only that they may be made a common thoroughfare for all the idle and curious—all the high and low vulgar of the land;—*these* paths cannot be paced (at least by those who have a jot of sympathy with either the strengths or the weaknesses of our human nature) without feelings and associations which are perhaps the more, rather than the less active, because they are not easily to be communicated or explained—in fact, they cannot be paced without what was, and must long continue, the *genius loci*, being ever present in imagination, under such form or image as the mood or recollection of the moment may invest it with. For our parts (who are, it is true, somewhat addicted to the romantic in such matters), we have seldom wandered alone through the mazes of this spot without fancying by the side of us an inhabitant of the Halls of Eblis, permitted for awhile to visit these Elysian fields; but still condemned to wear its right hand upon its left breast; or only allowed to lift it up now and then, to shew beneath, through the transparent flesh, the red heart burning like a flame of fire [*].

We must now positively take leave of Fonthill at once, by saying, of the grounds generally, that as far as the mere planning and arrangement of them goes, they strike us as being nearer to the perfection of this sort of spot than any thing else we are acquainted with, or had previously formed a conception of. The *spirit* of them, be it understood, is that of pure Nature; not unassisted indeed, but entirely unadorned, and almost uncontrolled. Every thing she is capable of producing, that will live under our skies, is here collected together; but scattered about with so artful a hand, that the art of it is entirely concealed. The usual natives of the forest, the heath, and the garden, here meet together in one spot, and form one beautiful and happy family; and all flourish and bloom together, by mutual consent. Roses blush from out the bosom of the heath furze; rhododendrons fling their gorgeous flowers at random among ferns and forest shrubs; the frail woodbine hangs its dependent clusters upon the everlasting laurel; and on the ground all sorts of rich (so called) *garden* flowers group themselves with those gentle families of the earth which we (happening to be " drest in a little brief authority" over them) have chosen to banish from our presence into the fields and hedges, and denominate *weeds*.

The above refers to particular spots that present themselves occasionally as you wander about. But the general character of the place,

---

[*] See the conclusion of Vathek.

as a whole, is that of one vast solitude, half wild, half cultivated, spreading itself over a plot of earth which includes every variety of natural beauty; here opening into rich lawns studded with lofty forest trees or low clumps of evergreens and underwood,—there stretching away into interminable vistas through lines of larches and pines—now descending abruptly, and shewing, from between the topmost branches of the trees beneath, lovely lakes basking in the still light, and reflecting all the beauty about them; and now opening suddenly at a turn of the green path, and permitting a rich expanse of distant country to burst upon the eye for a moment, only to be lost again, as you pass on, in the dark shadows of some deep fir-grove;—a solitude; but—(and this is one of its greatest charms,) " a populous solitude :"—for here, all the animal tribe, save their would-be lord alone, have had permission to wander, unmolested, and uncontrolled, but by their own wills; and for *them* at least it has been, until lately, a new Paradise. Even now, when the idle crowds that at present haunt and disturb this peace-hallowed spot have quitted it for a few hours, and in the sweet mornings before they have broken in upon it, we have seen the hares sporting about within a few yards of our feet like kittens, and heard the birds sing to each other upon the bough above our head, as if the place were all their own. For this alone, if for nothing else, we shall never cease to regret that any cause, but the inevitable one of death, should have laid bare the secret beauties of Fonthill Abbey, and divorced them from the only possessor who could be said to have a *natural* right in them, in virtue of their having been purely the work of his own hand.*

---

### SONNET, FROM FILICAJA,

#### *On the Earthquakes of Sicily.*

"Qui pur foste o Città, ne in voi più resta."

HERE, on the spot where stately cities rose,
  No stone is left, to mark in letters rude
Where Earth did her tremendous jaws unclose—
  Where Syracuse—or where Catania stood.
  Along the silent margin of the flood
I seek, but cannot find ye;—nought appears,
  Save the deep settled gloom of solitude,
That checks my step, and fills mine eyes with tears.
O thou! whose mighty arm the blow hath dealt,
  Whose justice gave the judgment, shall not I
Adore that power which I have seen and felt?—
  Rise from the depths of darkness where ye lie,
Ye ghosts of buried cities—rise, and be
A sad memorial to futurity.

---

* The Arabic figures in this paper refer to the numbers in the descriptive catalogue of the building.

### EXTERNAL APPEARANCE.

THERE are few particulars in which the present generation has
more decidedly established its superiority over the "wisdom of our
ancestors," than in the art of improving personal appearance. What
between the blessed advantages of vaccination for the young, and the
multiplied artificial resources of those more advanced in life, age and
ugliness have been completely banished from good company. Chesterfield's eternal "Graces" have now fallen to "rude mechanicals" and
country parsons. Instead of cultivating amiable manners, we task our
efforts to adorn the person ; and our improvements, for the most part,
regard much less the address than the dress. To be agreeable is nothing, unless at the same time we have an agreeable exterior ; and to
succeed in society, integrity of body is a point of much more importance than integrity of mind. Now-a-days, indeed,

Dente si nigro fieres, vel uno
Turpior ungui,

it is all over with you. in the world of bon-ton ; a wrinkle is the sure
mark of a quiz, and grey hairs a more infallible proof of rusticity than
the Yorkshire brogue, or the lisping Venetian Z of the county of Zo-
merzet. Whether this be one of the "death-despising" signs of the
times, I cannot say. I should have had some hesitation in touching on
the tender subject in the face of that scourge of reviewers, and Minos of
magazines, Mr. I——, if I had not heard some of those who frequent
"the Caledonian" hint that his Reverence was himself, at least as far as
regards his own person, an "elegans formarum spectator." Hoping,
therefore, to escape the bitterness of his censure, I must frankly own,
that I think this tendency to put a good face upon matters, meritorious.
I see no virtue in looking abominably, no self-denial in laying bare to
public gaze a concealable deformity ; no laudable forbearance in pale
cheeks and hollow eyes. I confess I prefer a patched face to a patched
conscience, and think a painted woman less morally offensive than a
painted sepulchre. Dare I add, that I would rather hear a good
preacher habited in that most happy imitation of luxuriant nature
technically called "a head of hair," than a dolt in a cauliflower that
would rival Paris, or give the fullest aid to "frowning a schismatic
into insignificance."

The Duc de Duras very properly placed the majesty of the French
throne in the royal kitchen ; and Dr. Gastaldy * esteemed cookery at
once the criterion and the end of civilization. Certain it is, if the gas-
tronomic science does not "come home to men's business and bosoms,"
it does to their stomachs ; and that is the next thing to it. Still, however, if we look to the history of inventions, and trace chronologically
the progress of human science, we shall be compelled to make the
dressing of our persons, rather than the dressing of our dinners, the
touchstone of our advance towards the goal of civilized perfectibility.
For men cooked beefsteaks before they wore breeches ; and à fortiori,
before they wore false teeth.

These matters were rolling in my brain the other day, precisely as
I entered Mr. Colburn's library ; and while I was deep in the perusal

---

* Almanach des Gourmands.

of a new pamphlet on political economy, my eye wandering from the
page to the well-filled shelves which surrounded me, I fell into a profound reverie. The shop was in considerable bustle. There were
half-a-dozen carriages drawn up in front of the door, all of whose inmates were eagerly petitioning for the newest novelties. Two members'
of parliament were calling for copies of " The Oracles ;" three country
ladies were desirous of putting down their names for Sir Walter's last
novel but two, the " sticking-place" of their actual stock of literature ;
and another demure-looking female was whispering the librarian in a
corner, something that I fancied had the sound of " the last Cantos of
Don Juan." These images, my previous thoughts, and the pamphlet
I was reading, all worked together in my imagination. The division of
labour, Adam Smith's pin-maker, the vast utility of Mr. Colburn's
establishment, the rapid diffusion of knowledge it occasioned, its political and moral influence on society, were vaguely floating through my
half-dormant intellect, when on a sudden, by the happiest association
of ideas, I was seized with the notion of a Circulating Collection of supplemental Limbs and Organs. The idea was novel; it was judicious;
it promised great advantage to the community, and no small profit to
the projector. How many individuals, I said to myself, does this
vast and overgrown metropolis contain, whose circumstances will not
allow them to purchase out and out a whole limb to themselves, who
would gladly subscribe for its occasional use! How many are there
that would be delighted to hire a cork leg to walk in their wife's funeral
procession ; or would be grateful for the opportunity of subscribing for
a handsome Irishman's calf, till they had married the widow! How
many would acknowledge the convenience to a " drapery Miss," when
far past her teens, of hiring a set of teeth by the ball-night! How
many a poor Lieutenant, turned out of a "hell," with his pockets as bare
as his upper lip, would rejoice to hire his whiskers for a single parade!
How many a city-piece of lath and plaster would be contented to remain as thin as a whipping-post all the week, could she sport a calli-
pyge in the Park on a Sunday! How handy for a "crop-eared pren-
tice" to step into his wig for a night on the return of the Kennington
Assembly ; or to mount a temporary eye-brow, when he would be critical in the pit of the Surrey Theatre! Thus also a cocked hat and an
ear for music might go with the seven-and-sixpenny ticket on opera
nights ; and an eye and an opera-glass might be let together, at the
doors of panoramas and picture-galleries.

Bright thoughts like these do not often occur in a man's life ; and if
they be not seized and acted upon at once when they pop into the head,
he may pine in obscurity in a back garret, or die in a workhouse, with
nobody to blame but himself. These are the " tides in the affairs of
men, which, taken at the turn, lead on to fortune," but which, when they
are suffered to pass unheeded or neglected, are followed by a rapid and
unvanquishable ebb, which infallibly

"Leaves us at e'en on the bleak shore alone."

For two hours I remained fixed on the spot where I stood, unconscious of all that was passing around me. I had, " with unremitting
diligence, long made the science of artificial" limbs and members,
" where mechanical contrivance is requisite, my peculiar study," and
" could supply any loss with an artificial or natural substitute in a

superior manner." I could make " belts to reduce corpulency and relieve and strengthen abdominal debility;" * in short, I understand the
whole art of man-mending, from a padded hip to a complete set of
ricket irons. So turning down Conduit-street into Bond-street, without hesitation I engaged for the first " elegant and well-situated shop"
that was vacant, which I mean to stock with a complete assortment of
every article in the personal line. There the judicious and discriminating world of fashion will be accommodated with the hire of every
qualification for genteel society, of which nature or accident may have
deprived them, either by the year, quarter, month, week, or single
night, and at the most reasonable prices.—Noses of every description,
from the Wellington hook to the Apollo Grecian, shall be fitted on in
an undiscoverable perfection, and warranted to carry spectacles, and to
stand a moderate pull undisturbed.—Eyes of all colours' and waters,
tastefully matched—the sentimental, the joyous, the leering, the pout-
ing, and the disdainful, in sets, right and left. · N. B. Eyes with tears
in them for funerals and melodrames. A superiorly constructed calf,
in sizes, warranted not to turn in a waltz, nor to change its position in
the most complicated quadrille.—Chicken-breasted busts *à la Russe*,
for the use of the army; and female forehands of all calibres. False
b—tt—ms let out by the single quarrel, warranted to bear kicking.—
Dandies completely made up by the year, at a considerable discount;
or by the single night. N. B. There will be a confidential agent at
each of the principal watering-places, and on the Chaussée d'Antin at
Paris, for the benefit of customers *only*. The founder of this establishment has likewise engaged one of the first Parisian artists in hair;
whose labours much exceed the products of the most approved dyeing
materials, or even the Macassar oil. All quantities of teeth, from a
single tooth to a complete set, furnished at half-an-hour's notice.—Particularly recommended to dispeptic aldermen, and sputtering members
of parliament, as an infallible remedy for indigestion and imperfect
delivery. The projector having imported many thousands of this article from the field of Waterloo in the greatest perfection, will provide sets, warranted from the French guard, for the jacobins and reformers, and real and genuine English, certified upon the spot by affidavit,
for the service of the thorough-going John Bulls, and of those renegadoes
and ultras who are too well paid for their loyalty to suffer any thing
to pass their mouth favourable to Napoleon. This is the more necessary, as we are given to understand, that some of the crowned heads
of Europe are, in more senses than one, indebted to the French Emperor for being able to shew their teeth and bite, and not only owe
their heads but their jaws also to him and his.—Rouge and white
paint shall be obtained at any price from abroad, and supplied by contract at a great saving; and every article connected with this branch
of business, shall be kept ready for service in the greatest abundance,
and of the first quality. Old heads will be taken in exchange, and a
liberal allowance made for second-hand legs and arms.—Thus will a
new branch of commerce be opened for the service of the public; and
so assured is the projector of the success of his plans for improvement, that he doubts not in a short time to be enabled to offer substi-

---

* See Advertisements in the Morning Chronicle.

tutes for the more essential viscera no less than the external organs.
Mr. Burke assumed, that the old democrats of France wore shreds of
parchment and scraps of the rights of man, in place of their usual internals; why, therefore, should I despair of supplying his Majesty's
ministers with brains, giving sound hearts to placemen and corruption-
ists, and a good liver to any reverend clergyman who has a good
living to pay for it?

Now, Mr. Editor, as I look upon you to be a man of some intellectual courage, and not to be browbeaten from the defence of truth and
justice because it may happen to be in a minority, I give you a preference over all other periodical artists, by committing this paper to
your care, and I trust, that by affording it a good place in your journal, you will shew that I have not mistaken my man.  For envy follows merit like its shadow, and I fear you may run some risk in proposing in such times such an overwhelming innovation on our glorious
constitution as in church and state established, as that now proposed
by your obedient servant, &c. &c. &c.                          M.

## MUSIC.

It comes—it comes upon the gale,
  That pensive voice of days gone by,
With early feelings down life's vale,
  On Arab airs as odours sigh.

Oh! on this far and foreign shore
  How doubly blest that song appears,
Long days and distance wafting o'er
  The sweetness of departed years.

The scene around me fades away,
  As at the wave of magic wand—
I see the glens and mountains grey
  And wild woods of my native land.

The summer bower, the silent stream,
  The scenes of youth are on the strain;
And peopled is my waking dream
  With forms I ne'er shall see again!

As on my wanderings when a child,
  That music comes at close of day,
Along the dim and distant wild,
  And wafts my spirit far away.

And o'er the heart as it distils,
  Dear as the dew-drop to the leaf,—
Oh! how the rising bosom thrills
  Beneath the mystic joy of grief.

So sweet—so hallow'd 'tis to feel
  The gentle woe that wakes the sigh,
That e'en in Heaven, methinks, 'twill steal
  Upon the spirit's dream of joy!

But hark!—that soothing strain is o'er,
  And broken is the lovely spell:
So fades from off our native shore
  The accents of a Friend's farewell.         M. M.

## PLEASURES OF DRAWING.

HUNGER, they say, will penetrate stone walls: alas, would it were the only thing that could find its way through brick and mortar; for, then should I not have begun this sentence fourteen times, mended my pen, bitten my nails, scratched my head, and wished the whole race of Tomkisons and Broadwoods at Jericho, because a young lady in the next house has been for three hours fighting the Battle of Prague. There has been as much wire spun at Nuremberg within these latter days, as would reach from here to Jupiter; and if all this music reaches the other spheres, heaven knows what they must think of their coadjutor in that concert which they are all performing.

Dr. Spurzheim says, that there is a lump of fibrous and cineritious matter in certain brains, allotted to this particular function, and that vain is mortal toil, should some other lump of brain have usurped its place. This may possibly be true of German brains; but I beg to inform the Doctor, that there is a distinct organ allotted to piano-forte playing, which is universal. How else should all our misses learn the piano-forte, and play on the piano-forte? how else should piano-fortes swarm from John o' Groat's house to the Land's-end, as frogs did erst in Egypt? and how should it be that if you retire from one corner of your house to avoid the "piano-forte next door," it is only to meet the other piano-forte at the other next door? How should it be else, that nine, or seven, or six hours of every day, from eight years of age to five-and-twenty, are occupied in thrumming the eternal wires, and drumming the endless keys? that every daughter of every shoe-maker, and innkeeper, and farmer, plays on her "piano?" that even the mahogany of Jamaica has not time to grow, and that the dentists of Africa cannot draw elephants' teeth fast enough? These unfortunate beasts complained, ages ago, that the great statue of Phidias (Pheidias, I beg your pardon,) had cost them one hundred and forty sets of teeth; but what is this to the depredations which are now to find beef and porter for an army of workmen that might have built the Athenian fleet, and claret and carriages for the whole race of Cramers and Kalk-brenners, and noise for all Great Britain?

Time must be occupied:—true. But as there are dumb bells, why cannot there be dumb piano-fortes? That indeed would be a meritorious patent. In the mean time, the sampler is thrown to the dogs; the honours of the ancient chair-bottoms are no more; our shirts are without buttons to the collar; our kitchens are left to the cook, and our children to the nursery-maid; and after fourteen years of hard labour, and four or fourteen hundred guineas transferred to the fiddler's pocket, besides the finish, which can only be given by the polishing powder of some Ries or Von Esch,—the end is, the Battle of Prague, perchance a Scotch reel, or two sonatas of Clementi, with a set of variations on God save the King, of which two or three must be skipped; and, among the rest of which, old Carey would be troubled to know his own again.

Life is a good deal too long, I admit. Something must be found to do, or how are we to wear out this long disease? We are all ambitious to be reformers. You want to know my scheme: it is contained in one word.—Drawing. This has many advantages.

In the first place it makes no noise. In the next, as I shewed at the beginning, you may shut your eyes if you do not like it. In the third, it is not a theatrical acquisition: it does not exhibit a tender female contending in a hot room for the applause of an unknown crowd; her bosom rankling with envy, or swelling with ambition: it does not make our wives and daughters public characters, nor infringe on the sex's first charm, its retiring modesty. Lastly, it does not cost so much money; and fourthly, as Dogberry says, it does not cost so much time; and seventhly, and to end, its produce is permanent, durable, lasting; it may be stored away for future pleasure, and is not whistled off into thin air, to perish and be forgotten like the taste of turtle, or last year's clouds.

But do not suppose that I mean by drawing, the manufacture of three pair of fire-screens and two card-racks, or a gentle swain making love to a shepherdess under the cover of Cupid and a bundle of painted and twisted matches; or that I intend, by drawing, a landscape framed and glazed and gilded; combed and brushed and sponged and plastered by the fair pupil and Mr. Glover in partnership, splendent in all such colours as never were seen but in the colour-box: the first, the last, the only one that ever is to result from the expenditure of three years, and ten or thirty times as many guineas. Unless, indeed, the fair should become ambitious to " sketch from Nature," and should, after a tour to "the Lakes," or to Loch Caterine, return with an exquisitely-bound marble and morocco book, filled with " sketches from Nature," which unhappy Nature would be at a loss to recognize, and where we only know that a house is not a mountain, because it has a door and a chimney; and that it cannot be a cabbage which we are contemplating, because cabbages have no branches; nor a pole, because poles do not bear leaves.

It is however a popular and absurd prejudice that the art of drawing is difficult or unattainable, that it requires genius, as the vulgar phrase it, and that it is fruitless, for those who have no genius, to attempt it. A young lady, or a young gentleman, for it is all the same, tries once or twice, or perhaps half-a-dozen times, to produce a drawing, the copy generally of some bad print; and because they do not at once rival Claude or Raphael, it is determined that they have no genius, and the pencil is thrown aside for ever. As if this art was to be attained without effort or study, and by inspiration; when a shoemaker must serve his years of apprenticeship, and even the genius of a chimney-sweeper is not elicited till his knees and elbows have acquired half a dozen new integuments.

I am not going to theorize on this matter so absurdly, as to say, that mere labour will make a great artist; or that all mankind may become painters by practice alone. But there is a great deal in all its inferior branches which may be attained in this manner, without much superiority of intellect, and by ordinary minds. Even in a professional point of view, this is true; far more, where amusement or mere utility is in view, where it may become the general pursuit of the people, as literature or general science is. Much of painting is merely imitative. In these inferior parts, all may attain a mediocrity which is valuable, or which may be a source of pleasure. But of all these branches, there is in kind, of a general nature at least, so attainable as landscape, and in which the produce is always, in some way, amusing.

It is a popular mistake also, that the education in this art is difficult, or tedious, or expensive. It bears no proportion to music in this respect, even where pursued in the most extravagant manner. It may be made expensive; as it is, as every thing is in England, where the trade of education is a lucrative one, where it is therefore rendered, as far as possible, a mystery, and where parents have agreed to shift off from themselves the labour of education, in every thing; where that which ought to be a pleasure has become a burden and a task, and all the duties of parentage are to be commuted for money. But all this is unnecessary. Children, generally, shew a desire to draw, and, when permitted, acquire it to a certain extent, with far less toil than they learn to write: doing the one, in fact, with pleasure, because they see the immediate results, and labouring unwillingly on that of which they cannot yet foresee the value. Habits can thus be acquired by them, with very little superintendence, and without expensive masters—without any masters indeed; and, even at a more advanced stage, it is almost sufficient to give them to copy good models, which cost little.

Even in advanced age, it is a great mistake which supposes that the art of drawing cannot be acquired: that, if not commenced in youth, it is too late to begin. It is never too late for any thing, unless where, as in music, muscles are to be taught habits which their rigidity or want of early training prevents them from acquiring late in life. This is not the case with drawing, which lies more in the eye and the mind than in the hand.

In a country like ours, where every one looks at pictures, and buys pictures, and talks of pictures, and travels in pursuit of the picturesque; and where every one reads every thing and talks of every thing; and where our ladies write reviews and treatises on political economy, and attend the Royal Institution, and make experiments, and study their *ologies*, nothing but such a prejudice could have prevented them at least from studying the art of drawing, as they do that of music. Why the gentlemen do not, or why drawing is not, for them, considered a branch of liberal education, I do not know; unless that they are too much occupied in driving barouches, corrupting Cornish boroughs, attending Newmarket, reading newspapers, and practising divinity, law, physic, and fox-hunting; while all the knowledge of art which is required for talking about it, may be acquired in a few hours, by reading Pilkington and Mr. Haydon's criticisms on the British Gallery.

Aristotle says of this art, " It ought to form a branch of education; not that it may prevent its possessors from being cheated in the purchase of pictures, but because it teaches them the art of contemplating and understanding beautiful forms."

To come nearer home, Lord Arundel says, that a man who cannot draw cannot be an honest man. Shakspeare has said pretty much the same about music: and the axiom came from a warm heart at least, in both. Castiglione, too, is not a very bad authority in matters that concern a liberal education; and certainly his view of the nature and education of a courtier, differed somewhat from that of my Lord Chesterfield. What he says of the utility of drawing, might indeed have been said a hundred ways;—so that I may pass it over: but what he says of landscape-painting, which is the only part of this subject in which I am about to intermeddle, is deserving of being said in his own words, which, not being Greek, may be safely quoted. " Et veramente chi non estima quest' arte, parmi che molto sia dalla ragione alieno : che la machina del mondo che noi veggiamo, con l' ampio cielo di chiare stelle tanto splendido ; et nel mezzo la terra da i mari cinta, di monti valli, et fiumi variata, et di diversi alberi et vaghi fiori et di herbe ornata ; dir si puo che una nobile et gran pittura sia per man de la natura et di Dio composta. La qual chi puo imitare, parmi esser di gran laude degno."

With respect to the utility of this art, two strokes of a pencil will often tell a tale of unknown length, and there are many tales which cannot be told at all for want of it.

Sir Joseph Banks ploughs the depths of old ocean for years, cutting through the bodies and souls of the myriad tribes by which it is inhabited, in vain. They will neither pickle nor preserve; the wealthy Baronet cannot draw them, and he and the world continue as wise as ever. Mr. Humboldt sweats himself to a thread on the Oroonoko, and freezes his beard to wire on the Andes; and lo! when he arrives at Jamaica, all his collections are in the maws of termites, and dermestes, and centipedes : all for want of a few scraps of paper and a halfpenny-worth of Indian ink properly distributed on them.

Our Parks (worthy man), and our Mackenzies, and our Hearnes, and Brownes, and uncounted thousands more, run all over the world to disenny themselves and bring home journals ; and when the journals have generated a quarto, or half-a-dozen quartos, nine-tenths, and the better part too, of the story is all to seek. There are beasts and buildings, and men and plants, and serpents and gorgons, and chimeras and countries of all kinds, architecture that we are dying to understand, monuments from the time of Nimrod, mountains whose heads do reach the skies ; and what is it all when told ?—nothing.

It is just the same at home. The same cowardly and indolent spirit has served to make taste a trade : and thus, in this commercial country of ours, we proceed on the principle of the division of labour; as if no one man ought to do more than one thing, as if he who twists the head of a pin is not to cut its carcase into lengths ; going to the proper shops, to buy a guinea's-worth of taste from one artist, and a thousand pounds'-worth from another. Thus the gentleman who has more money than wit, applies to him who has more wit than money, and who sets up a shop where he retails it to all those who are fools enough to buy. Hence the gardener, who has acquired a fortune of some kind, by the usual means, sets up for a Capability-man ; and those who, like the general mob, are led by high pretensions, flock to him, laying open their lands and their purses, till the one is emptied, and the other marred ; and thus doing, by a deputy, what they ought to have been far better capable of doing themselves, while also depriving themselves of what might have been a source of pleasure, as well as an employment. It is the same in architecture : as if taste could only be acquired by those who must live by it; as if he who has, or might have, the most general education and the most varied acquirements, must necessarily be inferior to all those who choose to assert their superiority, and to keep a shop for its distribution.

It will surprise those who are not accustomed to analyse and study their impressions and recollections, to find how little of accuracy their ideas of visible objects really possess; not only in remembrance, but even at the moment of the impression. But it does not surprise a painter to find that, even at the distance of years, he can recall a subject which he once intended to paint, or that he can give, at any time, the true character of objects once impressed on his mind. As far as painting is merely an imitative art, this is its essence—a correct notion of visible forms and colours; and he who cannot paint, differs far more from the artist in his eye for present observation, or in his memory for past ones, than he does in mere dexterity of hand. In truth, ordinary observers have but vague notions of forms, whatever they may imagine; and the test is, that they cannot draw them. When the eye has acquired its knowledge, the hand will not be long in learning to record it.

Were this art more generally diffused, the relations of travellers would differ far less from each other than they now do, even on ordinary matters; and would convey far more accurate, as well as more consistent ideas. It is the fashion, however, for every one to imagine that he can describe pictures and buildings; though ignorant of painting and architecture, and unable to mark on paper the outline of a column or the angle of a pediment. The public at large has no resource in these cases, but to submit with sad civility, or to believe and be deceived. But he who knows what art is, will pay the same attention to these tales as he does to the criticisms which he daily hears in picture-galleries; where a knowledge of all that belongs to art is supposed to be innate or inherent in those who do not possess one of its principles; but whose claims to knowledge consist in wealth to purchase, or in birth to dictate. Sir Joshua shifts his trumpet and takes snuff.

But I must return from utility to pleasure; which, nine times out of ten, is the better thing of the two. And here, also, I must limit myself to landscape; lest, if I went deeper into the subject, I should weary the patience of the reader. If the pleasures derived from any art—from painting, architecture, poetry, or music—are greatest to those who are educated—a truth which will only be denied on the general ground of the felicity of ignorance—then we ought to cultivate the art of drawing, to enable us to derive from natural scenery all the pleasures which it is capable of affording. Nature, as Castiglione says, is a great picture painted by the hand of the Creator: it is an endless collection of pictures, offering inexhaustible sources of pleasure and study and criticism; containing not only all that art ever executed, all its principles and all its details, but infinitely more than it can ever attain. If it requires deep and long study to understand art, if none can truly judge of it but he whose hand can follow his eye, or whose eye at least has acquired that knowledge which makes the painter; it cannot require less to understand nature. Nor must it be said that, in the study of art, any more than in that of nature, taste

may be independent of this accuracy of knowledge, or that a perfect
perception of beauty can exist without it. As well might it be said
that a perfect perception of the beauties of poetry or music may exist
without critical knowledge. I do not mean technical criticism, but
a distinct comprehension of all the sources of beauty, of their nature
and causes.

Applying this rule to the simple enjoyment of natural scenery, as
the object now before us, it is only the practical painter, he who is at
the same time every thing that a painter ought to be, who can derive
from landscape all the pleasures which it is calculated to yield. And
the ignorant or uncultivated spectator will receive less enjoyment from
it than he who, though not an artist, has studied the art of painting,
or who, from his practical knowledge of drawing, has learnt to observe and compare truly, to attend to a thousand minute circumstances
in colour, form, shadow, contrast, and so forth, which escape ordinary
spectators.

Among artists, also, each has his particular bent: each observes
something which another will overlook. While the eye of Claude
comprehends the whole extent of a rich or fertile country, dressed
up in all the luxuriance of art and nature, adorned with mountains
and rivers, and trees and temples, and teeming with life; that of
Cuyp will content itself with a sunny bank and a group of cattle; as
that of Berghem too often does with a few ruined walls: while the
degenerate taste of others is satisfied, where Nature spreads all her
beauties around, to grovel among hay-fields and pig-sties, to study
and detail the anatomy of a wooden bridge or a muddy wharf.

The critic in art finds other sources of enjoyment in landscape,
which are unknown, even to those whose acquired taste may, short of
this information, stand at a high point in the scale. In the accidents
of light and shade, he perceives beauties which those do not know
how to feel or value who are unaware of their power in giving force
and attraction to paintings. In the multiplicity and harmony of direct,
reflected, and half lights, under a thousand tones for which there are
no terms, he sees charms which are only sensible to a highly cultivated
and somewhat technical eye. It is only such an eye that can truly feel
the beauty of colouring—that is sensible to its innumerable modifications, to all the hidden links by which it is connected, and to all the
harmony which results from arrangement and contrast.

The mere art of omission in contemplating landscape is a most material one; nor is it to be acquired without study and technical knowledge. Nature is rarely, indeed, faultless; more commonly, she is
full of faults to counteract her beauties. And as the deformities are
commonly the most obvious, invariably so to the uneducated, so these
turn with neglect or aversion from scenes whence the educated and
the critic, without difficulty, extract beauties. The latter may, if
he practises drawing, fill his portfolio with subjects from countries
where others would not make a single sketch: or, if that is not his
object, he still travels in the midst of beautiful scenes where his
companions, if he has any, are dull and uninterested; with the additional satisfaction, if he thinks it such, that results from his consciousness of superiority, and with the much more legitimate one, that he is
enjoying the reward of his own exertions and studies.

This is the education which not only teaches us how to enjoy Nature, but which absolutely creates the very scenes for our enjoyment. This, too, is the education which is attainable by all. But the artist who is versed in the works of his predecessors, finds still farther sources of pleasure in comparison, as the critic does in comparing the several styles of authors. Thus he learns to look at Nature alternately with the eye of Poussin, or Claude, or Berghem, or Rembrandt, or Waterlo; detecting, by their aid, beauties that would otherwise have escaped him, and multiplying to an incalculable degree the sources of his enjoyment as well as of his studies.

It is of the character of one artist, perhaps, to dwell on all that is placid and rich in composition and colour; another delights in the foaming torrent, the ravine, and the precipice; the simplicity of rural nature exclusively attracts a third; and others yet, select for imitation the edifices of art, the depths of the forest, the ocean decked with smiles or raging with fury, or the merest elements of landscape—the broken bank, the scathed tree, or the plants that deck the foreground. Viewing with the eyes of the whole, stored with the ideas which he has accumulated from the study of their works, his attention is alive and his senses open to every thing; and not a beauty can pass before him but he is prepared to see it and to enjoy it.

I have supposed, at the outset of this little essay, that all the ordinary and mechanical part of drawing—that which consists in copying from works of art, from drawings, or even from nature, may be attained by all persons of moderate and ordinary talents, if they will but believe that it is attainable, and will make use of that moderate portion of exertion or industry which they bestow on other things. But, having still before me landscape as the most attainable and amusing branch of this art, it is necessary, if we would form the mind of the young artist, or even our own as mere idlers in art, so as to extract from Nature all the beauties she contains, and analyse and detect her inexhaustible stores, that we should become familiar with the works of all those painters who have excelled in their several ways, neglecting no style, but learning to appropriate to each his particular class of scenery, and to seek for these in Nature. Fortified with this knowledge, we can look at the objects she presents; and glancing over our treasured ideas, if we find not what Claude would have found, we may yet discover what would have formed the study of Both, or Suaneveldt, or Vanderneer; and thus multiply our enjoyments to an incalculable degree, by extracting something of form, or colour, or composition, from what is before us; by personifying the infinite variety of tastes that have preceded us, and for all of which there is enjoyment, when we choose to seek it, and know where it is to be sought.

In every thing the art of seeing is really an art, and an art that must be learnt. It must be learnt for the plainest of reasons. It is not a simple effort, nor the result of simple sensations; it is the consequence of short and quick, but complicated trains of reasoning, and is necessarily connected with, and dependent on, a thousand associations, without which it were the same if the objects were exhibited to the eyes of a child or a dromedary.

It is natural for us to imagine that we must know well and thoroughly that with which we are familiar, that we cannot fail to understand what we see every day. Thus the vulgar, which imagines itself a judge of music, forgets also that there may be more in this art than meets its own ear, and refuses to yield its judgment to the learned. As little can it comprehend the natural beauties which surround it; and thus also it disbelieves, as it dislikes, like Mungo in the Padlock, what it does not understand. Yet this taste is of slow growth, and is among the last to appear. If we doubt that, to be attained in perfection, it requires much and various study, much practice, and great delicacy of feeling, a warm and creative imagination, and many collateral acquisitions, we have only to examine our own progress, to compare our present state with any previous one, and, in admitting that there may be a much longer path before us than the one we have left behind, learn to be modest.

As to the public at large, we have almost ourselves witnessed the rise, the origin, of the present taste, such as it is, for the beauties of Nature—for landscape scenery. If it does not yet possess much, it is still a far other public than it was forty, nay, thirty years ago. And if I shall succeed in convincing your readers, whether male or female, that it may be yet a far different public from what it is now, I expect that Mr. Newman and Mr. Ackermann, and the remainder of this ingenious tribe, will join in a handsome subscription for a piece of plate, something better than the silver palette of the Society of Arts, to be presented through your hands, Mr. Editor, to the X. Y. Z. gentleman who has written this paper, and thus brought custom to their shops. I beg to assure you that I am neither a colourman, nor a paper-maker, nor even a drawing-master; and that the Ladies and Gentlemen, who are ambitious of learning more than they already know, need not " apply as above." I am, I assure you, a most disinterested, or uninterested, personage; and am only ambitious to add to the pleasures and accomplishments of the darling sex from which all our own pleasures and accomplishments arise, and to which they all tend.

But, as I am in danger of travelling out of the record, I shall only add, before I take my leave, that the great increase of domestic travelling, while it appears to originate in a taste for the beauties of Nature, is that which chiefly tends to generate it. The people begin by imagining that it sees, and admires, and understands; and it ends in doing what it had but fancied before—in seeing, and admiring, and understanding. If a taste for the art of design is also yet low in Britain, there is a certain moderate portion of it which is widely diffused, as is a species of rambling and superficial literature: and all this aids the cause, as it is equally an earnest of future improvement. Let us all strive for more; and, to attain it, begin by convincing ourselves of our ignorance. There are few pleasures better worth the pursuit, for there are few that cost less and produce less pain—few that yield more refined and delicate satisfaction, either in the present enjoyment or the future recollection. The contemplation of Nature is a perpetual and a cheap gratification; improving the heart while it cultivates the mind, and abstracting us from the view, as it helps to guard us against the intrusion, of those cares, against which it requires all our watchfulness and attention to shut the door.

## SKETCHES OF THE IRISH BAR.—NO. VII.

### Serjeant Lefroy.

"Read your Bible, Sir, and mind your purse."—DON JUAN.

THERE is something apparently irreconcileable between the ambition and avidity which are almost inseparable from the propensities of a successful lawyer, and any very genuine enthusiasm in religion. The intense worldliness of his profession must produce upon his character and faculties equally tangible results; and if it has the effect of communicating a minute astuteness to the one, it is not very likely to impart a spirit of lofty abstraction to the other. I cannot readily conceive any thing more sublunary than the bar. Its occupations allow no respite to the mind, and refuse it all leave to indulge in the aspirations which a high tendency to religion not only generates, but requires. They will not even permit any native disposition to enthusiasm to branch aloft, but fetter it to the earth, and constrain it to grow down. How can the mind of a lawyer, eddying as it is with such fluctuating interests, receive upon its shifting and troubled surface, those noble images which can never be reflected except in the sequestered calm of deep and unruffled thought? He whose spirit carries on a continued commerce with the skies, is not only ill adapted to the ordinary business of society, but is scarcely conscious of it. He can with difficulty perceive what is going on at such a distance below him; and if he should ever divert his eyes from the contemplation of the bright and eternal objects upon which they are habitually fixed, it is but to compassionate those whom he beholds engaged in the pursuit of the idle and fantastic fires that mislead us in our passage through "this valley of tears." To such a man, the ordinary ends of human desire must appear to be utterly preposterous and inane. The reputation which Romilly has left behind, must sound as idle in his ears as the wind that shakes the thistle upon his grave. An ardent religionist must shrink from those offices which a lawyer would designate as the duties, and which are among the necessary incidents of his profession. To play for a little of that worthless dross, which is but a modification of the same material upon which he must at last lie low, all the multiform variety of personation which it is the business of a lawyer to assume—to barter his anger and his tears—to put in mirth or sorrow, as it suits the purpose of every man who can purchase the mercenary joke or the stipendiary lamentation:—these appear to be offices for which an enthusiastic Christian is not eminently qualified. Still less would he be disposed to misquote and to misrecite—to warp the facts, and to throw dust into the eyes of justice—to enter into an artificial sympathy with baseness— to make prostitutes of his faculties, and surrender them in such an uncompromising subserviency to the passions of his client, as to make them the indiscriminate utensils of depravity. But how fallacious is all speculation when unillustrated by example, and how rapidly these misty conjectures disappear, before the warm and conspicuous piety of the learned gentleman whose name is prefixed to this number of the " Sketches of the Irish bar." This eminent practitioner, who has rivals in capacity, but is without a competitor in religion, refutes all this injurious surmise; and in answer to mere inference and theory, the sainted fraternity amongst whom he plays so remarkable a part, and who with emulative admiration behold him uniting in his person the good things of the Old Testament, with the less earthly benedictions of the New, may triumphantly appeal to the virtues and to the opulence of Mr. Serjeant Lefroy.

The person who has accomplished this exemplary reconciliation between characters so opposite in appearance as a devoted follower of the gospel and a wily disputant at the bar, stands in great prominence in the Four Courts, but is still more noted among " the Saints" in Dublin, and I think may be accounted their leader. These are an influential and rapidly increasing body, which is not wholly separated from the church, but is appended to it by a very loose and slender tie. They may be designated as the Jansenists of the establishment; for in their doctrines of grace and of election they border very closely upon the professors of the Port-Royal. For men who hold in such indifference the pleasures of the world, they are singularly surrounded with its fugacious enjoyments. Encompassed with innocuous luxuries and innocent voluptuousness, they felicitously contrast their external wealth with that mortification of the spirit of which they make so lavish a profession, and of which none but an irreclaimable sceptic could entertain a doubt. At the bar they are to be found in considerable strength, and are distinguished among their brethren for their zeal in the advancement of the interests of religion and their own. They are, in general, sedulous and well-informed—competent to the discharge of ordinary business, and free of all ambition of display—a little uncandid in their practice, and careless of the means by which success is to be attained— pursuivants of authority and followers of the great—gentlemanlike in their demeanour, but not without that touch of arrogance towards their inferiors, which is an almost uniform attendant upon an over-anxious deference to power—strong adherents to abstract principles of propriety, and vehement inculcators of the eternal rules of right, but at the same time not prodigally prone to any Samaritan sensibilities—amiable in their homes, and somewhat selfish out of them—fluent reciters of the scriptures—conspicuously decent in their manners, and entirely regardless of the apple-wenches in the Hall.

The great prototype of this meritorious fraternity is Mr. Serjeant Lefroy. It would do good to the heart of the learned member for Galway to visit his stables on a Sunday. The generous animals who inhabit these exemplary tenements, participate in his relaxations, and fulfil with scriptural exactness the sacred injunction of repose. Smooth as their benevolent master, they stand in their stalls amidst all the luxury of grain, and, from their sobriety and sleekness, might readily be recognized as the steeds of a prosperous and pious man. It is one of the Serjeant's favourite canons, that the lower orders of the animal creation should join in the celebration of the seventh day, and contribute the offering of their involuntary homage. Loosened himself from the rich wain of his profession, he extends a similar indulgence to the gentle quadrupeds, who are relieved on that day from the easy obligation of drawing one of the handsomest equipages in Dublin, to which, in all probability, the chariots of the primitive Christians did not bear a very exact resemblance. If you should chance on Sunday to walk near the Asylum (a chapel in Leeson-street, which, from the number of sanctimonious lawyers who inhabit it, is called " Swaddling-bar,") you will see the learned Serjeant proceeding to this favoured domicile of worship, near which he resides without any verification of the proverb, with a huge Bible bound in red morocco under his arm. It is a truly edifying spectacle. A halo of piety is diffused about him. His cheeks, so far from being worn out by the vigils of his profession, or suffused with the evaporations of the midnight lamp, are bright, shining, and vermilioned. There is a gloss of sanctity upon them, which is happily contrasted with the care-coloured visages of the profane. A serious contentedness is observable in his aspect, which indicates a mind on the best footing with heaven and with itself. There is an evangelical neatness in his attire. His neckcloth is closely tied, and knotted with a simple precision. His suit of sables, in the formality of its outline, bears attestation to the stitches of some inspired tailor who alternately cuts out a religion and a coat—his hose are of grey silk—his shoes are burnished with a mysterious polish, black as the lustre of his favourite Tertullian. As he passes to the house of worship, he attracts the pious notice of the devouter fair who flock to the windows to behold him, but, heedless of their perilous admiration, he advances without any indulgence of human vanity and joins the convocation of the elect. There his devotion exhales itself in enraptured evaporations, which nothing but the recognition of some eminent solicitor in the adjoining pew can interrupt. The service being over, he proceeds to fill up the residue of the day with acts of religious merit, and, as I have heard, with deeds of genuine humanity and worth. With him, I really believe that upon a day which he sets apart from worldly occupation, with perhaps too much Puritan exactness, " works of mercy are a part of rest." While I venture to indulge in a little ridicule of his sabbatarian precision, which is not wholly free from that sort of pedantry which is observable in religion as well as in learning, I should regret to withhold from him the encomium which he really deserves. It has been whispered, it is true, that his compassion is, in a great degree, instigated by his theological predilections, and that it has as much of sectarianism as of philanthropy. But humanity, however modified, is still humanity. If, in leaving the chamber of suffering and of sorrow, he marks with a bank-note the leaf of the Bible which he has been reading at the bed-side of some poorer saint, let there be given to his benevolence, restricted as it may be by his peculiar propensities in belief, a cordial praise. The sphere of charity must needs be limited ; and of his own money, it is a clear truism to say, he is entitled to dispose as he thinks proper. With respect to the public money, the case is different, and upon the distribution of a fund of which he and certain other gentlemen of his profession are the trustees, (so at least they have made themselves,) there appears less right to exercise a summary discretion. I allude to the Kildare-street Association, of which he is one of the principal members.

The street from which this association has derived its name has brought the extremes in morals into a close conjunction. The Pharisees of Dublin have posted themselves in a most Sadducean vicinage, for their meetings are held beside the most fashionable gaming-club in Ireland. Loud indeed and long are the oratorical ejaculations which issue from the assemblies held under the peculiar auspices of the illuminated associates of the long robe. Here they hold out an useful example of prudence as well as of zeal, and indulge their generous propensities at little cost. They receive, by parliamentary grant, an annual sum of six thousand pounds for the education of the poor ; and by a prodigious stretch of individual beneficence a hundred guineas are added through a private subscription among the elect. In the allocation of this fund they have established rules which are entirely at variance with the ends for which the grant has been made by parliament. They require that the Bible should be read in every school to which assistance is given. With this condition the Roman Catholic clergy (and the chief amongst the Protestant hierarchy concur in their opposition) have refused to comply. The indiscriminate perusal of the scriptures, unaccompanied by any comment illustrative of the peculiar sense in which they are explained by the Roman Catholic church, seems to be inconsistent with the principles in which that church is founded. The divines of Kildare-street have, however, undertaken the difficult task of demonstrating to this obstinate and refractory priesthood, that they understand the tenets and spirit of their religion much better than any doctor at Maynooth. A consequent acrimony has arisen between the parties, and the result has been that the few channels of education which exist in the country are denied all supply from a source which has been thus arbitrarily shut up. It is lamentable, that, in the enforcement of these fanatical enactments, so much petty vindictiveness and theological acerbity should be displayed. The assemblies held at Kildare-street, with the ostensible view of advancing the progress of intelligence among the lower classes, exhibit many of the qualities of sectarian virulence in their most ludicrous shape. A few individuals who presume to dissent from the august authorities who preside at these meetings, occasionally venture to enter their public protest both against the right and the propriety of imposing a virtually impracticable condition upon the allocation of the parliamentary fund. Lord Cloncurry implores them, with an honest frankness, to abandon their proselytising speculation. O'Connel too, who " like a French falcon flies at every thing he sees," comes panting from the Four Courts, and gives them a speech straight. The effects produced upon the auditory, which is compounded of very different materials from the meetings which the counsellor is in the habit of addressing with so much success, are not a little singular. Of the ingredients of this assembly it may not be amiss to say a few words. Aware of his purpose, the Saints employ themselves for some days before in congregating all those who hold his politics and his creed in their most special abhorrence. They accordingly collect a very motley convocation. In the back-ground are posted a strong phalanx of the ragged and ferocious votaries of Mr. Cooper. These persons belong to the lower classes of Protestants, of whose religion it would not be easy to give any more definite description, than that they regard the Plunket-street orator as on a very close footing with the Divinity, and entertain shrewd doubts whether he be not the prophet Enoch himself. Adjoining to this detachment, which is posted as a kind of *corps de réserve,* whose aid is to be resorted to upon a case of special emergency, the Evangelicals of York-street are drawn up. Next come a chosen band of Quakers and Quakeresses ; and lastly are arrayed The Saints, more properly so called, with the learned Serjeant and divers

oily-tongued barristers at their head.   The latter are judiciously dispersed among the pretty enthusiasts who occupy the front benches, and
whisper a compliment in the ear of some soft-eyed votary, who bears
the seal of grace upon her smooth and ivory brow.   It may not be
inappropriate to observe, that among the softer sex the Saints have
made very considerable way.   The cold worship of the establishment
is readily abandoned for the more impassioned adoration which cor-
rects the tameness and frigidity of the constituted creed.   The latter
is, indeed, a kind of Catholicism cut down; it is popery without
enthusiasm; and to remedy its want of stimulus, an exciting system
has been devised, the practices and tenets of which are endowed
with a peculiar pungency.   The Kildare-street meetings are attended
by some of the prettiest women in Dublin; and I should say, in justice
to these tender devotees, that they appear there with a peculiar interest.
There is a studied modesty in their attire that only excites the imaginations which it purposes to repress.

In this scene, thus strangely compounded, it is pleasant to see the
popish agitator engaged in a wrestle with the passions and antipathies
of his hearers.   The moment he rises, an obscure murmur, or rather
growl, is heard in the more distant parts of the room.   This discour-
teous sound proceeds from the Cooperites, who find it difficult to restrain themselves from any stronger expression of abhorrence towards
this poisoned scion of St. Omer's.   The politer portion of the audience
interfere, and the learned Serjeant entreats that he may be heard.
O'Connel proceeds, and professes as strong and unaffected a veneration
for the Holy Writings as any of them can entertain; but at the same
time begs leave to insinuate, that the Bible is not only the repository of
divine truths, but the record of human depravity, and that, as a narrative, it comprehends examples of atrocity, with the detail of which it
is, perhaps, injudicious that youth and innocence should become familiar.   Are crimes which rebel against nature, the fit theme of domestic contemplation? and are not facts set forth in the Old Testament,
from the very knowledge of which every father should desire to secure
his child?   If he were desperate enough to open the Holy Writings in
that very assembly, and to read aloud the examples of guilt which
they commemorate, the face of every woman would turn to scarlet, and
the hand of every man would be lifted up in wrath: and are the pages
which reveal the darkest depths of depravity fitted for the speculations
of boyhood and the virgin's meditations?   Will not the question be
asked, What does all this mean? and is it right that such a question
should be put, to which such an answer may be given?   The field of
conjecture ought not to be opened to those whose innocence and
whose ignorance are so closely allied.   Sacred as the tree of knowledge may appear, and although it grow beside that of life, its fruits
are full of bitterness and death.   Mr. O'Connel then insists that the
Scriptures ought not to be forced into circulation, and that a bounty should
not be put upon their dispersion among the shoeless, headless, shirt-
less, and houseless peasantry of Ireland.   Give them work and food
instead of theology.   Are they capable of comprehending the dark and
mysterious intimations of St. Paul, or St. John's Revelation?   Would
not the Apocalypse bother the learned Serjeant himself? and have not
his poor countrymen enough to endure, and are they not sufficiently

disposed to quarrel, without the additional incentive of polemics? Is it in a ditch school that his learned friend conceives that the mysteries of the Trinity, of the Incarnation, and not more embarrassing Sacrament, are to be discussed?

Kindling as he advances, the great demagogue throws himself into other topics, and charges his pious friends with a violation of their duty to the public, in the arbitrary imposition of conditions against which every Roman Catholic exclaims. He disputes their right to exercise a compulsion founded on their own phantasies in the execution of a solemn trust, and, at last roundly insinuates that proselytism must be their object. At this a mighty uproar ensues. The holy rabble in the distance send up a tremendous shout: their Bibles are brandished—their eyes gleam with a more deadly fire—and their faces become more formidably grim:—a thrill of indignation runs through the whole assembly—the spirit of Obadiah himself is moved within him, and even the ladies allow the fierce infection to make its way into their gentle and forbearing breasts. An universal sibilation is heard,— mouths that pout and mince their orisons with Madonna sweetness are suddenly distorted,—a hiss issues from lips of roses, and intimates the venom that lurks beneath. O'Connel struggles hard and long, but he is at length fairly shouted down. In the midst of this stormy confusion, the learned Serjeant appears, and the moment his tall and slender person is presented to their notice, a deep and reverential silence pervades the meeting. The previous tumult is followed by attention

" Still as night, or summer's noontide air"—

the ladies resume their suavity, and look angelical again; and the men chuckle at his anticipated triumphs over the far-famed missionary of Antichrist. To pursue their champion through his victorious reply would swell my pages beyond their fitting compass; suffice it to say, that he satisfactorily demonstrates the propriety of teaching the alphabet from the Prophecies, and turning the Apocalypse into a primer. He points out the manifold advantages of familiarising the youthful mind with the history of the Jews. The applauses of his auditors, and his own heated conviction (for he is quite sincere), inflame him into emotions which bear a resemblance to eloquence, and raise his language beyond its ordinary tone. The feelings nearest to his heart ascend to his mind, and communicate their effervesceuce. His phrase is struck with the stamp of passion. His eye becomes ennobled with better thought; he shuffles off for a moment the coil of his forensic habitudes. The universal diffusion of Christian truth fills him with enthusiasm. He beholds the downfall of Popery in the opening dimness of time. Every chapel is touched by that harlequin the fancy into a conventicle. The mass bells are cracked, and the pots of lustral water are shattered. A millennium of Methodism succeeds. A new Jerusalem arises. The Jews are converted (a favourite project with the Serjeant, who holds an annual meeting for the purpose); all Monmouth-street is illuminated; its tattered robes are turned into mantles of glory. The temple is rebuilt upon an exact model of the Four-Courts. The Harlot of Babylon is stripped stark-naked, and the cardinals are given over to Sir Harcourt Lees. At length the vision becomes too radiant for endurance. A third heaven opens upon him, and he sinks

exhausted by his enjoyments, and perspiring with ecstasy, amidst the
transports of auditors to whom he imparts a rapture almost equal to
his own.

Let me conduct the reader from Kildare-street to the Court of
Chancery. Here an utter transformation takes place in the person of
the learned Serjeant, which almost brings his identity into doubt. Instead of eyes alternately veiled in the humility of their long and downcast lashes, or lifted up in visionary devotion, you behold them
fixed upon the Chancellor, and watching with a subtle intensity all the
shiftings of expression with which the judicial countenance intimates its
approval or dissent. The whole face of the vigilant and wily pleader
is overspread with craft. There is a lurking of design in every feature
of his sharp and elongated visage. You will not perceive any nice
play of the muscles, or shadowings of sentiment in his physiognomy;
it is fixed, hard, and imperturbable. His deportment is in keeping
with his countenance. He scarcely ever stands perfectly erect, and
there is nothing upright or open in his bearing. His shoulders are
contracted and drawn in; and the body is bent, while the neck is pro-
truded. No rapidity of gesture, or suddenness of movement, indicates
the unanticipated startings up of thought. The arm is never braced
in the strenuous confidence of vigorous enforcement with which
Plunket hurls the truth at the Bench; but the long and taper fingers
just tip the green table on which they are laid with a peculiar lightness. In this attitude, in which he looks a sophism personified, he applies his talents and erudition to the sustainment of the most question-
able case, with as much alacrity as if weeping innocence and virtuous
misfortune clung to him for support. The doubtful merits of his
client seem to give a new stimulus to his abilities; and if some obsolete form can be raised from oblivion, if some preposterous precedent
can be found in the mass of antiquated decision under which all reason and justice are entombed; or if some petty flaw can be found
in the pleadings of his adversary, which is sure to be detected by his
minute and microscopic eye, woe to the widow and the orphan! The
Chancellor is called upon to decide in conformity with some old monastic doctrine. The pious Serjeant presses him upon every side. He
surrounds him with a horde of barbarous authorities; and giving no
quarter to common sense, and having beaten equity down, and laid
simple honesty prostrate, he sets up the factious demurrer and the
malicious plea in trophy upon their ruins. Every expedient is called
into aid: facts are perverted, precedents are tortured, positions unheard
before are laid down as sacred canons; and in order to effect the
utter wreck of the opposite party, deceitful lights are held up as the
great beacons of legal truth. In short, one who had previously seen
the learned Serjeant for the first time in a Bible Society, would hardly
believe him to be the same, but would almost be inclined to suspect
that it was the Genius of Chicane which had invested itself with an
angelic aspect, and, for the purpose of more effectually accomplishing
its pernicious ends, had assumed the celestial guise of Mr. Serjeant
Lefroy.

Let me not be considered as casting an imputation upon this able,
and, I believe, amiable man. In the exhibition of so much professional
dexterity and zeal, he does no more than what every advocate will

regard as his duty. I am only indulging in some surprise at the promptness: and facility of his transition from the religious to the forensic mood ; and at the success with which he divests himself of that moral squeamishness, which one would suppose to be incidental to his intellectual habits. Looking at him as an advocate, he deserves great encomium. In industry he is not surpassed by any member of his profession. It was his good fortune, that, soon after he had been called to the bar, Lord Redesdale should have been lord chancellor. That great lawyer introduced a reformation in Irish practice. He substituted great learning, unwearied diligence, and a spirit of scientific discussion, for the flippant apophthegms and irritable self-sufficiency of the late Lord Clare. He entertained an honourable passion for the study, as well as for the profits of his profession, and not satisfied with pronouncing judgments which adjusted the rights of the immediate parties, he disclosed the foundations of his decisions, and opening the deep groundwork of equity, revealed the principles upon which the whole edifice is established. The value of these essays delivered from the Bench was well appreciated by Mr. Lefroy, who, in conjunction with Mr. Schoales, engaged in the reports which bear their names, and which are justly held in so much esteem. Soon after their publication, Mr. Lefroy rose into business, for which he was in every way qualified. He was much favoured by Lord Redesdale, and now enjoys the warm friendship of Lord Manners, for whom he acts as confidential counsel. His great familiarity with cases, and a spirit of peculiar deference to his Lordship, combined with eminent capacity, have secured for him a large portion of the judicial partialities. He is in the fullest practice, and, taking his private and professional income into account, may be well regarded as the wealthiest man at the Irish Bar. His great fortune, however, has not had the effect of impairing in him the spirit of acquisition. He exhibits, indeed, as acute a perception of pecuniary excitement, as any of his less devout brethren of the coif.

' Serjeant Lefroy will in all likelihood be shortly raised to the Bench. He has already officiated upon one occasion as a judge of assize, in consequence of the illness of some of the regular judges, and gone the Munster circuit. His opinions and demeanour in this capacity are not undeserving of mention: they have attracted much attention in Ireland, and in England have not escaped observation. Armed with the King's commission, he arrived in Limerick in the midst of those dreadful scenes to which no country in Europe affords a parallel. All the mounds of civil institution appeared to have been carried away by the dark and overwhelming tide, which was running with a tremendous current, and swelling every day into a more portentous magnitude. Social order seemed to be at an end. A wild and furious population, barbarized by a heartless and almost equally savage gentry, had burst through the bonds by which its madness had been hitherto restrained, and rushed into an insurrection in which the animosities of a civil, were blended with the ferocity of a servile war. Revenge and hunger employed their united excitations in working up this formidable insanity. Reckless of the loss of an existence which afforded them no enjoyment, the infuriated victims of the landlord and the tithe-proctor. extended to the lives of others the same estimate which they set upon their own, and their appreciation of the value of human breath was illustrated in the daily assassinations which were devised with the guile, and perpetrated with the fury of an Indian tribe. The whole country smoked with the traces of devastation—blood was shed at noon upon the public way—and crimes even more dreadful than murder made every parent tremble. Such was the situation of the county of Limerick, when the learned Serjeant arrived to administer a remedy for these frightful evils. The calendar presented almost all the possible varieties which guilt could assume, and might be designated as a hideous miscellany of crime. The court-house exhibited an appalling spectacle. A deep and awful silence hung heavily upon it, and the consciousness that lay upon every man's heart, of the frightful crisis to which the county seemed rapidly advancing, bound up the very breath of the assembly in a fearful hush. The wretched men in the dock stood before the judicial novice in a heedless certainty of their fate. A desperate independence of their destiny seemed to dilate their broad and expanded chests, and their powerful faces gave a gloomy token of their sullen indifference to death. Their confederates in guilt stood around them with much stronger intimations of anxiety in their looks, and as they eyed their fellow conspirators in the dock, seemed to mutter a vow of vengeance for every hair that should be touched upon their heads. The gentry of the county stood in the galleries with a kind of confession in their aspect, that they had themselves been participant in the production of the crimes which they were collected to punish, but which they knew that they could not repress. In this assembly, so silent that the unsheathing of a stiletto might have been heard amidst its hush, the learned Serjeant rose, and called for the piece of parchment in which an indictment had been written. It was duly presented to him by the clerk of the crown. Lifting up the legal scroll, he paused for a moment, and said, "Behold! in this parchment writing, the causes of all the misery with which the Lord has afflicted this unhappy island are expressed. Here is the whole mystery of guilt manifestly revealed. All, all is intimated in the indictment. Unhappy men, you have not the fear of God before your eyes, and you are moved by the instigations of the Devil." This address went beyond all expectation—the wretches in the dock gazed upon their sacred monitor with a scowling stare—the Bar tipped each other the wink—the parsons thought that this was a palpable interference with my Lord the Bishop—the O'Grady's thrust their tongues into their cheeks, and O'Connel cried out " leather !" I have no room to transcribe the rest of this remarkable charge. It corresponded with the specimen already given, and verified the reference to the fabulist. So, indeed, does every charge delivered from the Irish Bench. Each man indulges in his peculiar propensities. Shed blood enough, cries old Renault. Be just, be humane, be merciful, says Bushe. While the learned Serjeant charges a confederacy between Beelzebub and Captain Rock, imputes the atrocities of the South to an immediate diabolical interposition, and lays at the Devil's door all the calamities of Ireland.

## THE LORD OF VALLADOLID.[*]

The Monarch of Arragon hied to the field,
  The flower of his warriors round,
When a stranger knight, with no arms on his shield,
  Approach'd from the distant ground :
Far flash'd his blue mail in the sunbeams bright,
  As his war-horse career'd the plain,
With foam-cover'd bit and an eye of light,
And nostrils distended, that breathed in their might
  Thick smoke round his bridle's chain.

The courtiers were still—not a whisper was heard—
  All eyes on the strange knight gazed ;
From his horse he alighted—no visage appear'd,
  His plume-shaded beaver was raised :
He moved t'ward the presence of majesty,
  With the air of a noble graced ;
All were awe-struck and dumb as he slowly drew nigh,
And, lifting his steel-cover'd fingers on high,
  His beaver and helmet displaced.

Peranzúles, the traitor to Arragon's king—
  'Tis he that stands hoary there,
Where the ancient oak, aloft wavering,
  Shoots its stately gnarl'd boughs in air :
And his knee to the monarch he lowly bends,
  His hand a vile halter bears ;—
Distrusted, alone, unsupported by friends,
On the rock of his courage and truth he depends,
  In the wane of his glorious years.

" O king ! I once swore to be true to thy cause
  With the blood in every vein, ‹
And I tender it now for my breach of the laws,
  To wash out the forfeited stain !
O king ! at thy footstool this worn life I lay,
  But thou ne'er canst take from me
That which I more cherish, my honour, away,
Not blacken a name with foul treachery,
  That ne'er hath been treacherous to thee.

" I was bound by my knighthood, by justice, by ties,
  More worth than these sinews dry ;
More worth than the fast ebbing tide that supplies
  This old heart with its pulses high :—
By the law of Castile and my country's command,
  When its Queen you divorced from your throne,
She took back the cities I held at your hand—
She took her dominion again o'er the land,
  Her forefathers' right and her own.

" I blush for my country !—this insult of thine
  To the blood of proud Castile
Might cancel all bonds of my vassals and mine,
  All service of homage and steel—
But Peranzúles no traitor shall shield with his name—
  Though faithless,—it was to be just !
To his Queen he has acted as duty became,
And now is before thee unsullied in fame,
  To pay with his life for his trust."

---

[*] See a striking Fragment of Spanish History, page 309 of this work.

The courtiers shrink back from the space where stands
  Valladolid's grey lord alone,
Grasping firmly the cord with his clinging hands,
  And his black bright eyes flung down ;—
As if o'er the waves of a stormy sea,
  He clung for his last inch of life,
To the only stay that on earth he could see,
That would save him from shame—from the agony
  Of his bosom's speechless strife.

When the King thus address'd him (unchanged was his mien,
  His sight on the ground yet lay :)—
" Peranzúles an upright judge hast thou been
  Of princes in open day—
Thou hast justly judged—but let none like thee
  E'er presume to cast a crown,
That dare not as boldly the loser see—
That dare not uphold his judgement free,
  In the shade of the Monarch's frown !"       J.

---

BRITISH GALLERIES OF ART.—NO. IX.

*Fonthill.*

A work of high art deserves to be traced and followed to whither-soever the chances and changes of time may carry it—its *biography* is worthy of being recorded and read, even when itself, from the perishable nature of the materials which form it, may have passed away from among existing things. We have few volumes more inte-resting than that would be which should duly trace the history of what once formed the treasures of the Louvre,—hinting, in its progress, at the causes and consequences of the events referred to ; and its value and interest would be greater rather than less, now that the principal objects of its notice are again scattered abroad over the face of Europe. It is on this account that I have thought it worth while to give a short notice of the Fonthill Gallery,—although, by the time this paper is before the public, it will no longer exist as such. But the few, the very few works which compose its principal ornaments, will exist, and will even (in imagination) keep their places on the walls where they have once hung, when nothing else belonging to the spot is cared for or remembered. I, for one, could walk up to the bare walls which the objects I am about to notice lately covered, and mark out with a pencil the identical space which each of them occupied. In fact, for me, and for those who have seen and duly appreciated them, *there* they will continue to hang, till we shall chance to see them in some other place ; as the image of a lost friend for ever occupies the spot where we *last* saw him.

It has been said that the works now forming the Fonthill Gallery are not the same of which it consisted before this singular spot was opened to public inspection. It may, or it may not be so. With this I shall not concern myself. The true lover of art cares not to whom a fine picture may *belong ;* he, and he alone, is the *possessor* of it, who is sufficiently impressed with its beauties to be able to enjoy the me-mory of them ; and he sees no difference in those beauties, whether they look upon him from the walls of a palace or of a picture-dealer's shop;—nay, he scarcely thinks the worse of them for having an auctioneer's lot-mark in the corner—since this does not oblige him to read the *description* appertaining to it!

A paper which appeared in the last number of this work has superseded any thing that I might have to say on the place which contains the Gallery I am now to notice. I shall, therefore, proceed at once to the pictures themselves;—arranging them without any reference to their relative situation, but merely in the order in which they may happen to present themselves to my recollection; which will probably be nearly correspondent with what I conceive to be their respective merits. In pursuance of this plan, the first that returns to me, in all the freshness of its beauty, and as if it were actually before me while I write, is one of almost miniature size, but for rich purity of colouring, severe sweetness of expression, and inimitable truth and delicacy of finishing, equal to any thing of the kind I am acquainted with. It is by Albert Durer, and represents the Virgin and Child, in an interior, with a distant landscape seen through a window on the right. The infant Jesus is eagerly looking out of the picture, and straining forward towards the point to which his eyes are directed; while the Virgin-mother is tenderly restraining him with one hand, which encircles his body, and presses into the soft flesh in front. This hand of the Virgin, and indeed the whole picture, may be offered as a perfect specimen of what *finishing* ought to be—of how far it ought to be carried, and at what point it should stop. We have here all the details of the actual object, in their most delicate minutiæ, producing all the force and spirit of general effect which is so usually frittered away, or diluted into mawkishness, in attempts of this kind. But the chief charm, in the detail of this rich little gem, is the expression of the Virgin: it is the perfection of a divine humanity; blending together, into one lovely whole, all the attributes with which the imagination invests this most interesting of historical characters.

The next picture that I shall notice, is one of corresponding and perhaps equal merit with the above, but in altogether a different class of art; the first being, notwithstanding its truth, all ideal, and the second being a piece of actual unmingled nature. But I place them thus, side by side, because they seem to have been dictated by the same spirit, and to proceed on the same principles: each being actually *true* in every particular; but the one being true to the imagination, and the other to actual knowledge and observation. The exquisite work to which I now allude is by Metzu, and represents a woman scraping fish on a table, before the door of a cottage; on the table are placed some parsnips, and a brass kettle, with a kitten seated on the top of it. Among all the specimens that I have seen of the Flemish school of finishing, this is without exception the very best, with reference to the ostensible *object* of all finishing—viz. to produce natural impressions. Any thing which proceeds beyond this—(which much of the Flemish finishing frequently does—that of Vanderwerf, W. Mieris, and G. Dow, for example)—is distinct from the purpose of *painting*—which was and is as 'twere "to hold the mirror up to nature." The reader will, perhaps, pardon me, if I direct his attention in a particular manner to this last illustration, because it precisely explains what I mean, with reference to pictures of the class now in question. Their perfection, in fact, consists in representing objects, not as they actually appear when presented directly to the eye, but as they would appear if *reflected from a concave mirror.* Looked at in this point of view, the little work before us is the most purely *natural* effort of the pencil that I have ever seen ; so much so, as to have required nothing less than *genius* to produce it —which is more than I should be disposed to say of any other similar work, that I am acquainted with, of the Flemish school.

As an illustrative contrast to these two charming works, I would have pointed out, had the collection remained entire, an execrable picture by W. Mieris, which was (strange to say) considered as among the chief boasts of the gallery. The subject is the Judgment of Solomon ; and the whole scene (with the exception of the real mother) is the ideal of what a work of art should *not* be—whether regarded as a composition, a piece of colouring, or an effect of high finish. To convey a notion of the spirit in which the work is composed, I will mention that the false mother is standing, with a smile on her countenance, holding out her apron to receive *her share* of the infant !

As a fine contrast to the above, in point of style, I will here notice a noble gallery picture, by Ludovico Carracci,—the only one in the collection, of this class, which is worthy of particular mention. It is a long low picture—the figures larger than life—representing the Libyan Sibyl, seated on the ground, and giving forth her oracles ; while youths are attending her on either side, with tablets, taking down what she delivers. The figure, attitude, and whole expression of the Sibyl, are grand in the highest degree ; but grand from the pure and severe simplicity of their conception and execution ; for any thing like the adventitious aid of art or refinement is totally abandoned. She is sitting on the ground,—self-collected, as it regards her attitude, and involved in a noble drapery, which seems to wrap itself about her like a solemn thought ; but her eyes are gazing forth into the void space before her, as if searching for inspiration from the elements or the clouds. The youths who are holding the tablets on which her words are to be recorded, are no less fine, but in a different way. As specimens of anatomical design, they are admirable ; one in particular —— that on the right of the Sibyl, holding the pen and looking round towards her—includes an astonishing union of power and truth. The colouring of this picture is correspondent with the conception and design ; and it is altogether a noble specimen of what truly merits to be called the grand style in Art.

In as highly imaginative a class of Art as the above, though at the very opposite extremity of the scale in point of style and subject, is the Temptation of Saint Anthony, by D. Teniers. This is one of those grotesques in which Teniers had no rival, and, indeed, no imitator ; and in which he displayed a force of conception, a vividness of imagination, and a truth and facility of hand, that have never been united in any other person, either before or since. The Saint, with a fine solemn, self-possessed, but anxious countenance, is seated in his cell, looking towards a seeming lady who is *gliding* onwards to offer him a cup of wine which she holds in her hand ; while all around him are seen nondescript creatures, composed " of every creature's *worst*," making the most hideous mops and mows, to " fright him from his propriety." It is in the expressions thrown into the faces of these creatures, that the wonderful power of the picture consists. Though any thing but *human*, yet unquestionably their effect arises from some recondite resemblance that they bear to something that we have either seen or dreamt of in human faces. Teniers must, I think, have been an opium-eater, or he never could even have imagined, much less embodied, such expressions as we find in this and some other of his pictures on the same subject; for " such tricks hath strong Imagination" only when she is under the influence of some adventitious circumstances. That these expressions do owe their power upon us to some resemblance they bear to what we have previously seen with the mind's eye, I am convinced from the fact, that upon general spectators they have no effect at all—except that of mere strangeness. To be affected by them, and consequently to appreciate the astonishing skill displayed in them, demands an imagination akin at least to that from whence they have sprung. Not that I am disposed to rank the value of this skill higher in consequence of its effects not being generally intelligible; on the contrary: but I merely refer to the fact as explanatory.—To shew the variety of his power, the artist has depicted the seeming lady, who forms the principal object in the picture, with a grace and dignity of deportment which cannot be surpassed, and which could little be expected to proceed from his pencil, by those who do not know that, whatever he could see, that he could depict—any one thing as well as any other; and that he adopted one particular line of Art, not because he excelled in it, but because he preferred it.

There is another picture in this collection on the same subject with the above, and of almost equal merit, but on a much smaller scale.—There is also one which deserves to rank with the very finest he ever painted, in his own peculiar class,—a Village scene. It is of a large size, and yet includes but few figures; but for skilful composition, truth and harmony of colouring, and rich touches of nature and character, it merits to be called a noble production. It represents a bagpiper standing on a tub before an alehouse door, and playing to three or four couples who are amusing themselves about him. I adopt the following passage from a Catalogue Raisonné of this collection, which has been printed but (I believe) not published; as I could not vary the description with any advantage. " The most conspicuous parts in the detail of this fine work are—first, the couple who are dancing in the centre. There is an indescribable expression of half shame-faced, half chuckling delight in the woman, which is peculiarly rich and striking; but so far from moving on ' the *light* fantastic toe,' she lifts up her feet as if weights were tied to them. The ' tipsy dance and revelry' that looks out from the face of her partner, is equally rich and fine. The figure next in merit, on account of the truth as well as imagination which its expressions combine, is that of the old man who is watching the young couples romping, and rejoicing over them as if the sight renewed the very spirit of youth within him, and made him able to ' fight his (love) battles o'er again.' The bagpiper elevated on the tub, and at once playing his tune and partaking in the game that is going forward below him, is also wonderful."

The next picture that I shall notice is perhaps, upon the whole, the most perfect in this collection, and, to my mind, the very best that I have ever met with of the master. Indeed it has raised my opinion of his talents to a height that it had never approached before. It is a picture by Berghem, which was formerly in the gallery of the Duke de Praslin, and known there by the name of *L'embarquement des Vivres.* The scene is the Gulf of Genoa, with various figures and cattle on the shore in front, about to embark in a passage-boat; and buildings and shipping occupying different points of the distance. The manner in which these latter are steeped in air, and as it were blended with it, is truly admirable, and in no degree inferior to some of Claude's best efforts in the same class; and the objects in the foreground are equally effective in a different way. There is a man seated at the head of the passage-boat, whose whole character might be written from his face and air. He cares no more about his customers than if he was to get nothing by them, because he knows that they *must* come to him; and instead of dancing attendance upon them, there he sits as if they were coming to his levee. In the centre is a woman counting her money, with a prospective eye to the amount of its increase by her marketing expedition. On the left are two men spelling the contents of a posting-bill; and near the boat are two boys, one pushing and the other dragging a goat that they want to embark, but that seems to feel an instinctive horror of its fate, and will not stir a step. The boys are urging it with an expression made up of half fun half anger. But, the general effect of this picture is its great charm; and this seems to arise chiefly from the extreme lightness and elegance of the handling, and the exquisite harmony and sweetness of tone that is preserved through the different gradations of the perspective and the colouring. This charming picture, if it does not evince so high and rare a degree of power as some others that I have noticed, is, I repeat, the most faultless work in the whole collection.

If I do not pass over Leonardo da Vinci's "Laughing Boy," it will be more in respect to its celebrity than in conformity with my own opinion of its merits—which strike me as being very limited indeed. It is a small upright picture, representing a very young child amusing itself with a toy; and the expression of infantine simplicity which beams from the happy countenance is extremely pleasing and appropriate. But to hold the picture up as a distinguished effort of high art, is to betray an ignorance or an indifference as to the true import of the phrase. It is a pleasing specimen of a natural expression most naturally depicted; and nothing more.

As it was not my intention to notice in detail any objects of the Fonthill Gallery but those of surpassing merit, I shall conclude this notice by merely naming a few others which remain upon my memory, and adding a few words on the general character of the whole collection.

Of the Flemish school of finishing there are several most exquisite specimens, and one or two that are perhaps unrivalled. Of these latter, a lady in a satin and fur cloak, feeding a grey parrot, by F. Mieris, is the best. There is another on the same subject, by the same master, which is extremely beautiful in its way. G. Dow's "Poulterer's Shop" is also inimitably rich and elaborate; and its expressions are more natural and characteristic than this master usually took the trouble of making them: for his care was chiefly applied to tangible things. Among the gallery pictures is an Adoration of the Shepherds, by Philip de Champagne, which possesses extraordinary merit in the design and the chiaro-scuro; among the portraits, there is an admirable one by Bronzino, and two by Sir Anthony More which are little inferior to Titian; and finally, there is a charming set of pictures by Watteau, representing the Four Ages of Man, and two others by the same artist in his usual courtly style.

In taking leave of the Fonthill Gallery, I should not give a fair impression of its character to those who have not seen it, if I did not add, generally, that it is (or, by this time, *was*) more miscellaneous in point of merit than any other great collection that I could point out. It contains (as I have shewn) a few fine works—but those, with one or two exceptions, not of the finest class; many that do not reach to mediocrity; and some that are totally bad. Whether this argues a want of taste, or only a want of means, is more than I shall determine. It must be confessed, however, that it might be difficult to say where four hundred fine pictures are to be found. In fact, the mistake of picture-buyers is to limit themselves in price rather than in number. Oh, for the two best rooms in Fonthill Abbey, and a hundred thousand pounds to furnish them with! With this space and this sum alone one might, even in the present day, collect together a finer private gallery than any one now in existence;—bartering his paltry gold for the " riches fineless" of truth and beauty; and (if *that* were his appetite) acquiring a lasting fame at the same time. The late Mr. Angerstein was known all over Europe, and will not soon be forgotten, for no other reason than that he possessed ten of the finest pictures in the world!

---

## SOLITUDE.

Seek not for loneliness 'midst leaves and flowers,
　But on the sands that void and voiceless lie,
Where not a shade reveals the passing hours,
　And Time seems lost into Eternity!
And where—like wrecks upon a sullen sea,
　Making the solitude more sad—we tread
O'er cities long lost from the things that be,
　Where, towering like tall phantoms of the dead,
Haunting their desert tomb dim columns rear their head.

But when the stars look down through night's dun veil,
　And o'er the Arab's slumber shed their beams—
As soft as Beauty's eye at Sorrow's tale,
　Then is the desert peopled with his dreams—
With fairy scenes creative fancy teems;
　He sees the blue-robed daughters of the skies
Wave on his spirit—where the crystal streams
　Stray through cool shades, and every air that sighs
Wafts o'er immortal bowers the songs of Paradise!　　　M.

## CONJUGALISM,
### Or the Art of making a good Marriage.

SUCH is the attractive title of one of those Parisian publications, which from their union of a refined and piquant style with great licentiousness of matter—from their abundance of caustic satire, or playful bantering, with the most barefaced want of principle—and from the employment of a cultivated, subtle, and even delicate intellect to inculcate the grossest sensuality, may be pronounced eminently and emphatically French. From the profligate romance of Louvet, down to that most heartless, and detestable of all productions *Les Liaisons Dangereuses*, the literature of France, however poor in other respects, leaves not a single niche unoccupied in what may be termed her national Temple of polished Libertinism: while England, so superior to her rival in all the nobler departments of mental power, has fortunately seldom deigned to compete with her on this unhallowed and forbidden ground. One remarkable coincidence between the prurient writers of both countries is the common hypocrisy and cant with which they set themselves up for moralists and saints whenever they are about to be particularly scandalous. We could mention certain British mawworms who never venture upon an indecent or abusive article without a preface of pretended horror at the irreligion, indecorum, and personality, of some unacceptable contemporary. Thus the Viscount de S——, which is the *nom de guerre* assumed by the author of " Conjugalism," while in the spirit of the misogynist Swift he wallows in the most revolting nastiness of detail, is careful to add, that there is no security for female virtue or conjugal happiness unless it be grounded upon our holy religion; and at the very moment that he suggests means of the basest artifice, fraud, and forgery, to lovers of both sexes, for the attainment of their object, he piously warns them that there is no medium so likely to succeed as the practice of strict honour and unsullied morality. Upon other occasions, however, he forgets all his theoretical integrity, inculcates falsehood, treachery, and cheating, without deeming them worthy of even a passing apology, or, if he condescends to excuse them at all, revives the controversy of Thwackum and Square; assures us that, if the end be the happiness of the parties, it completely sanctifies the means; quotes the old adage, that in Love and War all stratagems are allowable; and finally tells the reader very cavalierly, that if any objections be made to the sordid duplicity which he advises, he rests his whole defence upon the title of his book, which he has called *the art* of making a good marriage. Without farther stigmatizing the pernicious tendency of this unprincipled work, we shall proceed to give such extracts from its unobjectionable passages as may afford amusing specimens of the author's style and power of observation, as well as of the Parisian fashions, habits, and modes of thinking upon that universally interesting subject—Marriage.

The very first paragraph of the preliminary reflections is strikingly characteristic of the nation. Whoever is in the slightest degree conversant with French literature must have observed the slavish conceit with which every individual, for many ages, identified his own personal vanity with that of the *grand monarque*, to which we may attribute their custom of ransacking ancient and modern history for *bon-mots*

full of sensibility, do you know what remains of those marriages which are sneeringly termed the union of hunger and thirst?—mutual regrets—manuscripts of romances, and pawnbrokers' duplicates. Reflect, then, seriously, conjugalizers of both sexes, before you submit yourselves to the empire of a *sentiment*; anticipate the future fate of the Venus, or the Apollo, who has captivated you, and do not imagine that this firework of the heart can be of long continuance. Alas! after the fine Catherine wheel has been let off at Tivoli, there remains nothing but blackened scaffolding, scorched pasteboard, and the bad odour of sulphur; and to many husbands marriage, after the honeymoon, appears little better than a Tivoli firework."

Of the propriety of submitting to our parents in all matrimonial affairs, the following is adduced as an exemplary illustration:

"Edward, a handsome cashier, fell in love with the beautiful Olympia, only daughter of an opulent banker. Love had never more vehemently inflamed two hearts already united by the bonds of sympathy; nevertheless the father, having learnt the folly of his daughter, formally declared in an angry letter, that she must prepare to renounce her chimerical passion. Olympia replies, for lovers are never sparing of long-winded epistles, that Fate had pointed out as her husband the only individual who could secure her happiness, and concluded her high-flown and romantic letter with the following remarkable words—*Edward or Death!!!*—What did papa write under this theatrical and mournful declaration?—"*Neither the one nor the other.*"—And he was perfectly right. Edward had nothing but a good figure, a little talent, and a good many creditors. Olympia passing from opulence to penury, in a melancholy hovel, disinherited by her parents, and forced to make a little kitchen, in a little room, with little means, would soon have repented her melo-dramatic resolutions; love, who is a lover of good cheer, would as usual have flown out of the window, and our married couple, according to custom, would have recriminated upon their mutual folly."

Against the dupery of fortune-tellers and gipsies the following caution is given to all amorous damsels:

"I beseech all those young ladies, who, while they have the bandage of love or of the senses over their eyes, never see any thing except through the prism of illusions and desire, not to yield to the puerile superstition of consulting one of those Pythonesses of the highway, one of those sibyls of the garret, who, of their own plenary authority, read in the future every body's fate but their own, and in a game of cards spread out like a fan, in the white of eggs, or the grounds of coffee, shew you sweethearts as clearly as astrologers perceive inhabitants in the moon. Believe me, these sorceresses of the cellar, upon their modern tripods, with their black or white magic, their legerdemain and conjurer's tricks, know not a jot more of the matter than those porteresses who prophesy husbands for the chambermaids of their hotel, by signalizing the knave of hearts as *a fair lover*, the queen of spades as *a dangerous rival*, and the ace of diamonds as *a letter from the country*. Do you wish to know, ladies, the only method of securing a rich and good husband, who after love (which has an *immortality* of some months after marriage) will preserve for you an eternal esteem? It is by your good conduct, your manners, your prudence, that you will obtain this treasure."

It would have been well for our author, and better for his readers, had he never given more objectionable advice.

Upon the subject of education, he disserteth after the following fashion.

"In bestowing a brilliant education upon a girl whose whole fortune consists in the pride of her superficial learning, in her harpsichord, her musicbooks, and her fastidious purism in language, you are unconsciously preparing for her the most painful lot. Quitting her high-bred school with a complete varnish of fashion and scientific trumpery, she no sooner reaches home than she looks down with scorn upon her own mother, who is for ever breaking poor Priscian's head, and sometimes offends her ear by a pleonasm, and sometimes by a blunder in prosody. Even the chambermaid cannot ply her broom without doing an injury to grammatical sensibility; our precious blue-stocking reasons about rhythm and the rules of versification, composes somniferous novels upon the question ' *whether Love is a purely metaphysical or material being,*' and with all this gallimaufry of words, and of alembicized and ambitious phrases, will never be able to make any water-gruel for her husband in case he should fall sick. What have mythology, the Dryads and Hamadryads, Pan and the Fauns, Endymion and the moon, to do in a butcher's or a grocer's shop? and why should the daughter of such people be able to jabber a few words of Italian, or have her head loaded with the revolutions of the Lower Empire? Young persons, however, should make a serious study of dancing, which is to marriage what the candle is to the moth: it is the principal flame at which Hymen lights his torch. I recommend them, then, to frequent all balls, public and private; and if a perfumed billet-doux should be slipped into their hands, they should make a point of refusing the first, as the surest method of receiving a great many more. These little obstacles are the thorns of the moss-rose, which centuple its value. In your anxiety, however, to conjugalize, I beseech you, by the apple of your eye, not to imitate those husband-hunting *Nina Vernons*, who, perched in the balcony of an alcove or park-pavilion overhanging a high road, holding a book or a guitar in an affected attitude, seem to be fishing with a line for any husband who will nibble at the bait. I knew a young lady at Lille so possessed with this *matrimoniomania*, that it was impossible for a young man to pay her the commonest attentions without her considering it as an overture, and threatening him with an action for breach of promise when he undeceived her of her strange error. I recollect an unfortunate young man, who was imprudent enough to reply to some of her ridiculous missives. Heavens! he had no sooner arrived at Lille, than he was summoned to appear before the father and mother; the new *Nina Vernon* throws her arms around him with a frantic cry; calls upon him to realize his vows, and declares that she will only release him at the altar. A lucky falsehood enabling him to throw himself upon his horse, and gallop away from this nuptial cut-throat, I encountered him in the High-street of Bethune, still imagining that he saw at his heels all the evil genii and malevolent sylphs of Hymen.''

In a chapter devoted to the marriage-ceremonies of England, our author begins by stating, that " clandestine marriages are no where so prevalent, inasmuch as any two lovers have only to send for a Protestant priest, who, for a trifle, will give the sanction of the law to the caprices or desires of a momentary passion. It is not uncommon for the clergy," he adds, " to write upon their windows ' marriages performed here upon cheap terms ;' and we are informed that women have this great advantage, that, if they cannot succeed by other means, they may intoxicate their lover, who, on recovering his senses, may find himself the husband of the woman whom he most despises." With an unusual scrupulosity, he admits that these fraudulent marriages have lately been prohibited by an Act of Parliament. Guernsey is the new Cythera of conjugalism for which all those embark whose nuptials encounter any legal obstacle, and the throwing of the garter and other exploded ceremonies are described as indispensable accompaniments to every union. Among the anecdotes, we are told of an Englishman who suddenly resolved to be married before he had finished smoking his pipe, which he accomplished with some little difficulty; and of

another, whose wife confessing upon her death-bed that she had been
guilty of several infidelities—"Alas!" exclaimed her husband, "you
have no more reason to be satisfied with me; I promise therefore not
to preserve any remembrance of your misconduct if you in return will
forgive me whatever wrongs I may have committed towards you." Not
less surprised than overcome by this excessive goodness, she gladly
consented, when he informed her, that having discovered her gallan-
tries, he had taken the liberty of poisoning her, and that she was then
dying by his hand!—A Milord Anglais, of great wealth, lately arrived
at Paris, was so much smitten with the beauty of the poor woman's
daughter in whose house he lodged, that he cried with a sheepish air—
" *Moi epouser vous toute de suite.*" The damsel blushed. " *Volez-vs,
voi o no?*" *(oui ou non.)* The young woman being advised to decide
instantly, as this marrier *à la minute* might change his mind, very seriously cried out—" *Oui* ;" to which Milord replied, " *Une Gentelman
ne pas avoir qu'une parole,*" and the wedding was shortly solemnized
with great magnificence. Eight days after, a friend returning from
Italy gave him such an attractive account of Naples that he exclaimed
afresh—" *Toute de suite, toute de suite, dais chival de la poste, et à
Naples!*" and in a few days his new wife finds herself under the burning skies of Lombardy.—These most authentic anecdotes are wound
up by the marriage of a Parisian exquisite.

" Saint-Elme was charming, brilliant, witty, *fait à peindre ;* he fenced, and
wrote a billet-doux *en vrai Lovelace :* the Coryphæus of the side scenes, the
actresses contended for his favours, and liveried lacqueys brought him letters
perfumed *à la Vanille*, with appointments from ladies of distinction. Descending from his unpaid tilbury in the Bois de Boulogne, and ogling through
a diamond eye-glass, for which he was still in the jeweller's books, he was
the darling of those fashionable dames who parade their landaus in fine weather, scattering from their horses' feet clouds of ostentatious dust. Nothing
in appearance was wanting to the happiness of our ambered hero, since he
took his tea at Hardy's, on the Italian Boulevard, dined at Beauvilliers, employed an English habit-maker, wore a waistcoat of *Eau du Nil*, had his
pockets filled with orange-comfits, candied cherries, pastilles *au punch*, and
Nougat de Marseilles ; and was, moreover, often seen in the private boxes
of the theatres ; but alas! his prosperity was soon to end."

Besieged one morning by bailiffs and creditors who offered him his
choice—payment or a prison—he decided as firmly as Cæsar when he
crossed the Rubicon, and, accompanied by his father, betook himself
to the horrible Lady Formes, a Londoner, of a hundred thousand sterling a-year, whose hideous portrait is exhibited in the frontispiece to
the volume, and sacrifices himself to this ancient fright for the purpose
of paying his creditors. Our author, it will be observed, is about as
happy in the names of our nobility as Rousseau in his " Nouvelle He-
loise," and Madame de Staël in her " Corinne ;" and as to the clumsy
ridicule of his story and his caricature, we apprehend that it is much
less disreputable to possess the forbiding features of a *Lady Formes*,
than the sordid and profligate soul of a *Saint-Elme*.

After recommending the revival of a custom among the Babylonians,
who used to assemble all their marriageable young women in a public
place, and bestow the money which was bidden for the beauties in mar-

riage portions for those who were ugly, our author quotes from LEGOUVE—

> " Quand l'homme de la vie entreprend le voyage,
>    La femme avec douceur guide ses premiers pas ;
> Elle sait le charmer dans le fougue de l'age,
>    Et le console encore aux portes de trepas."

A sentiment which ought to have inspired him with a little more respect for the sex: and, when he ventures in another place to exclaim—

> " Mais pour moi dont le front trop aisement rougit,
>    Ma bouche a déjà peur de t'en avoir trop dit,"

he may rest assured that no decent reader, even in France, will accuse him upon the first line, or acquit him upon the second.　　　　H.

---

## LONDON LYRICS.

### *The Watering Places.*

> " AWAKE, arise," bold Neptune cries,
>    " It scandalous and base is
> To lag behind, when half mankind
>    Frequent my Watering Places."—
> " 'Tis passing odd, blue-bearded god,
>    That men should thus turn otters ;—
> With every due respect for you,
>    I never liked your waters.
>
> " If 'twere my lot to build a cot,
>    Or dome of Chinese pattern,
> It should not verge upon thy surge,
>    Joint Devisee of Saturn.
> The very trees, that own thy breeze,
>    Seem by the favour undone ;
> With inland bend, like me, they send
>    A longing look tow'rd London.
>
> " The man who stops in sea-side shops,
>    Like Donaldson's or Lucombe's,
> In hopes to find food for the mind,
>    Soon finds he's not at Hookham's.
> The libraries that edge thy seas,
>    Are fit for boys in short hose :
> Their gew-gaw shelves bear tops for twelves,
>    And paper kites for quartos.
>
> " Sandgate may do for those who woo
>    The leaden god of slumber.
> O'er Bognor Rock the sea-gulls flock ;
>    I 'll not increase their number.
> Who loves to hide should go to Ryde,
>    Full equi-dismal Cowes is :
> And poor Eastbourne appears to mourn
>    Her runaway 'Sea Houses.'
>
> " To Broadstairs they may post away,
>    Who think it famous cheer is
> With gun and shot o'er fields to trot,
>    Monopolized by Ceres.

Southend's too nigh, and they who hie
    To Scarborough too far get:
Worthing's all tides, and all Cheapside's
    Mud-carted into Margate.

" Tow'rd Rottingdean who walks the Steyne,
    A bold and jutting work sees,
Which aims, by spars, and chains, and bars,
    To fetter thee, like Xerxes.
But, Son of Ops, the pile that stops
    Thy waters in their gushing,
*May* quit its post on Brighton coast,
    And walk away to Flushing.

" See yonder yacht, with paddling trot,
    And rolling Lichfield Sam's gait,
Unload, at eight, its motley freight,
    To skim thy surf at Ramsgate.
I once swam near her Lighthouse Pier,
    Than moist Leander madder,
But, warn'd by Time, no more I climb
    For Angels Jacob's ladder.

" At Hastings, if her frisky cliff
    Would be more staid and sober,
The gods I 'd thank to pass, dear Frank,
    With thee a blithe October.
But from her brink new rocks may sink,
    The next time blows the wind bad :
And I below her chalky brow
    Be sepulchred like Sindbad.

" Thus, billowy god, my muse has trod
    Thy forelands, creeks, and mountains,
And, could I boot as light a foot,
    I 'd seek thy briny fountains.
But gout requires more inland shires,
    The limb, that last-night felt numb,
Instinctive clings to mineral springs—
    Adieu, I 'm off for Chelt'nham !"

---

### A WALK TO VINCENNES.

It was in the Spring season, a short time ago, that I walked to the chateau of Vincennes. The day was fine, and the pure cerulean sky, with that vivifying clearness of the atmosphere never seen or experienced in our metropolis, and of which the feeling is understood by most, but which it would be difficult to describe here, gave me more than a common susceptibility of enjoying a walk—it was the exhilaration of incipient inebriety without its deadening effect upon the faculties. The mind wore its keenest edge, and its perceptions were stimulated as forcibly as the fibres of the body were braced. Such a moment is favourable for enjoying the beauties of Nature, and it is then almost an offence against natural feeling not to walk forth and drink in the delight which creation offers us. My resolution was executed *sur le champ*. I had breakfasted at the Caffè Hardi in the *Boulevard des Italiens*, when I planned my ramble, and having crowned my *déjeuné* with a *petit verre* of brandy, about a good-sized thimble full, (for my breakfast, be it observed, was *à la fourchette,*)·I proceeded along those charming adjuncts to the French cities—the Boulevards, amusing myself with the endless variety of objects in my way, until I reached the *Barrier du Trone*. All who have been at the eastern end of Paris know this spot of ingress and egress by the two naked columns on each hand. The road from the barrier runs in a straight line to Vincennes and its pleasant neighbourhood, and is planted with a double row of trees the whole way. The ground on the right is level; on the left hand it begins to rise at a little distance off, forming the quadrant of a hill, on the side of which is the celebrated cemetery of Père La Chaise, with its white monuments and plantations. This hill is called Mont Louis. The cemetery is the site of the chateau and grounds of the Père La Chaise, the Jesuit confessor of Louis XIV. and his mistress Madame de Maintenon, who used to visit the Père La Chaise there, as a Frenchman of the Bourbon school would say, from motives of pure piety! The side of the hill without the cemetery, and some of the space intervening between that and the road of Vincennes, was occupied by peach-gardens, then in all their luxuriance of rich blossom. I walked at a slow rate over a road which presented a curious contrast to the busy scene of one situated near the British capital. I met few persons; a diligence with its grotesque accompaniments in pilotage, passengers and lumber, a *gens-d'arme* patrolling, and a *demi-tasse** or two, if I might judge from their soldierlike air, threadbare coats, and toil-worn aspects, were the most important in the scale of consequence. There were also a few country people with the produce of their ground, seeking Paris for its sale, and jabbering their *patois* with the accustomed volubility of their nation. No splendid equipages passed me; Paris seemed to have attracted and retained all; as it retains every idea that a Frenchman can possibly accumulate of beauty, excellence, and grandeur.

I must mention that before reaching the Barrier du Trone, I went a little out of the way to visit a spot, the associations with which presented the most painful aspect, and recalled the recollection of scenes which France must for ever blush to find in the records of her history. It is a piece of ground, not forty feet square, in the corner of what was once the garden of some canonesses of St. Augustin, in the Faubourg St. Antoine. It is scarcely credible that between the 24th June, 1793, and 27th July, 1794, nearly one half of all the corpses of unhappy persons decapitated in Paris during the "reign of terror," as the French denominate that period, were crammed into such a little space. This number amounted to 1298. Over each layer of bodies some inches in thickness of quick-lime were deposited. Little indeed is the room that mortals require for their last sojourn at this rate, much less even than our scanty London grave-yards can bestow! Though these remains must have constituted a mass of human putrefaction quite appalling, the lime effectually prevented any bad consequences to the living, and the decomposition was rapid and complete. Among the dead thus inhumed here, was the noted Frederick Baron Trenck, who was decapitated only two days before Robespierre.

After this digression, to return to my main object. I pursued my

---

* The half-pay officers, or demi-solde, who are supposed to possess only the means of paying for half cups of coffee.

route under the delicious green shade of the trees, until I reached the palace built by Catharine and Mary de Medicis; it contains nothing remarkable, and I passed it by to enter the fort or chateau, so celebrated as a state prison, having been in every respect the twin brother of the Bastile. It would have shared the same fate as that edifice, had not the patriotic La Fayette preserved it by calling out the National Guard. A young officer of *gens-d'armerie*, with whom I had been long acquainted, accompanied me. He wore the ribbon of the Legion of Honour given him by Napoleon, and therefore it is fair to suppose he merited it by his services. Yet he told me that having served the Emperor faithfully, he had now transferred his allegiance to Louis, and would equally devote his life for him, adding with all a Frenchman's levity and vehemence, upon my smiling at his pliancy of principle, " he would rather serve Louis than his God, for he had seen one but he never saw the other." This is too true a picture of modern political Frenchmen, and of numerous politicians in every country. Even erroneous principle may command respect, if it be inflexibly true to its pretensions, but who can respect those who studiously subject their principles to their interests! We crossed the drawbridges and entered the inner court. All seemed adapted to the purposes of arbitrary power, —moats and walls precluding any chance of escape; a gloom falling from the dark masses of stone the whole height of the keep, that flung over the mind, together with its dark shadows, a sadness weighing down every other sensation. The recollection of the mass of human suffering endured and enduring there, must have inflicted a death of hope in the mind of every newly-arrived victim. A *lettre de cachet* and a warrant for execution could have produced in him feelings very little dissimilar. No question was allowed to be asked by the prisoner on his introduction; *c'est ici*, he was told, *la maison de silence*. As I entered the door of the donjon, the walls of which are sixteen feet in thickness, I thought of the inscription over hell-gate in Dante,

> Lasciate ogni speranza, voi, che 'ntrate!

What a picture was before me of the old regime of France! From the palace to the dungeon was here indeed but a step. The groans and misery of the captives must often, from their vicinity to it, have been echoed back in return for the music and revelry of courtiers. Thus the pains of captivity were rendered more cutting, and a torture inflicted on the mind even more bitter than Louis XI. caused on the bodies of the unfortunate Princes of Armagnac, at Vincennes or in the Bastile. They were placed in holes in the masonry shaped like inverted cones, to prevent their feet having an easy resting-place, scourged twice a week, and a tooth was drawn from them every three months! The donjon is a square building, having round towers at the angles; it is surrounded by an inner ditch. The first door being passed, it was formerly necessary to open three more before entering the first apartment, though these are at present dispensed with. The cells of the prisoners surrounded this room, small and lofty, with very little light, owing to the enormous thickness of the walls. The lowest floor was of old used as a place of torture. The stone elevations still remain on which the prisoners were seated, with the places of the rings over them by which they were confined while they suffered. A staircase in one of the circular turrets led to the summit of the building; I ascended, and was charmed with the prospect. On one side me lay what remains of the wood of Vincennes, *riant*, as the French say, in the rich luxuriance of spring; at a little distance was the pleasant village of Saint Mandé, and in another direction the city of Paris, with the domes of the Pantheon and Invalids clear and minutely seen, under the lovely blue heaven; no black dinginess obscured the buildings; every thing was defined, and stood out in its minutest details. The soft air bore with it a spirit of voluptuousness that seemed to afford fresh excitation to enjoyment on every inhalement. It almost made me forget where I was standing, that beneath my feet was a place of sighs and groans, and woe, or rather had been such, and perhaps might soon be such again; and that, amidst the luxuriance of earth, air, and skies, man had even there erected a habitation for his crimes, deforming, as usual, the face of Nature with monuments of his iniquities. How painful must the feelings of a favoured prisoner have been, who was permitted to walk on the leads for an hour with his turnkey on such a charming day, and then forced to return to his dark cell amid solitude and heart-rending desolation! I descended the narrow stairs, which once had several iron-plated doors on them for additional security, more in love with freedom than ever, and with a greater detestation of the despotic will of "a little brief authority." My guide told me that there were many inscriptions on the walls, the labour of different captives, and wished me to view some dungeons below, but I was glad to hasten out of the horrible den. Such, however, is the happy nature of some temperaments, that calamity cannot depress them, nor danger alarm. Among numberless persons incarcerated at Vincennes by Cardinal Mazarine, was the great Condé, who sung, laughed, danced, and played the violin; being a prisoner of rank, he received indulgences unknown to plebeian offenders. Abandoned by his friends, he never gave way to sadness or anger, except when speaking of Mazarine, " *Le vieux renard qui jusqu'à présent a trompé Dieu et le diable, et ne se lassera jamais d'outrager les bons serviteurs de l'état, à moins que le parlement ne congédie ou ne punisse sévèrement cet illustrissime faquin de piscina.*" He studied much, being allowed books, and wrote epigrams upon his persecutors. The Abbé Fresnoy was many times incarcerated in the Bastile and Vincennes for his writings, at which latter place he terminated his days in 1755, at the age of eighty-two. So gay was he on going to his cell, and so accustomed to be sent there, that when the officer came with the king's order he did not allow him to speak first, but began himself. " *Ah, Monsieur! Bon jour!*" and turning to his housekeeper, " *Mon petit paquet, du linge, du tabac,*" and set off laughing. Such are happy dispositions. Goldsmith thinks it best to oppose the calamities of life by dissipation rather than reason. Alas! neither is a specific for all, since our constitutions, before the receipt will do, must be remoulded alike. When we consider the limited duration of human existence, nothing man can bestow on his fellow can atone for the loss of liberty to an individual for the comparatively short space of two or three years. By the *lettres de cachet* many were imprisoned at Vincennes for twenty and thirty years. Latude, whose story has been long published, was incarcerated thirty-five years for only affronting Madame Pompadour. Many a son of literature had languished away his days there in sorrow, and brave spirits, little deserving to be "kept in such a cage," as Prince Henry said of Raleigh, have worn out life in unmerited forgetfulness within its iron precincts. Madame Guyot, the enthusiastic and good, Crebillon, Diderot, Mirabeau, Morillet, and a long list of great names, were among the captives at Vincennes. Their captivity however took place openly in latter days, when public opinion began to have some sway. One half of the victims of regal vengeance, more to be pitied than these, were never known to the world by name or by their fate. Under Louis XIII. XIV. and XV. people were frequently taken from their dwellings in the night, and seen by their friends no more; for no one was ever permitted to enter the chateau, even the priests and physicians were inmates ; secrecy being an essential point in all these state imprisonments. I felt great pleasure on coming from this monument of suffering to the open air in the court of the donjon, round which I walked. Heavy cannon were mounted on the platforms, which had thundered on the allied armies advancing upon the same side of Paris in 1814, and kept them effectually in check on that point until the capitulation was signed.

I then visited the part of the ditch where the Duke d'Enghien was executed for his conspiracy against the French government. The revived regime erects expiatory altars and chapels at every spot which has been marked by any outrage against itself ; and here some superstitious ceremonies had been lately performed over the remains of the prince on their removal to St. Denis. It is astonishing how little wisdom was displayed in thus going back to ceremonies which could never again be regarded with reverence by an enlightened people. A peaceable removal and interment would have answered every purpose. No impartial Frenchman ever denied the participation of the duke in the plots carrying on : it was the violation of a neutral territory by Bonaparte that was chiefly blamed, and the violence with which his object was effected. I thought there was something strange and retributive in the duke's execution on the very spot where his ancestors had immolated so many innocent persons : it was almost the visitation of the sins of the fathers upon the children. One instance of this kind of oppression under Louis the Fourteenth I will give, curiously involving, too, a violation of neutral territory. A young man named Desvalons fought a duel at Paris, and fled to Manheim ; he was received kindly by one Cardel, a Protestant resident there, and soon made love to Cardel's sister, or rather to her fortune, but was unsuccessful, chiefly by the brother's interference. He determined on revenge, and sent a communication to Paris, that a person at Manheim, named Cardel, intended to kill Louis the Fourteenth. The French envoy was desired to aid in getting possession of his person. He was attracted to a village out of the city, carried off by a hundred dragoons of the garrison of Laudau, and finally conducted in chains to the donjon of Vincennes. He suffered most cruel treatment, and died in the Bastile after a confinement of thirty years, and after being claimed by all the European powers in vain. Even the family of this unfortunate man was thrown into a horrible prison, and endured the most terrible sufferings, having been unhappily in France at the time of his unjust caption. I must mention another anecdote relative to Vincennes, as it records the faithfulness of the most faithful race in creation. About the time of the last persecution of the Protestants, an officer of that persuasion was shut up in the donjon. He wished much to have his dog admitted with him; it was a greyhound, which he had reared. This innocent request being refused, the dog, though turned out of the fortress, watched an opportunity on the following day, and re-entered within the innermost court. His master was confined in one of the lower cells, the window of which was near the ground, and the animal appeared at it and was recognised. He came to the bars and visited his unhappy master, whose relatives knew nothing of his fate, diurnally for four whole years, in spite of cold or wet. At length the officer was set at liberty, returned home, and died in a few months afterwards. The dog again returned .to Vincennes, and repeated its visits, taking up its dwelling with an outer turnkey, and frequently going to the window, where it sat for hours gazing in vain for its master, until death terminated its career. These two anecdotes respecting Vincennes I met with on my return to Paris, and the latter is worthy of being added to our extant collections of animal attachment and sagacity. I now thought of extending my walk, and of seeking Paris by a circuitous route. I quitted the chateau with a feeling of pleasure, and congratulated myself, that though it was but a little time comparatively, not indeed forty years ago, since Vincennes sent forth the sighs of the captive, we had had no secret prison in England since the reign of Henry VIII., when the Tower of London was used as such. At no period after him for three hundred years, including the bloody proscriptions of Mary, have we such instances of incarceration and mean cowardly oppression acting in darkness and blasting for ever the hope of its victims, as the eighteenth century discloses among our neighbours. There have been instances enough of injustice, but they took place in open day. We never pounced upon our unoffending and unsuspicious prey amid the darkness of the night, and wrapped its fate in eternal oblivion. Our state oppressions were boldly perpetrated upon the most illustrious of our victims; and we could have no motive for acting otherwise with the meaner, about whom much less interest and partisanship would naturally be excited.

The village of Vincennes had nothing novel or worthy a pedestrian stranger's notice. Passing, therefore, some way into the Park by an indirect route, I.reached St. Mandé, a pleasant commune about the distance of a *petit pas*, as the French style every measure within a league. How often have I asked the distance to a chateau, or village, and been answered *un petit pas*, when an hour's walking, *à grand pas*, has barely brought me to my object! The Frenchman, like the Irishman, speaks often without reflection; he is eager to oblige and satisfy an enquirer, but he does not reflect that precision is of consequence at all. I found, however, that in the present instance a few feet and yards were of no moment, as the scene I had just quitted exchanged for the beauty of the vegetation, the smiling flowers, the freedom of the expanded horizon, and the springiness and elasticity they diffused over the frame, would have made me forget leagues of distance. I ran, hopped, and really think I danced along the path; I thought myself supernaturally gifted with the levity of the nation,—no balloon could be more buoyant. The excitement I felt was a delicious sensation, such as I imagine few dwellers in cities know any thing about. In this way I entered an hotel in St. Mandé, and encountered a pretty but *petite* girl, who looked the very picture of health and good-humour. Her dark locks were neatly dressed and arranged, and her light step, with that peculiar and captivating air which the sex in France always possess; completely fixed my attention, so that it was not until M<sup>lle</sup> Pauline, as she afterwards told me she was called, enquired if Monsieur would please to have some refreshment, that I recollected I had entered the house for that very purpose. M<sup>lle</sup> Pauline informed me that the grilled leg of a turkey or a mutton cutlet, could be got ready in a few minutes, and preferring the *dindon* to the mutton, with some *potage à la Julienne* and a bottle of Burgundy, I made a most excellent repast. M<sup>lle</sup> Pauline then insisted upon my taking some of her coffee, which she assured me was *superbe* in taste and flavour; and having swallowed it on credit of her recommendation and found it so, I walked back to my hotel in Paris, and concluded my day at the spectacle of the Opera Comique.　　　　　　　　　　　　　　　O.

---

### ADDRESS TO THE STARS.

Ye are fair—ye are fair—and your pensive rays
Steal down like the light of parted days;
But have sin and sorrow ne'er wander'd o'er
The green abodes of each sunny shore?
Hath no frost been there, and no withering blast,
Cold—cold o'er the flower and the forest past?
Does the playful leaf never fall nor fade,
The rose ne'er droop in the silent shade?
Say, comes there no cloud on your morning beam,
On your night of beauty no troubled dream?
Have ye no tear the eye to annoy,
No grief to shadow its light of joy?
No bleeding breasts that are doom'd to part,
No blighted bower, and no broken heart?
Hath death ne'er saddened your scenes of bloom,
Your suns ne'er shone on the silent tomb?
Did their sportive radiance never fall
On the cypress tree, or the ruin'd wall?
'Twere vain to guess, for no eye hath seen
O'er the gulf eternally fix'd between.
We hear not the song of your early hours;
We hear not the hymn of your evening bowers.
The strains that gladden each radiant sphere
Ne'er poured their sweets on a mortal ear,
Though such I could deem—on the evening's sigh,
The air-harp's unearthly melody!

Farewell!—farewell! I go to my rest,
For the shades are passing into the West;
And the beacon pales on its lonely height—
Isles of the Blest—good-night!—good-night!　　　　M.

## FIRST LETTER TO THE ROYAL LITERARY SOCIETY.

*" Our court shall be a little academy."*—SHAKSPEARE!

*"Doctor, I want you to mend my caeology."*—*Heir at Law.*

CANDOUR requires, Mr. Secretary, that I should commence my letter by confessing the doubts I once entertained as to the necessity of any such establishment as that which I have now the honour to address; for at a time when our booksellers evince such unprecedented munificence, that no author of the least merit is left unrewarded, while all those of superior talent acquire wealth as well as fame, it did appear to me that our writers needed no chartered patrons or royal remunerators. At the first public meeting, however, of the Society, the president having most logically urged the propriety of such an institution, because this country had become " pre-eminently distinguished by its works of history, poetry, and philology," without the assistance of any corporate academy; while they had long possessed one in France, (where literature has been notoriously stationary or retrograde from the period of its establishment), I could not resist the force of this double argument, and am now not only convinced that it is necessary to give to our literature "a corporate character and representation," but prepared, as far as my humble abilities extend, to forward the objects of the Society, by hastening to accept its invitation for public contributions. Aware that the model of the French academy should always be kept in view, and remembering the anecdote recorded by M. Grimm, of one of its members, who died in the greatest grammatical dilemma as to whether he should say—"Je m'en vais," or, "je m'en va, dans l'autre monde," I shall limit my attention to considerations of real importance, particularly to such as may conduce " to the improvement of our language, and the correction of capricious deviations from its native purity," such being one of the main objects proposed in the president's address. Not having time, in this my first letter, to methodise all my suggestions, I shall loosely throw upon paper such observations as have occurred to me in a hasty and superficial view of the subject.

Nothing forms so violent a deviation from philological purity as a catachresis. We sneer at the slip-slop of uneducated life, and laugh at Mrs. Malaprop upon the stage, yet what so common in colloquial language as to hear people talk of wooden tombstones, iron milestones, glass inkhorns, brass shoeing-horns, iron coppers, and copper hand-irons?—We want a substitute for the phrase going on *board* an iron steam-boat, and a new verb for expressing its motion; which is neither sailing nor rowing: these are desiderata which the Society cannot too speedily supply, considering the prodigious extension of that mode of conveyance.—Many expressions are only catachrestical in sound, yet require emendation as involving an apparently ludicrous contradiction; such, for instance, as the farmer's speech to a nobleman at Newmarket, whose horse had lost the first race, and won the second:—" Your horse, my lord, was very backward in coming forward, he was behind before, but he's first at last."—I myself lately encountered a mounted friend in Piccadilly, who told he was going to carry his horse to Tattersall's, whereas the horse was carrying him thither, an absurdity which could not occur in France, where (owing, doubtless, to the Academy) they have the three words *porter, mener,* and *amener,* which prevent all confusion of that nature, unless when spoken by the English, who uniformly misapply them.—All blackberries being of a wan, or rosy hue in their unripe state, we may with perfect truth affirm, that every blackberry is either white or red when it is green, which sounds like a violent catachresis, and on that account demands some new verbal modification.   Nothing is so likely to corrupt the taste of the frugivorous generation as any looseness of idea connected with this popular berry.—By the structure of our language, many re-petitions of the same word occasionally occur, for which some remedy should be provided by the Society.   " I affirm," said one writing-mas-ter, disputing with another about the word " that," written by their re-spective pupils,—" I affirm that that ' That,' that that boy has written, is better than the other."   Here the same word occurs five times in succession, and many similar examples might be adduced; but enough has been urged to prove the necessity of prompt interference on the part of the Society.

In our common oaths, exclamations, and interjections, there is much room for Academical supervision.   For the vulgar phrase, " All my eye and Betty Martin," we might resume the Latin of the monkish hymn which it was meant to burlesque—" O mihi, beate Martine!"   It may be doubted whether we could with propriety compel all conjurers to adopt the original "hoc est corpus," pronounced in one of the cere-monies of the Romish church, which they have irreverently corrupted into hocus-pocus; but we may indisputably restore the hilariter-celeriter, which has been metamorphosed into the term helter-skelter. It would be highly desirable to give a more classical turn to this de-partment of our language.   The Italian " Corpo di Bacco !" might be beneficially imported; and in fact there is no good reason why the Ædepol ! Hercle ! Proh pudor ! Proh nefas ! Proh deûm atque ho-minum fides ! and other interjections of the ancients, might not be brought to supersede those Billingsgate oaths, which are not only very cacophonous, revolting, and profane, but liable to what their utterers may think a more serious objection—a fine of one shilling each.

Some remedy should be provided for the inconveniences arising from the omission or misapplication of the aspirate H, to which some of our cockney tribe are so incurably addicted.   It is upon record, that a Lord Mayor, in addressing King William, called him a Nero, meaning to say a hero; and no longer ago than last season Miss Augusta Tibbs, daughter of a respectable slopseller in Great St. Helen's, entering Mar-gate by a lane that skirted the cliff, and calling repeatedly to the post-boy to drive nearer the edge (meaning the hedge on the opposite side of the road,) was so incautiously obeyed, that the vehicle was precipi-tated into the sea, and the poor young lady declared, by a coroner's inquest, to have died of Inaspiration.   Surely so melancholy an occur-rence will interest the humanity of the Society in making some provi-sion against similar calamities.

Under the head of Topographical Literature, I would earnestly re-quest the attention of the Institution to various anomalous and contra-dictory designations of locality, which would long ago have been cor-rected, if, like the French, we had possessed a special Academy of In-scriptions.   Thus we apply the name of Whitehall to a black chapel ;

Cheapside is dear on both sides; the Serpentine River is a straight canal, and the New River an old canal; Knightsbridge has no bridge; Moorfields exhibit no more fields; the Green Park was all last autumn completely brown, Green-street was in no better plight, and both, according to Goldsmith's recommendation, should be removed to Hammersmith, because that is the way to Turnham-green. Endeavours should be made to assimilate the names of our streets to the predominant character of their inhabitants, a conformity to which those lovers of good cheer, the citizens, have not been altogether inattentive, inasmuch as they have the Poultry, Fish-street hill, Pudding-lane and Pie-corner, Beer-lane, Bread-street, Milk-street, Wine-court, Port-soken ward, and many others.—If the mountain cannot be brought to Mahomet, we know there is still an alternative for making them both meet; so, if there be too great an inconvenience in transposing the streets, we may remove the householders to more appropriate residences. Upon this principle, all poets should be compelled to purchase their Hippocrene from the Meuxes of Liquorpond-street; those authors who began with being flaming patriots, and are now court-sycophants or treasury hirelings, should be billeted, according to the degrees of their offence, upon the Little and Great Turn-stile. Some of our furious political scribes should be removed to Billingsgate or Old Bedlam; those of a more insipid character, to Milk and Water Lanes; and every immoral or objectionable writer should illustrate the fate of his productions by ending his days in Privy-gardens. Physicians and surgeons might be quartered in the neighbourhood of Slaughter's coffee-house; the spinsters of the metropolis might congregate in Threadneedle-street, and all the old cats in the Mews; the lame-ducks of the Stock Exchange should take refuge in the Poultry or Cripplegate; watchmakers might ply their art in Seven-Dials; thieves should be tethered in the Steel-yard: all the Jews should be restored to the Old Jewry, and the Quakers should assemble in Hatton-garden.

Chancery-lane, which would of course be appropriated to the suitors of that court, should by no means terminate in Fleet-street, but be extended to Labour-in-vain-hill in one direction, and to Long-lane in the other. Members of Parliament, according to their politics, might settle themselves either upon Constitution-hill or in Rotten-row. I am aware that if we wish to establish a perfect conformity between localities and tenants, we must considerably diminish Goodman's-fields, and proportionably enlarge Knave's-acre; but the difficulty of completing a measure is no argument against its partial adoption.

In what may be denominated our external or shopkeepers' literature, the Society will find innumerable errors to rectify. Where he who runs may read, correctness and propriety are peculiarly necessary, and we all know how much good was effected by the French Academy of Inscriptions. Having, in my late perambulations through London, noted down what appeared to me particularly reprehensible, and thrown the various addresses of the parties into an appendix, in order that your secretary may write to them with such emendatory orders as the case may require,—I proceed to notice, first, the fantastical practice of writing the number over the door, and the names on either side whence we have such ridiculous inscriptions as "Bovill and—127—Boys," which would lead us to suppose that the aforesaid Mr. Bovill's tailor's bill must be of alarming longitude, though perhaps less terrific than that of his opposite neighbour, who writes up—"Thackrah and —219—Sons."

Not less objectionable is the absurd practice of writing the name over the door, and the trade on either side, whence we have such incongruous combinations as—"Hat—Child—maker,"—"Cheese—Hoare—monger;" and a variety of others, of which the preceding will afford a sufficient sample.

Among those inscriptions where the profession follows the name without any transposition, there are several that are perfectly appropriate, if not synonymous, such as, "Blight & Son, Blind-makers:"— "Mangling done here," occasionally written under the address of a country surgeon:—"Brewer, Druggist,"—"Wrench, Tooth-drawer," —"Sloman, Wine-merchant,"—"Waters, Milkman," &c. &c.—But on the contrary, there are many that involve a startling catachresis, such as, "Whetman, Drysalter,"—"English, China-man,"—"Pain, Rectifier of Spirits,"—"Stedfast, Turner,"—"Gowing, Staymaker;" while among the colours there is the most lamentable confusion, as we have "White, Blacksmith,"—"Black, Whitesmith,"—"Brown & Scarlet, Green-grocers," and "Grey—Hairdresser," which would erroneously lead the passenger to suppose, that none but grizzled heads were admitted into the shop. While remedying these inconsistencies, the Society are entreated not to forget, that the Pavement now extends a full mile beyond what is still termed "The Stones' End" in the Borough; and that the inscription at Lower Edmonton, "When the water is above this board, please to take the upper road," can be of very little use, unless when the wash is perfectly pellucid, which it never is. On a shop-window in the Borough there still remains written, "New-laid eggs every day, by Mary Dobson," which the Society should order to be expunged as an imposition upon the public, unless they can clearly ascertain the veracity of the assertion.

One of the declared objects of the Institution being the promotion of—"loyalty in its genuine sense, not only of personal devotion to the sovereign, but of attachment to the laws and institutions of our country," I would point out to its indignant notice, the following inscription in High Holborn—"King—Dyer," which is not only contrary to the received legal maxim that the King never dies, but altogether of a most dangerous and disloyal tendency.—"*Parliament sold here*," written up in large letters in the City-road, is also an obvious allusion to the imputed corruption of that body; and the gingerbread kings and queens at the same shop being *all over gilt*, suggest a most traitorous and offensive Paronomasia. I suspect the fellow who deals in these commodities to be a radical. Of the same nature is the indecorous inscriptions (which should have been noticed among those who place their names over the door), running thus, "Ironmongery—Parsons—Tools of all sorts;' while in London-wall we see written up, "Deacon & Priest, Hackneymen." A Society, which among the twenty-seven published names of its council and officers, contains one Bishop, two Archdeacons, and five Reverends, cannot, out of self-respect, suffer these indecent allusions to be any longer stuck up in the metropolis.

The French Academy having decided, that proper names should never have any plural, I would implore the Royal Literary Society to relieve the embarrassment of our footmen, by deciding whether they are authorized in announcing at our routs "Mr. & Mrs. Foot and the Miss Feet;" whether Mr. Peacock's family are to be severally designated as Mrs. Peahen and the Miss Peachicks; and also what would be the best substitution for Mr. & Mrs. Man and the Miss Men, which has a very awkward sound.

Concluding, for the present, with the request that the other gold medal of fifty-guineas may not be appropriated until after the receipt of my second letter, I have the honour to be, &c. &c. &c.    H.

---

### STANZAS.

Unread, and poor, and basely born,
  Why do I suffer your caress?
Your hopes are high, your friends would scorn
  To touch the hand you're pleased to press!

Why do you of a cottage talk?
  I know your wishes climb above
Your fortune;—they with whom I walk,
  Are poor, but honest,—like my love.

Honest!—Ah no! I own, my mother
  Has sinned, as you would sin with me:
Would you such children as my brother,
  As I, and my poor sisters be?

Content, my maiden pride, and youth,
  Are all I ever had;—and you
Have ta'en the first,—would you in sooth
  Pollute, and blight, the other two?

Marry!—I do not wish you should,
  I would not wrong you for your name!
You are too happy, young, and good,
  To be allied to me and shame.

Wed you some richer girl, whose face
  Deserves the praises I disown,
Far above me in mind and grace,
  Nor like me—save in love alone.

'Twere best if we had never met;—
  The next thing for us is—to part:
You're young, can change, and soon forget;—
  Not I—I have, or had, a heart.

In mercy go, while all is well,
  Or well for one,—before you share
The grief that clouds the eyes of Bell,
  Or Bell the guilt that brightens there.

No pledge I give, or ask:—each tree
  Whispers enough of thee, and thine:
Gifts cannot fix thy thoughts on me;
  None need I to keep thee in mine.    J. F.

---

## THE GOOD OLD TIMES.

Among the unreasonable and ridiculous prejudices which many people imbibe from those who go before them, is an admiration for old customs and things, and a belief in their surpassing excellence. I do not mean that feeling of love for our early years, and the melancholy affection we cherish for scenes of recollection, but the absurd credit which we implicitly give to certain crude notions of the advantages of the by-gone over the present time, in respect to religion, virtue, honour, talent, and so forth. Nothing modern can be good. Every recent improvement is an unwarranted innovation upon the sacred system of the past. Every scheme projected for the public benefit, every new invention, is the butt of censure and the object of a sneer. Instead of examining the practical usefulness of a recent discovery, or the rationality of an argument *per se*, the one, it is alleged, cannot answer because it is unlike any thing that has preceded it, and the other is contrary to former opinion, and cannot therefore be right. It is almost ludicrous to listen to the eternal encomiums lavished upon what the present age can know nothing about but by hearsay and tradition. If we are to believe these allegations, we have had the misfortune to be born in the most unfortunate era of the world ; when every thing relative to man has fallen to the lowest ebb. We are even a puny generation in stature, compared with our gigantic forefathers, whose longevity and strength at least doubled that of their ill-starred posterity. The moral depravity of the age is another theme of depressing comparison, echoed from the Rev. Mr. Irving's chapel to the hall of Westminster, and back again. We are gone deeper into the stream of turpitude than any preceding generation—we are altogether abandoned to crimes of which our forefathers never dreamed, and to opinions of which their sagacity would have instantly shewn the fallacy—which they would have contemplated with abhorrence. In short, we are on the very brink of perdition. In literature, also, we are in a state of retrocession. To sum up all, our condition is truly pitiable, and the blindness of too many to the immeasurable superiority of the old state of society, is operating to effect our irretrievable ruin. Such it is to take things for granted, to assent to received notions without examining them, to follow credulity instead of reason, and to be the incorrigible slaves of usage. This stays the ripening of many a useful discovery, protracting its perfection to a distant date ; hinders the true policy of a nation from being followed up, and prevents legislation from keeping pace with the circumstances of the age. It is from the injurious prevalence of this folly that in our law courts, and even sometimes in the senate, we hear arguments maintained that are open to refutation by the humblest capacity that will give itself the trouble to analyze them.

. That agreeable fable of a poetic imagination, the " golden age," probably gave rise to this prejudice in favour of retrospective excellence. We so naturally feel an admiration for the good that is beyond our reach, and are so apt to invest it with fictitious splendour, that it is not wonderful a pleasant illusion should depreciate the value of present things below the brilliant visions of past excellence, which imagination colours so highly, and the dreams of future good, of which hope is for ever holding up to us the shadowy semblance. A dissatisfaction with the present, independent of any merits in the past, tends to attach to the latter no inconsiderable value, and is a latent cause of the disposition of which I complain. Reason, however, is the touchstone by which the truth must be elicited ; and by having recourse to it we shall find that this prejudice is a senseless clamour, and that the same notion has been the burthen of complaint in every age of mankind. If there appear to have been some isolated advantages on the side of those who have gone before us, it should be recollected that we are obliged to credit their own story, that what they assert it is impossible we can controvert, when it relates to such a remote era, and that even the colouring of history is oftener laid on after the taste of the artist than with the correct pencil of truth. Still though we must judge by the accounts thus transmitted to us on the testimony of the interested party, even then I contend, that the charge is groundless, and that the moderns have, in almost every respect, the advantage. For some hundred years past there has been a progression in civilization, and human comforts have increased. I will not go beyond our own country, as it is more especially *our* forefathers who were so marvellously superior to their descendants ; and I find, judging from the mass of evidence before us, that we have gained immeasurably upon what preceded us. Three wonderful inventions—gunpowder, printing, and the steam-engine, are alone sufficient to have thrown into the back ground all of which our ancestors could boast. Of these, the press, in its modern state of freedom, is perhaps the most important, because it operates to prevent the world's retrocession in knowledge. Had the works of all the ancient writers been rendered eternal by this art, and been dispersed innumerably among the nations, the downfall of the Roman empire would never have been followed by the obscurity of the dark ages, as they are denominated. However the reins of empire might have been disposed of, the intellectual improvement of man would have increased. Enlightened nations, since the invention of printing, may suffer changes, and a temporary loss of liberty, but it will only be to arise out of their slumber, and, by shaking off the yoke, to become more free and powerful than before—to stand, like the aroused lion, invincible in their own strength. The time, however, which these changes may take in operating must depend upon contingencies ; I only mean to assert what must be the ultimate effect, the final result. Away, then, with the foolish notion that we are retrograding from the superiority of some departed and undefined period. The present may not be the best of all possible times, but is infinitely better, as a whole, than any that have gone before it. There are a greater number arrived at a high pitch of mental culture. There may be fewer Bacons, Miltons, Shakspeares, and Newtons, to attract by their sole refulgence the dazzled eyes of the world, but the aggregate of knowledge is dispersed far wider than it was in their time. Thousands have approximated, of late years, nearer to the summit, distant as it may be, on which these immortal men stand, than could be found a hundred years ago. There are more who read and reflect now than ever ; there are fewer now who will take the *ipse dixit* of another upon any subject of importance without thinking something about it themselves. Hence the diminution of credence in popular superstitions, ancient dogmas, and the absurd legends of priestcraft. In the " good old times" so much deplored, one Bible, after it was permitted to be read in the vernacular tongue, was chained to a desk lest it should be stolen, and served for the use of a whole parish. Before this period the book of the Christian's faith was not suffered to be read by the people, but was explained to them by artful ecclesiastics, who made it the means of rivetting the chains of temporal authority under the terrors of spiritual denunciation. Now it is placed in the hands of all without comment—a measure perfectly consistent with the object of a book which is designed to direct men to a better life by its own simple guidance. Let the political economist contrast the vast resources of the nation now with what they were a few centuries ago, when England had a population of two or three millions, and her revenue was not a quarter of one. Let him exhibit the state of agriculture and commerce, and compare it with what it was when our houses were built with mud and wattles, and the floors were of the bare earth strewed with rushes; few having chimneys to let out the smoke, or glass in the holes designed for windows. Let the feudal system and its barbarous customs be compared with the present horror of vassalage, and the contempt for pretensions grounded on the tawdry emblazonments of the Heralds' College,—with the manly spirit of freedom, which will brook no insult from fellow-man, let his rank be what it may, and which the superior in rank and fortune is, owing to the better spirit of the age, equally restrained from offering to an inferior. Let the Border-robbers be stripped of the gaudy colouring in which the deceptious charm of antiquity and the magic pencil of Scott have arrayed them, and what were they but lawless barbarians deeply dyed in blood, rioting in the plunder of the defenceless? Let the scanty population on the estates of these worse than Old Bailey villains, be contrasted with the flourishing fields and the healthy population that is now seen upon the borders of England and Scotland. Where are the chains and dungeons of the old baronial castles, for ever in a state of vigilance against the assaults of desultory warfare?—" the very halls of the justices of the peace," too, as Aubrey says, " dreadful to behold: the screen garnished with corslets, and helmets gaping with open mouths, with coats of mail, lances, pikes, halberds, brown bills, and bucklers?" Let the whole empire, which the narrow intellect of the " good old times" was unable to look upon, but in numerous petty divisions with an endless diversity of interests, be contrasted with the unity of object and easy working of the busy whole at present. Rivers, on which a wicker fishing-boat was now and then seen moving amid a scene of solitary desolation, are now loaded with vessels. The ocean is covered with the commerce of the nation, and to make the circuit of the world is a mere every-day occurrence. What were the cock-boats and light vessels of our ancestors to our men-of-war?—and the clumsy arms and system of former warfare, to those which have given battles more decisive weapons, mitigated the severity, and abridged many of the calamities of that human curse? The comparative advantage of ancient and modern times, in these respects only, is of itself a subject which would engross no little space, and might be rendered highly interesting. One thing is certain, that no one who is not insane will deny, that in these respects at least, we have left our forefathers in the " good old times" sadly in the back-ground.

I am aware there are some persons, who, with imaginations of no common levity, form to themselves pictures of the most romantic outline and enchanting colours in contemplating the manners of our ancestors, and believe their conceptions to be perfectly correct. They gaze so long at the rainbow-hued vapoury forms of fiction, that these become in their eyes embodied realities. They live in a sort of reverie, a dreamy abstraction from all present truths, and, hoping little from the future, they for ever brood over the impossible past. They move and breathe in our times, but their heated fancies are filled with the freebooters, dungeons, towers, dames, and foray-hunting lords, who are in their view the very *beau idéal* of human virtue. They invest their imaginary characters with every attribute that can confer honour on human nature, and place them in triumphant contrast with the world around. The worst is, they are seldom aware of the inconsistencies their illusions exhibit. In woman, for example, the utmost delicacy, grace, and refinement, are mingled up with the savage times of feudalism, and modern ideas of what constitutes the superlative of feminine attractions, are displayed in pictures of remote barbarism. All the characteristic elegance of modern times and manners is carried back to the filthy and smoky halls of our forefathers. But what is the fact? The ladies of the olden time naturally partook of the coarseness of their age. They breakfasted at six o'clock in the morning upon coarse beef, and that salted, during one-half of the year; and there being no agricultural societies and oil-cake then in fashion, it was doubtless not deficient in toughness. Their drink at the same meal was home-brewed and potent strong-beer. They worked hard in their household; and but few of them, any more than their lords and masters, at one period of our history at least, were proficients in the useful acquirements of reading and writing. The boisterous revelry of the hall, and the drunken broils of the household, vulgar jests and rough familiarities, were common to them. Few of the sex in the present day, even among the lower classes, exhibit a more masculine character than the ancient dames of high birth did. Even so late as the reign of James II. the court was so unpolished and ill-mannered, "that the ladies, even the Queen herself, could hardly pass the King's apartment without receiving some affront." In the ecstatic view of those who admire the " good old times," the ladies were all softness and gentleness, they possessed every accomplishment—they were all Juliets and Ophelias. As it was in respect to the female sex, it was with most other matters; but to go farther into manners, would require great space, and close and attentive reading, far beyond what I could bestow upon it.

Another cause of complaint with the lovers of the "good old times" is the immorality and irreligion of the present period; not but that there is sufficient mass of wickedness of every species at present, as well as in days of yore, that may justly form a subject for lamentation. But the question is not whether the present age is spotless, but whether the past exceeded it in virtue. Bright and noble characters have been sprinkled here and there in all ages, but at no period was there a greater number among the mass more moral or more rationally religious than now. Hypocrisy and cant are rife; but let us examine whether these vices in religion were not far overbalanced by the grovelling and swinish superstitions that formerly enchained the mind, and led the multitude captive to a blind and servile obedience, that made the worship of the Deity an obligation of fear, and even arrayed the parent

of man in the terrible garb of vengeance, for the neglect of some mis-
called religious form, by which monks and friars, "black, white, and
grey," or their mitred superiors, lost some temporal advantage. In
the "good old times" rational religion was rarely known; all belonging to it was dictated by others. It was too much the instrument of
designing or mistaken men, who rendered the doctrines of Christianity
obscure, believed persecution was doing God service, and confused
their own brains, and the faculties of all around them, by ridiculous
disquisitions upon points of doctrine, while they neglected the simple
and clear precepts which involved its great essentials. Persecution
was deemed a religious duty, and the different Christian sects nourished
the most baleful hatred towards each other. Now we see charity
widely diffused among all orders of Christians, though some still exist
in each who love persecution, because it savours of the "good old
times." We no longer see bishops sitting in judgement, and condemning to the fire those who will not yield assent to some incomprehensible
creed; but churchmen mingle with schismatics in promoting together
the essentials of religion. Have modern times no advantage here?

Benevolence and charity are now more extended than ever. The
order and decencies observed in society, the ornaments and luxuries
of life, exceed what the most imaginative persons of old could have
dreamed to be possible. Refinement is not more superior to barbarism
than is our present state to that of our forefathers. It is the ignorant
and wilfully blind who do not see this, as well as those who prefer
the past from mere feverishness, because they have determined that
nothing in modern days is, or can be, as they wish it. Excepting two
or three literary giants, who appeared in early times, not less the
astonishment of their own age than ours, many writers who were deemed phenomena then, are now only read with a smile of astonishment
that they ever could have been esteemed. The vilest ballad-writer of
the present day is far superior to them. A brilliant light now and
then appeared in a world of darkness, that we find illuminated with accumulating splendours. Literature is more diffused; our literary
spirit is become more liberal; and with the exception of one or two
publications of acknowledged bad character, preserves a tone of
moderation in argument and of mildness in discussion, which shows
that writers would much rather gain a point by reason than end an
argument by vituperation; the ultimate certainty of conviction being
now only reserved to the rule of good sense. The character of our
present literature is, as a whole, as high as it ever was before, and its
beneficial effects on society are more obvious.

How mighty is our national strength compared to that in the "good
old times," in spite of numerous causes, originating in too fondly
clinging to ancient prejudices, that have but tended to hamper it.
Formerly our display of power was more in appearance than in reality.
We exhibited an imposing front to an enemy, but we had no reserve;
all our resources were at once in the field of view. Like the soldiers
of Cadmus, they now seem to grow up from the earth; they multiply
with our necessities, and increase in proportion to our wants. The
island that a short time ago had an army of but a few thousands of
men, on whose first combat its fate depended, lately exhibited a million in arms, and bribed with her wealth nearly all the civilized nations
in the world. Add to this our astonishing mechanical inventions,

our progress in the fine arts, in the sciences, in public education, in liberality of opinion, and the principles of rational liberty, and then turn to the vaunted " good old times" with what appetite we may.

To examine and minutely enumerate our advantages under the foregoing heads would require a bulky volume, but it would be a lasting monument of triumphant fact over bald assertion and wearisome tautology. Let us justly appreciate the real benefits our ancestors possessed, at their due value, and we shall find what is the real worth of the " good old times." We shall find ourselves very unwilling to exchange ours for those of Henry VIII.—the dungeon and the block ; for those of Mary, with the rack and the faggot; for those of the heroic and splendid Elizabeth, with all her talents ; for the James or the Charles, or the remoter eras of seignorage and vassalage, of intestine broils, maddening factions, desolation, and civil war. It may be very well for Mr. Irving and others to invoke the names of brave men who sealed the cause of liberty or religion with their blood—who braved the red torture of martyrdom and bearded a tyrant in his strong hold ; but while we admire these glorious instances of the mind's victory over nature, what more can they be to us than subjects of admiration ? In these much-abused modern times we have no demand for similar *auto da fés*. Persecution dare not now pile her faggots in Smithfield, nor a king of England tax his subjects without the aid of a parliament. We can have no martyrs now even in bravado, and there is nothing that can warrant our making the country's " chivalry to leap," by displaying our " death-despising" prowess. It is the glory of modern times that similar exhibitions exist no longer, nay, that it is impossible they ever should exist again. Whatever religious intolerance and arbitrary usages remain, they are among the relics of the " good old times," and form the scandal of ours. Were there a necessity for men to show examples of constancy and bravery, they would not be now found wanting. Men can die at present as bravely as heretofore, either in the field or on the scaffold, and would smile as contemptuously at the burning stake as a victim of the fiendish Mary, bare their wrists before a bloody judge as coolly as Sidney, or sell their lives as dear in a good cause as any among their ancestors.

Glory then be to the progress of the human mind, to the enlargement of liberal opinion, to the march of freedom ! Let the advocates of old times, the sighers after martyrdom, the lovers of civil desolation, the admirers of feudal chieftains, and the advocates of old abuses, indulge a little longer in their mistaken notions, invest the attributes of the past in modern virtues, and supply themselves with unsubstantial arguments to cavil at substantial benefits. They will, by and by, see their error. They will in the end discover that they have been in a reverie, in which they have mistaken the images of fancy for real objects, and reasoned upon them as if they had been correct. Some of these lovers of the "good old times" are to be pitied rather than severely censured. There are others, however, who are too obstinate and ignorant ever to perceive the truth ; who know no criterion of the merit of a thing but its age, who combat reason with usage, common sense with the most cobweb sophistry, and the cause of freedom with the arm of power. These must be left as incorrigible, to the contempt of the present age and the scorn of posterity ! Y. I.

## TO THE EVENING STAR.

From the Spanish of Lupercio Leonardo de Argensola.

"Pura luciente estrella."

O FAIR and goodly Star
 Upon the brow of night,
 That from thy silver car
Shoot'st on the darken'd world thy friendly light:
 Thy path is calm and bright
Through the clear azure of the starry way,
 And from thy heavenly height
Thou see'st how systems rise and pass away—
The birth of human hopes, their blossom, and decay.

Oh! that my spirit could
 Cast off its mould of clay,
 And with the wise and good
Make wings unto itself and flee away;
 That with thy bright array
We might look down upon this world of woe,
 Even as the God of day
Looks on the restless ocean-flow,
And eyes the fighting waves that pant and foam below.

Alas! it may not be—
 For mortal fetters bind
 To dull mortality
The prison'd essence of th' immortal mind:
 Our course is too confined,—
And as, beneath the sun that blazed too bright,
 The Cretan's waxen wing declined,
Before the splendour of immortal light
Our failing pinions fall, and plunge us back to night.

Then let my course below
 To them be near allied—
 Far from the worldly show,
Through dim sequester'd valleys let me glide:
 Scarce be my step descried
Amid the pompous pageant of the scene;
 But where the hazels hide
Cool stream or shade beneath their leafy screen,
Mine be the grassy seat—all lovely, lone, and green.

Within those verdant bounds,
 Where sweet to ear and eye
 Come gentle sights and sounds,
The current of my days shall murmur by,
 In calm tranquillity;
Nor doom'd to roll o'er Passion's rocky bed,
 Nor slothfully to lie
Like the dull pools in stagnant marshes bred,
Where waving weeds are rank, and noxious tendrils spread.

## PHILOSOPHY ON THE ROAD.—THE YACHT CLUB.

—— " Navibus atque
Quadrigis petimus bene vivere."            HORAT

The comparison of life to a voyage is a mere common-place ; but if it has not the advantage of novelty, it cannot be refused the merit of truth. There is, in fact, no simile that runs more upon all-fours. Shakspeare has told us, that " all the world's a stage ;" but if he had said that the world was a stage-coach, he would have been nearer his mark. For not to insist upon the fact that each day of our " journey through life" is a post towards death (a verity perhaps too trite to mention), what can be more like the passive condition of a traveller on a journey, than the way in which we are hurried through existence, each in his own *tourbillon* of circumstance and condition as in a carriage, with the passions for coachmen, which drive us at the rate and in the direction they please : and in this last particular, the simile is the more perfect, inasmuch as we change the driver at almost every stage, and never part with him till we have paid a good smart *buona mano* for his whipmanship. A prosperous life may be compared to a journey on the Bath-road, while a struggling existence is all " up-hill work." The humbler classes are the outside passengers, exposed to all the pitiless pelting of life's storms, and all the perils of the road, while the happier few resemble the " insides," warm, snug, safe, and at their ease. A more extended view of the conditions of society shews some men as travellers in a post-chaise, some in their own coronetted travelling-chariots, and but too many, God help them! trudging through the mire on foot, bespattered by the wheels of their more fortunate fellow-citizens, and happy to escape being trodden under their horses' feet, and a coroner's inquest. Some few have the luck to pass free from all the more serious accidents of the journey, while others are upset on the road, and are sent into the next world with a broken neck, or a concussion of the brain. Some go the whole journey, and some are only " booked" for a certain place on the road, where they are set down to make room for other passengers.

But if life be like a journey, it is not surprising that a journey should be the very image of life ; and so indeed it is. We begin both with the same " pleased alacrity and cheer of mind," looking forward to every fresh post as a difficulty surmounted, a source of new sensations, or at worst as a step towards our object ; and we finish both with the same sense of lassitude, if not of disgust, with this only difference, that very few can make up their minds to the anticipation of being " put to bed with a shovel," with the same pleasure that they look forward to a warming-pan, and a smart chambermaid to tuck them up for the night, at the " Three Crowns," or the " Bird and Baby." In life and on a journey we are equally not masters to choose our own company, being in both cases alike compelled to associate with those who are booked for the same coach. In both cases, likewise, we are equally under the necessity of making the best of the lot which chance has given us ; and nothing can more strongly resemble the manner in which shyness ripens into acquaintance, and acquaintance into intimacy through the jolting of the leathern conveniency, than the friendships of the world in general.

In friendship, as in all the rest, we are the dupes of our own *amour-*

*propre*; and flatter ourselves that society hinges on our sympathetic tendencies, our kindness, tenderness, and forbearance. On the contrary, society is the pure creature of necessity and self-interest ; and, if these did not operate to bring mankind together, they would never come sufficiently within the sphere of each other's activity, to bring the finer feelings at all into play. Let him who doubts this truism turn his eyes upon the world, and see who and who are together ; let him look at that little knot of parsons congregated within the walls of a cathedral-close, or at the " Mrs. Generals" and " Mrs. Majors of ours," who are so intimate in a garrison-town. In what do such friendships differ from the casual acquaintanceship of a stage-coach ?

Another point of resemblance between life and a journey is the little intercourse which takes place between the inside passengers and the outsides of the same vehicle. In real life, it happens every day that two persons are brought to touch, or nearly to touch, in one or two points, and run parallel to each other, or approach, as if it were for the mere purpose of exercising a mutual repulsion, like two corks floating in a glass of water. Mrs. Mary Jones and Mrs. Dinah Bohea have long inhabited the same house. They meet every day upon the stairs without more acquaintance than a courtesy, because the one lodges on the first floor, and the other lives " up two pair of stairs backwards." In the same spirit, the inhabitants of the little villages round London regulate their intimacies with their neighbours in the row, those who keep their own carriages not condescending to associate with those who go to 'Change at sixpence a-time in the stage. The great and little green-rooms of a theatre are as immeasurably separated, as the commissioned and non-commissioned officers of a British regiment, or the in and out-door servants of a nobleman's family. In country towns, likewise, to keep a shop is fatal to all association with those whose business is conducted independently of such an arrangement ; or at least, if the families may occasionally dine together in private, they cannot publicly meet in the great room over the market-place, where aristocracy and *entrechats* centre in a master of the ceremonies, and dulness and mutton-fats combine to spread gloom and *ennui* over the company. We all know the rigid laws of the Bar against " hugging." Woe to the barrister who on circuit shakes hands with his own brother, if that brother happens to be—an attorney !

There is nothing about a stage-coach that has excited more frequent remark, than that little vanity which finds its account in a thousand artful innuendoes, such as, " A stage-coach is vastly inconvenient for them as is used to their own carriage," or, " I travels usually in a chay, but the post-boys are grown so extortionate." Travellers under the influence of this passion have always personal anecdotes of the owners of the great seats on the road, inferring considerable intimacy with the narrator : and they never fail to let drop, by pure accident, some little trait or other, proving their own consequence and elevated position in life, in which truth seldom so wholly presides, as utterly to exclude exaggeration. Now, though this seems mighty ridiculous, because, being committed by vulgar persons, it is done awkwardly, without measure, and *à propos des bottes*, yet it differs very little from the systematic impositions of higher life—from the swelling port which every one affects, when observed—from the dazzling a neighbour's eyes with Birmingham plate and Irish diamonds, or taking away his appetite by a disproportionately sumptuous dinner :—in short, from all those nameless details of occasional splendour and habitual meanness, discomfort, and parsimony, which make up the sum of existence, in a numerous assemblage of all classes in society.

Were all the parallels of this most apt and comprehensive metaphor duly set down and chronicled, the New Monthly would not be large enough to hold them. It is not, therefore, very surprising, that the present generation should have given birth to two sects of philosophers, whose systems are bottomed upon the resemblance of life to a journey; to say nothing of the modern peripatetics, who place the *summum bonum* in walking, and whose life is one perpetual " match against time."—The Four-in-hand Club, which is now somewhat on the decline, and the Yacht Club, which is usurping its place among the enlightened and reflecting, may be considered as the two most remarkable schools of morality, which the progress of civilization has produced. Of the former, the leading virtue was humility : to look like a coachman, talk like a coachman, and spit through a vacancy between two teeth like a coachman,* being the criterion of the sect. The rigour of their morality was evinced in the frequent question, " Is all right?" with its immediate answer "All right," without which no step in life could be taken. Their firmness to their party was manifested in their anxiety " to keep their own side," not less conspicuous in the House of Commons than on the road. That they were uncompromising in their principles, was proved by the strictness with which they excluded from their society, all who were not perfectly "bang up to the mark," while their punctilious attention to the smallest trifles in their " turn out," was not inferior to the stoical maxim of *nil actum reputans dum quid superesset agendum.* Sobriety, industry, and a patient endurance of the hardships of our inclement seasons, were absolutely necessary to a philosopher of this sect ; and so closely must he watch his passions, as never to let the reins out of his hands. His greatest triumph was over the vices of those he guided, and all his care went to prevent their deviating, either to the right or left, from the prescribed curse. Their magnanimity and contempt for death were daily exhibited, not only in the rapidity of their own fiery course, and the *sang-froid* with which they drove "like hell," but in the cool indifference with which they overthrew and run over whatever crossed their path— pigs, poultry, old women, or children. Nor was their sense of glory less conspicuous in the carelessness with which they passed a companion upset in a ditch, or worsted in a trial of strength between his axle-tree and a turnpike-gate. It is in schools like these that our senators could best acquire the passion for driving, which so advantageously superseded that *twaddling* habit, in which our ancestors indulged, of *leading* the people. There, too, the contempt for " the populace," " the mob," was practically illustrated, and the usage of dispersing assemblies collected on their lawful avocations *vi et armis*, and at the small expense of a life or two, familiarly taught. Another advantage of this school of philosophy lay in the expertness it engendered in money matters ; in which respect there were few of its scholars who

---

* One youth of high spirit and life actually had a tooth drawn, though one of the best in his mouth, for the express purpose of attaining to perfection in this elegant art. Horace's dust-collecting curricle drivers were mere chickens to lads like these.

might not have officiated as chancellor of the exchequer, borrowing as carelessly, and spending as profusely, as if they had all the paper-mills of the kingdom at their command.

Every thing, however, has its day ; and notwithstanding the moral and political utility of the Four-in-hand Club, it has met with its *Vingt de Mars* and given place to the usurping Yacht Club, which may be considered as reigning the most fashionable and popular school of the day, and dividing with the Musical academy, and the new Literary institution, the cares and the favours of the great fountain of all honour and distinction. At the present moment, in which all true patriots lament the decline of our naval power and consideration, this revival of nautical tastes and habits cannot but be most gratifying ; but it is as a school of odoeporic philosophers that they are interesting to the present discussion. The Argonautic expedition was, doubtless, a philosophic enterprise of a similar description, and the golden fleece a mere type of that great object of philosophic research, the το πρεπον.

Nor could a better theatre be well chosen than a ship, for the study of all the virtues which most dignify our nature. How refreshing to the mind, to pass at once from the slavish and fawning habits of a court, to the frank, manly freedom of the Ward-room !* How invigorating both to the senses and to the feelings, to exchange the luxury and the dissipation of the saloon and the supper chamber, for the fresh breezes, salt junk, and hard biscuit, on board the "Lively Kitty."—On the contrary, how heartily *sick* of all the vanities of the world must the pupil be while rolling in his cot in a gale of wind ! The benevolence of tars and their sympathy for human suffering is notorious ; and their love of liberty has been manifested too frequently in the course of English story to admit of denial. Who knows what Blakes may arise from the bosom of the Yacht Club, to assert the rights of the people in the two Houses of Legislature ? and who shall presume to say, that *all* the *professors* of that club will not return from a cruise with kinder feelings concerning the distresses of the people, and with more national notions, than Britons of late years have imbibed by their too close contact with Continental despots, and slavish ministers, in Royal congresses and Imperial progresses?—How, indeed, is it possible for mortal man to tread the quarter-deck of a British vessel, and breathe the free air that blows over the ocean, without swelling into all the dignity of manhood, and burning to assert that liberty which was the foundation of England's maritime and commercial grandeur? How mean, how paltry, how contemptible is the theatrical splendour of courts, to the proud pomp of a royal navy! how poor the utmost wealth of despotism, in all its "barbaric pearl and gold," to the displays of prosperous commerce in the crowded ports of Liverpool or London ! Yes, this is indeed a school for kings to study in, and for British senators to form themselves to the independence, the gravity, and the courage, their place in society demands. Who, with his hand made hard by honest labour, and his mind steeled by the dangers and hardships of a nautical life, will dare hold out the one

---

* " Is not the sea          Here are we slaves,
  Made for the free,           But on the waves
  Land for courts and chains alone ?     Love and liberty's all our own."
                                        *Moore.*

to receive the hire of corruption, or debase the other to the habitual practice of dishonesty? That the Yacht Club is also important to the national welfare, as a school of chastity, cannot be doubted.—The hot blood of our luxurious nobility will certainly be cooled down below the fever point, to which indolence and high living on shore heretofore raised it. At least, when a great man is " all alone by himself at sea," whatever may be his meditations, he cannot be practically attacking the *cara sposa* of a benchfellow in the Senate.

Subservient to this great society, which may be regarded as the Eton of nautical education, are those preparatory seminaries, the Funny Club and the Sailing Club, on the River Thames. Swift, were he alive, would insist that the former possessed many great " scullers," and that no "Roman" of antiquity could compare with them. All in these schools learn the labour of pulling against the stream, and acquire a practical knowledge of what may be done by perseverance. Here, too, they are taught the experience of *tacking in time*, the inconstancy of gales, and the uncertainty of all that depends not on a man's own exertions. With such establishments, we need not despair of the moral and political regeneration of Old England. With their aid things must go on "swimmingly," and the bark of the state be kept "afloat;" there will be no want of " pilots to weather the storm," and when all hands are piped, Britain shall again muster such a crew on her deck as will fill her enemies with dread, and carry the glory of her name to the remotest bounds of the earth. Valeant quantum valere possunt. **M.**

---

### TO THE LAST LEAF OF AUTUMN.

Frail child of Spring, that Summer's sun
Hath warmed, thy race is nearly run;
O'er thee with cutting chillness blow
Brown Autumn's blasts to lay thee low;
On the storm's wing thou soon must fly,
And hurled to earth decaying lie,
All one to thee, now, sun or shade—
'Tis night, thy last damp bed is made!
Once thou couldst flout thy sire the Spring,
In pride of green youth glorying;
Once thy fresh. verdure shaded me
From noontide's glowing sovereignty;
But now a zephyr makes thee sigh
And rustle as it passes by;—
Syllabling, while it marks thy date;—
" Fall! fall! sear wretch, and meet thy fate,
" Lone relic of the year's past prime—
" Dead nature's scutcheon—wreck of time!"

Forlorn, despised, and quivering,
A wasted, useless, outcast thing,
Drop from thy bough—it is not good
To live alone amid the wood,
Without a friend to share thy pain,
Demanding sympathy in vain.
Who 'd bear in solitude the blast,
And curse of friends, to die the last? *
Sad solitary, fall! what share
Canst thou in life or pleasure bear!

---

* Ultimus suorum moriatur!

No more wilt thou o'ershade the walk
Of lovers in their moonlight talk,
While happy from the eye of day
They breathe love's secret witchery :
Nor spread thy robe empearl'd with dew
In April morn to glittering view ;
Nor hide the ring-dove's downy nest ;
Nor fan hot summer's panting breast ;
Nor to the painted insect be
The shelter of its infancy.
No suns shall e'er again enfold
Thy glossy hue with beams of gold ;
For thy dry faded form is clad
Already in death's livery sad.
The storm that rages for its prey,
I hear it howl, is on its way.

O Nature ! when will man be wise,
And read thy book with thinking eyes ?
The bard can view the leafy bier,
The wintry triumph of the year ;
Snatch lessons from such trivial things,
Prompting strange thoughts and visitings
Of man's own darker destiny,
That vulgar visions never see.
The waving leaf his eye can mark,
Its hues so changed—its tints so dark—
Apply them to his kindred state,
And see them point him to his fate.
Lone ensign ! last of all the pleasures
The year late marshall'd to its measures
Sad flag on a wide ocean tost !
Thou tell'st me summer's pride is lost.
Rent as thou art and torn, in thee
The Sibyl's mystic leaf I see,
Where last, most prized, the lines declare
Too legibly what mortals are.
Yet if I sturdy should remain,
And bide one cruel storm again—
I still must crowd a heaped up bier,
Nor haply call, like thee, a tear ;
Pass unlamented from my place,
And make room for a greener race.
I 'll " bide my time," though small my gain,
A pensive verse, a mournful strain,
And hang a dead leaf by a thread,
With shrivell'd heart and aching head :
A withered scroll, a useless thing,
That may not see another spring ;
A tired, ragged scrap of life,
With winds, storms, seasons, time, at strife ;
Emblem'd in this poor leaf's decay,
The remnant of a brighter day.
Yes, I 'll too " bide my time" and dare
The tempests of the wintry year ;
Resign'd like thee, poor leaf, at last
To fall forgot beneath the blast ;
But fixed to live my utmost date,
And meet undauntedly my fate !

J.

## MARCO BOTZARI,

*The Achilles of the modern Greeks.*

THE Greeks have just sustained the bitterest loss which has befallen them during the whole of their short, but brilliant contest with the enslavers of their country. Marco Botzari, the Achilles of their cause—the Achilles in all things but his invulnerability—has perished prematurely in the flower of his age and his fame; and has left none behind him that can adequately supply his place. They have still many excellent leaders; but none who unite into one noble whole the various admirable qualities possessed by that distinguished person.

The following is extracted from a paragraph in the Morning Chronicle, which purports to give the substance of a letter just received from Missolonghi :—

" In the neighbourhood of Valto the Greeks had again assembled in considerable force, made a most determined resistance, and compelled the invaders to take the direction of Carpanesi. The Suliotes, having marched upon this place in the end of July, under the command of their illustrious chief Marco Botzari, and having been joined by other chiefs as they advanced, came up with the barbarians on the evening of the 8th of August; and on the next morning, by one of those daring movements for which this nation of Christians has always been so justly celebrated, they gained a great victory over the Turkish army. During this memorable engagement Marco Botzari placed himself at the head of four hundred of his countrymen, penetrated to the centre of a column of five thousand of the enemy, and by his example infused the greatest confidence into his small but determined phalanx of Suliotes. He was severely wounded in the groin, but concealed his situation until, in the heat of the action, he received a musquet-ball in the head, and instantly fell, &c."

" Another account states, that Marco Botzari penetrated to the tent of the Pacha himself, whom he slew, but was wounded by a black servant, faithful to the Pacha, while he was exhibiting the head to his soldiers."

As there is, unhappily, no reason to doubt the fact of the death of this distinguished patriot, it may be interesting to our readers, and, what is of even more importance, it may serve the almost sacred cause which he espoused, if we give a slight notice of his public life and character : and we do this the rather, as we have reason to believe that the source from whence we derive our information is the only one at present in this country that is capable of supplying it.

Marco Botzari was the son of the celebrated Kitzo Botzari, a member of one of the principal families of Sulei, and a head of his tribe during their long war with the late Ali Pacha. When this war was terminated, by the fall of Sulei into the hands of the Pacha, Kitzo Botzari retired to the Ionian Islands; but Marco, the subject of this notice, remained in Albania, with several other members of his family, and lived for some time in the most entire obscúrity. During this period, no circumstances occurring to call forth any peculiar traits of character, nothing was noted of him but that he was a young man of great personal courage, and with high notions of justice and honour. A trifling anecdote will here illustrate his views on the latter points. A particular friend of Marco's was playing at cards with two persons who were in the service of Ali Pacha, at the time the latter was at Prevesa; and this friend, in conjunction with one of the other players, had con-

trived to mark the cards, and thus make a certainty of winning the
third. But Marco, who was present, and observed what had been done,
openly noticed it; saying, " There is no true victory, my friend, but that
which is gained by fair skill and open courage."

It was at the time Ali Pacha was reduced to the last extremity, when
besieged in Joannina, (in the latter end of the year 1820) that Marco
Botzari first began to distinguish himself as a warlike leader of his
countrymen, the Suliotes. At this epocha the Suliotes had leagued
themselves with Ismael Pacha, the successor of the deposed Ali, in the
hope of recovering their country, which the latter had conquered,
from them. In this league, under the command of his uncle Noto
Botzari, chief. head of the Suliote tribe, Marco led several bold and successful attacks against the troops of Ali—chasing them to the very
gates of the fortress of Joannina. This league, however, was almost
immediately broken, on the discovery that Ismael Pacha,—jealous of
the Suliotes once more gaining any head in Greece,—had actually employed a company of his Albanian troops to take the field in the rear
of the little tribe of Sulei, for the purpose, if possible, of extirpating
them altogether.

On the discovery of this perfidy, the Suliotes made common cause
with Ali Pacha against the Turks; and in this league Marco displayed,
from time to time, the most conspicuous military talents, and became
the terror of all the Pachas, and of the Albanians. On one occasion,
in particular, with a little troop of about thirty followers alone, he succeeded in dislodging Hassan Pacha, of Negroponte, from the village of
Strivina, in the plain of Arta. And on another occasion, with a very
inferior force, he defeated and took prisoner a Bey of Gregaria, at the
foot of some mountains near Joannina.

Again, when the town of Arta was occupied by the expedition consisting of mixed troops—Greeks and Mahomedan Albanians—who
were acting for Ali Pacha, Marco, with a little troop of twenty-five
men only, night after night attacked the fortified dwelling of Combotti,
which is a place of great strength, and in which were posted the *Has-
nadar* (treasurer) of Chourshid Pacha, and Soultzo Kersca, with two
hundred men; and not a night passed that the enemy did not lose
several men, either by the boldness and suddenness of his attacks, or
by his dexterity in picking them out with his musquet through the
windows and other accessible points of the place. Twice, also, he
set fire to the building; and had nearly succeeded in mining and
blowing it up.

On the defection of the Mahomedan Albanians at Arta, which happened shortly after this, he retired with his own countrymen to the
mountains of Sulei.

At the period now alluded to, the distinguished talents and reputation of Marco Botzari had acquired for him the particular notice of
Prince Mavrocordato, and the uses to which he applied the influence
which these gave him, immediately cemented a friendship between the
two leaders; and at the time that the general rising of the Greeks
against their Turkish oppressors took place, Marco was the first to
submit himself to the regular government that was formed, and to use
his almost resistless influence with his countrymen to induce them to
follow his example. When it is considered that Marco was (unlike his

brother Constantine) an entirely uneducated man; in the flower and
heat of his youth; at the summit of a well-earned fame; and with unbounded influence over the sentiments and conduct of his countrymen;
his thus laying aside all personal and ambitious views, and submitting
himself wholly and unconditionally to a newly-formed government,—
seeking and desiring to hold no higher station in it than that of an
humble agent in fulfilling its plans for achieving the liberties of his
country,—evinces a self-devotion and simplicity of character rarely to
be met with even under circumstances which might seem more likely
to call it forth.

When Sulei was invested by a formidable Turkish force, and every
avenue of entrance or escape was shut up, Marco, who was there,
contrived, with a very few of his countrymen, to effect a passage
through the Turkish camp, and to reach Messolongio; where, after
having collected more troops, he took up a position at Plaka, and
the memorable battle fought on that spot again testified his extraordinary skill, valour, and devotion. He fought sword in hand for a
great length of time against a party of Mahomedan Albanians; when,
after having killed several of their officers, and been himself severely
wounded, he lost his horse and baggage, and was again compelled to
retire to Messolongio.

When the Suliotes afterwards made terms with their besiegers, he
was at Messolongio; and though, aware of the critical situation in
which they were placed, he did not disapprove of their resolution to
submit themselves conditionally to their enemies, yet he refused to
follow their example and retire with them, as he might have done with
honour, but resolved to remain with Prince Mavrocordato, conscious
that if *he* had left him, he would have lost that most efficient support
which he derived from the *opinions* of his fellow-countrymen as to the
state of their cause, and that the edifice of liberty, which seemed to be
just rising from its foundation, cemented by the blood of his fellow-
soldiers, would again fall to pieces and go to nought. He therefore
sent away his family to Ancona, to avoid the importunities which they
were urging upon him, and linked himself, for better for worse, to the
fortunes of Mavrocordato and his suffering country.

The most successful, distinguished, and important epoch of Marco's
exploits was that which included the siege and storming of Messolongio
by the Turks. At this period, when the town was invested on all sides
by a Turkish army of fifteen thousand men, he still kept possession of
the weak outskirts (for they do not deserve the name of fortifications)
in company with his friend Mavrocordato, and with a body of no more
than three hundred men—both of them determining to perish in the
ruins of the town, rather than willingly abandon it. And it may, perhaps, be attributed to this determination, that the cause of Greece at
present bears an aspect of hope instead of despair. In this campaign,
with the aid of some slight reinforcements, they occasioned the Turks
a loss of three thousand men, and finally saved the town. This latter
event was effected purely by a piece of personal valour and conduct on
the part of Marco Botzari. The Turkish troops had assaulted Messolongio, and actually gained possession of the outposts of the town,—
overpowering for a time the chief body of troops under the command
of Botzari, and compelling them to retire to the shore and endeavour

to escape in their boats, &c. Marco was compelled to follow them in this extremity; but he determined to make one gallant effort to rally them, which entirely succeeded. While they were retiring precipitately, he rushed in among them, flourishing his sword and shouting Hurras! and gave them to believe that their fellows had repulsed the Turks, and that they were flinging themselves from the walls into the ditch. His troops rallied at these sounds; he again placed himself at their head and led them unexpectedly on the enemy, and the place was finally abandoned by the Turks, leaving behind them an immense booty in artillery, ammunition, and baggage of great value.

Botzari was in no instance known to avail himself even of the fair spoils that were taken from the enemy, but suffered them all to be divided among his men, with whom, however, he invariably shared all the dangers and hardships of the campaign, being neither armed, attired, or fed in any way different from them. It is also well known, that he has in many cases refused large bribes offered him by the enemy, if he would retire into the Ionian Islands. Once, in particular, at Messolongio, five hundred purses * were offered to him if he would quit the place. The person from whose lips these notices of his life are collected, was informed of the above through an unquestionable channel.

But the most prominent and striking illustration that can be offered of the pure patriotism that actuated Botzari in all his views, is perhaps to be found in the following fact:—The father of Marco (Kitzo Botzari) was extremely obnoxious to Ali Pacha, on account of his being one of the heads of the Suliote tribes, against which Ali had so long made war. It was mentioned, in the commencement of this paper, that, on the fall of Sulei into the hands of Ali, Kitzo Botzari retired into the Ionian Islands. Shortly after this period, Ali made several underhand attempts on the life of Kitzo, one of which at last succeeded. Having occasion to leave the islands, and come to Arta, he was there privately shot by an agent of Ali. At the time the Greeks first rose on their oppressors, this agent in the death of Marco's father, (one Capitan Gogo, of Tzumeaka) was considered as an important aid to the cause, but he was reluctant to come forward in conjunction with Marco, knowing that the latter was aware of the part he had taken (by the order of Ali) in the death of his father. But Marco voluntarily sought an interview with this person, in which he assured him that this was an epoch at which he had thought it necessary to dismiss from his breast all passions but the love of country; and he urged *him* to do the same; adding, " It was not you who killed my father, it was Ali." And he actually endeavoured to bring about a marriage between some branches of their respective families, in order to strengthen the bond of union which he wished to exist between them on this occasion.

Only one more anecdote will be added, in illustration of the personal coolness and intrepidity of this distinguished chieftain. The relater of the foregoing was one day dining at the head-quarters of Marco's uncle, at Arta, and after dinner he was walking alone in the town with Marco, when several balls from the Turkish batteries fell at a very short

* A purse is 500 Turkish piastres, or about 10*l.* sterling.

distance from them. While the relater (who is no soldier) was endeavouring to conceal his sense of the danger that seemed to surround them, Marco observed laughingly, and pointing to the balls, " You see, *these* are the only kind of apples the Turks would send us for our dessert."

Marco Botzari was, at the period of his death, not more than thirty or thirty-one years of age, stout, but of low stature, with extremely fine bright black eyes, dark complexion, and a countenance altogether highly animated and expressive. His arms consisted of a musquet, a sabre, and a Turkish knife, and one small pistol of extremely inferior quality.

### HARP OF ZION.—N°. I.

Oh! how art thou fallen, thou City of God!—
He hath stricken the crown from thy brow with his rod—
On thy neck is the yoke—on thy garment a stain—
And the Lion of Judah hath bow'd to the chain!

The phial of wrath on thy forehead was pour'd,
Thou hast shrunk from the withering glance of the Lord;
Like the gourd of the Prophet, thy beauty is gone,
And thy cedars are blasted on proud Lebauon!

Thy temples are ruins—thine altars o'erthrown—
On the Hill of thy strength is the Infidel's throne;
And the wreck of thy glory, where'er it is hurl'd,
Is the scoff of the Gentiles—the scorn of the world!

O turn thee, our God! let thy mercy awaken,
And smile on thy Zion—deserted, forsaken!
Let the light of thy glory on Solyma burst,
And its lightning-glance wither her foes to the dust!

Oh, Zion! his smile shall dawn on thy night
Of sorrow and shame with a heavenly light,—
As the burst of the sun-beam comes over the sea,
When the dark cloud has past, and the thunder-storms flee.

W. C.

### SONG.

What absence from the heart can wrench
  The thought that haunts where'er we rove?
Or what can time avail to quench
  The enduring flame of youthful love?

Still, still, where'er we rest or roam,
  The spirits rise of brighter hours;
Love lingers round his early home,
  And strews the grave of Hope with flowers.  J.

### THE HERMIT ABROAD.*

Any one who has ever passed a September in London, a rainy day at Buxton, a winter-evening at an inn, or a week with a rich uncle in a small country town, must be feelingly alive to the virtues of an entertaining book, which may serve to dissipate some portion of that dreadful load of *ennui* which in such situations is found to "weigh upon the heart." It is only those persons who are acquainted with sufferings like these that can form any idea of the gratitude with which, upon its first publication, we received the precursor of the present work, "The Hermit in the Country," when it was forwarded to us per mail during a residence of some weeks with a relative,

—— A dowager
Of great revenue, and who hath no children,

in a distant and retired part of England. The mornings we had contrived to consume with the aid of the worthy old gamekeeper, but the evenings seemed as though they would, to use Macbeth's phrase, "stretch out to the crack of doom." In spite of the excellent old lady's library, which appeared to be formed on the model of the one catalogued in the Spectator; nay, even in spite of her conversation and backgammon-board, the nights (it was in autumn) were drawn out to an almost interminable length. It would be in vain to describe the joy with which we seized upon the cargo of amusement, wherewith in our distress the provident attention of Messrs. Colburn and Co. supplied us. We could have hugged the greasy knave who carried the parcel from the neighbouring post-town, and we actually bestowed upon him a gratuity, which, we fear, tended for ever to confound in his mind the due proportion between labour and remuneration. With what hot impatience, despising the sober lessons taught us by Miss Edgeworth in "waste not, want not," did we cut the string which bound the parcel, into twenty pieces, and how eagerly did we pounce upon the contents! Debarred as we had been of every thing like an entertaining volume for many long days, we devoured one half of the work with an appetite which astonished our respected relative—nay we even furtively conveyed a volume into our bed-chamber, and enjoyed the ineffable luxury of reading it after our *couchée*. We remember being particularly pleased with the paper entitled "An Elopement," in which, according to our apprehension, considerable knowledge of the human heart is displayed. The feelings of the two guilty lovers are described with a truth and simplicity which are not found in all the Hermit's writings, who occasionally sentimentalizes a little too much for our taste. As a painting from low life (though the assertion may seem somewhat Irish) "The Top of a Stage" has many claims to merit. We could particularize some other clever papers in the Hermit in the Country, were we not sure that our readers can tell what amuses them at least as well as we can.

Encouraged by a perusal of his peregrinations in the country, we resolved the other day to follow the Hermit Abroad, nor have we found reason to repent of our resolution. He has helped us to kill

* By the author of the "Hermit in London," and "Hermit in the Country." 4 vols. 12mo.

several heavy half-hours, of which we stood greatly in dread. We found him particularly useful in assisting us over those spare portions of the day which it is impossible wholly to avoid; and in filling up these crevices of life, a work like the present is of considerable value. Should dinner be delayed half an hour beyond the appointed period, it is in vain to attempt to beguile the time with any grave and weighty authors. The mind and body are both in a state of irritation which requires some lenitive to soothe them; and we have more than once on such occasions resorted to the Hermit's lucubrations with success. We hold that, in these cases, a work which like the Hermit's is composed of separate papers, is more to be desired than the regular novel, which, should it be a good one, requires a continuous perusal, and is not, like a flute or a friendship, to be taken up and laid down at pleasure. Who, for instance, could have the fortitude to read "The Bride of Lammermoor" by snatches? who could bear to break the wonderful chain of interest which binds together that heart-moving tale? When we meet with a production singularly attractive, we make a feast of it and consume it entire, despite of all its length; but the good Hermit has cut up his volumes into mouthfuls, of which we can swallow one or two at any spare season. Thus, when enjoying our Pekoe alone, we have sometimes enhanced its flavour by adding a few pages of the Hermit; for we hold it to be a high luxury thus to exhilarate at once both body and mind. Again, during the few agreeable sunny days with which we have been favoured this autumn, we found the Hermit a very pleasant companion beneath the shade of a certain oak-tree, whither, "as was our custom in an afternoon," we resorted at once for air and coolness. It is possible that the circumstances which have thus attended our perusal of these volumes, may, in some degree, have induced a bias in their favour. Every critic knows how much depends upon the humour he is in when he first reads his author, and that if an unfortunate writer happens to fall in with his reviewer when the gall of the latter is roused, he stands no small chance of suffering from that accident. What thief would choose to be tried before a judge impatient for his dinner, or what author would wish to fall into the hands of a reviewer in a fit of choler? But we shall now endeavour to award to the Hermit what the lawyers call *summum jus.*

The Hermit's writings, then, are well suited to their scope and object—the whiling away of a leisure hour, and the dispersion of vapours and *ennui.* They exhibit much good-natured observation, and a deal of good taste in matters of principle and feeling, which are very creditable to the anchorite. Sometimes they are dashed with a little affectation, and now and then, though rarely, they are slightly mawkish; but these faults are forgotten in the amusement they afford, and the improving lessons they frequently inculcate.

We hasten to select a short paper as a specimen of what may be expected from the Hermit's travels. Perhaps, "La Chaumière" will suit for the purpose.

" '*Etes vous seul, Monsieur?*' Are you alone, Sir? Will you have a cabinet, or will you be served in the garden? Do you belong to a *société,* or are you waiting for any one? Would Monsieur wish to have some refreshment before dinner, a *déjeûner à la fourchette,* or a *petit verre.*—Mercy! how many questions to a solitary elderly man in a black coat, without follower or precursor, sauntering from the boulevard *Mont Parnasse*, and wishing to take a peep at another scene in the environs of the metropolis!

"I had now three waiters about me; one asked me, if I was of the wedding party? 'Not a principal,' answered I, 'nor a party concerned in any way;' the second now winked at his fellow waiters, and said, in a low tone, 'the gentleman is waiting for some lady;' then, addressing himself to me, 'you can have this *cabinet*,' pointing to a pigeon-hole, where a brace of cooing doves might have been conveniently caged. 'You are wrong,' quoth I, showing the garçon that I understood him; 'I mean to dine in the garden,' taking at the same time a chair and laying my cane across it. '*Attendez, Monsieur*,' said the last speaker, 'you must not occupy that place, it is for the dancers.' 'And that large room?' enquired I. 'That is for the marriage party, and here the fiddlers are to sit; but are you really alone?' '*Comme vous voyez.*'—'Then,' observed another, 'I will get you a snug corner; will you have *du bifsteck aux pommes de terre?*' (What a proof that he held my taste cheap.) However, I begged leave not to have *bifsteck*, but called for the bill of fare, and chose a little dinner *à la française*, and a bottle of *château margot*. '*A la bonne heure*,' muttered a trio of waiters, as much as to say, this *n'entends pas* has not so bad a taste.

"The marriage party now arrived, sixty in number, of all ages, and whilst they sat down to a late *déjeûner*, I began to reflect on their wanting to *get me into the cabinet* (a thing I am not fit for), or to join the party in the grand saloon; or why the wondered at my sober, solitary visit. I now perceived that every face but mine was lit up with a smile, that snug *tête-à-têtes* moved together through the serpentine walks, that comfortable couples peeped through the lattices of closets, that the young and gay tripped it lightly in the dance, whilst veterans smoked their pipes under the bay or olive, and either went over the past campaigns again, or ogled their fat landlady or some buxom widow who might afford a solace after the rigours of war. A serious Englishman alone was a rarity in the place, and they seemed to pity me for not mingling in the surrounding mirth, for not belonging to some party or person, for not having some pursuit or other like the rest of the frequenters of the Chaumière. The dance now began, and I sat with my hat off reading the outlines of pretty faces, and watching the activity of well-turned ankles. I could easily make out the bride by her dress, and by the place which she occupied, as well as by the degree of attention which she gained. I could also discover bride-maids, relations, connexions, and mere acquaintances. The bride-maids had an arch look, not free from a feeling which, although not envy, was something like it; the sisters and near relations were discoverable by a warm look of regard thrown on the bride, meaning, 'May you be happy, but, ah! we are sorry to lose you!' The connexions flirted it through the dance, and hung out for a *partner after it;* brothers looked anxiously, parents had a tinge of melancholy overclouding hope, whilst the mere acquaintances gamboled and pranced, and clearly proved that they came there merely for amusement and good cheer. The bride and bridegroom had a difficult card to play in endeavouring neither to seem too distant nor too familiar. When the dance was over, the party retired to dinner, and I wondered on looking at my watch and discovering how many hours I had been engaged in a scene with which I had no connexion or interest: 'No interest or connexion!' seemed to whisper an invisible being; 'No interest in the felicity of your fellow creatures! no connexion with the chain of humanity, although only a small link thereof! fie, fie!' This monitor explained to me, that when we take pleasure in seeing others happy, we cannot be lonesome or forlorn ourselves; that the innocent diversion of a surrounding circle includes us in its sunshine; that, without having an assignation or intrigue, a party to join, or a festival to attend, there is no more rational pleasure than that of being a looker-on when youth and mirth form a party together.

"The selfish and cold-hearted man will turn aside from what he may proudly and unfeelingly term folly, from the relaxations of the people; but they will never be indifferent to          THE WANDERING HERMIT."

## ST. PAUL'S.

HAPPY is the man who on a fine bright morning steps forth from an hotel in a part of London which admits some of the charming freshness of early day, and full of health and strength and cheerfulness, feeling himself in good nerves, and dressed to his perfect satisfaction, unclogged with any ponderous, unmanageable, and inelegant companion, has London "all before him where to choose" pleasing occupation or rational amusement for the day. Happier still, if, for his companion in these feelings and these pursuits, he has some friend of similar taste, some man who hates the mere business and gravity, and all the pervading hypocrisy of life, and loves to partake of its allowable pleasures and advantageous elegancies when he can. With such a man there is no fear of being deluded into the city, or decoyed into the baleful outskirts of the town; he loves the western air, and doats on the growing magnificence of the capital; and whether in the morning, or afternoon, or night, lives only for the best parts of the great world of the metropolis. On such a morning, and with such intentions, and in such a happy state of mind and body, and above all, with such an enlightened and beloved friend, did I set forth on the second day of my stay in town; but we had not reached the bottom of St. James's-street before the provoking chances of the place clashed us with a man fresh from Lincolnshire, with all the odour of its fens about him; a man who from his youth upwards had passed his inglorious days in that pleasing part of England. It would have been cruel, heartless, utterly despicable, to meet the honest joy with which he greeted us by any coldness or affectation; and, not knowing how to avoid it, we allowed all our bright visions to be dissipated at once, and the whole design of the day to take its form and colour from our worthy but somewhat rustical companion. There was no time for reflection, and it was not without disappointment that I found in a few moments I had promised, or rather was sentenced, to see *St. Paul's* that very day, and already bending my steps away from the Eden of the West. The *Tower* itself, with all its armour and its beasts, was darkly hinted at; but happily for me *that* scheme Providence averted; for no suspected traitor ever visited that strange old pile of barbarous times and barbarous taste, that monument of regal crimes and monstrous tyranny, with more reluctance than myself, when "for some sin" I have been dragged thither by a sight-seeing friend.

The approach to St. Paul's, in spite of buildings which have no association with it, is a grand thing, and its aspect from Ludgate-hill full of magnificence. The passenger has scarcely time to catch more than a glimpse of this, such is the hurry of the corner of the church-yard. Of all thoroughfares this is the most crowded, bustling, and thought-interrupting; and to those who are fond of contrasts, I know none which may be more strongly recommended than that of which we are sensible, when, ascending by the broad steps of the Cathedral, a moment elevates us above the struggling and the racket of the city, and shrouds us in the silence of that vast and solemn sanctuary. Fifteen years had elapsed since I had before ascended those steps, and the events of them, their good and evil things, passed before me by some mental magic in

a single moment, all distinct and vivid and independent of time and
distance ; but London is not a place to indulge sentiment in, and abs-
tractions, however flattering to human pride, are but follies after all.
Fifteen years had made a difference in St. Paul's.   Not that in that
petty space of time its everlasting dome had shown symptoms of decay,
or any feature of its aisles had mouldered into dust; but there was a
rejuvenescence that startled one.   It dwelt in my recollection a
gloomy, dusty, and immeasurable place, and I found it enlivened in
colour, with marks of care and attention about it, and all its proportions visible at once.

The vastness of the church, as seen from the centre of the floor, is
most imposing; it is impossible not to be struck with its extent, its
length, its width, and the unbroken loftiness of the dome above, into
the recesses of which the eye ascends and penetrates until respiration is
thickened and the brain grows giddy, and we seek relief in the contemplation of objects nearer the surface of the earth and immediately
around us, the monuments of the illustrious dead.   It is disagreeable to
have to say that the general effect of these works of art in this building
is unpleasant, few of them being in good taste, and many of them so
overloaded with allegory as to be quite absurd.   The monument to
Picton can never be seen, without interest, by those to whom the most
devoted courage of a soldier is dear ; and there are many more to
proud names in military annals which revive the almost forgotten
glories of the stirring years so lately past.   The simple inscription
under the organ, to Sir Christopher Wren, is a happy instance of taste ;
and although I am far from disputing the propriety of its being in
Latin, it is still a pity that four-fifths of those who gaze and wonder at
St. Paul's should be unable to profit by it, and thus be reminded of a
tribute of gratitude to a name which should never be forgotten.   It
would be painful to enumerate the monuments disfigured by angels
and by wild beasts (howling " in dull cold marble,") and by Britannias
and by trumpets and all the noisy extravagancies which frantic allegory
has associated with the silent grave.   The monument to the immortal
Nelson is rather less unhappy in this respect than some of the rest ; but
I confess that to me the statue of the man, with its likeness to the figure
which he bore while on earth, would be more interesting and more
affecting without that undefinable female and the two little school-
boys, and yet more without that huge and very unconcerned looking
lion, which we are left to suppose means England.   Nay, I am so fastidious that I cannot admire the keys in the hand of Howard; by a
strange opposition to the will of the sculptor, they give the philanthro-
pist a sort of jailor-look, and sometimes cause him to be oddly mistaken
for St. Peter : his statue and his name would be sufficient, the keys
and the trickery about him are superfluous.   Every one must feel
more pleasure in contemplating that monument, in which an officer is
seen falling from his horse with a fatal wound into the arms of a soldier, than in beholding others in which dying heroes have some
fairy nymph about them, some goddess or equivocal female, standing
amid the dying and the dead, half-armed like a soldier and half-clothed
like a woman, sprung or dropt from nobody knows where to do nobody
knows what.   It is high time indeed that a purer taste should prevail

in these respects.   Let those who have contemplated some unadorned figure of a child by Chantrey, represented with all the loveliness of early death, uniting all that is sweet on earth with something borrowed from that purer world whither the spirit of the little innocent has fled ; let any one look at such a figure of a child sleeping in simple and unfanciful attire upon its marble tomb, and say whether figures of angels, or of all the birds of the air and beasts of the field could add to its touching interest, or make it more affect the heart.   It is in the want of this species of interest, and in the interruption of these sacred feelings, that we find the utter folly and emptiness of elaborate allegory.

The eyes of most people are so little accustomed to making an accurate admeasurement of heights, that the loftiness of St. Paul's can perhaps only be estimated justly from below.   If we ascend to the whispering gallery, a height far above the habitations of the people of London, the view downwards is overpowering, affecting various heads in various ways—producing vertigo in some, sickness in others, and an awful feeling of overthrow-*itiveness* in a few ; a sort of propensity to drop-through the passive air upon the hard marble below, a thought full of madness and horror : but when we ascend far above this point, and even to more than double its elevation, the fearful height does not seem proportionably increased, the feeling it inspired before seeming scarcely to admit of aggravation.   The whispering-gallery is indeed to many a fearful place.   The surpassing altitude of dome and tower above, the yawning and immense abyss below, the stern marble spread out to dash the mortal frame to instant dust, the narrowness of the circular gallery, the overshadowing of the superincumbent vault, the appalling loudness of every common sound, and the loud wind heard ever sweeping round the dome itself, produce an incredibly alarming effect on some individuals.   I am one of those happy and composed people who could look down from a balloon in its most ambitious ascent without a shudder ; and I could eat, drink, and sleep in the whispering-gallery as pleasantly as in any other prison from which the view of the sweet world was in the same way utterly excluded ; for confinement there would be a dreadful punishment on this last account, although I suppose the sage who many times a-day does there repeat his story of the birth, education, and extravagance of the church, feels *his* daily durance mitigated by the conscious pleasure of continually accumulating property.

It gave me much pleasure to see the banners, taken from many a vaunting foe, and among others the proud tri-color itself, by the mariners of England, all which were formerly scattered about the western division of the cathedral, ragged, black, and neglected, now ranged round within the dome, which has thus become, without any formal preparation, a receptacle of trophies, as the space below has become a vast mausoleum to worth, learning, and bravery.

The young, the aspiring, the new to London, can seldom be restrained from ascending to the airy gallery above the dome, and there, in describing a most limited circle, the eye takes in ten thousand histories. London, with all its vicissitudes, with all its generations, with all the present and all the past about it, is stretched beneath us, and almost every house visible.   Even from that height the eye cannot, in all directions, overleap the colossal city, and what is seen of green fields and hills is seen with the indistinctness of another world. The wind storms for ever round the cupola, blowing the fair and adventurous ladies about (" a chartered libertine !") to the greatest advantage ; whilst the spectator feels almost disposed to lose his confidence in the secure and eternal pedestal· on which he stands, and breathlessly enjoys the sublimity of apparent danger without the reality.

It is when we begin to descend from this immense elevation that we feel the fatigue which our over-excitement has caused us to incur ; and that man may be considered the favourite of fortune who begins to retrace the never-ending steps when the organ is pealing in the afternoon service ; for at such a time fits of melody will burst upon him at unexpected turns, and the piercing voices of the " full-voiced choir below" will penetrate the intricate recesses of the vast structure, and vibrations of harmony will meet him suddenly in unexpected angles and sinuosities of the building. Sweet sounds will be heard now near, now distant, as if borne to him by the soft and fitful breeze, and every thing will conspire to shorten his journey downwards. On leaving the building, and descending the broad steps which lead almost into the celebrated, and as it seems, perpetual pastry-cook's shop opposite, we again feel the contrast between the calm and silence of the solemn temple we have left, and the bustling, restless, and money-making world. Turning to its western grandeur as we descend the hill and re-plunge into all the hurry of London, it stands lofty, singular, and sublime, silent, unchangeable, impenetrable to all the noise which agitates the air around it, and is to the city what a towering mountain is to the plain beneath ; its grandeur unapproachable by the indolent vulgar, its atmosphere uninfected by commerce and turmoil ;—a place sacred from all the ordinary wretchedness of common-place life, presenting itself fearlessly and uninjured to the storm, the tempest, the lightning, and ever and anon holding mysterious and " dark communion with the cloud." Thus too, at night, seen from the river or the bridges, it rests in its gloomy vastness over the subsiding activity of the city, like some presiding and superior power, whilst its deep-toned bell sounds along the line of river

" Swinging slow with sullen roar,"

and awakening the imposing echoes of Westminster. Thus too, in approaching the capital, as in sailing up the Thames, long before arriving within the sounds of London, its awful dome and brilliant cross are often beheld lifted up as it were in mid air, floating on the thick and murky vapours in which the vast and invisible city is enveloped.

The opinion of my Lincolnshire friend on these subjects I may perhaps be induced to communicate at another opportunity.

C.

## PEREGRINATIONS OF THOMAS TRYATALL.

### NO. III.

IT is in vain to attempt a separate notice of all the Paris sights. They come, like blushing honours, "thick upon me;" and drive me out of my pitiful retail business into a line of wholesale combinations. Horse-racing, ballooning, drunkenness, La Rosière, and La St. Louis, make but an odd jumble, I must confess. It is, like that of a modern work, "rank confusion in the orders of precedence"—but no matter; symmetrical arrangement must not be expected from a head which the last month's varieties have set spinning like a merry-go-round. The sun, that so long refused to shine, has at length burst out, and warmed into life all the ephemeral enjoyments of France. Before their flutterings subside into the winter's inanity, I must endeavour to pluck a few of those innumerable feathers which compose their butterfly wings. I have been at about twenty fêtes and fairs within a month; and being completely disburthened of the friendship, and even presence, of my quondam associate De Vaurien, I was driven out upon the stormy solitudes of public places and suburban pleasures. I was for many days tossed about on "the multitudinous sea;" borne along the moving waves of the crowd; carried forward by the gale of the popular breath (not over "spicy," to be sure), like any other privateer or pleasure-barge running ready rigged before the wind. Continuing this maritime allusion to my pursuits, and at the same time adopting an epithet used by that exquisite equestrian Geoffrey Gambado, to designate such piratical marauders on the face of nature, I may call myself a cutter, i. e. daisy-cutter, and confess in this capacity my manifold offences in my cruise after curiosities. Many a thousand have I crushed of those

> Wee, modest, crimson-tipped flowers,

as Burns has it, or

> —— These floures white and rede,
> Such that men callen daisies,

according to Chaucer—when bringing myself to an anchor, on beds

> Of daisies pied, and violets blue,
> And ladysmocks all over white,
> And cuckoo buds of yellow hue,

as Shakspeare says—I have, upon getting under sail again, had the variegated reproaches of many a murdered flower, staring in the face—any one who happened to follow me. It really grieved me to the heart to witness and partake in these floral depredations; and it is positively one of the chief evils of that propensity for everlasting dance which entitles this nation to have St. Vitus for its patron, that there is not a spot of meadow or pasture-ground round the capital sacred from the trespasses of " Le Cavalier Seul," " Chassez deux," "La chaine Anglaise," and such like boisterous intruders. The fact is, that no man likes a fête better than I do. Once and away, a rural party of joyous peasants, or a group of gay grisettes, tripping it—not on the green, alas! but on "the russet lawn or fallow grey," if you will—is as pleasant a sight as one could wish.

I delight in dancing, but then I love moderation, and I hate excess, coupled with which pleasure is (like the punishment of What's-his-name, the tyrant of old) a living body joined to a dead carcase. Now the French, at this season at least, think of *nothing* but fêtes, and *do* nothing but dance. All the world goes capering, and there is no fear of treason certainly, for every one seems to have "music in his *sole.*" A working-day must be a delightful holiday, I am sure, when they can, without being singular, put their feet at full length upon the ground; for at present all, young, old, well or ailing, are from Sunday morning to Saturday night "on the light fantastic toe"—except one hideous fat old woman, who nearly crushed the corn of my left foot with the *tread*-mill pressure of her heavy heel the other day, at the horse-races in the Champ de Mars. And this reminiscence brings me round quite naturally to my subject.

Horse-racing, then, in France, is precisely what opera-dancing is in England, or opera-singing in America. None of them are indigenous to the soil; the natives are not cut out for such exercises of the arm, the leg, or the voice. The performers must all be imported; for the home-breed, in their various ways, are too much or too little refined for the several accomplishments. It will ever be thus in countries so remote in manners and institutions. The social soil can never be ploughed, nor the national feelings harrowed up, so as to bring forth the fruits, which are looked on as the productions of a barbarous or a degenerate clime. Would John Bull give his Newmarket for L'Academie Royale de Musique—for which last word read *la danse?* Not he! any more than an independent Yankee would barter his hard-earned liberty, for the emasculated refinement that

"Squeaks and gibbers in the Roman streets."

For my part, I am always happy to see a people gazing with pleasure, in the heart of their capital, on an exhibition of foreign skill, which they nevertheless most heartily despise. It is a proof of independence of feeling; of a notion of self-superiority in matters of importance, without which no people can be great; and, above all things, it satisfies me that, in my time at least, there is no danger of those distinctive features being rubbed off, which keep all countries from becoming (the most abhorrent of *improvements* to my mind) one great, undistinguishable, monstrous family. I love to hear an Englishman allow the French to be the best dancers, and a Frenchman acknowledge us to be the best boxers in the world. There is something so *naïve* in the first, and so unsophisticated in the latter! and the admission is always made with so truly national a toss of the head or shrug of the shoulders, as the case may be! Vestris and Paul, kicking their heels against the fly-scenes of the opera-house, are objects of high delight and deep contempt to the applauding English audience—while Tom Cribb or Randall, making their best display in the Champs Elysées, would amuse the Parisians while they pronounced the pugilists to be barbarians. These national incongruities are all as they should be. What we are proud of, the French despise, and *vice versâ.* We are, like our roast beef, too underdone and too plain for their palates; and they, like their fricassees, too unsubstantial and too *saucy* for ours. It is just as *morally* impossible for John Bull and Monsieur de Grenouilles to have the same notions of politics and pleasures, as it is *phizically* impossible that they could resemble each other in features or complexion. As to horse-racing, in which we excel, it is a matter of *course* that the French should botch it. To succeed in such a pursuit, men must, of all things, love the country, and have a relish for rural pleasures. Of them the French gentry know little or nothing, beyond transplanting their natural productions to the towns; and probably the greatest burlesque existing is the annual exhibition of horse-racing in the capital of France,—from the simple reason, that the actors and the spectators have no sympathy in common. The place, too, appropriated, but not adapted, for the race, is enough to destroy all enjoyment in it; and has been chosen only from a stupid revolutionary imitation of the ancient Romans, who held their Fasta Equiriæ in the Campus Martius. Instead of a smooth and level turf, against which, with us, the noble animals strike their elastic limbs, and bound along in grace and beauty to the goal, here they plough through an immense bed of sand, labouring and panting, and covered with a coat of dust and sweat, jaded and disheartened, and looking any thing, in short, but what one expects in a "high-mettled racer." Such as the thing is, it is almost wholly in the hands of Englishmen. A French jockey rarely appears; and the only gratifying object, to my eyes, in the display, was the knowing air with which the riders mounted their steeds, and gave them their preparatory canter through the ranks of gaping *spooneys* about them. It was amusing too (though somewhat humiliating from its anti-English look) to see the winners of the prizes, two thorough-bred horsedealers, with all the blunt, and rather slangish, air of their profession, lead their respective horses up to the foot of the balcony, (from which the Duchess of Berry superintended the scene) preceded by a band of music, and escorted by a troop of horse-grenadiers. I did not much like to see my two countrymen twirling their hats in one hand, stuffing the other into their breeches-pockets, and looking altogether so confoundedly *gauche* in the presence of "les augustes personnages." I could not help smiling, however, when they took their silver coffee-pot and ewer away in triumph under their arms; and as they gave their several scrapes of the foot, and bobbed their bows up to the balcony, and turned off upon their heels, I thought I distinguished on each of their countenances an expression that seemed to say, "All my eye, Betty Martin!"

Next came Mademoiselle Garnerin and her balloon; and they were much more to the taste of the spectators—she gracefully bowing and looking gaily; *it* moving along, gaudy, inflated, and "full of emptiness." Up she sailed upon her aërial voyage, not to go round the world, but merely (a hard task, alas!) to get above it; and if a man may judge of his fellows by his own feelings or their faces, (most uncertain tests I allow,) there was scarce a looker-on who did not, in the enthusiasm of the moment, wish to be yoked in the car with the adventurous nymph, "fat, fair, and forty," as she looked to be.

I had long had a desire to *assist* (as we say in France) at *la fête de la Rosière.* Early associations, boyish imaginings, Madame de Genlis, and other delusions, had fixed this passion deep in my mind. Pasto-

rality and purity, and innocence and ingenuousness, and such animating alliterations, floated before me, and, as might be expected, prepared
me for—an utter disappointment. I had gone to the *Champ de Mars*,
my brain crammed, like a Yorkshire newspaper, with the anticipated
joys of horse-racing, and I came away knocked up like a sorry hack—
there are various kinds, reader, as the booksellers could tell you. I
went to the fête of the Rosière, my head as full as a flower-pot of bloom
and fragrance, and I returned with every expectation as withered as
the faded wreath that adorns the image of the Virgin over the porch of
Suresne's Church. There never were such cruel pains taken by a Curé,
with or without the commands of his superiors, to render common-place
and unpopular an institution full of sense and sentiment, as have been
taken in the present instance by the Curé of Suresne. The fête of
la Rosière, established on the basis of national feeling and true morality,
was in its origin meant to reward with a garland (full as honourable
*per se* as a blue ribbon) the girl of the village who combined the best
life with the most graceful demeanour. To-day the whole matter, if I
am rightly informed, (and I beg that this clause may be a *saving one*,)
has become an affair of paltry intrigue and party prejudice. The fortunate maiden last year was the daughter of the Maire! Now, though
I would no more exclude the progeny of a *Maire* from the right to the
Rosière any more than the prize of the horse-race, I think the public
functionary ought not to have let his daughter enter the lists, lest the
people might suppose *his* situation to have some influence in *her* success.
They think so at Suresne, I can assure him; but the discontent is at its
height this summer, from the Curé having refused the claims of all the
girls of the village who could be convicted of having gone *to* a fête or
a dance during the year! Imagine this, in France—on the banks of
the Seine—within sight of Paris! It is the most preposterous innovation of modern *epurations*, for it strikes at the very root of national
manners and character. A French girl entitled to be crowned Rosière
in proportion as she is ignorant of " Balancer and Rigadoon!" why it
is worthy of John Knox, who did not deal harder with Mary, his gay-
mannered and French-hearted Queen, than this Curé with his virgin
parishioners. There were, as may be supposed, scarcely any candidates, for the favoured maiden, instead of being " one in a hundred,"
was, of course, only one *out of* four or five; and these, no doubt, the
pious *wallflowers* of former ball-rooms, who, unable to get a flesh and
blood partner in a mortal quadrille, have been forced to waltz through
the year with the memory of some dead-and-gone saint of the second
century. Mademoiselle Julienne Something-or-other may, therefore,
arrange her garland before the looking-glass, without exciting the least
envy in the majority of her fellow-villagers.

As for me, I turned from the contemplation of these puny conten-
tions to the overwhelming enjoyments of " *La Saint-Louis.*" Here,
thought I, I shall see something worthy of the genuine fête of religion
and royalty combined. Saint Louis and King Louis are to be celebrated together to-day—the throne and the altar—regal splendour with
Christian piety—all the national virtues consecrating a few of the
national vanities—civility and sobriety walking hand-in-hand with
gracefulness and gaiety! That was something like a combination for

an amateur of fêtes ;—so away I trudged in the hot sun of the 25th of August, glowing with expectation, and determined to be pleased:—and a dogged fellow he must have been who was not pleased with the sight of the Champs Elysées at noon of that day. Every thing that could give pleasure (to an unthinking people at least) was gathered together. Merry-andrews, mountebanks, rope-dancers, bands of music, games of all kinds, and every kindly gaiety, were collected on the spot. I really wandered through these Elysian fields, something in the mood of the happiest of the shades. A thousand vagaries crossed me at every turn; but that, I think, which caused me to moralize the most, was the poor devils climbing up immensely high poles to come at the reward of their aspirings—a silver watch, a pair of buckles, or some such ornament. It was painfully amusing to see these climbers straining upwards; the earliest cleaning off the greasy unction, with which each pole was larded half-mast high, then slipping down to earth, and followed by others, all with their pockets filled with sand to fling upon the pole above them and give them a chance of clinging to it the better in their ascent. I thought of the strange contrast presented by this road to wealth and fame to all the others in life. Instead of being harsh and rugged, the only fault of this was being too smooth; and the only effort of the adventurers was, not to level obstacles, but to roughen their way to fortune. Here, too, were no sharp turns or short cuts. This was plain, straight-forward, up-pole work; and so far from a needy aspirant being, as in common cases, the most looked down upon, the fellow the most *in-kneed*, on the present occasion, had the best chance of getting above the world. Then came the *associations*—those whirlwind disturbers of the nicest train of philosophical speculation. I bethought me of barbers' poles, and the Polish lancers, and the North Pole, and Capt. Parry, and so on—until I was roused by the noise of wheels, and the shouts of the human animals that were dragging along the body of a cart, with a huge empty barrel thereon.

The group that presented itself was frightful. It consisted of a couple of dozen ragged, villain-visaged fellows, with about as many atrocious specimens of female degradation, coming forward towards the place where the wine was to be distributed. It was as if a band of demons had stolen into Paradise. They came on with gestures and exclamations fitting their appearance; brushed through the dancers; broke in upon the sports; and, as if under the special protection of the police, took up a position in front of one of the dépôts of provisions, which were to be immediately scattered gratis to the crowd. As every eye turned on these savages, each tongue exclaimed—"*Ah, voila les gens des Faubourgs!*" Aha! (said I to myself, like the Lord Chamberlain, in Henry VIIIth.)—

> " There's a trim rabble let in ! Are all these
> Our faithful friends o' the suburbs ?"

And I moved forward for the purpose of inspecting this odious deputation from all that is most odious in France. I shall not detail the result of my observations, but merely state, that every stage erected for the *distribution* was guarded at foot by a band of those miscreants, who are as anxious to wallow in wine to-day, as their fathers (or themselves perhaps) were to bathe in blood this day thirty years. At two o'clock the distribution commenced. Bread, meat, sausages, &c. were showered down on the multitude, in a profusion that would have reminded me of the pleasant times when

> " Streets were paved with penny rolls,
> And houses thatch'd with pancakes ;"

if my memory had not been pre-occupied by painful recollections of a more recent epoch, and all my feelings in revolt against the demoralizing spectacle. But when the edibles were exhausted, and the wine-giving began—then, indeed, I blushed for the profanation of the day, and the degradation of my species. When I looked on the struggling wretches, raving, raging, and deluged in the flood, rushing forward with pots, kettles, and cans, to catch the streaming liquor, and convey it to the barrels provided by each Faubourg as a common reservoir; while others, the great majority, glutted themselves into instantaneous drunkenness, rolled in the mud, and uttered yells, and songs, and blasphemy—it was then that all my indignation was up,—it was then that I cordially cursed the policy which debases and brutalizes a people, to give their rulers a better chance of crushing them. Then it was, that viewing the national sobriety and decorum violated, as it were, at the foot of the throne and by the royal ordonnance, I marvelled how a king could be honoured, or a saint be glorified, or man be bettered, or Heaven be pleased, by such a scene !

I pondered all this so deeply, walked so fast, and used such energetic action as I inwardly debated, that I saw I had attracted the remarks of some of the agents of that multocular monster—the Police; and fearing to be taken up for a malcontent, I wheeled away through the trees, and took French leave of the place.            T. T.

---

#### ANSWER TO THE POEM ENTITLED
#### " WHY DO WE LOVE ?"

**Which appeared in the 33d Number of the New Monthly Magazine.**

> Oh ! is it not because we love
>   (Far more than Beauty's fleeting worth)
> *The kindred soul* which soars above
>   The fair yet fading flowers of earth ?—
>
> Because Affection shuddering shrinks
>   From the cold dust left mouldering here ;
> And 'midst his tears the mourner thinks
>   Of Hope—beyond this troubled sphere?
>
> Yes—if, when Beauty's dazzling mask
>   Is gone, no *other* charms remain,
> Well may the heart desponding ask—
>   " *Why* do we love—if Love be vain ?"
>
> But 'tis not so :—when we behold
>   Death's faded victim, once so fair,—
> The eye is dim,—the lip is cold,—
>   But *all* we valued *lies not there*.        T.

### REGINALD DALTON.

WE have already taken occasion[*] to give vent to a slight movement of impatience at the overwhelming rapidity with which the anonymous author of the, so called, "Scotch novels" proceeds in his literary career—a career, in which the panting reviewer toils after him in vain, and the most voracious glutton of circulating lore that ever "gave his days and nights" to the Clarindas and Theodosias of the Minerva press, can hardly avoid being distanced. To what extent our readers may have sympathized in this pettishness of our criticism, we know not; for critics are a waspish sort of personages, and when tormented with the necessity of thinking for others, (it is bad enough to be obliged to think for ourselves,) may fall into fits of spleen, unfelt by the happier being whose "gentleness" is not disturbed by such considerations, and who has nothing in life to do with a book but to read it, to consume his aliquot portion of literature with thankfulness, and be satisfied with what is prepared for him. Of this, however, we are more assured, that if the public be ready to take the productions of the "great unknown" from his bookseller's hands as fast as he can bring them into the market, the case is not quite the same with every imitator, whom the speculating activity of the "north countrie" may engender; and we are quite convinced that something more is necessary to the production of a good novel, than the free use of the Scottish dialect, and an assortment of names for places and persons which no mortal man born south of the Tweed can hope to pronounce. We are, indeed, very much mistaken, if the frequent repetition of the *mannerisms* of even a good model will not affect the popularity of the original, and the "crambe repetita" of parodists and copyists, bring to a premature close a style of composition, which has perhaps contributed more largely to the public stock of innocent amusement, than any other description of fictitious narrative that has yet lent wings to time, or soothed the anguish of suffering or sorrowing humanity.

To this subject we propose very shortly to recur ; and for the present we shall confine ourselves more strictly to the work the title of which stands at the head of the present article. Reginald Dalton, we are told in its title-page, is the production of the author of Adam Blair ; and we confess ourselves indebted for the information. In no other part of the volumes have we been able to discover the slightest trace of the fact, there being little of that *vraisemblance*, that Defoeish accuracy of portraiture, and painfully minute delineation of sentiment and situation in the new novel, which characterizes so forcibly its singular predecessor ; and we frankly own, that but for the friendly hint in question, with all our critical acumen and lynx-eyed perspicacity, we should never have dreamed of such a thing " in our philosophy."

To complain that the story is totally defective in interest, may be deemed hypercritical ; for though the story *used* to be considered the most important particular in a good novel, now-a-days " *on a changé tout ça*," and it goes for little or nothing in the affair. Provided an author can muster a few melodramatic situations strongly conceived, and a few picturesque groupings clearly delineated, the vehicle, or to use

---

[*] Review of Quentin Durward, page 82.

the apothecary's phrase, the "*quitis idoneus vehiculus*," in which they are to be gulped down, is a matter of perfect indifference.

This observation equally applies to the characters; if characters they can be called, that character have none. An insipid dawdle of an heroine with nothing indicative of her sex but her petticoat, and a lackadaysical *tay-drinking* sort of a gentleman, as Paddy happily expresses it, for a hero, are amply sufficient to carry the most rebellious and recalcitrant reader through three goodly volumes of that "pure description," which in these latter times holds the place not only of sense, but of wit, humour, adventure, pathos, and philosophy, to boot. The defect of moral interest in the writings of the Scottish novelists, which we have already noticed, in our examination of Quentin Durward, as the result of design rather than of accident, of deliberate volition rather than of defective power, is carried to an extreme in the execution of Reginald Dalton,—a work from which it would be difficult to collect that any thing great, or noble, or generous, existed in our common nature. Aristotle*, good easy man, was of opinion, that the agents of fictitious narrative should be marked by decided qualities, good or evil ; and in admitting the wicked to play a part, he required a certain decency and moral shading which should relieve as far as possible, and give elevation even to the worst. He little imagined the possibility of weaving into a story, with any hope of pleasing, the no-characters of that commonplace existence the feelings and motives of which are all grovelling and mean; an existence divested of the energy of passion and the impulse of sentiment, which rarely rises even to the dignity of crime, and is immeasurably removed from the mere apprehension of virtue—at least, of virtue in its more exalted and resplendent phases. It cannot but strike the reader as a circumstance sufficiently extraordinary, that the writers of the Scotch Tory school should have so closely adhered to the *médiocre* in character, as not even to exempt their own countrymen; whom, in defiance of all nationality (that bright feature in the Scottish character) they have represented under the meanest and most selfish traits of low cunning and close prudence, which are said peculiarly to belong to narrow fortunes and narrow educations in the northern part of these dominions.

This defect of character, which, in the writings of the original of the school, is relieved by the merits of the narration, and to which, splendid exceptions must occur to every reader's recollection, is the more conspicuously revealed in the novel now under examination, by the almost total absence of a lively interest in its situations and adventures. So much is this the case, that it is impossible to escape, even for a single page, from the conviction of a *malus animus* seeking to lull the public to sleep, to wean it from all the finer feelings, and more expansive generalizations of sentiment and of views which encourage a love of freedom and predispose to patriotism. As long as the public taste can be fed with an idle literature, that rouses no emotion, forces no thought, awakens no passion, but, like the drowsy hum of distant waters, stupefies with a continuity of monotonous impressions, corruption is safe from invasion, and the work of national degradation goes on in unobserved security. This truth, if not perceived as a sentiment, is no less

---

* Poetics.

felt as an instinctive impulse; and similar writers, among whom the author of Reginald Dalton is evidently ambitious to be classed, labour hard to write down the tone of popular feeling to a right loyal and legitimate standard of insipidity. In every page of the work in question, we perceive the author's conviction, that exaltation of character is jacobinical, and high feeling dangerous to the state. In the estimation of this gentleman and of the school to which he belongs, the staple virtues of social life are—eating and drinking. To listen to their *élans* on this subject, we might fancy them of that creed, of which Margutto declares the dogmas in the Morgante Maggiore

> Io non credo più al nero che al azurro,
> Ma nel cappone o lesso o voglia arrosto,
>    \*    \*    \*    \*    \*    \*
> Ma sopra tutto nel buon vino ho-fede :—

Their faith is in "capons and cups of sack ;" and provided the heroes of their romances go drunk to bed every night, they seem very little solicitous that they set an example of any other virtue. In Reginald Dalton, no opportunity is lost of recommending intemperance; and that the reader may judge of this fact for himself, we subjoin one passage of very many in the work illustrative of the point :

"There is nothing in which the young sinners of a debauch have so decidedly the better of the old ones, as in the facility with which their unshattered constitutions enable them to shake off the painful part of its immediate consequences. I say the *painful* part—because really when the sickness and the head-ache are gone, the feverish fervour which remains about the brain, is with them neither a pain nor a punishment. A sort of giddy, reckless delirium lies there, ready to be revived and rekindled by the mere winds of heaven ; and in fact, when such excitements as air and exercise are abundantly supplied, a sort of legacy of luxury is bequeathed to them even by their departed carousal ; and it is in this point of view, I apprehend, that any charitable person will ever interpret old Tom Brown's glorious chaunt of

> Wine, wine in the morning
> Makes us frolic and gay,
> That like eagles we soar
> In the pride of the day."—Vol. 2. p. 10.

To what good purpose, it will be asked, can these fascinating portraitures of debauchery be directed? What benefit can be sought by informing youth that the first steps in vice are less painful and less dangerous than the last? or by encouraging boys to enter upon a train of riot and excess, which, when once it has become habitual, can seldom be thrown off? Can these scribes be really afraid that a sober and diligent youth leads to a maturity of radicalism and resistance? or that, to ensure the triumphs of legitimacy, it is necessary that man should be not only ignorant, but brutish, sensual, and besotted? There is something so odious in this eternal recommendation of the pleasures of the table, this chanting of the delights of locked dining-rooms and "no daylight," this fulsome eulogy of sound principles and sound corks, of the good old loyalty and good old port of other times, —coupled too as it is with hypocritical pretensions to superior virtue and sanctity, of the same class of writers, upon other occasions,—that we cannot but mark it with a strong expression of disgust. Let the reader observe also, that one of the coarsest debauches in which Reginald is made to participate (and he is never insensible to the claims

of a bottle of Champaigne) is supposed to occur after he has ruined
his father, shot his friend in a duel, been expelled from college, and is
on the point of sailing for India without a hope of again seeing the object of his devoted attachment! If this new school of philosophy
should take root, we shall have the rising generation staggering through
our streets at noon-day; and as the German youth turned banditti
after the example of Schiller's robbers, and the English lads knocked
down watchmen in humble admiration of the exploits of Tom and Jerry,
so we shall see a jovial band of stripling Tories riot through the land,
obedient to the canons of good fellowship laid down in the Reginald
Daltons, the Peter's Letters, and the other productions of the *clique*, putting down Whiggery and water-drinking by club law, and forming in
every village associations for the propagation of passive obedience to
rulers and toast-masters.

But to return to the story. Reginald Dalton, a common-place sort
of youth, educated in the seclusion of a north country parsonage, is
the son of a clergyman, the cadet of an ancient family, from which he
has estranged himself in consequence of a very silly disappointment in
love. Left to the solitude of his parsonage-house, the victim at once
of *ennui* and pique, the worthy divine marries a farmer's daughter,
who, *Dieu sçait pourquoi*, is represented as a Catholic. This fair tran-
substantialist has a sister, who runs off with a seducer, and is privately
married according to the succinct forms admitted by the Scottish law.
The seducer, after the most approved usages " in that case provided,"
endeavours to hush up the transaction, and marries again. Of this
transient union a daughter is the fruit. The mother dies, and the
orphan is quartered on a Catholic priest, who takes her abroad.

The gay deceiver, the cause of all this mischief, is the half-brother
of the elder Dalton's cousin and first love; who, to comfort her in her
afflictions, instead of looking for another husband, turns Methodist:
and her brother, to conciliate her affections and become the legatee of
her property, adopts, or rather affects to adopt, her religious predilections also. At the opening of the novel, Reginald's father renews
his intimacy with his family, and the problem to be solved in the
progress of the work is, whether his old flame shall suffer the family
estate to follow the legal course of descent, or will it out of the family
to her Methodist brother. *En attendant*, Reginald goes to Oxford;
and the larger and the most amusing part of these volumes is occupied
with details of college life, wine-parties, hunting, fights with the town-
folks, debts, duns, and drunkenness. On his road to the university,
Reginald meets in the coach with an odd sort of Scotch attorney, who,
" for the better carrying on of the plot," goes at once out of his way
and his character to introduce the young man to a Catholic priest, resident in Oxford; who is, of course, the protector of Reginald's neglected and disowned cousin. Love, in the usual routine, follows; which
thrives the better for the mutual poverty of the parties (Malthus on
Population at this time probably not forming part of a college course).
Meantime the hero's dissipation plunges him in difficulties, and he
utterly exhausts his father's slender finances. Notwithstanding a very
edifying repentance, he becomes involved in a duel, is expelled from
college, and has a new life to seek. Just at this time the *dignus vin-
dice nodus* of the piece is solved, by the death of the virgin heiress;

who leaves the estate,—not to her canting brother, but to his daughter by the second marriage, a lady one degree more cunning and assiduous than her father. Forthwith the honest attorney *ci-dessus nommé*, who was "*particeps criminis*" of the clandestine marriage, determines to turn his knowledge of that transaction to account, by forcing the father of the rich legatee to give her and her estate to his own son. His power to effect this purpose is increased by an error in the wording of the will, which, giving the property to his friend's *eldest* daughter, of course, if her claim were made public, would assign it to the little Catholic *perdue*. The negotiation to keep this secret, very happily commenced, is abruptly broken off by the supposed heiress choosing for herself and running off with a third party. The attorney, thus foiled, embarks in a new speculation to produce the "true Simon Pure," and marry his son to her. Upon the point as he imagines of carrying this design into successful execution, he is again thwarted by the old Methodist father, who, seeing no other means of avoiding the snare, and touched moreover in his conscience, brings to light a forgotten entail which nullifies the will, and settles the property on Reginald, who, as in duty bound, marries his cousin, and the curtain falls.

Such are the very flimsy materials out of which the author of Reginald Dalton has contrived to spin three very closely printed volumes, by dint of descriptions and details à la Walter Scott, (if W. Scott be the "great unknown")—descriptions and details, which, though of the most ordinary and trifling incidents and situations, are still, by force of writing, endowed with considerable interest to the reader. It is this circumstance, indeed, which alone renders the work worth five lines of criticism. It is this faculty of engaging an half-alive sort of attention, and pinning the mind down to details which tend to enfeeble the intellectual powers of the reader, which aim at affording amusement without rousing thought or interesting the nobler passions, and which familiarize the imagination with selfish and narrow notions and motives,—that we would deprecate as debasing literature and degrading the national tone of feeling. Whatever openings the story affords for energy and dignity of character in the better personages of the tale, are utterly lost by the author. Reginald and his father are both more amiable than otherwise, but both are nearly ruined; the one by his thoughtless extravagance, and the other by want of paternal vigilance, or rather of common prudence. Both are *weak*,—and accident alone prevents them from being *miserable*. There is, indeed, an attempt at the portraiture of an old lady of sense and goodness, but nothing is made of the character, either in the story or as a character. The moral interest which might spring out of the religious peculiarities of the personages, is left wholly aside, and no use whatever is made of the circumstance.

The most interesting and amusing part of the book is occupied with a very vivid description of a night brawl in Oxford, which, though a mere parody of the prentices' row in the Fortunes of Nigel, is executed with considerable force. **M.**

### THE RELEASE OF TASSO.

THERE came a Bard to Rome: he brought a lyre,
Of sounds to peal through Rome's triumphal sky,
To mourn a hero on his funeral pyre,
Or greet a conqueror with its war-notes high ;
For on each chord had fall'n the gift of fire,
The living breath of Power and Victory!
—Yet he, its lord, the sovereign city's guest,
Sigh'd but to flee away, and be at rest.

He brought a spirit, whose ethereal birth
Was of the loftiest, and whose haunts had been
Amidst the marvels and the pomps of earth,
Wild fairy-bowers, and groves of deathless green,
And fields, where mail-clad bosoms prove their worth,
When flashing swords light up the stormy scene.
—He brought a weary heart, a wasted frame,
The Child of Visions from a dungeon came.

On the blue waters, as in joy they sweep,
With starlight floating o'er their swells and falls,
On the blue waters of the Adrian deep,
His numbers had been sung: and in the halls,
Where, through rich foliage if a sunbeam peep,
It seems Heaven's wakening to the sculptured walls,
Had princes listen'd to those lofty strains,
While the high soul they burst from, pined in chains.

And in the summer-gardens, where the spray
Of founts, far-glancing from their marble bed,
Rains on the flowering myrtles in its play,
And the sweet limes, and glossy leaves that spread
Round the deep-golden citrons ; o'er his lay
Dark eyes, dark, soft, Italian eyes had shed
Warm tears, fast-glittering in that sun, whose light
Was a forbidden glory to his sight.

Oh ! if it be that wizard sign and spell
And talisman had power of old to bind,
In the dark chambers of some cavern-cell,
Or knotted oak, the Spirits of the Wind,
Things of the lightning-pinion, wont to dwell
High o'er the reach of eagles, and to find
Joy in the rush of storms ;—even such a doom
Was that high Minstrel's in his dungeon-gloom.

But he was free at last!—the glorious land
Of the white Alps and pine-crown'd Apennines,
Along whose shore the sapphire seas expand,
And the wastes teem with myrtle, and the shrines
Of long-forgotten gods from Nature's hand
Receive bright offerings still ; with all its vines,
And rocks, and ruins, clear before him lay—
—The seal was taken from the founts of day.

The winds came o'er his cheek ; the soft winds, blending
All summer-sounds and odours in their sigh ;
The orange-groves waved round ; the hills were sending
Their bright streams down ; the free birds darting by,

And the blue festal Heavens above him bending,
As if to fold a world where none could die !
And who was he that look'd upon these things ?
—If but of earth, yet one whose thoughts were wings—

To bear him o'er creation! and whose mind
Was as an air-harp, wakening to the sway
Of sunny Nature's breathings unconfined,
With all the mystic harmonies that lay
Far in the slumber of its chords enshrined,
Till the light breeze went thrilling on its way.
—There was no sound that wander'd through the sky,
But told him secrets in its melody.

Was the deep forest lonely unto him
With all its whispering leaves ?—Each dell and glade
Teem'd with such forms as on the moss-clad brim
Of fountains in their sparry grottoes play'd,
Seen by the Greek of yore through twilight dim,
Or misty noontide in the laurel-shade.
—There is no solitude on earth so deep
As that where man decrees that man should weep !

But oh ! the life in Nature's green domains,
The breathing sense of joy! where flowers are springing
By starry thousands, on the slopes and plains,
And the grey rocks!—and all the arch'd woods ringing,
And the young branches trembling to the strains
Of wild-born creatures, through the sunshine winging
Their fearless flight!—and sylvan echoes round,
Mingling all tones to one Eolian sound!—

And the glad voice, the laughing voice of streams,
And the low cadence of the silvery sea,
And reed-notes from the mountains, and the beams
Of the warm sun—all these are for the Free !
And they were *his* once more, the Bard, whose dreams
Their spirit still had haunted !—Could it be
That he had borne the chain ?—Oh! who shall dare
To say how much man's heart uncrush'd may bear?

So deep a root hath hope !—But woe for this,
Our frail mortality ! that aught so bright,
So almost burden'd with excess of bliss,
As the rich hour which back to summer's light
Calls the worn captive, with the gentle kiss
Of winds, and gush of waters, and the sight
Of the green earth, must so be bought with years
Of the heart's fever, parching up its tears !

And feeding a slow fire on all its powers,
Until the boon for which we gasp in vain,
If hardly won at length, too late made ours,
When the soul's wing is broken, comes like rain
Withheld till evening, on the stately flowers
Which wither'd in the noontide, ne'er again
To lift their heads in glory !—So doth Earth
Breathe on her gifts, and melt away their worth !

The sailor dies in sight of that green shore,
Whose fields, in slumbering beauty, seem'd to lie

On the deep's foam, amidst its hollow roar
Call'd up to sunlight by his fantasy !—
And, when the shining desert-mists that wore
The lake's bright semblance, have been all pass'd by,
The pilgrim sinks beside the fountain-wave,
Which flashes from its rock, too late to save.

Or if we live, if that, too dearly bought
And made too precious by long hopes and fears,
Remains our own; love, darken'd and o'erwrought
By memory of privation, love, which wears
And casts o'er life a troubled hue of thought,
Becomes the shadow of our closing years,
Making it almost misery to possess
Aught, watch'd with such unquiet tenderness.

Such unto him, the Bard, the worn and wild,
And sick with hope deferr'd, from whom the sky,
With all its clouds in burning glory piled,
Had been shut out by long captivity,
Such, freedom was to Tasso !—As a child
Is to the mother, whose foreboding eye
In its too radiant glance, from day to day
Reads that which calls the brightest first away.

And he became a wanderer—in whose breast
Wild fear, which, e'en when every sense doth sleep,
Clings to the burning heart, a wakeful guest,
Sat brooding as a spirit, raised to keep
Its gloomy vigil of intense unrest
O'er treasures, burdening life, and buried deep
In cavern-tomb, and sought, through shades and stealth,
By some pale mortal, trembling at his wealth !

But woe for those who trample o'er a mind—
A deathless thing !—They know not what they do,
Or what they deal with !—Man perchance may bind
The flower his step hath bruised; or light anew
The torch he quenches; or to music wind
Again the lyre-string from his touch that flew !
But, for the soul !—Oh ! tremble, and beware
To lay rude hands upon God's mysteries *there !*

For blindness wraps that world !—our touch may turn
Some balance, fearfully and darkly hung,
Or put out some bright spark, whose ray should burn
To point the way a thousand rocks among !
Or break some subtle chain, which none discern,
Though binding down the terrible, the strong,
Th' o'ersweeping passions! which to loose on life,
Is to set free the elements for strife !

Who then to power and glory shall restore
That which our evil rashness hath undone ?
Who unto mystic harmony once more
Attune those viewless chords ?—There is but One!
He that through dust the stream of life can pour,
The Mighty and the Merciful alone !
—Yet oft his paths have midnight for their shade—
He leaves to man the ruin man hath made !        F. H.

## De Lamartine.

THE higher order of poetry in France was considered as almost extinct for some time before the fall of Napoleon. The impulse which the Revolution gave to genius is sufficiently attested by its prose productions, its specimens of eloquence, and the progress of painting. But that species of boisterous excitement which inspires the orator and the artist with subjects fitting to such times, and strengthens the faculties in their immediate display, seems the very reverse of that which is most favourable to the poet. His art is pre-eminently one that demands repose. His talent lives on recollections, and grows in retrospect. The images which flit before him escape as soon as observed. They are impalpable, though powerful, and can rarely be described when first conceived. Their presence is as unreal as the shadows of a dream, but the impressions they make sink as deeply in his mind; and it is in leisure and retirement that he embodies forth the notions, the vividness of which is not injured by time. The interval between inspiration and composition is therefore much greater than is commonly supposed; and we think that extempore productions are in most cases but the utterance of ideas long before received. It must be obvious that we do not refuse belief in those improvisatore effusions which are frequent and sometimes good. We do not deny the hurried production of verses possessing considerable merit, nor undervalue the various *pièces de circonstance* for stage or closet; but we speak of *the higher order of poetry;* and glance at, rather than examine, one great cause of its decline in France. Another obviously presents itself, in the slavery that succeeded to the fury of the Revolution. The storms of that event, which rocked the cradle of Despotism, were chilling to the bright but delicate flower of poetry. It opens gladly to the breath of Freedom, but is shrunk and withered by the noxious blast of Tyranny. Every one of the productions under the reign of the Emperor was forced and unseemly. They had, perhaps, the florid bloom of poetry, but it was unhealthy; and what they gained in colouring they lost in perfume.

It is, therefore, but little astonishing that from the days of Delille and Parny until the Restoration, no poet of any eminence appeared in France. But no sooner did that event take place, and political convulsions subside into something like the calm of comparative freedom, than literature resumed its influence; and however political sentiments might vary, there seemed a common accord in relation to poetry. The general feeling was, that it had arisen from its long sleep; that it had returned, as it were, from its term of exile; and that, however little other emigrants had profited by their banishment, it at least had gained new vigour from repose, and came back regenerated and revived. The inspirations of the Muse were deeply and generally felt, and she scattered her favours neither like a niggard nor a partisan. Amongst men of every political opinion she found votaries; and she denied her smiles to no party in the state. Royalists, Republicans, and Constitutionalists produced alike their poets, of various degrees of merit and in different walks of the art; but none took his station on a prouder eminence than Alphonse de Lamartine.

A volume of poetry, the leading qualities of which were religion

without intolerance, piety without cant, and elevation without bom-
bast, was a novelty in France; but it was still more strange to see a
young and ardent author discarding every aid of popular prejudice,
and writing to the minds instead of the passions of his countrymen.
Such were the " Méditations Poëtiques," the title of the book, and M.
de Lamartine, its author. This work appeared anonymously in the
spring of 1820. Its success was instantaneous, and the name of the
author became immediately known. The second edition bore it on the
title-page, and it was at once enrolled among those of the most distinguished of the national poets. This success was chiefly the combined effect of the merit and the novelty of the work; but another
principal cause was the strict avoidance of political opinion or allusion.
Poetry, purely abstracted and imaginative, spoke to all parties in a
tone of feeling, but to none in that of hostility. The aristocratical
class of society (and literature was distinguished like it) was satisfied
that it had gained a powerful adherent; while there breathed through
the verses of De Lamartine a strain of high and liberal thought, dissi-
pating the doubts suggested by his name, which announced nobility,
and his general tone, which savoured so deeply of religion. In thus
noticing the feelings of modern France, it is not our intention to enter
into the question of their prejudice or their propriety. Political discussion would be misplaced here. But blended as it is with every
thing relating to modern French literature, it is impossible to separate
allusions to the one from a notice of the other; and it is too true that
nothing is looked on with more distrust by the nation at large than religion as now professed, and nobility as formerly composed.

De Lamartine, thus dear to the hopes of the powerful minority, and
not obnoxious to the distrust of the larger, and perhaps the more enlightened, portion of the public, found favour on all hands, and was
read only to be admired. His triumph was not gained over party-
feelings, to which he was not opposed, but over national prejudices,
less virulent, but full as strong; for he struck with a vigorous hand at
the root of chill correctness—that family-tree under the branches of
which French poetry had so long reclined. He came to the exercise
of his art at home, prepared for it by the study of foreign models. He
shewed himself to be well acquainted with the classical authors of antiquity; and, what was of much more value in the present day, he displayed a deep knowledge, and frequent imitation, of English writers.
In this particular point of view he stands at the head of all his contemporaries; and, even had his talents been less than they are, he
would have thus rendered one of the best services to the literature which
he in other respects so eminently adorns. We say this without arrogance or even vanity. It is, in fact, but an echo of the general opinion
of the best qualified judges among the French themselves; for while
they reject as *outré* and ridiculous the metaphysical extravagance of
German poetry, they acknowledge in the boldness of that of England
the best model for the enfranchisement of their own. The tribute
which M. de Lamartine has thus paid to this country has been returned
in the reputation he has acquired among us. A light but well-aimed
blow at almost the only part of his "Méditations" open to the
assaults of ridicule, retarded for some time our knowledge of his merit;
but from the same source which gave vent to that witty effusion a full

stream of eulogy has lately flowed, and carried away, no doubt, the memory of the attack.*

The biography of our author affords but little food for curiosity or remark. He was born about the year 1790 at Macon, was educated at the college of Belley, and obtained in 1820 the situation of secretary to the French embassy at Naples. In the early part of 1822 he was attached to that at the English court, and occupied the same situation at the period of M. de Chateaubriand's arrival in London. We have heard it remarked by friends of our author, that from some cause unknown to them, the literary ambassador never shewed a great cordiality towards his celebrated subaltern; and it is certain, that on his elevation to the ministry, M. de Lamartine was wholly passed over. He consequently, and by reason of a delicate state of health, lives a life of literary retirement, rarely visiting Paris, and residing chiefly at his old family château of Pierre-Point, in the province of his birth. He keeps utterly apart from all political intrigues, and is of too much moderation in his principles to be ranked with any of the conflicting factions. It was chiefly during the leisure time snatched from his official duties at Naples, that he composed his poems; and he was absent from France at the time when their publication gained him so much fame. They were announced by the Editor as " les premiers essais d'un jeune homme qui n'avait point en les composant le projet de les publier;" but he, nevertheless, ceded to the " advice of his friends," and was one out of a hundred in finding such a course to be a wise one.

Among the most extraordinary, and by far the most interesting, effects of his verses, was the fact of their having captivated the heart of a young English lady of small but independent fortune, who immediately transferred to the author the admiration which his poetry had excited. We must go far back into the history of poetry and real love to find a parallel for this interesting fact, which even there is not furnished by the female sex. In the dawning of French literature we may discover the record of something similar; and the reader of Millot's History of the Troubadours will probably call to mind the adventures of Geoffroi Rudel, who became enamoured of Melinsende Countess of Tripoli, merely from hearing a report of the surpassing beauty which he had never seen. The unfortunate result of his passion has happily no counterpart in the instance we at present relate; for our amiable countrywoman, instead of meeting such tardy sympathy as only came

---

* We allude to a passing mention of the " Méditations Poëtiques," in the Edinburgh Review, soon after their appearance, in which an amusing though rather exaggerated translation was given of the following passage:

> Lorsque du Créateur la parole féconde,
> Dans une heure fatale, eut enfanté le monde
> Des germes du Chaos,
> De son œuvre imparfaite il detourna sa face
> Et d'un pied dédaigneux le lançant dans l'espace,
> Rentra dans son repos.

Which to the air of burlesque in the action attributed to the Deity, adds the absurdity of giving to the All-wise the blame of a bungling mechanic! This was indeed a weak point in the poetry of De Lamartine; but it was the heel of Achilles, and was struck by an arrow from *Paris.*

In No. 74, of the Edinburgh Review, M. de Lamartine is placed, we think justly, at the head of the French living poets.

to join itself to the death-sighs of the hapless Troubadour, received, after a chance-acquaintance formed at Chamberry in the South of France, the reward of her affection, in the gratitude and admiration of a faithful husband. She has been for some years united to M. de Lamartine; and for the interests of literature (beyond which we do not presume to touch on these domestic topics) we may be allowed to rejoice in a union, which must advance the poet's knowledge of our language, and do honour to it in strengthening the poetical diction of his own.

In the preface to the " Méditations Poëtiques" a continuation of the poems was promised, should those first published meet success. This pledge can be scarcely said to have been redeemed, as only three more short effusions were added in subsequent editions; so that the fame of our author rests at this moment on a thin *brochure;* a new illustration (we hope and believe) of Voltaire's assertion, that a heavy baggage is not necessary to enable an author to reach posterity. Be M. de Lamartine's chance for enduring fame what it may, he at least has the best security for the acceptance of his drafts, in not having exceeded a moderate extent of credit; and if he goes on as he has done hitherto, writing carefully and publishing sparingly, we think he runs little risk of the sentence of his own age being reversed by the time to come. This has pronounced him to be the first of the living poets of France; and we, at least, are well disposed to join our opinions to that oracular decree. His chief title to the first place is in the nature of his subjects, which are generally of the most elevated nature, and which have at once raised him above every reliance on support from the prejudices of mankind; and this distinctive trait is borne out by almost every one of his productions. There is throughout a startling tone of independence—a continued spurning of the trammels of academical rules—a hardy innovation nowhere else to be found in French poetry. His versification is quite original. Unlike the majority of his contemporaries, he never seems to look for models in his own language. His thoughts, in themselves of the boldest range, seek a clothing unknown to the limited formalities of the Academy. The brocaded and touped confinement, assorting well with the habits of a century back, would sit ill upon the muse of De Lamartine. She comes robed in a costume more suited to the region she inhabits. Cities and palaces are not the scenes of her resort. She wanders abroad in fields and forests; plunges into the mysteries of Nature; and sometimes, in a more ethereal ambition, wings her way into illimitable space. It is in flights like these that De Lamartine becomes occasionally vague and vapoury. Out of the sphere of common feelings, we "toil after him in vain;" and it is in his discursive reveries that he partakes the fate of writers of his stamp, who, seeking no sympathy from others, are left to their self-formed solitude.

It is, in fact, a hard effort for common readers, immersed in worldly pursuits and unfit for metaphysical wanderings, to mingle with the poet, whose meditations take so high a range. It requires a rare analogy in spirit to make a fellowship such as this; and did not our author appear before us with the proofs of deep reality in every line, we must infallibly attribute to an affected extravagance, much that we are convinced is the honest language of the heart. This is a distinction that supremely marks the poetry of De Lamartine. It bears the stamp of truth, which never can be counterfeited; and so much is nature evident throughout, that it presents those continual shiftings from abstract speculation to familiar feeling, which we apprehend are the best touchstones for distinguishing between art and nature in composition.

Religious sentiment with all its best associations, are the principal features in the "Méditations Poëtiques." We find, however, something more soothing to the heart in a tender and impassioned strain of affection, lavished on some real or imaginary object; in sweet descriptions of the face of nature; and many fine passages of sound philosophy. But the piety which blends in those verses with the warmest expression of love, seems to raise the passion to a height too great for common sympathy, and we are apt to think the expression too much refined; that none of the lees remain, which reason tell us to be inseparable from human passion; and from which the purest stream of mortal feeling can never be wholly cleared without being *over*strained. Tormented unceasingly by the involuntary desire to plunge into the secrets of nature, De Lamartine seems almost always oppressed by a mysterious inquietude. Thus his style is a continued mixture of elevation and melancholy. He has nevertheless contrived to avoid a dangerous rock, on which the reputation of an inferior writer would have infallibly split. In the continual utterance of thoughts relative to an unknown world, and abandoning himself to the language of faith mixed with conjecture, his style never wants precision, nor do his expressions savour of that vagueness which is the very spirit of his subject. His lines are always sonorous and full; and we are frequently astonished to find, on reaching the end, sufficient room for a sentiment or an image which does not, nevertheless, appear to overload the phrase. His rhyme is varied, and generally harmonious; and while among those daring turns which we think his greatest merit, many repetitions and other negligences may be found, his versification has no trace of effort, is highly energetic, rarely inflated, and never common-place.

Having said thus much in the way of general criticism, it now only remains for us to afford some short illustrations of our remarks, in specimens of this author's productions. The nature of our work, and indeed of our design, limits these within narrow bounds. We shall merely give the *Golfe de Baya*, near Naples, in the original; feeling how inadequate translation is, to afford a perfect exemplar of his style and merits.

*Le Golfe de Baya, près de Naples.*

" Vois-tu comme le flot paisible
   Sur le rivage vient mourir !
Vois-tu le volage zéphyr
   Rider, d'une haleine insensible,
L'onde qu'il aime à parcourir !
   Montons sur la barque légère
Que ma main guide sans efforts,
   Et de ce golfe solitaire
Rasons timidement les bords.

Loin de nous déjà fuit la rive.
Tandis qu'une main craintive

Tu tiens le docile aviron,
Courbé sur la rame bruyante
Au sein de l'onde frémissante.
Je trace un rapide sillon.

Dieu! quelle fraîcheur on respire!
Plongé dans le sein de Thétis,
Le soleil a cédé l'empire
A la pâle reine des nuits.
Le sein des fleurs demi-fermées
S'ouvre, et de vapeurs embaumées
En ce moment remplit les airs;
Et du soir la brise légère
Des plus doux parfums de la terre
A son tour embaume les mers.

Quels chants sur ces flots retentissent?
Quels chants éclatent sur ces bords?
De ces deux concerts qui s'unissent
L'écho prolonge les accords.
N'osant se fier aux étoiles,
Le pecheur, repliant ses voiles,
Salue en chantant son séjour.
Tandis qu'une folle jeunesse
Pousse au ciel des cris d'alégresse,
Et fête son heureux retour.

Mais déjà l'ombre plus épaisse
Tombe et brunit les vastes mers;
Le bord s'efface, le bruit cesse,
Le silence occupe les airs.
Ce l'heure où la mélancholie
S'asseoit pensive et recueillie
Aux bords silencieux des mers,
Et, méditant sur les ruines,
Contemple au penchant des collines
Ce palais, ces temples déserts.

O de la liberté vieille et sainte patrie!
Terre autrefois féconde en sublimes vertus!
Sous d'indignes Césars maintenant asservie,
Ton empire est tombé! tes héros ne sont plus!
    Mais dans ton sein l'ame agrandie
Croit sur leur monuments respirer leur génie,
Comme on respire encore dans un temple aboli
La Majesté du Dieu dont il etoit rempli.

          *       *       *       *       *

Colline de Baya! poétique séjour!
Voluptueux vallon, qu'habita tour-à-tour
    Tout ce qui fut grand dans le monde,
Tu ne retentit plus de gloire ni d'amour.
    Pas une voix qui me réponde,
    Que le bruit plaintif de cette onde,
Ou l'écho réveillé des débris d'alentour!"

Since the above paper was prepared for the press, we have seen two
very recent publications from the pen of M. de Lamartine, one entitled
*La Mort de Socrate;* the other a second volume of the "Méditations."
He *has* thus redeemed his pledge; and we can only now observe, that
these works have all the characteristic beauties and defects of his first
productions—highly imaginative and powerful passages, with lines prosaic and negligent in a remarkable degree. Had we seen these late

poems before our article was written, it would not have caused any variation in the observations there contained; so we have committed no injustice, either to our author or our readers. One thing has struck us as odd. "La Mort de Socrate" bears on its title-page the name A. Lamartine, the *de*, distinctive of nobility, being left out. We know not what this omission means; but it is rather curious to see De Béranger preserving this important particle, while he writes a poem *(Le Vilain)* disclaiming all pride in it; and his contemporary and rival discarding it silently in print, and even, as we have seen, in the signature by his proper hand. De Béranger always omits it in writing his name. It is not, after all, in either case an affair of much moment.

---

### TABLE TALK.—NO. IX.
#### *On Sitting for one's Picture.*

THERE is a pleasure in sitting for one's picture, which many persons are not aware of. People are coy on this subject at first, coquet with it, and pretend not to like it, as is the case with other venial indulgences, but they soon get over their scruples, and become resigned to their fate. There is a conscious vanity in it; and vanity is the *aurum potabile* in all our pleasures, the true *elixir* of human life. The sitter at first affects an air of indifference, throws himself into a slovenly or awkward position, like a clown when he goes a courting for the first time, but gradually recovers himself, attempts an attitude, and calls up his best looks, the moment he receives intimation that there is something about him that will do for a picture. The beggar in the street is proud to have his picture painted, and would almost sit for nothing: the finest lady in the land is as fond of sitting to a favourite artist as of seating herself before her looking-glass; and the more so, as the glass in this case is sensible of her charms, and does all it can to fix or heighten them. Kings lay aside their crowns to sit for their portraits, and poets their laurels to sit for their busts! I am sure, my father had as little vanity, and as little love for the art as most persons: yet when he had sat to me a few times (now some twenty years ago), he grew evidently uneasy when it was a fine day, that is, when the sun shone into the room, so that we could not paint; and when it became cloudy, began to bustle about, and ask me if I was not getting ready. Poor old room! Does the sun still shine into thee, or does Hope fling its colours round thy walls, gaudier than the rainbow? No, never, while thy oak-pannels endure, will they inclose such fine movements of the brain as passed through mine, when the fresh hues of nature gleamed from the canvass, and my heart silently breathed the names of Rembrandt and Correggio! Between my father's love of sitting and mine of painting, we hit upon a tolerable likeness at last; but the picture is cracked and gone; and *Megilp* (that bane of the English school) has destroyed as fine an old Nonconformist head as one could hope to see in these degenerate times.

The fact is, that the having one's picture painted is like the creation of another self; and that is an idea, of the repetition or reduplication of which no man is ever tired, to the thousandth reflection. It has been said that lovers are never tired of each other's company, because they are always talking of themselves. This seems to be the bond of connexion (a delicate one it is!) between the painter and the sitter—they are always thinking and talking of the same thing; the picture, in which their self-love finds an equal counter-part. There is always something to be done or to be altered, that touches that sensitive chord—this feature was not exactly hit off, something is wanting to the nose or to the eye-brows, it may perhaps be as well to leave out this mark, or that blemish, if it were possible to recall an expression that was remarked a short time before, it would be an indescribable advantage to the picture; a squint or a pimple on the face handsomely avoided may be a little of attachment ever after. He is no mean friend who conceals from ourselves, or only gently indicates, our obvious defects to the world. The sitter, by his repeated, minute, *fidgetty* inquiries about himself may be supposed to take an indirect and laudable method of arriving at self-knowledge; and the artist, in self-defence, is obliged to cultivate a scrupulous tenderness towards the feelings of his sitter, lest he should appear in the character of a spy upon him. I do not conceive there is a stronger call upon secret gratitude than the having made a favourable likeness of any one; nor a surer ground of jealousy and dislike than the having failed in the attempt. A satire or a lampoon in writing is bad enough; but here we look doubly foolish, for we are ourselves parties to the plot, and have been at considerable pains to give evidence against ourselves. I have never had a plaster cast taken of myself: in truth, I rather shrink from the experiment; for I know I should be very much mortified if it did not turn out well, and should never forgive the unfortunate artist who had lent his assistance to prove that I looked like a blockhead!

The late Mr. Opie used to remark that the most sensible people made the best sitters; and I incline to his opinion, especially as I myself am an excellent sitter. Indeed, it seems to me a piece of mere impertinence not to sit as still as one can in these circumstances. I put the best face I can upon the matter, as well out of respect to the artist as to myself. I appear on my trial in the court of physiognomy, and am as anxious to make good a certain idea I have of myself, as if I were playing a part on a stage. I have no notion, how people go to sleep, who are sitting for their pictures. It is an evident sign of want of thought and of internal resources. There are some individuals, all whose ideas are in their hands and feet—make them sit still, and you put a stop to the machine altogether. The volatile spirit of quicksilver in them turns to a *caput mortuum*. Children are particularly sensible of this constraint, from their thoughtlessness and liveliness. It is the next thing with them to wearing the fool's cap at school; yet they are proud of having their pictures taken, ask when they are to sit again, and are mightily pleased when they are done. Charles the First's children seem to have been good sitters, and the great dog sits like a Lord Chancellor.

The second time a person sits, and the view of the features is determined, the head seems fastened in an imaginary vice, and he can hardly tell what to make of his situation. He is continually overstepping the bounds of duty, and is tied down to certain lines and limits chalked out upon the canvas, to him "invisible or dimly seen"—on the throne where he is exalted. The painter has now a difficult task to manage—to throw in his gentle admonitions, " A little more this way, sir," or " You bend rather too forward, madam,"—and ought to have a delicate white hand, that he may venture to adjust a straggling lock of hair, or by giving a slight turn to the head, co-operate in the practical attainment of a position. These are the ticklish and tiresome places of the work, before much progress is made, where the sitter grows peevish and abstracted, and the painter more anxious and particular than he was the day before. Now is the time to fling in a few adroit compliments, or to introduce general topics of conversation. The artist ought to be a well-informed and agreeable man—able to expatiate on his art, and abounding in lively and characteristic anecdotes. Yet he ought not to talk too much, or to grow too animated; or the picture is apt to stand still and the sitter to be aware of it. Accordingly, the best talkers in the profession have not always been the most successful portrait-painters. For this purpose it is desirable to bring a friend, who may relieve guard, or fill up the pauses of conversation, occasioned by the necessary attention of the painter to his business, and by the involuntary reveries of the sitter on what his own likeness will bring forth ; or a book, a newspaper, or a portfolio of prints may serve to amuse the time. When the sitter's face begins to flag, the artist may then properly start a fresh topic of discourse, and while his attention is fixed on the graces called out by the varying interest of the subject, and the model anticipates, pleased and smiling, their being transferred every moment to the canvass, nothing is wanting to improve and carry to its height the amiable understanding and mutual satisfaction and good-will subsisting between these two persons, so happily occupied with each other !

Sir Joshua must have had a fine time of it with his sitters. Lords, ladies, generals, authors, opera-singers, musicians, the learned and the polite, besieged his doors, and found an unfailing welcome. What a rustling of silks ! What a fluttering of flounces and brocades ! What a cloud of powder and perfumes ! What a flow of periwigs ! What an exchange of civilities and of titles ! What a recognition of old friendships, and an introduction of new acquaintance and sitters ! It must, I think, be allowed that this is the only mode in which genius can form a legitimate union with wealth and fashion. There is a secret and sufficient tie in interest and vanity. Abstract topics of wit or learning do not furnish a connecting link : but the painter, the sculptor, come in close contact with the persons of the Great. The lady of quality, the courtier, and the artist, meet and shake hands on this common ground ; the latter exercises a sort of natural jurisdiction and dictatorial power over the pretensions of the first to external beauty and accomplishment, which produces a mild sense and tone of equality ; and the opulent sitter pays the taker of flattering likenesses handsomely for his trouble, which does not lessen the sympathy between them. There is even a satisfaction in paying down a high price for a picture—it seems as if one's head was worth something !— During the first sitting, Sir Joshua did little but chat with the new candidate for the fame of portraiture, try an attitude, or remark an expression. His object was to gain time, by not being in haste to commit himself, until he was master of the subject before him. No one ever dropped in but the friends and acquaintance of the sitter—it was a rule with Sir Joshua that from the moment the letter entered, he was at home—the room belonged to him—but what secret whisperings would there be among these, what confidential, inaudible communications! It must be a refreshing moment, when the cake and wine had been handed round, and the artist began again. He, as it were, by this act of hospitality assumed a new character, and acquired a double claim to confidence and respect. In the mean time, the sitter would perhaps glance his eye round the room, and see a Titian or a Vandyke hanging in one corner, with a transient feeling of scepticism whether he should make such a picture. How the ladies of quality and fashion must bless themselves from being made to look like Dr. Johnson or Goldsmith! How proud the first of these would be, how happy the last, to fill the same arm-chair where the Bunburys and the Hornecks had sat! How superior the painter would feel to them all! By "happy alchemy of mind," he brought out all their good qualities and reconciled their defects, gave an air of studious ease to his learned friends, or lighted up the face of folly and fashion with intelligence and graceful smiles. Those portraits, however, that were most admired at the time, do not retain their preeminence now: the thought remains upon the brow, while the colour has faded from the cheek, or the dress grown obsolete; and after all, Sir Joshua's best pictures are those of his worst sitters—*his Children.* They suited best with his unfinished style; and are like the infancy of the art itself, happy, bold, and careless. Sir Joshua formed the circle of his private friends from the élite of his sitters; and Vandyke was, it appears, on the same footing with him. When any of those noble or distinguished persons whom he has immortalised with his pencil, were sitting to him, he used to ask them to dinner, and afterwards it was their custom to return to the picture again, so that it is said that many of his finest portraits were done in this manner, ere the colours were yet dry, in the course of a single day. Oh! ephemeral works to last for ever!

Vandyke married a daughter of Earl Cowper, of whom there is a very beautiful picture. She was the Œnone, and he his own Paris. A painter of the name of Astley married a Lady ———, who sat to him for her picture. He was a wretched hand, but a fine person of a man, and a great coxcomb; and on his strutting up and down before the portrait when it was done with a prodigious air of satisfaction, she observed, "If he was so pleased with the copy, he might have the original." This Astley was a person of magnificent habits and a sumptuous taste in living; and is the same of whom the anecdote is recorded, that when some English students walking out near Rome were compelled by the heat to strip off their coats, Astley displayed a waistcoat with a huge waterfall, streaming down the back of it, which was a piece of one of his own canvasses that he had converted to this purpose. Sir Joshua fell in love with one of his fair sitters, a young and beautiful girl, who ran out one day in a great panic and confusion, hid her face in her companion's lap who was reading in an outer room, and said, "Sir Joshua had made her an offer!" This circumstance, perhaps, deserves mentioning the more, because there is a general idea that Sir Joshua Reynolds was a confirmed old bachelor. Goldsmith conceived a fruitless attachment to the same person, and addressed some passionate letters to her. Alas! it is the fate of genius to admire and to celebrate beauty, not to enjoy it! It is a fate, perhaps not without its compensations—

> " Had Petrarch gain'd his Laura for a wife,
>   Would he have written Sonnets all his life ?"

This distinguished beauty is still living, and handsomer than Sir Joshua's picture of her when a girl; and inveighs against the freedom of Lord Byron's pen with all the charming prudery of the last age.[*]

The relation between the portrait-painter and his amiable sitters is one of established custom : but it is also one of metaphysical nicety, and is a running *double entendre.* The fixing an inquisitive gaze on beauty, the heightening a momentary grace, the dwelling on the heaven of an eye, the losing one's-self in the dimple of a chin, is a dangerous employment. The painter may chance to slide into the lover—the lover can hardly turn painter. The eye indeed grows critical, the hand is busy: but are the senses unmoved? We are employed to transfer living charms to an inanimate surface; but they may sink into the heart by the way, and the nerveless hand be unable to carry its luscious burthen any further. St. Preux wonders at the rash mortal who had dared to trace the features of his Julia; and accuses him of insensibility without reason. Perhaps he too had an enthusiasm and pleasures of his own ! Mr. Burke, in his *Sublime and Beautiful,* has left a description of what he terms the most beautiful object in nature, the neck of a lovely and innocent female, which is written very much as if he had himself formerly painted this object, and sacrificed at this formidable shrine. There is no doubt that the perception of beauty becomes more exquisite (" till the sense aches at it") by being studied and refined upon as an object of art—it is at the same time fortunately neutralized by this means, or the painter would run mad. It is converted into an abstraction, an *ideal* thing, into something intermediate between nature and art, hovering between a living substance and a senseless shadow. The health and spirit that but now breathed from a speaking face, the next moment breathe with almost equal effect from a dull piece of canvass, and thus distract attention : the eye sparkles, the lips are moist there too ; and if we can fancy the picture alive, the face in its turn fades into a picture, a mere object of sight. We take rapturous possession with one sense, the eye ; but the artist's pencil acts as a non-conductor to the grosser desires. Besides, the sense of duty, of propriety interferes. It is not the question at issue : we have other work on our hands, and enough to do. Love is the product of ease and idleness : but the painter has an anxious, feverish, never-ending task, to rival the beauty, to which he dare not aspire even in thought, or in a dream of bliss. Paints and brushes are not " amorous toys of light-winged Cupid;" a rising sigh evaporates in the aroma of some fine oil-colour or varnish, a kindling blush is transfixed in a bed of vermilion on the palette. A blue vein meandering in a white wrist invites the hand to touch it : but it is better to proceed, and not spoil the picture.

---

[*] Sir Joshua may be thought to have studied the composition of his female portraits very coolly. There is a picture of his remaining of a Mrs. Symmons, who appears to have been a delicate beauty, pale, with a very little colour in her cheeks; but then to set off this want of complexion, she is painted in a snow-white satin dress, there is a white marble pillar near her, a white cloud over her head, and by her side stands one white lily.

The ambiguity becomes more striking in painting from the naked figure. If the wonder occasioned by the object is greater, so is the despair of rivalling what we see. The sense of responsibility increases with the hope of creating an artificial splendour to match the real one. The display of unexpected charms foils our vanity, and mortifies passion. The painting *A Diana and Nymphs* is like plunging into a cold bath of desire: to make a statue of a *Venus* transforms the sculptor himself to stone. The snow on the lap of beauty freezes the soul. The heedless, unsuspecting licence of foreign manners gives the artist abroad an advantage over ours at home. Sir Joshua Reynolds painted only the head of Iphigene from a beautiful woman of quality: Canova had innocent girls to sit to him for his Graces. I have but one other word to add on this part of the subject: if having to paint a delicate and modest female is a temptation to gallantry, on the other hand the sitting to a lady for one's picture is a still more trying situation, and amounts (almost of itself) to a declaration of love.

Landscape-painting is free from these tormenting dilemmas and embarrassments. It is as full of the feeling of pastoral simplicity and ease, as portrait-painting is of personal vanity and egotism. Away then with those incumbrances to the true liberty of thought—the sitter's chair, the bag-wig and sword, the drapery, the lay figure—and let us to some retired spot in the country, take out our portfolio, plant our easel, and begin. We are all at once shrouded from observation—

> "The world forgetting, by the world forgot!"

We enjoy the cool shade, with solitude and silence; or hear the dashing waterfall,

> "Or stock-dove plain amid the forest deep,
> That drowsy rustles to the sighing gale."

It seems almost a shame to do any thing, we are so well content without it; but the eye is restless, and we must have something to show when we get home. We set to work, and failure, or success, prompts us to go on. We take up the pencil, or lay it down again, as we please. We muse or paint, as objects strike our senses or our reflection. The perfect leisure we feel turns labour to a luxury. We try to imitate the grey colour of a rock, or of the bark of a tree: the breeze wafted from its broad foliage gives us fresh spirits to proceed, we dip our pencil in the sky, or ask the white clouds sailing over its bosom to sit for their pictures. We are in no hurry, and have the day before us. Or else, escaping from the close-embowered scene, we catch fading distances on airy downs, and seize on golden sunsets with the fleecy flocks glittering in the evening ray, after a shower of rain has fallen. Or from Norwood's ridgy heights, survey the snake-like Thames, or its smoke-crowned capital;

> "Think of its crimes, its cares, its pain,
> Then shield us in the woods again."

No one thinks of disturbing a landscape-painter at his task: he seems a kind of magician, the privileged genius of the place. Wherever a Claude, a Wilson has introduced his own portrait in the foreground of a picture, we look at it with interest (however ill it may be done), feeling that it is the portrait of one who was quite happy at the time, and how glad we should be to change places with him.

Mr. Burke has brought in a fine episode in one of his later works in allusion to Sir Joshua's portrait of Lord Keppel, and of some other friends, painted in their better days. The portrait is indeed a fine one, worthy of the artist and the critic, and perhaps recalls Lord Keppel's memory oftener than any other circumstance at present does. Portrait-painting is, in truth, a sort of cement of friendship, and a bias to history. Mr. C****r, of the Admiralty, the other day blundered upon some observations of mine relating to this subject, and made the House stare by asserting that portrait-painting was history or history portrait, as it happened, but went on to add, "That these gentlemen who had seen the ancient portraits lately exhibited in Pall-mall, must have been satisfied that they were strictly *historical;*" which showed that he knew nothing at all of the matter, and merely talked by rote. There was nothing historical in the generality of those portraits, except that they were portraits of people mentioned in history—there was no more of the spirit of history in them, which is *passive* or *active*, than in their dresses.

I was going to observe, that I think the reviving the recollection of our family and friends in our absence may be a frequent and strong inducement to sitting for our pictures, but that I believe the love of posthumous fame, or of continuing our memories after we are dead, has very little to do with it. And one reason I should give for that opinion is this, that we are not naturally very prone to dwell with pleasure on any thing that may happen in relation to us after we are dead, because we are not fond of thinking of death at all. We shrink equally from the contemplation of that fatal event or from any speculation on its consequences. The surviving ourselves in our pictures is but a poor consolation—it is rather adding mockery to calamity. The perpetuating our names in the wide page of history or to a remote posterity is a vague calculation, that takes out the immediate sting of mortality —whereas, we ourselves may hope to last (by a fortunate extension of the term of human life) almost as long as an ordinary portrait; and the wounds of lacerated friendship it heals must be still green, and our ashes scarcely cold. I think therefore that the looking forward to this mode of keeping alive the memory of what we were by lifeless hues and discoloured features, is not among the most approved consolations of human life, or favourite dalliances of the imagination. Yet I own I should like some part of me, as the hair or even nails, to be preserved entire, or I should have no objection to lie like Whitfield in a state of petrifaction. This smacks of the bodily reality at least—acts like a deception to the spectator, and breaks the fall from this "warm, kneaded motion to a clod"—from that to nothing—to the person himself. I suspect that the idea of posthumous fame, which has so unwelcome a condition annexed to it, loses its general relish as we advance in life, and that it is only when we are young, that we pamper our imaginations with this bait, with a sort of impunity. The reversion of immortality is then so distinct, that we may talk of it without much fear of entering upon possession: death is itself a fable—a sound that dies upon our lips; and the only certainty seems the only impossibility. Fame, at that romantic period, is the first thing in our mouths and death the last in our thoughts

## STANZAS

To the memory of the Spanish Patriots latest killed, in resisting
the Regency and the Duke of Angoulême.

BRAVE men who at the Trocadero fell—
Beside your cannons conquer'd not, though slain,
There is a victory in dying well
For Freedom,—and ye have not died in vain,
For come what may, there shall be hearts in Spain
To honour, ay embrace your martyr'd lot,
Cursing the Bigot's and the Bourbon's chain,
And looking on your graves, though trophied not,
As holier, hallow'd ground, than priests could make the spot!

What though your cause be baffled—freemen cast
In dungeons—dragg'd to death, or forced to flee;
Hope is not wither'd in affliction's blast;—
The patriot's blood's the seed of Freedom's tree:
And short your orgies of revenge shall be,
Cowl'd Demons of the Inquisitorial cell;
Earth shudders at your victory,—for ye
Are worse than common fiends from Heaven that fell,
The baser, ranker sprung, *Autochthones* of hell!

Go to your bloody rites again;—bring back
The hall of horrors and the assessor's pen,
Recording answers shriek'd upon the rack;—
Smile o'er the gaspings of spine-broken men:—
Preach, perpetrate damnation in your den;—
Then let your altars, ye blasphemers, peal,
With thanks to Heaven that let you loose again,
To practise deeds with torturing fire and steel
No eye may search—no tongue may challenge or reveal.

Yet laugh not in your carnival of crime
Too loudly, ye oppressors—Spain was free,
Her soil has felt the foot-prints, and her clime
Been winnow'd by the wings of Liberty;
And these even parting scatter as they flee
Thoughts—influences, to live in hearts unborn,
Opinions that shall wrench the prison key
From Persecution—show her mask off-torn,
And tramp her bloated head beneath the foot of Scorn.

Glory to them that die in this great cause!
Kings, Bigots, can inflict no brand of shame,
Or shape of death, to shroud them from applause:—
No, manglers of the martyr's earthly frame,
Your hangmen-fingers cannot touch his fame.
Still in your prostrate land there shall be some
Proud hearts, the shrines of Freedom's vestal flame;
Long trains of ill may pass unheeded, dumb,
But vengeance is behind, and justice is to come.

## FELLOW TRAVELLERS.

"And do you travel alone?" is a question that has often been proposed to me in a tone of surprise mixed with remonstrance, when I
have opened the project, or described the past incidents, of a journey in which I had no companion. Accident, or the humour of the
moment, have in general been the best reasons I could adduce, and
perhaps they are as solid ones as most people can assign for their practice in matters of the like importance. But the kind objector is seldom
satisfied with this reply, for he thinks (though perhaps he is too polite
to say) that a man who rambles forth without any comrade, must be very
fastidious, or very unfortunate in his acquaintance. I certainly do not
fall within the latter predicament; and if the first imputation be well
founded, I may claim some excuse as an old traveller, (not to say an
elderly man,) who has, either by choice or chance, associated with way-
farers of almost every character, who knows well how the pleasures of
travel and the enjoyments of society may, under propitious circumstances, enhance and recommend each other, but who has also tasted
pretty largely of the mortifications that arise in this, as in greater undertakings, from an ill-judged alliance.

If society be requisite on a journey of pleasure, it will be generally
agreed that company on a very large scale is not always advantageous
to such an expedition. Whether six or six-and-twenty persons go to
Blackwall together for the purpose of eating white-bait, is, perhaps,
not very material as a question of sentiment; but I would not willingly
join a pic-nic party under Stonehenge, or appoint a rendezvous of carriages on the quiet margin of Grasmere. Our Northern neighbours,
indeed, have established a steam-boat on Loch Lomond, and the passengers are regularly disembogued where they may take a view of
Rob Roy's cave: a very business-like arrangement, by which twenty
families at once may be booked for a day's felicity, and enraptured,
pursuant to contract, at so much per head; children, I suppose, at
half-price. Most persons will say that the promoters of this undertaking have rather signalized their commercial activity than the delicacy of their taste; and yet, if the steam-boat enthusiasts are mistaken
in their mode of paying homage to Nature, they do but err a little
more palpably than the multitude of prouder tourists, who pour their
"select parties" upon every sequestered and romantic country in more
aristocratical conveyances. I suppose there is no sober solitary traveller who cannot, like myself, remember some provoking occasion,
when his reveries have been put to flight by these gregarious pilgrims
of Nature. I had once established myself very luxuriously at a small,
convenient inn, standing by itself in the wilds of Cardiganshire, and
was listening to the melody of some neighbouring waterfalls, among
which I proposed to spend a long summer's evening, when suddenly a
different sound broke in upon my meditations; a rumbling of wheels
was heard, and, with infinite bustle and commotion, there arrived at the
inn-door, two carriages, a gig, and three horsemen. The party alighted: four ladies, an old gentleman and two young ones, two little
boys, a valet-de-chambre, two grooms, a lady's maid, a poodle, and a
couple of terriers. The gentlemen claimed an old watering-place acquaintance with me, and were polite enough to think it a piece of good

fortune that we should see "the Falls" in each other's company. A vast deal of arrangement, however, and enquiring, and expostulation with the people of the house, was to be gone through before the Falls obtained any share of attention ; nor were our thoughts and conversation of a very romantic character when we at last set out for the cascades. One of the horses had suffered a strain ; a bottle of fish-sauce had been forgotten ; the boys would not keep in their mother's sight ; and an old maid, who had been studying Malkin's Tour, strove vigorously to convince our Welsh guide that he had taken the wrong path. When we came to the waterfalls, the old gentleman was disappointed, the mamma was frightened, the maiden lady, armed with note-book and ink-horn, occupied the foreground of the view ; the young men spouted parodies of Gray's Bard, and the terriers hunted a rat. As for me, my companions, as I have since heard, discovered me to be a peevish old bachelor, and to have no taste for romantic scenery.

It is the common misfortune of travelling parties, to be clogged with some unblest spirit, who by the peculiarity of his humour, or by some undefinable fatality, never fails to blight the enjoyment and damp the cordiality of his associates. The perfection of this character consists, not in a mere passive sullenness (like my own upon the occasion I just mentioned), but in a wakeful, assiduous, and self-complacent ill-nature. Men of this disposition are particularly fond of travelling in company, and they are just such companions as the "Little Master," who followed Sintram through the haunted valley, or the Dæmon in the Ars Moriendi, who besets a gentleman with the kind suggestion—"Interficias teipsum." He is the most diligent of travellers ; he scrupulously sees every thing, and sees only to disapprove : like a dog that ranges far and wide for objects of curiosity, and bestows the same mark of contempt on all.

In a journey I once made with some friends through Switzerland, I was, by evil hap, induced to wait upon a gentleman of this humour with a letter of introduction. We were proceeding to the celebrated Lake of the four Cantons, and he, with great politeness, offered to bear us company, and afford us the benefit of his local knowledge. He entertained us, at starting, with a careful enumeration of the things we should *not* see to advantage at this particular time. The morning was undeniably fine, and one of our boatmen expatiated on its splendour with a profusion of bad French and bad German, till our friend put him to silence by telling him, with a sneer, that if he had the day to sell, he had better leave off puffing and name his price. The skies, as if resenting this affront, became overcast, and a drizzling rain attacked us, re-inforced by icy blasts from between the mountains. We had proposed to visit several places adjoining the lake, which are connected in tradition with the romantic history of William Tell and the Austrian governor ; and our kind cicerone insisted that we could see all these spots as well in the worst weather (which he owned we were but too likely to encounter) as in clear sunshine. On, therefore, we went, and our companion, though drenched and chilled like ourselves, and exposed, with us, to some slight danger, became, after his manner, perfectly joyous, and expatiated eloquently upon the sublime piles of rock, the magnificent Alpine vistas, and the variety of lake prospects that *might* have been visible at each point of our course, if the clouds had not circumscribed our view. With inexorable complaisance he insisted on escorting us to every spot marked out in our morning's plan, though he confessed they did not deserve so much pains; and as to William Tell, he laboured both long and learnedly to convince us that the adventures of that worthy were at least half fabulous; that it was probable he never slew Gesler at all; that if he did slay Gesler, there was not so much merit in the affair as people imagined; and that, for any thing we knew, neither Tell nor Gesler had ever come within a league of the places we were examining. He dismissed us, at the end of the day, in a state of chagrin and dissatisfaction, which became absolute dismay when he told us that he proposed making such arrangements as would enable him to accompany us in our journey to the Alps of Berne. We exclaimed with one voice that we could not possibly remain another day, and we precipitately quitted his neighbourhood the next morning. He came to bid us farewell, and, when he saw us actually on the road, very cordially expressed his regret that we could not devote a little more time to the lake, since it never appeared to so much advantage as the day after a fall of rain.

I lately made a short journey in the West of England with one of these amiable humourists; a man remarkable for a very sweet voice, an ungracious smile, and a malevolent near-sighted eye. His practice was, if any object drew the admiration of his companions, to disparage it by introducing some superior wonder of the same kind which he had visited in his travels, I believe for the sole purpose of mortifying those who had not. " My good Sir," he would ask, in a scornfully compassionate tone, " have you seen Palermo? Have you been in the Crimea? Have you ever happened to look into the port of Scio?"—" My good Sir," said he to an honest Somersetshire gentleman, who had led us to a prospect of uncommon beauty and extent, " did you ever see Cintra?" At the same moment he stepped backward and fell into a deep dry ditch; the western man assisted him in getting out, and seeing that he fretted and bustled, and endeavoured to magnify the accident, addressed him in his own phrase and manner, " My good Sir! did you ever tumble down Chedder cliffs?"

A fellow-traveller of this disposition is a wasting disease, and should be shunned accordingly. But there is a contrary habit of mind which a splenetic man finds almost as difficult to tolerate, though it is connected, no doubt, with honest and amiable qualities—I mean that proneness to wonder and be delighted without any known reason; which is usually a sign of great animal spirits and very little experience. I had once passed through Berwick with a gentleman of this lively character, very early in a dark and cheerless morning; the road is celebrated as one of the dullest in Great Britain, and I had carefully composed myself to sleep. Suddenly my friend recollected that we had crossed the Tweed; he sprang up, thrust his head out of both the carriage-windows, and then shouted aloud, " Well, Sir, we are in Scotland! Scotland—' land of the mountain and the flood, land of my sires!' (he was an Essex man)—And it really is a romantic country— you do not see Nature on such a scale as this in England! Tell me candidly whether it equals your expectations." I saw a flat, open country, adorned with one cottage, two or three stone dykes, and a few patches of oats. " It is night and I am alone," (sang my companion,)

" forlorn on the hill of storms."—" I wish you were, from my soul," was my peevish answer.  A pedlar came up and asked our driver if we had met the mail; which incident threw my friend into a new rapture at the originality of the Scottish character.—I was a fellow-passenger of the same gentleman in an Ostend packet; he appeared on deck for the first time when·he heard that we could see our place of destination. " Ostend! ay, there it is.  A wonderfully strong place!  Ostend, that cost the Spaniards seventy thousand men in one siege.  And I do not doubt it at all.  Any body may see that it is one of the finest fortified towns in Europe!" I borrowed his telescope, and found we were just near enough to distinguish half a dozen house-tops, three windmills, and a bank of sand.

This unreflecting eagerness to admire is a very innocent error when it extends only to an idle wondering at inanimate objects, the appearances of nature, or the exhibitions of art: but it is more than ridiculous, it is a source of incalculable dangers, when it leads the travelling novice to adopt false estimates of human character; to fashion his conduct after depraved models, and to draw his information from disreputable sources.  I could illustrate this reflection by the history of a simple, sanguine young Englishman, my relation, whom I last saw at Heidelberg, cultivating a thin crop of mustachios, and a wiry handful of flaxen tresses, with a view of entering the University; his imagination being captivated by the habits and manners of the Teutonic youth. Some time before, he was at Aix-la-Chapelle, compiling·a history of Bonaparte's return to France in 1815, from the information of a Colonel Count L'Escroc, (or some such name,) who professed to know all the secrets of that amazing enterprise, and to have enjoyed peculiar opportunities of observing it in all its stages.  The Colonel was so pleased with my kinsman that he concealed nothing from him, not even his own pecuniary difficulties.  In a little time it began to be rumoured at the Redoubt, that M. L'Escroc was neither Count nor Colonel, and that his alleged opportunity of watching the transactions between France and Elba in 1815, consisted in his having resided at that time on board the gallies at Toulon.  My novice of course took measures to rid himself of his noble acquaintance, and desired the return of a sum of money for which the Colonel had consented to " become his banker;" the Colonel sent for answer a note of hand enclosed in a challenge, and we never heard of him more.  Again I found my foolish relation at Naples, affecting to talk mysteriously of his *liaison* with a literary Marchioness, a robust elderly woman, or, as he expressed it, a matronly specimen of Italian beauty, who taught him to recite sonnets in a vile Neapolitan dialect, and persuaded him that he was wearing the chains of another Corinne.  The poor youth imagined himself an accomplished wit and debauchee, and assumed a sheepish swagger, while he barbarously mouthed the old saying, *Inglese italianato è diavolo incarnato.*

But I forbear to dwell upon adventures of this kind, as they belong to a more extensive subject, and are connected with a more serious train of reflection than I have undertaken to deal with in the present trifling disquisition.  Such anecdotes would be appropriate to a different kind of work, which I should gladly see commenced, a modern Gull's Hornbook for the use of British travellers on the Continent.

There is not a more common source of disagreement between asso-elated in a tour of pleasure, than their different opinions with respect to the time and pains which ought to be bestowed on objects of curiosity. I myself am a leisurely traveller, but I was compelled in mere despair to abandon my old friend Job Furlong, who persuaded me a few years ago to make a journey with him in the north and west of France. Our intended route was through Normandy, Brittany, along the Loire, and so to Paris, where we were to consider how the rest of our time should be disposed of. After we had lingered three days at Dieppe, I was obliged to dislodge him by stratagem before he had half completed his inventory of remarkable things in the church of St. Remy. This caused him so many regrets that I did not venture to rebel while we hovered eight and forty hours about Neuchâtel and the Château d'Arques. On the ninth day we arrived at Rouen, and in three more we had taken a particular survey of the custom-house, the great clock-tower, the Marché-neuf, and seven of the principal fountains; and we had actually digested a plan for viewing the cathedral. It then occurred to me to calculate the time we were likely to spend in surveying the whole city, and I found that with good health, fine weather, and unabated activity, our task would probably engage us thirteen weeks. I represented this to my companion, who very calmly took the spectacles from his nose and the pen from his ear, and mildly answered that he had already been hurried more than was consistent either with health or with improvement; adding, in his quaint way, that travelling was one thing and steeple-hunting another, that he did not come into France to gallop over it like a Cossack, that he considered a foreign country as a book, and he, for one, would not turn the leaf till he had finished the page. Upon this explanation we parted; I left him, one fine day in September, pondering and pensive on the bridge of boats, and on the bridge of boats I found him again when I returned through Rouen from the tour we had proposed making together. He had by this time conquered six of eleven departments into which he had divided the remarkable objects of the city, but as winter was now beginning, he agreed to suspend his operations and return with me to England. Twice again did Job cross over to Normandy, and still the bridge of boats formed the boundary of his excursions; at last, in a moment of energy, upon a fourth visit, he boldly pushed across the Seine and proceeded as far as Evreux, but precipitately retraced his steps on recollecting that he had always omitted, while at Rouen, to taste the mineral spring of St. Paul. He had not finished criticising the smack of this water when he discovered a capital mistake in his measurement of the butter-tower; and in rectifying this, he was led to make some further speculations on the famous bell, said to be the largest in Europe, except one which is or was at Moscow. "When I complete my tour of the Continent," said Mr. Furlong, "I shall, of course see Moscow; and it is a satisfaction to judge for oneself, even between two pieces of bell-metal." Winter, as usual, found him in the midst of his labours, and he carried home his note-book enriched with a voluminous supplement, and seven divisions of new queries, to be resolved on the next excursion.

But I prefer even the conscientious plodding of my friend Job, to the senseless activity of persons who flit from object to object, without taste or even curiosity, in a rapid and business-like discharge of what they conceive to be their duty as gentlemen on their travels. I refused to dine with an Englishman at Paris, who told me (in a jargon which he affected) that he had " done" the picture-gallery of the Louvre in five hours and thirty-seven minutes without missing a number, and would engage to " knock off" the marbles in half that time. And I have never felt duly grateful for the hospitality of a well-meaning city gentleman, who once, when I was very young, insisted on my taking a corner of his carriage from Mayence to Dusseldorf. " I will shew you all the fine scenery of the Rhine," he said, " for I go this way on purpose, and I make it a point to miss nothing in travelling." To do him justice, we made easy journeys, and fared sumptuously. A servant was always sent on early to the place where we proposed resting for the night, and my friend piqued himself on arriving as punctually to dinner as if he had only driven down to his own house at Tooting. He carried with him what he called a " *rout*;" a written list of the objects and places to be noticed in each stage; and it was evidently the greatest pleasure he enjoyed, to cross out the names with his pencil, as we despatched the successive portions of our task. He never allowed a halt but with manifest uneasiness, except once, when we drew up to the inn-door at Bacharach to taste the wine. " Stop," he would say reluctantly to the postilion—" but you need not dismount. What is that town with the castle ?"—" Caub." " And that odd building in the middle of the river ?"—" The Pfalz." " And that high place with the fortification ?"—"The Rheinfels." " Drive on—be brisk. Come, we have seen Caub," (striking out the names as he spoke) "Pfalz, and Rheinfels, and we have only lost three minutes and a half—too much time—but it takes so long to make these Germans move again if they once stop." At Coblentz (which was one of our resting-places) I suggested that we should cross the river to visit the renowned fortress of Ehrenbreitstein. " Why," said he, " we saw it for a good quarter of an hour as we walked up that hill to the Chartreuse." " But that was such a distant view." " Well—stay—they will be ten minutes putting the horses to—run down to the water-side and look at it, and you shall have my telescope." When we approached the celebrated Seven Mountains, we were told that two of the eminences before us were Drachenfels and Rolandseck; both scenes of romantic legend. " And which is Drachenfels," said I, " and which Rolandseck ?" " What does it matter?" answered my companion, " we are sure we see them both:" And thus did we pass through the scenery of the Rhine, that

> " Blending of all beauties ; streams and dells,
> Fruit, foliage, crag, wood, corn-field, mountain, vine,
> And chief-less castles breathing stern farewells
> From gray but leafy walls, where Ruin greenly dwells."

It was my fortune many years afterwards to meet the same gentleman a second time on the banks of the Rhine. We encountered each other at Cologne. He had just been " seeing," in his manner, all the notable things of this ancient city, from the skulls of the three Wise Men to the rival manufactories of scented water, and had completed his task within a quarter of an hour of dinner-time. I asked him whether he had seen the famous Crucifixion of St. Peter, one of the masterpieces of Rubens, lately replaced in the church for which it was originally painted. He had not heard of it, and far from receiving the suggestion with pleasure, he looked at me with as much mortification as if I had told him of a great loss at sea, or an elopement in his family. " Well," he said at last, " I suppose I must see the picture. I am sure I thank you for mentioning it. How far did you say it was to the church? You are certain the painting was in the Louvre? So unlucky! the thing happening at this time of day. Well! it is useless to say more. You know I am an enthusiast for Rubens—have a Rubens myself at Tooting." So the poor gentleman bustled away to St. Peter's Church, and I charitably followed to assist him in his homage to the Fine Arts. We arrived; he entered with his watch in his hand, and made directly for the altar. The great picture is concealed from view by an imperfect copy which supplied its place while the original Crucifixion was detained at Paris: the visitor is allowed at first to cast his eyes upon the rude imitation, which is then withdrawn, and discloses one of the most astonishing works achieved by modern art. My friend, however, did not wait for this shifting of scenes; he briskly walked up to the external canvass—" Ah!" he cried, " a very fine thing indeed! Rubens all over! Ten minutes past six, I declare. Well, I am glad I have seen the Rubens." And without waiting for remonstrance or explanation, he fled the church as precipitately as if the painted executioners had been alive and marking him out for their next victim.

A worthy Londoner whom I once met at the Lakes was as much a man of business as my good friend of the Rhine, and carried his love of method still farther. We had passed each other on the banks of Windermere, and I had begun to climb a hill near Bowness, which seemed likely to afford an extensive view of the surrounding region. I had mastered two-thirds of the ascent (which in a sultry summer's day was no light task), when I observed my acquaintance looking after me in a violent fret and agitation, and I presently perceived that he had sent his servant to overtake me. The man begged I would come back and speak to his master. I returned. " Sir," said the good citizen (who was a plump, fatherly man, and evidently overheated with anxiety on my account,)—" Sir, you must excuse the liberty I am taking; but I believe you have not seen this book. I have travelled all round the Lakes, Sir, with it in my hand, and it has saved me from many mistakes, such as you were about to make just now— Sir, do you know you were going to Station V. before you had been at Station IV.? Look what the book says—' Station IV. Rawlinson's-nab is a peninsular rock of a circular figure, swelling to a crown in the centre.'" I believe, in the first energy of my reply I sent my kind monitor and his book, and Rawlinson's-nab—farther than was consistent with strict politeness; and I shut myself up in my inn, determined not to leave it till he had gone the round of his stations according to the rubrick, and finally evacuated the country.

My recollections would supply many other sketches of travelling society, but I pause for the present, lest the reader should refuse to proceed any farther in mine. If we part in kindness now, he will perhaps resume the subject with me hereafter.

## ON LIEUTENANT HOOD. *

The Briton lies low on a wreath of snow,
  From his Island home afar,
And the bright ice sheets and the wild storm sleets
  Round the rest of the gallant tar.

He had spread his sail to the Arctic gale,
  On a course that no mortal knew;
With a spirit brave he had plough'd the wave,
  While the freezing tempest blew.

Where the flinty North sends its terrors forth,
  And life is in man alone—
Where the insect that plays in the short summer rays
  Is in winter a thing of stone.†—

There long had he been, and with wonder seen
  In a circle the sun career,
And flash through the night in his radiance bright
  In the June of the Polar year.

And a wintry night by the snow-beams' light
  He had worn for dull weeks away,
And the north lights had shed on his hardy head
  Their gleam, in day's mockery.

And his task was o'er, and he sought the shore—
  The shore of his native Isle:
And his bold heart burn'd, as he homeward turn'd,
  At the thought of its green fields' smile.

And he counted with joy that his brave employ
  Had won him his Country's praise :
And he fondly dream'd, as the prospect gleam'd,
  On an hour of toil-purchased ease.

And cheerful he past over antres vast,
  While the deep snow hid the ground,
At night 'twas his bed, and pillow'd his head
  Mid the horrors reigning round.

But the famine came, and he dragg'd his frame,
  Hunger-stung and wearily,
Over morass and stone of that frozen zone,
  To his cold log hut to die.

They have laid him there in their hearts' despair,
  Where the stunted pine-trees grow,
Where alone the sky with blue canopy
  Covers the bold heart low.—

Where no breath is heard—where no wing of bird
  Cleaves the desolate atmosphere ;
Where the softest sound is a thunder-bound
  In the hush of the fear-struck air.

Oh there he is laid !—but no time shall shade
  The worth of his honest name :—
Though the life of the brave may set dark in the grave,
  There's a dawn for their glorious fame!

                                J.

---

* See Captain Franklin's Narrative of his Journey to the Polar Sea.

† Insects, such as spiders and others, are frozen hard during the Polar winters, and may be thrown about like stones without injury. On being brought to a fire, they recover animation, and move their limbs as actively as in the summer season.

## ON THE CHARACTER OF LOUIS XI.

Louis XI. to whom the public attention has lately been drawn in "Quentin Durward," like most of those men of extensive power and extraordinary character in whose hands lay the fate of nations, has been variously represented by historians. Some have confined themselves to a recapitulation of his cruelties, his treacheries, his tyrannical conduct, his superstitious practices, and the sad and desolate termination of his career; while others appear to have been more struck by his fortitude, his prudence in the conduct of the important enterprises he undertook, the success of his efforts in abolishing the power of the great vassals of the crown, augmenting the royal prerogative, and aggrandizing France. Under this last point of view, that country has been more indebted to him than to any other of her monarchs; for he augmented her territory and influence by the important addition of the Duchy of Burgundy and the States of Provence, Anjou, and Maine. Amongst those who were nearest his person, and in whom he most confided, he has found an admirer in Philip de Comines, who has held him up to posterity as almost an excellent king. Duclos, also, who, though historiographer, possessed independence of mind and elevation of character enough to dissuade him from any false adulation, towards at least a deceased monarch, concludes the two volumes of his Memoirs of Louis XI. in these words.

"Although Louis XI. was far from being without reproach (for few monarchs have deserved more severe ones), yet it may be said that he was celebrated equally for his virtues as his vices, and all things considered that he was a *king*."

Notwithstanding this grave dictum, it is not unreasonable to doubt, whether the talismanic word *king* be possessed of such sovereign virtue as to obliterate the deep-dyed crimes which stain the character of this despot. Fenelon, whose candour and rectitude of mind furnished him with no other criterion for judging of kings than the happiness or misery of the people under their sway, represents Louis XI. in his Dialogues of the Dead, " as a wicked and ferocious being, the scourge of mankind." The virtuous prelate puts the following bitter reproaches into the mouth of the Cardinal de la Balue, who was very little less of a villain than his master.

"The fundamental maxim of all those counsels, which you (Louis XI.) took such pains to instil into those that surrounded you, was, that every thing they could do was to be done for you, and you alone. You reckoned as nothing the princes of your blood; nor the Queen, whom you kept at a distance from you and in captivity; nor the Dauphin, whom you had brought up in ignorance and confinement; nor the kingdom, which you desolated by your harsh and cruel policy—the interests of which were always sacrificed to the jealousy of your tyrannous authority. You even set no value upon your most devoted favourites and ministers, whom you made use of merely to deceive others. You never had the least affection for, nor put the least confidence in any one of them, unless when driven to it by the utmost necessity. It was your delight to deceive them in their turn, as you had employed them to deceive others; and they were sure to become your victims on the slightest umbrage, or when the most trifling benefit could result to you from their destruction. There was not a moment of security for any one within your sphere. You played with the lives of men. You never loved a human being,—how then could you expect that any one should love you

You delighted to deceive every one,—how could you hope then that any one should confide in you from motives of esteem or friendship! Such disinterested fidelity, where was it to have been learned? Did you deserve it, or dared you to hope for it? Could it have been practised towards you, or within the precincts of your court? Was it possible to preserve an upright and sincere heart for the space of eight days passed under your influence? Were we not forced to be scoundrels the moment we approached you? Were we not declared villains by the very circumstance of gaining your favour, as the only way of attaining it was by villainy? Those who wished to preserve their honour untouched, and their conscience unstained, took care to keep far away from you. They would have gone to the remotest bounds of the earth sooner than live in your service."

Voltaire has, with his usual perspicacity, distinguished in the character of Louis XI. those traits which may claim the approbation of posterity, from those which are calculated only to excite their horror; he remarks,

"The life of Louis XI. offers a most singular contrast; and as if for the purpose of humiliating and confounding virtue, we are obliged to regard as a great king, a being whom history has handed down to us as an unnatural son, a barbarous brother, an unkind husband, a bad father, and a perfidious neighbour. He filled with bitterness the last years of his father's life, and was the cause of his death. The unfortunate Charles VII. as is well known, died through fear of being made away with by his son; he chose starving himself to death to being poisoned by his own child! The mere dread of such an event by a father, proves that the son was at least considered capable of perpetrating so horrible a crime."

Duclos also proves, in a more detailed manner, that the conduct of this prince exhibited qualities of the most opposite and conflicting nature: at one time giving way to the impulses of cruelty, pride, jealousy, and vindictiveness, while at another he acted with perfect *bonhommie*, trusting confidence and even kindness. An author of the present day, Dumesnil, in a work on Louis XI. has hazarded the surmise, that the extreme mistrust observable in Charles VII. and the sombre melancholy and cruelty of Louis XI. had come to them with their blood as descendants of Charles VI. who had fallen into a state of complete mental alienation, in the paroxysms of which he shewed himself equally suspicious and cruel. It may be that Charles VI. left this "heritage of woe" to his descendants: a surmise that becomes the more probable when we examine with attention, the last years of the life of Louis XI. When, shut up in the chateau of Plessis les Tours, and hemmed in by numerous guards, he was terrified by the appearance of every new face; when he delivered over to the murderous hands of his executioner and favourite Tristan the Hermit, those who, however innocent, excited his suspicions, whilst he sought to dissipate his thick-coming fancies and black melancholy, by viewing from the walls of the chateau the simple dances and amusements of the shepherds and villagers; when he had recourse to all the relics that it was possible to procure; when he caused himself to be anointed from head to foot with the oil of the *holy Ampoule*, kept at Rheims, in order to prolong his life; when he conferred the title of Countess of Bologne upon the Virgin Mary; when he drank the blood of young children, in order to renovate his strength and bring back his youthful vigour;—when, I repeat, we think upon these facts, we can scarcely hesitate to recognize a taint of insanity in the singular compound of this monarch's mind, similar to that with which Charles VI. was afflicted. It is, at all events, the only, or at least the best excuse, that can be offered in his favour. However, Charles VI. did not display these propensities before the period of his madness; while on the contrary, Louis XI., during the full vigour of his faculties mental and corporeal, while he was conceiving and executing vast and well-organized plans for the aggrandisement of his power, shewed himself always suspicious, false, treacherous, and cruel. A certain portion of this cruelty must, in fairness, be put to the account of the barbarity of the times in which he lived; few if any of the princes of that period being exempt from charges of this nature. Knowing or employing no other means than terror and cruelty to quell the turbulence of their subjects, they took vengeance for barbarous insurrections by still more barbarous punishments. In the long struggle between Louis and Charles the Bold, the famous Duke of Burgundy, a struggle which renders the annals of this reign so interesting, we are presented with a regular trial of skill between the bad faith, treachery, and cruelty of the two rivals. It has been pretended that Charles the Bold was naturally good and generous, and that it was the vices of Louis XI. that forced him to adopt the use of similar weapons. But this, we think, is giving too great an extension to charitable surmise. It would be a strange effect of rivalry to make Charles thus adopt the crimes and bad qualities of his adversary. A more reasonable supposition is, that the unprincipled and atrocious conduct of both was the result of the savage sentiments so generally prevalent at that period, pushed to excess under the baleful influence of violent passions and uncontrolled power.

Dumesnil, who has been already cited, has remarked some extraordinary coincidences between the lives of Louis XI. and Tiberius. The commencement of the career of both these princes began by a long exile. Louis at the court of Burgundy practised an equal degree of dissimulation with Tiberius during his sojourn at Rhodes. They were both equally addicted to astrology, and put a like faith in superstitious practices and relics. They were both equally anxious to avoid war, not from motives of humanity, but that they considered the conquests or acquirements made by political intrigue, as reflecting more personal credit upon them, and the honour of which they were not obliged to divide with their military forces. After a harsh and tyrannous reign, both these princes precipitately retired into seclusion, and sought to shun the sight of their subjects, except those chosen from amongst them to be immolated as victims before their eyes. It is also said, that Louis, like Tiberius, divided the last hours of his existence between alternate debaucheries and cruelties. Notwithstanding these points of resemblance, these two tyrants are widely distinguished from each other by the different motives of their dissimulation, their cruelty, and their seclusion. The moving principle of Tiberius was, hatred and scorn of mankind; that of Louis, an insatiable love of sway. The latter retired into seclusion for the purpose of building up an artificial power, capable of resisting the approaches of old age and infirmities. He confounded and astonished the neighbouring princes by the rapidity of his negotiations, by the number of ambassadors and political agents that he sought to multiply in foreign courts. When there was no treaty on the tapis to countenance their presence, he took care to employ them in administering to his fancies or caprices. He sent agents all over Europe to purchase the most celebrated coursers and the rarest dogs. Sweden and Denmark were put under contribution for the wild beasts of their forests; lions and leopards were brought at an immense expense from the burning deserts of Africa. Nothing was talked of but the magnificence and spirit of the monarch: which was the object he had in view, as he was desirous of concealing the approaches of death by the affectation of youthful sports and caprices.[*] This pretended trait of policy may, however, have been nothing more than an access of folly that developed itself in solitude. Happy would it be for their people, if the follies of kings were only exhibited in such harmless vagaries. It is, however, certain that a remorse of conscience weighed heavily upon Louis towards the close of his life, and this might have been one of the means he employed to escape from it. He ordered an enquiry to be made, whether his subordinate agents had not abused the powers intrusted to them: a rather extraordinary scruple on the part of a prince who had delivered thousands of his subjects into the hands of the hangman. He exhorted the parliament to be less free in receiving accusations. About the same time he made a bargain for his monument with Conrad de Cologne, a goldsmith, and Laurence Wear, a brass-founder, to whom he engaged to pay a thousand golden crowns. And in order that his bust might be an accurate resemblance of him in his best days, he ordered the artists to examine his former portraits, and add from them whatever old age might have altered or effaced in his features.

Some modern authors, in seeking an excuse to extenuate the crimes of Louis XI., have chosen rather untenable ground for their approbation. Duclos, for instance, asserts, that Louis XI. was, of all the French monarchs, he who best knew how to manage or turn to his own advantage, the *States* who then represented the kingdom, and eulogizes him for his prudence in not convoking them but when the malcontents and the factions pushed their enterprises to excess. He admires the policy of Louis in inflaming the choice of the deputies, and by thus making sure of their suffrages beforehand, being enabled in some measure to dictate the decisions of an assembly, of which he wished to make an instrument and not a partner in power. This, in the present day, would be called, and properly so, a corrupting of the national representation. Under Louis XV. when Duclos wrote, they must have entertained but very loose and erroneous ideas of the dignities and duties of the representatives of the nation, for Duclos thus to hold up as an object almost of eulogium, one of the greatest crimes which the French nation has to lay to the charge of the despot of Plessis les Tours. Louis corrupted the judges as well as the deputies of the people, and enriched them with the spoils of those whom they condemned. An

---

* It would be endless to enumerate the absurdities to which he had recourse to ward off death, which he so much feared. We shall merely mention two. He had brought from Cologne some of the pretended bones of the three Eastern Kings who are said to have visited the infant Christ, and which bones were supposed to be of sovereign virtue in the cure of royal ailments. In a letter of Louis's to one of the Priors of *Notre Dame de Salles*, he vehemently entreats of Our Lady to grant him a *quartan fever*, as his physicians assure him that this is the only malady which is good for the health.

author little known out of France, *Pierre Mathieu*, who had the impudence to write an eulogium of Louis XI., says of this monarch, " that justice put her sword more frequently than her balance into his hand, which he made many of the nobles severely feel, whose trial was generally preceded by their execution." This, notwithstanding Pierre Mathieu's admiration for his royal master, sounds more like an epigram upon him than any thing else. Some authors have set down as a trait of profound policy, Louis's familiarizing himself with the people, visiting obscure citizens, enquiring into their family affairs, sitting at their tables and partaking of their humble fare, and in turn permitting them to appear at his own royal banquets. As he wished to lessen the influence of the nobles, it was good policy, as they suppose, on his part, to make himself beloved by the people and give them consideration. But it is probable that there was more of fancy and whim than of policy in these familiarities; and that, being naturally affable, inquisitive, and anxious to discover the truth, he had adopted an equal condescension towards every class of his subjects. If he had been so desirous of securing the good will and affection of the middling and lower classes, he would not have caused to be thrown into the Seine, bound in pairs, several citizens of Paris, whom he suspected of a correspondence with his enemies. He would have treated with less barbarity the unfortunate inhabitants of the towns and cities that he conquered. The most striking peculiarity of his character is, perhaps, the ascendancy which he allowed some of those in menial situations about his person to acquire over him. Some of these so captivated his confidence, that he intrusted them with several most important missions and affairs of state. But still more extraordinary and altogether odious was the degrading familiarity which existed between him and his prevot, the atrocious Tristan the Hermit, a wretch who took a ferocious delight in executing the cruel orders of his master. This horrid being he called his *gossip*. With the exception of the barbarian Czar Peter I. of Russia, the history of modern times offers no other example of a prince who took a pleasure in witnessing with his own eyes the executions he had ordered, and who afterwards amicably pressed the hand of the executioner, still dripping with the blood of his victims. Louis may be more easily pardoned for having conferred the title of Count de Meulan upon his barber Olivier le Dain, who served him faithfully and proved himself a brave captain. But unfortunately this valiant barber had a spice of the villain in him, like most of those who enjoyed the favour or confidence of Louis: he was hanged in the following reign for having, during the time of his power and credit, caused to be strangled, the husband of a lady, whose life he had promised to spare as the price of the wife's submission to his desires. This trait proves him to have been a worthy favourite of such a despot. It is difficult to imagine how Jaques Coittier, his physician, contrived to inspire Louis with so wholesome a fear of him; he obtained from him any thing and every thing he wished; he spoke to him with arrogance, and even insolence, without bringing down upon himself the wrath of the tyrant. He often said to him, " I know that you will serve me some fine morning as you have served so many others, but I swear to you that you shall live but eight days after." By this extravagant threat he worked upon Louis's credulity and fears,

It was owing to the same causes that he spared the life of an astrologer, whom he had doomed to death, but, wishing to prove the fallacy of his art, he asked him if he could foretell the period of his own death, to which the wily juggler replied with apparent *sang froid*, that it would take place exactly three days before that of his majesty. The King's dread of his physician will appear the less surprising, if we recollect in what continual fear of death the monarchs of that day were; when their distrust and dread of treachery were such, that at their interviews they were separated from each other by strong bars of wood or iron, through the intervals of which they passed their hands. It was thus, that Edward of England and Louis met at Pequigny. "On the middle of the bridge," says Comines, "was erected a strong palisading of wood, similar to that of which the cages of lions are made, and the distances between the bars were only large enough to allow an arm to pass through." In like manner it was with a strong grating between them that Louis and the Constable of France met to treat of their differences. Louis and his brother monarchs knew too well the danger of putting confidence in each other's honour. It was for having blindly confided in the word of the Duke of Burgundy, that Louis found himself a prisoner in the chateau of Peronne, and was obliged, as the price of his liberty, to assist the duke in exterminating the revolted inhabitants of Liege. Louis, however, seemed to have had as little regard to his word as the Duke of Burgundy : he judged of others by himself, and in that age he was not often mistaken in so doing. A favourite expression of his was, "he that knows not how to dissemble, knows not how to reign." If this be true, few kings knew better how to reign than he. It was only when he swore upon the true cross of *St. Lo*, that he considered himself bound;—as for all other oaths, he held himself dispensed from observing them, unless when it was his interest to do so. Louis is the first of the French monarchs, who took the title of "*Most Christian*," though there is scarcely one of the number who had less of the spirit of Christianity, but, as a compensation, no one could be a more scrupulous observer of devotional practices and the dues of the church. In 1481, he visited for seven days successively the tomb of Saint Martin, and gave an offering, each time, of thirty-one golden crowns : this was his usual donation when he visited a church, or heard mass, in company with the Queen. On Assumption day, he gave three times as many golden crowns as he was years old ; and during the last years of his life, he was so profuse of donations to the churches, that the greater part of his domains passed into the hands of the clergy.

Notwithstanding his tyranny and superstition, France was near being indebted to him for a general code of laws, and a unity of weights and measures, of which he had conceived the idea. But these wise and useful intentions did not receive their execution till the revolution at the close of the last century. The posts for the conveyance of letters, which he established for his own personal service, have become a general advantage. It was Louis also, who first introduced Swiss stipendiaries to serve as his life-guards, as if Frenchmen were not the fittest guardians of the throne and monarch of France.          D. S.

## HARP OF ZION.—NO. II.

### *The Song of Deburah.*

On the wing of the whirlwind Jehovah hath past,
And the turrets of Harosheth shook to the blast,
And the mountains of Edom were crumbled to dust,
As the lightnings of wrath on their proud foreheads burst !

The Canaanite came like the grasshopper down—
Like the grasshopper *now* that the tempest hath strewn—
And the pride and the pomp of his battle array
Hath past like the chaff in the tempest away!

Oh proudly the war-horse was pawing the plain
And proud was the boast of the warrior-train !
But the red-star in Heaven hath wither'd their force,
And Kishon hath swept them away in his course !

And his bride look'd forth from her latticed tower,
When the soft dew was sinking on tree and on flower ;
And she thought as the gust of the night-wind swept by,
'Twas Sisera's chariot in triumph drew nigh.

And she watch'd till the last dim star of the night
Had faded away in the morning light—
" Why tarry his chariot-wheels thus ?" she cried,
"O haste with thy spoils to the arms of thy bride !"

But far from his bridal bower away,
In the tent of the stranger proud Sisera lay—
With the dust for his couch—and the worm at his side,—
All headless he lies—he hath Death for his bride !

W. C.

---

### BISHOP BLAISE, THE ASH-WADDLER.

Strolling one morning in the Spring of 18— through a village in the north of merry Devon, I observed young Isaac Wall (better known by the name of Bishop Blaise,) the roving ash-waddler, in hot argument with his worship the Justice. Isaac was mounted on a fine athletic ass, garnished on all sides with tinker's tools and bags of wood-ashes. On the beast's withers crouched a young otter snarling at the Justice as he flourished his staff at the waddler ; who, with the end of a long, brown, polished, and rudely-carved pastoral crook, restrained his little amphibious friend from attacking his worship. He occasionally took the mitre from his head, and shook it in the Justice's face ; and ever and anon shed a cloud of dust from his patched clerical gown on his worship's garments. These were quite in the old fashion—quaint, bizarre, imposing, and affected. The style is now perhaps rooted out from its few strong holds even in the heart of Devon. He wore a blue coat, bedecked with silver coins, cuffed and collared with rich crimson velvet. His vest was a long-flapped flowery brocade —a cravat of fine muslin, with a running pink border, encircled his neck. His nether garments were greasy buckskins and yarn stockings of the old card pattern, wherein kings, queens, and knaves shouldered each other, ace shouldered deuce, diamond flamed cheek by jowl with spade, and every card in the pack flaunted 'twixt ankle and knee-band.

His worship was about fifty years of age, fat and unlettered : one who loved the ways of old, and had not been a score of miles from his secluded domains (as he often boasted) above thrice in his life.   When I approached, he was loud in interrogatories.   " How dare you, Sirrah ?" quoth he, " How dare you travel the county in that guise, with a pedlar's pack on your back too, when the maggot for illicit dealing bites ?   How dare you keep an alehouse by Exmoor yonder without a licence ?   What warranty hold you ?   Where's your conscience ?"

" Shut up your worshipful head," replied Blaise, drawing himself proudly up, and exhibiting a large woolcomb as he spoke.   " A man's conscience must have a broad pair of shoulders in these days ; and many do that without authority which I do by statute.   Talk to such men of conscience.   I am a woolcomber's son, Sir !   Who does not remember Sampson Wall, my father ?   Did he not parade in proper trappings as Blaise the good Bishop's representative, for nine successive years ?   He died, Sir, while officiating in the old rite, with his friends and the fellow-craftsmen who honoured him as their chief around him, in an open street of his native town—a woolcomber to the last, with this mitre on his head, this comb in his left and this crook in his right hand, and these robes flowing about him, as the proxy of the trade's patron saint.   I have worn them ever since ; and while a rag of them hangs to its neighbour I 'll not cast them off, for the good old man's sake, who impoverished himself to school such a truant, wandering, ungrateful, tinker-loving rogue of a fellow as I was.   I am a woolcomber's son, Sir, and therefore, thanks to Billy Pitt's Act, can carry on any art, trade, or mystery whatsoever, and wheresoever, without let or hindrance from any dweller in the land, beyond the University precincts.   I bite my nail at your worship.   You have been wooing and hankering after Jacob Shapcot's daughter Ally these three years ; but, mark me, to spite your worship much and please myself a little, I 'll set about a lusty courtship to her at once, and if I do not ferk you out of all likelihood of ringing the beauty, why mandamus me !"—" Pooh ! pooh !" pettishly ejaculated the Justice, while Blaise struck heels into his " palfrey's" sides, and went off at a strong gallop through the village.

About a year after, I met with the waddler again, and inquired if he had succeeded in his wooing.   " Sir !" said he, " it was a whole month before I was cheered with a single glance of my lady goodluck : thus it happened.   It's a custom with us here in Devon to cure a broken lip by stealing unperceived behind the door at new-moon-tide, and then and there with closed eyes devoutly singing certain old rhymes, which you shall hear anon, 'twixt the intervals of bussing.   Sweet Ally had bitten her lips so fiercely at my warm courtship one evening, that when I came to see her the next night, my damsel's mouth was sore and rough.   The young moon had just then broken up from her soft cloudy pillow, so that I suspected what the lass was bent on by her attempting so often to creep to the doorway unseen.   I marred her project thrice by a roguish glance, and, having a pleasant quiddit in my pate, suddenly bade the hearth-group good night.   But deuce a step stepped I across the threshold.   Ally had darkened the doorway for her own purposes, and I taking advantage of the cunningly contrived murkiness, slipped into the nook unperceived, instead of passing out. Anon comes my lass, with lid kissing lid, stealthily and lightly as fawn going to brook, when somewhat scared by the low patches of cloud, that swiftly scudding 'twixt sun and glade, chequer her verdant path. My cheek was lowered to the height of her mouth, and dextrously did I contrive on her approaching, directed only by her warm, short, fluttered breathings, to be saluted—thrice saluted by the comely lass. 'Wall! Wall! I love thee! And may thy virtue now cure me!' sang she, and the words floated to my pleased ear, soft, low, and indistinct, as the gentle talk of a dreaming birdlet. She bussed again, and then chaunted loudly and triumphantly

> 'Wall! Wall! I've kissed thee, Wall!
> Wall! Wall! I've wooed thee, Wall!
> And none have seen my love to Wall!'

'Say you so, darling?' cried I, suddenly clasping her up in my arms, and kissing her warmly,—'Say you so, bird, to Wall's face?' And I danced out into view with her as I spoke; while Ally shrieked, her mammy frowned, and her stout brothers crowded about us, dancing, gibing, and frightening the caged blackbird's head from beneath his wing, by their peals of jollity. 'Now, Ally, lass,' continued I, as the roar abated, 'you said last night, that you would be wooed willingly by Blaise, if ever you gave his sooty cheek a salute. Henceforth, I am a free suitor! But come, folks, who says a clear floor for a fall?' 'I'll vell any o' my buoys upo' the lime-ash that do zay noa?' cried old Shapcot, shaking his stick. This was enough. One of the youths immediately doffed woollens, and slipped into his corded jacket, and shin-facers. Our shoes were then rigidly inspected by the old man, who was chosen 'tryer,' and neither nail being found in the bottoms nor tinplate inserted atween the soles, we tippled a cup of cider to each other's health, shook hands, and manœuvred for a grab. In two minutes I felled the youngster by a twist of the wrist and toe-touch. While gratulations were showered upon me for this feat, I cast my eye round, and in the winding of the staircase, detected Ally peeping over her sister's shoulder at the sport. She drew back the moment she encountered my glance, but little Admonition boldly kept her place. I had another of the sturdy youngsters down in a twinkling; but Michael, the nestletripe of the sons, baffled me long. I threw him once on his side, again on two joints; and had almost brought him to another half-fall, which would have won me the bout, when the fellow slipped aside, and wiped off one from his score, by turning my own strength so cleverly in his favour, as to tilt me on the hip. I was up and at it again with a hot brow and a beating heart in a moment. He was a stiff one, and the time we had agreed upon for fair collar and elbow play, passed off in striving, and wheedling, and tempting, and kicking; still he was on his legs. I marvelled! Ally's eye was again upon me. I saw it not, but felt it, or fancied I felt it, on my flaming cheek. Anon, in came Mike for a grip at my belly-band, or a kidney-hug. But I was 'ware of him, and whipping out my gam, clutched him by shoulder and brisket. He went over, flying horse-fashion in a trice. Well! upon this, forth totters old Shapcot himself, from his elbow-chair, to play me out. The dusty protectors which he drew from a dark nook by the chimney-side were of rough bark; for he cleaved to the fashions

of his foresires, and preferred the skin of a stout oak to guard his
shins, rather than the tough hide of a bull. They were cosily lined
with thick flannel, but still lacked padding to fit them to his waning
withershins. ' Look tha there, Ikey,' said he, as we pledged the preparatory health,—' Look at them trovies. I won thic pair o' leathern
at Southmolton nineteen year. agone come Yeaster; thac uns at
King'snympton, the month avore Ally were bwoarn'd; and thac
othern at Yemmacott, the day I were married. ' Win me, and wear
me,' thou zeez't zamplered upo' th' band o' um, wi' green and red
zilk; but there they ha' hung, and there they shall hang untouched,
zo long as ever Geakup Shapcot do zuck wind. Now come on oot. I
drowth un lads by the vore hip vor a virkin o' yeal. Come on Ikey.
If I dwoant scat tha, christen me twoad.' Lord love you! I could have
carried him, poor withered rogue, to my hut by Exmoor, easily as
crow does dry elm-twig to her nest. But I dallied with him—pretending to put out all my craft and strength; and at last, when the old
man sweated and blowed nigh to bursting his wrinkled hide, let myself
sink gently down beneath him as a matter of policy. And then to hear
the breathless old body trying in vain to squeak Victoria! oh! 'twas
fine! The boys chuckled; the dame chirruped; and down came the
girls with kisses and condolements. When the first burst of his joy
was over, he sat cool, solemn, and dignified; affecting to treat his conquest as a mere matter of course. I was certainly, he said, one of the
best players he had ever mated with; but few could evade his back-
clamp: it was no disgrace to be levelled by Jacob Shapcot. The sons
laughed again; and he mistaking the cause of their mirth (for I feigned
to be chapfallen, though Mike and his brothers knew how the affair
was managed), reproved three, and whacked the fourth for scoffing at
a beaten man.

" Supper, drink, and nutty mirth succeeded; but Alice was icy, and
the Justice's bags sat heavy on the mind of the dame. Little Admonition, my trusty ally, after long noting her sister's deportment, at last
stole out, winking to me as she went, and returned in about half an
hour, with a few ashes in the corner of her bib, which she slily managed
to empty unseen into my palm. ' It's the web o' th' ould gander's
voot,' whispered she; ' she died a Monday. I've a burned it for tha
—Dooey just gie't to th' cretur in her drink, and I'll warrant she'll
love'e. It's a sure charm, and ha' been tried scaures o' times. If you
do but offer zider to her, wi' th' ashes in't, she's witched by't, and will
she, nill she, the twoad can't but drink—once down—and job's auver
—she's thine for zertain.' I pretended to laugh at her for a little
fool; but warm was the kiss which I pressed on the sun-burnt curls
that shaded her brow, and I seized the first opportunity to sprinkle a
half-filled jug with a few of the ashes. I had not the least hope that
the proud hussy would take drink from my hand, and advanced trembling with liquor and anxiety to Ally's seat. Judge of my wonder, when
she not only eagerly clasped the jug, but, instead of sipping like bird
at flowery dew-cup, according to her usual custom, she smilingly
quaffed off the whole contents. There's virtue in an old gander's foot,
thought I, and who knows the luck of the looby calf? Justice, your
worshipful hopes totter. The ashes left a grey bow above Ally's
upper lip, and ere her smooth round arm reached it, the brothers' eyes

were one and all fixed on her. She stared at her arm, after she had passed it lightly across her mouth, and blushing deeply, looked about, to see if any one had observed her. The youths, as well as Ally, suspected what I had accomplished, and burst into an uproar of laughter, the moment Ally's eye was fearfully bent on them. Little Admonition said, that I had succeeded in fixing a crooked pin in her sister's skirt too, and the poor maiden deeming herself witched to have me, ran out of the kitchen, to search her garments for the obnoxious pin. Addy told me that she could not find it, and while my lass fretted in her chamber, I, spite of the frowns of dame, rejoiced at the hearth-side. My otter, Tommy, soon after crept into the place, with a live fish in his mouth; and while I was caressing the obedient and well educated little beast, Bob, ' Gentleman Bob,' the farmer's eldest son, proposed an otter chase at day-break. The motion was carried by acclamation; orders were issued to the prentices for a gathering of efficient dogs among the neighbours; and after a little lingering, and peeping into the empty jugs, we all staggered bedward.

" The doze of age after a tipsy frolic is shorter than the sleep of youth —the married man who has been merry and wild overnight, leaves his bed the next morning long before the bachelor—Jacob Shapcot, with cracked voice, rheumy eyes, and sage long visage, was the first of the family that appeared in the kitchen at day-break. He cast a rueful and repentant look at the reliques of the night's revelry, and hurried up his people, so that the hunt might be finished early enough for them to set about their usual avocations, within an hour, at the latest, after the customary time. He was just as sparing of his morning cups, as he had been lavish of his liquor overnight. After a single draught each, the young men speedily equipped themselves in baragan jackets, laced boots, stout hose, and straw hats, for the sport. Ally, with her nightcap awry, peeped out of her woodbine-shaded lattice; but seeing me in the yard below, blushed, tittered, and drew back again in a moment. At length, armed with pikes, dung-forks, hoes, and poles, with farmer Grane's Towler, Toby Abbott's Brandy, a couple of hounds that were billeted on Bob, his own private professional tykes, and some dozen yappers and yellers of all shapes and breeds, we started to the number of a score and half towards the neighbouring stream.

" We turned off at the boundary bridge of the good Squire's park, through which the water flowed. The old hunters that sauntered about beneath the oaks in the lawn, pricked up their ears at Towler's first joyful note, when freed from the coupling leathers, and galloped down at full speed towards the palings, over which they stretched their necks, and watched our proceedings, apparently with the most intense longing and interest. A meek doe had stolen charily down to the bank within the park, from whence she was scared in the midst of her draught, by the sudden plash of a leaping fish; and ere she had tripped thrice her length up the hill-side coppice, Towler's voice struck her motionless with fear. The hares forgot their gambols, and scampered away to cover, from which a few of them immediately stole out again, some few bounds, and sitting erect on their strong haunches, with extended ears and searching eyes, peered anxiously around. The rooks in the wood behind the old mansion-house began to caw most querulously, and flapped about the tops of the elms for many minutes after, while the watch-dogs far and near responded in hoarse gruff tones to Towler's musical bay.

" The banks were rugged and beetling; some of our dogs pried warily beneath them with nose and eye, while others beat landward round, and we, with pole and pike, searched about the roots of every old tree that bathed in the water,—disturbing the lurking Jack from his lair, and driving the mottled trout like arrows up the stream. In less than half an hour old Brandy, the mother of the subscription pack, spoke in a gleeful and decided tone! Every eye and ear was turned towards such prime authority; those who were on the opposite bank dashed into the stream, and in a few moments men and dogs were all assembled round the pack-mother. Meantime she was driving her clear, melodious voice into a hole about the size of a barley-straw, some four feet or so from the water's edge. There was evidently an otter's haunt beneath, and we sturdily set about thwacking and thumping the ground with our poles. The true dogs parted off again : some betook themselves to the stream, paddling cautiously about within a yard or two of the bank; others posted themselves along the margin, all joyfully giving tongue and anxiously waiting for the *burst.* Out he came at last, and a chain of strong bubbles showed his course and velocity of dash, down the stream. There was a moment! There was a time of shouting, hurrying, cheering, and heart-beating! Away went the dogs after the game, swimming with all their might on the track of his ventings, or following in full cry along the banks. Some of us cheered on the pack, while a few of the most active cut across to the shallows, and plunging hip deep in them, with ready poles and erected spears, waited the diver's approach. Onward he bore in gallant style, maiming the dogs who headed him, snapping at spear and pole, and evading every jaw-clutch and thrust by dip or parry. Finding us drawn up in such formidable array on his course, he rose for a moment, opened his strong jaws, gasped convulsively, grinned at the nearest hound, and diving again dragged him by the leg under the water. The victim was brave Towler, a rough and a rigid-toothed dog, but what chance has tyke with otter in the bed of a river? I hooked him up with my pastoral, when almost at his last gasp. He was hurt in twenty places, bleeding from heel to wither, water-blind, deaf, and lame ; but his nose was still alive, and on the otter's getting away again, spite of his disaster—

   ' Brave Towler led the cry.'

Our game soon after took refuge under a shelving bank. There he kept the bravest at bay. He sallied forth occasionally, marked mementoes of the day on the legs of six of us, drowned two of our hounds, disabled five, and sent several with their tails curled under their bellies disconsolate, sorry, and yelping, towards home. Thrice did he 'scape us after we mooted him from the bank, and as often did our high-nosed dogs reveal him again. At last, with Towler somewhat recovered, and hot with revenge, hanging on his gorge, while his own sharp teeth were making ribbons of Brandy's lug, I speared him. He was mine by the laws of brook and fen. I carried him to Shapcot's, and after laying the spoil at Ally's feet, in the presence of the frowning Justice, I dried my robes, adjusted my mitre, mounted palfrey Ned, slung Tommy across his withers, and trotted merrily away.

Within a week I cut the bark off Hosea Butt's nose, after he had opened the pates of Mike and Bob at a single-stick match, and from that time who but Blaise the waddler was king paramount at Shapcot's, with all but the dame and Ally. I solaced them during the first three days of March—the *deaf days*, when they fear to sow corn (seed never growing that is buried at such time) and none lifted up so loud a voice as Ikey Wall at their harvest-home, when the old man, with sons, servants and assistant-neighbours about him, according to ancient custom, raised the garlanded oak-bough from earth towards heaven, in token of thanksgiving for his plentiful crops. Dozens whooped as the green branch was elevated, but my whoop was heard above all. The lass grew more kind, but she warmed to me slowly. The Justice I made a fool of, in the presence of Ally, regularly once a month; and whenever he sneaked down to the farmer's, I, to the horrible discontent, fretting, and fuming of the dame, was found perched upon the seat of honour allotted to his worship, from which, refusing to wag an inch, with gibe and song, I flouted him most respectfully. He never could find occasion to quarrel with me openly, so well did I manage my taunts and girds. But the bee stings sorely through his rose-leaf—the Justice felt my thrusts, though prettily veiled, and hated me most bitterly. One night, when the dame expected his worship, she persuaded Ally to hang the rind of a turnip, which she had contrived to pare off without fracture, on the latch of the door. Whoever first enters is fated to be the bridegroom of the lass who fastens up this charm; and the old woman was desirous of doing away with the idea in Ally's mind, that, having quaffed the gander's-foot-ash cider, she was doomed to be linked to Blaise—by his worship being notified, under the influence of a cantrip of equal power, as the future lord of her hand. I was at the next farm moulding spoons of the bits of metal which the women had hoarded, when my little ally warned me of my peril. You may wonder why Admonition was so true to my interest. Gratitude made her my friend. She had the hooping-cough three years before, and I, in pity to the child, plucked a few hairs from the brown streak that adorns my donkey's shoulder, sewed them up in a rag of my gown, and hung the charm with my own hands about her pretty neck. She was well in a week. But to proceed, his worship had already ambled down the hill from the village church when Addy came to me, but by a cross-path and good speed I reached the door before him. Oh! Saint Botolph! how she stared, the old dame did—and how she blushed, my beauty did—when I entered, and taking the rind from the latch unbroken to Ally's lap, snatched a hearty buss for my fee. Shortly after in rolled his worship, and the first thing he heard was little Admonition's tale, maliciously and shortly told, of the turnip charm. Sore was he at heart, though he affected to despise such follies; and I remember well, that on the same evening I gained a peg upon him thus: Ally, by accident, laid the bellows on the table whereupon his arm rested, and well the fat gentle knew, that she who places such an utensil on the board will be unlucky for three days after if she take it up again herself. Well he knew, too, that whosoever relieves the slut of that duty removes the ill-chance from her shoulders to his own; but fast he sat as roopy turkey-poult. I afforded him a fair opportunity to be gallant, but, finding him utterly currish, tripped at last across the floor and taking the bellows from his elbow hung it on its peg in the chimney. He repented when I touched it, but he was then too late. Thus obtained I a smile from my rose of the valley, and many a thorny look did she afterwards inflict on her cowardly suitor. The dame foamed, but I was merry with little Addy, and basked in the warm sunny looks of my love. Justice, thought I, to-day have I dealt thee a pong in the midriff.

"He was a miserly rogue, and once when I came to his house in the way of my profession, on putting a handful from the heap which he warranted to be ashes of wood into my mouth, I knew, by the smack they left on my tongue, that they were vilely adulterated. ' Your worship,' said I, ' to every seam of your wood, you have burnt nine days gathering of cowdal from the moor, a hundred of turf, and many a square of tanners' leather-chips, as well as niggardly bricks of blended clay, small coal, and cinders—my palate tells me this; and yet you warrant the heap to be all hard-wood and coppice ash. Did you think my tongue was ignorant as a quarry-slate ?—Fie! fie !' This lie of his got abroad; he was nick-named for it, and I, by him, more hated than ever. He has a fish-pond in his grounds which, tradition saith, is the abiding place of a furious water-pixy for twenty days current at the conclusion of every century. I had heard of the sprite's tricks in the days of our grandads, and on the time of his re-appearance approaching, posted myself, night by night, near the pond, to watch his pranks. By way of amusing myself, I gutted the water, with the aid of Tommy, my otter, and feasted my friends with the spoil. They knew not where I obtained the fish—it was enough for them that they had it to prey on. Meantime I daily heard tales about the Pixy of Blackpool. He was described in a thousand different ways, and such feats were assigned to him as ear never heard before. I still fished in the waters— Tommy and I—but deuce a smiggott of aught wonderful saw we, save and except only a colossal carp now and then, during all our watchings. At last, his worship, while wandering with dame Shapcot about his lands to astound her with his rich possessions in beeve and fleece, unconsciously neared (about sunset) a hedge that fringed the bank of Blackpool. In the heat of an eloquent sally on the rare wool of his chilver-hogs then present, suddenly drops the uplifted cane from my gentleman's hand, he roars like a town-bull, and takes to his heels, most uncourteously leaving the dame to settle with his honour the Pixy in the best way she could. I was up to my belt in water when I heard his shout (he shouts well, his worship does), aiding Tommy to capture a fine fish. I was busied, to be sure, but I looked suddenly and carefully about me, and no pixy saw I—deuce a bit of one. The dame, however, vowed she did, and sorely terrified she was. I found her sprawling and praying on the ground—and most superfluous of kisses and kindness she became when I raised her up. As we walked towards home, she lavished curses, bitter as the words to which women are restricted could make, on the cowardly brutal Justice, for leaving a helpless woman in such a situation ; and lauded me to the skies as a mirror of goodness and manhood. Ally despised his worship, and looked upon me as a living wonder, for my daring hardihood in rescuing her mother from the jaws of the terrible Blackpool goblin. I said nothing, but eh! me! how I chuckled! The Justice never showed his ruby nose at Shapcot's again, and matters went on swimmingly in favour of Blaise.   One night Ally stole out with some other maids to sing—

> ' New moon! True moon—tell unto me,
>   Who my love and husband shall be.'

I was standing at her elbow when she concluded.   She stuck the heart of one of Bob's game-cocks, that had been killed in battle, with new pins, placed it under her pillow in a stocking which had been thrice washed in fountain water, and bleached as often in moonlight: that night she confessed I was the subject of her dreams.   The charm worked in favour of Blaise.   She went to see the sun and moon jig together in the brook on Easter morning, with her true love's face laughing at the fun.   She glimpsed the peak of my mitre in the waters, and shrieking fell—into my arms!   If she loitered in the church-yard at nightfall to chaunt—

> ' Hemp seed I set, and hemp seed I sow,
>   Let my bonny boy come hither to mow,'

I was accidentally passing that way with a scythe or a bill on my shoulder, after assisting her brothers a-field.   Could she but love me?   Or was she to fight fate?   When each of us present at a merry-meeting threw a lock of hair on the fire (I need scarce say that the owner of the lock that frizzles without flaming is doomed to die within the year) she grew pale as a lily when mine created no blaze.   Then I was sure she loved me!   It was a bit of my palfrey's mane, but I could not bring the colour to her cheek again, nor would she be easy until she plucked a curl from my brow, and it threw up a lusty flame when she cast it on the burning log.   Then she moaned for my beast, and he, poor palfrey, has lived five months of his allotted time.   I look forward with grief to the hour of our parting ; but die he must at the year's end—that's fated.   We played at shord and pancake last Shrove-tide, Ally was lady of the door, and caught me as I was dropping my bit of crockery on the threshold.   Nevertheless she did not black my cheeks with the frying pan, as by the law of custom she was entitled to do, but gave me a kiss and a cake, as if I had succeeded in laying down my shord, and escaping without detection.   In fact, we are now as fond as two turtles, and to-morrow Alice will be made the bride of the roving waddler.   Long may she live to vex the eye of his worship by her beauty, and to cheer my heart by her loving tones !   My cot by Exmoor is fitted for her reception, and I shall hereafter limit my wanderings to a day's tramp; but never while I am able, and she is willing, will I discontinue my profitable and merry occupation of gathering ashes for the soap folks.·  The hill-side shall still ring with my song—the metal be fashioned in my moulder—the wood-ash darken these the robes of my good old father—and young and old from village and homestead, crowd forth to greet and employ their boon-friend, their comforter, and champion,—Bishop Blaise, the ash-waddler."        A.

## ANGLO-GALLIC SONG.

### *The Exposition at the Louvre,*

BEHOLD how each Gallic improver, in science, mechanics, and arts,
As he roams the Bazaar of the Louvre, snuffs, shrugs up his shoulders, and
    starts;
*Mon Dieu!—c'est superbe—magnifique!—les Anglois eux-mêmes diront cela—*
*O Ciel! comme c'est charmant—unique!—L'Angleterre est mise hors de*
    *combat—*
    And its oh! what will become of her?   Dear! what will she do?
    England has no manufactures to rival the wonders we view.

Here is a patent *marmite pour perfectionner* pumpion soup—
The Gods on Olympus complete—*tout en sucre*—a classical group;
*Quatre flacons de produits chimiques*—a clarified waxen bougie,
A Niobe after the Greek, and the Grotto of Pan—*en bisquit.*
    And its oh! &c.

*Voilà des chapeaux sanitaires* with a *jalousie* cut in the hold,
To let in a current of air, and give hot-headed people a cold;
Six irons with which boots are heel'd, so no modern Achilles miscarries,
For he now gets his tendon and shield where the Greek got an arrow—
    from Paris.
    And its oh! &c.

A ham and a head of wild boar in a permanent jelly suspended,
*Cinq modèles de chaises inodores pour un cabinet d'aisance* intended;
The elixir term'd *odontalgique*, which can stubbornest tooth-aches controul,
*Et les poupées parlantes* which can squeak "papa! and mamma!"—*comme*
    *c'est drole!*
    And its oh! &c.

For heads without ringlets or laurel, *Regnier* fashions wigs like a wreath,
While *Desirabode* cuts out of coral false gums and unperishing teeth;
Here's a lady in wax large as life, with all the blonde lace she can stick to,
And an actual Paris-made knife which will cut—*O mirabile dictu!*
    And its oh! &c.

A gross of green spectacles—nails—a stick of diaphanous wax,
A Faunus—one Pan and two pails—account-books with springs in their
    backs;
A spit, wheel, and flyer, all forged in France, with a jack-chain complete;
A bladder with eatables gorged—a portrait of Louis Dixhuit.
    And its oh! &c.

*Pour vous dire en detail toutes les choses* there's no time, so we'll lump as
    we pass,
Caps, corkscrews, cheese, cucumbers, clothes; glue, gingerbread, ging-
    hams, and glass;
Pianos, pipes, pipkins, pots, pattens; rouge, rat-traps, rings, ratafie, rice,
Salt, sofas, shawls, sugar-loaves, satins; dolls, dredgers, delf, dimity, dice.
    And its oh! &c.

Through the fifty-two rooms on a floor, now you've seen all the sights in
    your tour,
*Et si vous en voulez encore vous les verrez là bas, dans la cour;—*
*Oui, pour leur commerce de la mer, c'est fini—enfin, c'en est fait,*
*Et la Grande Nation, il est clair, a ecrasé les pauvres Anglois.*
    And its oh! what will become of her?   Dear, what will she do?
    England has no manufactures to rival the wonders we view.    H.

## THE PHYSICIAN.—NO. XI.

### Of the Nature and Dietetic Use of Water.

WATER-DRINKERS imagine that they are drinking a perfectly pure element; but the enquiries and experiments of natural philosophers have demonstrated, that every drop of water is a world in miniature, in which all the four elements and all the three kingdoms of Nature are combined. Woodward, who took particular pains to examine our English waters, found none of them free from extraneous matters. Boerhaave called the water which the clouds send down to us the ley of the atmosphere, because it is intermixed with so many foreign matters which it envelopes in its descent through the air: nay the very water that has been purified by art still contains a large proportion of such matters. Distill, or filter water as often as you please, and it will nevertheless in time turn putrid in the sun, and by its bubbles, scum, sediment, and taste, afford evidence of its impurity.

Let not the reader suppose that I deal in exaggeration, when I term every drop of water a world in miniature, a compound of all the four elements, and all the three kingdoms of Nature: for I can prove the accuracy of this definition in every point.

Besides water itself, as the primary element, all water contains a variety of earthy particles. Pure water, when distilled, yields an earth; and Boyle found, that after it had been distilled two hundred times, it still contained this kind of matter. We know from experiments, that a tea-spoonful of water, ground in the cleanest glass mortar, becomes turbid in a few minutes, and in half an hour quite thick, and as it were a solid body. Pott conjectured that this earth proceeded from the friction of the glass, because he found that it was vitrified by a high degree of heat: this notion, however, is refuted by Eller; and not only did Wallerius find the earth of water ground in mortars of iron or other metals of precisely the same nature as that from glass-mortars; but the presence of earth in water may be proved by other experiments, to which this objection of the friction of the glass will not apply. A few drops of oil of tartar dropped into water, will instantly detect its earthy particles. Woodward says, that we need only let water stand a few days in a clean closely-covered glass, and abundance of earthy particles will not fail to appear. If we, moreover, consider how much earthy matter water every where meets with in the air and in the ground, which it partly takes up and carries away with it, and partly dissolves, we cannot for a moment doubt its presence in water. In the ancient Roman aqueducts were deposited thick incrustations of tuff-stone or marble-dust, which in time became quite solid: and I shrewdly suspect that there are very few tea-kettles in constant use in our immense metropolis, but exhibit the same phenomenon. In short, all rain, river, and spring-water, if left to stand any time, deposits an earthy sediment.

Among the earthy matters in water, I include every thing that belongs to the mineral kingdom: a calcareous earth, a selenitic matter, nay even real iron are found in it. Water contains also several species of salts. In rain and snow-water we discover an acid, arising from common salt and nitre. Pliny, of old, regarded snow-water as more fertilizing than any other on account of its salts; and for the same reason Bartholin ascribed to it certain medicinal qualities. It is also owing to the presence of particular salts that washerwomen find rain and snow-water fitter for their purpose than spring-water; and as it has been ascertained that water, like all salts, crystallizes under a certain invariable angle, since the icy particles always form under an angle of sixty degrees, we might almost be tempted to consider water in general as a species of salt, if the other properties of the salts did but coincide with this. In spring-water we find real sea-salt and nitre: and it is a remarkable fact, that water can absorb all these salts without occupying on that account a greater space. The warmer water is, the more salt it is capable of holding in solution; boiling water will dissolve nearly its own weight of salt; while freezing water, on the contrary, deposits ever so small a portion of salt that it may have taken up.

This, however, is not all. Water contains also inflammable or sulphureous particles, which manifest themselves in its sediment, in its putrefaction, and in many chemical experiments which are recorded by the best writers. It must not be imagined that I here allude to the mineral waters only, some of which actually take fire. Common putrid water frequently inflames in the same manner; and moreover, the existence of caloric, or fiery particles, in water, cannot be doubted; for without them it would not be a fluid but a solid body. As soon as water is deprived of all its caloric, it contracts, becomes more ponderous, and acquires the solidity of stone. Muschenbroeck and Eller found that heat expands water about a twenty-fourth or twenty-sixth part; and that in passing from the freezing point to the degree of heat at which it begins to boil, it becomes about a sixty-fifth part lighter. As then it is the caloric or fiery particles alone which keep the particles of water so slightly connected that they form a fluid body; the presence of caloric in all water must be incontestable. On this account Boerhaave called water a sort of glass, which melts at the thirty-third degree of heat, and the vapours of which are wholly composed of small glass globules.

That water contains air, is a point which no one will dispute. It has been observed that this air is expelled from the intervals between its particles, at a heat of 150 degrees of Fahrenheit's thermometer; but that it does not begin to boil under 212 degrees. As water, deprived of its air, occupies no smaller space than before, the air, like the dissolved salts, cannot take up any perceptible space in water, but must insinuate itself into the minutest interstices. Hence probably it is, that the intermixture of air with water takes place so slowly; for if water that has been deprived of all its air, is exposed to the atmosphere, it takes several days, and even weeks, before the air again combines with it: and to this end no shaking or agitation is required. This has been fully demonstrated by the most careful experiments of many eminent natural philosophers, as Mariotte, Boerhaave, Muschenbroeck, Nollet, and Hamberger; and Eller has calculated that the natural proportion of air contained by common water, amounts to a hundred-and-fiftieth part.

As then common water comprehends earth, salts, caloric, and air, it is evident that all the four elements are combined in every drop. But, methinks, I hear the inquisitive reader exclaim, how do you make out the three kingdoms of Nature?

The mineral kingdom I have already introduced. Earth, lime, chalk, selenitic matter, sea-salt, nitre, inflammable matters, caloric, iron, are all associated in a drop of water. We now want nothing but vegetable and animal matter.

All water must contain a vegetable principle, because all vegetables are solely and alone generated and nourished by it. That the earth contributes nothing to this effect, is almost incontestable. Many natural philosophers have found by accurate experiments, that a vessel full of mould, after a large tree has grown in it, loses none of its original weight; and hence it follows, that the water used in watering it, must have exclusively operated the developement, growth, and nourishment of the tree. This observation is very old, and has merely been confirmed by the moderns. As then it is inferred, that the earth contributes nothing to the principle of vegetables, philosophers have also proved that water, considered *per se*, is not transformed into the substances of plants, or converted into a solid body, but that it is only the vehicle of the vegetable particles, and merely conveys them to the plants. Woodward, who thoroughly investigated this subject, has demonstrated that water itself, nourishes plants no more than earth, but that it is only the vehicle of the vegetable matter; and it is in this way that we must understand the principles of the philosophers, of Thales, Seneca, Cicero, Van Helmont, and others, when they regard water as the primary element of all things, or assert with Palissy, that without water nothing can say —I exist. As then water is capable of communicating to all vegetables that by which they become what they are, it must be considered as the parent of the whole vegetable kingdom, and every drop of it must comprehend the elements of thousands of different plants.

The animal kingdom alone now remains: and this, too, inhabits the water. I shall say nothing of the fish, and the large aquatic insects that dwell in it by millions; for the very smallest drops of water have their inhabitants, which may be discovered with suitable optical instruments. Every body knows also how soon animalculæ are generated in stagnant water. In long voyages, the water on board ships becomes putrid, perhaps three or four times, and then contains innumerable small worms, which, when they have accomplished the period of their existence, die, and then the water again becomes drinkable. Soon afterwards, other species of similar animalculæ are generated, and the water again becomes foul. If we would preserve it from this impurity, or destroy the worms which infest it, we must have recourse to the assistance of art; and either burn sulphur in the vessels before they are filled, or drop into the water a few drops of vitriolic acid, which kills the animalculæ. There are good grounds for suspecting that the generation of these worms in water is chiefly owing to heat, and to the influence of air; for it is remarked in ships, that those butts which are placed in the warmest situations, generate worms the soonest; and that water, which is inaccessible to air, keeps perfectly sweet for many years. Clavius kept water sweet for twenty years in a retort, the neck of which was closed up by its accidental melting, without perceiving the smallest diminution. In the subterraneous city of Herculaneum, water was found after the lapse of nearly as many centuries in strong crystal vases. The water of the Rhone is kept at Arles eighty years in earthen vessels placed in cool cellars. These observations, however, prove nothing more than that the developement of the spawn of worms in water may be prevented by external circumstances, by cold and by the exclusion of the air. The principle of these worms, the elementary matter of them, which belongs to the animal kingdom, nevertheless indisputably exists, though in a dormant state, in the water.

From all this it is evident how egregiously they are mistaken, who imagine that in water they are drinking a perfectly pure element. It is true, that if water were perfectly pure, it would be one of the finest beverages, and its indissoluble elementary parts would produce scarcely any medicinal effect on the human body. But when we consider in what manner water nourishes plants, we may easily infer, that in animals also it is not transformed into the rudiments of their bodies, but rather communicates to them the few nutritious organic particles which it contains. Hence it is that water, if pure, possesses no particular nutritious property ; but, by means of its peculiar subtilty, it dissolves the nutritious parts of the alimentary substances, and conveys them into the minutest vessels. Of this subtilty of water some notion may be formed, when it is known, that a drop of water, when converted into vapour, occupies, according to Eller's calculation, a space 13,000 times greater than before ; and that, as Leuwenhoeck found, the pores of the skin, by which water, in the form of vapour, is secreted in perspiration from the blood, are 24,000 times smaller than a grain of sand. By means of this astonishing subtilty, water can convey the alimentary particles, which it absorbs to the remotest points of the body ; and so far it produces an incomparable effect in diet. We observe this effect in beer, which is nothing but water saturated with animal nutriment. At the same time, it is obvious how necessary it is to mix our solid food with a sufficient quantity of liquid in the stomach, that it may be subtilized by this solvent, and carried along with it into all quarters. In this point of view I regard water, with Pindar, as the most useful thing in life, because it is the vehicle that conveys our nutriment to its proper place ; but of itself I do not imagine that it contributes in the least to the nourishment of the body, since it is not at all probable that it should change into a solid body, or that its pure particles should dissolve.

I consider water as an inestimable benefit to health, not as water, but inasmuch as it is a fluid. Without fluids we should not be able to digest any thing, and with a superabundance of the most nutritious, but perfectly solid food, we should dry up and inevitably perish. Fluids dissolve our food, and the water saturated with the liquefied animal particles of food is the chyle, which insinuates itself with this vehicle into the most secret channels and minutest interstices of all our parts. Here this viscous nutriment combines with the solid parts of our bodies, and the remaining water, leaving its companion behind, pursues its course into the most delicate vessels, till it arrives beneath the epidermis, where the air imbibes it, as it were, from the skin in the form of an infinitely subtile vapour, and gives it back to the world at large, as it does also in the case of plants. In this manner water promotes perspiration and urine.

I have already observed that water also absorbs salts, and even contains something oleaginous in its composition. Hence it is easy to conceive, how the water that mingles with our juices, imbibes a superabundance of acridity which exists in them, and laden with this fresh burden, must be voided from the body to return to its general home. The sweetest water, which passes off again in urine in the space of a few minutes, with scarcely any change of colour, nevertheless betrays, both in taste and smell, traces of salt and animal oil, and the perspiration carries with it a large proportion of both. Hence water is a good beverage for those who eat much salt meat, or who have upon the whole a superabundance of sharp humours. It is better for them than beer or any other liquid that is already saturated with extraneous particles of a different nature, and herein consists the chief pre-eminence of pure water over other beverages.

A liquid, already saturated with particles of any kind which it is capable of dissolving, will not take up so large a proportion of particles of a different kind, as it would otherwise do. Eight ounces of water, in which nine ounces and a half of green vitriol have been dissolved, will be completely saturated with it: the water will nevertheless be still capable of taking up one ounce and a half of Epsom salt, two drams of refined saltpetre, and three ounces of refined sugar. But if the water is not previously saturated with vitriol, it can hold in solution five ounces and a half of Epsom salt, four ounces of pure nitre, &c. Any water, therefore, which is already saturated with particles of a certain kind, is not so well adapted to the purification of our juices from insoluble impurities as that which is not so impregnated; consequently, no beer, no broth, no wine, and perhaps, too, no decoction for cleansing the blood, is so efficacious for this purpose as the very purest water.

As water can perform such great things, and at the same time, because it has no taste, it neither stimulates the appetite to excess, nor can produce any perceptible effect on the nerves, it is admirably adapted for diet, and we ought, perhaps, by right, to make it our sole beverage, as it was with the first of mankind, and still is with all the animals. Pure water dissolves the food more, and more readily, than that which is saturated, and likewise absorbs better the acrimony from the juices— that is to say, it is more nutritious and preserves the juices in their natural purity; it penetrates more easily through the smallest vessels, and removes obstructions in them; nay, when taken in large quantity, it is a very potent antidote to poison.

From these main properties of water may be deduced all the surprising cures which have been effected by it in so many diseases, and which I shall here pass over altogether. But as to the dietetic effect of water, I shall recommend it to my readers for their ordinary beverage on three conditions.

The first is, that they drink it as pure as possible. Impure water is of itself impregnated with foreign matters which may prove prejudicial to health. Hence it loses all the advantages which I have in the preceding pages ascribed to water; and it would in this case be much better to drink beer or any other such beverage that is saturated with

nutritive particles rather than impure water. We must leave the
stomachs of camels to answer for the preference given by them to muddy
water; for we are assured by Shaw, that these animals stir it up with
their feet and render it turbid before they drink. The human economy
requires, on the contrary, a pure beverage.

The signs of good water are, that it easily becomes hot and cold;
that in summer it is cool, and in winter slightly lukewarm; that a drop
dried on a clean cloth leaves not the faintest stain behind; and that it
has neither taste nor smell. It is also a sign of good water that when
it is boiled it becomes hot, and afterwards grows cold, sooner than
other water. But this sign is far more fallible than the evidence of the
quality of water obtained by feeling. Singular as this may sound,
it is very possible to distinguish the properties of water by means of
this sense. A soft or a hard water is synonymous with a water the
parts of which adhere slightly or closely together. The slighter their
adhesion, the less they resist the feeling, and the less sensible they are
to the hand, because they may be so much the more easily separated.
A gentleman of my acquaintance has for many years used two different sorts of water, which are equally pure and limpid, the one for
drinking and the other for washing his hands and face. If his servant
ever happens to bring the wrong water for washing, he instantly discovers the mistake by the feeling. Our cooks and washerwomen would
be able to furnish many other instances of the faculty of discriminating
the properties of water by the touch, which would show that this faculty depends more on the excitement occasioned in the sensible parts
than on any other cause. Hard water, for instance, makes the skin
rough; soft, on the contrary, renders it smooth. The former cannot
sufficiently soften flesh or vegetables; the latter readily produces this
effect. The difference of the extraneous matters which change the
qualities of water, naturally makes a different impression on the feeling; and in this there is nothing that ought to astonish a person of
reflection.

The water of standing pools and wells is in general extremely impure, and is accounted the worst of all. River water differs according
to the variety of the soil over which it runs, and the changes of the
weather; but though commonly drunk, it is never pure. Of all impure
river-waters, those which abound in earthy particles alone are the least
injurious, because those particles are not dissolved by the water. In
Auvergne, near the villages of St. Allire and Clermont, there is a stream
of a petrifying quality, which constructs of itself large bridges of stone,
and yet it is the only water drunk by the inhabitants of those places,
and that without the slightest inconvenience. If we consider that a
stony concretion is deposited in all our kettles, we shall readily conceive, that a water which carries stone along with it cannot be very pernicious to health, since it is constantly drunk by men and animals.
This stone in our kettles is really a calcareous earth, which may be
dissolved by boiling in them vinegar, or water mixed with a small
quantity of nitric acid; and as the water deposits it, and does not hold
it in solution, it can of course do us very little injury. I cannot, therefore, imagine how the celebrated Dr. Mead could believe that water
which leaves such a deposit in culinary vessels may occasion stone in

the kidneys or bladder, merely because Pliny has said so; though he was well acquainted with the great difference between animal calculi and mere calcareous earth.

Next to well and river-water, both which are always impure, rain-water follows in the scale of preference. It is very impure, and a real vehicle for all the pernicious matters that are continually floating in the atmosphere. Snow-water is much purer. Snow is formed of vapours which have been frozen before they could collect into drops. It is in the lower region of the air that these drops in falling absorb most of their impurities. The vapours floating in the upper atmosphere freeze before they reach the mire of the lower. This water is seldom to be had. That which I would most strongly recommend for drinking, is a spring-water, which descends from lofty hills, through flints and pure sand, and rolls gently along over a similar bed or rocks. Such water leaves behind all its coarse impurities in the sand; it is a purified rain and snow-water, a fluid crystal, a real cordial, and the best beverage for persons in good health.

The second condition which I attach to water-drinking is, that such persons only choose it for their constant beverage, to whom warming, strengthening and nutritive liquids are hurtful; and that if they have not been in the habit of drinking it from their youth, they use some caution in accustoming themselves to it. Many suffer themselves to be led away by the panegyrists of water, without considering that even good changes in the system of life, when a person is not accustomed to them, and when they are abruptly or unseasonably adopted, may be productive of great mischief. Hence arise the silly complaints that water-drinking is dangerous, pernicious, nay fatal, and the inapplicable cases quoted from experience. Those who have been in the habit of drinking water from their youth, cannot choose a more wholesome beverage, if the water be but pure. Many nations, and many thousand more species of animals, have lived well upon it. But for an old infirm person, a living skeleton, with a weak stomach that can scarcely bear solid food, to exchange nourishing beer or strengthening wine, with the water of his brook, would be the height of absurdity. Let such adhere to their accustomed drink. Water is an excellent beverage, but beer too is good; it is also water, more nutritious than the pure element, and therefore more suitable for the persons to whom I am alluding.

The third condition which I require of my water-drinkers is—that they take cold and not hot water for their habitual beverage. I mean not to prohibit their boiling or distilling it if they suspect it to be impure. Boyle drank nothing but such distilled water, and most delicate people of good taste in Italy still do the same. It must not, however, be drunk warm, but cold. The ancients, it is true, drank hot water. Various passages in Plautus and other ancient writers clearly prove that so early as their times it was customary to drink the water of warm springs; and there are frequent instances of common water warmed. Thus, in Dio, we find Drusus, the son of Tiberius, commanding warm water to be given to the people, who asked for water to quench their thirst at a fire which had broken out. Seneca says (*De Ira*, ii, 15,) that a man ought not to fly into a passion with his servant, if he should not bring his water for drinking so quickly as he could wish ; or if it should not be hot enough, but only lukewarm ; and Arrian says the same thing, but more circumstantially.  The drinking of hot water must of course have been a common practice with the Greeks and Romans ; but it should be observed, that even in their times it was held to be an effeminate indulgence of voluptuaries.  Stratonicus calls the Rhodians " pampered voluptuaries who drink warm liquors."  Claudius, when he attempted to improve the morals of the people and to check luxury at Rome, prohibited the public sale of hot water.  When on the death of the sister of the Emperor Caius, he had enjoined mourning in the city of Rome on account of this, to him, exceedingly painful loss, he put to death a man who had sold hot water, for this very reason, because he had thereby given occasion for voluptuousness, and profaned the mourning.  So dangerous an indulgence was the drinking of hot water considered, that the trade of water-sellers was interdicted by the Censors.  Some writers publicly satirized this species of voluptuousness.  Ammianus complains that in his time servants were not punished for great vices and misdemeanours, but that three hundred stripes were given them, if they brought the warm beverage either not promptly enough or not hot enough : and from that passage of Martial's in which he says, that at entertainments the host was accustomed to pay particular attention that during the feast there should be an abundant supply of hot water, it appears that this beverage was an essential requisite at the tables of the luxurious.

---

### STANZAS.

In glowing youth, he stood beside
His native stream, and saw it glide
Shewing each gem beneath its tide,
   Calm as though nought could break its rest,
   Reflecting heaven in its breast,
   And seeming, in its flow, to be
   Like candour, peace, and piety.

When life began its brilliant dream,
His heart was like his native stream :
The wave-shrined gems could scarcely seem
   Less hidden than each wish it knew ;
   Its life flow'd on as calmly too ;
   And Heaven shielded it from sin,  ·
   To see itself reflected in.

He stood beside that stream again,
When years had fled in strife and pain ;
He look'd for its calm course in vain—
   For storms profaned its peaceful flow,
   And clouds o'erhung its crystal brow :—
   And turning then, he sigh'd to deem
   His heart still like his native stream.

C. L.

*"Quand li œil pleure, li cuer rit."*—*La Bible Guyot.*

"I HAVE no doubt, Sir, but your will will be my pleasure," said a graceless nephew to a good-natured old uncle, who announced the intention of leaving him a fat legacy; and let sentimentalists say what they please of "tender pains," "soft sorrows," "the pleasures of melancholy," and the "joy of grief;" there are no tears half so satisfactory as those of a legatee. In this sense, at least, most people will feel shocked at Sterne's jocular commencement of a sermon,—"*that I deny*,"—and will, in Yorick's despite, freely and at once acknowledge with the preacher of antiquity, that "it *is* better to go to the house of mourning than to the house of feasting."

The merriest faces, it has been said, are to be seen in mourning-coaches; and though a ride in a mourning-coach (as my own woful experience has too frequently testified), does not necessarily imply a legacy, the circumstance can hardly fail to put the idea into a man's head; the *memento mori* reminding him of his legitimate expectations in some other quarter, and forcibly impressing on him the conviction, that, notwithstanding the man may still live who stands between himself and an estate, yet "in him nature's copy's not etern,"—of which truth the mourner's corollary, like Macbeth's, ("then be thou jocund") follows, "as ready as a borrower's cap." This hypothesis for explaining the paradoxical combination of "inky suits" and "broad grins," will prove sufficient, I imagine, for the latitude of England: in Ireland, as we all know, "*it's the whiskey does it;*" and what necessity can there be for looking farther into the causes of that country's excessive population, since it is well known, that one man is never interred beneath the shamrock, without giving occasion to the production of at least two—*uno avulso non deficiunt plures?*

As a zealous disciple of the doctrine of final causes, which has a why for every wherefore, I firmly maintain that legacies exist *in rerum natura* for no other purpose than to dry our tears, to reconcile us to the loss of friends, and prevent that sinful despair which might otherwise unfit us for the business of life; and this will explain the cause of lachrymatories falling into disuse, and giving way to bottles of sal volatile, the pungency of which may supply the place of our gold-stifled sensibilities. Franklin does not mention of the lady, who, he said, "had not forgiven God Almighty the death of her husband," that she was handsomely provided for by will, or that she succeeded to a large jointure; but if this was the case, she must have been of a singularly unforgiving temper, a living monument of morosity and *rancune*, and an impugner of the decrees of Providence, beyond the ordinary temerity of human discontent and perverseness. In the silence of authority, I should rather imagine, that, like many other widows, she had been sacrificed to the heir, and that, with the man, the lady also missed his comfortable establishment. Although when death takes place in families, "some natural tears" are shed by the most obdurate heirs-at-law, and some tender regrets are indulged by men of the worst dispositions for those with whom they have long associated, yet, when the first quarter's rents are coming in, it may be doubted whether the most pious and affectionate of us all would not hesitate to accept the resurrection of our lost friend, if that resurrection implied a resumption of his testamentary donations. The closing of the grave, like that of the sea over a sinking ship, leaves no trace behind it. As each man drops from among the living, the ranks close over him, his place is supplied, and if a Prince Hohenloe should contrive to bring him back to life at the end of a week, it is but too probable that he would find "no standing-room" upon the whole face of the earth. I am not of Hamlet's philosophy, who thinks building churches the way to make "a great man's memory outlive his life half-a-year." No, no; let him who would really be regretted, take his money with him to the next world; and who knows what the force of association may then do for him? Such is human nature—"'Tis true 'tis pity, pity 'tis 'tis true;" but we must even accept of it upon its own terms.

This being the lamentable truth, need we be surprised to find legacy-hunting the vice of all nations, or to see among the landed aristocracy, father and son considering each other as natural enemies? The savage, no less than the civilized man, is desirous of living at the expense of his neighbour, and with a characteristic impetuosity he knocks his friends on the head without scruple, in order to obtain the reversion of their good *properties*,—a practice wisely enough forbidden in Christian communities, lest estates should exist perpetually *in transitu*, and possession, instead of being nine points of the law, should become nine posts towards the next world. For if the savage goes to such extremities to procure the sense, spirit, and physical force he envies in his neighbour, what would not the *auri sacra fames* effect in the civilized animal! The song says

"L'uom senza denaro è un morto che cammina,"

"the man without money is a mere walking corpse;"—but if the savage notion prevailed among Europeans, the reverse would be the truth; and every man of wealth might be considered, if not dead in law, at least, in the language of the common people, *all as one.* · Proletarians would have it all to themselves, a landholder would have scarcely time to bespeak his own coffin, the world would no longer be "a stage to feed contention in the lingering act," but "heir" would indeed

"Urge heir like wave impelling wave," *

"inexorable death" would "level all" with a vengeance; and however it might fare with the "trees and stones" no proprietor's life would be worth three days' purchase.

The Romans, who are celebrated among nations as the first in recorded story who reduced legacy-hunting to a system, did not hesitate, under the Tiberiuses and Neros, to denounce their dearest friends and relations, for the purpose of hastening the succession—an example sometimes imitated during the calamitous period of the French revolution. Of this practice, however, there is the less reason for vaunting, inasmuch as it partakes largely of the savage *knock-me-down* method above mentioned, and can in civilized life rank only with George Barnwell's commentary upon testamentary law—

---

* Pope.

" Make nunky surrender his dibs,
  Rub his pate with a pair of lead towels,
Or stick a knife into his ribs,
  I 'll warrant he 'll then show some bowels.
      Rum ti iddle ti, &c." *

*Cætera quid referam?* Why should I mention the elder Hamlet, who
was " murdered in his garden for his estate?" or Philippe Egalité,
who helped, if common fame be not a common liar, Louis XVI. to
the scaffold, for the sake of a reversionary interest in his crown? this
mode of legacy-hunting being too common in aristocratical families to
need illustration in these pages. Esau's " Jew's trick" upon his brother
is, however, of more importance, both as the type of modern Hebraical
dealings in the *post obit* line, and the model of that species of legacy-
hunting in which Mother Church in her younger days was a perfect
Nimrod. The passion of churchmen for legacies is of so violent a
nature, that no English parliament was ever strong enough to contend
with it, or cunning enough to draw up a statute of mortmain, through
the meshes of which the church could not slip. It must be owned that
their " *adveniente mundi vespero*" was a capital hit in this line; and the
getting men to part with their property, under the notion that all property was about to be instantly destroyed, without causing their own
rapacity to bring the plea into suspicion, was a *tour de force*, which
shames the *droit d'Aubaine* of old France, and throws all regal and imperial schemes of legacy-hunting to an immeasurable distance.

This remnant, however, of the good old times, as well as the savage
method of doing business, is gone by. Since the invention of the
funding system, men do not care to place their money out in so long
an adventure as the " twilight of the universe;" or perhaps, as Swift
has it, they don't like the security, or peradventure they think more of
their money than their souls, (and Heaven knows, a good many of them
are just enough in their appraisement of the commodity); although,
therefore, the Holy Alliance may succeed in restoring the church to its
old possessions, it is not probable that all the committee of right-lined
extinguishers, with all their ribbons and baronies to boot, could persuade the bulls and bears in 'Change-alley to give a Benjamin's share
of their loans and debentures to the parsons.

But to descend from these sublimer speculations to mere private
adventure, it may be observed, that the *état* of a legacy-hunter belongs
exclusively to an advanced state of civilization, and to a rich community. Where the forms of society are simple, and the labour of supporting life is small, every body marries, and every body has children.
There are no miserly bachelor uncles, no servant-starving maiden aunts,
who, by dint of celibacy and tremulousness, acquire dominion over
all who approach them. In this state of society, too, every one loves
his own kin; and if accident or constitution now and then deprives a
man of offspring, it is rare that he will *chouse* his collateral descendants, or disinherit even a third cousin once removed, in favour of a
flattering apothecary, or cajoling attorney. On the other hand, nobody
is willing to undergo the hardships and restraints of expectancy, and
submit to the drudgery of currying favour, where the rewards of pro-

---

* Rejected Addresses.

ductive industry are at all proportionate to the labour. Who, indeed, (if a spade or a shuttle would support existence,) would give up twenty of the best years of life to the abnegation of self, to the curbing of every wish, to the hiding of every opinion—in one word, to the simula- tion and dissimulation of dependency, to eating the viands they detest, coaxing the cat, the monkey, or the parrot they abhor, flattering the lady's-maid they fear, or the valet of whom they are jealous? Who would voluntarily incur the paroxysms of anticipation, the cold fits of apprehension, and the hot fits of hope, which recur with every varia- tion in " the old man's" mood? Who would consent to diminish his own little funds, by incessant presents to Volpone and his *atours*, upon the forlorn hope of an unknown will; or would endure the ceaseless anxiety of watching his cough, divided between the certainty of his death and the chance that he may not yet have signed his will? who would do and suffer all this, and much more indeed than my paper would contain, if he could hold up his head, and breathe the fresh air of heaven in independence?—I had almost said, " when he could his quietus make with a bare bodkin!" Blessed (says Pope in one of his letters) are they who expect nothing, for they shall not be dis- appointed; and blessed, doubly blessed, say I, are they, for they are masters of their own house, keep their own hours, rule their own ser- vants, vote as they please for the county, order their own dinner, and eat their share of the brown, without reference to the whims and ca- prices of " *ame qui vive:*" that is, provided always that they have not a shrew for a wife.

To live in the constant desire for another man's death, if it be not a misprision of murder, is a baseness beneath the dignity of a free man, and incompatible with the integrity of an honest one. But these ca- suistical refinements in morals, I admit, though amusing enough for the elder children of Fortune, are too expensive for the poor and lowly. In these Malthusian days, in which population drives so hard against— *taxation*, (for *voilà le mot de l'énigme*,) and in which wealth and poverty, like the galvanism of Sir Humphrey's great pile, accumulate round the opposite poles of society in an all-destructive intensity, there must be rich old bachelors to be courted, and poor young bachelors to be cor- rupted: so that it is as plain as $x = \frac{a+b-c}{2\sqrt{3\,ab}}$ that legacy-hunting will increase till Pitt and paper, notes and non-representation, shall be for- gotten; and those " martyred saints the five per cents." shall be fol- lowed by their other kindred stocks into that abyss of by-gone things, into which they must all finally sink, and "leave not a—*dividend* behind."

Of all modes of trading adventure, legacy-hunting is the most provokingly uncertain. Depending on the caprice of sickness and of age, a vapour or a whim may overturn the expectations of a long life; and the most artist-like combinations, after years of patience and perseverance, may be defeated by a sly hussy with a warming-pan, a methodist parson, or a fit of the blue devils. Nor is this without some appearance of poetical justice; for let a man make his will as he pleases, it is ten to one that he does not please any one else. Even when he gives all to one universal legatee, the heir may grudge the servants their mourning, and the corpse its funeral honours; or he may be angry that the testator has tied him down in some particular in which he wishes to have been free. Not many years ago, a Scotch gentleman, who had realized a large fortune in India, died, and bequeathed all his wealth to two brothers, partners in a mercantile house in the city, on the condition that he should be buried in great state in his native village, and how, think you, did the heirs comply with the letter of this injunction? Why, they packed up the dead man in a cask of damaged rum, and shipped him on board the Lovely Kitty, bound, God willing, for the port of Leith: there a cart waited to receive this singular item of invoice, (upon which it must have puzzled the customhouse folks to fix the *ad valorem* duty,) and to convey it to the markettown nearest the place of sepulture. The body was then taken out of pickle, put into a sumptuous coffin, and conducted to its final abode with the customary paraphernalia: and thus the charge of a funeral procession from London was saved, and the function performed "in the cheapest and most expeditious manner :"—and so much for the spirit of trade!

Pliny well observes (Lib. viii. Epist. 18.) that the vulgar opinion, which regards a man's will as a reflection of his disposition, is wholly false. It is, in fact, a mere reflection of the particular moment in which it is written; and much depends whether it be dictated before or after dinner. When the making a will is deferred to a late period of life, it is more usually a contradiction than a corollary to the testator's habitual modes of thinking and feeling. This remark of the Roman letter-writer is *apropos* to an old gentleman, who, after lending himself to the legacy-hunters, taking all their bribes, and accepting all their adulation, died, and left his property, as he ought, to his own relations. "Upon this occasion," says Pliny, "the town-talk was considerable; some said he was ungrateful, some said he was false, some that he forgot his old friends, thus betraying their own unworthiness by their open expression of disappointment :" (*seque ipsos, dum insectantur illum, turpissimis confessionibus produnt :*) others, on the contrary, praised him for thus cheating the cheaters, and reading them "*a great moral lesson*" on the prevalent vice of the day. Of all the uncertainties of human life, the uncertainty of a legacy is the greatest. The extent to which the vice of legacy-hunting prevailed among the Romans is among the most extraordinary moral phenomena which the political combination of their day presents. The coarseness of the methods employed betrays an inconceivable relaxation of the social affections, and developes a selfishness the most disgustingly revolting. One man comes into the house of a dying woman, with whose family he had lived in constant variance, and by the help of a few grimaces, an affected zeal for her recovery, a sacrifice, and a declaration that the victim predicts long life to the patient, he worms himself into a good legacy. Another meddles in the dictation of all his neighbours' wills, on the speculation (which rarely failed) of insinuating an item in his own favour. In our days the world is grown something wiser, if not better, and a man must play his cards much more dextrously if he hopes to win any thing at this game. Indeed, it is now the expectant who is most generally the dupe in these transactions; and we more frequently hear of old folks quartering themselves upon some credulous and greedy family, and pestering them through life with their maladies, whims, and caprices, (or, as Winifrid Jenkins calls them, their "*picklearities*"), and then dying intestate, or, what's worse, willing their property away God knows where,—than of great fortunes derived from obsequiousness. I remember a man, who, after having failed in trade, retired to a remote country-town at an advanced period of life, with little or nothing but his wits to live upon. After receiving the civilities of his neighbours, in virtue of an imposing exterior, a few well-applied innuendoes, and frequent dissertations on the relative value of landed and funded security, he gradually began to express his regard for his new friends, his satisfaction at his reception among them, the pleasure he derived from their society, and his admiration at their several virtues ; and, at length, sending for the attorney, he dictated the sketch of a will, in which he inserted the names of the most considerable residents in the environs. To some names he put two cyphers, and to others three, leaving the prepositive numeral which was to give value to the whole—a blank. This will he ordered the man of law to draw up in form, of course with the strictest possible injunctions of secrecy. The secret was *of course* confidentially betrayed to every one of the interested parties, with a friendly hint "to stick to the warm old fellow, without a relation of his own on the face of the earth." Thus the testator contrived to pass the rest of his life very comfortably from house to house ; and from that day forward never wanted a hare, or a brace of pheasants, a basket of fish, or of grapes, when he chose, for the sake of appearances, to dine at his own lodgings. At the day of his death he very honourably divided all he had equally among these numerous expectants ; bequeathing to each, in the strict fulfilment of his implied promise, just £00 0s. 0d.

Against frauds like these, the poor legacy-hunter cannot be too guarded ; for there is no tread-mill to punish this species of vagrancy—unless, indeed, the devil, the true inventor of that anti-English species of legal torture, has a round-about of his own, where, by the by, he cannot at least punish the prisoner *before* trial and judgment.—Indeed, old folks in general have an unlucky pride in thus overreaching their prey, and chuckle heartily (in their sleeve) at the idea of the disappointment which the opening of their will will produce. When the party is a female, and not within the prohibited degrees of kindred, the best means of proceeding is to marry at once ; and then the law and the usage combine to leave the lady no longer a will of her own. If this be not possible, the case is too often all but desperate. Waiting for dead men's shoes is at best but a tedious business ; and the bailiffs of this world may be more expeditious than their great prototype of the next, who, being always sure of his man, is very often most provokingly forgetful, and keeps the writ a long while in his pocket. All things, in short, considered, as long as lotteries and little-goes exist, I would not advise a friend to take to legacy-hunting. Even gambling in foreign securities, or joining the Poyais or the Cape of Good Hope settlers, may be made a better trade, or at all events a pleasanter one, than dodging the whims or watching the growing decrepitude of a fellow who continues to exist long after he has ceased to live, for the mere pleasure of balking your most reasonable expectations, laughing at your agonies, and making your life an "eternal renewal of hope, with an everlasting disappointment."        M.

## ELEGIAC STANZAS.

I WANDER'D when the shadows fell,
  'Till darkness brooded o'er the deep ;
And thoughts of her, I loved so well,
  Came o'er me—but I could not weep.

The night was silent as the grave—
  I thought of her who slumber'd there :
Of her I would have died to save—
  The young, the beautiful, the fair.

I could not weep a single tear,—
  The wave of ocean roll'd below,
And evil thoughts were gathering near—
  But oh, thank God ! it was not so.

I wept not still—but when the light
  Was kindled on the beacon tower,
And stream'd on ocean through the night,
  I felt an influence from the hour:

My better feelings, that had slept,
  Gush'd like the water from the rock
When Israel's leader smote—I wept
  Such tears as can the heart unlock.

They were not tears of bitterness,
  But such as contrite spirits shed ;
For thus Religion comes to bless
  The darken'd hour, when hope is fled.

I wept—but they were tears of balm,
  And soon was felt throughout my frame
A blessed, and a holy calm—
  And call'd I then upon his name.

" Oh God ! be thou the mourner's stay,
  " My refuge on life's troubled sea ;
" Thy word the light that guides my way
  " To her I love, to Heaven and thee."

                                    W. T.

---

## SOCIAL AND SAVAGE LIFE.—DANIEL BOON.

An attachment to what is called civilized life, is considered to be interwoven with our existence ; but perhaps it is not so much so as we in general suspect. Like an attachment to the locality where we spent our earliest years, the value which we feel for it arises less from its intrinsic superiority over savage life being properly estimated by us, than from the effect of habit. Local attachments we owe to accident, they relate to things, and therefore there can be no interchange of regard, no mutual tie between them and ourselves, beyond what may arise from fancy and the associations that they may recall. They offer us nothing like the affection we feel towards friends and relatives who receive our kind offices and render us theirs in exchange. Local attachments are experienced in their greatest intensity by those who live remote from large cities and great congregations of men. Inhabitants of mountainous districts, however unpolished in manners and less advanced in civilization than those of plains, feel much stronger the charm that binds them to the scenes of their early life—the countryman much more than the citizen. Climate seems in this respect to make little distinction; the Laplander, the Swiss, and the Negro whom we steal from among his native mangroves and his pestilential marshes to steep in slavery, are alike strongly sensible of its influence. In great capitals it is almost obliterated; the early habits of their inhabitants being singularly unpropitious to its operation. The endless change of objects, the soul-engrossing traffic, and the bustle and turmoil of London, for example, soon stifle every trace of the feeling, if the smallest portion of it exist at all among its natives. In truth, what local attachment, in the sense I allude to, can be experienced by him who was born and resided two or three years in Smithfield, lived two or three more in the purlieus of Fleet-street, or among the dirty alleys of Holborn, his residence for ever shifted as the calls of business might require? The local attachment of a Londoner is a very general and indefinite thing, and perhaps only consists in his regard for the name of the city itself, and its high claims upon public estimation, and because he will have every thing with which he is connected, to be better than any other. His early removal into the shop or manufactory, his artificial mode of life, his associates, and the demoralization around, make him incapable of feeling any of the sensations experienced by the unsophisticated inhabitant of the country, who has spent his youth amid the charms of nature, gazed with a delight of which the Londoner is utterly ignorant, upon the blue stream, the craggy mountain, or the tufted wood, from the door of the tenement in which he was born, and which has sheltered his ancestors for ages—who has noted every tree in the landscape on which he has looked with fondness for years, and has completely identified with his own heart "the hill that lifts him to the storms:"—his neighbours are all in his horizon of view; it is his little universe, and he would exchange it for no other. Thus, what may be called the highest congregated state of man, tends to obliterate local attachments, which will be found strongest in that state of society which approaches nearest to the simplicity of Nature.

It has been remarked, that those who have been educated in civilized society, if they have at any time been forced to quit it by some accidental circumstance, and mingled with the Indian tribes in the forests of America, adopting for any considerable time their mode of life, and ranging unrestrained through the vast domains which have never yet submitted to the plough, have found it extremely difficult to return again and yield obedience to its restraints and institutions. A Mr. Hunter has lately published a most interesting work, containing an account of his life and residence among the Indian tribes of North America, having been made captive by them, when an infant, in one of their attacks upon the White settlements. According to their custom, they adopted him into a family, and reared him up in their own mode of life. He wandered with them across the vast territory of the Missouri to the Pacific Ocean, and back again to the western states of America. He made his escape from them to one of the American cities, where he attracted much notice. This gentleman has stated to his intimate friends, that, particularly since he has been initiated into the forms of polished life, he has felt at times an almost irresistible inclination to return and join again his former associates; every thing seeming beyond measure cramped and restrained when contrasted with the liberty and ease of his former mode of life. Mr. Hunter's work contains much interesting matter for the consideration of the philosopher, and indeed of all who make the history of the human mind their study. It discloses many traits of Indian character, which must tend to raise rather than depress them in the scale of being. The fondness of the savage for ranging the forest and leading the life of a hunter, arises from the same love of liberty which is engrafted in the nature of civilized man, and is diminished, but never utterly annihilated, in the bosom of the citizen. Every attempt which has been made in Canada to amalgamate the aboriginal inhabitants with Europeans has failed. A chief here and there has been found, after long intercourse, to join occasionally the colonial society, and conduct himself in a very superior manner, so as to demonstrate that he was able, if he pleased, to support the artificial accomplishments of those whom he visited; but soon afterwards he has resumed his Indian habiliments, and rejoined his countrymen in the forest, with a delight that seemed to have derived a higher value from the contrast it afforded him to the manners he had just quitted. The village of Jeune Lorette in Canada is entirely an Indian residence; but though every method has been taken to make them adopt European customs, even with the children, who have been instructed in reading and writing, the effort has appeared insurmountable. By the aid of the strong liquors and diseases imported from Europe, they will by and by become extinct, owing to the rapid diminution of their population, but they will never disappear by being blended with those who have conveyed to them these baleful plagues. The stream of Indian life will be dried up, pure to its last dregs, without commingling its waters and repairing its diminution from foreign sources. Yet these Indians have the sagacity to discover that knowledge is strength, and to shelter themselves under our protection, some of them even tilling small plots of ground after the mode they have learnt from us. But nothing can obliterate their affection for their own mode of life. After all, considering them abstractedly from the part they constitute towards the whole body politic, a considerable portion of the inhabitants of every civilized state have little of which to boast over the Aborigines of Canada, either in the employments in which they spend their time, the moral innocence of their lives, or the elevation of their pursuits. The free Indian has the advantage in many high and romantic qualities; he is brave, content, and independent, while the former cannot be said to be either.

But there may sometimes be motives for the freedom of the woods and forests being adopted by civilized men. The injustice and oppression that man often receives from his fellow, from bad laws, or from the shafts of calumny, may appear in themselves sufficiently strong to justify him in adopting the simplicity and uncontrolled state of natural life. To men of particular dispositions, of high spirit, and keen feelings, whose minds have been deeply wounded, a life spent apart from scenes which they cannot contemplate without pain, has been felt to be grateful. They have determined that the social compact is dissolved: that the boasted protection which was held out as the price of restraint, and for which freedom and property were sacrificed, was no longer a shield held over them. They hear statesmen talk of citizenship, and the duty of every man to bear evil and injustice, and even to sacrifice himself for the sake of the community—that the bundle must not be weakened by abstracting a single stick. They hear lawyers boast of the excellency of laws that bar that exercise of his free will which inclines him to withdraw from their power, and declaring that his fealty, arising from the accidental circumstance of birth, can never be violated under any pretence;—that he must bear every evil life can inflict, but has no right to withdraw himself from that society which has a paramount claim on him and his. He considers, reflects, and at last presumes to differ from these very politic but sophistical principles. What is society to him? has he power over his own property, and shall he have none over a choice of country? Shall he not resign that which in his feelings is guilty of injustice towards him, and endeavour to spend the remainder of life in the mode most congenial and soothing to a wounded spirit? He demurs a moment, forms his resolution, rushes into the woods, and becomes a hunter for the rest of his days, far removed from the footsteps of civilised man. Who can blame such an individual, or with justice contend that he has no moral right thus to dispose of himself? Who can blame him for not submitting to a state of life full of disgust, and that would drench the remainder of his days in suffering?

Such was, in all probability, the reasoning of Colonel Daniel Boon, whose name was unknown in this country until it was lately brought before the public by Lord Byron.* His history is still a novelty. Accident made me acquainted with some incidents respecting him by means of an American friend. Memoirs of this extraordinary individual, or rather of part of his singular career, have been published on the other side of the Atlantic, but I believe have never yet reached England. Boon originally belonged to the state of North Carolina, where he cultivated a farm. In company with five other individuals, he left that province in 1769, and journeyed to a river that falls into the Ohio,

---

* The passage alluded to, by Lord Byron, is as follows :

Of all men, saving Sylla, the manslayer,
　Who passes for in life and death most lucky,
Of the great names which in our faces stare,
　The General Boon, backwoodsman of Kentucky,
Was happiest among mortals any where ;
　For killing nothing but a bear or buck, he
Enjoy'd the lonely, vigorous, harmless days
Of his old age in wilds of deepest maze.

Crime came not near him—she is not the child
　Of solitude ; health shrank not from him—for
Her home is in the rarely-trodden wild,
　Where if men seek her not, and death be more
Their choice than life, forgive them, as beguiled
　By habit to what their own hearts abhor—
In cities caged. The present case in point I
Cite is, that Boon lived hunting up to ninety ;

And what's still stranger, left behind a name
　For which men vainly decimate the throng,
Not only famous, but of that *good* fame,
　Without which glory's but a tavern song—
Simple, serene, the antipodes of shame,
　Which hate nor envy e'er could tinge with wrong ;
An active hermit, even in age the child
Of nature, or the Man of Ross run wild.

with a view of settling upon it. The spot which he chose was situated in the state of Kentucky, in which he thus became the first settler. He began by erecting a house, surrounded by a stockade or close palisado, formed of the square trunks of trees, placed close together and sunk deep in the earth, a precaution absolutely necessary to be taken in a frontier settlement continually exposed to the attacks of the native Indians. This fort, as the Americans call such defences, was situated about seventy-five miles from the present town of Frankfort, and the party gave it the name of Fort Boonsborough; and thus was formed the primitive settlement of the state of Kentucky, which now has a population of 564,317. He entered his lands and secured them, as he imagined, so as to give him a safe title, and was completely established in them in the year 1775. He seems, however, to have experienced various attacks from hostile tribes of Indians. At this place, with no common resolution, and with a fortitude that argued him to be of the order of superior men, far removed from military succour, in a wild and savage forest, and with a constant fear of attack from a ferocious enemy, he steadily and undauntedly proceeded to mature his plans. When his little fort was completed, he removed his establishment to it from North Carolina, conducting thither his wife and daughters, the first white females that had ever trod on the shores of the Kentucky river. He was soon joined by four or five other families, and thirty or forty men settlers. They had several times repulsed the attacks of the Indians with bloodshed; and at length, while making salt from some brine springs at no great distance from his home, he was surprised, together with twenty-seven of his settlers, by upwards of a hundred, who were on their march to renew their attacks on his infant colony. He capitulated with them on condition that their lives should be spared, and they were immediately marched away to an Indian town on the Miami river, a long distance off, and finally conducted to the British governor, Hamilton, at Detroit, the Indians scrupulously abiding by the terms on which Boon had surrendered to them. These sons of nature, however, got so attached to their prisoner on their march, that they would not resign him to the British governor, nor even part with him for a hundred pounds generously offered for him by the British officers, in order that he might return home to his family; but leaving his fellow-settlers behind, they took him away with them again, adopted him into the family of one of their chiefs, and allowed him to hunt or spend his time in the way most agreeable to his inclination. One day he went with them to make salt, when he met with four hundred and fifty warriors painted and armed, and ready to set out against Fort Boonsborough. He immediately determined, at a great risk of his life, to make his escape, trembling as he was for the fate of his family and settlement. In four days he reached Boonsborough, a distance of one hundred and sixty miles, making only one meal by the way. Not a minute was to be lost, and he began to strengthen his log defences and fortify himself as strongly as possible. The Indians, finding he had escaped, delayed their attack; and having received a reinforcement of men, in which were a few troops, he determined to brave all dangers and defend himself to the last. At length a ferocious Indian army made its appearance. Boon encouraged his little garrison to maintain an obstinate defence, death being preferable to captivity, though his hope of resisting with success was but faint. The cruel and savage enemy also, they might well calculate, would become doubly enraged by a protracted resistance; but like brave men, determined to let fate do its worst and think nothing of final consequences, they let the Indian chief know their resolution. Upon this the latter demanded a parley with nine of the garrison; articles were proposed for an arrangement without bloodshed; but on signing them they were told it was the Indian custom to shake hands with each other by way of sealing their engagement. On complying, each Indian grappled his man in order to make him prisoner, but, by a miracle, eight out of the nine succeeded in extricating themselves, Boon being among the number, and they got safe into their garrison. A furious attack was now made upon the fort, which lasted nine days and nights, during which only two men were killed and four wounded by the besiegers, who in return suffered severely, and the logs of the fort were stuck full of the bullets which they fired. At length hostilities ceasing, Boon's wife, who on his first captivity supposing him killed, had set off with her family on horseback through the woods a long and dangerous distance into North Carolina, was fetched back by her husband a second time to his new residence, where he hoped for the future to pursue his peaceful occupations unmolested. His sufferings and perils had been great, but his courage and constancy had surmounted them all, and he had just reason to calculate at last upon a period of repose.

Boon, however, was not to end his days amid the advantages of social life. His horoscope had been cast, and discovered no common portion of malign influence. His courage and constancy, under the severest trials; his long and unremitting labours, in perfecting his infant settlement, almost entitled him to a civic crown; but how different was his reward! After his exemplary labours, after spending the best part of an honest life in rearing and providing for a numerous family, and having arrived at that period of existence when he might reasonably expect to enjoy the fruit of his exertions, and obtain some return for the fatigues and hazards of his preceding life; too old to begin another settlement, and that which he had begun so many years before in the heart of the wilderness, looking smiling around him, the prop of his old age, the pride of his hoary years, his family's hope when he should be laid low—he suddenly finds that he is possessed of nothing, that his eyes must be closed without a home, and that he must be an outcast in his grey hairs. His heart is torn, his feelings are lacerated by the chicanery of the law, which discovers that there is a defect in his title to the land of which he was the first settler, even in a state where no white man had put in the spade before him. Perhaps his thriving farm was envied by some new adventurer. The discovery was fatal to his happiness. While he fondly believed that his title was indisputable, his land was taken from him, his goods were sold, and he was deprived of his all. The province had been rapidly settling by his countrymen, and encreasing civilization was accompanied by those vices which are its never-failing attendants. Knavery, in every form, marched with it; interest, at any sacrifice of honour and justice, became the reigning principle. The law, which in all countries inflicts nearly as much evil as it prevents, was made an instrument to dispossess him of his property, and he saw himself a wanderer and an outcast. His past labour, even to blood, had been in vain. Cut to the soul, with a wounded spirit, he still showed himself an extraordinary and eccentric man. He left for ever the state in which he had been the first to introduce a civilised population—where he had so boldly maintained himself against external attacks, and shown himself such an industrious and exemplary citizen; where he found no white man when he sat himself down amid the ancient woods, and left behind him half a million. He forsook it for ever; no intreaty could keep him within its bounds. Man, from whom he deserved every thing, had persecuted and robbed him of all. He bade his friends and his family adieu for ever; he felt the tie which linked him to social life was broken. He took with him his rifle and a few necessaries, and crossing the Ohio, pursued his track till he was two or three hundred miles in advance of any white settlement. As the territory north of the Ohio was taken possession of, and peopling fast from the United States, he crossed the Missisippi, and plunged into the unknown and immense country on the banks of the Missouri, where the monstrous Mammoth is even now supposed to be in existence. On the shores of this mighty river he reared his rude log hut, to which he attached no idea of permanency, but held himself constantly ready to retire yet farther from civilized man, should he approach too near his desert solitude. With the exception of a son, who resided with his father, according to some accounts, but without any one, according to others, his dog and gun were his only companions. He planted the seeds of a few esculent vegetables round his fragile dwelling, but his principal food he obtained by hunting. He has been seen seated on a log at the entrance of his hut by an exploring traveller, or far more frequently by the straggling Indian. His rifle generally lay across his knees and his dog at his side, and he rarely went farther from home than the haunts of the deer and the wild turkey, which constituted his principal support. In his solitude he would sometimes speak of his past actions, and of his indefatigable labours, with a glow of delight on his countenance that indicated how dear they were to his heart, and would then become at once silent and dejected. He would survey his limbs, look at his shrivelled hands, complain of the dimness of his sight, and lifting the rifle to his shoulder take aim at a distant object, and say that it trembled before his vision, that his eyes were losing their power, rubbing them with his hands, and lamenting that his youth and manhood were gone, but hoping his legs would serve him to the last of life, to carry him to spots frequented by the game, that he might not starve. It does not appear that he talked much of the ingratitude of mankind towards him. He perhaps thought regret and complaint alike unavailing, and that his resolution of exiling himself in the back woods and the territories of the Indians was the best way of demonstrating the high-spirited contempt and indignation he felt towards his countrymen, by whom he had been so unjustly treated. Boon seems to have possessed a great mind; congregated men had treated him with injustice and with cruelty, considering his claims upon them; he sought not to retaliate his injuries on individuals—he felt not the passion of revenge, nor the wish to injure those who had injured him irreparably, but he viewed social man with the scorn of ill-requited merit, and he determined to withdraw from his power. He felt that he could not be happy amid the heartless vices of society; that the desert and the forest, the Indian, the rattlesnake, and the Juagar, were preferable associates; that they bore no feigned aspect of kindness while they were secretly plotting his destruction; that they rarely inflicted evil without just provocation; and that the uncontrolled child of Nature was a preferable companion to the executors of laws, which to him at least, however beneficial they might in some cases be to others, were most cruel and unjust.

Thus he passed through life till he was between eighty and ninety years of age, contented in his wild solitude, and in his security from injustice and rapacity. About a twelvemonth ago, it is reported, he was found dead on his knees, with his rifle cocked and resting on the trunk of a fallen tree, as if he had just been going to take aim, most probably at a deer, when death suddenly terminated his earthly recollections of the ingratitude of his fellow-creatures, at a period when his faculties, though he had attained such an age, were not greatly impaired. Boonsborough is now a thriving town, and its name will ever remain as a testimony of its founder's sufferings, and the conduct of his fellow-citizens towards him, in the midst of the freest nation of ancient or modern times. Y. L.

---

## THE LOST PLEIAD.

"Like the lost Pleiad seen no more below."—LORD BYRON.

AND is there glory from the Heavens departed?
  —Oh, void unmark'd!—thy sisters of the sky
    Still hold their place on high,
Though from its rank thine orb so long hath started,
  Thou! that no more art seen of mortal eye!

Hath the Night lost a gem, the regal Night?
  —She wears her crown of old magnificence,
    Though thou art exiled thence!
No desert seems to part those urns of light,
  Midst the far depths of purple gloom intense.

They rise in joy, the starry myriads burning!
  The Shepherd greets them on his mountains free,
    And from the silvery sea
To them the Sailor's wakeful eye is turning;
  —Unchanged they rise, they have not mourn'd for thee!

Couldst thou be shaken from thy radiant place,
  Ev'n as a dew-drop from the myrtle-spray,
    Swept by the wind away?
Wert thou not peopled by some glorious race,
  And was there power to smite them with decay?

Why, who shall talk of Thrones, of Sceptres riven?
  —It is too sad to think on what *we* are,
    When from its height afar,
A world sinks thus! and yon majestic Heaven
  Shines not the less for that one vanish'd star! F. H.

## THE PROGRESS OF COXCOMBRY.

*"Nemo repente fuit dandissimus."*

THE transformation of the chrysalis into the butterfly is not more complete or surprising than that of the slovenly schoolboy into the finished civil, academic, or military dandy. The last metamorphosis is, however, more gradual than the former. The nice observer can easily mark the successive stages of its developement, from the superstitious tie of the cravat and scrupulous "brushing of the hat o'mornings," to the minute observance of the entire ceremonial of foppery, and faithful discharge of the whole duty of dandyism.

The passion for dress is, generally speaking, stronger in the fair sex than in ours, and is in them infinitely more excusable. But when it has once thoroughly laid hold of an unlucky wight, it carries him into much greater and more ridiculous excesses than we ever witness among the ladies. Dandyism, at first, is like the small speck in the cloudless azure, which to the eye of the experienced mariner presages the gathering·storm. In its birth it is scarcely noticed by common observers, or noticed only to be despised. But it gradually increases by fresh accessions of vapour, until the intellectual horizon becomes completely overcast, and the sun of reason

——" from far peeps with a sickly face,
Too weak the clouds and mighty fogs to chase."

The late Hugh Peters was a striking instance of how far the genuine dandymania could carry a man, who in other respects was not destitute of natural good sense. In Hugh, indeed, this disease appeared to be constitutional; he evinced evident symptoms of it at a very early age, and it continued with increasing violence to his dying day. This master-passion was not to be controlled by sickness, poverty, imprisonment or exile. It burned with as much fervour in age as in youth, and was scarcely extinguished by that universal damper—death.

Hugh, as I have said, began dandyism at an early age. His parents were "of the straitest sect," Methodists. They, of course, reprobated all vain adornment of the outward man, considering the gauds of dress as the ensigns of Satan, and so many badges of subjection to the kingdom of darkness. They were careful that Hugh should be arrayed with the utmost plainness, in clothes of the coarsest texture, and the most ungainly fashion. The style of his habiliments was singularly ludicrous, and afforded infinite diversion to his young companions. Instead of being dressed in the fashion of boys of his own age and rank, he was attired like an old man. He usually wore a blue coat with covered buttons, which fitted him like a sentry-box, and exhibited a latitude of skirt that would have done honour to George Fox himself. You would swear that he had been measured by the tailors of Laputa, or the ingenious artist who works from hasty observations taken on the body of M. Rothschild, during its transit to the Stock-Exchange. His waistcoat was of a sober brown, with pocket-flaps "five fathom deep," that overhung a pair of scanty corduroy inexpressibles, scarce covering the cap of his knee. Grey yarn stockings, shoes, or rather brogues, two inches in the sole, and a broad-brimmed hat, completed the exterior of the elegant Hugh Peters.

The system pursued by his parents produced an effect diametrically opposite to their intention. It turned the boy's regard to the subject of dress, and generated and fostered the desire of decoration. He ventured, as he grew older, though with a trembling hand, to make some slight reform in his costume. He disfranchised his enormous coat-flaps, and succeeded in cancelling a few sinecure pockets. This he managed by cultivating a good understanding with his tailor. But all his efforts were fruitless, to oblige his corduroy breeches to vacate their seat, or to prevent the annual return of the broad-brimmed beaver to the presidency of his pericranium. He managed, however, to procure a pair of buff leather-gaiters as a counterbalance to the corrupt influence of the one, and in some degree to alter the constitution of the other, by cocking it up at the sides with black pins; a measure, which would have rendered him a prime favourite at the Court of St. Petersburgh, when Paul, the hater of round hats, was autocrat of all the Russias.

It is not to be imagined that even these changes were effected without considerable opposition : in fact, they gave birth to continual explosions of present wrath, and fulminations of wrath to come, on the part of his father. His mother, too, added her mite of zeal in predicting the eventual perdition of her only son ; for who, as she acutely remarked, could escape hell-fire, that wore a cocked hat and sulphur-coloured gaiters ? But Hugh had arrived at that age and stature where flagellation ceases to be practicable, and exhortation to be efficient. His parents could not succeed

> " with wind
> Of airy threats to awe, whom now with deeds
> They could not."

Their only resource was to deprive him altogether of money ; and though this could not wither his dandyism in the bud, it yet checked its growth for a season, and imparted to it a stunted character of original and ludicrous peculiarity.

Necessity is the mother of invention, and some of Hugh's devices at this period to put off the clown and put on the dandy were sufficiently ingenious, though often productive of ridiculous results. He turned tailor in his own defence, but his earlier attempts to modify his habiliments, were, like the infant efforts of every art, rude and clumsy to a degree. He reduced the latitude of his skirts without any very strict observance of mathematical proportion, and finished his work with no particular neatness of stitching. The partial alterations in his dress, harmonized very ill with its general character, and often exhibited the most ridiculous contrasts. The flaming gaiters, for instance, were not well assorted with the clumsy shoes and corduroy-breeches deeply bronzed by the relentless finger of time. The tail of his coat, cropped short by his rash hand in evil hour, gave to the otherwise too ample garment, something of the look of a fireman's jacket destitute of the badge and made by a most ill-conditioned tailor. A red waistcoat, second-hand, trimmed with old fur, and, in the fashion of the day, ridiculously short, which he purchased of an honest Israelite, seemed within the prodigious lappels of his external habit, like a flea in St. Paul's, or Gulliver in the embraces of Glumdalclitch. His neck enveloped in muslin manifold, rose above his humble collar, "like the tower of Lebanon which looketh towards Damascus." But an invention which he hit on, for the decoration of his nether limbs, was indeed a *chef-d'œuvre*. Entertaining a high opinion of the symmetry of this part of his person, he longed to reveal its graceful proportions in the seductive transparencies of stocking-web. His uncle, who was something of a dandy, gave him an opportunity of gratifying this penchant by the present of a pair of cast-off *tights*. These, though somewhat large, Hugh contrived, by his sartorial dexterity, to adapt tolerably well to his own person. But on trying them on, though highly gratified by the contemplation of the femur and tibia, he found that something was still wanting to the perfection of their developement. Our desires increase with our possessions, and every new gratification gives birth to a fresh necessity. Hugh soon discovered that tight pantaloons without Hessian boots were as preposterous as a haunch of venison without currant-jelly, or a leg of pork without peas-pudding. They were, in truth, natural correlatives, coefficient quantities, mutually attractive, conductors to each other,—their separation was violent, dangerous, improper, sacrilegious! But how to effect the desired union? Boots were dear, Hugh was poor; his uncle had no Hessians to spare, and his father's heart and purse were equally closed against him. He must either wear the pantaloons without boots (a thing not to be thought of) or steal a pair. Dire dilemma! diabolical alternative! But the genius of dandyism descended kindly to his aid, and opportunely rescued her ardent votary from the hazard of crime and the mortification of disappointment. As Hugh cast around

> " His baleful eyes,
> That witness'd huge affliction and dismay,"

he suddenly espied his buff-leather gaiters, which hung upon a peg above his head. An idea flashed across his brain like lightning—one of those felicitous conceptions of genius, perfect as if matured by years of thought, sudden as inspiration! He seized the gaiters, posted to a cobler, had them cut out into the shape of Hessian boots at top, blackened, polished, decked with tassels. What need of more words? Nothing could be more complete. The following day was Sunday. He appeared at church in complete costume,—cocked chapeau, pudding-cravat, red waistcoat, fireman's jacket, brown-coloured tights, and gaiter-boots,—the admiration of himself—the derision of many—the astonishment of all!

But the hour was at hand when Hugh was to cast his slough, to unfold his glittering scales in the sunbeam, to burst the dark prison of his chrysalis for ever, and issue forth an airy butterfly in all the colours of the rainbow. His father, who was much more sincerely devoted to Mammon than to God, undertook a voyage to Smyrna in quest of gain. The prince of air, who thought it high time to appropriate his destined prey, raised a storm and plunged the Methodistic merchant in the deep. Hugh was sole heir of all his wealth, which was considerable, and as the trustees of the property did not pretend to

any control over his conduct, this hopeful youth was left at the age
of seventeen

"Lord of himself, that heritage of woe."

His first step was to enter the army, a measure of which he would
not have dared to whisper during the lifetime of his father. He got
into a dashing regiment of light-infantry, and soon became distinguished
for the most extravagant foppery. Not contented with the costume of
his corps, which was elegant and splendid, he was perpetually making
such alterations and additions as his own whim suggested. His capricious taste in this way subjected him to frequent reprimands and arrests
for the violation of the regimental orders. His offences became at last
so frequent and so flagrant, that the colonel, much of a martinet, told
him that he must leave the regiment unless he thought proper to conform to its regulations of dress. Hugh promised obedience, and for a
while was less open in his transgressions. But his ruling passion was
too strong to be controlled for any length of time. He went to a
garrison-ball in a fantastic costume which bore a caricatured resemblance to the uniform of his corps. The first person he met there was
the colonel, who insisted on his leaving the room immediately; and as
colonels seldom experience much difficulty in the removal of an obnoxious subaltern, his exit from the regiment very speedily followed
his exit from the ball. He was, in fact, *advised* to tender his resigna-
tion; and he had too much knowledge of the army not to feel the propriety of following this judicious counsel.

Hugh was not very seriously concerned for the loss of his commission, as it left him "fancy free" to pursue his devious courses through
the fields of foppery and fashion. He repaired to London, and soon
became the very mirror of fantastic coxcombry. He had his day like
other dogs, and the time has been when the promenades of Bond-street
and Hyde-park would have been deemed to want their most essential
attraction in the absence of "the original Hugh Peters." But, alas
for human eminence, and the degeneracy of present times! The
"lights of the world and demigods of fame" have quitted the stage for
ever, and the fashionable, like the political horizon, is left in a feeble
twilight, the precursor, it is to be feared, of a long night of Egyptian
darkness. Brummel is extinct, Van Butchell in his grave. Sir L—,
like another Ovid in Pontus, is exiled to the ungenial climate of St.
George's, where he pours his unavailing "tristia," and *stoops* indeed,
but, alas, no more to conquer! Baron Geramb is gone, and the gallant
gay "Lothario" is sobered down into "Benedick, the married man."
We listen in vain for the rattling of his chariot-wheels, and the high-
crested cock has now become an empty name. Finally, Hugh Peters
himself hath passed away, and the flags of Bond-street have forgot his
steps!

Hugh was, at this time, more remarkable for the singularity than the
taste of his costume. He delighted in glaring colours, and a close fit
he considered the "summum bonum." His motions were dreadfully
constrained by the tightness of his dress, and the various organic functions seriously impeded. To button his coat required an effort almost
superhuman. His inexpressibles (horresco referens) were perpetually
yielding to the force of pressure, and leaving him exposed in some
vital part. The tarsus, metatarsus, and toes, sustained infinite damage
from the compressive action of the boot, and the uncomfortable pro-

jection of a heel three inches high. His feet became pleasingly variegated with corns and bunnions, and were soon reduced to a state of premature superannuation.

I shall not speedily forget the first time I had the honour of beholding Hugh Peters. He was in full dress for the pit of the Opera. His coat was of the genuine Pomona-green, with a collar reaching to the crown of his head, basket-worked buttons made of silver, and skirts lined with white silk. His waistcoat was white, richly embroidered, and studded with three rows of small yellow buttons. Inside this were two more, cushioned and quilted, the one of scarlet silk, the other of sky-blue. Canary-coloured small-clothes, with flesh-coloured silk-stockings, decorated his nether limbs; and a pump, which might emulate a vice, with a diamond buckle, showed his almost Chinese foot to exquisite advantage. His cravat, which at the least he took an hour to adjust, was fastened in the centre with a large emerald, and beneath it a waving banner of frill sported in the wanton zephyrs. A gold eye-glass with a red riband, white kid-gloves, and inordinate *chapeau-bras*—the portrait is finished.

Hitherto Hugh had given more attention to his person than his face; and, coxcomb as he was, he had still much to learn in the minuter details of dandyism. Critically nice in the cut and fashion of his apparel, he was but a novice in the mysteries of the cosmetic art, his practice in this way scarcely extending beyond the more ordinary processes of ablution. He had, besides, certain prepossessions to overcome on this score. Notwithstanding the latitude of his foppery, he conceived that there was a fixed boundary beyond which it must not extend, and where manliness would say, "thus far shalt thou go and no farther." He would wear, for instance, a coat tight enough almost to check respiration, but would shudder at the thought of a pair of stays. He might employ an hour in brushing his hair, but he would turn with loathing from the idea of painting his face. But it is the character of every folly, and of every vice, to increase, unless the growth be timely and effectually prevented. The incipient gangrene must be met with the knife and the cautery. Hugh's attention was first directed to his visage by some one remarking that his eyebrows were rather light. There could be nothing unmanly in adding to the expression of the countenance, to which dark eyebrows so materially contributed. He began first by pencilling, next proceeded to painting, and lastly to staining his brows, with a variety of deleterious composts. He became the dupe of advertising impostors, and the most absurd distresses were the frequent result of his ill-judged experiments. In the course of a few months his brows had successively assumed all the colours of the rainbow, to the vast amusement of his friends, and his own ineffable inconvenience. He persevered, however, with a constancy worthy of a better cause, and at last hit upon a composition which produced the proper hue; but after a few applications utterly destroyed the hair, and left him literally *browless!* His only resource was a pair of artificial eyebrows, which formed, as may be supposed, but an imperfect deception, and an insecure substitute for the natural.

Hugh's next discovery was, that a smooth skin and clear complexion were essentials of beauty. His toilet was soon loaded with cold cream, milk of roses, botanic bloom, eau de Cologne, and soaps of all sono-

rous titles borrowed from " the rich orient," and of a variety of shades
of colour and degrees of fragrance.   His hands now came in for their
share of attention, and be consumed immense quantities of almond
paste and white wax.   Not satisfied with topical applications for the
purpose of improving his appearance, he used warm baths, had himself blooded and physicked regularly with the same view.   He consumed three estates, which he inherited, in the expenses of the toilet.
When destitute of money, he ran in debt to gratify his vanity; and for
some years previous to his death he supported his elegant appearance
by certain financial measures, to which, peradventure, a fastidious
moralist might attach an impolite epithet.   Confined in the Bench,
he used to saunter about, in a rich *robe de chambre*, green velvet-cap,
and red slippers, with an immense Turkish pipe in his mouth, from
which he exhaled not " Mundungus' ill-perfuming scents," but green
tea!   He debilitated his frame by the use of medicine, and contracted complaints in his side and chest from continual pressure.

Dandyism is in youth only ridiculous; in age it is contemptible.
We have attempted the portrait of Hugh in his earlier days.   At fifty
he was the most artificially constructed being in existence; he was
made up from head to foot.   He wore a wig, false eyebrows, false
whiskers, and false mustachios.   He had a complete set of false teeth,
his cheeks and lips were painted, and the furrows beneath his eyes
were filled up with a white paste.   His clothes were stuffed out at the
chest and shoulders, his waist was tightened in with stays, and he had
false calves to his legs.   He was altogether a walking deception—a
complete lie from top to toe—a finished specimen of that most despicable of all animals—the superannuated dandy.                Π.

---

THE SLEEPER ON MARATHON.

I LAY upon the solemn plain,
    And by the funeral mound,
Where those who died not there in vain,
    Their place of sleep had found.
'Twas silent where the free blood gush'd,
    When Persia came array'd,—
So many a voice had there been hush'd,
    So many a footstep stay'd!

I slumber'd on the lonely spot,
    So sanctified by Death!
I slumber'd—but my rest was not
    As theirs who lay beneath.
For on my dreams, that shadowy hour,
    They rose—the chainless Dead—
All arm'd they sprung, in joy, in power,
    Up from their grassy bed.

I saw their spears, on that red field,
    Flash, as in time gone by!
Chased to the seas, without his shield,
    I saw the Persian fly!
I woke—the sudden trumpet's blast
    Call'd to another fight:—
From visions of our glorious past,
    Who doth not wake in might?                F. H.

## On Application to Study.

No one is idle, who can do any thing. It is conscious inability, or the sense of repeated failure, that prevents us from undertaking, or deters us from the prosecution of any work.

Wilson, the painter, might be mentioned as an exception to this rule; for he was said to be an indolent man. After bestowing a few touches on a picture, he grew tired, and said to any friend who called in, " Now, let us go somewhere!" But the fact is, that Wilson could not finish his pictures minutely; and that those few masterly touches, carelessly thrown in of a morning, were all that he could do. The rest would have been labour lost. Morland has been referred to as another man of genius, who could only be brought to work by fits and snatches. But his landscapes and figures (whatever degree of merit they might possess) were mere hasty sketches; and he could produce all that he was capable of, in the first half-hour, as well as in twenty years. Why bestow additional pains without additional effect? What he did was from the impulse of the moment, from the lively impression of some coarse, but striking object; and with that impulse his efforts ceased, as they justly ought. There is no use in labouring, *invitâ Minerva*—nor any difficulty in it, when the Muse is not averse.

" The labour we delight in physics pain."

Denner finished his unmeaning portraits with a microscope, and without being ever weary of his fruitless task; for the essence of his genius was industry. Sir Joshua Reynolds, courted by the Graces and by Fortune, was hardly ever out of his painting-room; and lamented a few days, at any time spent at a friend's house or at a nobleman's seat in the country, as so much time lost. That darkly-illuminated room " to him a kingdom was:" his pencil was the sceptre that he wielded, and the throne, on which his sitters were placed, a throne for Fame. Here he felt indeed at home; here the current of his ideas flowed full and strong; here he felt most self-possession, most command over others; and the sense of power urged him on to his delightful task with a sort of vernal cheerfulness and vigour, even in the decline of life. The feeling of weakness and incapacity would have made his hand soon falter, would have rebutted him from his object; or had the canvass mocked, and been insensible to his toil, instead of gradually turning to

" A lucid mirror, in which nature saw
All her reflected features,"

he would, like so many others, have thrown down his pencil in despair, or proceeded reluctantly, without spirit and without success. Claude Lorraine, in like manner, spent whole mornings on the banks of the Tiber or in his study, eliciting beauty after beauty, adding touch to touch, getting nearer and nearer to perfection, luxuriating in endless felicity—not merely giving the salient points, but filling up the whole intermediate space with continuous grace and beauty! What farther motive was necessary to induce him to persevere, but the bounty of his fate? What greater pleasure could he seek for, than that of seeing the perfect image of his mind reflected in the work of his hand? But as is the pleasure and the confidence produced by consummate skill, so is the pain and the desponding effect of total failure. When for the fair face of nature, we only see an unsightly blot issuing from our best endeavours, then the nerves slacken, the tears fill the eyes, and the painter turns away from his art, as the lover from a mistress, that scorns him. Alas! how many such have, as the poet says,

> " Begun in gladness ;
> Whereof has come in the end despondency and madness"—

not for want of will to proceed, (oh! no,) but for lack of power!

Hence it is that those often do best (up to a certain point of common-place success) who have least knowledge and least ambition to excel. Their taste keeps pace with their capacity; and they are not deterred by insurmountable difficulties, of which they have no idea. I have known artists (for instance) of considerable merit, and a certain native rough strength and resolution of mind, who have been active and enterprising in their profession, but who never seemed to think of any works but those which they had in hand; they never spoke of a picture, or appeared to have seen one: to them Titian, Raphael, Rubens, Rembrandt, Correggio, were as if they had never been: no tones, mellowed by time to soft perfection, lured them to their luckless doom, no divine forms baffled their vain embrace; no sound of immortality rung in their ears, or drew off their attention from the calls of creditors or of hunger: they walked through collections of the finest works, like the Children in the Fiery Furnace, untouched, unapproached. With these true *terræ filii* the art seemed to begin and end: they thought only of the subject of their next production, the size of their next canvass, the grouping, the getting of the figures in ; and conducted their work to its conclusion with as little distraction of mind and as few misgivings as a stage-coachman conducts a stage, or a carrier delivers a bale of goods, according to its destination. Such persons, if they do not rise above, at least seldom sink below themselves. They do not soar to the "highest Heaven of invention," nor penetrate the inmost recesses of the heart; but they succeed in all that they attempt, or are capable of, as men of business and industry in their calling. For them the veil of the Temple of Art is not rent asunder, and it is well: one glimpse of the Sanctuary, of the Holy of the Holies, might palsy their hands, and dim their sight for ever after!

I think there are two mistakes, common enough, on this subject; viz. that men of genius, or of first-rate capacity, do little, except by intermittent fits, or *per saltum*—and that they do that little in a slight and slovenly manner. There may be instances of this ; but they are not the highest, and they are the exceptions, not the rule. On the contrary, the greatest artists have in general been the most prolific or the most elaborate, as the best writers have been frequently the most voluminous as well as indefatigable. We have a great living instance among writers, that the quality of a man's productions is not to be estimated in the inverse ratio of their quantity, I mean in the Author of Waverley ; the fecundity of whose pen is no less admirable than its felicity. Shakspeare is another instance of the same prodigality of genius ; his materials being endlessly poured forth with no niggard or fastidious

hand, and the mastery of the execution being (in many respects at least)
equal to the boldness of the design. As one example among others
that I might cite of the attention which he gave to his subject, it is
sufficient to observe, that there is scarcely a word in any of his more
striking passages that can be altered for the better. If any person, for
instance, is trying to recollect a favourite line, and cannot hit upon
some particular expression, it is in vain to think of substituting any
other so good. That in the original text is not merely the best, but it
seems the only right one. I will stop to illustrate this point a little. I
was at a loss the other day for the line in Henry V.

> " *Nice* customs curtesy to great kings."

I could not recollect the word *nice :* I tried a number of others, such
as *old, grave*, &c.—they would none of them do, but seemed all heavy,
lumbering, or from the purpose : the word *nice*, on the contrary, appeared to drop into its place, and be ready to assist in paying the reverence required. Again,

> " A jest's *prosperity* lies in the ear
> Of him that hears it."

I thought, in quoting from memory, of " A jest's *success*," " A jest's
*renown*," &c. I then turned to the volume, and there found the very
word that, of all others, expressed the idea. Had Shakspeare searched
through the four quarters of the globe, he could not have lighted on
another to convey so exactly what he meant—a *casual, hollow, sounding
success!* I could multiply such examples, but that I am sure the
reader will easily supply them himself; and they show sufficiently that
Shakspeare was not (as he is often represented) a loose or clumsy writer.
The bold, happy texture of his style, in which every word is prominent, and yet cannot be torn from its place without violence, any more
than a limb from the body, is (one should think) the result either of
vigilant pains-taking or of unerring, intuitive perception, and not the
mark of crude conceptions, and " the random, blindfold blows of
Ignorance."

There cannot be a greater contradiction to the common prejudice that
" Genius is naturally a truant and a vagabond," than the astonishing
and (on this hypothesis) unaccountable number of *chefs-d'œuvre* left behind them by the old masters. The stream of their invention supplies
the taste of successive generations like a river : they furnish a hundred
Galleries, and preclude competition, not more by the excellence than
by the number of their performances. Take Raphael and Rubens
alone. There are works of theirs in single Collections enough to occupy a long and laborious life, and yet their works are spread through
all the Collections of Europe. They seem to have cost them no more
labour than if they " had drawn in their breath and puffed it forth
again." But we know that they made drawings, studies, sketches of
all the principal of these, with the care and caution of the merest tyros
in the art ; and they remain equal proofs of their capacity and diligence.
The Cartoons of Raphael alone might have employed many years, and
made a life of illustrious labour, though they look as if they had been
struck off at a blow, and are not a tenth part of what he produced in

his short but bright career. Titian and Michael Angelo lived longer, but they worked as hard and did as well. Shall we bring in competition with examples like these some trashy caricaturist or idle dauber, who has no sense of the infinite resources of nature or art, nor consequently any power to employ himself upon them for any length of time or to any purpose, to prove that genius and regular industry are incompatible qualities?

In my opinion, the very superiority of the works of the great painters (instead of being a bar to) accounts for their multiplicity. Power is pleasure; and pleasure sweetens pain. A fine poet thus describes the effect of the sight of nature on his mind:

> ——— " The sounding cataract
> Haunted me like a passion : the tall rock,
> The mountain, and the deep and gloomy wood,
> Their colours and their forms were then to me
> An appetite, a feeling, and a love,
> That had no need of a remoter charm
> By thought supplied, or any interest
> Unborrow'd from the eye."

So the forms of nature, or the human form divine, stood before the great artists of old, nor required any other stimulus to lead the eye to survey, or the hand to embody them, than the pleasure derived from the inspiration of the subject, and "propulsive force" of the mimic creation. The grandeur of their works was an argument with them, not to stop short, but to proceed. They could have no higher excitement or satisfaction than in the exercise of their art and endless generation of truth and beauty. Success prompts to exertion; and habit facilitates success. It is idle to suppose we can exhaust nature; and the more we employ our own faculties, the more we strengthen them and enrich our stores of observation and invention. The more we do, the more we *can* do. Not indeed if we *get our ideas out of our own heads*—that stock is soon exhausted, and we recur to tiresome, vapid imitations of ourselves. But this is the difference between real and mock talent, between genius and affectation. Nature is not limited, nor does it become effete, like our conceit and vanity. The closer we examine it, the more it refines upon us; it expands as we enlarge and shift our view; it "grows with our growth, and strengthens with our strength." The subjects are endless; and our capacity is invigorated as it is called out by occasion and necessity. He who does nothing, renders himself incapable of doing any thing; but while we are executing any work, we are preparing and qualifying ourselves to undertake another. The principles are the same in all nature; and we understand them better, as we verify them by experience and practice. It is not as if there was a given number of subjects to work upon, or a set of *innate* or preconceived ideas in our minds which we encroached upon with every new design; the subjects, as I said before, are endless, and we acquire ideas by imparting them. Our expenditure of intellectual wealth makes us rich : we can only be liberal as we have previously accumulated the means. By lying idle, as by standing still, we are confined to the same trite, narrow round of topics : by continuing our efforts, as by moving forwards in a road, we extend our views, and discover continually new tracts of country. Genius, like humanity, rusts for want of use.

Habit also gives promptness; and the soul of dispatch is decision. One man may write a book or paint a picture, while another is deliberating about the plan or the title-page. The great painters were able to do so much, because they knew exactly what they meant to do, and how to set about it. They were thorough-bred workmen, and were not learning their art while they were exercising it. One can do a great deal in a short time if one only knows how. Thus an author may become very voluminous, who only employs an hour or two in a day in study. If he has once obtained, by habit and reflection, a use of his pen with plenty of materials to work upon, the pages vanish before him. The time lost is in beginning, or in stopping after we have begun. If we only go forwards with spirit and confidence, we shall soon arrive at the end of our journey. A practised writer ought never to hesitate for a sentence from the moment he sets pen to paper, or think about the course he is to take. He must trust to his previous knowledge of the subject and to his immediate impulses, and he will get to the close of his task without accidents or loss of time. I can easily understand how the old divines and controversialists produced their folios: I could write folios myself, if I rose early and sat up late at this kind of occupation. But I confess I should be soon tired of it, besides wearying the reader.

In one sense, art is long and life is short. In another sense, this aphorism is not true. The best of us are idle half our time. It is wonderful how much is done in a short space, provided we set about it properly, and give our minds wholly to it. Let any one devote himself to any art or science ever so strenuously, and he will still have leisure to make considerable progress in half a dozen other acquirements. Leonardo da Vinci was a mathematician, a musician, a poet, and an anatomist, besides being one of the greatest painters of his age. The Prince of Painters was a courtier, a lover, and fond of dress and company. Michael Angelo was a prodigy of versatility of talent—a writer of Sonnets (which Wordsworth has thought worth translating) and the friend of Dante. Salvator was a lutenist and a satirist. Titian was an elegant letter-writer, and a finished gentleman. Sir Joshua Reynolds's Discourses are more polished and classical even than any of his pictures. Let a man do all he can in any one branch of study, he must either exhaust himself and doze over it, or vary his pursuit, or else lie idle. All our real labour lies in a nut-shell. The mind makes, at some period or other, one Herculean effort, and the rest is mechanical. We have to climb a steep and narrow precipice at first; but after that, the way is broad and easy, where we may drive several accomplishments abreast. Men should have one principal pursuit, which may be both agreeably and advantageously diversified with other lighter ones, as the subordinate parts of a picture may be managed so as to give effect to the centre group. It has been observed by a sensible man *, that the having a regular occupation or professional duties

---

* The Rev. W. Shepherd, of Gateacre, in the Preface to his Life of Poggio.

to attend to, is no excuse for putting forth an inelegant, or inaccurate work; for a habit of industry braces and strengthens the mind, and enables it to wield its energies with additional ease and steadier purpose.—Were I allowed to instance in myself, if what I write at present is worth nothing, at least it costs me nothing. But it cost me a great deal twenty years ago. I have added little to my stock since then, and taken little from it. I "unfold the book and volume of the brain," and transcribe the characters I see there as mechanically as any one might copy the letters in a sampler. I do not say they came there mechanically—I transfer them to the paper mechanically. After eight or ten years' hard study, an author (at least) may go to sleep.

I do not conceive rapidity of execution necessarily implies slovenliness or crudeness. On the contrary, I believe it is often productive both of sharpness and freedom. The eagerness of composition strikes out sparkles of fancy, and runs the thoughts more naturally and closely into one another. There may be less formal method, but there is more life, and spirit, and truth. In the play and agitation of the mind, it runs over, and we dally with the subject, as the glass-blower rapidly shapes the vitreous fluid. A number of new thoughts rise up spontaneously, and they come in the proper places, because they arise from the occasion. They are also sure to partake of the warmth and vividness of that ebullition of mind, from which they spring. *Spiritus precipitandus est.* In these sort of voluntaries in composition, the thoughts are worked up to a state of projection: the grasp of the subject, the presence of mind, the flow of expression must be something akin to *extempore* speaking; or perhaps such bold but finished draughts may be compared to *fresco* paintings, which imply a life of study and great previous preparation, but of which the execution is momentary and irrevocable. I will add a single remark on a point that has been much disputed. Mr. Cobbett lays it down that the first word that occurs is always the best. I would venture to differ from his authority. Mr. Cobbett himself indeed writes as easily and as well as he talks; but he perhaps is hardly a rule for others without his practice and without his ability. In the hurry of composition three or four words may present themselves, one on the back of the other, and the last may be the best and right one. I grant thus much, that it is in vain to seek for the word we want, or endeavour to get at it second-hand, or as a paraphrase on some other word—it must come of itself, or arise out of an immediate impression or lively intuition of the subject; that is, the proper word must be suggested immediately by the thoughts, but it need not be presented as soon as called for. It is the same in trying to recollect the names of places, persons, &c. We cannot force our memory; they must come of themselves by natural association, as it were; but they may occur to us when we least think of it, owing to some casual circumstance or link of connexion, and long after we have given up the search. Proper expressions rise to the surface from the heat and fermentation of the mind, like bubbles on an agitated stream. It is this which produces a clear and sparkling style.

In painting, great execution supplies the place of high finishing. A few vigorous touches, properly and rapidly disposed, will often give more of the appearance and texture (even) of natural objects than the most heavy and laborious details. But this masterly style of execution is very different from coarse daubing. I do not think, however, that the pains or polish an artist bestows upon his works necessarily interferes with their number. He only grows more enamoured of his task, proportionally patient, indefatigable, and devotes more of the day to study. The time we lose is not in overdoing what we are about, but in doing nothing. Rubens had great facility of execution, and seldom went into the details. Yet Raphael, whose oil-pictures were exact and laboured, achieved, according to the length of time he lived, very nearly as much as he. In filling up the parts of his pictures, and giving them the last perfection they were capable of, he filled up his leisure hours, which otherwise would have lain idle on his hands. I have sometimes accounted for the slow progress of certain artists from the unfinished state in which they have left their works at last. These were evidently done by fits and throes—there was no appearance of continuous labour—one figure had been thrown in at a venture, and then another; and in the intervals between these convulsive and random efforts, more time had been wasted than could have been spent in working up each individual figure on the sure principles of art, and by a careful inspection of nature, to the utmost point of practicable perfection.

Some persons are afraid of their own works; and having made one or two successful efforts, attempt nothing ever after. They stand still midway in the road to fame, from being startled at the shadow of their own reputation. This is a needless alarm. If what they have already done possesses real power, this will increase with exercise; if it has not this power, it is not sufficient to ensure them lasting fame. Such delicate pretenders tremble on the brink of *ideal* perfection, like dew-drops on the edge of flowers; and are fascinated, like so many Narcissuses, with the image of themselves, reflected from the public admiration. It is seldom, indeed, that this cautious repose will answer its end. While seeking to sustain our reputation at the height, we are forgotten. Shakspeare gave different advice, and himself acted upon it.

> —— "Perseverance, dear my lord,
> Keeps honour bright. To have done, is to hang
> Quite out of fashion, like a rusty mail,
> In monumental mockery. Take the instant way;
> For honour travels in a strait so narrow,
> Where one but goes abreast. Keep then the path;
> For emulation hath a thousand sons,
> That one by one pursue. If you give way,
> Or hedge aside from the direct forth-right,
> Like to an enter'd tide, they all rush by,
> And leave you hindmost:—
> Or like a gallant horse, fall'n in first rank,
> Lie there for pavement to the abject rear,
> O'er-run and trampled. Then what they do in present,
> Though less than yours in past, must o'ertop yours:
> For time is like a fashionable host,
> That slightly shakes his parting guest by the hand,
> And with his arms outstretch'd as he would fly,
> Grasps in the comer. Welcome ever smiles,
> And farewell goes out sighing. O let not virtue seek...

Remuneration for the thing it was; for beauty, wit,
High birth, vigour of bone, desert in service,
Love, friendship, charity, are subjects all
To envious and calumniating Time.
One touch of nature makes the whole world kin,
That all with one consent praise new-born gauds,
Though they are made and moulded of things past ;
And give to dust that is a little gilt
More laud than gilt o'er dusted.
The present eye praises the present object."
                              *Troilus and Cressida.*

I cannot very well conceive how it is that some writers (even of taste
and genius) spend whole years in mere corrections for the press, as it
were—in polishing a line or adjusting a comma. They take long to
consider, exactly as there is nothing worth the trouble of a moment's
thought; and the more they deliberate, the farther they are from deciding : for their fastidiousness increases with the indulgence of it, nor
is there any real ground for preference. They are in the situation of
*Ned Softly*, in the "Tatler," who was a whole morning debating whether a line of a poetical epistle should run—

             " You sing your song with so much art ;"
or,
             " Your song you sing with so much art."

These are points that it is impossible ever to come to a determination
about ; and it is only a proof of a little mind ever to have entertained
the question at all.

There is a class of persons whose minds seem to move in an element
of littleness; or rather, that are entangled in trifling difficulties, and
incapable of extricating themselves from them. There was a remarkable instance of this improgressive, ineffectual, restless activity of
temper in a late celebrated and very ingenious landscape-painter.
" Never ending, still beginning," his mind seemed entirely made up of
points and fractions, nor could he by any means arrive at a conclusion
or a valuable whole. He made it his boast that he never sat with his
hands before him, and yet he never did any thing. His powers and
his time were frittered away in an importunate, uneasy, fidgety attention to little things. The first picture he ever painted (when a mere
boy) was a copy of his father's house ; and he began it by counting the
number of bricks in the front upwards and lengthways, and then made
a scale of them on his canvass. This literal style and mode of study
stuck to him to the last. He was put under Wilson, whose example
(if any thing could) might have cured him of this pettiness of conception ; but nature prevailed, as it almost always does. To take pains to
no purpose, seemed to be his motto, and the delight of his life. He
left (when he died, not long ago) heaps of canvasses with elaborately
finished pencil outlines on them, and with perhaps a little dead-colour-
ing added here and there. In this state they were thrown aside, as if
he grew tired of his occupation the instant it gave a promise of turning
to account, and his whole object in the pursuit of art was to erect
scaffoldings. The same intense interest in the most frivolous things
extended to the common concerns of life, to the arranging of his let-

ters, the labelling of his books, and the inventory of his wardrobe. Yet he was a man of sense, who saw the folly and the waste of time in all this, and could warn others against it. The perceiving our own weaknesses enables us to give others excellent advice, but it does not teach us to reform them ourselves. " Physician, heal thyself!" is the hardest lesson to follow. Nobody knew better than our artist that repose is necessary to great efforts, and that he who is never idle, labours in vain!

Another error is to spend one's life in procrastination and preparations for the future. Persons of this turn of mind stop at the threshold of art, and accumulate the means of improvement, till they obstruct their progress to the end. They are always putting off the evil day, and excuse themselves for doing nothing by commencing some new and indispensable course of study. Their projects are magnificent, but remote, and require years to complete or to put them in execution. Fame is seen in the horizon, and flies before them. Like the recreant boastful knight in Spenser, they turn their backs on their competitors, to make a great career, but never return to the charge. They make themselves masters of anatomy, of drawing, of perspective: they collect prints, casts, medallions, make studies of heads, of hands, of the bones, the muscles; copy pictures; visit Italy, Greece, and return as they went. They fulfil the proverb, " When you are at Rome, you must do as those at Rome do." This circuitous, erratic pursuit of art can come to no good. It is only an apology for idleness and vanity. Foreign travel especially makes men pedants, not artists. What we seek, we must find at home or nowhere. The way to do great things is to set about something, and he who cannot find resources in himself or in his own painting-room, will perform the grand tour, or go through the circle of the arts and sciences, and end just where he began!

The same remarks that have been here urged with respect to an application to the study of art, will, in a great measure, (though not in every particular,) apply to an attention to business: I mean, that exertion will generally follow success and opportunity in the one, as it does confidence and talent in the other. Give a man a motive to work, and he will work. A lawyer who is regularly feed, seldom neglects to look over his briefs: the more business, the more industry. The stress laid upon early rising is preposterous. If we have any thing to do when we get up, we shall not lie in bed, to a certainty. Thomson the poet was found late in bed by Dr. Burney, and asked why he had not risen earlier. The Scotchman wisely answered, " I had no motive, young man!" What indeed had he to do after writing the " Seasons," but to dream out the rest of his existence, unless it were to write the " Castle of Indolence!"*

---

* Schoolboys attend to their tasks as soon as they acquire a relish for study, and apply to that for which they find they have a capacity. If a boy shows no inclination for the Latin tongue, it is a sign he has not a turn for learning languages. Yet he dances well. Give up the thought of making a scholar of him, and bring him up to be a dancing-master !

## MY SECOND LETTER TO THE NEW ROYAL LITERARY SOCIETY.

*De omnibus rebus et quibusdam aliis.*

" A rebus upon all things, and on several others."—*Free Translation.*

In my first letter I did not advert to one department of literature, that, for the abuses and corruptions with which it is defiled, may be termed the Augæan stable of the Muses, and calls aloud for the cleansing interposition of a Society which will not shrink from any labours, however Herculean. I allude to the present state of Logic. It is true that this science is not so severely studied as it was formerly, but it still forms a regular part of every classical education : and as many avail themselves of its subtleties and labyrinths for the purpose of puzzling others or making their own escape, to the great detriment of all truth, precision, and simplicity, and the manifest subversion of human reason in general, no more solemn or imperious duty can devolve upon the Society than the correction of so enormous and crying an evil. The whole sixty-four different modes of syllogism should be instantly abolished by act of parliament ; for what benefit can ever be derived from a study which will admit of such undeniable falsehoods, impossible truisms, and conclusive contradictions, as are exhibited in the following well-known dilemma of the Greek logicians?—Epimenides said all Cretans were liars—Epimenides was himself a Cretan—therefore Epimenides was a liar—therefore the Cretans were not liars—therefore Epimenides was not a liar—therefore the Cretans *were* liars, &c. I am willing to believe that the great majority of the Society I am addressing are fully impressed with the importance of atmospherical variations, as an inexhaustible subject of colloquial originality ; yet what is to become of our social enjoyments, if this most pregnant and delightful topic is to be rendered unavailing by such a *reductio ad absurdum* as the following ?—Either it rains, or it does not rain—but it rains—therefore it does not rain : or by reversing the position, you may prove that it does rain, and so strike at the very root of rational and instructive conversation. In the succeeding trite quatrain a most unfounded and illiberal imputation is cast upon the filial affections of a respectable class of his Majesty's subjects—the venders of turnips.

" If the man who turnips cries,
Cries not when his father dies,
'Tis a proof that he had rather
Have a turnip than his father."

When the perversion of logic is thus made a vehicle for private scandal, the legislature should provide some means of redress for the party libelled, provided he be proved to have taken out a regular hawker's licence.

In the Musarum Deliciæ an instance occurs of logical subtlety, which the Society may, perhaps, be disposed to think venial, and even laudable, since it was directed against the great enemy of mankind. A friar is stated to have sold his soul to the Prince of darkness, upon condition that all his debts were paid :—money was supplied in abundance ; and when the contracting party was extricated from all his pecuniary difficulties, and Satan appeared, saying that he came to claim the soul which was due to him,

> "The Friar return'd this answer:—If I owe
> You any debts at all, then you must know
> I am indebted still:—if nothing be
> Due unto you, why do you trouble me?"

This dangerous weapon is, however, sometimes applied, with a culpable Jesuitism and casuistry, to the evasion of the spirit, by adhering to the letter, of the most important moral enactments. Thus it has been urged that we are ordered to forgive our enemies, but not our friends; not to bear false witness *against* our neighbour, but we may do so *for* him: and he who had been accused of an improper intimacy with his valet's spouse, replied, that the offence was only forbidden against another man's wife, whereas this was his own man's wife. Such slippery subterfuges should be declared, by the paramount authority of the Society, to be senseless and irreverent mockeries. It might be advisable also that they should pass a severe censure upon a certain logical, or rather punning executor, who having three bank notes of a hundred pounds each to divide among five legatees, of whom he was himself one, said, "There is one for you two, one for you two, and one for me too." In cases of this nature, property, literature, and logic, unite in claiming the protection of the new Society.

It may also be most beneficially consulted as an umpire in cases that do not fall properly within the jurisdiction of any of our established courts: such, for instance, as the question whether the rustic was guilty of perjury, for swearing that at a certain hour a man on horseback stopped at his house, when it was clearly proved to have been a tailor upon a mare:—whether the common dictum, that the best side of a plum-pudding is the left side, (i. e. that which is left,) can be logically said of a piece cut from the centre;—whether you may legally object to paying for candles, as of bad quality, because when they are half burnt they will not burn any longer, but on the contrary burn shorter:—all these are most important considerations, which ought not to be left in their present state of cavil and uncertainty. Perhaps it might be advisable to offer prizes for the best essays upon subjects of general interest and clear unquestionable utility; such as the still unsolved problem,—"An chimæra rimbombans in vacuo poterit edere primas intentiones?"—for a solution of the old metaphysical crux of the jackass between the two bundles of hay;—for an enquiry into the much-disputed point, whether the philosopher Bias really invented the game of bowls, and Eusebius spectacles; whether Posthumus Leonatus was actually born again of a lion after his burial; and whether the surgical essay of Taliacotius, entitled "De Curtis Membris," may fairly be considered a prophecy that a well-known city baronet and his son should both become members of parliament. Much good may be effected in this way; but the questions selected should be of an importance as manifest as those which I have ventured to suggest.

The preservation of our language in all its purity being one of the main objects of the Institution, its attention cannot too earnestly be directed to an abuse of terms which is of much more serious importance than its mere philological inaccuracy, since it is calculated to injure morality and confound all our notions of right and wrong, by substituting certain silken phrases and taffeta terms precise for the most grave offences. Thus killing an innocent man in a duel is called—an affair of honour; violating the rights of wedlock—an affair of gallantry; adultery—a faux pas; defrauding honest tradesmen—outrunning the constable; reducing a family to beggary by gaming—shaking the elbows; a drunkard, that worst of all livers, is—a bon-vivant; disturbing a whole street, and breaking a watchman's head—a midnight frolic; exposing some harmless personage to insults, annoyances, and losses—a good hoax; uttering deliberate falsehoods—shooting the long bow: and various other polite epithets will occur to the Society, which, affecting to be used as synonymes for vice, not unfrequently assume the language of virtue. It is not beneficial to the monarchical principle that a female of bad character should be termed a courtezan; nor to morality that she should be described as a woman of pleasure. Such lenient periphrases are of most injurious tendency; and if the Society for the Suppression of Vice have failed to interfere for their discontinuance, I am confident that the Institution which I have the honour to address will not shrink from the full performance of its duty.

Perhaps I may be subjecting myself to the imputation of a Hysteron-proteron, if, after noticing the abuses and perversions of words, I proceed to those of individual letters; but the importance of the conclusions to which it leads induced me to reserve this subject for my own conclusion, and so end where most people begin—with the alphabet. So obscure and incomprehensible is the origin of letters, that many authors have been glad to solve the difficulty of their invention by referring it to divine inspiration. In that case, however, there would have been some conformity of character, number, and sequence; whereas there is a marked difference in all these constituents among the various nations of the earth. The learned author of Hermes informs us, that to about twenty plain elementary sounds we owe that variety of articulate voices which have been sufficient to explain the sentiments of such an innumerable multitude as all the past and present generations of men; and of course our alphabet, assuming this hypothesis to be true, might be much contracted. Yet there are others still more numerous, embracing all numbers up to the Chinese, which reckons by thousands, and assuming every variety of collocation, without any one people being able to assign reasons for deviating from the order of its neighbours. An elucidation of this curious subject is well worth the most serious attention of the Society.

The Scholiasts upon that ode of Anacreon which describes Cupid's being stung by a bee, state him to have been at that moment learning his letters; and that in perpetual remembrance of the pain inflicted by his winged assailant, he decreed that the alphabet should ever after commence with A B. Others suppose the whole ode to be allegorical, expressing how much Cupid felt stung and nettled at being compelled to undergo the drudgery of learning those letters. The precedence of B to C has been explained upon the principle that a man must be before he can see; but these, I apprehend, are plausible and ingenious conjectures, unsupported by any great philological or lexicographical authorities. Many curious discoveries have already been made in the hidden properties of letters, and the number might be indefinitely increased by the stimulating patronage, and ingenious researches of the Society.    But for the ingenuity of recent investigators, we should never have known that the letter S was of most essential service at the siege of Gibraltar, by making hot shot; that the letter N is like a little pig, because it makes a sty nasty; that the letters U V can never go out to dinner because they always come after T; that the letters o a s t are like toast without tea (T); and that a barber may be said to fetter the alphabet, because he ties up queues and puts toupees in irons.    These most important additions to our philological science are a happy foretaste of what may be accomplished by a chartered company expressly instituted for the encouragement of letters.

My limits not allowing me to enter at length into the subject of our hawkers and pedlars literature, vulgarly denominated the London Cries, I shall content myself with hinting that much of it is so alarmingly dissonant and cacophonous, as to need a thorough emendation. The wretches who yell—"Hi-aw-Marakrel!" and "Owld Clew!" should be compelled to articulate in a sweet and gracious voice—"Here are Mackarel"—and "Old Clothes." Our murderous dustmen's bells have converted many invalids, by depriving them of rest, into fit materials for their cart; and as their cry is at least as discordant as their clapper, I would have all these noisy nuisances converted into euphonious melodists by an immediate decree of the Society. The postman, as a man of letters, will of course receive a licence to bear the bell wherever he goes; and the muffin-man's tinkle is too inoffensive to require regulation. The great majority of our cries demand revision; but I would have no innovation upon the milkwoman's —'mi-eau! (probably handed down to us from the Norman times,) which is not only valuable as an antiquity, but as a frank confession that one-half of the commodity she vends is water.

From words, which are the signs of ideas, the Society may turn their attention to the signs of our public-houses, in which a very barbarous taste and a Gothic predilection for gorgons, and monsters and chimæras dire, is still but too visible. Since the recent discoveries in the interior of Asia, we are warranted in retaining the unicorn for our national arms; but the good taste of the Society will induce them to visit our public-houses, and procure the suppression of all such preposterous symbols as the Phœnix, the Griffin, the Green-dragon, the Blue-boar, the Red, Silver, and Golden Lions, with a hundred others; nor will they allow the continuance of such anomalous conjunctions as the Green Man and Still, which a recent French traveller has very excusably translated " L'homme vert et tranquille."

Presuming that my former letter has secured the first gold medal of fifty guineas, I have merely to hint in conclusion of my second communication, that my name is left with the publisher, and that the two medals may now be sent together to No. 50, Conduit-street.    H.

## PENSHURST CASTLE, AND SIR PHILIP SYDNEY.

DOES the reader, perchance not yet arrived at "years of discretion," love to sigh forth sweet breath over the sorrows of old romance, or feel his heart's blood dance in unison with its joys ?—or does he yearn to act those joys and sorrows over again in fancy—to melt his soul into bright thoughts, and coin those thoughts into burning words, and pour them forth, clothed in the purple hue of love, into the reluctant or not reluctant ear of some ideal lady, with a Greek visage and mellifluous name, beneath the shade of " Arcadian forests old," or in some rich glade of Tempé, where he may lie at her feet on the green turf by the hour together, without the previous precaution of wrapping himself up in lamb's wool ?—Or is he albeit a year or two older, but still in the rear of those "years of discretion" aforesaid) smitten with the love of the chase—not as it is pursued in these base and degenerate times, when the hunters and not the hunted are the beasts of prey—but when there was glory in the sport, because there was good in the end of it and danger in the means ?  Or, best of all, perhaps, does he believe and exult in those times—whether imaginary or not, no matter—when men held their lives but " at a pin's fee," and were content to see their best blood flow from them like water, in search of " that bubble reputation"—not indeed " in the cannon's mouth,"—for the cannon and its cursed kindred had not then blown courage into the air, and made skill a mockery—but when nothing but courage might cope with courage, and nothing but skill could hope to overthrow skill ?—Does the reader, I say, chance to possess any or all of these propensities, and seeing that they are proscribed and exploded in practice, would fain practise them in idea?  Then let him forthwith close his eyes to all things about him, and plunge headlong into that sea of sweet words in which are floating, like flowers in a crystal fountain, all high thoughts and beautiful imaginations—" the Countess of Pembroke's Arcadia."

But perhaps the majority of my readers *have* arrived at " the years of discretion" just referred to ; in which case they neither possess nor desire to possess the above-named amiable weaknesses: so that I must not urge *them* even to embark on the ocean I have named ; lest, having neither " youth at the prow," nor " pleasure at the helm,"—neither Passion to fill the sails of their vessel, nor Fancy to endue it with a self-moving power within itself—they may presently chance to find themselves becalmed and lying like a log upon the water, unable either to proceed or to return.  But even these persons, though they may have outlived the sentiment of intellectual beauty, which was born and lies buried within their breasts—though they may have ceased to consider mental love as any thing more than a subject of belief, or honour as any thing else than a word made up of mortal breath, or beauty as any thing less than " an association of ideas"—still they may like to recall the time when "nothing was but what was not,"—as the grown man loves to remember when he was a schoolboy, not because he liked to be what he then *was*, but because he *dis*-likes to be what he now *is*—still they may not object to look upon the express images of what *cannot be*, by " the light that *never was*," rather than remain for ever the discontented denizens of that darkness which they believe to exist *because they feel it*, though they refuse to believe in the brightness that is passed away·from them,·for the·same reason. If, I say, the·above class of persons choose to renew their intercourse with these "airy nothings" in default of those substantial somethings which cannot fill their place,—let them fly to the Astrophel and Stella—to the songs and sonnets—and above all, to the Defence of Poesy, of Sir Philip Sydney.

When the above-named classes of persons have followed this first part of my counsel, I shall probably have little occasion to urge upon them that to which it is intended to lead—namely, that they pay a visit, either by themselves or with me, to Penshurst Castle. But there is still another class for whom imaginary realities, so to speak, are not enough—but they must have tangible ones in addition; they are not satisfied with Mr. Coleridge for having written the Ancient Mariner, and the Stanzas to Love, but they would have had him distinguish himself at the Battle of Waterloo! To them, the most convincing proof that Lord Byron has written poetry is, that he has swam across the Hellespont. And they did not believe that Mr. Kean could play Lear till they heard that he could play Harlequin! But as my charity somewhat exceedeth, and as moreover I hold that our reason is never better employed than when it is accounting for the unreasonableness of others, I can excuse even *these* persons, and·would willingly entice them to perform a pilgrimage with me through the desolate courts, the deserted halls, and the mouldering chambers of Penshurst· Castle. I must therefore remind them, that the distinguished person· in virtue of·whose birth these halls have become sacred enclosures, and these courts classical ground, was not only one of the most accomplished scholars and writers of his day—(of which day the like has not been seen, either before or since)—but that he was "the observed of all observers" in all other things "that may become a man:"—that he not only *wrote* a story that young hearts may alternately sigh and smile· over till they grow old, and old ones till they grow young again, but that his whole life was employed in *acting* such an one:—that whether in the court or the camp, in hall or in bower, in the council or the·field, Sir Philip Sydney bore the palm from all competitors—or rather all competition, for it ceased to be so when *he* came among them, and· waived their claims in token of his undisputed supremacy;—that, in fact, if it were asked, by an enquirer into that most brilliant period of our· English annals, who was the most finished courtier and gentleman of· the day?·who was the wisest counsellor? who the bravest soldier? who the pink of knighthood and the flower of chivalry? who the favourite of a monarch whose favourites were her *friends?*—In short, who was· *par excellence* the glory of England, and the admiration of surrounding nations?—The answer to all must be—Sir Philip Sydney. Let us then pay a visit to his birth-place with the same reverence that we should feel in standing beside his grave; but without a tinge of that· melancholy which his grave, however triumphant a one, might inspire.

Penshurst Castle is situated in a lovely valley lying at the foot of a range of the Kentish hills, near Tunbridge Wells, and forms one of· those delightful morning rides, with which the neighbourhood of·that most romantic of English villages abounds. But the approach to·· Penshurst from the London road is even still more beautiful than the· above; and it has the additional merit of being the one by which, in·

all probability, Sir Philip Sydney himself passed in his passages between his paternal walls and that court of which he was the brightest ornament and the best support.   This road turns to the right out of the great London road, about three miles on this side of Tunbridge Wells, and lies the whole way along the topmost edge of that range of high ground at the foot of which is the valley I have just named; so that the lovely valley itself lies within the traveller's view at every point where the road-side trees open to admit the sight of it.   Nothing can be more charming than these various vistas that salute you through each opening; and what on the present occasion adds to the charm of them is, that they are all purely and exclusively *English* in their character; as all ought to be, that in any way connects itself with one, who, with all the variety of his accomplishments, made it his boast and glory to be an Englishman in them all.

Passing along for about three miles of this almost private road, (for it leads only to the little village of Penshurst,) the views that present themselves from time to time, though varying in detail, are all of a similar kind,—consisting of, first, the delicious declivity of the hill in the summit of which the road is situated,—sweeping down abruptly for a space, and then gently, till it meets the meadows that lie at its feet, and everywhere clothed with a rich garment of trees of every variety of hue, interspersed at intervals with bright spots of pasture, or rich corn-fields; and then the valley itself, presenting one wide flush of cultivation, studded here and there with little villages embosomed in groves of trees, and looking, at a distance, like summer-houses erected in a rich garden.

Passing along this lovely road for about three miles, at the end of that distance the little village of Penshurst is seen terminating the prospect of the valley, and in the midst of it the Castle rises, overlooking all around it with an air of modest superiority, as if, like its once illustrious inhabitant, it were anxious to be above those about it, not that it might look *down upon*, but only *beyond* them.   Beside, and as if forming a part of it, the village church lifts its unpresuming walls; as if to remind us that he, whose fame has attracted us here, was no less good than great—no less pious than wise and kind and brave.

The building is of an irregular construction, and presents no particular points for description, or even for admiration.   Neither does it, from the distance that we are now contemplating it, present any marks of decay.   It may, for any thing we can see to the contrary, be exactly in the state that it was at the period we are now connecting it with; for it was then an antique building, and was granted to the Sydneys by Edward VI.—having been forfeited to the crown by its former possessors.   This being the case, we may do well, now that the road before us begins to descend and wind down towards the castle, to think of it as it was when *he* inhabited it who would have equally illustrated it to the imagination, whether it had been the humblest cottage that it now overlooks, or the palace of a prince.   We shall thus, on reaching it, add a zest to our visit, which nothing but *contrast* is capable of producing.   Let us think of it, then, at the period when it stood here alone, the lord of the rich valley which its topmost windows overlook; when its courts were thronged with gay attendants and pampered menials, and its halls were alive with the noise of the ban-quiet; and its chambers echoed to the light footsteps of the revellers; and its bowers were conscious of the lover's whispers, or were whispering their own sweet music into the poet's ear :—for here Spenser meditated his rich lays, and Waller sighed in sweet rhymes to his Sacharissa. Let us, as we descend the steep declivity that leads to the castle, and lose sight of it in passing over the little bridge and through the village, think of it under the above aspect, and connect it with the kind of associations there alluded to; and then, passing through the church-yard, an ominous road! and over the little stile that divides the latter from the park, approach the great gate of entrance, and knock, with an undecided hand, for admittance.

The scene is somewhat different from that which we have just looked at in fancy. The knocker falls a dead weight upon the decaying door, and there is no answering sound within to say that it is heard; all is silent as the graves that we have just passed by to arrive here. We may venture to knock again, and less gently ; but not without waiting more than the due time between,—for we are not beneath the portico of a modern mansion in May-fair, and there is no sleek porter seated in the hall within, who has mistaken our modest rap for that of a poor relation, and therefore waits to have it repeated. But hark! a lumbering tread upon the stone pavement of the inner court proclaims that we have been heard—and see! the wicket opens slowly and we are invited to enter. But who is it that offers us this courtesy?—Is *this* the sole warder of Penshurst Castle—this fine hale old countryman, who looks fresh from the plough,—in his trim smock-frock, his blue worsted hose, his hobnailed shoes, and his slouched hat doffed to no one? Is it by him that we are to be led through the halls that once echoed to the tread of the Sydneys, the Pembrokes, and the Leicesters? No matter—as all is changed that we are to see, perhaps *this* is not the worst change we shall encounter before we leave the spot. But let us be content; for one thing, at least, nothing can change : these *are* the halls of the Sydneys—of THE SYDNEY—every stone of this court, and every plank of the chambers that we are about to pace, " prate of his whereabout," and the very winds that whistle through the broken casements, and behind the tattered tapestries,

" Pipe to the spirit ditties of no tone :"

so let us brace up our thoughts, and cheerfully complete the object of our visit—which was to look upon what remains, not to lament what has passed away.

Passing through the wicket-door which is cut in the great arched gate of entrance, we find ourselves beneath a lofty vaulted gateway, which leads to a square paved court or quadrangle; and traversing this, we reach another lofty door which leads into a narrow dark passage, a few paces on the right of which is the entrance to the great baronial hall. This is the largest and most interesting portion of the building; because that which is most characteristic of the times in connexion with which we are disposed to think of it, and probably more in its original state than any other part. In length it occupies the whole side of the court through which we have just passed; and its height is proportionate—the pointed roof being supported by great oaken beams, black with the smoke of the fire that occupied the centre spot of the hall. The floor is of red brickwork ; on either side from end to end stand massive oaken tables and benches—apparently as old as the hall itself, and witnesses of all that has passed in it; the tall pointed windows ascend nearly to the roof, commencing at about half the height of the walls, and between them, on these damp-stained walls, are painted, in black and white, rude gigantic figures of armed warriors; and finally, over the entrance door, at a great height against the wall, is placed a suit of armour—black with age—(as indeed every thing is which this hall contains.) This armour is said to have been worn by Sir Philip Sydney at the battle where he received his death; but we shall do well to pay but little attention to *on-dits* of this kind. In regard to objects of this nature,—where there is the slightest room for doubt, no satisfaction can be felt in the contemplation of them. And it is on this account that, while *relics* of every kind excite but little attention, however interesting the circumstances or the persons with which they may be said to have been connected—the *locales* that are in any way associated with similar circumstances, are always worth exploring; for *these* cannot be changed, or tampered with, or destroyed. I would not give a penny fee to see this armour, which is said to have clasped the body of Sir Philip Sydney, and to have been present (as it were) at the closing scene of his noble life. And yet I would not have missed pacing the courts where he has trodden, and passing through the halls where he has breathed, for more—than any one would have given me to stay away.

Passing out of the great hall (in which our innocent attendant wonders what we can have found to admire, since *he* has seen it so often and found nothing to admire in it yet—) we are led up a narrow staircase, to what is called the ball-room. This is a long spacious apartment, without furniture, except a few faded pictures, the tattered hangings of the walls, and some broken mirrors that serve to multiply the desolation on which they look. A portrait in this room, of Lady Elizabeth Sydney, is the only one worth attention. Without much beauty, it blends, in a very pleasing manner, a calm courtly dignity, with the mild sweetness of nature. An ante-room adjoining this apartment leads us to another, called Queen Elizabeth's drawing-room. In this room the mixture of remnants of antiquated splendour, with bareness and decay, produce even a more desolate effect than the entire emptiness of the other apartments. Here a few faded pictures, set in tarnished frames, hang, as if in mockery, on the mouldering walls, and round the room are placed a set of old chairs and a sofa, of gold and crimson velvet, every one of which is falling to pieces, and strewing with its mildewed fragments the bare worm-eaten floor. Two or three of the pictures, however, are worth attention; one, in particular, of the Countess of Pembroke—she for whom the Arcadia was written—she whom Ben Johnson celebrates as " the subject of all verse"—is very interesting. With even less of actual beauty than her relative in the last room, there is that about her look, of mingled wisdom and goodness, which makes us feel that she was not unworthy of the immortality she has gained. There is also a portrait of the young Lord Lisle, when a boy, which is very airy, elegant, and lordly.

There are two other apartments, each in a similar state with the foregoing, one of which is called the Tapestry Room, and the other the Picture Gallery. The walls of this last are nearly covered with paintings, most of them in a wretched state of decay, and many of which seem to have deserved a better fate than to be left to rot on the damp walls when all things else were removed. There are two, however, in the recess of the window, by Rembrandt, which are of great merit, and in a tolerable state of preservation; and also one by Holbein, which is exceedingly fine.

Let us now take an abrupt leave of this spot, lest the condition in which we find it should tempt us into a train of reflections unsuited to the feelings which should alone occupy the mind, when thinking of the illustrious person whose fame has attracted us hither. If the descendants of the Sydney (who are still in possession of this domain) think fit to cherish the memory of their ancestor elsewhere than on the spot which he has illustrated by his works and beautified with his actual presence, who has any right to complain of them? Perchance they think that, in thus abandoning the spot to the mercy of Time, and leaving it free to the visits of poor pilgrims like myself, who go to it once in their lives as they would to the shrine of a patron-saint,—they better evince their sense of the self-preserving qualities of their ancestor's name and fame, than if they made it the scene of modern " Christmas festivities," shooting-parties, and the like. And I do not know but they are in the right. His memory had better be left to itself than cherished unworthily. And, to say the truth, I scarcely know by what *outward* manifestations that memory *could* be worthily cherished, in times like these, in which he himself could not have existed, and in which he would not if he could.

I have not thought it necessary to lengthen this paper by recalling the details of Sir Philip Sydney's life, as the records of it are accessible to most. But still the reader may like to have a brief *note* of it at hand, instead of being compelled to trace such a one for himself out of the various extraneous matters that are usually connected with memoirs of persons of whom so few facts are known.

He was born at Penshurst in the year 1554, and before the age of twelve years he had shown so extraordinary a precocity of talent that in 1569 he was entered at Christ Church college, Oxford. His tutor here, Dr. Thomas Thornton, afterwards considered it so great an honour to have had him for a pupil, that he caused it to be mentioned on his tomb, now in the church of Ledbury in Herefordshire. It is not known exactly at what period he quitted Oxford for Cambridge, or at what college he belonged in the latter university; but he was certainly there—" probably at Trinity," Zouch says; and Fuller speaks of his parts and learning in the loftiest terms. Certain it is, however, that in 1572—that is, when he was only eighteen years of age—he had completed his studies; for in that year he went abroad on his travels, and was at Paris during the dreadful massacre of the Huegonots, and very narrowly escaped their fate himself—having been evidently marked out as a sharer of it. Here he became acquainted with Henry the Fourth, then Henry Bourbon, King of Navarre. During 1572 and the two following years, he pursued his travels through France, Italy, &c. becoming acquainted, among other distinguished persons, with Tasso; and in 1775 he returned to England, and became the delight and glory of the court and council of Elizabeth—being universally hailed and acknowledged as " the president of noblenesse and chevalrie."[a]

---

[a] See Spenser's Dedication to him of the Shepherd's Callender.

Another notice of him by that exquisite poet, written after his death, when the imputation of flattery or the hope of patronage were out of the question, will convey a striking idea of the estimation in which he was held.

> " Remembrance of that most heroicke spirit,
> The heavens' pride, the glorie of our daies,
> Which now triumpheth thro' immortal merit
> Of his brave virtues, crown'd with lasting baies
> Of heavenlie blisse and everlasting praise;
> Who first my muse did lift out of the flore
> To sing his sweet delights in lowlie laies,
> Bids me, &c."

Little is known with certainty of the detail of his life, from the time he returned to England in 1575 till he left it finally in 1585; except that he was sent on an important mission to Vienna, and that while at home he held the office of Cup-bearer to the Queen. It was, however, during this latter period that he wrote his works, the principal of which (the Arcadia) was not published till after his death, and was not intended by him to have been published at all—being merely written for the amusement of his beloved and accomplished sister, the Countess of Pembroke.

In 1585 he was appointed governor of Flushing; and almost immediately after this, being also general of horse under his uncle the Earl of Leicester, he received a wound in the thigh at the battle of Zutphen, of which, after remaining some time in a precarious state, he died. The story of his having given to a common soldier, who lay dying near him on the field of battle, a cup of water which had been brought to him to quench the feverish thirst arising from his wound,—saying, " This man's necessity is greater than mine,"—is well known.

There are two circumstances worth mentioning in conclusion : while lying on his death-bed he composed an ode referring to his feelings and situation (which, however, is not extant); and on his death there was a general mourning in England among the gentry, and I believe it was extended to several other courts of Europe.  **Z.**

---

## THE EMIGRANT.

> WHEN fire sets the forests on blaze,
>   It expires on their desolate track ;
> But the love which has lighted our days,
>   Still burns when our prospects are black.
>
> I must go to the Huron's wild grounds,
>   Whilst thou bloom'st to thine own native sun ;
> Oh, the ocean that parts us has bounds,
>   But the grief of our parting has none.
>
> Can the eagle fly home to his mate ?
>   Can he build by Niagara's foam ?
> And are we interdicted by fate
>   From a spot of the world for our home ?
>
> Thou art lost to me ev'n as the dead,
>   And our tears unavailingly flow ;
> Yet to think they could cease to be shed,
>   Would be worse than this burden of woe.

### STATE OF PARTIES IN DUBLIN.

#### *In a Second Letter to a Friend.*

My last letter concluded with the trial of the Orange rioters. While the public mind was agitated by the forensic contest, a new and more abundant source of bitterness was unsealed. The death of Mr. Hans Hamilton (of whom I know nothing except that I have seen him read his speeches from his hat) occasioned a vacancy in the representation of the county of Dublin. Sir Compton Domville, who always voted against the Catholics, but of whom it was said that he was ready to pledge himself that he would never speak against them, was persuaded to leave the retirement of private life, for the silent tranquillity of which he seems to be eminently fitted, and upon the strength of the Orange party, backed with twenty thousand pounds a year, to offer himself as an appropriate successor, which he certainly was calculated to be, to the "late lamented member." Circumstances appeared to have combined for his success. The Catholic interrest which centered among the middle-men, had seemingly been annihilated by the peace, and Protestant ascendancy was seised in fee-simple of the whole county. The political epidemic, which had broken out like a moral typhus, raged through all classes, and almost every landed proprietor had caught the infection. Calculating upon the entire subserviency of their tenantry, the gentry of the county entered into an apparently invincible combination in favour of Sir Compton, who started as the champion of Orangeism. The certainty of a triumph produced a premature intoxication, and the anticipated election of Sir Compton was held out as a test of their supremacy as unequivocal as if he were already seated in the House. This preposterous vaunt wounded the pride of the opposite party to the quick, and Luke Whyte was not slow to perceive that the moment had at last arrived for the achievement of the darling object of his ambition, in the advancement of his son to the representation of the county. You have not, perhaps, heard of Luke Whyte, but he is well worth a glance, and in this desultory outline, I propose to give you rather a sketch of the individuals engaged in the passing incidents, than a grave and formal detail of the events in which they were involved.

Luke Whyte is in Ireland a person of considerable importance, although in England he would in all likelihood have been almost unknown. So many strange and sudden productions of fortune are thrown up by the rich commercial soil of England, that they seldom attract a very peculiar notice; while in Ireland the means of acquisition are so limited, that the wealth of Luke Whyte is regarded as prodigious. The pouch and paunch of the hugest alderman of Cheapside are not beyond the emulation of the humblest tenant of a desk, who, in the nipping of his pen, casts through a dusky window an aspiring glance at the ponderous citizen, and cheered by the golden model, bends with alacrity to his work again; but when the spare figure of Luke Whyte glides like the ghost of Crœsus through College-green, where is the Hibernian shopboy who ever dreamed of compassing his portentous treasures? In truth, the amazing fortune of this singularly prosperous man defeats all conjecture of the means by which it could have been accumulated. Some forty years ago he would have furnished matter for the ecstasies of Mr. Wordsworth. If the profound author of the Excursion had seen him in one of the peregrinations incidental to his itinerant profession, he might have derived many valuable hints from so interesting a prototype, and added to the sublime beauties of that admirable poem. Its hero and Mr. Whyte were of the same craft, or, to speak more appropriately both with respect to Mr. Whyte and Mr. Wordsworth, of the same mystery. To avoid the use of an ignoble word from which the poet has studiously abstained, and express the fact with circumlocutory dignity, Mr. Whyte was no more or less than

A wandering merchant, bent beneath his load.

The latter consisted of books which he carried through various parts of the country ; and I have heard old men say that they remember to have seen him with his cargo of portable literature upon his back, toiling upon a blustering day along the road, and driving a hard bargain for Cordery or Cornelius Nepos at the door of a village-school. When he had acquired a sufficient sum, through dint of his vagrant industry, to dispense with the necessity of travelling, he fixed himself in more permanent importance at a stall in a small alley called Crampton-court, and soon afterwards purchased a shop. Book-piracy was at that time legal in Ireland, and the buccaneers of literature drove a profitable trade. Luke Whyte accordingly became a publisher. He next engaged in speculations in the lottery, from the lottery he plunged into the funds, and turned the rebellion to good account. Farther I am unable to trace his progress to the golden summit on which he stands ; but it is enough to say that he is now worth a million of money. He is largely endowed with good sense ; and so far from blushing at the former inferiority of his station, he looks back from his elevation with a sentiment of honourable pride upon the road which has conducted him to such an eminence. It is not a little remarkable that his manners are wholly free from vulgarity, and not only unaffected, but highly polished, and not without a cast of the court. Strongly as he is attached to gold, he is still more fond of power, and never allows his avarice to interfere with his ambition. Previous to the Dublin election he had already secured the representation of the county of Leitrim for himself. He next aimed at putting his son in parliament for Dublin. He had failed on two occasions in a contest with Colonel Talbot, and expended an immense sum of money in the adventure. The popular feelings had been enlisted by Colonel Talbot, and bore down the thousands of his competitor, who now perceived that in opposing Sir Compton Domville, he might marshal the very means upon his side, to which his former defeat might have been attributed. Accordingly he proposed his son at the hustings—threw his coffers open, and announced himself the champion of the Papists. The popish party, seeing the treasures of Luke Whyte unclosed, took heart at the sight, and their leaders formed themselves into a committee for his support. The most efficient amongst the latter was a gentleman of the name of Murphy, commonly called Billy Murphy, in the mercantile parlance of Dublin. His history may be told in three words :— he started in life without a guinea—was in the secret in 98—fled the country—came back when all his associates had been hanged—engaged in the trade of a salesmaster, and is now worth ·10,000*l.* a-year. Billy is one of the shrewdest and most energetic men in Dublin. He has been turned into an aristocrat by circumstance, but is by nature a republican, and looks so shrewd, so bold, and dark, that he may be regarded as a kind of *beau ideal* of Captain Rock. Among the Catholics he affects moderation, from a certain affectation of gentility, but the old leaven of 98 occasionally breaks out. He felt a just indignation at the insolence of the ascendancy faction, and embarked with honourable ardour in the cause of Popery and Whyte. With a bag of gold in one hand, and with the cross in the other, Billy Murphy was irresistible. His eloquence was of a tangible sort, and was immediately felt through the whole county. The patriotic rhetorick of Mr. O'Connel was blended with the more palpable logic of the great potentate of Smithfield. The great popular orator, not contented with an harangue to the multitude upon the hustings, went a kind of circuit through the chapels upon the sea-coast. Great numbers of the freeholders of Dublin are fishermen, who, even near the metropolis, exhibit the wildness, and almost the mood of the tempestuous element from which their livelihood is obtained. They of course had heard of the renowned O'Connel, but the real presence of the orator had never before been presented to them. He addressed them in their native tongue, and infused all the artifice of a long-practised pleader into its rude and barbarous strength. To these efforts the co-operation of the Catholic clergy was united. It was urged as a matter of reproach to them that they interfered; but it was forgotten that every Protestant clergyman in the county was enthusiastically devoted to Sir Compton Domville, with the single and signal exception of Sir Harcourt Lees, who, true to his nature, if not to his opinions, gave his vote to the Popish candidate. This union of gold, patriotism, and religion, was attended with its legitimate results; nor is it to be much wondered at, and still less perhaps is it to be deplored, that the Irish peasant should, under these combined incentives, have been debauched from that subserviency to his landlord, which, in the estimate of every petty squire, should be as uncalculating as the allegiance of the ox to the driver who goads him to the stall. So highly wrought was the enthusiasm of the people, that in the space of a few days the opulent, and hitherto absolute proprietors of the county, were left destitute of all influence, and without the power of commanding a single vote. The friese-coated patriots, who were sent in droves to the election-booths in order to vote for Sir Compton, under the very eye and to the beard of their astounded masters, flourished their shillelahs and shouted for whisky, religion, and Colonel Whyte. The scenes exhibited at the hustings were full of ferocious drollery. The moment a freeholder appeared at them, who intimated an intention to support Sir Compton, he was assailed upon all sides with a strange confusion of appeal. A tremendous cry was sent up by the multitude —O'Connel, with a stentorian voice and brandished arms, bade him remember Ireland: Father M'Farland exclaimed, "Will you sell your religion?" while Billy Murphy, seizing him with his brawny hand, and whispering "five guineas" in his ear, completed the seduction, and set him down in triumph upon the tallies of Colonel Whyte. Vainly did the ominous landlord, a prophet who accomplishes his own predictions, bid him remember the 25th of March—vainly did he foretell the sale of his blanket, the starvation of his children, the howling of his wife, and the freezing of the winter night. Inflamed with patriotism and whisky, and heedless of these portentous auguries, the half-emancipated enthusiast leaped heroically into the gulf. Then rose a peal of acclamation which "frighted chaos and old night," or in plainer speech, astounded Lord Norbury, and appalled the Corporation. The events of even a Westminster election can give you but little notion of the grotesque character of a Dublin one. I have often been present at an English contest, but never witnessed so fantastic a scene. The native ardour of the national temperament was roused into its wildest excitation—every countenance glowed with passion—every gesture was informed with emotion—every movement was a tumult—and every sound an exclamation. They shouted, cursed, and stamped—their hands were clenched, their eyes were on fire, and their mouths in foam. The whole assembly would have looked like a great collection of maniacs to some sober English spectator, who, however, in retiring from the uproar, would have been inclined to attribute a still higher degree of delirium to the men who nurture the fatal discords which generate such calamitous results.

It was not alone to the hustings that the visible results of the election were confined. The streets of the city were filled with uproar, and while the Orangemen were rejoicing at their victory in the Four Courts, the Papists were indulging in an equally ferocious exultation at their Kilmainham triumph. At length the friends of Sir Compton advised him to relinquish the field, and Whyte was proclaimed the member for the county, after an expense which none but his father could have sustained. But the collision of party was not destined to terminate with the contest. The populace insisted upon chairing the successful candidate. An enormous mass of people moved through the streets of Dublin with Colonel Whyte at its head. The vast procession extended as far as the eye could reach. The living body rolled like a great tide through the metropolis. No tumult or interruption occurred until the people had reached the gates of the College, and suddenly a large quantity of stones and bricks was flung from the roofs of the building upon the multitude below. Several severe wounds were inflicted in the performance of this academic exploit. The mob, infuriated at the unprovoked aggression, burst through the iron railing which divides the area before the College from the street, and seized upon certain unhappy loiterers, who would probably have been sacrificed to their fury, had not some of the more respectable persons in the crowd interfered for their preservation. This circumstance may appear trivial in itself, but it was one of the many symptoms of the inveterate detestation which was rapidly growing up, and has been since matured between the two parties in Ireland.

I pass from the election to the Beef-steak Club—singular transition! and yet it scarcely illustrates the art of sinking. Whatever bathos may be in its title, the Beef-steak Club is not without importance in a country where the most momentous results originate from the obscurest source. This society was established in Dublin by a Mr. M'Caskey. The love of music was the ostensible object of the association, but the rites of Apollo were speedily blended with the adoration of a more exhilarating god. These fanatics in music soon exhibited an enthusiasm of a very opposite kind:—as was natural in Ireland, the professors of harmony became the propagators of discord. A few years ago the political feelings of the club were manifested in rather a remarkable way. A nobleman, so distinguished at the Kilkenny theatricals for the fidelity of his representations in the parts of ostlers and of grooms, that it was supposed that Nature and Fortune must have quarrelled at his nativity, proposed from the chair of this society, in the midst of one of its boisterous orgies, a toast, the malice of which can only be surpassed by its absurdity. It ran to this effect—" The Pope in the pillory, pelted by the Devil with the brains of priests," together with other concomitants, which I shall not soil the paper by inditing. The publicity given to this piece of malignant buffoonery excited great sensation, and fixed upon the club the character of an Orange lodge. The noble Earl (for he is one at present, and was selected as a person deserving to be raised to a higher grade in the powerless peerage of Ireland) was afterwards obliged to apologize to the galleries at Kilkenny, when enacting his favourite part of David in the Rivals; and by imputing to the superabundance of his potations the aforesaid effusion of constitutional sentiment, obtained permission from the gods to proceed with his faithful personation of a shoe-boy. In Dublin, the recollection of his offences did not so easily pass away, and the Beef-steak Club became an object of popular aversion. Of this society the Lord Chancellor is a zealous and conspicuous member. This nobleman is the creature of impulse, and having been educated in England in high-church principles, and surrounded upon his arrival in Ireland with the menials of the Castle, derived an unhappy confirmation in his impassioned biasses, from those whose interest it was to bring forth the seeds of Orangeism which had been originally deposited in his mind. His ardent temperament abandoned itself entirely to their seductions, and he became the chief and avowed protector of the anti-Irish party in Ireland. He is by nature and by habit an inveterate Tory; and, indeed, has so strong a cast of the Stuart family, with which he is connected, and is withal so spare and spectral, that he looks like the phantom of the departed dynasty. Upon his qualifications to fill his high judicial situation, it would be foreign to my purpose to pronounce; and to enter into any minute investigation of his character and habits were to trespass upon the rights of the author of the " Sketches of the Irish Bar," who intends, it is said, to extend his portraits to the Bench. It is enough to say, that he is an unqualified supporter of Protestant prerogative; that he has a horror of " Popery and wooden shoes," and that, while he discards the miracles of Prince Hohenloe*, he would not, for the Chancellorship of Great Britain, sit down at dinner with a party of thirteen. The meetings of the Beef-steak Club being free from this numerical omen, Lord Manners readily consented to join their political festivities at a moment when the spirit of faction raged with the utmost intensity, and virtually presided at one of the Orange fasti, which was held in the midst of all the uproar of party which I have just described. How far his asso-

---

* In a late pamphlet written upon the Miracles, and universally attributed to Baron Smith, the fact in the text, of which there is no doubt, is alluded to. Of this ingenious essay some account will, upon a future occasion, be given.

ciation with the proselytes of Mr. M'Caskey may be consistent with the dignity of the house of Rutland and the keeper of the seals, I shall not venture to decide; but it did certainly appear not a little singular that a man having so large a share in the government of the country, and an influence almost co-extensive with that of Lord Wellesley himself, should in such a crisis have descended to a convivial familiarity with the political zealots who frequented this obnoxious club; and should by his presence have extended an implied approbation to the principles and feelings which they unequivocally expressed. A very numerous assembly of the subscribers was convened; Champaigne and claret circulated with rapidity, and when the votaries of Apollo had been roused to the just level of enthusiasm, the chairman proposed as a toast "The exports of Ireland." The rumours which had previously prevailed of the contemplated removal of Lord Wellesley, suggested to every person present that the toast was given in allusion to that measure, and it was hailed accordingly with votive acclamation. There is a passage in the letters of Lord Essex, written when he was Lord Lieutenant of Ireland, so immediately appropriate to the state of Protestant feeling at this moment, that I cannot forbear from transcribing it. It falls, indeed, into a very remarkable coincidence with the situation of Lord Wellesley. Lord Essex, in page 35 of the volume of his letters, says, "The reports which every day are transmitted hither from England of my remove, is the principal cause of their stubbornness; and, indeed, it is a misfortune to his Majesty's affairs that such rumours are spread, for I do not believe that under the sun there are a people more apt to despise their governors than some here are, and will, if they have any imagination that they are to be recalled." This sentiment, which appears to be almost indigenous in Ireland, was illustrated at the period of which I am speaking; and when "The exports of Ireland" was given as a toast from the chair of the Beef-steak Club, it was loudly and rapturously cheered by those who found in the toast an occasion for venting their gratification at the anticipated exportation of the noble Marquis, which was more strenuously desired by the Orangemen than his demi-measures and oscillating policy appeared to justify. There could be no doubt that it was intended to apply to Lord Wellesley, although the Chancellor afterwards stated, in his own defence, that it admitted of a different interpretation. If the question of construction had been regularly discussed in his Lordship's court, it would in all probability have afforded a field for the exercise of much ingenious ratiocination: but in the public mind no doubt existed as to the intent of the parties. The anger of the noble Marquis at this immediately personal affront, was said to be unbounded. The viceregal irritation was speedily embodied in a measure of domestic and summary retribution. Three ill-starred officers of the Castle happened to have attended at the obnoxious club, when the anti-Wellesley toast was given. I have forgotten the name of one of them, which has nothing to fix it in the memory. Sir Charles Vernon, the gentleman-usher, and the *ex-officio* fan-holder to the Ladies Lieutenant (we are now happily relieved from these mock and mob-led queens), and Mr. Stanhope, the brother-in-law of the Duke of Leinster, were the other unhappy wights who had the misfortune to attest these symbolical expressions of dislike. On the day following they were dismissed. This proceeding produced a singular sensation. Familiarized as the

Orangemen were with the tameness of the administration, they were astounded at what appeared to be so bold and adventurous a step. Those who held no place were loud in their invectives against the autocratic character of the Marquis's resentment. They forget, or rather they affected not to remember, that under the constitutional administration of the Duke of Richmond, the brother of the very Mr. Stanhope (who was now discharged) had been deprived of the very same office, for attending a dinner given by the Roman Catholics of Dublin, at which nothing offensive had taken place. Such are the incongruities of faction. This expulsion of three placemen produced upon their brethren in office a different effect. While those who had nothing to lose were loud in their reprobation, the underlings of authority—the petty tenants of office—the menials of the Custom-house and the Post-office, stood silent and aghast. The name of Lord Wellesley, which had before been a standing jest, and furnished matter for relaxation among the clerks in every public office in Dublin, was no longer pronounced in those abodes of alternate insolence and subserviency. There prevailed over those domiciles of inferior Orangeism "a death-like silence and a dread repose." Nor was this sentiment confined to the humble dandies of the quill. It extended itself even to the parasitical expectants at the Bar; and the birds of prey, whose vulture sagacity had long scented the demise of some paralytic chairman of a county, or of some apoplectic Master in Chancery, moulted many a feather. It was supposed that farther dismissals would take place, and the apprehension produced a dismal taciturnity for a considerable time. But at length the countenances of the Williamites began to clear up—they resumed the use of the organ of invective, and were gradually restored to the enjoyment of that factious loquacity which serves to exhilarate the labours of the fiscal desk. They saw that Lord Wellesley had indulged in a just resentment of an individual affront, but that his indignation was not tinged by any political vindictiveness; and relied upon the evidence of impunity afforded in the example of a gentleman who had been engaged in the theatrical riot, and who continued to hold and still enjoys many lucrative situations, from which the government did not dare to remove him.[*] The passions which had been repressed by a temporary barrier, burst through it with an augmented force. The imperfect effort at independence made by the Irish government was designated as an act of Oriental autocracy, and the fate of Sir Charles Vernon afforded an ample field for reprobatory exclamation. He had acquired the liking of the ordinary frequenters of the Castle, and possessed all the talents requisite for his vocation. The motley personage, who charmed the melancholy Jaques in the forest of Ardennes, could not surpass him in his adaptation to his office; and so wide and genuine was his popularity amongst a certain class, that it might have been aptly said upon his dismissal,

—— Mimæ, balatrones—hoc genus omne  
Mœstum et solicitum est.

---

[*] The forbearance of Lord Wellesley's administration is remarkable. The instance above mentioned deserves notice, but a circumstance which recently occurred is still more singular. Lord Wellesley lately dined with the Corporation, and among the persons officially employed to preside at the dinner and lead his Lordship into the banquet-room, was one of the chief rioters at the theatre!

The solicitude for the fate of the Dublin Tigellius was not, however, confined to persons of this cast, but reached to nobler bosoms. A certain conspicuous octogenarian dropped tears for rheum upon hearing of his fate, and vowed by her widowhood that she would never enter the Castle again. Lord Manners also expressed an equally unqualified resentment. The natural good-nature of his lordship was moved by Vernon's misfortunes, and he also felt this discharge from the viceregal service as an indirect rebuke to himself. It was said that his lordship expressed great and loud irritation, and rumours were dispersed that either Lord Wellesley or Lord Manners would leave the country. It is certain that the latter wrote letters of bitter complaint to the heads of his own family and to the leaders of the high-church party in England. I have heard from good authority that the Duke of Rutland, Lord Lonsdale, and one or two of the other great proprietors in the House of Commons, held a meeting in London, and deliberated upon the means of effecting the removal of Lord Wellesley, but that, having felt the sense of the lower house, they abandoned the proposed measure, and determined to compromise the differences between the noble lords. Neither of the latter could afford to indulge in any very practical resentment, and consented to retain their stations upon the pathetic and conclusive plea of Shakspeare's apothecary. Accordingly a fantastic kind of accommodation was effected between them. Poor Sir Charles, however, was not included in this prudential negotiation, and fell gradually into oblivion. The bells upon his cap were no longer heard at the Castle. His practical jokes, his innocent caricatures, and innocuous buffooneries, were no longer remembered; and what is much more deserving of regret, his domestic virtues were forgotten in the reconciliation of the great contending personages. The latter readily compromised their differences under the salutary influence of reciprocal convenience. The facility of the adjustment excited some surprise; but much greater astonishment was produced by the event which almost immediately succeeded.

The insult offered to Lord Wellesley was marked and unequivocal. So deeply had it penetrated into the very core and vitals of his pride, that he had instantaneously dismissed the dependents upon whom his resentment could be practically exemplified. What, think you, was the issue of the viceregal exasperation? You will start at the bare mention of the fact. The brother of the Duke of Wellington, the conqueror of Tippoo Saib, the moving spirit of the Spanish war—the lofty statesman, the impassioned orator, and the philosophical politician—he who upon his first arrival in this country, had united the suffrages of the British empire, and seemed to be of all men the best qualified for an undertaking in which sagacity and elevation were to be combined—he, galled and blistered as he was by a wanton and deliberate offence, selected this convocation of wassailers for an especial mark of favour, and uninvited, announced his intention to dine with the Beef-steak Club. This communication from the Castle was at first received as an idle rumour. The liberal party exclaimed, "It is impossible! True it is that he made a baronet of the man who was the first to violate the King's commands; it is true that he shook hands with Alderman Thorpe; it is true that he has flattered, without cajoling the Corporation; and for all this there is, perhaps, an extentation, if not an excuse: he has been driven by the exigency of circumstances to a thousand acts, from which his principles as a statesman, and his own noble instincts, must have made him shrink. But that he should dine with the Beef-steak Club! the thing's impossible." With such expressions of indignant incredulity this report was received. Yet it gradually gained ground upon the public disbelief, and at last the day on which these novel festivities were to take place, was formally and authentically proclaimed. The day arrived, and Lord Wellesley sat in the midst of the Orange orgies, by the side of the very man with whom he had just declared that he could no longer act in concert in the government of Ireland. The triumph of Lord Manners was complete. Even his accustomed urbanity could not prevent him from indulging in some partial expression of superiority. His black eyes glistened with more than their usual fire; a deeper shade of Orange was infused into his complexion; his Stuart smile assumed a more lordly courtesy. With the exception of the immediate suite of the Lord Lieutenant, there was scarcely one friend of his in the whole assembly—the tables were lined with men who eyed the noble Marquis with an expression, in which hatred appeared to have given way to a less vehement emotion. The evening passed slowly and heavily away, and in place of the usual bustle and clamorous jocularity which accompany such assemblies, a certain dulness, arising from the consciousness of restraint, prevailed over the meeting. Lord Wellesley affected high spirits, but it was easy to perceive that he was personating a part, which he felt at last that he ought not to have undertaken. He was not actually insulted to his face, although he took a sudden offence at some phrases of the Lord Chancellor, who, in pronouncing judgment upon the excellence and utility of the Beef-steak Club, congratulated Lord Wellesley upon the opportunity which he enjoyed of relaxing, amidst these recreative convocations, from the rigour and austerity of his political labours. The latter imagined, but I believe erroneously, that something disrespectful was intended, and suddenly started at the banquet at the ghost of his own dignity. The Chancellor assured him that he was under an erroneous impression; and he rested apparently contented with the explanation. Nothing remarkable occurred until the hour for Lord Wellesley's departure, which was anxiously expected by the company, had arrived. They had entered into a stipulation that "The exports of Ireland" should not be drunk in his presence, and waited for the moment of his departure to indulge in this contumelious toast. At length he signified his intention to retire:—the whole assembly rose—he walked through the files of Orangemen upon each side, and bowed as he passed along. He reached the door, while every glass was filling to the brim; and scarce had he crossed the threshold, when "The exports of Ireland" was given, and received with loud and vivacious acclamations. The noble Marquis hurried down stairs, with the shouts of laughter, which proceeded from the meeting, ringing in his ears, and returned to the Castle after an effort at conciliation, which, whatever may be thought of it in a political point of view, must be regarded as a pattern of Christian virtue, in which the precept of forgiveness was carried to a point of perfection that excited as much wonder as admiration. Those who had formed an estimate of his character from his Oriental achievements, expected that his descent in the West would be attended with a scarcely inferior lustre. It was hoped that he would leave behind him a track of illumination which would be long reflected by his country. It is possible that some beam of light may yet break through the dimness in which he is enveloped, but hitherto we have only had occasion to contrast his glory in the East with the clouded setting of his renown.

While these incidents were taking place, the Ex-Attorney-general, Mr. Saurin . . . But I have exceeded my limits, and must postpone a detail of the events which were produced by the agency of that once important, and still remarkable person. Mr. Saurin, Bradley King, the Archbishop of Dublin, and the church-yards, will furnish me with materials for another letter. CRITO.

---

## THE HUNTER OF THE PYRENEES.

LIGHT o'er the lea the hunter bounds,
  With buoyant heart and brow unclouded ;
Shrill answer to his bugle sounds
  The hill, with its peak in thick mists shrouded,
And the baying of his hounds.
He quickly clears the deep ravine,
  Treads with firm foot the blue-flower'd heath,
But leaps those spots of treacherous green
  Which hide the shaking moss beneath—
  Like life's allurements veiling death.
His pointers through the scrubwood rush,
Or hasty lap the torrent's gush,
Or busy snuff the quarry's trace,
And yelp the music of the chase.

The game is up, and away he goes !
  The Izard springs from its leafy lair—
  Cleaves, with a panting plunge, the air—
A moment breathes—and backward throws
One glance at the yelling foes.

The eagle from her crag-form'd rest
  Eyes the fierce chase, and onwards soaring,
  With eager ken the prey exploring,
Flaps her flight o'er the mountain's breast,
And fancies food for her hungry nest.
She marks from her height the fusil's flash—
  The death-struck Izard tumbles down,
  And blood-drops blush on the rock-weeds brown.
Straightway she stoops with rapid dash—
But the hunter's stern fix'd aspect fearing,
In gloomy grandeur upwards steering,
Sweeps slowly through heaven's solitude
To hover again o'er her screaming brood.

G.

CIVIC SPORTS, NO. II.

Extracted from the Journal of Simon Swandown.

### The Wedding Day.

First they kiss'd,
Then shook fist,
And look'd like two fools just a-going to marry.—*Old Song.*

*Saturday, Nov.* 15, 1823.—9 A. M. Dressed myself in my new blue coat, white waistcoat, diamond shirt-pin, sea-green small clothes, and white silk stockings, not forgetting a pair of white kid gloves, to attend celebration of marriage of Betsy, third daughter of my old friend Benjamin Blueball, the pawnbroker in Fleet-street, with Richard Highdry, son of Ezekiel Highdry, the tobacconist in Long-lane, Smith-field. Waited half an hour for my wife, who had solemnly engaged to " get on her things" at nine precisely. No time for breakfast; but as Blueball had promised us a magnificent one in Fleet-street, that did not much matter. To save time, walked down stairs to shop, and served Clutterbuck's clerk with two quire of foolscap and a quarter of a pound of red sealing-wax; he evidently all the while much puzzled to account for my early finery. Wife's flounces being at length ad-justed, set off as gay as larks, in a hackney chariot, up from Bush-lane toward place of appointment. Stopped by a coal-waggon at corner of Cannon-street, while carter was throwing down empty sacks, and bawling one, two, three, four! Wife thrust out of window her head, covered with a white beaver hat, ornamented with white ostrich feathers tipped with scarlet, and told counting man that we were in a hurry. Carter grinned, and answered, " Then you had better wait till your hurry is over!" Wife drew back in anger, observing, however, that the fellow really had not a bad set of teeth. Coalheavers and chimney-sweeps always have white teeth. Val. Verjuice says, it pro-ceeds from the blackness of their faces; as a Drury-lane message-bearer looks a capital actor when planted among the sticks on Rich-mond-green. Drove through Lombard-street, and got a nod from my banker, Sir Daniel Discount, who was seated at a pulpit-desk punching holes in old checks, super-enlightened by a fat mould candle four to the pound. Wife looked up at Mansion-house windows, but could not catch a glimpse of her bran-new ladyship, or either of the honourable misses. Drove, at an easy rate, along Cheapside; feeling a serene complacency at being well dressed. Turning toward St. Paul's, when wife gave a loud scream as if she was stuck, and, with a pull at the check-string that almost brought the driver's little finger into her lap, exclaimed that she had quite forgotten a toy for little Sally Blueball. Deviated to corner of Paternoster-row, and stopped at Dunnett's toy and Tunbridge warehouse, with rocking-horses enough to stock both theatres. Paviours and passengers made an awe-struck alley to let us pass. Much deliberation before final decision. Leaden rope-dancers, tumble-down London cries, nut-cracking human heads, and wax dolls with moveable eyes, successively chosen and rejected. Wife at length pitched upon a little white dog, who, on being earnestly pressed, barked under his fore-paws. Had a private opinion that it sounded more like a cuckoo, but was too prudent to give it utterance.

10 A. M. Arrived safely in Fleet-street, Wife desiring Blueball's shopman to be particularly careful of her shawl. Ushered up stairs, and introduced in form to the assembled company. Heard my own name repeated above twenty times, and longed for Bishop to set the serenade to music: "Sir Christopher Contract, Mr. Simon Swandown; Mr. Simon Swandown, Sir Christopher Contract; Mr. Simon Swandown, Sir Samuel Suffrage; Sir Samuel Suffrage, Mr. Simon Swandown." Ditto (*wicy warcy*, as the man has it in "Sweethearts and Wives,") with Mr. John Blueball and Mr. Peter Blueball, brothers of our host. Ditto with Mr. Prune and Mr. Pob-joy, brother and half-brother of Mrs. Blueball. Head hardly settled, when it was set dizzy again by similar changes rung between my wife and the wives of the aforesaid. Observed three old ladies, dressed, poor creatures! in white muslin at this inclement season, seated near the fire, and staring at the hearth-rug. Asked Blueball, in a whisper, who they were? was answered, in another whisper, that they were maiden aunts of Mrs. Blueball, who had come up to London on purpose; that he did not at this moment recollect their names, nor where they came from; he knew it was from some place beginning with an M. It might be Malton, or Maidstone, or Margate; no, that was not it: he was pretty sure it was either Malmsbury, Manchester, or Mauritania: at all events, it began with an M. After the storm of introduction, sea settled into a dead calm, nobody knowing what to talk about. Mrs. Blueball hereupon pulled nursery-bell, and a shower-bath of brats ensued. Wife now produced white dog, which was received by little Sally, who, in the hurry of possession, quite forgot the requisite curtsey. That homage being performed at the instigation of mamma, wife put urchin up to the barking process, and the whole house ere long echoed "cuckoo:"—odd overture to a marriage festival! Every body habited in white: could not help thinking of the Miller and his Men. Much whispering and getting into holes and corners. Walked to the window: saw an old woman cleaning Waithman's upper casements, and thought of Whittington and his Cat. Two of the little Blueballs, in their passage near the hearth-rug, unluckily pounced upon by two of the maiden aunts from the place beginning with an M. Little innocents forced to stand like stocks to have their heads smoothed down by two venerable paws. Did not see the necessity of this, their pates being previously sufficiently glossy, but said nothing, the family having, I found, expectations in that quarter. Felt a gnawing in my internals, and looked about sharp for tea and toast. Hinted my feelings to Bob Blueball, and was greeted with a horse-laugh, appended to "You'll get no water here, great Rusty Fusty. We don't breakfast till we come from church."

11 A. M. A knock at the street-door announced the advent of the bridegroom, and brought Betsy the bride into the room, supported by Emma and Harriet, her two elder sisters. A general rising, accompanied by that sort of compassionate attention which is bestowed upon gentlemen in the press-yard while their fetters are being knocked off. Betsy's eyes red; dressed in order to look particularly well, and consequently never looked so ill. In two seconds, in stalked Richard Highdry. Ribbed white silk stockings, and breeches of the colour of

our Elizabeth's canary-bird: hair auburn, according to the Miss Blueballs; but had he come upon any errand short of courtship, I am convinced they would have dubbed it red. A hurried bow and a blush
denoted the iniquity of his object. Seated himself, as in duty bound,
next to his mistress upon a music-stool. Offered him a chair; but he
answered, in a tone of affected indifference, " No, thank you—this will
do very well !" vibrating and creaking all the while like a tin chimney
cap in a high wind. Another knock, and an announcement of two
dingy-looking trustees under the marriage-settlement. Blueball in
high spirits, snapping his fingers, jingling his keys in his breeches
pocket, and darting his physiognomy into every body's face, like one
in quest of his wits. Mrs. Blueball communicated apart with one of
the dingy trustees, who thereupon thus addressed the company: " It
is time to go to church. Saint Bride's being such a mere step, it is settled that we go on foot." Bride now applied sal volatile to her nostrils,
and groom, in my humble opinion, looked like a decided ass. Written
paper produced by other dingy trustee, setting forth order of precedence, viz. Mr. Blueball and bride, Mrs. Blueball and groom, Sir
Christopher Contract and Lady Suffrage, Sir Samuel Suffrage and
Lady Contract, Bob Blueball and my wife, myself and Mauritanian
aunt No. 1, Peter Blueball and ditto No. 2, Mr. Prune and ditto
No. 3, the two dingy trustees with Emma and Harriet Blueball, and
Mr. Pob-joy with the French teacher. Troops filed off, and descended
to street-door. Order of march much impeded by a string of Meux's
drays extending from Temple Bar to the Hand-in-Hand Fire-office.
Three first couple darted between two drays, remainder left on pavement in front of door. Mauritanian aunts thus separated, to their no
small terror. Forces at length congregated safely in St. Bride's
church. Rank and file ranged round the altar. Audible sobs from
mamma, and serious symptoms of hysterics from Emma. Bridegroom
fumbled in his waistcoat pocket for ring; would gladly have given him
mine, but wife would not let me. On being questioned whether he
would take Betsy Blueball for his lawful wife, groom waited half a
second, as if to deliberate, and at length out bolted " I will !" like a
pellet from a pop-gun.

12 M. Order of return impeded at corner of Bridge-street, by
Bethel Union charity-boys, in dwarf leather breeches, headed by Lord
Gambier, and tailed by Mr. Wilberforce, singing a suitable hymn in
duetto. Hundreds of servant-maids looking out of garret windows.
Safe back at starting-post. Magnificent breakfast in the mean time
set out in drawing-room. Found juniors of family busy in making up
packets of bride-cake, with little bits drawn through the ring for special
favourites. Wife made me cram ours into my coat pocket: grease
evidently oozing through: did not quite approve of having my new
blue coat pocket made a buttery hatch, but thought it expedient to say
nothing. Coffee handed round by simpering maid. Bridegroom,
having one hand round bride's waist, reached his cup too carelessly in
the other, and consequently tilted half its contents upon his own Canary
shorts. The latter, in the parts thus deluged, assumed an autumnal
tinge not ill suited to the season. More finger-snapping and tomfool-
ing from Blueball, who exhibited in triumph the key of the street-door,

swearing that, on a day of such fun and jollity, nobody should depart till midnight. Looked about for the fun and jollity: Momus's writ returned *Non est inventus.*

1 P. M. Affairs at a dead stand-still. Piano opened by Emma. Three aunts reinstated near the hearth-rug. Two of them beckoned their former captives, but youngsters hung fire, as not approving of any more head-patting. Bride tried her hand at " She loves and loves for ever," but burst into tears at the second line, and finished the business with a glass of water. Two dingy trustees began to pore over draft of marriage settlement; the words " 3 per cents—vested—body—issue, if any—then to such only child—*toties quoties*," being distinctly audible. Flattened my nose against window-pane, and betted sixpences with Bob Blueball upon passing hackney-coaches : if number above 500, I was to pay him; if below, he me. Hack chaise and pair drove up to door, to convey happy couple, accompanied by Nancy, to Star and Garter, at Richmond. Kisses, tears, and farewells. Bridegroom's asinine aspect in no way diminished. Had he been ridden by Balaam, Martin of Galway's bill would have protected him from ill usage. Tried to get a kiss from the bride, and got my mouth full of Brussels lace.

2 P. M. Ennui banished by political discussion. Great abuse of the Cortes by Mr. Pob-joy for cowardice : proposition denied by Sir Christopher Contract, who swore that Spain owed all her prosperity to that quarter. Found at length that they were talking of two distinct people, Mr. Pob-joy alluding to the submissionists at Cadiz, and Sir Christopher to the gentleman in armour personated by Mr. Cooper at Covent-garden theatre. Wife much occupied in shewing Lady Suffrage the mode in which the scarlet tips were made to adhere to her white feathers. Lord Mayor's-day dinner discussed ; three men in armour criticised ; and many causes assigned for the absence of the nobility. General opinion that they were all deep in civic magistrate's books, and dreaded being dunned. Another political storm. Sir Christopher contended that Lord Holland ought to be thrown into the sea ; and Sir Samuel Suffrage swore that Mr. Canning deserved to be hanged. Thought to soften down matters, as I do at home ; so I suggested that Mr. Canning should only be half hanged, and that Lord Holland should be sunk only up to the middle in Probert's pond. Proposition treated by both parties with an indignant frown, as proceeding from a wretch who knew nothing of the matter. Took up Morning Chronicle, and read for the fourth time account of sale at Gill's-hill cottage. Mr. Prune, a great collector of curiosities, shewed me a feather from the bed that Miss Noyes slept in the night of the murder ; knocked down to him yesterday by Page the auctioneer at £4. 10s. Had nearly finished that article, and was setting about reading the whole paper, beginning with No. 17,028, and ending with " Printed and Published," when old Blueball whisked the paper out of my hand, and exclaimed, " What! reading ? No reading to-day. This is, as Tom Thumb says, ' a day of fun and jollity.' " Wondered when the fun and jollity was to begin. Looked out of the window, and envied the black sweeper officiating at the base of Wilkes's pedestal.—N.B. Idleness a very laborious trade. If any youth has no objection to a fatiguing occupation, let him be bound apprentice to a nothing-to-do man.

3 P. M.—Determined to stand it no longer. Watched opportunity, when host was chuckling and poking the ribs of trustee at the window, to open parlour-door softly. Stole down stairs on tiptoe; rushed out of back door; put my foot upon an inverted pail; used mop as school-boys do a leaping-pole, cleared Mother Mangle's railway; got safe into Flower-de-Luce-court; bolted out into Fleet-market; walked briskly up Ludgate-hill; and on turning up Ave Maria-lane, heard a hard breathing in my rear. Heart palpitated like the woman's in Ovid, who was turned into a holly-bush. Quickened my pace; and on entering Paternoster-row, bobbed swiftly to the left, and dived into the viscera of Newgate-market. Slackened my pace, no longer dreading pursuit: walked leisurely along Cheapside, the Poultry, and Cornhill; and, with great delight, on full 'Change, mixed myself with Jews, jobbers, brokers, and Turkey merchants. Talked with Moses Tresorio, whose splashed black satin breeches, boots, and spurs, denoted the muddy state of the road from Stamford-hill. Chattered with Cringe the broker about yellow pine timber, Zante fustic, masquash skins, tub bark, and gum arabic: was in the very act of looking at stonemason chipping the smut from the dilated nostrils of George the First, when somebody gently touched my elbow, and on turning round, to my great consternation! beheld Blueball's shopman, who, touching his hat, exclaimed, " Beg pardon, Sir, but master says you must come back." Gave him a shilling to promise to say he could not meet with me. Went home, and caught Peter Pencil, my foreman, practising the jumping waltz with Betty, with a blind fiddler aiding and abetting upon a two-stringed kit.

5 P. M.—Went back to dinner, and mollified Blueball with a story about a returned acceptance of Colonel Palaver's, and the necessity of giving notice to the drawer. Ladled out the peas-soup, sitting between maiden aunt No. 1, and Lady Suffrage. Long story from the latter about dead bodies found in a cave under Manchester-buildings, with dice-boxes in their hands. Conversation during dinner rather miscellaneous,—the subjects being length of leases in Long-lane, Lilliput-pavement in St. James's-square, massacre of Mr. Barber Beaumont in his ground-floor study, price of a couple of Dorking fowls, Miss Waithman's feathers, Letitia Hawkins, Clara Fisher, Moore's " Fly not yet," and Edwin's " Fal de ral tit."

6 P. M.—Hints from old Blueball to me to propose health of bride and bridegroom: trembled as I filled my glass: had the requisite speech quite by heart yesterday, having been heard by wife without missing a word. Got upon my legs, and transposed a dozen initials, viz.—said that " I rose to toast a propose, which I had no doubt the company would delight with a great deal of drink; that I was not much used to spublic peaking, and therefore should merely health the drink of Mr. and Mrs. Richard Highdry, and may they be a cappy hupple!" Speech received with great applause, notwithstanding the hey contrary sides of its consonants. Mrs. Blueball burst into tears in order to return thanks—felt highly flattered by the flattering manner in which, &c.; that she had lost the flower of her flock, (here the eldest survivor reddened)—she should never see her equal, (here the second survivor bridled)—she hoped and trusted she never should lose another. (Here Emily, just come out, giggled and cast a glance upon her flirting asso-

ciate Peter Prune, as much as to say "I would not be a good offer in her way.") She hoped the company had been feasted to their satisfaction (applause) : she left the management of the wine to Mr. Blueball, but in justice to herself, she must say she bought the almonds and raisins from Groom's opposite, and blanched the former with her own hands. (Great and continued applause.)

7 p. m.—Sad symptoms of music. Heard Bob Blueball squeaking a preparatory tenor, and Mr. Peter Prune, who piques himself upon his base, grumbling in his gizzard. Anticipated with horror the accustomed routine, viz. "Hark the lark," the "Loadstars," "When shall we three meet again," and "Drink to me only," for the ninety-ninth time. Entertained an apprehension that the parties might even be "Deserted by the waning moon," when providentially a cry of "Fire !" saluted our ears from the street. Ran to the window, threw back the curtain, and found it to proceed from two butcher's boys, who with pop-guns were playing at duels. Said nothing, but walked back with a grave face. Wife in hysterics already. Beheld the Albion engines pumping in at the parlour-window. Insisted, if I loved her, that I should call a hackney-coach, greeting me with accustomed rondeau, "Do make haste, do." Threw up the sash and shouted "Coach," in a voice that might have drawn one from the Pavement in Moorfields. Wife darted into vehicle in an access of terror, quite forgetting the shawl which she had given shopman for safe custody. Hasty adieus, and tea and toast in Bush-lane.

If nobody marries till Simon Swandown again attends the ceremony, Malthus will have no reason to grumble at excess of population.

### SONG.

Oh how hard it is to find
The one just suited to our mind ;
　　And if that one should be
False, unkind, or found too late,
What can we do but sigh at fate,
　　And sing Woe's me—Woe's me !

Love 's a boundless burning waste,
Where Bliss's stream we seldom taste,
　　And still more seldom flee
Suspense's thorns, Suspicion's stings ; ·
Yet somehow Love a something brings
That 's sweet—ev'n when we sigh Woe's me !　　C.

### STANZAS TO ——

Do you call my religion unlawful and light ?
　　No, believe me, the creed that I cherish,
Is that souls, which are sparks from the fountain of light,
　　With their perishing dust shall not perish.

For I cannot imagine my love quench'd in death,
　　Though the dross of our being should sever,
And the thought of thee rivets a chain on my faith,
　　That there is an hereafter for ever.

　　　　　　　　　　　　　　　　　　N.

# INDEX

## TO THE

## EIGHTH VOLUME.

---

2 Q

Lightning Source UK Ltd.
Milton Keynes UK
UKHW020605120219
337137UK00005B/766/P